The Appearance of Things

THE APPEARANCE OF THINGS

Vernon S. C. Castle

The Appearance of Things

Dynasty Press Limited
36 Ravensdon Street
London SE11 4AR

First published by Dynasty Press Ltd.

ISBN 978-0-9935780-9-0

Copyright: © Vernon St. Clair Castle 2016

Vernon S.C. Castle has asserted his right under the Copyright, Designs and Patents Act 1988 to be identified as the author of this work.

All Rights Reserved: No part of this publication may be reproduced, copied, stored in a retrieval system or transmitted, in any form or by any means without written permission.

Cover artwork design by **Rupert Dixon**.

Book Design by **Biddles Books**

To my darling, Renee.
Your love and encouragement
made this possible.

Table of Contents

Chapter 1 – Bali 1
Chapter 2 – Sumatra 23
Chapter 3 – Java 89
Chapter 4 – Tanjung Benoa 167
Chapter 5 – Thaipusam 209
Chapter 6 – Phuket 235
Chapter 7 – Thai Time 275
Chapter 8 – Laos 315
Chapter 9 – Calcutta! 369
Chapter 10 – Darjeeling 385
Chapter 11 – Kathmandu 391
Chapter 12 – Back to Mother India 431
Chapter 13 – Afghanistan 483
Chapter 14 – On to Greece 509
Epilogue 545

Chapter 1
Bali

"Odd travel suggestions are dancing lessons from the Gods."

Graham Greene

"Oh hell, they're putting their bow line right across our exit channel."

Rod stood up on the bow of *Moonshiner*, his thirty-three foot racing hulled sloop, as the crewmen on the huge Chinese junk *Hong Kong* set their mooring lines.

The small harbor at Tanjung Benoa, Bali hosted a baker's dozen of boaties, sailors of small vessels from all over the world enjoying a layover. The shallow anchorage kept out the cruise ships so we pretty much had it to ourselves, along with a few dozen local fishermen.

The junk was troubling though. From *Moonshiner* we could make out a lot of the crew. They looked like something out of central casting for "Pirates of the South China Sea." These were lean faced men - Chinese, Malay, maybe Vietnamese - hardened by life at sea. These were the marauders that preyed on the small boats of refugees fleeing the hell of a collapsing Vietnam and Cambodia.

More than a few of the crew looked us over as we lay in our homemade drydock near the sandy shore. It wasn't a hostile visage I saw - more of a chilling appraisal of us, *Moonshiner* and our gear. The cold eyes of a wholesale buyer at the slaughterhouse.

One of the men on the deck was shouting orders and Rod called out to him, now that they were about fifty feet away.

"Ahoy, Captain……Captain!"

The Appearance of Things

Rod had a Midwestern wholesomeness that the tropics had rusted but not completely degraded. Blue eyes and a freckled face stood out under a thatch of sandy colored hair. He was lean after his years of knocking around in the South Seas. It made him appear taller than his six foot frame.

The captain of the junk approached the rail near the bow, and looked us over.

"What you want?!" The voice clipped and staccato, higher pitched than I would have expected. His wispy beard and moustache pushed slightly downwind by the gentle sea breeze, eyes narrow. Not friendly.

"Captain," Rod began, "we need free passage when the tide comes up."

With his outstretched arm Rod indicated the line from *Moonshiner* that now ran under the bow of the junk. *Moonshiner* was at this point completely out of the water, supported by the crossed timbers of four logs of giant bamboo. Early that morning, on the highest tide, Rod and I had pulled the boat into the beach channel as close as we could get to the shore, the keel inches above the white sand bottom. Once there we had lashed the bamboo posts under the boat, forming two huge "exes" so that when the tide withdrew *Moonshiner* would be supported high and dry. Instant dry-dock!

The reason that we wanted *Moonshiner* out of the water was to paint the wooden hull with a toxic compound I had bought to keep boring worms from putting holes in the hull and sinking her. It turned out that this paint was volatile and the poison part would dissipate in the air in short order. We had to refloat her on the next tide and get back out into deeper anchorage or we'd waste all our labor and my hundred bucks.

The captain of the junk looked us over and in his choppy alto called back, "OK, when you ready call over and we pass the line around."

He turned and went back to directing his crew. Satisfied, Rod turned to me. "Vern, let's get the paint buckets closed up and make ready for later." There wasn't much of the antifouling paint left, maybe just enough for a touch up around where the bamboo logs kept us from reaching the hull, near the gunwales.

The early afternoon was clear and fresh, a few clouds clinging to the twin volcanic peaks that defined our northern horizon. I had come to appreciate the sundown, sitting forward on the boat in a beach chair, sipping White Label scotch. It was surprising how fast darkness could fall in the tropics. The sky would blaze golden as the sun descended to the shoulder of the volcano, then sink behind with unexpected rapidity. We'd often see the shafts of light and shadow which softened the golden brilliance into shades of tangerine and a startling blue green. On occasion, delicate clouds clinging to the peak would catch the light show, and the whole would be a swirled watercolor rainbow. Then a lovely peacefulness would settle over the little harbor, the still water reflecting the sky as it was transformed from red and orange into the violet and indigo of the night.

This evening, as we made ready to exit our small channel into the deeper bay, I noticed that the usual calming of the sea breeze had not occurred. The water remained ruffled. I took a sip of my scotch and felt a slight sway as the incoming tide floated *Moonshiner*. The sun was still about 10 degrees above the slope of the volcano. Looking west, everything appeared tranquil. Behind me, a low rumble drew my attention to the east, and in the distance a wall of dark clouds. I saw a flash of lightning between the slate grey sea and the darker mass of cloud roiling above. There was an unmistakable veil of falling rain, a vertical smear of dark striation below the cloud mass.

Rod was coiling ropes on the bow. We had placed our bowline anchor out in the channel earlier in the day. The plan was for Rod and me to pull on the anchor line and edge *Moonshiner* out as soon as we were floating clear. We'd worry about the big bamboo cross pieces once we were away at depth. The 'fly in the ointment' was the *Hong Kong*, whose bowline was straight across our path out of the channel. The bow of the *Hong Kong* was pretty much directly over where our anchor was so, for a moment, we'd be nose to nose as we passed. I'd never done this before, but it seemed reasonable for the *Hong Kong* crew to release their bowline and hand it down to us, then we'd run it around to the stern of *Moonshiner* and toss it back. I imagined that Rod would run it back from the bow to the stern and I'd keep pulling to get us by. That was the plan anyway. By 6:00 pm, the breeze had grown to a gusty wind. The approaching gale flashed menacingly and I could hear the wind making a rushing, whistling sound in the fringe of palms at the head of the bay.

Rod was looking tense as he moved quickly around the topside, checking lines and looking down over the edge of the boat. He started the small motor in case we needed a power assist.

"We're bouncing a bit. Come on, let's start the pull."

As the wind had picked up, so too had the wave action. Instead of a lovely calm sunset and smooth glide out of the channel, the small swells were lifting us, then dropping us back. I could feel the boat shiver each time we hit the bottom.

"Come on!" yelled Rod, and I felt the first drops of rain hit my face. A real tropical downpour was moving across the entry of the bay, coming at us way faster than I had thought. I could see whitecaps as it pushed into the little harbor and bore down on us. We were maybe ten feet from the *Hong Kong* when the wind and rain lashed into us. *Moonshiner* was bucking in the swells and the wind, while the much more massive *Hong Kong*, turned into the wind, seemed to be riding serenely.

"Ahoy!" Rod called from the bow. "Ahoy, Captain!" We were both soaked to the skin as the heavy rain poured down. Flashes of lightning lit us up like strobe lights, the explosion of the thunder on top of us. "Ahoy, Captain! Come on deck!"

Nothing.

"God damn it!" Rod shouted into the wind, and turned back, cupping his hands. "Ahoy, Captain of *Hong Kong*. On deck!"

Nothing.

By this time we were pretty damn close. The *Hong Kong* had a rope webbing draped over both sides of her bow. Rod yelled over to me, "Can you get a hand on the net and reach up to the bow line?"

I looked down at the surges smashing between the boats. Falling down into that looked like a very bad idea. We were bobbing under the bow of the *Hong Kong* and their bowline was beginning to scrape along the front cable of *Moonshiner*.

Shit.

"OK," I shouted and reached out to the webbing. My hands were wet, but the rough rope of the net felt solid and secure. As *Moonshiner* bobbed up, I got a foot into the webbing and was suddenly airborne, clinging to the bow of the *Hong Kong*. I'd learned a bit about sailing knots during the last few weeks aboard *Moonshiner* and after a few seconds I was actually able to loosen their bowline at a slack moment.

"Hand it to me," shouted Rod.

I knew the plan. He'd run it to the stern and pass it back to me for reattachment. So I slipped the last loop and tossed the line to his waiting hands. He pulled in the slack and the loose end whipped past my face. As he made to run astern with the rope coil, the *Hong Kong* and *Moonshiner* began to slide apart. The gap widened to three feet, then to four feet.

"Fuck this!" I thought, and made my leap back to *Moonshiner* before it was too late.

The squall was way too intense for this sort of thing. Halfway to the stern, Rod saw I was back on board. He quickly grabbed loose one of his floats, looped the rope he was holding and dropped it overboard. He leapt down into the pilot's seat and gave the motor some throttle. The anchor line tugged us down for a moment, then came free.

"Pull it up!" he shouted over to me, and I began, as best I could, to haul up the line without falling head first into the heaving water. At that instant, I heard the high-pitched voice cut over the water, "You son bitch!" The captain of the *Hong Kong* glared at us over the bow of his boat as the distance between us increased. The wind caught the *Hong Kong* and it began to drift in a great arc, with its stern line as the apex. "What you do my ship?!" he shrieked.

Now sailors were on deck, scrambling all over *Hong Kong*, fierce eyes towards us, scrambling to make ready and set a new bowline in the chaos of the storm. Rod stood in the cockpit, steadying himself on the boom of the mainsail and shouted back, "We called for you to come out and pass the line, but you wouldn't come."

"You son bitch. I kill you!"

Rod drew himself up.

"You're no Captain," he bellowed. "We asked for your help and you ignored us!"

The two men glared at each other over the widening gap.

The gusting wind seemed in that moment to be holding its breath.

"We asked for your help. I'll see you in Maritime Court!"

There was an instant of pause. The captain of *Hong Kong* said, through gritted teeth: "Dare no court out here."

Rod started to say more, but then turned back to the cockpit, took the wheel and increased the throttle. "Is the anchor on board?" he asked in a tight monotone. I was still up front, hanging on to the rope, but I could see the small anchor maybe five feet below the surface. "No, but I can see it. It's clear."

The storm seemed to drop away as fast as it had appeared, and with the reduced bobbing I successfully pulled the anchor up the rest of the way without dinging the boat. I lay the anchor back into its slot and went astern. "That was pretty weird," I said, and Rod nodded.

"He's a bad captain. When we asked for help, they were just keeping dry."

Rod stared ahead and we putted over to the small colony of other boats. I could make out the silhouette of the *Hong Kong* in the lingering lightning flashes as the squall moved on over the land to the west. They had set another bowline, but the ship was not riding easily, no longer turned into the direction of the swell. I thought I could make out people on the deck looking at us, and felt both exhilarated with the adventure of it all but also ill at ease.

"I kill you!"

I heard the voice again in my mind. Yeah, he kill us alright, if he get the chance.

***

The harbor at Tanjung had a lot of types in it. Everybody seemed to tacitly acknowledge that *Hong Kong* was really a pirate boat, but as long as we all behaved ourselves the government of Indonesia, at least here, was content just to let things be.

Frankly, I was amazed to even be on *Moonshiner*. Rod was a character, for sure. I had come to know him a few weeks earlier as I sat alone in a juice bar in Denpasar. It was just after the New Year and already blisteringly hot by 9:00 am.

I am not a little guy, six foot three with more than a little meat on my then 23 year old frame. I guess someone who looked at me would see a person who might be of Irish or German ancestry, but who was now obviously an American. Both my mom and dad had blue eyes, so I did too. I'd grown a reddish beard over the last summer when I was vagabonding around in Europe and North Africa, but had shaved off everything except the moustache when I landed in Singapore. It was just too hot and humid to sport a beard, so I compromised with a pretty decent moustache that framed the sides of my mouth - an Eric Clapton look, I liked to think. On that bright and muggy morning, I stood out from the more diminutive Balinese around me on the stools at the juice bar.

I heard a voice speaking English at the far end and looked over. "You an American?" It was a friendly inquiry, made in a friendly American accent.

"Yeah," I said. "California."

The stranger stood up and walked to where I was sitting. "Mind if I join you?"

I'd been on the road in Asia for about two months, having flown by myself from London to Singapore. I'd gone up through Malaysia to Penang, crossed over to Sumatra and gone overland down through Java to Bali. There were wonders and great people and beauty, but also times when I had never felt more alone. My own story about myself had developed a number of cracks, but maybe that's one of the reasons we hit the road - an innate wisdom to break up the storyline we build before it hardens into a prison. For now I welcomed the chance to talk to a fellow American. There weren't very many of us in Southeast Asia - at least not very many who weren't in the military.

"No, sit down," I said. "I'm just sitting here enjoying my mango and pineapple smoothie."

"Rod McKinley," he said. "Out of Seattle."

He extended his hand and as I took it, I replied, "Vern Castle, out of LA."

"What brings you to Bali?" asked Rod.

"Well, I spent pretty much all of last summer with a couple of friends banging around in Europe. They went back to the States in September, but I wanted to keep going." I took a cool sip of my smoothie. Rod nodded and looked at me expectantly. "So I got a one way ticket out to Singapore in London. I'd heard really good things about Southeast Asia from kids in Europe, Australians and New Zealanders who'd come all the way overland. I figured it would be cool to take that way myself."

Rod reflected, "So you're going all the way back to Europe, huh?"

"Yeah," I replied, "but no particular timeline."

"How long are you planning to stay in Bali?"

I was thinking about that myself. Sumatra had been fantastic, so exotic and not like anything I'd ever imagined. Java was good - Jakarta, Yogakarta, the highlands with their volcanoes and ruins, good people, good food. Amazingly filled with humanity. Stopping to piss by the side of a hiking trail, thinking I was all alone, a dozen faces had appeared, giggling in the woods around me. But Bali had held a sort of mystical sway in me, and I had been mentally holding it out as the "cherry and cream" on the top of my Indonesian travels. I remember as a kid growing up near to Hollywood in Los Angeles, and going to see the film "South Pacific." I was nine years old at the time, and listening to Juanita Hall sing her heart out on 'Bali Hai' pulled at my imagination.

The reality on the ground was, thus far, pretty much a letdown. Denpasar was noisy, crowded and filthy. Nearly all the travelers were staying in the cheap *losman* scattered around Kuta Beach and Legian. It was what I was coming to recognize as the usual travelers' scene – cooking magic mushroom omelets, smoking ganja, and swapping lies and travel stories. Not that all the stories were bad. Some of them were turning out to be my best source of information about what might lie ahead or what might be worth a look. It was a mixed bag and left me a little blue. I remembered the old song that asked, "Is that all there is?" So far my only adventure here had been with large spiders. After dark the narrow paths between the small bungalows would be crisscrossed with newly woven spider webs holding thin-legged black spiders as big as my hand. I'd walked into a few of these at night on my way home and felt the spider run across my chest and jump back into the bushes off my shoulder. These babies had some weight and felt like someone galloping their fingers across my skin. It scared me and creeped me out at the same time.

Outside of Denpasar were mostly muddy roads and with the rains nobody was going very far. In the forest around me I had seen temples and beautifully dressed people carrying offerings of intricately stacked fruit and flowers, or woven palm frond trays laden with sweet burning incense and more tropical flowers, hibiscus and frangipani. I watched them file up the temple steps and into the compounds, heard the jangle of the gamelan music within and wanted to follow, but felt like an interloper in my flip-flops and shorts. Their elegance demanded my respect, so I stayed outside. Yes, I'd only been on the road in Asia for a short time, but the travelers' watering holes had a sameness that was already growing less enchanting.

"How long in Bali?" I returned Rod's gaze, "Not really sure. It's not quite what I was hoping for. I need to buy a ticket back to Singapore so I can head up towards Thailand and I haven't done that yet." A heavily laden truck roared past and we both winced at the noise and exhaust it kicked out. "I'm not really seeing that much to stay for."

I'd developed the notion that when I found a paradise, I'd stay awhile. This didn't seem to be it.

Rod took in my answer, nodded to himself, and seemed to make a decision.

"Well, let me make you an offer. I've got a boat in the harbor. My girlfriend Brenda and I parted company back in Australia. I'm pretty much flat broke. If you'll pay for food for both of us you've got a berth if you want it."

It was a sudden and surprising offer. I wasn't in love with Kuta Beach so I said, "OK, sounds alright to me. What I'm paying for room rent can go towards food. I guess your boat has a kitchen?"

Rod smiled, "A small galley. I've got a kerosene stove that boils water and works ok."

I wanted to check his offer out before pulling up stakes at my bungalow, so we finished up our drinks and hailed a *bemo* heading down to the crescent shaped natural harbor, maybe two miles across. There was a spit coming off the mainland from the north, low and with numerous palms. It didn't seem very wide, less than a hundred feet, a few small stretches of white sand beach. Beyond the sand I could see breakers spending their energy on a reef about a quarter of a mile out. The harbor swept around to the south, with dense vegetation right down to the water along much of its shoreline. The far point looked like the mainland, with larger trees and the characteristic wispy, giant bamboo bending in the sea breeze. I spied a few small houses with corrugated tin roofs, and a dozen or so boats of differing shapes and sizes lay in the turquoise blue waters, sheltered in the crescent that was straight across from where we were standing.

Rod and I sat down at a rough table built from the sawn slabs of palm tree trunk. An old woman, grinning and nearly toothless, came out of a tiny shed and cackled at us: "Bir?"

Rod shook his head 'no' but I stepped in with, "*Ja, dua, terimah kasih.*"

Rod raised his eyebrows. "Didn't know you could speak Indonesian."

"I can't, not really, but I have picked up some basic traveler speak in the last few months. You know, the twenty question game - what's your name, where do you come from, where do you go, are you married, numbers - not really conversant."

The old gal brought out two bottles of Bintang and an opener. She sat down with us, eyes filled with good humor. Her worn brown and purple sarong had seen better days. I popped open the beers and handed one over to Rod. Mine was cold and tasted good.

"Which one is your boat?" I asked, looking towards the collection that rested at anchor in the crescent.

"See the one with the single mast, white on top and a yellow hull?"

At over a mile away about half the boats looked to fit that description.

"Not exactly," I mused.

"On the far right, called *Moonshiner*."

We could see a tiny boat leaving the sandy beach beyond the crescent. "That's going to Tanjung Benoa, the village behind my anchorage. We'll take that boat over when it gets here." He nodded out towards the little motorboat making its way across the bay.

I enjoyed a long draught of my beer.

"You sailed all the way here from Seattle? When did you start?"

II
Rod's Story

Rod took a sip of his beer.

"I left Seattle in April of 1972, heading towards Japan. *Moonshiner* is a thirty-three foot racing sloop and I can handle her by myself. I was planning to go first to Japan, and work my way down towards Okinawa, and then maybe Manila."

"Long way to go in a small boat," I said.

Rod smiled. "I love sailing and I'd been planning this trip for a long time. If you go at the right time of the year there's no sea in the world you can't sail." He took another sip of his beer. "That's generally true, but there can always be unexpected weather and that's what happened to me. About half way across I hit a hell of a storm, late season. I lost my mast - it was snapped right off - lost a bunch of gear too. Almost lost it all there."

He looked thoughtful, touching his near death in that instant of reflection.

"I crippled down, finally, to the outmost of the Solomon Islands. The people there were wonderful. Together with them I was able to fabricate and set a new mast. With no electricity or power tools we had to do it all by hand. It took about a year. And I'll tell you, we were out of touch. It was like we were the only people in the world. I didn't see one single jet trail or big ship go by, not in the whole year I was there. Anyway, I was finally able to sail out and down to Bougainville, New Guinea where they've got a copper mine. I'd talked to a few people along the way, once I'd set sail again and got back into the so-called world. I heard they needed English speaking help at the mine, and I needed money, so I went."

"God, that's incredible. Sort of a Robinson Crusoe story!"

"Yeah," Rod whispered to his beer.

"When I got to Bougainville, they had a telephone so I called home. My parents hadn't heard from me going on a year and a half. They were happy as hell to hear from me, but then my mom said, "Oh Rod, my god! We thought you were dead. They found your lifeboat and other things of yours after that storm. Oh Rod, we thought you were dead so… so we collected the life insurance policy you had, the one before you left. Rod, we paid off the house and got your sister into college. Oh god Rod, if you come back we'll have to pay all that money back and we can't, now that dad's not working."

Rod looked at me ruefully, trying to keep some humor in his eyes like it was a big joke. I was thunderstruck.

"So what did you do?"

"Well, the statute of limitations on this stuff is seven years. I've got to stay gone another four years. There can't be a hint I'm still alive or it's fraud. I went down to Darwin to find work after that," he said grimly. "That's where I met Brenda. But like I told you, we just broke up and I headed over here from Darwin."

The little shuttle boat beached, and a laughing gaggle of women in sarongs piled out barefoot into the water. They grabbed large bamboo baskets off the bow and balanced them on their heads, drifting past us, talking and laughing. A few coy looks at us as we sat watching them pass.

"*Lapan ratus rupiah!*" the old woman said, pointing to our now empty beer bottles. I paid up the eight hundred rupiah, and we waded over to the tiny boat and climbed in. A whiff of wood smoke wafted out of the dark shed the old woman had disappeared into with the empty bottles. Another older woman appeared, stepping out from behind the shed, topless, carrying a basket on her head. She had the blood red mouth of a betel nut chewer and spat a healthy portion of rust colored saliva into the water before joining us in the boat. Her rheumy eyes looked us over, and then she started fussing with her basket.

The Appearance of Things

I turned to Rod, "That's an incredible story. So you can't go home for at least four more years."

He nodded, "And right now I'm broke. The Darwin money I earned was mostly spent getting re-outfitted. But I think that when the winds turn I'll go back up to Bougainville. There's work there, if I want it." He smiled wanly.

The boat operator, a small man wearing a headscarf, torn green t-shirt and sarong, shoved off and set to, hoisting a sail. No need for a motor on the way back with the wind. The air lost its humid weight as the shoreline fell away and we swung towards the far point. It was serene. We were silent in our own thoughts, the susurration of the smooth water on the hull the only sound. I was still internally shaking my head at Rod's story as we pulled into the landing beach of Tanjung Benoa. The fine coral sand stretched for about a hundred feet and extended maybe twenty feet up before the thick undergrowth closed it off. At several points there were openings and there was evidence of a trail retreating back into the forest. From the opening nearest us a sturdy man of about thirty five emerged, wearing khaki shorts and nothing else. As he strode across the short stretch of white sand, he smiled broadly, his short cropped black hair shining in the sun.

"*Selamat soré*, Rod."

Rod greeted him with a handshake.

"*Selamat soré*, Wayan." He turned to me. "Wayan, this is Vern."

Wayan turned his smile on me and energetically pumped my outstretched hand. "*Selamat datang*, Ben."

He turned back to Rod. "Come with me Rod. Kerosene!"

"Oh, great!" exclaimed Rod, and they marched into the jungle. I followed and was surprised to find myself standing on the sand street of a wooden village after only a few dozen paces. Rod and Wayan crossed the small street to a two story building with no visible windows. Wayan lifted out a wall panel to reveal an entry, disappeared inside and then momentarily reappeared holding a white plastic one gallon container. Rod reached into his pocket and handed Wayan a fifty rupiah coin, then came over to where I was standing.

"Let's head out to *Moonshiner*," he said, and we set off back to the beach the way we had come. "Wayan is the village headman. He's a good man. His English is fairly good as well. Because I've got the boat I'm a headman too, and we get along just dandy." Rod put the kerosene down in the sand. "Help me with my canoe," he said, turning towards a sleek little white craft resting near the edge of the vegetation, "I got this in the Solomons."

A type of rowing shell, about twelve feet long but only about eighteen inches wide and eighteen inches deep, Rod's canoe appeared to be hand carved from a single piece of wood, and when we lifted it towards the water, I was dazzled how light and streamlined it was. A beautiful piece of work.

"You get in," said Rod, steadying the little craft. "It's a great canoe, but I guess it can seem a little tippy if you're not used to it." He handed me the kerosene and we shoved off into the clear blue water. I reached for a paddle, but Rod said, "Don't worry about it - we're just going over there." He indicated a boat about a hundred feet in front of us. *'Moonshiner'* it read across the stern, and when we drew alongside a small platform at the rear waterline Rod held the side bar to steady us as I climbed out of the canoe and onto the big boat, hefting the kerosene with me. Rod tied the little canoe off with a yellow poly line, hopped nimbly out, and we climbed up into the pilot's nest. I was surprised at the compact little space. It would be pretty cozy for two, even if they got along ok, and I wondered what I might be letting myself in for.

Rod took the kerosene and dropped down the short ladder into the interior cabin. "Come on down!" he invited. The dominant smell of salt water and canvas was not unpleasant. The main part of the cabin had a bench seat against the port side hull, and a small table that was maybe two feet wide and five feet long. Opposite was a galley with a compact sink and a table-top kerosene stove. The interior was about seven feet wide and barely deep enough for me to stand up straight. Forward there was a bulkhead with a toilet on the left and storage cabinets on the right. I moved past and found two bunks, one on each side, growing narrower towards the bow. The space at the end was stuffed with what I took to be sails.

"It's a racing hull." Clearly proud of his boat, Rod ran his hand along some of the wooden structure as we made our way back to the galley. "She doesn't have a broad beam but it makes for better sailing. Have a seat."

I dropped down on the bench and looked up through the entryway at a blue sky with a few clouds. "It's great," I said, then qualified it with, "I guess it will work ok with the two of us, huh?"

"Aw, yeah, I mean there's plenty of room. When Brenda was aboard, we made the bow into a double bed and used the bunks for storage. It's not like you spend a lot of time up there." He cocked his thumb forward and I wondered if he was remembering good times with Brenda.

Decision time.

It looked like a good deal to me if Rod was as he appeared - a pretty normal guy with a really weird story. I wasn't impressed with Kuta, but Tanjung Benoa seemed like the real deal, maybe the Bali I was looking for. If it got too crowded, or if Rod turned out to be a nutter, I could bail out and no harm done. And then there was the courage thing. I'd already come up against some fearful elements in myself - the time across Sumatra, the trip over to Java in the hold of a rust bucket - new people and situations where I had to take a chance. The cautious me was often in a pitched argument with the adventurous me and I was actually getting to enjoy the freefall feeling of allowing insecurity, of trusting. I'd read a book a while back by Alan Watts called *The Wisdom of Insecurity*, in which he suggested that if you really pay attention, there is virtually no guarantee in life of anything. Life is short, death is certain. *Carpe diem!*

"Tell you what, Rod - this seems great to me. If the offer is still open, I'll head back to my guesthouse and pack up."

My words broke through whatever reverie Rod was lost in and he looked up.

"What? Oh, yeah, of course. Welcome aboard."

We shook hands, and I saw that he was taking a chance too.

III
Boaties

Our floating neighborhood off Tanjung was by necessity a transient one. I'd met nearly everyone who was anchored out, either at Cassie's, the little hut at the harbor road where Rod and I shared our first beer, or at The Chinaman's, the closest thing we had to a restaurant. In general, dining out was a luxury most Balinese eschewed, eating in the family compound when the spirit grabbed them. Today, it appeared, nearly everybody was on shore and The Chinaman's was as full as I'd seen it since my arrival nearly three weeks ago.

Rod was talking to Art while I listened in. I liked Art. He was about thirty-eight years old, but his face was already lined from the salt and the sun. Art always looked like he needed a shave, his dirty blond hair disheveled from bathing in the sea and just toweling off. He had the appealing air of an adventurer and reminded me of Kirk Douglas, even down to the cleft in his chin and the laughing, pale blue eyes. From the stories he shared, he'd been all over the South Seas for the last eight years, sometimes with company but mostly not. He referred to his boat as 'The Banana' and with its yellow and blue low slung middle it did look rather like a floating banana.

"She's sound, I can tell ya' and we've been through a lot."

I found the boaties to be a fascinating group of people, mostly a decade older than me and way more experienced. At twenty-nine, Rod was relatively young. And here was me, twenty-three years old and out on the road, really on my own for the first time.

I surveyed the low wooden room. Jan and Moe, the Danish couple, were huddled in low conversation with the French, Laurent and Jessie. They were all in their late thirties, except Laurent who was a bit older. I liked him too, with his beat-up sheepskin coat in the tropics. I wished I would grow into the kind of guy who could make that coat look as good as Laurent did. Jessie looked at him with love in her eyes and a slightly sardonic smile which said, "Here you go again," as he waved his hands in animated conversation with Moe. Moe smiled at his story, her truly beautiful face alight with interest and engagement - Ingrid Bergman as a child, or at least that was how I imagined her. Jan was being cool, supervising the interaction. There weren't too many single women knocking around, none around here at any rate.

John and Angelina sat at a creaky table near The Chinaman's family shrine. All kinds of little porcelain pots and small flowers, a plate of rice and a few pieces of fruit - a banana and a mandarin orange - supervised by a stiff, black and white photo of an older Chinese man in a western suit. His expression was that of a guy who couldn't wait to get going.

John looked downcast as Angelina was talking to him, her long slim fingers tapping at the table as she spoke. Her red nails made a clicking, but I could only make out the singing tone of her voice, not her words. I was knocked out by Angelina. John had met her in Hong Kong and they had sailed the *Baroness* down here together. I liked John too, maybe in part because he was vulnerable and seemed guileless, but Angelina was a true beauty whose long black hair was piled on her head, and today a few curled strands played about her temples as spoke. She was like a Chinese movie star with those crossover looks that worked everywhere, flawless skin and the healthy glow that life on the sea confers. With her cover girl looks and exquisite figure it was all I could do not to drop to my knees and start panting. Angelina was friendly and open with me and didn't act like she knew she was beautiful - part of her charm. I liked it that when we spoke she didn't make me feel like a kid.

John was about five foot ten with a medium build and a smooth, pleasant face. His wavy hair was well kempt and he was obviously fit, but not in a jock sort of way. I both admired him and felt sorry for him. His ship, the *Baroness*, was a beautiful piece of teak craftsmanship; single-masted, but still the largest boat in the harbor. If *Moonshiner* was thirty three feet, the *Baroness* was at least sixty feet, with a wide beam. Rod and I had paddled over and visited a few times, and I'd never seen anything finer. The salon was sixteen feet across and a spacious twenty feet long. There was a wet bar at the far end, carpeting, comfortable chairs and two sofas. I delighted in the stereo system, a real high fidelity rig, with tons of music I liked in the cassette collection. All we had on *Moonshiner* was me and my harmonica.

Besides being beautiful, Angelina was a masterful chef and we enjoyed some fine meals she prepared in their little galley. Forward, there was an inviting stateroom with blond wood paneling, a queen bed and full on bathroom - shower, toilet, sink. I'd seen it all one time when the little head off the salon was in use and John told me to use the master suite.

John, with the help of on board automation, had sailed the *Baroness* by himself all the way from San Diego. I'm not an experienced boat guy and I've seen the fuss we've been through on *Moonshiner* just to get repositioned. It would be daunting to sail a boat like *Baroness* alone. When I said I admired John, his seamanship was only one part. He seemed to be accomplished in mechanics and was able to help Rod resurrect a little Yamaha outboard that looked way too far gone. He'd made good money as an attorney, but was very much the Renaissance man and had walked away from it all last year in order to roam the South Seas.

The reason I felt sort of sorry for him was that in spite of all his talents and accomplishments he didn't believe in himself. Most of the boaties I met were pretty fearless, but with John I'd get the feeling that my approval mattered to him, that he needed to be affirmed by those around him. Yet there could never be any approbation that would quell his restive doubts about himself. I'd say something like, "It blows me away that you could manage a ship like the *Baroness* by yourself," and he'd reply, "It's not so much really. I can run all the sails from the cabin. Got good radar but my nav skills are nothing special. I was mostly just lucky." He'd always knock the wind out of his own sails. This staggered me. I mean, how could he not be proud of himself? I've met people who act self-effacing or humble when it's only a manipulation to get more praise, but this was different. Like he had a little demon on his shoulder whispering, "You ain't got it, man!" no matter what he did. Like he was broken hearted.

Art, on the other hand, with his little banana boat and crusty, old salt mannerisms, impressed me as far wealthier in himself. I'd seen how Angelina looked at him, how they played off each other and laughed in a sort of sexy, teasing dance of words and gestures. I saw the hurt and the withdrawal in John's eyes as he watched them play, right in front of him. I'm not one of these guys who gets a charge out of seeing other people's spirit ground down. I don't know exactly why, but it hurt my feelings for John, watching those two flirt in front of him. Maybe I could relate to the fear of never being enough. I told myself that most of these folks had ten or fifteen years on me and the fearlessness they conveyed was a function of getting older, but I didn't quite believe it was that automatic. I knew plenty of adults back in LA who didn't seem to have any wisdom. They were fearful about jobs or the news or a million other things.

A burst of laughter from the table where the Danes and the French were sitting pulled me back into the present.

Art suggested to Rod, with a nod to me, "You should come to the gamelan tonight. I'm thinkin' the whole village will be there and if you haven't seen the dance in Bali, you gotta come." After a moment's thought he added, "You've got sarongs, don't you? You need to wear a sarong when you enter a temple."

Both Rod and I nodded. The ubiquitous garment was the Southeast Asian traveler's best friend - you could wear it, use it for a towel, make it into an instant hat, use if for a cover on long bus rides. Hell, I suppose strain coffee, if it came to that.

"I talked to Wayan," Art continued, "and he said to come to the first courtyard at the Pura Desa by five thirty."

We finished off our spicy *mee goering* fried noodles, and the Chinaman came to the table wiping his hands on a small greasy checkered towel. I guessed he was about fifty, but it was hard to tell. He certainly didn't have the cheerful, outgoing openness and easy smile I was coming to love in the Balinese. The word curmudgeon comes to mind.

"*Barapa harga, bapack*" How much father? I asked.

He eyed us, not unfriendly, but all business. "*Lima ratus rupiah*" 'Five hundred rupiah.' Art pulled out two hundred rupees and I paid the three hundred for Rod and myself. I appreciated that the tipping thing was not an issue here. People with restaurants were just glad you decided to patronize their establishment.

We stood to go and the Chinaman shuffled back towards the small smoky kitchen.

"*Sampai jumpa lagi, Bapak,*" I said in farewell, and waved to the old man. He turned slightly and acknowledged my 'see you later' with a creased smile and nod of the head.

As the evening approached I stood outside the *Pura Desa*, the main temple in Tanjung Benoa, in my sarong and clean, short-sleeved white shirt. Each of the stonework corners of the ornate entrance had a winged creature with huge pointed teeth and fierce bulging eyes. Sitting astride the wings, like a horse jockey, was a human figure wearing an arched headdress. Above each rider was another gargoyle creature, also with serious teeth and protruding eyes.

I climbed the first two stone steps to where I could see within the compound. Men and women were mounting the steps, then gliding down into the courtyard like some brilliantly costumed ancient ballet. The women were balancing elaborately decorated, woven boxes on their heads. Each engaged in a small personal ritual when placing their offering on the ledge of the central temple, lighting a few sticks of incense and offering a dedication. A rather lovely older woman, wearing a striking green and orange sarong topped by a purple lace blouse, placed her gold foil adorned box on an altar ledge fifteen feet in front of me. She removed the woven lid, extracted a small bowl of cream yellow frangipani flowers, and set it within the removed lid. Within the basket I could see pieces of fruit, more flowers, little baked cakes and something that looked like a cooked, flattened chicken. She lit a few sticks of dark incense and placed one in the food basket, along with a folded hundred rupiah note. I admired her long straight black hair as she lifted her offering basket from its platform and found a place for it on the surrounding ledge, amongst the growing numbers of other baskets. The woman placed her palms together and made a small bow towards the altar platform, then collected the lid with the flowers she had left on the edge and made her way into the throng in the center of the courtyard. With my eyes I followed her to the grassy center of the complex where she sat down in a kneeling position and placed the flower bowl on the ground before her. Many others were kneeling and placing lighted incense sticks near their own flower offerings. The air was truly perfumed with the sweet smoke and the profusion of fresh blossoms.

A beautiful young woman approached the steps with her basket atop her head and we smiled at each other. Her luxuriant black hair was tied in a loose ponytail that flowed to her waist. She hesitated on the steps and turned her lovely oval face, large dark eyes and full lips towards me. With a nod of her head she indicated a young man mounting the steps beside us.

"*Tidak ada udung Anda?*" which I think meant 'You do not have *udung?*' I must have looked confused because she touched her head and then pointed to a boy who was descending the steps into the temple. It dawned on me that while I was focused on the offering baskets, the white headscarf was the thing most of the men were wearing and no, I didn't have one.

"*Tidak, ma'af. Saya tidak ada,*" 'No, sorry, I don't have.'

She handed her basket to a little boy who was standing behind her, maybe her little brother, and disappeared into a nearby house. The little boy looked up at me, silent and stoic. She reappeared moments later with a square of white cloth, and folded it in half to make a large triangle. As she began to roll the long edge, it reminded me of how I used to roll my neckerchief when I was in the scouts. She bade me sit on the step and bent forward, wrapping the cloth completely around my head, bringing the ends forward to tie a double knot over my forehead. I inhaled the perfume of her skin as she stepped back to appraise the *'udung'* she had created. There was merriment and, maybe my wishful thinking, flirtation in her glistening eyes.

"*Bagus!*" 'Good,' she exclaimed, examining her handiwork. Then she turned and collected her basket from the little boy who had mutely watched the whole scene. As she ascended the stone steps to the interior I found my voice, "*Siapa nama anda?*" 'What's your name?'

"Ketut," she replied with a generous smile. She inclined her head towards the temple, inviting me to follow.

Ketut stepped over the threshold and descended into the courtyard, not looking back. The little boy stared at me for a moment longer, his large, dark eyes curious, but maybe a bit cautious too. He turned and entered the courtyard as well.

"Well, OK." I said to myself. "Here I go."

The view was enchanting as I descended the steps into the grassy temple field. The women were all arrayed in multicolored sarongs and lacey tops, with glowing silk sashes about their waists. The men with their varied *udungs*, white shirts and sarongs tended towards the sober compared with the brilliant hues and textures of the women. I reflected that in the bird world it was usually the male that was the more gaudy. Quite a few of the men had black and white checkered sarongs - some special function? And maybe half the men also wore what looked like a yellow apron that was put on backwards, with the tie and opening towards the front. All in all, it conveyed a formality like a school prom, with the guys in rented tuxedos and the girls in fancy dresses, but more ancient and dignified. We were all barefoot, and intricate streamers woven from pale palm leaves stretched over our heads, suspended from long bamboo poles arching out from the walls. Flowers were everywhere, decking the multiple altars around us, the offering baskets crowded together amidst the orange marigolds and sweet smelling frangipani.

Occupying a larger, covered platform, over on the far left a group of musicians played a jangling music using what appeared to be giant xylophones and horizontally mounted brass gongs. A man dressed all in white sat ringing a small golden bell and chanting quietly at a small table at the far end. Honest to god, I felt like I was in the middle of a National Geographic Special and the electric thrill propelled me forward into the throng. Nothing had prepared me for this.

Looking to my right, I saw Ketut kneeling on the grass. She met my eyes, and with a nod of her head indicated I should join her. My chest felt like it had just got thicker as I moved forward and sat down beside her on the grass, Indian fashion. She slid the small basket of flowers she had before her in my direction, and as she did so the gamelan orchestra stopped playing and the few people who had remained standing found a place to settle. Long, informal rows formed and we sat in expectant silence.

Coming out of another courtyard, beyond the one in which we sat, a group of men and women all in white moved into our crowd, each carrying a small pot with a spout and a shallow bowl. At no signal that I could see, people reached into their flower baskets, selected a blossom, then held it aloft with the tips of their pressed-together fingers. A gentle touch on my hand and Ketut passed me a soft, yellow frangipani, then pressed her palms together and held her own blossom above her dark hair.

I gazed for a moment at her closed, downturned eyes and along the smooth brown skin of her cheek and neck. Wow.

I held my own flower up in the same way, not sure of what I was doing, but loving the sweetness of the supplication. Then everybody lowered their hands and placed the flower in their hair or behind an ear. How did they coordinate?

I slipped my flower into a fold of my *udung*, as I saw some of the other men do, and looked over at Ketut. Again she reached into her basket, this time pulling out a sprig of red bougainvillea that she held up to her forehead in her pressed palms. Everyone around me did the same thing, but with no particular type of flower, so I grabbed another frangipani and followed suit.

The third time, I was feeling more confident. I reached for a blossom and I think I saw a little smile play across Ketut's lips.

The small group of people dressed in white fanned out into our midst. Stopping before a kneeling group of three or four people, they would pour a small splash of water into the upturned right palm of each. The recipient would then sip the water from their palm. This was repeated until the fourth pass, when they'd bring their hand over their own head, dripping a bit of the scented water on to their hair. Lastly, each person would reach into the shallow dish and extract a few grains of moist rice that they affixed to their forehead and throat.

I watched, and when they stood before Ketut and I and we both received the water and brought the rice to our foreheads I didn't feel like a phony, even though it wasn't my ritual. I'd attended Catholic masses with friends and even an Ash Wednesday ceremony, participating always seemed to me a way of honoring people I cared about, and here in Bali, I realized, I was falling in love with a people and their way of being.

The music had begun again sometime back, but I only noticed it just now. Ketut gracefully arose from the ground with her small basket top and moved to retrieve her offering from the altar. She looked back at me once when she placed the basket on her head and then exited with a group of brilliantly garbed older women. Her eyes were friendly, but not what I'd call suggestive or inviting, so I turned and found Rod, Art and some of the others sitting on the stoop of one of the altar platforms over on the right.

As I approached, I caught a glint in Rod's eye.

"Becoming a Hindu?" he asked wryly, looking at my rice dappled forehead.

I grinned and felt proud for some reason. "I like to be part of things."

Wayan Krieg, our village Banjar headman, approached our group with a small tray laden with short squat glasses of steaming tea that were handed around. I could still taste the perfumed water from the ceremony, and now the warm, jasmine steam from the tea fitted right in with the incense laden air. The music picked up tempo, becoming more jangling and insistent, a whole line of young men rhythmically striking then damping the line of brass gongs. Others from the village took seats on the ground until we were a group of perhaps a hundred, forming a semi-circle around the musicians' platform. Elaborate kerosene torches cast a glimmering orange light over the assembly. At a sudden stop in the music, Art leaned over to me and roughly whispered, "The gamelan band is really good. Wayan told me that the Legong dancers are all village girls. This is going to be the real deal."

The band began to play again, now with a more melodic progression. I'd heard this sort of music when I was first staying in Legian, coming over the walls from distant temples and hanging in the humid thickness of the night. Now, from an ornate stone gate in the wall on the right side of the courtyard, a group of exquisitely costumed dancers began to file colorfully into the open space. For a moment I thought I recognized Ketut, but then saw the dancer was significantly taller. Her eyes looked left then right, without moving her head, her extended, decorated fingers bent upwards and moved in patterns I found both beautiful and disturbing. Her long, slim fingers bent the wrong way at the joints, pointing up in pronounced curves when the hand made a flat sweep in the dance. I looked down at my own hand and tried to duplicate the back-bending fingers. No way! Not even if I used my other hand to try and push them back.

The hypnotically precise movements of the dancers pulled us in and I felt I was outside of time. Not outside exactly, but 'back' in time, like I had somehow been transported back a thousand years and was in the honored presence of an ancient story from a time before words or writing. I was in another age, in a place unimaginably far away.

The dancers made their graceful exit, the gamelan orchestra playing triumphantly before falling silent. I felt stunned, and in the twinkling golden light of the kerosene torches people's eyes glowed and the light reflected off their teeth as they laughed and spoke to each other.

"What d'ya think?" asked Rod.

"Amazing! I'm blown away!"

I walked up the exit steps and turned to look back over the temple compound.

I felt in love.

Chapter 2
Sumatra

> "Security is mostly a superstition. It does not exist in nature, nor do the children of men as a whole experience it. Avoiding danger is no safer in the long run than outright exposure. Life is either a daring adventure, or nothing."
>
> *Helen Keller*

I
Lake Toba, two months earlier

The harbor at Medan in the northeast of Sumatra had the feel of a Mexican port called Ensenada where I visited a lot with my mom as a kid growing up in Los Angeles. Unlike Ensenada however, the majority of the boats resting at anchor were small sailing boats rather than motorboats.

We approached the main wharf slowly, threading our way through to the tie up. I was anxious to get going since the plan was to try and make it all the way up to Lake Toba today. This was the so-called "fast boat" from Penang in Malaysia and there were about forty of us getting ready to disembark. As far as I could see I was the only Western person around. Everybody on our little boat had bags and stuffed baskets and the majority were workers, bringing home money and goods from the prosperous island of Penang or maybe a bit further afield on the mainland.

I hoisted my pack and was again pleased with the slim, frameless design. Rock climbing packs were a new thing to me and I liked the way my little green Outward Bound hugged my back. It made my progress through the jostling crowd a lot easier. I guess being a foot taller and heavier than the diminutive souls around me helped too, but I made an effort not to step on toes, both literally and figuratively.

The noonday sun was brutal. My grey baseball cap, emblazoned with 'Nietzsche' in red lettering gave my noggin some protection, but my ears and neck felt the sting of the radiation. Under my tee shirt my skin was dripping as if I'd been running around the track at school in my gym clothes. A small man in a uniform made a downward wave with his hand, which I took to mean come this way and I followed the disembarking crowd towards a low building, cream colored with a brick red corrugated tin roof. Over the double-wide doors a hand painted sign proclaimed, "Imigrazi." As I walked, I fumbled around with my leather side pouch, trying to get it open and extract my passport folder. It had seemed like a good idea at the time of my trip planning to get a hippie leather worker in Venice, California to make this cool leather pouch that attached to my belt. I figured that there couldn't be any "snatch and run" if I was physically attached to my cleverly closed pouch with a tough leather belt. Mostly it was a pain in the ass. Too big to sleep comfortably with on overnight trains or bus trips, always clunking around on my side. Live and learn. I needed a better way to carry my passport, medical papers and traveler's cheques.

"Passport!" Official eyes across a worn wood counter surface. He was obviously standing on a stool behind the counter so as to be taller and look down on the incoming passengers. That put us just about equal, eye-to-eye as it were.

I handed him my passport and yellow inoculation booklet, but he pushed the booklet back, waving it away, and began to leaf through my passport. He stopped on the Indonesian visa which I'd had issued in London. He looked up at me once, stamped the page and handed it back to me with a wave that I should just keep moving. Welcome to Indonesia.

Blinking in the bright sun and dust in front of the harbor house, I saw a bunch of guys lounging in their bicycle rickshaws. It was a warm afternoon and most sat under the passenger canopy, their legs crossed on top of the side fender. A few were smoking the big fat clove cigarettes that went "snap, crackle, pop" when you inhaled on them. While we waited for the boat to leave back in Penang the air had been perfumed by a delicious clove tang and one of my fellow passengers had offered me one to try.

"*Kretek. Bagus,*" he had beamed.

It was a smooth smoke with a spicy clove aftertaste I liked, but I'm not much of a smoker and the dizzying rush that came from the strong rough tobacco made me feel nauseous. I didn't finish it.

I looked expectantly at the row of rickshaws and they all motioned at once for me to take my place on their passenger seat, moving on to the driver's seat and beginning to pedal towards me and the other travelers emerging from the building. A bus clattered past leaving a blue cloud of dust and oily exhaust in its wake.

The first rickshaw guy reached me and with a missing tooth smile and bright dark eyes asked, "Where you go?"

"Bus station," I replied, *"Términal bis."*

"OK!" he grinned and motioned that I should climb on to the bench. He was off his bike in a flash and behind me, holding my pack as I slid it off my shoulders.

"Barapa harga?" I asked – 'How much?' He rattled off a number, but it was too fast for me and he saw my lack of comprehension.

"Five hundred rupiah, very cheap," he nodded affirmatively, compelling me to agree that it was indeed very cheap.

Just on general principle, I pulled back my pack and started to re-shoulder it, saying, *"Tidak. Ini majal,"* 'No, this is expensive.'

I had no idea if it was too expensive, but so far it seemed like everybody hi-balled me when we talked prices. For anything, even a cup of tea. I wasn't yet solid on the numbers in Indonesian. From banging around in Europe and North Africa last summer I'd figured out a short list of basic things I needed to say in Greek or Italian like, "How much?" or "Where is?" or "Do you have?" It got tricky trying to understand the answers sometimes, but it was a starting place. Numbers were mostly pretty basic, but a lot of counting systems had quirks and I hadn't yet learned enough in Bahasa Indonesian to navigate well.

So I said in English, "Two hundred rupiah is enough." That was about half a dollar.

The rickshaw driver gave me his missing tooth grin and parried, "OK, three hundred," while pulling on my backpack.

"OK," I smiled back, "Three hundred, *tiga ratus.*"

I'd tried the bicycle rickshaws my night on Penang, around Georgetown.

The Appearance of Things

There, the driver was in front and I could lean back and watch the people and traffic circulate around us. The Indonesian version had me sitting on the bench facing forward with the bicycle driver sitting behind me. It was pleasant to feel the air washing over my face and not looking at somebody's butt. On the other hand, I was out there. I was the bumper if we ran into something. I leaned back, held on to my pack and just hoped for the best. They do this all the time, right?

We wound along the strand, the harbor on our right. There were food carts along the walkway and I smelled the sesame oil and garlic on the air. I was hungry and the aromas from the stalls made my stomach start to grumble. I looked over and made a motion towards my mouth, pointing at a cart we were passing. A stout looking man wearing a white skullcap was orchestrating with a stir-fry spatula in front of a smoking wok. In the little glass case on the right side of his cart piles of shredded vegetables and noodles along with a white ceramic bowl heaped with raw meat cut into small strips awaited his pleasure. We pulled to the side and my driver, with his constant grin, tapped his lips with his pinched forefinger and thumb, then pointed at the chef. I sighed and when the cart owner looked over I held up two fingers. I hoped this meant two plates of stir-fry. Casting a look at my driver I found him nodding in affirmation. Today we all eat.

A small hand lettered sign affixed to the top of the cart read *"Mee Goering Spesial 100 Rps."* As we watched, the chef deftly scooped the pile of noodles and vegetables he was cooking into a white plastic bowl and passed it to a man sitting on a thin rattan stool at the end of his cart. On the stall counter a drinking glass held light duty spoons and forks, and the customer grabbed one of each and tucked in. The garlic oil and the chili aromas set my mouth watering.

The eyes of the chef turned to me and I again held up two fingers. He glanced at my rickshaw driver and I caught a look of amusement pass between them. Using a small ladle he dipped a couple of good tablespoons of oil into the steaming wok and reached into the glass cabinet with his right hand. Fresh peeled garlic, chopped onions and a small handful of the meat sailed into the pan and immediately began to sizzle and hiss. He flipped it all with a large rounded spatula and, as he did so, pulled out what looked like an old Coke bottle filled with a dark liquid and shook a few squirts into the mix. The bottle cap had a hole punched in the center and dried sauce was crusted around the edge. The cook made a comment to my chauffeur and they both laughed.

An aromatic cloud of steam wafted from the wok. God, I was more hungry than I thought. Shredded cabbage and thin sliced stalks of something else went in followed by a generous handful of the soft noodles. More sauces and a chili paste flew in and then the whole mass skillfully whirled. A cloud of sizzling steam mushroomed up and I had a coughing fit when the chili oil hit my lungs. A last few swirls with the spatula and our *Mee Goering* slurped into the two waiting bowls. The chef passed one to me and the other to my driver, who stood chatting with him while I seated myself on an available rattan stool. The savory garlic sesame ginger exploded in my mouth and I gasped involuntarily, "God, this is fantastic!"

I would have probably licked the bowl if they weren't watching, but it didn't seem well mannered so I simply finished my bowl and gave the chef a thumbs-up he seemed to appreciate and acknowledged with a tip of his head. I fished out two hundred rupiah notes and handed them over.

"*Terimah kasih, enak sekali,*" I said. 'Thank you, very delicious.'

The chef regarded me with a small smile and nodded. I think I pronounced it right, but I found the pronunciation guide in my little Indonesian phrase book and dictionary to be pretty useless. I'd taken to writing the words I learned in my own sort of pronunciation key. Like "Tree mah kah see. Ee nahk seh-khali."

I hopped back into the rickshaw and looked at my driver, who made an exaggerated patting of his belly. We both laughed and off we went.

The bus station was away from the harbor road by two long blocks. The dusty streets were lined with bleak, two storey tall, unimaginative cement buildings that reminded me of cellblocks from prison movies. The ground level rooms were occupied by various shops and services - plastic buckets, electrical cables, bags of rice or maybe fertilizer, an incongruous ladies fashion shop with banged up plastic models sporting Islamic head scarves. The upper floors were apartments and I saw TV antennas and curtains in many. A few women, their heads covered in black cloth, stared grimly down at our progress along the street.

I paid my driver the three hundred rupees as he unloaded my pack and placed it on the ground. That grin again. He seemed like a pretty happy guy. Hey, I guess with lunch thrown in, he made out ok after all.

"*Selamat jalan!*" he cried, as I waved and disappeared into the station.

I'd been hearing good things about Lake Toba from other travelers and in my little "Trailfinders" guide so I made my way to the ticket counter and looked at the posted destinations. No Toba. The ticket seller, a small man with a trim moustache and wire framed glasses, looked at me expectantly.

"Lake Toba?" I stammered. No reaction, just a quizzical face looking back at me. Phrase book. I want to go… *"Saya mau purgi ke Toba."* Apparent understanding flooded the fellow's face and he nodded to the signboard behind him on the wall. He touched the destination "Prapat" and said, "Go Prapat."

From the drawer before him he extracted a thick yellow ticket and wrote the number 16:30 and said *"Empat ratus rupiah,"* four hundred rupees. I counted out the four notes, handed them over and noticed from the signboard that the 16:30 was meant to arrive at 21:40 so I was looking at a five hour ride and a night time arrival. So it goes. I also felt a little stupid for having just paid three hundred rupees for my ride from the harbor, maybe two miles. But, what the heck, I'd had fun, a good meal and at the end of the day we're talking less than two bucks - not a major expenditure. Some of the folks I'd met on the road had "getting the cheapest price" as their Holy Grail. I wasn't there yet. Maybe when the money ran lower.

It was not quite four in the afternoon so I had half an hour before the bus left. Toba sounded like a pretty interesting place to start in Indonesia, a huge fresh water lake in the center of Northern Sumatra, an ancient caldera maybe eighty miles long and ten to fifteen miles wide with a large island in the center called Samosir. When I'd bought my ticket out to Singapore in London at a shop in Earls Court called Pathfinders they had given me a homemade packet of tips and information about Southeast Asia, and in my Trailfinders guide I'd read that Samosir Island was the home of the Batak people, a tribal group that had been converted to Christianity by missionaries during the colonial times. I wonder if I'll meet any Bataks with blue eyes.

The afternoon grew thicker with the heat and humidity, and when our bus pulled out of the station the dark clouds that had been accumulating against the mountains began to drop a light rain on the dusty streets and the coolness of the moist air washed over my gritty face. I could smell the warm wet asphalt through the open windows of the bus as we rolled out of town towards the green mountains behind the city. The bus entered the agricultural countryside in very short order. Rice paddy extended on each side of the road and palm trees laden with bright green coconuts were scattered about. Dry palm fronds roofed the houses with simple, woven bamboo walls, mud filled yards, and children with large eyes that stared out at us as we rumbled past. Three men walking alongside the road had cut huge heart shaped tropical leaves from the lush stands of nearby plants and were using them as umbrellas to shelter from the rain, which was increasing in its intensity. Their reaching out into nature for a useful item that cost nothing and did no harm when discarded tickled me.

We began ascending into the mountains and the pond-like rice paddy fields gave way to smaller farms with terraced fields creeping up the hills around the simple homes. I could recognize bananas and tapioca as we climbed, but it was getting dark and soon details were becoming difficult to discern. Every once in a while we'd pass a more substantial structure, with cement or grey brick walls and the thick, corrugated asbestos roofing, but most of the dwellings were of the type we'd passed back in the low lands - palm frond roofs and the interlaced flattened bamboo walls. Now that it was darker the interiors were illuminated with the yellow gold light of kerosene lanterns and grey blue smoke from cooking fires drifted out of simple doorways and open windows.

About 8:00 pm the rain had slackened off to a light drizzle and our driver pulled into the parking lot of a large, well-lit building. I really needed to follow the red WC signs around the corner of what was apparently a roadside restaurant. I relieved myself into a cement trough that lined the far wall, along with about half the men on the bus. The urea ammonia cloud billowed up in the humid, close air, and I was glad to make my escape back around to the front of the restaurant. I washed my hands at a sink in the corner of the dining hall and took a seat alone at a small table amid a few curious glances by some of the other passengers. I tried to smile in return. Several tables were filled by groups of young women whose faces were framed by colorful scarves, their chatter and laughter filling the room. I couldn't see their hair, and it felt odd, like being with a group of young nuns. In Europe, in a crowd, I took for granted seeing a variety of hair colors and styles. The absence of that vista here was striking. The majority of men had dark hair, except a few older men who were grey or balding. More than a few wore the small white or grey skull cap associated with Islam, but there were also incongruous Nehru style black hats made of fur or felt. They looked hot.

I expected a menu, but as people seated themselves a busy cadre of service men and women began to load the tables with small white ceramic bowls of food. A large piece of trimmed banana leaf was placed before me and a serious looking young man deposited a molded scoop of white rice in the center. Two young ladies, smiling shyly, began to load my table with the array of bowls and plates I saw on the table of others - peeled hardboiled eggs in a rich looking chili sauce, green beans cut short topped with shredded toasted coconut, a plate of what I took to be portions of meat in a thick brown sauce redolent with ginger and garlic, deep fried things and oddly shaped things, green vegetable patties and fired fish and battered shrimp on bamboo skewers. Smaller bowls came, containing various sauces with spoons - I recognized chili seeds in a red sauce and one that looked like soy sauce, but was syrupy and had a molasses odor.

Taking my cue from those around me I began to select portions from the bounty placing them against my rice. On solid items I used my right hand and, like the other diners, kept my left hand off the table and in my lap. One of the oddly shaped deep fried things turned out to be a delicious corn fritter and I grabbed a second. I noticed how my fellow passengers skillfully worked small portions of the rice and other food into bite sized balls with one hand and then picked up the whole moistened wad and popped it into their mouths. It wasn't rocket science and in moments I was delighting in the fantastic array of flavors and textures. I loved touching my food. The dark chunks of meat were my favorite, a wild curry of ginger and chili and maybe camphor, flavors I couldn't name but that conspired together into one of the best dishes I'd yet had in Asia. I ate three portions, tearing it into shreds and hand mixing it with my rice. The green beans were cooked but still crisp, toasted coconut enhancing the fresh bean flavor. I must have consumed about 70% of what they laid out. Indonesian food was a knock out.

The bus motor started and the hall passengers made ready to depart, washing hands at one of the nearly sinks along the walls while the staff ran bills and change quickly to and fro. An older woman sitting behind a high counter was keeping an eagle eye on each table, totaling up what was eaten. She had a pile of flimsy white papers before her and with shrewd eyes sized up my meal, quickly writing the ticket. She passed the paper to the young man who'd served me the rice and he quickly came over.

"*Empat ratus rupiah*," he said, and handed me the paper. 'Four hundred rupia.' Not cheap, but an amazing meal, and as I pulled out the exact change I added a forty rupiah tip. The young man seemed startled and pointed to the 400 rupiah written on the cheque and pushed the two extra coins back to me. Tipping wasn't the thing here.

I settled back into my seat as the bus ground off into the misting night and must have fallen asleep because a bump jarred me awake. I saw we were headed downhill. Ahead the faint lights of a small town. The rain clouds had thinned and a half moon shown down, reflecting off an inky black, vast body of water that spread away from the town. The lake shimmered in the dim silver light. It wasn't late, but Prapat seemed to have rolled up the sidewalks. Our bus slowly groaned and rolled along the pitted lakefront road. The wet pavement of the road glistened in the weak orange light of the few scattered street lamps. At what must have been the market square, now abandoned in the dark of night, our bus came to a halt.

Immediately the jumble of passengers were on their feet, hoisting bundles off the floor, grabbing small bags and coats out of the flimsy net that constituted the overhead rack. There was a reek of vomit in the close atmosphere of the bus and getting out into the night air became a priority. I squeezed out the side door and waited at the rear of the bus while the baggage men removed the tarp protecting the bags on the roof. The laughter and chatter that had marked the start of our journey out of Medan was gone, more than a few of my fellow travelers were nauseous on the curving trip down the road into the caldera. The sour smell of the vomit coating the side of the bus reached me. In the upturned faces looking for their parcel to come down off the roof I saw grim determination and patience as well as fatigue that I too felt. It had been a long day of travel and the bright morning in Penang seemed ages ago. The passengers retrieved their belongings and disappeared into the night, slogging up darkened alleys away from the square.

There were a few reunions as passengers found family members or friends waiting for them, but my backpack was almost the last thing handed down and I found myself looking blankly around the nearly deserted square. The busmen had re-secured the tarp and departed in a cloud of exhaust. I rested my backpack on my foot to keep it dry and off the ground and scanned the fronts of the buildings for a hotel sign. There was nothing. Just a light drizzle, closed wooden doors and two light posts with small orange colored lights burning dimly in the quiet of the night. Great. I shouldered my pack and began to trudge in the direction the bus had exited. Nothing had caught my eye on the way in. Maybe the hotels were away from the square along the lake road. I'd walked about two hundred feet when light coming through the wooden wall boards of a looming, two story building ahead caught my attention. Stepping up on to the boardwalk in front I could hear muffled voices and some scratchy music coming from a small radio. Over the front entry a hand painted sign read, "Makan-Kamar". *Makan* meant food or eating and *Kamar* meant "room". I pushed the door open and three men standing around a counter stopped talking and looked at me. Their faces were neither friendly nor hostile, more curious than anything. I pulled out one of my phrases and hoped for the best.

"*Selamat malam. Ada kamar untuk malam ini?*" 'Good evening. Do you have a room for tonight?'

A rotund, balding man with a whisper of moustache and a wet look returned my greeting.

"*Selamat malam. Demana?*" 'Good evening. From where?'

"*Di Medan. Saya datang bis.*" 'From Medan. I come by bus.' At least, I hoped that was what I was saying.

He cast an eye towards the other two men and then back to me.

"*Ja, ada. Dua ratus rupiah.*" 'Yes, I have. Two hundred rupiah.'

As far as I could see, it was the only game in town. It was after ten at night and I was beat.

"OK. *Bagus. Terimah kasih.*" 'OK, good. Thank you.'

The proprietor called out to the next room. I took it to be the kitchen, pots and plates visible on a table within.

"Ali," he said and a couple more sentences I didn't understand.

A young man, maybe twelve or thirteen, emerged from the back and stared at me. The proprietor rattled off more Bahasa and the young man nodded, went back into the kitchen and then returned with a flashlight. He approached me and made to lift my backpack but I waved my hand and lifted it myself.

"*Tidak apa apa.*" 'No problem,' I said.

He glanced at me with wide dark eyes that held a hint of amusement, then, with a nod of his head, led the way towards a flight of wooden stairs at the far end of the room. When we reached the top of the landing Ali moved quickly down the hall with the flashlight and flipped a light switch, illuminating our path by a single bare bulb hanging loosely from a ceiling wire. He opened the door to a room half way along the corridor. I peered in and found it reasonably sized and apparently clean. The place was maybe fifteen by twenty but very sparsely furnished. The bed, if I could call it that, was a wooden platform about a foot off the floor with several pieces of flattened cardboard for a mattress. A small, rough wooden table, about two foot square completed the furnishings. Through an open window I could see the lake shimmering below. Not the Ritz but it would do for tonight, I'd head over to Samosir Island in the morning. Ali said something that I took to be an inquiry if I wanted the room. I didn't see a bathroom or toilet and I needed both so I asked, "*Demana kamar kecil?*" Where is the bathroom?

Ali stepped back into the hall and pointed to a door at the far end. I walked down, opened the door and found the light. The usual squat toilet and a tiled area with a tank of water and a dipper.

"*Ja, bagus. Terimah kasih,*" Yes, good. Thank you.'

We walked back to the room and he came in with me, saying, "*Dua ratus rupiah.*"

Pay in advance. Ok, fair enough. I pulled out the money and handed it over. He looked at me and grinned widely, and I was grateful for the friendly face. Ali nodded and walked out, closing the door behind him.

I contemplated the bleak little room. With a sigh I lifted my pack on to the bed, unzipping the lower compartment and carefully extracting my bottle of duty free Glenfiddich, protectively wrapped in my sleeping sack. I was pleased with my sack. I'd made the thing at home out of light-weight flannel to serve as my tropical weight bag. As I removed it and rolled it out it felt familiar and reassuring. Nestled at the bottom of the pack I had the thin canvas Blackwood rainfly, my floorless travel tent, and an old crunched down, war surplus sleeping bag. Too warm for that one tonight. In my clean well-ordered world back in Los Angeles, I'd imagined a layered approach and the flannel bag could go into the old sleeping bag when it got cold. I was thinking "Himalayan trekking" but the combo had served me well last summer when banging around in the Alps. I pulled out the old bag and gave it a shake. At least it could serve as extra padding. The cardboard looked a bit firm.

I was shaking out the flannel bag when there was a light tap on the door. Ali was standing there, holding a tray with a small pitcher of water and a glass. He placed it on the table and eyed the bottle of Glenfiddich.

"Whiskey!" he said brightly, and gave me a big-toothed smile.

"Whiskey," I replied in turn and fumbled in my pocket for a coin to give him. I was glad of the water and the glass.

Ali walked over to the door of the room, but instead of exiting he slowly closed the door and came back over toward the bed and table. I smiled to myself. The kid wants a drink of Whiskey. He moved to the bedside and sat down on the edge and looked up at me. Then he reclined, bringing his legs off the floor and stretching back, one arm behind his head, and looked at me with a sensuous, inviting glint in his eyes.

What the hell? Is this what I think it is?

As I stood looking down at him in my confusion, he rolled a bit on his side and brought one leg up, presenting an open shot at his buttocks. He hooked a thumb under the edge of his shorts and hiked the waist down a few inches, showing the coffee brown skin and the beginning of a plump curve.

I was stupidly shocked, like the time I stopped to pick up a young woman hitch-hiker. She was standing on the street in front of a cheap motel in North Hollywood. I opened the passenger door and said, "Hi, where you goin'?" then noticed she was wearing house slippers. She must have been all of fifteen, but looked at me like I was the biggest dope in the world. "Do you want to do it?" she spat, looking at me coldly. I think I turned a shade of red and I stammered, "Oh! Gosh! Sorry, no, uh, I thought you wanted a ride." She looked disgusted, stepped back from the open door, slammed it and stalked away, muttering to herself.

I felt that same shock and embarrassment right now, looking down at Ali's supine presentation. He looked back over his shoulder at me, questioning, and I shook my head back and forth and managed a, "*Tidak, terimah kasih,*" no, thank you. Ali sat up on the bed and shrugged as I stood uncomfortably to the side. He moved lugubriously across the room to the door, opened it and exited without looking back.

I had the butterflies in my stomach and sat down on the bed myself. The water pitcher looked inviting and god, I was thirsty. I poured a glass and sipped it – cool, tasted purified. I downed the glass and opened my bottle of whisky, pouring three fingers into the now empty tumbler. I felt sad about Ali. The view of the lake out my little window was lovely and I let my gaze wander over its shimmering surface. I had a sip of the malt scotch, feeling the liquid warm my throat and stomach. Its rich aroma and peaty taste brought back memories of good times with friends last summer in Scotland.

I took another sip and a flash of movement drew my attention. A wet spot on the wooden floor, darker than the blond grey wood of the dry planks. Then another drop fell away and I watched it descend in slow motion, all the way down, to where it hit beside the other.

I touched my cheek and it was wet. How could I be crying and not even know it?

I wiped my face with the back of my hand and had another sip of the scotch. The lake rippled and the scudding clouds revealed, then hid again, the rising half-moon. I had never felt more alone in my life. It startled me. My home and the people I loved were all on the other side of the world. The people who loved me. I had another sip of whisky and felt the odd tickling of the twin rivulets of water leaking down my face. Inside I was quiet, not sobby, not whipping up a drama. I touched the aloneness like it was a soft, dark fur and wondered at it.

The light of morning spilled into the room. The clouds had dissipated and the sky was a clean and brilliant blue. My mouth felt sticky and I poured some water. The lingering smoky smell of the whisky in the glass was not unpleasant. I put on my shorts, grabbed my towel and dop kit, then padded down the hall to the *Kamar Kecil*, the little room also known as the bathroom. I relieved myself in the squat toilet and wished I had worn my sandals.

I'd neglected to wash the day off last night and felt much in need of a bath. The *'mandi'* was a large blue plastic barrel, open at the top and filled with water by a wall spigot. A cream colored plastic dipper floated inside. I pulled off my shorts and reached into my dop kit for a bar of Dial soap. The water was chilly and an involuntary gasp escaped as I poured the first dipper over my head and shoulders. Cold fingers of water ran down my back and chest. One more dipper and I lathered up. It's the tropics, a fact that generally means warm and pleasant, but being up in the mountains made for cooler temperatures. For every rise of one thousand meters, you drop something like ten degrees Celsius. I rinsed off, dried and went back to my little room. It took me all of ten minutes to get dressed and packed up.

The stairs creaked as I descended and saw the proprietor in basically the same position I'd left him in - standing at the high counter and leaning on one arm.

An explosion outside caught me by surprise and I jumped. Sounded like a cherry bomb. The man at the counter didn't even turn his head at the sound so I figured, ok.

"Makan?" he asked.

This didn't seem like a place for good food so I shook my head "No" and said, *"Tidak. Terimah Kasih."*

He shrugged and had a sip of what looked like hot tea from a steaming tumbler on the counter.

"You going to Samosir?" he asked in English. His expression was of mild interest, just making conversation.

Before I could answer another explosion rocked the room and I looked in the direction of the sound.

"Christmas cannon," he shrugged. I must have looked surprised since he laughed and held me in his friendly gaze.

"You speak English?" I inquired.

"Little bit," he responded, waggling his right hand in a way I took to mean "so-so."

"Well, yes, I do want to go over to Samosir Island. Is the boat to the island near here?"

He nodded, walked to the door and out on to the boardwalk. I hefted my pack and followed him out. We both squinted in the sun and he pointed down the road I had come in the drizzle of last night.

"Go this road to the harbor. Many boats."

He smiled slightly and I had the feeling of talking to a sympathetic uncle.

"Thank you—uh, *terimah kasih*," I offered. He touched the middle of his chest with his right hand and wordlessly returned to the salon.

I set off down the now busy avenue. Another explosion to my left, a group of young men collected out on a small stone jetty, maybe a hundred feet off. They had a sizeable bamboo log braced in the rocks in which I could make out a small side hole cut in the lowest bamboo segment. They were laughing and shoving each other good-naturedly. One young man, wearing a white headband, had a wire about two feet in length with a dark wad of something burning on the end. As the others grinned and waited, he brought the burning wad over the hole and another "Kaboom" hurtled out over the lake. A small, white, smoke donut roiling after it from the mouth of the cannon. The Christmas cannon!

It reminded me of the carbide cannon my cousin Ted had to make noise with out on the ranch each Fourth of July when we were kids. Memories are funny things. I hadn't thought of Ted in a while. He was five years my senior and for most of my childhood, my hero and older brother surrogate. I was twelve years old and Ted was seventeen. We were out on the ranch where my uncle lived with his wife and two children. It was my semblance of normal family life since my dad had been killed in a plane crash when I was one year old and my mom hadn't remarried. She wanted me to feel like I had family. Most of the time, we felt pretty much alone, living in a suburb of Los Angeles. Coming out to the country was her going back to her roots and trying to give me some at the same time.

Ted and his buddy Dale were going to walk out to what we all called The

Sumatra

Auction House, a structure at the far end of the ranch built to handle the business of buying and selling cattle during the roundup. It was out in the open, near some of the stockades but far removed from the actual ranch house. Think flies.

The walk out there, through the shady canyons with their overhanging oaks and the small meandering creek was cool and pleasant on a hot day. I'd made the walk many times over the years. But I didn't like the night out there. Maybe it was that Halloween a few years back when they did the "fright walk." It had frightened me. Those cool glades were fear filled at night, the near complete darkness under the thick canopy of trees, the night sounds of scampering and growling, my imagination filling in the details.

Ted and Dale planned to do a guys' camp out at the Auction. I'd wished they would've invited me. I wanted so much to be like Ted, who seemed almost perfect. He and I would sometimes wander around the vast acreage of the ranch with our own .22 caliber rifles, doing target practice on the side mirrors of old cars that had been dumped in the river bed to control erosion. When I was thinking of learning to play the violin at age nine, Ted, who played the trumpet in the school marching band, said to me, "Violin! Violins are for weak sisters! Play a trumpet. That's a man's instrument."

I wanted to be a man so I took up the trumpet. Got pretty good on it too.

Well, it was clear that Ted and Dale had their own agenda on their overnight and it didn't include me. I was sitting with my disappointment on the porch of the ranch house, gazing out past the tall eucalyptus windbreaks, when Aunt Kay came out through the swinging screen door drying a glass measuring cup.

"You kids be careful with fire up there tonight. It's a dry time."

I looked up in surprise but didn't say anything except, "Um, ok."

A little while later Ted and Dale caught up with me while I was throwing some bread to the peacocks that roamed the yard with their strange, screaming cry.

"My dad says we gotta take you tonight so let's get one thing clear. You gotta do what we say if you're comin."

I looked at Ted. His eyes looked angry, his face petulant and annoyed. Dale stood back behind him and stared out at the windbreaks and the orange grove bordering that side of the ranch.

"Sure," I agreed, glad to be included.

Ted looked resigned and pointed back up to the porch.

"Ok, so you got to carry that black duffel. Dale and I will bring the rest."

Not long after we set off.

It was about three miles walk out to the Auction and the sun was low in the sky when we opened the door and dropped our bags on the floor. Four army bunks with thin mattresses were arrayed along the far wall and a small, cast iron stove stuck out towards the middle of the room, its bent and rickety chimney snaking up through the roof. There would have been electricity except that a tree had knocked the line down a few months back and my uncle hadn't got around to fixing it. Not Auction season.

"Too bad there's no refrigerator for these," crooned Dale, extracting two six packs of Rainer Ale from one of the bags. Ted pulled a third out of his bag and set it beside the others.

Dale nodded with satisfaction at the beer. "I'll go down to the creek and bring up a bucket of water to cool them down."

Ted looked at me again, that look without warmth, and I felt bad. They had been forced to bring "Little Vern."

"Let's get unpacked and let useless here get the water."

Ted handed me a bucket from the corner and I scuttled out the door towards the creek. I wasn't supposed to know about the beer. My uncle was very anti-alcohol after an unfortunate experience in his youth when he tore apart a local restaurant after the waitress got him drunk. "Big handsome boy like you ought to be able to handle a little liquor." My family blamed the waitress. I wasn't so sure.

I returned with the bucket of cool water and pulled back into myself a little bit, trying to stay out of the way as the big boys had their fun. I wanted so much to be included though. Ted got the wood stove going and the growing chill of the room was vanquished. He and Dale opened cans of beer and bags of potato chips.

The dusk turned into darkness and the flicker of fire from the open door of the little stove illuminated the room. Ted looked at me uncomfortably. He was on his fourth Rainer Ale.

"You are along with us and the beer's a secret. Do you get it?"

Dale took a long pull on his beer and glowered at me over the top of the can. Our faces glowed gold in the firelight, hard eyes on me.

Sumatra

"Yes, I get it," I said, a little defensively.

More beers. Ted burbled, "Come on. You got to have some beer so that we're in this together."

He winked at Dale who toasted him with an upraised can. I took the proffered beer and tipped it up. I'd tasted beer before, when my mom had parties or we went to somebody's house. Bubbles, kind of a weird flavor but ok. Not Coca Cola. Strange aftertaste.

As I began to take another drink Ted reached out and pulled back the can. "Whoa! We just brought enough for us."

Dale turned to me and said, "I've got a challenge for you. Think you can tie me up in a way I can't get free from? How about that! I'm like Harry Houdini and can get free from anything."

His words slurred slightly.

Ted laughed a wet, sloppy laugh. I knew they were both high. At the parties my mom gave, I'd seen plenty of adults get high. Usually they talked too loud and acted funny silly and everybody had a good time. I enjoyed all the cigarette smoke in the air.

"Yeah, that's a good one. What do we got here?"

Ted stood up a little unsteadily and began pulling ropes and leather straps out of a tack box in the corner.

"Plenty of stuff here, Vern. Come on, let's see what you can do."

He laughed again and waved his Rainer can at me.

I eyed the pile of straps and ropes, even a little piece of chain. I didn't want to do this.

Dale pulled an army cot in front of the fire and sat with his back to the light of the open door. Ted threw a couple more pieces of wood in and pushed them around with the iron poker. It was a broken branding iron and he left it nestled in the firebox.

"Come on," Dale coaxed. "We'll have a time limit. I've got to get out in less than half an hour or you win."

What did I win?

I started with his feet, making multiple figure eights with the thinner ropes. Dale used his free hands to pour down a fifth beer.

"Ok," he announced, "my hands are behind my back."

He folded his arms back and interlaced his fingers.

I tied the thinnest leather strap around his left wrist and then began to interweave. I used up three more straps and said, "Ok, now you got to lie on your side."

When cowboys tied up cattle they would have all four legs bound together in front, like tying up a bouquet. I figured if I tied a rope from the hands to the feet from behind that it would be pretty effective.

So there was Dale, trussed up and lying on the cot. I stood back, not liking the game. Ted took a long drink of his beer, weaving slightly.

"Thirty minutes, starting now."

He took off his watch and placed it on the bed next to Dale's head.

Dale burped, "Well, what do I get if I win?"

Ted and he looked at each other and then Ted looked at me, a sort of malignant light glowing in his eyes.

"If you get out, Vern here will give you a blow job."

I felt a stab of fear and horror course through me. I knew what that was. My mom was an interior designer and she would sometimes speak disdainfully of some of the men she worked with going down on each other. It was a wrong thing.

I stood up and blurted, "No! I don't want that," and made a move towards the door.

Ted was on his feet and he reached into the fire, pulling out the now red hot iron. He pointed it at me.

"You'll do it or we'll burn off your little pecker!"

He and Dale both laughed together. I felt sick in my heart. This was my older brother. My hero.

In the years that followed I asked myself why I didn't just leave. I was scared. It was like a mental paralysis, the fear of the dark all around me.

I huddled in the corner while Ted and Dale chuckled drunkenly. Dale slowly and inexorably freed himself. Ted glared at me from time to time and turned the poker in the fire. Maybe he won't get loose. Maybe I did a good job with the knots.

With seven minutes to go, Dale's hand came free and he straightened his legs, sighed, and began to undo his feet.

I was in hell, petrified, nauseated as Dale unzipped his trousers and lay back on the bed. His erection was sticking straight up in the firelight.

"I'm really going to enjoy this," he moaned.

"Come on," Ted growled at me, "we do this all the time. This is the cleanest part of your body."

Ted pushed me down beside the cot, so I was on my knees facing Dale's erection.

I slowly leaned forward and down, a tidal wave of humiliation engulfing me as my lips touched the glans. From within me the start of an involuntary wail and Ted's hand pulled me back. He looked a little sick himself.

"You make too big a deal outta this," he slurred.

I escaped back to my corner and hid my face in the crook of my arm. I heard Ted and Dale open more beers, the "kush" of the can as the pop-top was pulled. They talked quietly. My arm was wet with tears when I fell asleep, huddled in the corner.

Funny where thoughts can lead! I shook my head to clear the recollection and moved towards the busy harbor. The aroma of fried noodles and rice reminded me that I'd had nothing in me except water and whiskey since the bus ride from Medan.

The little market square in front of the harbor was a riot of multicolored movement. One of the small docks had a sign that read "Samosir - Tuk Tuk - Tomok." A little motor skiff, maybe thirty feet long and five feet wide was about half full of passengers. I noticed four people that looked European. Where had they come from? I was thinking I was the only foreigner in town.

I walked the short distance out along the pier and hailed them. "Hello. Are you all going out to Samosir?"

An attractive, curly haired blond smiled up at me. Nice smile.

"We're heading back to Tuk Tuk. We just came over for market day." She nodded back at the busy square. Australian or Kiwi accent.

"Any accommodation to be had over there?" I inquired.

"Oh, plenty. We're all staying at Brenards. Come on in, I'll show you when we get there."

She slid over on the bench, making room for me. I handed my pack to the boatman who placed it forward and settled down on the bench seat with my new companion.

"I'm Jacinta," she said. The other three stopped talking momentarily and looked over. Friendly faces.

"This is Penny," Jacinta continued, "and John and Louise."

Penny had a small but lovely face framed by a sort of dark pageboy cut. She smiled but seemed uninterested and turned back to her conversation. John looked like a Three Dog Night rocker with big hair and a dense moustache goatee affair. He was holding forth about something and didn't look back after the introduction. Louise, who was apparently with John, looked me over appraisingly. She had straight red hair hanging past her shoulders and a rather thin-lipped smile that tilted to the side. Her current expression suggested a wry amusement with life in general and right now in particular.

Samosir Island rose up in the center of Lake Toba. The near vertical escarpment that formed its backbone was emerald green with ferns and bushy palms. It was easily over a thousand feet tall and apparently stretched the length of the island. From the base of the escarpment the land was largely cultivated and sloped gently down to the lake. The slope itself was maybe half a mile wide at the settlement our boat was headed towards. Mists swirled at the lush, green summit and whirling birds supported themselves on the updraft. It was like approaching the Lost World and I could imagine dinosaurs roaming just out of sight beyond the escarpment.

As we got closer, I could make out a number of A-frame structures scattered about. They had a graceful, upturned arch to their roofline, as if a quarter moon was resting upside down in a jewel box. Their rectangular bases gave the impression of boats at anchor. Rice paddy terraced up the slopes, with all the soft shades of green imaginable.

Our boat pulled into a small pier with a sign announcing Tuk Tuk. On the way in, we had passed a lovely cove with a sandy beach. Jacinta had waved to a few of the people swimming and sunning themselves.

"That's our beach at Brenards," she informed me.

I followed the small group off the pier and on to a wide dirt path running along the lakeside. John, Louise, Penny and Jacinta were engaged in an animated conversation and I brought up the rear enjoying the warmth of the morning sun and the sense of fellow travelers.

Brenards itself was a cluster of the exotic A-frames, which Jacinta referred to as "The Batak Houses", as well as a scattering of bamboo huts with the palm frond roofs, similar to what I'd seen from the bus on the way up here. The difference was that these huts were built off the ground, raised up maybe three feet in the air with front porches and woven bamboo flooring.

In the center of the compound a covered area sheltered a long table with benches on each side. It looked large enough to seat forty or fifty people. The long roof extended over a ground level bamboo hut from which thin blue smoke curled and dissipated skyward. A woman in an orange and brown printed sarong stood in the doorway, surveying the scene.

John turned to me.

"That's Pepy. She pretty much runs the show around here…chief cook and bottle washer. She's the one to talk to about a room." He grinned at me and followed with, "See ya' later, mate!"

Pepy was an attractive, Polynesian looking woman, maybe early thirties. She had long, brownish red hair that didn't look natural but her wide face radiated joy and good humor. She was laughing with a seated group of westerners, all of whom were eating aromatic bowls of fried noodles, eggs and vegetables. My stomach growled at me that it was way past breakfast time, but first things first. Pepy turned her smiling countenance to me.

"*Selamat datang.* Looking for room?"

She studied my backpack and wiped her hands on a towel she wore around her waist like an apron. I returned her smile and nodded towards the bamboo huts.

"*Selamat pagi!* Good morning. How much do the bungalows cost per night?"

Pepy looked at the bamboo huts and back to me. Her high, elegant cheekbones reminded me of some of the Hopi Indians I'd seen on a trip through Arizona when I was a kid.

"All full," she said, matter-of-factly. "Batak house has place. Share with three other."

After the loneliness of last night the prospect of sharing with others actually sounded welcoming.

"May I look?"

Pepy nodded and led me towards the A-frame on the far left of the property. It too was built off the ground, maybe five feet in the air. Its upswept front had carved wood detailing with a Polynesian look, a Tiki Room for real. The frieze depicted four figures engaged in pounding rice in a central mortar. We ascended a wide set of steps and entered the generous space of the house. Four simple beds, one in each corner and plenty of space. The multiple open windows allowed good airflow and light. The place was clean and just felt good so I turned to Pepy and asked, *"Barapa harga satu malam?"*

She giggled at my attempt with Indonesian and held up her slim hand, a single finger extended and replied in English, "One hundred rupiah, one night."

About twenty five cents!

"Great," I exclaimed and set my pack down beside an unoccupied bed. It looked like two of the other beds had tenants, judging from the backpacks resting on the sturdy tables at the end of each bed. One held a guitar as well.

"You want lunch?" Pepy smiled. "Pancake, *mee goering*, what you like?"

Her smile was infectious and I laughed. I felt really happy for the first time in a while.

"Mee goering," I replied. Pepy headed towards the door, speaking while she walked, "You want egg or chicken?"

"Yes, thank you. Both."

I sat down on the bed. Not bad. I lay my pack flat on the end table, unzipped the lower compartment, pulled out my sleeping sack and spread it on the thin mattress. I felt relaxed.

Wandering out to the common area, I took a seat on the bench at the long table. A few others in groups of two or three were finishing up their food and the aroma of marijuana filled the air along with the garlic and chili. As in Europe, my fellow travelers tended to roll large, multiple paper joints with a mixed load of ganja and tobacco. I was accustomed to straight marijuana in California and it took me awhile to get accommodated to the European style of smoking. On one hand, it did make for a smoother, longer burn. Usually they had little rolled paper tubes in the end that acted as both filter and a holder as it was passed. On the other hand, I'm not a regular tobacco smoker and didn't like what it did to the flavor or my head. The tobacco made me feel a bit nauseous and dizzy so I'd usually use my little traveling pipe from Amsterdam. That meant not smoking what was passed which could be perceived as being anti-social. So far, most people were ok with it when I explained my tobacco sensitivity.

"Hello Vernon. Settling in?"

The mellifluous English accent belonged to Louise and she smiled down at me. She really was quite lovely with her aquamarine eyes and tropic tanned skin.

"Yes. Yes I am, thanks. I'm in the Batak house over there." I indicated with a nod of my head.

"Oh, then you'll meet Mike and Tony. That's where they're holed up as well."

A burst of laughter drew both our attention. John was again holding court with a group at the end of the table, waving a cigar-sized joint while he spoke.

"And then they'd have all us little ones in a line. The old Sister used her walking stick from behind."

John was either from Australia or New Zealand. My American ear had trouble discerning the nuances. His slightly nasal twang was fun to listen to and somehow made his stories that much more engaging. I had heard some of his commentary on the boat ride over and liked the incisive wit and his good sense of timing.

Louise smiled at him. He caught her eye and winked back, but didn't miss a beat with the story he was relating.

"So we'd all be the little ducks in a row and she's walking behind, talking about how so and so had been a naughty little whelp and running her cane up the outside of our trousers."

He paused for effect and took a long puff on the joint, pressed and exhaled.

"So Artie was looking a bit green about the gills and sister sets up right behind him and says, 'but little so and so wasn't alone was he?' And she runs the stick up between Arties legs and gives it a snap. Artie shouts out 'Bloody Christ!' and grabs the family jewels. The old girl grabs his ear and pulls him out of the line. We were all holding it in but crikey, it was funny!"

"John likes to tell stories about the sadistic nuns who ran his boarding school in Christchurch," Louise confided. I gathered from her measured tone she'd heard the stories before but didn't mind the retelling.

Pepy emerged from the kitchen with a steaming bowl of fried noodles and veggies and set it before me. "*Selemat makan,*" she sang. *"Minum?* Drink?"

"Lemon ice, *silakan.*"

My Bahasa needed a lot of work but Pepy seemed to appreciate my effort.

Louise had drifted over to John and they made ready to leave. John looked over to me, "Vernon, when you finish your tea come down to the beach and join us."

A goofy twinkle in his eyes.

I've always felt a bit odd about being named "Vernon." In grammar school my peers had regular, normal names - Mike, John, Tommy, Ned, Mark. There weren't any other Vernons. I was called Vern by most of my friends and relatives. It was new to be called Vernon by someone with an English accent. When Louise or John said it, it sounded rather nice, distinguished even.

"Will do," I called back and waved.

The beach was a short walk along a grassy path behind the last bamboo bungalow. Toba is a fresh water lake, and in my experience in California and Europe, fresh water lakes tended to range from cold to very cold. The surface waters of Toba were a silky 82 degrees Fahrenheit. Cool enough to take off the heat in the tropical sun, but warm enough to jump in and paddle about without catching a chill. The beach was carpeted in a lovely golden sand that stretched for at least a hundred feet along the shore. At the place where I joined the small, seated group I'd say it was about twenty feet wide. After the rains of yesterday the sand had compacted, but the surface was dry and it made a comfortable seat.

I spotted John and Louise sitting with a couple of guys, one playing guitar. John caught my eye and motioned that I should join them.

"Vernon, these are your bunk mates. Mike," nodding towards the guitar player, "and Tony."

I stretched out a hand, "Vern Castle."

Mike had a bit longer than shoulder length blondish-brown wavy hair. With his thin beard, moustache and soulful eyes set in an elegant face he reminded me of a young David Niven. That impression was reinforced when he gracefully stopped playing and took my outstretched hand.

"Hello Vernon. Where do you hail from?" the voice cultured and almost London but the little bit of nasal twang said more likely Australia.

"LA, Los Angeles, California," I replied, "How 'bout yourself?"

"Well, lately from Darwin, but I was raised up outside of Sidney."

I turned to Tony. He transferred the joint he was holding to his left hand and we shook.

"Tony Regan," he grinned, "out of Sydney."

Tony looked to be a bit shorter than Mike but more solidly built. His nearly round, pleasant face had a quality of eagerness I found appealing and his oddly turned out upper incisors lent his smile a slightly goofy Little Rascals kind of look. His blue eyes were a little bloodshot at the moment, his sandy colored hair was wire straight and sat on his head like a thatched roof.

"Pleased to meet you," I replied and accepted the proffered joint. "I guess we're house mates in the Batak house."

I looked around at the assembled sunburned faces and felt suddenly very much at home.

"How long have you all been here?"

Mike took the lead.

"Tony and I, what…" he looked over at Tony, "maybe ten days now?"

Tony looked a little confused then shrugged his shoulders, "Aw yeah, at least that."

Mike looked at John and continued, "John, you and Lou got here about two days before us, I think?"

John nodded, "Yeah, on December 10th, I'm pretty sure."

"We all came up from Darwin to Bali on the same flight last month," Mike explained, "but John and Lou flew to Medan from Jakarta. Tony and I took the boat."

He rolled his eyes and Louise began laughing.

Tony earnestly chimed in, "I wish we'd taken the plane. The boat was like one of those childhood torture tales you go on about," looking at John.

They all laughed. This was old news.

"So you don't recommend the boat from Medan to Jakarta?" I asked.

"Worst three days of my life," Tony lamented, his voice thick as he warmed to his tale.

"We had pretty rough seas," Mike added with a touch of humor. "The boat was packed chock-a-block and a lot of Indonesians don't do too well with motion."

I flashed back to bus ride down into the caldera last night.

"I think," Mike hesitated, looking around at us, "there was no part of the ship that wasn't drenched in shit and vomit by the time we got to Medan."

"I wore shoes the whole time and wouldn't set my pack down," Tony smiled.

A general groan, head shaking and laughter from our little group.

This was interesting news. I'd been thinking of taking the boat south myself. My little rough travel guide from Trailfinders said it was likely a better bet than the Trans-Sumatran Highway since there was no Trans- Sumatran Highway, despite what the government tourist office said. Overland travel to the south was possible, but not reliable. I thought to pick up more from other travelers here at Toba, see if somebody had come up that way.

"Do you think it's possible to go overland to the Java crossing?" I asked.

John nodded his head affirmatively.

"Yeah, there was that guy Greg, the German guy who was through here last week. He did it, came up from Pandjang."

John reached for the joint, "Said that there was a pretty good train from the port up to Lubukklinggan. There were minibuses between the towns, all the way to here, to Prapat."

He winked and said wryly, "If it was me, I'd go that way if I was headed back south. See the country."

A smile passed between him and Louise and I wondered if his advice was in the vein of the jokes that travelers sometimes played on each other. I remembered back to Cadiz, Spain, last summer, getting ready to go over to Morocco. An English guy had told us that when we get to Fez, ask around in the medina for Mooley Idris. He described him as a very cool guy who would be invaluable to know, would really show us the best of the medina. Of course, being historically illiterate about Morocco, we went to the medina in Fez and asked around for Mooley Idris. We found out the hard way that Mooley Idris was a historical fighter a hundred years back and asking for him was like going up to people and saying, "Please fuck with me. I'm a chump."

John took a hit on the joint and passed it to me. It was the tobacco mix again, but never mind. I took a deep hit.

"Heading down to Oz?" he inquired.

"No," I wheezed and exhaled. "Last summer I was banging around in Europe and I met quite a few travelers who'd come across from Australia and New Zealand. This guy from Melbourne was on fire about Thailand and India and was working in Europe, trying to save enough money to go back. I flew out to Singapore from London and now I'm starting to work my way back."

Tony looked puzzled.

"Why didn't you just come overland from Europe to here?"

"Well, my air ticket back to the States is out of London, for one thing."

I took another hit of the joint and passed it along to Louise. Mike plucked a couple of strings on the guitar. I was getting pretty loaded and it looked like they were too.

"And I guess," I continued, "Asia sounded more interesting. North Africa was OK but I came down with cholera in Morocco and felt a little burned out on the Arab and desert thing. Maybe it will seem better to me on the way back." I shrugged.

Mike strummed another chord on the guitar and looked around with a sly if slightly stoned-out grin.

"We had a chicken," he sang, "No eggs did she lay." Another chord, nice singing voice.

"We had a chicken...... no eggs did she lay......one day a roosta' come into our yard....and caught that chicken......right off her guard...."

On that cue, John and Louise joined in, eyes brimming with merriment,

"She's laying eggs now......just like she use tah.....ever since that roosta'...... come into our yard."

Guitar fanfare from Mike, laughter and applause.

"Who's for a swim?" asked Louise and without waiting, stood up, dropped her sarong and moved gracefully towards the water. I appreciated her lovely, athletic figure from behind as she glided into the lake. I guess we all did.

After our swim and the sun bathing and the ganja I was feeling pretty beat. I withdrew to the Batak house and stretched out on my bunk. I blinked my eyes and it was suddenly dark. Mike had knocked into his table. The clunk was what awakened me.

"Hey there. You were down for the count. Sorry I wakened you."

He smiled and continued his preparations in the dim, kerosene lamplight.

"That's ok," I mumbled. "I lay down for a minute and must have dropped off."

I blinked at the darkness and at the small, orange flame in the lamp.

"Some of us are going down to Tomok for dinner, sort of a pre-Christmas eve thing. Got an appetite?"

Mike's question startled me into the present. Now that I thought about it, yeah, I was famished and thirsty. I grabbed my canteen, had a long drink of cool water and made a mental note to line up more as my water jug seemed to be getting perilously low. I hated being without drinking water.

"Yeah," I replied to Mike's inquiry, "Where's Tomok?"

Tony stumbled up the steps and into the room.

"Got to find my torch."

He began rooting around in his rucksack.

"Tomok is the next little village down. It's about one klick, maybe a twenty minutes' walk. There's a restaurant we like called Mongoloy's. Good fish, from the lake."

I sat up, rolled my feet on to the floor and rubbed my face.

"Let's go."

Mongoloy's was good. The little restaurant was built out over the lake and the boards of the floor were set wide enough apart to see the water glimmering beneath us. It was a warm evening and the lake smell, a pleasant muskiness of herbs and a bit of fish, permeated the air. I took a sip of my beer and surveyed the company.

We were seven strong with John and Louise, Mike, Tony, me and the two girls from the boat this morning, Jacinta and Penny.

The fried fish and French fries were dynamite! Mongoloy, a youngish looking man of maybe 30, had a small kitchen on the shore and his pretty helper Betty would carry out steaming plates of food and cold bottles of Bintang beer. Betty didn't seem like a Sumatran name but the missionaries who converted the Bataks to Christianity obviously left more than bibles behind when they fled the Japanese. Towards the end of the meal, John used his fork to tap an empty Bintang bottle. Eyes turned to him.

"Louise and I would like to make a modest proposal," he announced. "The day after tomorrow is Christmas and tomorrow is a market day in Prapat. We spoke with Pepy and if we all throw in and buy the ingredients, she'll help us to make a proper Christmas dinner."

He smiled at Louise and she back at him. "The proposal is tabled."

"I second it!" cried Louise

"I third it," Mike and Tony said almost simultaneously.

There was something charming and touching that we strangers in a strange land were coming together to make a Christmas. We were all a long way from home.

Walking back to Tuk Tuk, the moon had not yet risen and the velvety black of the sky, with its glowing Milky Way, appeared as a vast dome over our heads. The bowl of the caldera defined the edges, but no city lights compromised the starlight. I felt my harmonica in my pocket, a G Blues harp, but wasn't tempted to pull it out. Too intrusive and I felt a bit shy. Then Mike, our resident minstrel, began to sing Silent Night. It was corny, but I guess we were all feeling a little corny. Others joined in so I pulled out my harp after all. This was, oddly enough, a song I knew how to play and I softly joined in as we walked. Jacinta didn't seem to know the words, but she hummed the melody with us. We went through "Joy to the World" and "O Come All Ye Faithful" then fell silent for the last bit of the walk, each of us wrapped in our own thoughts.

Next day, December twenty fourth, John, Louise and a Dutch guy named Ewoud caught the public launch over to Prapat to buy the ingredients for our communal Christmas dinner. Louise had collected five hundred rupiah from everyone, about eighteen of us all together, so we had a tidy sum. The plan called for four chickens and a couple of good sized lake fish that Pepy would deep fry. The rice, potatoes and other vegetables would be served up Indonesian style, which I hoped meant spicy and with coconut.

We had all volunteered for some part of the work. I noticed Jacinta had her name on the vegetable prep list so I discreetly signed up for that as well. I liked the way she'd smiled at me when I got on the boat to come over the other day.

The majority of the Batak people on Samosir were nominally Christian so us travelers having a Christmas feast was the most natural thing in the world. I was not sure what sort of denomination they were but, in talking to Pepy, I gathered it grew out of the Dutch colonial times. I asked Pepy, "Are you Catholic?" The sparkle in her eyes diminished slightly, "*Tidak!* No catholic." She managed to convey disapproval and I dropped it.

I'd walked up to a pretty little cream colored church on the hill above Tuk Tuk and had appreciated the jungle themed stained glass windows. The people depicted in the windows were all brown skinned and reminded me a bit of the Gauguin paintings after he'd moved to Tahiti. No naked breasts though.

"Hey! Let's go down for a swim."

Mike and his cheerful invitation snapped me out of my reverie. It was one of those crystal blue days when the humid air felt silky soft on my bare skin. Tony, Jacinta, Penny and a few others sat in an informal circle in the shadow of a palm passing some ganja. Mike and I plopped down and joined in as well. It seemed that the majority of our rag tag community were here, swimming, reading, lounging and generally enjoying the warm afternoon.

Tony walked out into the water and pushed the big log that served as our informal canoe further out into the small, clear bay. He flashed a zany grin back over his shoulder, "Mike, Vernon, up for a lumberjack roll?"

A stoned game of trying to stand upright on the log had developed and it was a good excuse to fall into the cool water.

Mike and I waded out and held the log steady at each end while Tony clambered aboard and rose unsteadily to a standing position in the middle.

"Ready?" and we let go. Tony's downward gaze had the fixity of a drunk fumbling for the right key at his front door, and we laughed and shouted encouragement.

I heard an odd clicking and whirring behind me and turned to find a group of Japanese tourists ogling us from within the undergrowth that rimmed the beach. What the hell? They were all wearing little tan colored cloth caps, dark glasses and sports clothes, Izod Lacoste. They were exclaiming amongst themselves, pointing cameras at us and obviously taking pictures. A slightly louder voice, a tall man talking to the woman beside him. It was all in Japanese except I heard the word "hippie" a couple of times. In my slightly intoxicated state it seemed hilarious that we were the local wildlife and I burst out laughing. Mike looked away from Tony on the log, took in the scene and shook his head.

"I reckon it's a slow day on Lake Toba if we're the best show they've got."

At that moment the log rolled and Tony flew off into the water with a yelp and an ungraceful backflop. Laughter, pointing and clicking erupted from the Japanese. It was brought up short by a staccato bark from one of the men and, as a group, they all turned and filed off through the undergrowth. On to the next stop on the tour I guess.

Christmas Eve came and in my blurred and sentimental consciousness, a romantic notion caught hold of me. "I am a citizen of a floating nation! A country with no borders, peopled by a drifting, churning population of travelers. We come from all over the world and speak many different languages yet we recognize each other, a Pythagorean society on the road to find out." The refrain from the Cat Stevens song rolled around in my head. I accepted the proffered joint and looked about myself with a deep appreciation. It was just days ago that I had touched the most profound loneliness I'd ever known. Now, like a whiplash, reality turned on its head with a heartfelt experience of deep connection and belonging. Being home.

My personal narrative swept me onwards and my eyes were damp with the beauty of it all. Penny sized me up and slid the nearly empty bottle of White Label over towards me. I refilled my glass. This ganja with tobacco stuff was pretty good. I had a long sip and gazed at the small group sitting on low benches, out beside the smoky little campfire. Mike and the Spanish guy were playing their guitars and the J.J. Cale melody and words drifted back to me, like the smoke.

"Call a doctor, and tell him I'm ill," Mike sang the words.

God, I was so tired. I started to stand up, but since I was on the bench at the long table the impact of my thighs against the bottom of the table sat me right back down again. I smiled at my mistake and swiveled my body out from under the table. I steadied and wobbled to my feet. The suddenly far away Batak house and my bunk beckoned to me. Penny looked over at me from a place that was also very far away. I wiggled a little tah-tah with my finger and set off for bed. And a very merry Christmas to us all.

I wasn't the only one to sleep in late. Emerging into the light of Christmas day, my mouth tasted like I'd been eating dirt.

"Morning," Pepy crooned soothingly, "*Selamat pagi.*"

The detritus of the night had been cleared off the table and a few of my comrades were hunched over cups of muddy Sumatran coffee, poking desultorily at banana pancakes covered in honey.

"What you like?" Pepy stood before me beaming.

"Um, hi Pepy. *Saya mau kopi dan pankek, silakan.*" 'Coffee and pancake please.'

Pepy gave me a thumbs up and winked, "*Bagus Bahasa Indonesi,*" turned and disappeared into the smoky kitchen hut.

I tentatively made my way over to the bathhouse and did what I could to shake off and wash out the crust of the night. Yeah, we all got pretty loaded but the insight of Christmas Eve was still with me, still felt true. We are a nation and the world is our home. My mind and heart wrapped around that story, like cupped hands guarding a flame.

II
Prapat to Java

I changed my mind about taking the boat from Medan down to Jakarta. It wasn't just the horror show that Mike and Tony had described, when I looked at Sumatra on my Southeast Asia map the huge tract of land between Lake Toba and the port at Pandjang called to me. Names like Brastagi and Bukittinggi and Buket Luan evoked romantic visions of tribal life and wild, exotic landscapes.

I wished John and Louise, Mike and Tony well on their journey and readied myself to step back on board the ferry to Prapat.

"So maybe I'll see you all down the road. When are you all heading out?"

Mike and Tony exchanged a look with each other and a shrug.

Mike replied, "I reckon we'll be here for a while longer. At least through New Year."

Tony nodded in agreement.

I looked at John and then Louise.

"That was the best Christmas dinner I've had in years. Thank you guys so much for the inspiration and all the hard work."

John smiled at Louise and took her hand, "I was just another hungry mouth to feed. Let's lay laurels where they belong."

Louise almost blushed, but the cosmopolitan stepped forward, "You just think you'll get lucky if you put a shine on it."

She reached out quickly and pinched his chest. He cried out in mock pain and everybody laughed.

It had been a wonderful Christmas dinner, the cherry on the top of my time here on Samosir. The water sliding past the gunnels of the little boat was a friendly, bubbling melody that sang "you belong" to my open heart. I inhaled the cool morning air cruising over the lake and looked back at the dock and to where my new friends still stood. Louise waved again and I waved back. I took a deep breath and felt the expansion of my lungs matched by an expansion of something else inside me. I didn't know what it was, but I like it.

Penny and Jacinta trailed their fingers in the water and spoke quietly together. They had decided to go south overland as well and we were unofficially traveling together. I liked the sparkle of interest I fancied I saw in Jacinta's eyes when she looked at me and wanted to know her better. Increasingly Penny impressed me as a bit of an odd duck and I wasn't sure what the basis was for the friendship between them. Maybe nothing more than being school chums and growing up together in some place called Paddington, around Sydney. Jacinta was the driving force, as far as I could tell, wanting to get to what she called "civilization" in Europe. It made me smile when she referred to it that way.

"Don't get me wrong," she'd say, "Oz is a great place to be from, but it's rather like being on an extended camping trip. One is glad to get back to civilization, take a bath and be back in the center of things."

I asked about her name.

"Jacinta? My mother is English and met my Aussie father in Spain. I think I was conceived there so I'm their little Jacinta, the souvenir from the good old days in Barcelona."

She laughed and I could hear both pride and amusement in her voice. I asked Penny if she wanted to throw in her two cents and she just scowled at me.

"Australian born and bred," she said crisply. End of conversation.

Our bus was an odd affair and must have been a local production. It had the aspect of a large sedan, something out of the 1930s but puffed up so that they could seat five people across on the wooden benches that crammed the interior. Only the front seat, with the driver, had a backrest. The other four rows were open seating so we'd all just lean on each other. Our first stop was a hill town called Bukittinggi and we'd be there by about ten in the morning tomorrow.

As the vehicle filled up it was all I could do to keep a space for Jacinta and Penny. I was sandwiched between the window and two smaller men in sarongs, wearing brown and black batik headbands and all smoking Gudang Garams, a popular brand of the clove cigarette. They were chattering together but I couldn't make out the language. It didn't sound like Indonesian, any more than Batak did. My efforts to save a place on the bench for the ladies were all for naught. Penny and Jacinta looked stricken as they surveyed the packed bus and the space I had saved for them. Then, the driver leaned out the window and motioned for them to join him in front. Score one for the pretty girls. The front seat was further filled by the baggage man and a neatly dressed woman in long sleeves wearing a headscarf. It was way too close and humid for that get up to be comfortable, but there she was. So our bus bounced south out of Prapat, finally getting underway about two in the afternoon. My bent knees already hurt and I sat up straighter, trying to relieve the pressure. It was going to be a long night.

The road south was paved for about an hour then gave way to gravel. Apparently shock absorbers were not part of this design because every bump and jolt transferred directly from the axels to the frame to my spine and ended at my teeth. I learned to keep my jaw slack and my tongue behind my incisors. Finally, I figured out why everyone around me appeared to be asleep and leaned myself sideways so that the banging stopped rattling my jaw. Take the vertebral column out of the equation. I watched out the window as the jungle closed in on the road and darkness fell. I was cramped and felt that if I couldn't stretch out, the ache was going to kill me. But I couldn't stretch out. I apologized to my wracked body and began to dissociate, trying to mentally escape the discomfort. At a certain point in the night, I must have drifted from a half dream state into a half sleep state because when I next opened my eyes night was ending. The growing dawn light rendered the dark roadside vegetation into a blue green shadow presence. We were compacted together by the many turns and bumps of the night passage through the mountains. I shifted my left shoulder and set off a wave of repositioning in the slumbering bodies around me. Miraculously, I felt rested and relaxed. The cramped torture my body told me was unbearable had evaporated. What was that about?

Gazing out the dusty window, I felt relaxed and light, as if I was flying. The red orange fire on the eastern horizon intensified until the disk of the sun burst over the edge of a far mountain ridge. We slowly descended a long valley and I could make out small, cultivated areas wrested from the jungle. A thin mist of smoke hung stratified in the morning air. My fellow passengers began to stir as well, stretching as best they could and blinking in the ever brightening light flooding into our little ark. The corrugated tin roofs of Bukittinggi poked out of the verdant forest and my bladder anxiously anticipated our arrival.

The town was neater and apparently more prosperous than Prapat. People streaming out of a green painted mosque stopped to observe our passage. Our bus halted in front of a ramshackle three story wooden building. "Grand Hotel" read the sign above the apparent front door. The sagging wooden steps didn't look too grand to me but I guess everything is relative. I unfolded myself and crawled out the open back door of the bus. Quickly ascending the short flight of steps I entered the hotel. I really needed a toilet. From the front desk a tired looking, dark skinned man with a thin black moustache looked me up and down. I imagine that I looked as rumpled as I felt.

"*Kamar kecil*?" bathroom, I inquired. He pointed to my right and I saw the "WC" sign. After I relieved myself I splashed water on my face to wash off the sleep. Great, no towels. I used the side of my hand like a squeegee and returned moist faced to the front desk.

"*Ada kamar, Pak*?" Have a room.

The compact little man nodded and said "Yes" in English. "How many nights, sir?"

The thought of getting back on another bus anytime soon made my heart shrink.

"Two, maybe three."

He nodded and opened a ledger on the counter.

Holding up one finger I said, "A moment. I need to collect my bag," then turned and headed back down the stairs to the bus. The luggage man had the tarp folded back on the roof and was untying the cross ropes that secured the pile of gear. I looked behind me and spotted Jacinta and Penny a few feet away, staring haggardly up at the baggage.

"Good morning!" I chirped, "That was quite an ordeal!"

Jacinta looked at me, blood shot bleary eyed.

"Oh yeah. Great morning."

Not great, I decided.

The baggage guy handed down my backpack. I hoisted it over my shoulder and moved to head back up the steps.

A bright idea. Turning to the ladies, I smiled charmingly.

"They've got rooms here. Would you be interested in sharing with me?" Hope springs eternal.

Penny flashed me a dark look and Jacinta blurted, "I just want to get out of this fucking country."

I fell back on a sympathetic response since the hostility in her voice made me wonder what was going on. What had happened since Toba?

"It was a hard night, all cramped up," I offered lamely.

"Hard night!" Jacinta almost spit. "Hard night pushing that bastard's hand out of my crotch every time I fell asleep," she nodded towards the luggage man who leered down at the two girls. "We had to take turns staying awake to keep the monkeys off us," Penny shot in her clipped staccato.

The baggage guy hoisted Jacinta's rucksack over the edge. I reached up and grabbed it for her. Penny's black bag followed immediately and he dropped it down the two feet into her arms. She glared up at him and whirled around, knocking an elderly woman in the head with her bag. The old woman raised a thin arm to fend off the bag, but Penny couldn't be bothered and pushed past her. I passed Jacinta her bag and we all retreated to the sagging wooden steps of the hotel. As if no intervening time had passed, Jacinta said to me, "No thanks on the room. We're not staying here. Going straight on down to Padang and getting the first flight out of here. Singapore maybe."

Penny stared down at her dusty sandals, nodding affirmation, her face a grim mask of fatigue and anger. I didn't know what to say but my foot is never very far from my mouth, especially when I'm trying to impress a woman.

"I'm really sorry to hear those guys were idiots. Is there anything I can do to help you?"

Penny's glower deepened and I saw the flashing fury in Jacinta's eyes.

"Yeah. You can break the neck of every Allah praising fucking tit grabbing Muslim bastard in the world."

That was a conversation stopper so I stopped, almost.

"Well I hope you can get down to Padang OK today," I lamely offered. "If not they've got rooms here that you could, um, have just together. You two."

Jacinta looked daggers at me and I bowed slightly, retreating up the steps into the hotel. So much for that fantasy.

The little man at the counter looked up expectantly as I closed the door behind me.

"I'd like a room please, away from the street"

"How many night?"

"*Satu*," one, I replied.

He looked past me at the door, then back.

"How many people?"

"Just me, sorry to say."

"Pardon?"

"Just me. *Satu orang.*"

The clerk made a notation in his book and turned it towards me.

"Write name, passport, where you come from and where you go. Seven hundred rupiah. With breakfast."

I filled in the required information and reached into my pouch for my wallet but he waved his hand and breezily said, "When you go." He passed across a key attached to small red plate, emblazoned with "Kamar 7". Room number seven, a lucky number I've heard, was on the second floor at the rear of the building, and the two windows gave a nice view of the mountains. The bed seemed clean and the little washbasin even had a white terry towel draped beside on the wall. The bathroom was two doors away, tucked into a corner of the old building, and boasted a generous mandi done in white tile with a full basin of cool, clean water and a dipper.

Something about a bath makes me feel that I'm washing away more than road grit. I stripped down and had a welcome bath and a shave with the bracing water. After the long bus ride and the cramped sleeping, the cold bath was a rejuvenation. Donning a clean set of clothes I headed down stairs to see what Bukittinggi had to offer. I was famished and the little restaurant on the ground floor of the Grand Hotel actually looked cheery and cared for. A clean-shaven young man, maybe my age, stood formally near the entrance and greeted me with a "*Selamat pagi.*" I chose a table in the corner with a good view out over the street and the open plaza across from where the bus had stopped. On a small rise towards the back of the plaza there was a tall, white clock tower looking incongruous in the midst of the surrounding hill town architecture. The tower was about fifty feet tall, the uppermost roof a nod to the Indonesian long house with its upturned corners. The rest could have come out of a small Dutch town, angular and solidly familiar. The clock face caught my attention because its Roman numerals were standard except for the number four. Instead of being a "one, vee" it was shown as four vertical lines, incorrect for Roman numerals but surely not a mistake?

The waiter approached me holding a small tray upon which rested a plastic wrapped menu and a napkin wrapped fork and spoon. He placed the wrapped utensils before me then stood back, a friendly curiosity in his expression.

"*Kopi?*" he inquired.

"*Jah. Terima, Kasih. Kopi susu manis,*" 'Coffee with sugar and milk.' I had grown to like the thick, mud like coffee with a generous dose of sweetened condensed milk at the bottom and right now, it was just what the doctor ordered.

He returned promptly with a tall, steaming drinking glass filled with the finely ground Sumatran coffee, a thick ivory colored layer of sweet milk on the bottom. I unwrapped my spoon and began to stir the mix.

The photo in the menu of fried noodles and vegetables topped with an egg looked tasty so I pointed and gave my best shot at the Indonesian name.

"*Mee goerin dan telur, silakan,*" I said. My waiter smiled at me and gave a thumbs-up.

"*Bagus Indonesi!*" he grinned and walked smartly towards the kitchen.

The rich coffee aroma filled my little world. I continued stirring the glass, suspending all the condensed milk. A few moments to let the coffee grinds settle out a bit, then a sip. Sometimes a good cup of coffee is what it takes to feel that all is right with the world.

A commotion on the street below drew my attention. Jacinta and Penny were heading up the hotel steps pursued by a small man in a skullcap, waving a paper folder at them and gesticulating. They burst through the hotel door and entered the restaurant holding their bags. Jacinta saw me sitting at the table and hesitated. I stood and opened my palm, indicating the three unoccupied chairs at my table. They both harrumphed over, laying their bags against the wall and flopped down into two of the chairs, Jacinta nearest me.

"You look refreshed," observed Jacinta. Penny eyed my coffee.

"Nothing like a shower and a shave after an all-night bus ride."

"How's the coffee?" Penny asked.

"A bit muddy, but I like it."

The waiter appeared from the kitchen and looked at the three of us. I pointed at my coffee and held up two fingers. The waiter acknowledged and returned to the kitchen. I knew from our time at Toba that they both took it the same way.

"So what," I ventured, "did you find out about the Padang bus?"

Jacinta was calmer, the fire that had burned in her eyes now replaced by fatigue.

"We've got tickets on the twelve o'clock. With any luck we'll be sleeping tonight in Singapore. There's meant to be a flight out from Padang at nineteen hundred, if we can get tickets."

I felt bad about her "good riddance" attitude towards Indonesia, but to be fair she and Penny were not alone in being hassled by the Muslim men here. Back at Lake Toba, quite a few of the women travelers, even those traveling with boyfriends, related tales of obnoxious, even violent confrontations with third world men. It wasn't just Muslim men either. A Dutch woman, Katje, said she'd had to pull a knife out when a Hindu guy in India had followed her off the street and into her hotel and tried to force his way into her room. It was apparently a lot more of a challenge than I understood to be a woman traveler in Asia.

"Well, I hope it works out for you, that you get the flight," I offered. "Where will you head from Singapore?"

The two coffees arrived and Penny gratefully embraced hers with both hands. No eye contact. Jacinta stirred her coffee glass and looked vaguely out the window, into the distance.

"I'm……we're not certain."

She shifted her gaze to me, not aggressive, just tired.

"When we set off on this trip, going across Asia to Europe seemed a good bit of fun. About the only part I've liked was Toba and that was because we weren't getting hassled left, right and center."

She took a thoughtful sip of her coffee. "Um, good. I needed that."

"At any rate," she continued, "we're keen on getting to Europe. Penny has family in the south of France and I've got relatives outside of Barcelona, in Spain."

Penny looked up then and said, "Y'know Cin, we'd better have some tucker here because it's going to be a long day. I need to fill my water bottle too."

The waiter arrived with my aromatic fried noodles and set the steaming plate before me. Both women's eyes followed it down.

"God, that smells good!" exclaimed Jacinta. Penny nodded and Jacinta said to the waiter, "We'll have two of those. Oh, and two water."

The young waiter stared at her for a moment and looked at me with confusion showing in his eyes.

My chance to be cool. *"Dua mee goering telur, silakan,"* I said as suavely as I could. *"Juga, dua bottle air minum. Besar."*

"Big water?" asked the waiter in English.

"Yes, *terimah kasih*."

Jacinta watched him go then turned back to me, some of the old anger in her eyes.

"That's what I mean!" she sputtered.

"I ask him for food and water and he turns to you! It's like I'm not here with these people."

"Got that right," grumbled Penny.

I saw what she meant. I was so busy trying to be 'the man' I didn't get how it must feel to be 'the woman'. Not much fun. I started to say something and then just closed my mouth. What was there to say? Instead, I picked up my fork and spoon.

"Mind if I start?"

Both women were in their thoughts and didn't respond. I spooned in a mouthful of noodles and enjoyed the burst of savory chili and garlic. As I ruminated on the noodles, I also ruminated on a memory from my childhood.

Sumatra

I heard weeping coming down the hall from my mom's room. It was just she and I, growing up. My dad had been killed in a plane crash when I was one and at nine years of age I was the man of the house. She hadn't remarried although she could have.

"I loved your father," she would tell me. "I don't want just another man. Your father was the love of my life and he loved us both so much."

That was that and so she worked as an interior decorator, independently and at a big department store called Bullocks, over in Westwood near to UCLA. I had a morning paper route, getting up early and delivering the *Valley News and Greensheet*. After, I'd head to school. When I came home, I'd do my chores - maintaining our big yard and taking care of our two Beagle hounds, Rebel and Scarlett, whom I loved dearly. I'd always try to have the lights on when she came home from work and as I got older sometimes I'd even cook up some dinner. It was the 1950s so I'm talking about Kraft Macaroni and Cheese or Uncle Bens Converted Curry Rice with hot dogs. It was good.

On this night, she'd come home after 7 p.m. and it was dark out. I was watching Dobie Gillis on the TV when the door opened and she came in with a few shopping bags. We said 'hi' and I heard the reassuring sounds of her unpacking and putting things away, the sound of a can opener and some water being run in the sink.

Dobie Gillis ended and I turned off the TV and walked out of the living room into the kitchen. There were salad things on the sink and a small pot warming on the stove held some Gebhardt's Tamales from the can. I thought they were great and was looking forward to dinner when I heard her suppressed sobs filtering down the hall. I pushed open the door of the bedroom and found her sitting on the side of the bed, face in her hands, long black hair hanging loosely across her forearms.

"What's the matter mom?"

Her tears always tore at my heart, and frightened me too.

"Stupid men," she hissed fiercely. "Stupid men on the floor at Bullocks." She looked up at me, her blue eyes with the little gold ring around the iris. "I'm sorry honey. God, sometimes I wish I were a man. I'd knock those bastards down." There was vehemence in her voice.

I put my hand on her back and I felt like crying too. "I'm sorry mom," I whispered.

She looked at me then, her moist eyes a bit swollen but changed now, the reassuring love in them.

"Oh, I'm proud of you," she said gently. "Come on, let's go have some dinner."

It wasn't the first or the last time that a window in my soul opened to her struggle to keep her chin up in a Man's World.

The plates arrived for Jacinta and Penny. The waiter also put two glass liter sized bottles of water on the table, and I saw that slight honey color and a small bit of floating tealeaf that assured us the water had been boiled. We finished our meals, making small talk about Toba and Australia. Most of the water disappeared into their canteens and we looked at each other. Time to go.

"Hope you make the Singapore flight," I said. "That's where I flew into when I came out from Europe. It's pretty cool. There's an area down near the waterfront they call The Satay Club with tons of food stalls. You could even go to the old Raffles Hotel and have a Singapore Sling."

Jacinta smiled, "Yeah, I hope we make it today. If not, tomorrow."

She studied me for a moment. "I can't believe you were in Europe and you came all the way out here….. for this!"

Her upturned palm moved left and right, offering me the current real estate.

"I'm thinking seriously of flying out of Singapore straight to Paris or London or Amsterdam, whichever is cheaper."

She glanced over at Penny who looked back at her, nodding affirmatively.

"We've about had it with the mysteries of the orient," Penny groused.

I'd loved my time in Asia so far and I was on fire to keep going. But my natural tendency to talk up things I like was not the order of the day. They were having a really different experience so I bit my tongue and tried to put myself in their shoes.

"After all the crap I've heard women have to put up with, from people back in Toba, I can't say you ought to do any different. John and Louise had some god awful stories from Java, don't know if you heard any of them?"

Jacinta smiled sadly, "Ah yeah, we heard them and others too."

The waiter arrived with our tab and we all paid up and made ready to leave.

"Maybe we'll go up Thailand way. Friends told us that it's a fantastic place, Buddhist and all that. Not such a hassle for women."

Jacinta looked at Penny who shrugged, non-committal. They hefted their bags and we headed out the door of the hotel and down to street level.

"Good luck," I said and offered my hand. "Who knows, maybe we'll run into each other when I get back to Europe."

Jacinta took my hand and looked at me with warmth and maybe a little amusement.

"Who knows. Worlds collide, don't they."

Penny shook hands perfunctorily. "Bye," she said, then took Jacinta's hand and they were off down the street. A touch of melancholy as I watched their receding backs. Alone again.

A hand on my left forearm.

"Hello Baba!"

I recognized the little man who had earlier been trying to hand Jacinta and Penny the paper folder.

"I am Hakim, the number one guide for tourists," he beamed at me. His brown, moist forehead glistening in the sun almost as brightly as his toothy grin.

Out came the folder.

"The Sianok Canyon is a fine thing to see, to begin. And here we have a fine museum from the Hollander times."

He shuffled the papers to reveal a yellowed photo of a colonial style building.

Looking down the road at the retreating backs of the two girls it surprised me to realize that the "alone again" feeling felt liberating and somehow spacious inside. I turned to Hakim and his broad, hopeful smile.

"Hakim, I've got a question for you."

"Yes, please, mister..... mister...."

"Vernon."

"Yes, please Mister Vernon, what is your question?"

I pointed at the odd clock tower across the street.

"What is the story of that?"

Delightedly, Hakim launched into his subject.

"Our city administrator had the tower built to commemorate the coming of the railroad in 1926. Mr. Jan van der Seet even had his six year old son lay the cornerstone."

This news surprised me. "I didn't know there was a railroad out of Bukittinggi." My information was that I'd have to go all the way down to Lubuklinggan for a southbound train. Hakim looked somewhat abashed and apologetic.

"Well the line is in somewhat of a disrepair and is not currently in service."

He shrugged his shoulders and his upward turned palms suggested that he too was frustrated with the state of affairs.

"When did it go out of service?" I asked.

Again, with a slightly apologetic downcast of the eyes, "When, in about 1947. After the Japanese departed."

"The Japanese?"

"Yes, yes, we had them here with us until 1945. They chased out the Hollanders."

He pointed to the bell tower, "Do you see the two carved rabbits on the front? Those were added in the Japanese time. They are Shinto religion figures," he said proudly. "Then the Hollanders came back but they did not do too much fixing up on the railroad. They left again in 1948."

The clock face reminded me of my earlier observation.

"Hakim, all the hours are Roman Numerals except for number four. That isn't how to write four in Roman Numerals."

Hakim looked up at the tower. "Ah, Mr. Vernon, *pintar* eh? That not a mistake. The Hollanders brought Java men to do the building work. In the making of this tower four Java men killed and Tuan van der Seet make this memory of their death. You see, the one, two, three, four that is for the Java men who died."

Knows his stuff, give him that, "So Hakim, I'm here alone. How much to show me the wonders of Bukittinggi?"

Hakims face beamed, "Oh, I'm the number one guide and we will see many fine things!"

He whirled and made a downward scooping motion sort of wave to a man across the street sitting languidly in a horse cart. The cart was a worn blue and yellow wooden box mounted on what looked to be the rear end of a pick-up truck, worn rubber tires on an axel. The slack jawed old horse had a "seen it all" look of resignation on his face. The driver sat up straight at Hakim's signal and shook the reins.

"Just a moment, please, Hakim. Before we start I want to know how much you will charge to see these many fine things. How long do we go?"

Hakim turned his round face to me, his open palms outstretched as if he as checking for rain, "As you like!" then an extra big smile and he started to turn back to the approaching horse cart.

I wanted to laugh at the absurdity of the interaction but my inner businessman stepped forward, "Hakim, I want a fixed price and a plan. No price, no plan, no deal."

Hakim did not respond so I turned and began walking up the street. I wasn't really sure where I was off to but deciding to let go of this slippery interaction before it went any further.

"Mr. Vernon! Mr. Vernon!" Hakim raced behind me and caught at my departing elbow.

"Price five thousand rupee, all day going. We will visit the canyon, a very fine and natural place. And also Colonial Museum and city historical places. Five thousand rupiah, OK?"

His eager face implored me to agree with this very fine price.

"Two thousand rupiah," I countered, "including taxi," and cocked a thumb at the horse cart.

Hakim's face fell and he shook his head at the terrible news, "Oh, not possible Mr. Vernon. Not possible two thousand rupiah."

He hesitated and his face brightened, "OK, morning price, you are the first customer of the day. Four thousand rupiah, best price. We go." He started to turn again towards the cart and I placed my hand on his shoulder, "Hakim, we go for three thousand rupiah. *Tiga ribu cucup.*" Three thousand is enough. He tilted his head to the side, his face less happy but he agreed, "Three thousand rupiah, ok. We go!"

We climbed into the cart and he gave rapid-fire instructions to the driver, who nodded and shook the reins of the old horse. As we rolled up a gentle slope away from the hotel and clock tower, Hakim recovered his good spirits, happy at least to actually have a customer. "That is the colonial office," indicating a long two story building painted a light blue and protected with a red, corrugated metal roof. "Now it is the library and office of the administrator."

The morning stretched into the afternoon and by the time we returned to the plaza the shadows were lengthening and my butt ached from bouncing along on the wooden seat. We'd enjoyed a sumptuous lunch of spicy roasted chicken at a little restaurant overlooking the canyon. I had a cool Bintang, the local beer. When I offered Hakim a glass, he held up his hand, "No, thank you very much. I am Muslim and no alcohol."

Later, we stopped on our tourist pilgrimage at a simple neighborhood mosque that Hakim called a "moss-key." He invited me to sit within while he did his prayers. There was an appealing, meditative silence inside that attracted me. The ornate arched entryways and geometric designs on the walls with Arabic script reminded me of Morocco. I had been impressed there with the elegance of the architecture and the single mindedness of the men at prayer. Here, the ambience of a tropical outpost from a desert culture added a layer of charm. Still, it was also an outpost of another western, theistic culture and seemed to me not all that different from the intrusive and self-righteous Dutch colonials of whom Hakim was critical during our museum visit.

I stepped down from the horse cart and passed Hakim the agreed three thousand rupees. Although I'd paid for his lunch I added an extra five hundred rupiah. He acted a bit surprised and looked up at me with his broad smile.

"Thank you Hakim for the tour of Bukittinggi. It was a most excellent time."

"Oh yes, Mr. Vernon. Here," he fumbled in his small folder, "take my cards and recommend me to your friends. I will be most happy to see them."

I wished Hakim, the driver and the horse a fond "*Selamat jalan,*" and mounted the steps into the Grand Hotel. Hakim's words, to "tell my friends" had evoked a touch of gloom. The sense of being a stranger in a strange land, which had evaporated in our little instant community at Lake Toba, shadowed my awareness. Time to move on, I decided.

"Excuse me," I addressed the desk clerk, "where can I find out about a bus to Lubuklinggan?"

The man behind the desk hesitated and then seemed to recognize me.

"Bus to Lubuklinggan?"

I nodded in the affirmative.

He walked towards the door and motioned for me to follow. We stood on the porch, blinking in the dusty, late afternoon light and he pointed off to the right.

"You see big tree and *Kantor Pos?*"

I did.

"There, other corner." A red and green single story building. Parked in front a Toyota pick-up truck, fitted out with bench seats. A small crowd was milling around, unloading bags from the roof rack.

"*Terimah kasih*," I thanked him.

He saw I understood, bowed slightly and returned to the interior of the hotel lobby.

The "bus" to Lubuklinggan departed at 8:00 am. I'd spent a quiet evening in my hotel room reading *One Flew Over the Cuckoo's Nest* and was up early, breakfasted and waiting in front of the ticket office by 7:30 am. My fellow passengers sat on burlap bundles, most wearing the colorful, long Sumatran sarongs and chatting contentedly. Many sipped coffee and smoked Gudang Garums, the clove cigarettes that went "snap, crackle, pop" when you inhaled. The morning air was cool and the clove-spiced smoke, an incense I was coming to enjoy. It smelled like Indonesia.

The clattering drew all of our attention when our bus came around the corner. The vehicle was a small flatbed truck that had been fitted with the now familiar wooden benches and topped with a sturdy pipe and sheet metal roof and a luggage rack. A narrow ladder on the rear gave roof access and two men wearing dark Nehru hats sat on top, grinning down at us. That it was an open-air affair actually reassured me. Nobody was going to vomit against a closed window and stink up the joint.

I joined the crowd at the back of the bus and handed up my pack then located a good spot on the middle bench, over on the right side where I had a backrest and a wide view of the world outside. Amidst the chattering and laughter, the limp ghost of loneliness from last night evaporated and I had that sense of excitement and wellbeing that precedes the beginning of a new adventure. That's what made being on the road different. The rolling forward, stopping for a while when in paradise or moving on when it wasn't. I could reinvent my own existence every day and while there could be loneliness or fear, there could also be great joy and freedom, the kind of freedom I sometimes touched when backpacking in the High Sierra. I could be miles from the nearest road, deep in the high wilderness, in the high lonesome, yet not lonely. As though I was enfolded in the gentle, loving essence of life itself. The deep quality of freedom I knew at those times was similar to this moment - heading out on a weird truck bus into the jungles of Sumatra, surrounded by a new people and language - alone but not alone. There have been times in my life when I could literally feel myself growing. Alice eats a cookie and begins to grow larger. She was expanding into an unknown universe and so it felt to me, when the bus ground its gears and we bounced out of Bukittinggi.

The rainforest of Central Sumatra stretched away from the road on both sides. The tumble of trees and vines, the dense broadleaf understory limited my visual horizon, but still tantalizing glimpses of the forest floor punctuated our passage. Ahead and to the rear a canopy of tall tropical hardwoods arched over the road which wasn't really a road. In the wake of our passage, muddy water refilled the ruts cut by the truck tires. I leaned out and looked ahead, wondering at the multihued green wall before us. What road? It really impressed me as more of a glorified footpath cut through the undergrowth.

A little past noon we squished to a halt on a red mud riverbank. Pee stop. We tumbled out to relieve ourselves in the undergrowth. Don't get bit in the nuts by a cobra. Do they have cobras in Sumatra? I didn't stray too far in my quest for privacy and I noticed that none of my fellow passengers did either. Returning to stand by the front of the truck, we looked out over a dauntingly wide brown river that was flowing at a pretty good clip. Three sets of thick ropes spanned from our side to a station on the far side of the river, maybe a hundred and fifty feet away.

A barge constructed from multiple layers of crisscrossed bamboo was moving towards us. Perched atop was a Toyota pickup truck and a small team of men wielding long bamboo pushing poles. The sides of the barge had large metal eyes through which two of the spanning ropes passed. The third rope was affixed to the middle of the barge and I followed it down to a platform on the riverbank below us. It was wrapped several times around a large drum that was turning slowly, a diesel motor spouting black exhaust. A team of three men was pulling on the rope to keep it tight on the drum and feeding it behind them. They looked like they were working as hard as the motor to keep up the tension. The chugging motor was noisy, even though it appeared to have a muffler in the line of its six foot tall smoke stack.

The barge slowly approached the riverbank. I could make out a complementary line running back to the station on the other side of the river. It was pretty far away but it appeared that a similar engine and drum was installed over there. Quite an operation.

Some movement in the trees, up river on our side, caught my attention. A troop of large monkeys with blondish white short hair and black faces cavorted in the branches of the canopy. Some of my fellow passengers looked towards their noisy screeching, but then turned back to the more interesting river crossing action below us. The scene was striking, beautiful, with the curved sweep of the river coming down to us, the clear blue of the sky and leaf filtered sunlight dancing on the forest floor, the graceful bodies of the tall trees and hanging vines.

With a wet suck, the barge impacted the soft red mud bank. Men moved forward to place runner planks for the truck to exit. The Toyota roared to life, a plume of oily blue smoke wafting out and over us. The truck gingerly rolled off the barge on to the shore. The driver waved to all and sundry, disappearing along the jungle path from which we had come.

Our bus was a lot bigger and top heavy with all the gear stowed in the roof rack. Our driver gunned the motor and began to creep down the muddy slope. Lots of shouting and frenetic activity as the bargemen positioned and repositioned the runners to be the right distance apart. As the bus began to climb up the ramps the nose of the barge bowed and creaked, settling deeper into the water until it was almost awash. Finally, the barge must have touched rocky bottom because it stopped its descent. The bus now eased itself on to the front of the raft. I was wondering how the hell I'd get my backpack if the whole thing just flipped over and sank. Slowly, the rear wheels passed from the ramp on to the barge and the bus moved to the center of the platform. That shift allowed the swallowed front of the barge to resurface out of the mud. The sound reminded me of a toothless old man sucking on a Fudgesicle. More shouting, and the bargemen pulled the ramps aboard and began leaning into their bamboo poles to push out into the river.

We all watched silently while the barge slowly made its way across to the far side and a few of us cheered when it successfully negotiated the landing. It

The Appearance of Things

must not have been a busy day since there was nobody waiting on the other side and the barge made its return trip unladen, except for the pole men.

Now it was our turn to board the raft. I stepped out the ramp and on to the barge without much fuss. Some of my fellow passengers were not at all pleased about the gangplank over the water, eyes full of apprehension. One older woman, wailing and clutching her chest, needed to be pulled from the front and pushed from behind by her relatives. When she was finally aboard her fear turned to anger and she swatted at the man pushing from behind. He dodged the blow artfully and the people around them laughed.

Pulling away towards the center of the river everyone was seated on the raft, a colorful pile of scarves and sarongs and Nehru hats. There was a tension. People were silent as if a collective breath was being held until we were across. When the raft bumped the far shore there was a palpable relief in our little group and we began to pile off the gangplanks on to the riverbank.

I was about thirty feet up the bank when a woman's piercing shriek startled me and I whirled around. A young man of maybe twenty five had stumbled on the plank and fallen sideways into the river. His young wife was screaming and being held from falling herself. The fellow came up gasping for a moment, eyes wide with panic and lashing out with his thin arms for any support. Finding none he disappeared under the water again. I began to move down the slope, wondering why he didn't just stand up, being three feet from shore. Before I got close a boatman leapt into the water and came up with the limp and sputtering swimmer. The current began to carry them away from the shore and everybody was screaming. A second boatman thrust his long bamboo pole at an angle between the barge and the shore and the rescuer was able to grab on to it, leveraging himself and the other towards the riverbank. A small mob of shouting men grabbed them both, hauling the pair unceremoniously on to the muddy bank. It all happened so fast I felt rooted to the ground where I stood. The young man was on his stomach, muddy and coughing, arms stretched out before him, fingers dug into the riverbank. His wife was hysterical, still crying and wailing, shoving through the gathered crowd over towards him. He heard her and sat up now, sagging and wasted on the sodden earth. Time started again and he was standing and his wife was weeping and holding his hand, alternately squeezing and tugging at his arm. A few of the women put comforting hands on her back. An older man with a bald head and grey moustache came up from behind and threw a green cloth over his shoulders. The young man looked stricken, more I thought from mortification than from any physical damage. He and his wife were bundled into our waiting bus and we set off again. I couldn't understand what was being said, but everybody around me seemed to be either telling a story or listening to one.

In that agitated hubbub, we soon pulled into a small village that, to my untrained eye, looked to be made completely of found materials from the jungle. It lay beside a small river of clear, flowing water that looked black owing to the leaf litter on the bottom. We halted aside a fairly spacious open-air building and everybody poured out. Lunch stop. The driver and the luggage boys used buckets to heft clean water from the stream and wash the mud off the wheels and low sides of the bus. They spoke animatedly and I imagined they were talking about the near drowning.

The little *warung* had low walls of woven bamboo, palm frond roofing and fixed tables and benches also made from bamboo. If there had been a fire, there'd be nothing left but ash. A few of the passengers had ordered food from the small, dark woman who now looked at me guardedly from the kitchen hut. Most of the others pulled out triangular packets of banana leaf that contained a variety of vegetables, rice and maybe fish or eggs or meat. They chatted contentedly, eating with their right hand.

I smiled at the woman in the kitchen and made the scooping "come hither" motion I had seen others employ. She approached tentatively, staring, as if undecided whether to stay or run. I sort of wanted to shout "boo!" but figured if I was going to get a bite to eat I'd better not joke around. When she was a few yards away, I asked in my best Indonesian, *"Ada mee goering?"* 'Do you have fried noodle?'

Her expression told me she was surprised I could speak and she answered cautiously, *"Jah, ada."*

I added, *"Dengan daging o telur?"* 'With meat or egg?'

Again she replied, *"Jah, ada"* but now with less hesitation.

I held up my index finger, *"Satu, silakan,"* 'One please.' *"Dan the,"* 'And tea.'

I was thirsty but I wanted to be sure the water had been boiled.

She withdrew into the kitchen and I heard rattling and banging.

The little stream had a friendly look, as did the town, really just a wide spot in the road with maybe a dozen simple huts along the riverbank. Still, it was my first real jungle settlement and looking around I noticed paddocks out through the undergrowth and cleared areas with neat rows of leafy green plants. A plow made completely from hardwoods leaned against the wall of one of the sheds. I sat musing, my right arm draped on the railing of the restaurant wall. An old man had come around one of the huts and was looking me over. I smiled towards him. He began to walk slowly towards me, his face tentative like the woman in the kitchen, fearful apparently. Did I look like I was going to bite? What was going on here? First the lady cook and now this. I guess I'm the scary foreigner. Maybe they didn't get out much.

The old man now came up across from me, eyes on mine and slowly reached out his hand. I was wearing short sleeves and my forearm was exposed, resting on the railing. Keeping his eyes on mine, which I hoped looked friendly to him, he began to touch the hair on my arm. It startled me but I made the effort to keep a friendly engagement with my eyes, *"Apa kabar, bapak?"* 'How are you father?' I asked.

He relaxed and smiled back, rubbing the hair on my arm more vigorously. What is going on? Then he held a pinch of hair and looked over at the other passengers and said something. Everybody began to laugh and he looked back at me, his eyes merry. He patted my arm and bobbed his head up and down. My Indonesian wasn't that great, but what he said didn't sound anything like that language. He patted my arm some more, smiling at me, then turned and shuffled away. Some of the other passengers were still grinning, but it didn't feel malicious. Wow! They really don't get out much!

My banana leaf arrived with a pile of steaming noodles, vegetables and meat bits. I recognized the onions but the other leaves were new. The taste was delightful, herb and spice combinations I didn't recognize with a sort of camphor and mustard back flavor. The meat was a bit stringy but had been previously cooked curry style and it added to the overall richness of the dish. Jungle noodles!

We made ready to go and I walked over to the little kitchen hut to pay up. The cook was squatting in front of a small fire on the ground. A tripod of round rocks supported a spherical metal pot bubbling away with something savory. This was the first and only metal I'd seen in the village.

"Barapa harga?" 'How much?' I asked. She held up two fingers, *"Dua ratus rupiah."*

I dug into my billfold and noticed a child sitting on a mat in the darkened corner. A pair of small black puppies tumbled on the floor beside the child, a little girl. She giggled and held up one of the puppies by the front right leg and it began to screech in pain. Then she dropped it. Extracting two hundred rupee notes, I looked back to the seated woman. My eyes, now more accustomed to the dim interior, caught the small black pelt, with bloody paws still attached, beside the bubbling pot.

I swallowed, handed over the bank notes and retreated from the cooking shed. The texture of the curried meat leapt to mind. "Oh shit!"

My mind told me to be repulsed, but another voice said, "Well you're out in the world. New things are going to happen." I shrugged and headed for the bus.

The multihued greens and browns of the forest flowed past as the bus rolled on and I felt dreamy, full after my lunch. Puppy chow will never sound the same.

It was interesting, this feeling of confidence that was tangibly expanding within me. It had been some time since I felt confident about anything. I'd left UCLA twelve units short of my degree in Zoology, pre-med. A dream had yanked my youthful self-confidence out from under me while I was studying for the MCATS, the medical school entrance exam.

I was standing in front of a Parthenon-like building at midday. Wide white marble steps led up to the thick Doric columns framing the entrance to the building. Looking down at my right hand I found that I was gripping a power drill with a sharpened bit fixed in place. I pointed the drill at the building and charged up the steps, the drill motor whirring. I found a cavernous room with a vast number of small white marble tables flanked by small benches on each side. Men sat opposite each other engrossed in chess games and I realized that I needed to play too. I took a seat at one of the tables and the man opposite passed me a stack of black and white squares with a welcoming nod. He had a sandy colored beard and glasses and indicated I should do what he was doing, laying out the squares to form my half of a chessboard. As I began to deal out the alternating black and white squares my stomach tensed and a rising sense of panic engulfed me. I didn't know how many squares across I should put out.

I was ripped out of my sleep as by a thunderclap. My heart was beating rapidly and there was an overwhelming nausea of being unprepared, unprepared for the game of life. Here I was, not quite twenty one years of age and preparing for med school. That meant four more years of school beyond my Bachelors and at least another year or two interning. Since everybody I spoke with told me the future lay in specialization, that meant at least two more extra years of med school and another year of internship. I'd be thirty years old before I got out of school. I knew nothing of life and yet I was about to embark on a course that would consume that life.

It was a vital dream, a wake-up call from the Id. I was forced to see that I was making life choices based on an academic conveyor belt that led from high school to college to grad school to career. Becoming a doctor was noble and I loved the science. But what kind of doctor would I be if I didn't know anything real about life? I'd had a mind blowing journey to Europe in 1971, after high school. The camel had got its nose under the tent of my worldview and I was dazzled with the intimation of something grand and profound being possible in this life. I'd returned from Europe and jumped into my program at UCLA. Yet something, some parting of the fabric, stayed with me.

A bump in the road jerked me out of my reverie and looking forward I saw another river. It was getting to be late in the afternoon and the golden light was liquid, painting the leaves and the trees around us. The air had the moist fecundity of a green house and I drank in this place, this moment.

We all knew this drill this time and our passage across was uneventful, save for a vast cloud of fruit bats that poured down the river and passed over our heads, not ten feet away. I could see their little foxlike faces and the light filtering through the translucent brown skin of their wings. It was a river of life flowing over a river of water and the spectacle took my breath away.

Darkness falls like a sudden curtain on the equator, maybe because on a rotating sphere the equator is going the fastest. It was my first time south of the equator, which we had crossed just before Bukittinggi. I strained to look up at the stars as the bus rumbled along but the covering canopy of trees didn't offer any broad vistas. This night's passage was more comfortable than the Bukittinggi run since the benches were farther apart and we could all stretch out a bit. The man who had nearly drowned rested, his wife's shawl-covered head on his chest, her arm flung over his shoulder. Our little ship of souls sailing through the warm jungle night.

A few sleepy nods from my fellow passenger as we all made ready for our arrival. The sunrise had been spectacular, but as the day wore on the wild jungle fell away and we were again back in civilization. Away from the sheltering forest the day heated up quickly and the humidity felt like a blanket. We were all ready for the bouncing and jostling to be over, or so I imagined. I was at any rate. We'd had a couple of breaks but none as dramatic as the jungle village. The broad valley was well developed with agriculture and the rest stops were uninteresting cement block affairs. I stuck with the fast food of rice and egg wrapped in a banana leaf for breakfast and lunch. My guts felt a little wonky and it just seemed best.

Lubuklinggan had a boomtown industrial feel and I didn't see much that invited me to stay. The train down to the port of Banjar left from here so when our bus pulled in, I grabbed my backpack and walked down the main road to the station. Two trains a day, one at seven in the morning, the other at six in the evening. It was almost three in the afternoon so I bought a second class ticket on the six o'clock. Another overnighter. Ugh! I was starting to get used to it but the constant motion since leaving the laid back relaxation of Toba wasn't what I'd call fun. I could smell myself, so upon leaving the train station I began to look around for a bath and some dinner.

Half a block down I spotted a sign "Losman-Warung Molly." *Losman* meant lodging and *Warung* was a word for eating place. A tall, thin faced man at the counter inside sold me a *mandi*, the dipper type shower, for a hundred rupees. He didn't look like a Molly but what do I know, other than that I really needed to bathe. The bus from Bukittinggi to here had taken about thirty hours and I smelled to myself like a wet straw mattress mixed with manure, my dank clothes sticking to me in the extreme humidity.

The cool water was luxurious. I poured it over my head and down my back and soaped up. In this heat, the last thing I wanted was hot water on my body, but it would have been useful for my shave. Still, soaped off, shaved off and gloriously clean was deliciously rejuvenating. I pulled a clean blue t-shirt out of my pack and a pair of khaki shorts. Funny how something as simple as a bath and some fresh clothes can shift mind states. Placing the grubbies in my nylon laundry bag, it was obviously way past time to stop somewhere and do some clothes washing. I wondered idly where that stop would be. The little *warung* looked inviting so I grabbed a seat and ordered fried chicken, French fries and a cold Bintang beer. Later, heading back up towards the train station, I felt whole and very human.

I should have popped for first class on the train. The second class carriage was open air with lattice like park benches facing each other, room for three across on each bench. Where the benches were back to back luggage racks sprouted towards the low wooden ceiling. Even though it was not yet five o'clock, many of the benches were already packed with passengers, the luggage racks crammed to capacity. Burlap bags and hemispherical bamboo cages stuffed with fighting cocks cluttered the aisle. I worked my way down the carriage and found an open seat beside a very rotund man eating rice and meat from a folded banana leaf. I wedged my pack into the overhead, again grateful for the slim, rock-climbing configuration. I settled into my seat, wishing I had the window but the fat man was up against it, having a conversation with a vendor who stood outside. My seatmate scooped up the last finger full of food from the leaf and unceremoniously dropped it out of the window at the feet of the vendor. Then he reached both arms out of the window, as if he was being handed a watermelon or something. The man outside tilted a large aluminum teakettle and the fat man washed his greasy hands in the stream that poured out, on to the platform.

Across from me a family of three made expressionless eye contact so I smiled and greeted them with a good evening, *"Selamat malam."* They sprouted smiles, the woman in her light blue head scarf nodded and her husband replied, *"Selamat malam."* He and the little boy shared the same thin face, high cheek bones and ebony hair.

I settled myself against the aisle side post and pulled out *Cuckoo's Nest*, picking up where I'd left off. Nurse Ratchett reminded me of some of the characters I'd known at UCLA, in the biomedical building. It was nearly dark when the train pulled out of the station. The dim lights of the coach were scarcely bright enough for me to read by. Twenty minutes later, when I looked up from my book, most of the people I could see appeared to already be asleep. Amazing how the locals just drop off when transport starts moving. I saw the same thing every time I took a bus. I was growing accustomed to the slumped sleeping position myself, perhaps because the constant motion since Toba had left me subtly exhausted. It was easy to nod off with this rocking motion of the train and in what I experienced as the blink of an eye it was dawn and a cultivated green plain stretched away from the train on both sides. The golden morning light caught and reflected in the thin mist floating over the rice paddy. Stretching, I found the family across from me already awake and bright eyed. We tipped our hats to each other, figuratively, and the little boy handed me my book. It must have fallen from my hands when I dropped off to sleep.

"Terimah kasih," I said.

"Sama, sama," he grinned back.

The fat man slumped against the window corner. His mouth hung loosely open, still asleep. I rose and picked my way to the end of the carriage into the pit toilet bathroom. The clack-clack of the train on the rails sounded louder through the open hole in the floor. There was a small sink and I splashed some water of dubious quality on my face and the back of my gritty neck. Our descent into the southern plains was accompanied by a further increase

Sumatra

in temperature and humidity. Now, just past sunrise, I was already coated in a layer of sweaty moisture. I relieved myself down the hole, making a game of not hitting the sides and watched the golden stream bend backwards in the airflow beneath the speeding train.

Returning, the fat man was awake and rinsing his mouth with liquid from an old metal thermos. We visually greeted each other as I settled back on to the bench. An old woman with a pink terry towel piled up on her head worked her way down the carriage carrying a bamboo basket. Passengers paid her fifty rupees for the triangular banana leaf of breakfast rice and whatever. When she passed I opted for a packet, as did my seatmates. A good portion of rice with half of a hardboiled egg and very piquant green leafy vegetables makes an excellent breakfast. This eating with my hands thing was very satisfying. I enjoyed the texture of the rice and working a bit of egg and vegetable into a bite sized ball. I glanced to the opposite side of the carriage as I chewed and saw another family similarly engaged with their own banana leaf breakfast. The mother supported a very young child, maybe two years old, in her lap. I watched the baby reach out towards the banana leaf with its left hand. As a group, all the adults grabbed the baby's hand and jerked it away from the food. Somebody barked, "Ah!" The startled child began to cry but the mother soothed it, placing a small piece of ripe banana in its right hand.

How odd to have such a different relationship with one's own hands. The right hand for things clean, the left for things unclean. Enforced from birth. I still forgot sometimes and touched food with my left hand. With a shared food, non-westerners would tend to sit back and stop eating. With body contact the other would shy away, as if my hand was covered in shit. And I guess this wasn't far from the truth. Most toileting facilities were squat toilets with a knee level water tap and a plastic dipper. An upscale version might have a tile basin filled with water on the right side that one could easily dip into with the right hand while washing off with the left. I took to carrying a small, hotel sized soap bar in a plastic wrap so that I could wash both hands when the need arose.

My round seatmate, whose name turned out to be Zul, spoke considerably more English than I did Indonesian. He was a businessman supplying hardware to the companies drilling for oil around Palembang and was heading back home to Jakarta. He informed me that there was a ship leaving that evening for Java.

"Do you think I'd be able to get a ticket for tonight?" I asked.

"Oh yes, it is a very large ship. I cannot imagine that you would not find a place."

We pulled into the station at Lampung at about half past three in the afternoon. I wished my traveling companions good afternoon, *Selamat sore*, and hauled myself from the carriage into the moldering old Victorian steel station and out on the street. I needed to get down to the harbor and secure passage, but before that I wanted a *mandi*. Freshen up my sweat. The afternoon was again stiflingly hot and humid, and even though I used some deodorant my shirt and shorts were soaked through with stinking sweat. Maybe it was the amount of garlic and some combination of the oils and spices in my diet. I felt self-conscious since the people around me didn't stink. Most didn't even look sweaty.

Like Lubuklinggan, Lampung was certainly not a tourist destination. It was discouraging to see the unattractive grey cement and wood utilitarian buildings of the port town. Medan was also a port town, but it had trees and broad avenues and parks. And Bukittinggi was a town of cute alpine chalets compared with this mess.

The thin-faced man from the train, who had introduced himself as Abdulla, passed me with his family in tow as I stood blinking on the street. He looked back, stopped and approached me.

"Hello. You have friend here?"

The look of genuine concern on his face took me by surprise. We'd spoken briefly on the train, the usual twenty question game - what's your name, where you from, where you going, are you married? My low proficiency in Indonesian was masked by the fact that these were the usual questions and I was practiced with intelligible responses. "I'm from California, in America. I am coming from blank and going to blank. No, I'm not married. I am twenty three years old."

The downside was this often gave my inquisitor the impression I was conversant and they'd launch into a rapid monologue. I'd hold up a hand and smile, "*Ma'af, saya tidak bisa becara bagus Bahasa Indonesian.*" 'Sorry, I can't speak Indonesian well.'

When I hit that point with the man on the train, he had shifted into a stilted but understandable English. Now I stood on the street looking into his concerned countenance.

"No," I replied to him, "no friend here. *Saya tidak ada teman disini.*"

We had already covered that I was heading to Java in our train conversation. He placed a gentle hand on my arm, "Please, you come to my house. Meet family. Bathe."

The magic word. Yet inside of me fear reared up. I didn't know him. What if it was some kind of "lure the foreigner into a trap" sort of thing? I hated that in myself but since I'd started to travel on my own how far to trust was a constant internal battle. "I like what I know and I don't like what I don't know." Hardly a good game plan for a guy who wants to explore the world and find out who he is. If I was going to play it safe all the time I might as well have stayed home, followed the program and finished school. It required an effort of will to voluntarily make myself vulnerable to the unknown, and this battle raged in my chest, a physical contraction. I turned to Abdulla and said, "Yes. Thank you Abdulla. I would be very grateful."

I imagined that he had seen the fear and doubt in my eyes, but he smiled broadly, clapped me on the shoulder and said, "We go!"

We wound down a dirt street together. I carried a bundle for Fatima, his wife, and within about ten minutes' walk we arrived at a door in a cinder block wall. Abdulla pushed it open and we entered a walled compound, maybe fifty feet wide. A small group of older men sitting on an open air covered platform looked up as we entered. Two white chickens ran past our feet, clucking with alarm. One of the men stepped off the platform and came forward to meet us. The bright, intelligent eyes in his wizened brown face stood out like searchlights. He clasped both of Abdulla's hands in his and then touched his heart with his right hand.

"*Asalam Malekum,*" he intoned.

"*Malekum salam, bapak,*" returned Abdulla, who then turned and indicated to me with a nod, "*Ini pak Bern, di Amerika. Tamu saya dan akan purge ke Djakarta malam ini.*" 'This is Mr. Bern from America. He is my guest and will go to Jakarta this evening.'

Then to me in English, "This is my father, Pak Interam."

I shook hands with the old gentleman. With his black hat and white shirt he looked rather like photos I had seen of Nehru, distinguished grey hair on his temples.

"*Salam malekum,*" I said, touching my chest as he had.

Pak Interam's eyes crinkled with amusement, but he returned my greeting with a solemn *"Malekum salam,"* and in English, "Welcome to my home."

The Appearance of Things

We moved further into the compound and the two other men stepped off the platform. Abdulla introduced me to the tallest of them, "My uncle, Pak Hari."

He didn't offer his hand but touched his chest and bowed slightly. The white skull cap and his thin moustache and chin beard looked scholarly to me. Formal but not unfriendly. In the light, the second man startled me with his daunting visage.

"My friend Yap."

Yap was shorter than any of us and immediately made me feel wary. He had the usual Nehru type hat but it covered a wide, thick head of orange brown, wiry hair that looked more like a pelt. His eyes had a yellowish brown iris and were set deep in his skull, a pronounced simian shelf of a forehead extended out past the bridge of his wide, flat nose. Combined with almost no chin he looked to me like a Neanderthal cousin. The fearful effect evaporated, however, when we made eye contact and I saw the goodwill shining out. He extended his wide, short-fingered hand. We both smiled broadly at each other as we shook hands.

"Yap is going to Jakarta on the boat tonight also. He will show you the way to a ticket." Abdulla looked down at Yap with obvious affection. Abdulla's son, Umar, came over and took Yap's right hand and pulled at his arm, laughing. Clearly a trusted favorite in this house.

"Please, I will show you the *mandi*. When you have washed, we will have tea."

Abdulla led me towards the rear of the compound where the bathhouse and toilet were located. I put down my pack and fished out my toilet kit. I was dirty, I needed a shave, and I stank. A first class good impression, I'm sure.

"*Terimah kasih banyak*, Abdulla," thank you very much.

Abdulla inclined his head, then turned and retreated back towards the others.

The clean, sweet water felt miraculous as I washed off the travel. I pulled out my little mirror and stood naked, shaving. Incredible! Here I was in the welcoming home of someone I didn't know twelve hours ago. I'm met with warmth and generosity. I felt a twinge of guilt and embarrassment for my earlier hesitation and mistrust. How do I go through life - with an open hand or a clenched fist? In my protected Los Angeles world it is so easy to be the "urbane fellow." Most of the people I knew probably thought I was happy and comfortable in my own skin. It was dawning on me how I worked to cultivate that story. And that's what it was, just a story, and I knew it suddenly, standing here naked in Sumatra, shaving and bathing from a barrel in the rear yard of people I scarcely knew. Lake Toba had shown me what a fake I was, alone and lonely that night in Prapat. A different kind of naked. And when I got to Tuk Tuk and the other westerners, my storyteller jumped right in, fabricating a new identity for a new set of people.

At this moment, I felt disgusted with myself. OK, enough. You're on the road to find out, right? So quit the wallowing. There was something new beginning, a real courage, a willingness to start showing up for this life, unconditionally, here and now. This really is a good bath!

I toweled off and rolled the aromatic, sodden travel cloths into a ball and stuffed them into my bulging laundry bag. I extracted one of my few remaining t-shirts and sniffed at a pair of shorts. Not too bad, go with it. Dressed and refreshed, I turned to go. In the glow of my new found take on life I felt a squish under my bare left foot. I hoped it was mud but when I lifted my foot the smell was unmistakable. Symbolic. I went into the squat toilet and using the dipper and my left hand, I cleansed my soiled sole. Back to the *mandi* area where more soap and water gave the illusion of having handled things.

I laughed quietly and put on my sandals. What's the moral here? Be brave but watch where you step?

We enjoyed tea on the open platform. Fatima brought out a tray of cut banana leaves and everyone got a scoop of rice. We added from small bowls fried tempeh, onions, coconut and chili and a tender spicy ginger beef. And iced tea that was refreshingly cool with the piquant foods. At the end of the meal, I thanked everyone in my fractured Indonesian, as best I could. How do you say "kindness" and "grateful"? I intended to learn. A painting in the shelter was in a golden Arabic calligraphy on a black background. I leaned over to Abdulla, "What does that say?"

"Allah akbar," he replied. "God is great."

In the growing darkness, we sat on the platform lit by a small, hanging, bare yellow bulb. The noises of the city and the croaking of frogs drifted in over the compound wall. I looked at the circle of faces - Abdulla, Fatima, Pak Interam, Yap, Pak Hari and Umar, grateful for much more than a bath and food and conversation. I was on the road to find out and for the first time in my journey I touched the possibility of the man I could become. It startled me.

Yap and I were now travel buddies, at least as far as Merak in Java. He spoke virtually no English and we were both painfully aware of my limited Indonesian. And yet, as we trundled down the lane away from the house and towards the port, I felt I was in the care of a friend. We stopped in front of a low-slung bungalow with a red sign on a white background. It read, *"Tempat Penjualor Karcis"* and Yap beckoned to me to follow him up to the window. He extracted an ancient leather folder from his tunic and produced a ticket that he showed to the man behind the window. The ticket seller asked a question and Yap turned to me, indicating that I should come to the window. The agent's face was sweating in the warm, airless room and his face glistened in the glare of the bare bulb over his head. He looked at me doubtfully then said, *"Empat ribu rupiah,"* 'Four thousand rupees.' I passed over the money and he slid a pink and tan colored card out to me through the window slot. He said something to Yap and they both started laughing.

"Terimah kasih," I said to both Yap and the ticket seller. I could feel his eyes on my back as we walked away from the window and towards the tall chain link fence that delineated the port entry.

It was a far more varied port than Medan with many large steel vessels, cargo ships. Men swarmed around the cranes and rope-bound crates that cluttered the docks. To the left, resting a bit further out, a fleet of wooden boats. Some I recognized as fishing boats, similar to what I'd see in San Francisco bay at the wharfs. The majority were sailboats, hundreds of them, of all different shapes and sizes. Their masts and rigging rocked gently on the incoming tide, but not in unison. It was a vast kinetic sculpture spreading away from the shore until darkness and distance rendered it invisible.

Yap pointed at a white metal post with a large number six painted in black and beyond, to the ship. My heart dropped when I saw our boat. Cranes were busily engaged lifting pallets aboard from the dock. The ship had large rust streaks dribbling down its sides and the eyes on the bow for the anchor chains were completely eroded away. Two metal walkways were thronged with passengers, slowly shuffling upwards towards the ship. Hundreds of others milled about on the dock, awaiting their chance to board. The name on the bow *"Surabaya"* might as well have been *"Patna."* I was one of the Muslim pilgrims in "Lord Jim", trustingly boarding the rust bucket that would carry me to my fate on the high seas.

It's almost mystical how life automatically says, "Oh yeah?" when I think

I've learned something. My new-found confidence, my willingness to trust to new situations, evaporated like the morning dew. I began my ascent up the gangplank. Aboard, we crowded along the narrow passage, the fetor of metallic salt and humanity closing in like a fog. I followed Yap to a corroded metal staircase and began to feel a deep dread as we descended into the bowels of the aging vessel. Down one floor, then another, then another, the air now dank and humid. There were no port lights to bring in fresh air but we did pass ventilator tubes. The cool air flowing in from these skimpy vents was woefully inadequate. We passed halls and holds, dimly lit with glowing red ceiling lights. Finally, Yap turned into one of the holds and I followed. The red-lit metal room was maybe forty feet wide and extended into a dark distance, blocked by pallets of cream-colored bags. Small groups and individuals had spread out squares of cloth, as if they were getting ready for a rock concert or a picnic, but they were just settling in for the night on the stark metal floor. In the red light all colors seemed to be either black or reddish, including the dark eyes in the upturned faces as we passed.

Even with the heat I felt a chill in my guts. What happens if we hit something or a leak allowed the sea just beyond the corroding steel to flood our chamber? I was pretty sure we were below the water line. There was no scenario I could imagine that ended in survival. I pushed down the sick foreboding that wanted to engulf me. I never thought of myself as claustrophobic, but Jesus Christ!

Trust this. It's going to be ok. I was internally whistling in the dark when Yap put down his bundle beside a pallet of the large bags. In the weak light, I could make out lettering in Indonesian and a recognizable "Van Houton Flour Mill" insignia. A child was crying down the hall, sharp against the murmured background noise of people in low conversation. Somebody was smoking a kretik cigarette and in the close, humid air I suddenly didn't appreciate the cloying clove scented smoke. It was like being a refugee, fleeing some turn of the century Asian war. I rolled out my tropical weight sleeping sack across the top of the flour sacks and made my backpack into a head rest. I lay on top of the sleep sack, staring up at the rusting rivets and red metal ceiling not three feet from my face. It felt like ages since I had stretched out to sleep. Amazingly, I dropped off almost immediately and slept soundly and deeply. The movement and shuffling around me is what woke me up. My fellow refugees were already streaming out and up. We were there! Yap watched me with silent patience as I re-stowed my gear and shouldered my backpack.

The bright morning and the blue dawn sky felt infinite, huge, after the dark hold of the *Surabaya*. I literally breathed a sigh of relief as we crossed the last threshold out into the open salty freshness. I was back in the twentieth century. Or I thought I was until the harbor at Merak came into view. All of the hundreds of ships rocking at anchor were sailing ships. Many were over a hundred feet long and boasted three tall masts. A few, already under sail and pulling away, looked like paintings of merchant ships from the seventeen hundreds. Vast numbers of smaller vessels, some only a few yards long, bobbed at anchor or moved silently along in the slight morning breeze. The boats that had a single mast from which was suspended a single "V" shaped sail were the most numerous. Their brightly colored hulls and sails filled the early morning harbor and there was an elegant beauty in their slow ballet.

Movement on the docks, hundreds of human hands and backs ferrying the freight, a line of leaf cutter ants made large. The twentieth century fell away and I looked out over a bustling Asian harbor of the 1750s. The absence of machines and diesel smoke was stunning and deepened the preindustrial flavor of the scene. I stood taking it in, somehow knowing that this moment would never happen again, feeling grateful and happy.

Yap and I made it down the gangway and followed the crowd along the pier to the shoreline. I appreciated his sturdy frame as I walked behind him. He easily hefted his two solid cases. I knew they were heavy, having moved one of them last night as we set up our camp in the belly of the "Patna."

The open-air bus terminal had no ticket office and we wandered about, reading the signs on the front of each bus. Finally, one that read "Djakarta." Yap stood by as I passed my bag up to the luggage man, but when I reached down to pick up one of his he placed a restraining hand on my arm.

"*Tidak, terimah kasih,* Ben."

This surprised me and I asked, *"Apa kabar?"* 'How are you?'

"*Saya tinggal disini,*" he said with a gentle smile. 'I stay here.'

I didn't understand so I tried again, *"Anda tidak purge ke Djakarta?"* 'You do not go to Jakarta?'

"*Munkin besok,*" 'Maybe tomorrow.'

I understood then that he wasn't coming with me and a twinge of disappointment appeared, like a little electrical shock. We really had been through something together. At least, that was how the ordeal of the boat passage seemed right now. Maybe for Yap it was all just what he was accustomed to and no big deal. I thought it was a big deal.

"Selemat jalan, Ben," 'Good travels,' and he touched his chest with his right palm.

"Selemat tinggal," I returned, sort of a "good where you stay" farewell.

Yap gave me one of his big-toothed smiles and I boarded the bus. I took a seat on the right side and looked out the dusty window. Yap had picked up his bags and was walking away through the crowd, his short frame and broad shoulders setting him apart. Being on the road had a lot of "hello goodbye" in it, a wistfulness I didn't expect.

On to Java!

Chapter 3
Java

> Irrigators guide the water.
> Fletchers shape the arrow shaft.
> Carpenters shape the wood.
> The wise control themselves.
>
> *The Dhammapada*

I
Jakarta

Jakarta started before we ever entered the city, or so it seemed. Young men began to appear, standing on corners, shepherding two or three glass bottles filled with a honey colored liquid. I saw a woman on a scooter give one of these boys a rupee after he poured a bottle into her small gas tank. These kids with bottles were gas stations!

The simple single-floored cement and wooden buildings we were passing became two and three story buildings and grew closer together. The number of people on the streets multiplied logarithmically. As we drew closer to what I imagined was the center of town, scooters and bicycle rickshaws and little motorized things that looked like golf carts swarmed around us on the streets. It was a flowing river of vehicles, pouring people into the heart of Jakarta.

Around Gambir Station, from where the trains left for eastern Java, had been recommended as the best place to find traveler's lodging. John and Louise had been here and suggested a place on Jalan Jaksa street called Hotel

The Appearance of Things

Melodee. I walked over from the bus terminal, maybe half a mile, and it felt good to be moving my body after all the sedentary travel. It was hot but the canopy of trees over the streets kept the temperature manageable, barely. I turned on to Jalan Jaksa and immediately saw there was no shortage of lodging places. If Hotel Melodee didn't have a room there was plenty to choose from.

Hotel Melodee was easy to find and I liked the garden entrance of the place. An attractive girl at the desk smiled up at me as I entered the little courtyard.

"Hello. You like room?" she inquired.

"Yes, please, *silakan*. Not on the street side. Near the back if you have it."

Asia was always noisy.

She turned to a large rack hung with keys, paused thoughtfully then reached for one on the upper right.

"Eight hundred rupee one night. How many nights you stay?"

Expensive. I took the proffered key. It was heavy, with a metal plate attached that had the number sixteen painted on with red nail polish or paint.

"Maybe two nights," I replied.

"You pay first night now."

Usually, I'd want to see the room first but I wanted a shower and I really needed to use the *kamar kecil*.

"OK," I said and handed over the rupiah. Turning to go, my backpack knocked into a westerner who'd come up behind me at the desk.

"Whoa!" He took a step back and peered at me.

"Sorry, I didn't see you."

"Nice pack. Where's that from?"

I looked over my shoulder at my increasingly battered bag. "From the States. It's an Outward Bound. Frameless rock climbing pack. A place out in Chatsworth, near Los Angeles makes them."

"You from LA?"

He seemed open, friendly, a good sort - reddish hair, freckles, about my height

"Yeah. San Fernando Valley, if you know it."

Big grin. "Sure I know it. I'm from Encino," and he stuck out his hand. "Matt Franco."

We shook hands. I really needed to go. "Vern Castle," I replied.

"Funny! Wherever you go in the world, you always meet somebody from the valley." He laughed and that made me smile.

"I guess a lot of us couldn't wait to get out, huh?" I liked the valley well enough but as soon as I started at UCLA I moved out and into a commune in Beverly Glen Canyon with my girlfriend. The canyons behind Hollywood and West LA were cool. Frank Zappa and his band were over in Laurel Canyon, two over from us. It was understood that the valley wasn't cool.

I had to get to the toilet so I said, "Look, Matt, I've really got to see a man about a horse, if you know what I mean, but if you want to get some food later I'd like to hook up and hear about where you've been and stuff."

"You bet. How about we meet back here," indicating the garden area, "in around an hour?"

"Great. See you here."

I headed towards the stairs and noticed the girl at the desk grinning at me. Hmm. The best information came from other people on the road. We all had our own twenty question game too, but it was useful.

Room sixteen was small but it felt clean and had the dual virtues of being back from the street and possessing a bathroom. I had my own *mandi* and squat toilet. The mirror on the wall above the small sink had a sticker that read, "Smile - God Loves You." Higher up was another sticker, a drawing of a naked girl viewed from behind, her buttocks appealingly displayed as she looked back at me over her shoulder with a wink.

"Allah akbar," I murmured, kissed my index finger and touched her butt. It had been a while.

Settling in, I bathed and unpacked a few things. My laundry bag was now occupying half my backpack. The unrelenting southward push across Sumatra had left me no time to do a wash. I was down to one Hawaiian shirt and a pair of khaki shorts. My towel was pretty foul too. The front desk had a sign on the wall that caught my attention when I was checking in, "Laundry Service." I donned my shirt and shorts, feeling clean as a whistle, and hauled my laundry bag down the steps, back into the little garden lobby. The same girl at the desk glanced over at me and my bag and immediately reached for a short paper form.

"You write name and what you got - how many piece."

She handed me the order form and a BIC pen.

I didn't know how many piece so I retired to a bench on the opposite side of the lobby and pulled everything out, the aromatic pile reeking like a gym locker with overtones of ammonia. I did my accounting, putting each piece back in the bag as I noted it on my form. I was nearly done when a voice behind me boomed out, "Hey Vern!" and I turned to find Matt grinning at my labors and beside him a well-fed young man of apparent Chinese ancestry.

"That's a pretty ripe load," chided Matt. I felt self-conscious for a moment when I caught the eye of the girl behind the counter but then I just laughed.

"Yeah, from my job at the cheese factory."

Matt nodded towards his acquaintance. "This is Chung. He's from Malaysia and we're headed out for New Year's on the town. Care to join us?"

New Year's! I hadn't even thought about it. The journey down from Toba was like something out of time and I felt startled. My confusion must have shown on my face because Matt looked at me quizzically for a moment then laughed.

"Chung knows Jakarta like nobody's business. We've been talking about going for some great food and then hitting a few clubs he knows. How does that sound?"

It sounded terrific. I looked over at Chung. He smiled but his eyes were on my dirty clothes. I didn't offer to shake hands since he appeared to be making an effort not to recoil from the earthy aroma and here was me handling the stuff.

"Hello Chung. Pleased to meet you. I'm Vern. Yeah, ok, great, thanks for thinking of me. Let me just get this wrapped up and over to the desk."

I lugged my re-stuffed bag over and the girl pointed at the floor to the side of the desk. She delicately reached for the pen and the record I'd written with her thumb and forefinger, as though she was selecting a particular jellybean out of a bowl.

It amused and irritated me a little bit. These were just sweaty clothes, not radioactive waste. But taking the hint I crossed the lobby to the small sink near the fountain and washed both hands with soap. Nobody said anything, yet I sort of expected the denizens of the lobby to erupt in applause at my cleanliness.

Java

I rejoined Matt and Chung and we stepped out on to the noisy street. Matt eyed me appraisingly, "Well, you're not dressed for the Ritz but what the hell. Let's go celebrate the last day of 1974!"

By now it was almost 3 pm and I was feeling pangs of both hunger and thirst. The two small bananas I'd had on the bus ride weren't much of a breakfast but the heat and the humidity were appetite killers and I hadn't thought much about food until now. The warm water from my travel bottle kept me hydrated but it didn't put the thirsty feeling to rest like a cold something.

"I'd appreciate some food right now. We could talk about New Year's in Jakarta over a beer and a *nasi goering*." I looked hopefully at my two new comrades for agreement or a better idea.

"Do you like Chinese food?" asked Chung.

Both Matt and I said yes at the same time.

"I've been here three times and the best I've found is the Shanghai Palace, down on the edge of Chinatown."

It startled me for a moment to hear Chinatown when I was already in Asia, but I was beginning to understand that Asia is as different and varied as Europe, maybe more so. Chinese people in Indonesia were as distinct as Swedes in Italy. Although there is no Swedentown in Rome, so far as I know.

We hailed one of the passing golf carts and Chung haggled a bit with the driver in Indonesian. Matt said they were called "*tuk-tuks*" but I heard other travelers call them "*bemos*". Chung gave the driver directions and we all piled into the back. None of us were small people and we hunched over laughing as our driver sped out into the traffic flow. It was my first ride in a *bemo* and the noise and rush of air was exhilarating. I looked out at the huge tires of a truck, inches away from us. We're in a tin can. I tried not to imagine what would become of us in a collision. Mass always wins. We rocked and dodged between buses and trucks and cars and motorcycles, my fear and delight about equally balanced. Ok, so what the heck. The guy driving this thing does it all day and he's still alive.

We ripped to a stop in front of a row of drab, multi-storey buildings and tumbled out, the clown car at the circus. I caught Matt's eye and we both cracked up. Chung paid the driver the hundred rupiah and turned to us. The neighborhood had a rather worn, dingy feel, with black and rust stains on the facades of many of the structures. The whole place looked in need of a paint job it was never going to get. We looked up towards the second floor of the building we were in front of, where a large window sign proclaimed "Shanghai Palace" in red and white and gold.

Chung smiled, "Here we are!"

He proceeded through the glass doors of the lobby and bounded up the wide staircase. We followed and found ourselves in a vast room with dozens of large round tables, red and gold columns covered in black Chinese calligraphy and a noisy crowd. It was more of a social club than a restaurant, and many of the tables had games that looked like dominos or checkers in progress. The bank notes on the tables and the shouting, gesticulating patrons said it wasn't just for fun.

Chung spoke to a waiter and we were seated at a table near the long bank of windows, overlooking the street and parts of the downtown skyline in the distance. I looked at the menu, which was in Chinese but had photos of each plate with a number beside it. A drawing of a fish at the top of one column, a rooster at the top of another. There was a happy pig column. I realized that I hadn't seen pork on the menu anywhere since I arrived in Indonesia but its absence hadn't occurred to me until just now. The picture of the BBQ spare ribs looked good.

Matt and Chung were apparently not as hungry because a large bottle of Johnny Walker Red appeared on the table along with three glasses, a little bucket of ice and an old fashioned seltzer water bottle with a silver spout and a black handle. First things first. We each grabbed a glass and poured ourselves a good two fingers, added ice and a tiny shot of the soda.

"To 1974," Matt toasted and we raised our glasses. The scotch was a warm wave in my empty stomach. Matt picked up the bottle and looked at it sentimentally, "It was a very good year."

Chung and I grinned at him. I motioned to a waiter standing nearby and indicated by pointing at the menu that I wanted to order the ribs and a plate of something that looked like Chow Mein. Chung said something to the waiter. He stopped writing on his order pad and looked up.

"Tell you what," Chung said, looking archly at Matt and I, "let's order their Mandarin Feast. They do a great job here and you won't be sorry. But only if you're hungry."

Chung looked at Matt and me and we both shrugged. Who would know better? And we were hungry. The scotch had got the juices flowing.

"For the three of us, it will cost six thousand rupees but it's a real feast, like something you'd get in Hong Kong."

That was going to be two thousand rupees a head, plus the scotch but I'd been living cheaply for weeks. It was New Year's and time for a splurge.

"Sounds good to me," I said.

Matt nodded, "I'm in."

Chung rubbed his hand together, gleefully I thought, and spoke to the waiter who listened gravely, bowed and headed for the kitchen.

As plate after plate went from deliciously full to satisfyingly empty, I got to know more about both Matt and Chung. Matt was from my neck of the woods, a valley boy from Los Angeles. His folks had a place in Encino, south of Ventura Boulevard, up in the hills. He knew and I knew that was the right side of the street. Fancy. It surprised me to find out that he was 31 and still lived at home.

"I've got this sweet little scene in the guest house, out by the pool."

I couldn't understand why he'd be proud of living off his parents, in their back yard.

Chung was more interesting to me. He was born in Malaysia, in Georgetown on Penang and his family had multiple businesses on the island. He was studying engineering at the university in the capital Kuala Lumpur and had the goal of getting on with a well-known architectural firm.

"I want to have my own company but you know, you got to get started first. One of my uncles there is going to take me on when I finish at KL."

I couldn't help from contrasting my two dinner companions. One, a privileged American, apparently content to drift goallessly through life on somebody else's nickel. The other, a young man about my age whose passion for his architectural future gave me a twinge about walking away from my medical school path.

"Come on!" declared Chung. He rose to his feet a bit unsteadily and waved the waiter the waiter over. "We're gonna go have some fun!"

I thought I was having fun. While we paid the bill, Matt stumbled toward the *kamar kecil*, the toilet.

Reflecting back on previous New Year's Eves made me feel sort of blue, how everybody tried so hard to have a good time. When Matt came back from the loo we sort of walk-staggered downstairs to street level. I felt pretty done. Was it only this time yesterday I was taking a *mandi* at the house of Abdulla?

"You like girls?" Chung grinned and tapped the side of his nose, like we were all in on a big surprise. Matt's drifting eyes made me wonder if there was anybody home at the moment. Not needing any encouragement from us, Chung waved down another yellow *bemo* and we were off again. I was in a bit of a haze myself and didn't have a strong feeling either way. The breeze on my face felt good as we sped off into the Jakarta night. Our destination was a brightly lit neon alley. We piled out of the transport, paid up and followed Chung as he negotiated the crowds. Groups of young men and women flowed into and out of the various clubs that lined the street. A few older men leaned against walls, smoking and watching the action with veiled eyes. I noticed some of those eyes tracking us.

A double door opened and two attractive women in short skirts, clinging to a tall, older western man moved past us. They were all laughing. The thumping disco music and flashing lights spilled out behind them until the doors swung shut on their own. Matt was gawking around and we made eye contact.

"Remind you of Encino?" I asked. It was just a joke but Matt's eyes grew wide and he stammered, "No, no, there's nothing like this in Encino!"

I gave up and followed Chung towards a club called Bronco Billy's. The scotch had worn off a bit now and I felt a second wind. Ok, so let's give this a try.

A rather beautiful woman who I imagined to be Indonesian was strutting back and forth on the stage wearing a cowboy hat and pretty much nothing else. A group of men stood chest high near the floodlit stage walkway, some moving in time to the music, others clutching a drink in one hand while the other was draped around a nearby female. The girls looked pretty bored but their dates didn't seem to notice or care. On each side of the stage, other striking young Asian women sat astride hobby-horses, all in the same non costume as the main dancer. They cried "Yippee!" and swung their cowboy hats in a circle, their naked breasts bouncing merrily as they rocked on their horsies. I found myself giggling, looking at the scene. It was more funny than erotic. The main dancer, now that I was closer, had seriously caked on eye make-up and a harder edge than I thought at first blush. Still, a few of them had an alluring twinkle.

The largely male crowd was maybe three quarters western men and older than Chung or me. They didn't seem like travelers. Maybe businessmen connected with some international bank or something. Matt stood off a bit, closer to the stage. He was entranced by the woman dancer and she zeroed in on him, moving to where he stood gaping. She bent down towards him, her pendulous breasts almost brushing his face.

"Hey you, cowboy.... You want to ride the pony, huh?" She lowered her gaze on him and ran her hand up from her ankle toward her crotch. Matt was grinning from ear to ear when she reached down and seemed to draw him on to the stage. Oh no. I moved towards him. If it was me, I'd want to be pulled back by friends. There must have been some kind of railing or step for him to push off on because before I could cross the ten feet separating us, he was up on the stage with her, looking like a deer caught in the headlights. The dancer took Matt by the front of his shirt with both hands and began to sink towards the stage floor, pulling him down with her until he was down on all fours, his face almost buried in her bosom. The revelers whooped their approval. At that instant I felt sorry for him and humiliated too. In one smooth move, the dancer swung around, still holding his collar with her left hand, hiked her naked leg over him and mounted his back. The confusion on Matt's face, glistening in the spotlights, was painful. The crowd cheered and she whipped her hat back and whacked Matt on the butt. "Giddy up, cowboy." Huge laughter erupted.

Seconds later whatever spell held him frozen in place suddenly broke and he pushed off the floor to a standing position. The cowgirl felt him going and deftly stepped back and off. He whirled and stared at her for a stricken moment, his disheveled shirt sporting the wet stains of her vaginal sweat in the middle of his back. The crowd howled and more than a few shouted things like, "Go get 'em, cowpoke!" He fled to his right, to the edge of the stage, down the steps and pushed out through the crowd to the red-lit exit door. I didn't see Chung anywhere but the right thing to do was follow Matt out. He looked like a guy who needed help.

I found him outside, maybe twenty feet from the door, leaning against a wall vomiting. I went over to him but he waved me to go back and convulsed once more. Mandarin Feast wallcovering. Chung came out of the door of the club and saw us. He came over and I said, "Matt had a little too much Johnny Walker." He nodded and we looked at each other. Then we both burst out laughing. To his credit, Matt looked over at us from his pit of misery, wiped his mouth and began laughing too. Happy New Year, Jakarta!

The Appearance of Things

***

January 1st was bright as a new penny and well underway by the time I got downstairs. The little café next door, which was really part of the hotel, had coffee and a decent omelet with toast. I was enjoying my third bite when Chung walked in. We exchanged a friendly nod and he pulled up a chair at my table.

"How'd you sleep?" I asked.

Chung smiled again. "Good. Very good. But I'm ready for coffee."

A moment later Matt came around the corner, saw us both at the table and stopped, his face maybe a little guarded.

"Morning Cowpoke," I grinned, "Pull up a chair. How'd you sleep?"

Matt looked sheepish but pulled up a chair anyway.

"I was dry. Must have drunk three quarts of water last night. I was up and down with my pitcher twice."

The hotel provided purified water but you had to do your own footwork with the pitcher from the room.

I chewed a bite thoughtfully while Chung and Matt told the girl what they wanted off the menu.

"I was thinking to take the train up to Bogor and see the Botanical Gardens. Heard they were cool and it's a bit higher. Might be cool in more than one way. Either of you guys interested?"

I wasn't that surprised when both declined.

"I'm going to keep it close to home today," replied Matt, examining his spoon.

Chung said, "I'd go tomorrow. Today I want to go the big market. It's supposed to be something else on the first day of the New Year. I want to buy some gifts to take home." He paused then added, "The gardens are probably closed today anyway."

I was already planning to take the train down to Jogjakarta tomorrow and going shopping or hanging out didn't appeal to me. It was a new experience, how traveling alone made me increasingly enjoy being on my own. That night of loneliness in Prapat had changed the math somehow, like I'd come through to the other side of a wall I didn't know was even there. Back in what I thought of as my youth, I'd sit around with friends on a summer afternoon and the conversation went something like, "What do you wanna do? I dunno, what do you want to do?" Even then it was mind numbing. I came to dislike the paralysis of groups. People thought I was bossy or pushy when all I wanted to do was break the inertia. I finished off my omelet, paid and wished Matt and Chung a good day.

"I'm heading out to Jogjakarta tomorrow so I'm going to give it a try. It's supposed to be a good train ride up so even if it's closed I see a little bit of what's around here before I go."

Maybe I'd see them when I got back. Maybe New Year's Eve was all we were supposed to do together. I remembered a bit of graffiti from a toilet stall in West Hollywood. "May the warm tongue of freedom lick your inner ear" and smiled to myself as I walked to Gambir Station. A tiny kiosk with a sign reading "Tourist Information" huddled near the entry hall and a small dark man with his hair parted neatly in the middle and thick glasses sat within, looking down into his lap. As I approached, he closed the book he was reading and met my eye.

"Selamat pagi," I greeted him, "English ok?"

"Yes, yes. How may I help you?"

"Can you tell me if the botanical gardens at Bogor are open today?"

"The gardens are open daily for public viewing from 8 am until 6 pm."

He tugged at a drawer and removed a folded, single page glossy flyer that he handed over to me. Across the top it read The Royal Botanical Gardens."

"Thank you," I said, accepting the flyer. "But today is New Year's Day. Would they be open today?"

He looked at me like someone being patient with a child.

"The gardens are open daily. That would include today."

"So New Year's Day is not a holiday here?"

"News Year's Day is a holiday here. The gardens are open daily, including holidays."

He reached out and took back the flyer, turning it to the back side and underlined with his finger "Holidays included".

I took the flyer back and nodded my thanks, *"Terimah kasih, bapak."*

"Gate number two."

He leaned out of the kiosk and pointed to a row of windows.

"Purchase your ticket at that window. There is a train leaving every thirty minutes."

He sat back down, opened his book and looked at me over the top of his glasses.

"*Selamat jalan*," he said, and smiled broadly.

I had twenty minutes until the next train so I searched the signs over the ticket windows for Jogjakarta and finding it, went to the end of the short line. I'd sort of had it for a while with sleeping sitting up so I booked a ticket for the early morning train for tomorrow. That would get me in by early evening, time enough to find a hotel and have a decent bath, bed and a meal.

I wandered about the departure hall and found myself watching two boys, maybe seven or eight years old poking around in the ashtrays at the end of each row of waiting benches. They trawled through the filthy sand with their fingers, collecting extinguished cigarette butts and storing them in an old plastic bag. I watched surreptitiously as they withdrew to the base of one of the big columns supporting the roof and began to process their butts by rolling them between thumb and forefinger. The unburned tobacco scraps that fell out were collected into another, smaller plastic bag. It suddenly dawned on me what I was seeing. Yesterday, as we had roamed around Jakarta, I had seen boys on some of the corners with small bags of tobacco attached to old cardboard display boards, selling to passersby. This must be the source, or at least one of the sources, of that tobacco. I flashed back to the corner "gas stations" of soda pop bottles filled with petrol.

There's a concept in Ecology called "Niche." It's the idea that in any natural system all the life forms have someplace where they fit into the whole. The main idea was that life finds a way to fit into the environment and in so doing, alters the environment. You couldn't tease apart the life from the environment and have them be the same. One of my old professors at UCLA, George Bartholomew, led us on collection trips out into the high deserts near Los Angeles. We saw directly that if an environment presented an opportunity, a life form would arise to exploit that opportunity. It seemed to me that the desert offered plenty of opportunities that weren't being exploited. When I mentioned this observation to Dr. Bartholomew he just smiled and said, "Not yet anyway. Ecosystems work in time and space."

So the fascinating "human ecology" of Jakarta had revealed a few facets to me - in the glass bottles holding gasoline for sale by the pint, in the children unrolling cigarette butts for resale, the girls of the "Bronco Billy's" dance bar - a million ways to find a niche to survive another day. Then there was my well-fed American life. A lot of niches left to be filled there. I tried to shake off the foreboding of an America where all the niches filled, like what I see here in Java. Time and space. I know there are areas like Appalachia where many people are just scraping by or not even. There are probably plenty of people in the USA, maybe even my hometown, that are living on the edge. But it was so raw and in the open here that it touched my passage. I was insulated from the desperate lives in America and didn't give them much thought. I wonder if getting to see how the other half lives here in Asia will change the way I see things at home? Probably. I hope so. Once somebody points out the Big Dipper in the night sky it's hard not to see it.

Bogor was already worth the trip. The train ride out through the foothills was tranquil, a million shades of green glowing in the late morning sunlight. The town and gardens were at about twenty five hundred feet elevation which made it about eight degrees cooler than in Jakarta. Still, the tropical sun was fierce, and it was pretty darned hot and humid when I stepped off the train. I followed the crowd out through the station and onto the street. A large sign with an arrow to the left indicated the direction to The Botanical Garden. The shade trees along the way offered protection from the sun and the houses we passed reminded me a bit of the area outside of Amsterdam, a reminder of the Dutch colonials.

I paid my 50 rupiah at the white, Victorian looking entry building and wandered into the gardens. Around me families strolled together. A small group had plopped down on the trimmed lawn and pulled out breakfast, the ubiquitous triangular packets wrapped in banana leaf. As I passed, the aromas of curry and chili and garlic made my stomach growl. There ahead, below the sign proclaiming "Orchid House" was a little stall with a stack of the compact green pyramids and large jars of colored drinks.

"*Selamat pagi*," I greeted the seller, a young woman with dark eyes and a powder blue scarf covering her head. She looked at me shyly but held my gaze.

"*Selamat pagi, bapak.*"

I indicated the packet, which I knew was called a "*nasi campur*" and asked how much.

"*Barapa harga nasi campur itu?*"

The Appearance of Things

She gave me a dazzling smile. Made me wonder if I sounded like an idiot and she was amused.

"Dua ratus rupiah dengan minum," she replied and nodded towards the jars of fruit juice. 'Two hundred rupees with a drink.'

I held up one finger and said, *"Satu, silakan,"* 'One please,' and pulled out my money. She placed a green banana leaf pyramid on the little counter and inclined her head towards the drinks. I had no idea what they were but the red one looked pretty so I pointed at that jar. She nodded and pulled out a small plastic bag, deftly scooped a ladle of red juice into the bag, added a short straw and in one smooth move tied the whole thing off with a rubber band and handed it to me with an outstretched finger. I put my index finger through the rubber band and she handed it off, like one of those string games we'd sometime amuse ourselves with when we were kids.

"Terimah kasih," I said and retired to the nearby lawn to enjoy an early lunch. Unwrapping the leaf and folding it flat like a paper plate, I reached down with my right hand and smooshed a bit of curry and rice together and popped it into my mouth. I liked this touching the food and feeling its texture and temperature. Chili and camphor, hot and delicious. A sip of the red stuff, which was cold and sweet but no flavor I recognized, tropical punch maybe.

The gardens rolled away on all sides, beautiful and well cared for. I've always loved growing things. The exuberant flowers and exotic leaves were all new to me and I finished my *nasi campur* and continued my stroll through the gardens. It was a relief to walk through such a place after my rather strange New Year's Eve. I followed the signs to the Orchid House and was rewarded with a staggeringly vast collection of blooming orchids - reds, blues and maroons and bizarrely spotted yellow slippers. The translucent roof broke the direct sun and created a luminous patina on the waxy leaves and flowers. So many orchids stretching in all directions made me feel odd, like I was wandering in a mausoleum. Even though they were beautiful I had an overarching sense of death and felt better when I was back out under the sky. Odd.

This morning I'd felt sorry for Matt. The horrified, haunted look in his eyes as he had descended the stage and fled outside was replaced with a look I knew - embarrassment and maybe disappointment in himself. Maybe everybody knows that one at some point in this life. For all I know, maybe Matt has had a string of humiliations and that's why he's a guest in his parent's back yard in Encino at thirty one. Still, here he was in Indonesia traveling on his own. I wonder how many people just curl up and call it quits inside their hearts?

Java

A few large fruit bats circled above a magnificent tall hardwood. The living river of those bats passing overhead in Sumatra was vivid in my memory. Now, what I had taken for foliage came into focus and I saw that the tree was in fact loaded with bats, pendulous animal fruit hanging from the branches like ripe, brown pears enshrouded in leathery leaves.

Continuing deeper into the garden, a group of pretty schoolgirls passed me and I caught a few sly looks. When I smiled back the lookers would cover their mouths and chatter to their friends. More giggling. Ahead, the canopy of a broad-leafed tree shed an inviting shade on a little circular fountain, a few comfortable looking benches fringing the pool. I'd been walking around since morning and a little rest seemed in order. The tropical heat and humidity, while less intense here than back in Jakarta, still made me feel a bit groggy. Maybe last night's Johnny Walker played a part too. At any rate, the bench was comfortable and I settled down. I pulled out *The Illustrated Man*, an old sci-fi I'd traded for *Steppenwolf* with a girl back at Toba. I think she got the better deal. No matter. I had a slug of water from my bottle, braced my day sack against the bench arm for a pillow and lay back. Just read for a little bit.

My consciousness was claimed by fatigue. It was payback time for all the days and nights coming overland. The Illustrated Man lay open on my chest. I'd been awakened by the shouts of a family passing by and sat up with a start. I dug my watch out of my pack. Almost five p.m. When was the last train back? I collected myself and followed the flow of departing people along to the main gate. The 5:30 train was pretty full but I got a window seat. The sunset over the western horizon was almost a rainbow.

It was going on 8:00 pm as I trudged up the street from the station to the Hotel Melodee. It's funny how fast a place can seem like home. I walked into the lobby and the young lady at the desk said, "You friend leave note." She swiveled on her stool to the key rack and pulled off a folded paper. She held it out to me and said, "Laundry there," with a nod toward the shelves on the opposite wall.

"Four hundred rupee."

"*Terimah Kasih*," and I took the paper. Before reading the note, I pulled out my billfold and handed over the rupee notes. She took the money, slid open the drawer in front of her and deposited the cash.

"*Sama sama*," she said listlessly and went back to her magazine. Glossy photos of models showing off some fashion.

I went over to the big water bottle, refilled my own and opened the note. I had to stand up next to the wall light in the dim lobby to read it.

"Hey Vern, Chung and I waited around until about 7:00. How were the gardens? We're going over to the fried chicken restaurant up the street if you get this in time and want to join us. If not maybe see you in the morning before you leave for Joga. Matt."

I was sweaty and ripe from the day's travel so I folded the note, put it in my shirt pocket and went upstairs for a *mandi*. I wasn't that hungry since a vendor on the train came through with packets of *nasi goering*, fried rice with vegetable and a few shreds of chicken. I'd enjoyed two of them. Still, last night in Jakarta and a couple of friends. We had fun last night. So I opened up my laundry load and got the bulk of it stowed away in my backpack, leaving out a clean shirt and shorts. I thought I'd live it up so I put on clean underwear too.

The fried chicken place was about two blocks in the other direction from the train station. The air had cooled off a bit and the humidity was bearable. I threaded my way along a sidewalk that had been transformed into an open-air food court. Dozens of little pushcarts illuminated by white gas lanterns were serving up Javanese noodles and chicken satay and fried rice, all manner of things. Each cart had a semicircle of stools and the patrons were laughing and socializing and eating with an unselfconscious joy. If I hadn't already eaten, this is where I'd be for the rest of the evening.

The chicken place way brightly lit and a red neon sign over the door read *"Ayam Goering."* A hand painted graphic on the wall beside the door showed a cartoon rooster who looked like the cartoon character Foghorn Leghorn from Saturday morning TV, bowing to a line of baby chicks and pointing the way inside. They were all happily trooping into the restaurant. Seemed a little bizarre.

I leaned in the door and scanned the tables. The place wasn't that big and clearly Matt and Chung weren't here or had moved on. Oh well, I thought, back to the food cart that was making what looked like giant sugar donuts. Maybe there was room for one of those.

I'd walked about four steps when I heard, "Hey, Vern!" and turned to find Chung and Matt walking towards me, each of them with an arm around a dark haired girl. The girls were not made up like at Bronco Billy's and although they were smiling there was a demureness, as if they were slightly embarrassed. The lady that Matt was clinging to was the most attractive to me, with long black hair and a petite nose, beautiful dark eyes and full lips. The dress wasn't so modest either, with a longish leg slit and showing off her breasts enticingly. There was a twinkle in her that I immediately liked. The girl with Chung was a bit shorter and more round of face but she apparently spoke Chinese and said something to Chung. He said something back and then we were all standing face-to-face.

"Hello. I went past the restaurant but I didn't see you guys. What's happening."

Matt, looking proud of himself said, "We went on down the street to the Bintang Club. This is Gita," nodding towards the girl he held, "and this is Yingluk."

I smiled at the two young ladies and said, *"Selamat malam. Nama saya Vern,"* and bowed, maybe a bit awkwardly.

Chung jumped right in, "Yingluk asks me if you would like to meet her friend back at the Club. Right now, we're going to take a taxi to the Sheraton and go up for drinks on the roof garden. We could go back to the Club though and Yingluk could introduce you."

His tipsy good nature made me grin.

"It looks like you guys are already launched. I've got an early morning train. And, I'm still recovering a bit from last night. But thanks."

"Suit yourself. Hey, if I don't see you in the morning, have a great time in Joga."

"Thanks Chung. Have a great time yourself. I think you're going in the right direction. Good meeting you."

We shook hands and I turned slightly to face Matt.

"Maybe I'll run into you in Encino?"

Matt looked pleased with himself and maybe a little boozy too.

"Sure, why not. Had to come to the other side of the world to meet you here." He gave Gita a little hug.

"Have fun at the Sheraton. Don't do anything I wouldn't do," I added.

Matt gave me an exaggerated lascivious wink and they all began to move down the street together. Gita looked back at me once over her shoulder and for a moment, I envied Matt.

The Appearance of Things

II
Jogjakarta

The train clattered and banged into the switchyard of the Jogjakarta station. I tucked away "The Illustrated Man", lost in that funny transition zone when I move from being absorbed in a written world to moving in the material world. I lifted my pack down from the rack and shuffled with the departing crowd towards the carriage door. Brakes squealed, metal on metal protest. While I stood there, I felt for the scrap of notepaper in my pocket on which I'd written half a dozen hotel recommendations. I was getting into the habit of keeping a journal of my days and it was a good place to record the various travel tips I gleaned from others along the way. John and Louise had liked a place called the Borobodur, not far from the university. Mike and Tony had seconded this one. The Hotel Melodee in Jakarta had been a good call so I leaned towards checking out the Borobodur first. I also had the Hotel Bunga, suggested by the English guy George at Lake Toba. And Matt had said the Hotel Rasi, near the train station, was good, cheap and clean but sort of noisy.

The bicycle rickshaws were lined up in front of the station and I signaled to a driver who had looked my way. He gave his rig a running push then jumped on top of his pedals and moved towards me. The rickshaw was a trishaw, like in Medan, a three foot wide bench seat mounted on an axle between two bike wheels. The driver sat behind and pedaled, his seat over a single wheel and a one-speed drive chain. The handlebars were welded to the back of the bench seat and he turned by cranking the whole front seat assembly. The passenger seat had elaborately painted fenders and an accordion type canopy that could be deployed to protect from rain or sun if needed. Same basic design as an old-fashioned buggy, but sort of in miniature. As the trishaw drew closer, I could discern that the mural on the fender was of a Mt. Fuji, snow-capped volcano with a pastoral scene in the foreground, rice paddy and workers threshing the harvest. The driver pulled to a stop in front of me, his face glistening in the late afternoon light.

"*Di mana, Pak?*" 'Where to?'

I decided to start with the recommendation from John and Louise.

"Hotel Borobodur. How much, *berapa?*"

"OK," he said and jumped off his bike to grab my bag. I restrained it and repeated, *"Berapa?"*

"Dua ratus." 'Two hundred.'

I made a sour face and turned away to seek another cab. He pulled at my pack and said in English, "How much you pay?"

I felt I was finally starting to get the hang of this bargaining for everything so I looked at him sternly and said, *"Seratus rupiah cecup."* 'One hundred rupee is enough.'

He looked pained then suddenly broke out into a grin.

"OK," he agreed and made to lift my pack into the passenger seat. He was small and wiry but I felt better about doing it myself. I placed a hand on his shoulder and said, *"Saya"* and hoisted my bag up on to the bench then climbed in beside it. He grinned again and said, *"Bagus!"* and gave me a thumbs-up. He tapped the muscle of his upper arm and pointed at me. "Strong!"

He went behind and gave the whole contraption a push. I heard a "humpff" as he leaned into it, more of an effort this time with all my mass aboard, but we were rolling and set off down the street. The way was cheerfully lit with strings of lights on poles and in the trees. As the day darkened into evening I felt a wash of pleasure when the breeze cooled my skin. Dozens of rickshaws flowed in both directions, people on bicycles and small motor bikes weaving around us. There was a salt tang in the air. I leaned back, delighting in the parade of colored lights and aromas of stir fry and laughter. Joga felt like a happy place. I spotted the Hotel Rasa on the left. It looked decent but not inviting. I could see into the brightly lit reception room through the double glass doors. A woman reading with her legs crossed, industrial décor. Then we were past and a gold banner with "Happy New Year" caught my attention, draped across the front of a Padang restaurant. The front window had shelves displaying bowl after bowl of prepared food of a sort that I recognized from Sumatra. My favorite was called *"Daging Gulai"* an incredibly rich, dark brown curry cooked meat. I noted the location, just in case.

The Borobodur was set back from the street about twenty feet, a well-tended garden of colorful flowering shrubs and a neat little lawn filled the gap, effecting an air of hominess and order. Fronting the street, a wide white veranda offered guests a cozy vantage over the garden, a place to enjoy a beer and supervise the passing street life. Half a dozen travelers were doing just that. I off loaded my pack and passed over the hundred rupees.

"You like go to Water Palace tomorrow, I take you. See the bird market."

My rickshaw driver eyed me hopefully.

"Maybe, *bapak*. *Munkin*," I replied. "But right now I want to see if there is a room. No room, we go to Hotel Bunga. Wait a minute?"

He nodded and pushed his rig over to the edge of the curb, climbed aboard and gazed at me patiently. Hoisting my pack over one shoulder I crossed the small garden, following the brick path leading to the front steps, and began to ascend towards the lobby.

"Hey, Vern, you made it!" a female voice, Aussie accent, bright, friendly, familiar. I glanced toward the group of travelers lounging nearby on the veranda and a red-haired woman detached herself and came towards me, smiling. A pleasurable flash of recognition. "Hi Bernice! Wow, I'm happy to see you." Bernice gave me a clumsy hug over the pack and stood back, surveying me.

"How was your trip down from Toba?"

Bernice had been there on Samosir Island but departed with a small group before Christmas. They were heading for Australia via Bali. She appeared glad to see me. When I looked into the spinning blue pinwheels of her laughing eyes, I felt more than a little glad to see her too. Her curly red hair tumbled down past her shoulders and my darling memory provided me with a quick reminder of her figure from the lakeside beach days. Modestly dressed now in a red and black checkered man's shirt and blue jeans, she was still tall and provocative.

"Amazing, really!" I gushed. "I went all the way to the south and crossed over to Java aboard The Patna.'" I didn't see any recognition of my little Lord Jim joke so I continued, "Did you make it to Bukittinggi?"

"We did. Beyond, in fact. Some of those river crossings!" she rolled her eyes with amusement. "We went down to Padang and took the boat here. None of us wanted to do Jakarta again."

"Hey, come join us," a voice behind her called out. We both swiveled towards the small group enjoying their beers on the veranda. I recognized two others from Toba. A guy, I think called Alex, and brown haired girl named Francine. "Join the party, mate," from a seated man I didn't know.

I offloaded my backpack and leaned it against the frame of the door. I glanced over towards the rickshaw man and held up my index finger in a "give me a moment here" signal. I hope that's how he saw it. Eyes impassive.

I followed Bernice over to the group, smiles all around. I liked that about being on the road, how we'd all just fall in together without a lot of fuss. Bernice made the intros.

"You remember Alex and Franny from Toba?" I nodded hello and held up a hand in a small "howdy" wave. They nodded back, Alex arching his eyebrows too. "This is Paul from Adelaide and Becky and David from Sydney." Paul was what I guess people called "ruggedly handsome", athletic, square jaw, sandy colored hair. His eyes went from me to Bernice and back to me, less friendly than they were a second ago.

Becky and David sort of smiled a hello but they did not look healthy. Becky was thin of face and body. Her limp, straight hair framed a rather pallid countenance and dark areas under her eyes made her look very tired. David was apparently her boyfriend since he was holding her hand as they slumped beside each other in the wide wooden deck chairs. He had the visage of a poet, at least my idea of a poet. A dark Van Dyke beard that was too sparse for his face, awaiting manhood. He was pallid too. They both looked like wilted lettuce.

Bernice noticed my gaze and filled in, "Becky and Matt picked up a wog in Padang. They've just come out of hiding. Been a hell of a time." She looked sympathetically over to Becky who nodded in agreement. I saw that their glasses didn't hold beer but a clear brown liquid that was probably cool tea.

"Glad to hear you're on the mend," I offered and they both smiled wanly.

Paul grabbed the floor, "Aw well, you know how it goes out here. We all get a tummy wog from time to time. That's just part of the joy of travel."

He looked around the group for agreement and got a mumbled assent, nobody too thrilled about it.

David coughed and said simply, "I had blood coming out of my arse."

Becky gaped at him for a moment and the group burst out in laugher. I blinked.

"I had that one in India," offered Alex.

Stories about intestinal or other health problems were fairly common and in any group of travelers it was invariably a topic of conversation that would come up. I didn't have any stories of my own. Yet. Knock on wood.

"Are you all going to be here for a little while?" I asked. "I want to make sure I've got a place to sleep tonight before it gets too far down the road."

Bernice chimed in, "I reckon we'll be here all evening tonight. Except for the Maliboro, this is the best restaurant we've found around here."

She looked at Alex and Francine who agreed.

"So see if they've got a room and then come back and join us." She looked thoughtful for a moment and added, "If they don't we've got a big room with three beds. You'd be welcome."

This last drew a quick look from Paul that I read to be a mix of surprise and irritation. Francine didn't look too enthusiastic either.

"Thanks. That's great, just in case." I held up an open palm to the group and said, "See you in a bit."

I walked with my pack towards the front desk and again acknowledged the waiting rickshaw driver. I felt a twinge of guilt that he'd been waiting so long but it was only a few minutes and I didn't see anybody knocking down the door for a ride. Behind the counter, two men were engaged in rolling fork and spoon settings into paper napkins. For the restaurant, I guessed. The one nearest me, with a wide nose, looked up at my approach.

"*Selamat sore,*" he greeted.

"*Selamat sore, bapak. Saya mau kamar.*" 'Good afternoon sir, I want a room.'

He switched to English and said, "How many nights?"

I knew from my Trailfinders rough guide that Joga was supposed to have a lot to offer. A university town with good music, local history and some archaeological sites not far from town. Supposedly a good beach was just down the road too. Matt had talked it up, back in Jakarta. I wanted to go out to the namesake of the hotel, the ruins called Borobodur from a time when Java was Buddhist. I'd heard too that the batik workshops near a place called the Water Palace were really worth the time.

"Three, maybe four nights, *pak.*"

The clerk passed me a paper form and a pen. "Passport and name, please."

I handed my passport across the desk as he added, "Five hundred rupees per night. Pay the first night now please."

I dug a five hundred out of my wallet, lay the note on the counter and finished filling out the registration forms. He opened my passport and looked up at me. "American," he said. It wasn't a question so I made what I hoped was a pleasant face and nodded. He gazed at me a moment longer, as if considering something then turned and removed a key from one of the wall boxes and laid it on the counter. "Room twenty seven, second floor. Please enjoy your stay."

He went back to rolling place settings.

I snagged the key and made a decision to employ the patient rickshaw driver for tomorrow morning. When I went down the steps, he was perched on the handlebars facing me.

"You stay here, *bapak*? I know very good hotel. Much cheaper than here."

He was a go-getter. "*Jah*, I'm staying here but I will go to the Water Palace tomorrow and bird market." His face lit up and he said enthusiastically, "What time I come? Good to go early. Very hot later." He made a gesture of fanning his face with his hand.

"What's your name. *Siapa nama Anda?*" I asked.

"I am Birdy," he replied, touching his chest with his right hand. He tapped the painted fender, which read "Berdi Suwata".

"My name."

"Well hello Berdi," I responded. "*Nama saya* Vern."

"Mr. Bern" he said. Close enough.

"So Berdi, how much to go and come from the water temple?"

"Three hundred rupee. Far from here, *jao*, and I wait for you."

"Two hundred is better," I offered.

He shrugged and said, "Ok, ok. We start at eight in morning."

I thought he was right about the heat so I said, "Ok Berdi, see you tomorrow at eight."

"*Sampai jumpa*," he called as he got the rig rolling and hopped aboard. I waved him off and turned to go upstairs. I noticed that Bernice was watching me.

Room twenty seven was on the east side of the building and I could make out tree tops in the distance picking up the last orange light of the fading sunset. Set amongst them a collection of two storied buildings, like a barracks. The university maybe?

Down the hall I found the *mandi* and bathed, redressed and headed downstairs. Paul and Alex were gone, their empty beer glasses and green

Bintang bottles still on the table. The ashtray was full of butts. Business opportunity for somebody. Becky and David sat listlessly, peering down on the street scene below. Frannie's face looked more at ease, now that I had my own room, or maybe I was just imagining.

"Well cobber, fancy a beer?" Bernice giggled. I pulled out a chair and joined them at the table.

"Sounds good. Can I get one for you two?"

Frannie smiled at Bernice, "Now 'ees a proper gennelman, 'int he?" and looked over at me. She was attractive when she smiled.

About halfway through our beers, Becky and David tottered to their feet and wished us a good night.

"I'm still fucked," lamented Becky. "Those pills we got are helpin' but not fast enough."

David said nothing but gave us a weak wave as they went inside.

"What pills?" I asked.

"Oh, the one's they sell at the chemist's shop. Everybody swears by 'em," said Franny. "I've used them a couple of times but you have to find fresh curd to eat after, when you're done, or they bugger up your insides."

Must be some kind of GI sterilizer. Yogurt would replace the beneficial bacteria that get killed off.

We ordered plates of Java noodles with chicken and an order of fried fish with vegetables. Aromatic and delicious with the cold beer.

"They'd get better faster without the morphia," mused Bernice darkly. She and Franny exchanged a look. It surprised me but I didn't ask further.

"So how did you like *Steppenwolf*?" Bernice was the girl I traded with for *The Illustrated Man* back at Lake Toba. She made a face.

"Aw, I tried it for a while but it was too thick. You Americans like that sort of thing, I reckon, but it's not for me."

She looked at me warily for a moment, then asked, "Did you like *The Illustrated Man*?"

I felt suddenly awkward. To me, *Steppenwolf* was brilliant and transformative. Hermann Hesse had held up a mirror in his magic theater for my mind and spirit. I couldn't understand how she could dismiss it all so out of hand. Didn't read it, is how.

"I like Bradbury. I think my favorite is still *Fahrenheit 451* but *The Illustrated Man* was enjoyable. I liked how each tattoo was a story."

Bernice nodded. "I've heard of that one. What's it about?"

"Well, the title refers to the temperature at which paper starts to burn and…"

A clatter in the lobby gave us a start and we all looked over towards the door. Paul appeared from around the corner, brushing the front of his shirt, Alex just behind.

"…well the stupid bastard should look where he's going," a surly expression writ large across his meaty face. He looked up and saw us at the table and the aggressive face disappeared, the sun coming out from behind the clouds. He strolled over and looked down at Franny and Bernice.

"And how would you little beauties like to go dancing?"

He wasn't talking to me.

Bernice looked enthused. "Same place as last night?" she asked.

"Aw yeah, only game in town that I know of," crooned Paul.

Bernice turned to me, a playful gleam in her eye, "How about it, Vern. Night life in Joga. It's fun. They were playing "Mr. Natural" last night."

"Mr. Natural from *ZAP* comics?" I asked, feeling a bit confused.

"No, the new album from Down Under. Our local boys, the BeeGees"

I felt my heart drop at the mention of the BeeGees. The last thing on my list was listening to bubble gum from Barry Gibbs while smarmy Paul came on to the ladies.

"I'm not much of a dancer," I offered lamely, "but don't let me stop you."

Paul responded with what I'd call a self-satisfied smirk.

"Well, we'll miss your company," he said smoothly and offered his arm to Bernice.

"M' lady."

She was a little looped now and giggled as she stood. Frannie was up and ready to go as well so I settled back in my chair, topped off my beer and toasted them, "Don't come home too late." They all laughed and were off. How could she like the BeeGees? How could she not like *Steppenwolf*? I sighed, finished my beer and headed for bed.

The Appearance of Things

Berdi was stationed in front of the hotel at seven thirty in the morning. When I emerged on to the veranda with my bowl of salty gruel and a cup of tea, he waved cheerfully. I waved back, pulled out a chair and tucked in. I liked this *"bubor"* breakfast of soupy oatmeal with crisped onions and chilis. Round it out with a splash of the soy sauce stuff called *kecap asin* and spicy was a good way to start the day. There weren't any other westerners abroad at this hour. I imagined the dancers were all sleeping it off. I paid up and strolled down to the street level.

"Selamat pagi, Berdi."

"Selamat pagi, pak Bern."

Berdi touched the center of his chest with his right palm. His light brown Nehru hat was the same color as his eyes, his slight but wiry body loosely swathed in a button down shirt that extended almost to his knees. His trousers, of the same khaki toned cloth, had cuffs at the ankles buttoned closed. He looked well dressed.

"You are dressed very fine today," I observed, to which he replied, "Pak Bern, while you go about the *Taman Sari*, I go to the masjid." He was going to the mosque while I poked around. OK, fair enough.

The morning air was cool as he pedaled down the boulevard towards the Water Palace. Berdi had called it the *Taman Sari*. Make a note to find out what that means. The mild spice of morning cooking fires perfumed the air and I leaned back in the carriage seat enjoying the yellow-orange freshness of the rising sun. To the left those barracks building I'd seen from my room. A white wooden sign, about the size of a door on its side proclaimed, "University of Gadjah Mada" with the red, white, black and yellow Garuda seal of government conferring official endorsement. The campus had a park-like ambience, shaded by trees with a roughly cut under cover, green but not a lawn. A few knots of young people clutching bags and notebooks strolled between buildings in the distance.

I thought of the Bruin Walk, the wide sidewalk at UCLA that went uphill from the student store, effectively dividing the campus. I was a science nerd and we nerds inhabited the south campus, towards the hospital and biomedical buildings. Chemistry, engineering, botany and so on, all with their own modern complexes. North of the Bruin Walk was the liberal arts campus. We science people tended to view that side as the basket weaving crowd. They looked at us as the unenlightened crowd. The anti-war rallies all happened from the Bruin Walk north. That was where Jane Fonda had addressed a passionate gathering of students and faculty a few years back. The war in Vietnam was on the news nightly, pouring into the living rooms of America with body counts and horror stories. In my sophomore year, the government cancelled student deferments. When I received my draft card and instructions to report to the Selective Service center for my physical my solidarity with the anti-war, anti-Nixon crowd moved up a few notches.

Now it was the start of 1975. Mr. Nixon was on his way to obscurity and the Vietnam War was coming to its conclusion. I wondered what the passionate causes were for students here in Indonesia, in Java.

"*Taman Sari*," said Berdi, pointing in the distance. I followed where he indicated and could make out tall bamboo poles, most having a small square box, like a flag, situated on the top of the pole. A ruined wall complex, higher than the sea of surrounding rooftops, defined the horizon.

"*Pasar Ngasem*, the bird market," Berdi smiled, "Very good to see. Biggest bird market in Java."

We came to a halt near a faded blue building. The ornamented arches, the open floor plan, the gold crescent and star roof vane, all told me that this was a *masjid*, a mosque. "When you come back, I'm waiting here," Berdi said brightly. I slung my daypack over my shoulder and nodded, "Ok, see you here."

The big wall in the distance must be the Water Palace ruin so I plunged into a narrow alley leading in that direction. An elderly woman wearing a sagging turban sat in a doorway, picking at a scrap of cloth. Her wizened face and rheumy old eyes followed my passage. A house with one of the tall bamboo poles around the next corner, delicate basket at the top of the pole. Peering upwards against the bright blue of the sky I could make out a small yellow and black bird flitting back and forth in the basket. Ahead, more poles, each topped with a cage. The lines descending allowed for the cages to be raised and lowered like flags. Large round cages, square cages, even conical cages, held birds up into the morning air. Many of them were singing and I found that if I focused on one cage and watched carefully, I could tease out that particular song from the growing cacophony around me. The chattering of hundreds, maybe thousands of birds swelled as I pushed deeper into the web of alleys radiating from the base of the big wall. Dozens of finely made bamboo and rattan cages lined the passage. I found my camera at the bottom of my day sack and focused in on a dark blue and yellow mynah bird, round red eyes holding me as I approached. Impressions - the forest of poles with their hanging cages, two older men straddling a bench involved in an intense negotiation, an orange and white cat slinking along a wall. I was getting some good shots. Then a stone archway to my left, rough cut steps leading up into the wall of the ruin. Once atop the wall, I was rewarded with a multicolored vista out over the bird market neighborhood. Stepping into the open, to get a better shot over the rooftops, I smelled the sweet clove cigarette smoke wafting in from somewhere. Behind me a group of young men sat talking, taking in the view whilst they smoked. One boy looked over at me, a bit wary for some reason.

"*Selamat pagi,*" I said and smiled. 'I'm friendly, don't worry.'

His face relaxed. His two friends looked my way and inclined their heads in a return greeting. I snapped my photo of the market vista and stowed my camera back in the day sack. The passage way led past the small group and when I was abreast of them, the first young man, neatly dressed in a white tunic, spoke to me.

"*Darimana, pak?*" 'Where are you from?'

"*Dari* California, Los Angeles."

The speaker broke into a grin and said in English, "An American!"

His associates eyed me too and there was no unfriendliness I could discern. Some European or Australian travelers would offer opinions about Vietnam when I said I was American but mostly people were cool. They didn't hold me personally responsible for some of the bad choices my government had made over the years. Most people I met were more positive about America than young Americans. The only place anybody really gave me any shit was at a pub in London, a loudmouth showing off for his buddies.

"May I speak English with you?" The eagerness of the young man who had asked me where I was from was plain to see. I smiled and held out my hand, "*Nama saya Vern. Siapa nama anda?*"

It was his turn to grin and he took my hand, "Good Indonesian! My name is Luli. This my friend Sapon," indicating the boy who sported a thin Fu Man Chu beard, "and Dani." His confederates touched their chests with their right hand, a respectful gesture I was coming to appreciate and emulate.

Luli noted that I had looked at his cigarette and he reached into his shirt pocket, producing a yellow and red packet of *Djam Sam Soe*, the filterless *kreteks* that were the best, or so I thought.

He held the pack out to me. "*Anda mau merokok?*" then in English, "Would you like to smoke?"

"Yes, thank you."

I extracted one of the small cigars from the proffered pack. Dani produced a box of wooden matches and struck one on the box, extending the light out to me.

"*Terima Kasih*," I said and leaned over the light with the cigarette and drew in. The sweet smoke almost made me cough but I exhaled in a controlled manner. Coolness preserved.

"I really like the *kretek* of Indonesia."

All three young men smiled broadly and a place was made for me to sit beside them. We smoked contentedly, silently, for a time. Then Luli cleared his throat and asked, "How long you come to Java?"

It wasn't the first time that an Indonesian wanted to practice their English with me, but there was something here that went beyond the usual twenty question game and it drew me in, focusing on Luli's earnest expression.

"I came to Java only three days ago, to Jakarta. But I came from Sumatra. I was in Sumatra for four weeks. *Empat minggu.*"

Luli's silence invited me to ask a question.

"Luli, do you go to the university here in Yogyakarta?" They looked like students.

Luli smiled and nodded.

"Yes, we all go to the university."

He said something I didn't get in Indonesian. Both Dani and Sapon looked over and affirmed that yes, they too were students.

We sat and talked and smoked, mostly small talk. Then Luli asked me, "In America, you are allowed to protest, yes?"

I suddenly felt a twinge of apprehension creep into my spine. Was this going to be the Vietnam conversation?

"Yes, we can protest. At my school there were protests against the Vietnam War. Also, protests in favor of things. Civil rights for black Americans."

All three were focused, looking at me intently.

Luli almost whispered, "Here in Indonesia, if we protest the army kills us. Put us in jail. No freedom."

He was shaking slightly when he spoke. The darkened brows of Dani and Sapon told me they understood what Luli had said. They agreed with him.

Luli continued, almost pleading, "You have freedom. You are very...... fortunate to have freedom."

A feeling of pride about the USA surprised me. I realized I wasn't accustomed to feeling pride, not for a long time.

"Do you know Malari?" asked Dani.

I thought he meant malaria so I said, "Yes. Very dangerous. I have medicine against malaria."

Dani looked confused for a moment and turned to Luli, who said, "No, not malaria. Malari. A big protest last year in Jakarta."

I shook my head, no, I did not know.

Luli eyed me for a moment then went on, "To protest foreigners taking away from Indonesia. The Japanese ambassador came. Japan takes away so much from Indonesia."

Both Dani and Sapon bobbed their heads in affirmation, their eyes downcast.

"Students protest for three days. Then army came, shooting many students, many dead and hurt. They arrest more than a thousand people. Now," and he lowered his voice, as if we might be overheard, "Suharto says no more protests. No more student politics." He looked up at me with pain searing his eyes, "No more freedom now."

We all sat quietly for a time. Sapon got up and went down the stone stairwell, returning a few moments later with four small glass bottles of cool, sweet tea.

We shared another cigarette. I felt at a loss to offer any wisdom or advice. We take it as a right in the USA that we can protest what we want. Sometimes, I reflected, it doesn't work out too well, like the students shot dead by the national guard at Kent State. Or the beatings and murders around the civil rights marches. They killed Martin Luther King in 1968 but we keep on going. The army doesn't come in and say, "You're done now." Sitting with these young men, I really began to wonder what freedom is.

Luli shifted and stood. He seemed to make a decision and swiveled to face me.

"Pak Bern, please come with us for *makan siang*, for lunch. I will meet some friends... you would like, I think."

A small anxiety spike followed by a "sure, what the heck" feeling.

"*Terima kasih*, Luli. I would like to join you."

We filed down the stone steps and made our way back along one of the multitude of alleyways, different than the one I entered. Emerging into a small plaza shaded by a huge, gnarled broadleaf tree, I spotted the blue mosque where Berdi awaited.

"Luli," I touched his arm, "I have a trishaw waiting there."

I pointed towards where Berdi was now reclined on the passenger bench. He perked up when he saw us approaching. Luli spoke rapidly to Dani and Sopon, then to Berdi.

"OK... we will go to Maliboro," and he climbed into the trishaw. Dani waved over another trishaw waiting expectantly nearby and the four of us set out towards the university. I felt taken in hand and a flush of pleasure to be in the company of Indonesians rather than other travelers.

The Maliboro restaurant occupied a well-maintained white colonial era building. The dining area was settled in the open central garden, protected from the street noise. A number of white shirted students were already enjoying meals in the cool, tree shaded atrium.

"Hey, Luli!" a greeting from a table of young men and women. Plenty of open seats and we steered towards them. A very beautiful young woman met my gaze as we approached the table. She was my idea of a Polynesian princess or at least my fantasy. Thick, straight black hair cascaded down her back and framed the sides of her perfect oval face. Her lips were full but with a sensual slight depression in the middle, coy black bedroom eyes set wide apart, Asian islander nose, flattened but not pug. Radiant smile as we arrived at the table. I tried to shift my eyes to the others as Luli introduced me, nodding and trying to be gracious, but my gaze was yanked back again and again to this exotic beauty who met my eyes full on. She smiled demurely as Luli introduced her.

"Eva Simbolon, Pak Bern"

"*Selamat dating*," she cooed and I was entranced. Did she just flutter her eyes?

We seated ourselves at the long table and Luli jumped into a discussion with those nearest him.

"You are from America?" a voice on my left. A man in a black Nehru hat, thin black rimmed glasses, pressed long sleeve white shirt with a Mandarin collar. His expression mildly amused, fine features, dark brown intelligent eyes.

"*Jah. Dari* California."

"Oh," he smiled, "you are speaking Indonesian." His accent was English, cultured.

"Trying," I offered, "barely succeeding." His eyes crackled in a wry amusement. "My name is Jodo. I have the advantage of a diplomatic family and growing up in London. We can speak English, if you like." A small flush of relief. It was fun to be with a group of Indonesians but my Bahasa wasn't much and I was feeling a little out of it language wise.

"Thank you," I said, and then asked, "Are you a student as well?"

Jodo nodded and steepled his fingers as if he was about to deliver a lecture. "A student of sorts," he intoned. "I am studying law here at the university but I am also teaching English. Many of these," he indicated students around us at the table, "are engaged at one level or another in my courses."

A tinkle of laughter drew my attention and the lovely Eva looked in my direction. We smiled at each other.

"Hello Eva," Jodo called, "Have you met our American friend?"

Her eyes sparkled with amusement and she replied in clear English, "Just a quick introduction. May I join you?"

Not waiting for a reply, she rose and moved around the table carrying her iced tea, pulled out a chair from a nearby, unoccupied table and settled herself obliquely to Jodo and myself. As she sat her mane of dark hair wafted towards me, the aroma of some tropical flower and something more earthy, more disturbing.

"Let's try again," she smiled and extended her hand, "Eva."

Her hand was sexy.

"Vern," I replied.

Jodo looked at us, neutral, amused? I could see now that he was older than most of us at the table.

"Eva is one of my best students in English," the shadow of a smile directed towards her.

"You are more than generous Pak Jodo," her voice deep, throaty. She turned a little towards me.

"So Pak Vern, where are you from in America. Such a big place!"

When she spoke to me I felt like an ice cream cone getting licked, getting enjoyed, and I wanted to be the best.

"I'm..." my voice cracked. Clear my throat, start again. "I'm from Los Angeles, North Hollywood, really."

I wanted to get some name recognition in there. North Hollywood was a crap place but maybe I'd get points for the Hollywood part. She leaned into me, about to share something intimate.

"And what has brought you so far from home?" soft as silk.

I very nearly blurted out, "To meet you!" but at least some self-control was still functional and I fell back on a home baked, corn-fed boy sort of sincerity.

"Well, I wanted to know more about the world and myself before I, you know, got myself locked into a career path. I was going to school to become a doctor but now," I hesitated, "now I'm not sure that's what I want to do."

"A doctor is a good thing to be," she reflected. Then unexpectedly, "Are you married?"

"No. Not married. How about you?"

She looked down at her hands and quietly said, "No, not married yet."

Jodo's face was impassive during all of this. He looked from Eva to me and back again, bracing his hand on the arms of the chair, preparing to rise.

"Well, I need to get back to the University. A pleasure to make your acquaintance. How long will you be with us in Yogyakarta?"

"I don't have any plans to leave yet. I do want to visit Borobodur and spend some time getting to Yogya better."

Jodo rose to his feet and both Eva and I stood with him.

"I would also urge you to visit Prambanan, a Hindu temple quite as ancient as Borobodur. It is very much worth the candle."

Jodo and I shook hands, following it up with touching our respective chests.

"I see you are learning some of our ways," he said, with a side look at Eva. "I hope we shall meet again." Then he was gone.

I looked at Eva but before I could get my mouth working Luli called over, "Pak Bern, do you like to try the *Jawa mee goering?*"

A waitress was standing beside the table. Luli, Sapon and Dani were looking at me expectantly. Oh yeah, we had come here to eat.

"*Ja, terima kasih, mee goering* for me. And ice tea."

The waitress made a note and moved away from the table. Luli said, "Eva, join us here," and indicated two empty seats. Eva spoke to him in Bahasa. He nodded and shrugged, turning back to his conversation with the others.

"My family is going to Borobodur tomorrow. I would be happy for you to join us," she said.

Are you kidding? "Yes, that would be great. Thank you. How should I find you?"

"Where do you stay in Yogya?"

"Do you know the Hotel Borobodur? I'm there."

"Yes, I know the place. Shall we say nine o'clock tomorrow then?"

She stood then, making ready to go and I rose as well. The dancing light in her eyes was as inviting as it was erotic, illuminating her lovely face. Standing, she was about a head shorter than me. There, in the warmth of the early afternoon, the perfume of her young womanhood swirled between us and I felt like a compressed spring.

"Nine o'clock would be wonderful. I look forward to the day."

She said nothing more but simply nodded, turned gracefully and slipped towards the entry salon. My impression was that people in Yogya moved more slowly, were more relaxed. Her black hair hung past her waist and she was every inch a princess from my point of view.

The noodles were delicious, a spicy garlic, ginger and chili background with crisp green stalks, a fried egg and bits of chicken redolent of peanut sauce. Luli took a sip of his ice tea and said something to Dani, who frowned, then said, "*Ja, baik.*" Sort of a "yes, ok."

"Pak Bern, I would like to show you *pantai* Parangtritis. Not far and Dani say you can use his moto." I looked up at Dani who smiled wanly and nodded his head in a "yes."

Pantai meant "beach" so Luli was inviting me to ride down to the local beach with him on a motorcycle. Vision of a tropical white sand beach, coconut palms, crystal clear blue water, yeah!

"Yes, *bagus*, excellent! Thank you," I enthused.

We finished up our lunch and I paid for everybody. At two dollars for the whole thing generosity was affordable here. It wasn't expected and they started to protest but I said please, I wanted to give back a bit. I could see they were delighted and I felt good too.

Sapon excused himself as we departed from the Maliboro and began walking back towards the university campus. Dani, Luli and I strolled up a shaded side street to a house that had multiple small motorcycles parked in front.

"We live in this house," proclaimed Luli, "Many students here."

He indicated up and down the street and I could see that it was a Java version of student housing, like we had around the environs of UCLA. Bicycles, motos, young people walking, lots of comings and goings. Luli stopped in front of a yellow motorcycle that was a little worse for wear but the tires looked good. Dani reached into his pocket and pulled out a small silver key and placed it in my hand.

"*Hati hati*," he said, careful.

The bike was a Honda. It had a 90 on the small gas tank so I assumed it was a 90cc. For a time I rode a 125 cc to school and it was good fun. I liked romping around on the fire roads and building pads in the hills behind UCLA, where we lived. It wasn't exactly a dirt bike but it had enough spunk to do the steep stuff. More than once I went flying through the air. I had a small burn scar on the inside of my right calf from when the bike went out from under me in some loose sand and briefly pinned my leg under the hot exhaust pipe. I'd stopped riding after an unexpected fall on Sunset Boulevard nearly put my skull under the wheels of a truck. It was so weird. I was riding along down Sunset and about two hundred feet ahead, the traffic light changed. It was a clear, dry Los Angeles day. I braked, like always and the next thing I knew I was on the ground, sliding, wrapped up in the bike. A screech of tires and I turned my head to see a large truck tire inches away from my face. Freaked me out so I stopped street riding and just kept to country trails with no traffic. That bike died when I loaned it to an unskilled friend who accidentally popped the clutch and jammed it into a wall. Bent the front forks way back and wasn't worth fixing. The memory helped me appreciate Dani's apprehension in loaning me his bike

"*Hati hati*," I agreed with Dani. I turned the key and kick-started the little beast. It sputtered then caught. The motor sounded good and Dani nodded approvingly. I guess he felt more confident since I looked to be competent.

Luli walked down another thirty feet and pulled his bike out and into the street. He started up and buzzed down to join us. Luli's bike was a Yamaha and had that funny "wing ding ding ding" voice.

"Thank you, Dani. *Terima Kasih banyak.*" Dani smiled now. Luli and I pulled out into the street and headed south. The road leading from Yogya down to Parangtritis was two lanes of pitted asphalt. There were a few resurfaced sections bisecting rice paddy and what I thought were peanut fields. The afternoon sun was fierce but the breeze as we rode kept us cool. I was out in front for a time. The warm light of the day flickering past the tall palms, the roar of the little motor, the whipping wind making my eyes water a bit, all flowed into and around me and turned into a smile. This was freedom, riding a motorcycle to the beach in South Central Java.

When we pulled into Parangtritis though, my tropical beach fantasy took a hit. Dozens of ramshackle huts crowded the shore. The instant we arrived hawkers descended on us with fruit drinks, necklaces made of seashells and cold coconuts. Luli was clear with them and they backed off but the beach was littered and tired looking. The ocean was lovely and I had a swim while Luli watched from the shore. I waved for him to join me but he shook his head. When I came out of the water I asked him what was wrong and he smiled sheepishly, "No swim." I was embarrassed that I hadn't figured that one out on my own.

We walked up to one of the better looking shacks. I had a fresh water *mandi* in the back and Luli ordered us a couple of cold coconuts. I liked how they whacked off the end of a large green coconut, scraped the inside with a sharp spoon and threw in a dose of "syrup." It was both a drink that refreshed and a satisfying snack, the soft baby coconut flesh having a texture like firm jello.

On our ride back, the fire light of the sunset filtering through the jungle made the paddy glow, the orange gold light causing the multitude of greens to pop brilliantly. A Vermeer landscape set in the tropics. I opened up the throttle on a miles long straight stretch. I was probably going forty five miles an hour but I felt like a rocket ship approaching warp speed. For no reason,

I howled "Yeee haww!" as I flew over the road. A clutch of small children gaped as I roared past with my yell. They must have thought I was a demon!

At eight thirty the next morning I sat on the veranda of the Borobodur enjoying my bowl of spicy, salty gruel and tea. Luli and I had wished each other well and agree to meet at the Maliboro again this evening for supper. I filled the gas tank of Dani's bike as a thank you. It was my first time patronizing one of the soda pop bottle gas stations and the kid seemed in awe that a westerner, an "*orang utan*", would stop and buy gas from him.

Bernice and Frannie were on the deck too. We nodded to each other but didn't get cozy. I didn't see any of the others from that first night. A tall, thin French guy was talking animatedly to a woman who looked bored. I heard the word "shit" a lot but couldn't make out much else through the thick accent.

Just before nine, a white Toyota van pulled up in front of the hotel. I'd already paid up and was waiting, hoping the offer from Eva was going to come to fruition. Hoping that more than that was going to come to fruition actually. The passenger door slid open and Eva stepped into the early morning light. Her hair was down and she wore a slightly frilly white top that accented her figure. A tan skirt followed the line of her legs, modest but provocative. She looked stunning. Spotting me on the veranda, she waved as I rose and moved towards the stairs. I descended the steps and Eva moved to meet me. She came forward and we hugged. My hands felt the smooth sinews of her back and I was ready to keep going but she took my forearms and extricated herself. A coquettish grin. "Ready to go?" she asked.

"Yes, very ready. Thank you for coming."

We walked the short distance back to the waiting van and Eva climbed into the middle seat, beckoning me to follow. I braced myself on the edge of the roof and slid into the small vehicle. Happening to glance up as I was settling into the seat I caught Bernice's face. I don't know why but I gave her a thumbs-up. Poker face, no response, door closes. We pull away from the curb and the journey begins.

A woman who reminded me of Imelda Marcos sat in the front passenger seat and she swiveled to face me, smiling.

"This is my mother," Eva introduced, "and this is my brother Jaki."

The driver caught my eye in his rear view mirror and made a little wave.

"I'm pleased to meet you," I responded. Then to Eva, "How would I say that in Bahasa?"

Eva looked at me evenly and pronounced, "*Saya senang bertemu dengan Anda.*" I repeated the phrase, adding "Ibu Simbolon" at the start, to her mother who smiled and said in English, "Pleased to meet you too. But call me Maria."

"Of course, thank you. Maria is a lovely name but it doesn't sound Indonesian." I was curious.

Eva chimed in, "We are Toba Batak, Christians. There is even a Portuguese ancestor on my father's family." I hadn't noticed when we met but now the small golden cross suspended from a fine gold chain around her lovely neck caught my attention.

"I was at Lake Toba in December," I said. "It's a very beautiful area. I stayed out on Samosir Island for Christmas."

Maria smiled. "A lovely place to spend Christmas," she agreed. Then, "Are you a Christian, Vern?"

The question caught me off guard. I tend to look at things from a scientific perspective these days. When I was younger, I was exposed to Sunday school Christianity at a local congregational church. Mainly I just looked forward to seeing Gretchen Voth, who would lean back in her chair so I could see her underwear. We liked each other. I'd also attended some summer camps sponsored by the local YMCA where they did their best to corral us into a morning chapel. The camp counselors were usually dads from the community. I appreciated the "dad" energy since my father had been killed. A few counselors, however, were real keen on bringing us to Jesus. I observed that the more preachy they were, the bigger assholes they were along with it. It didn't win me over and maybe sent me in the other direction. I didn't give it much thought these days.

"Well," I stammered, "I come from a ranching family. I guess you could say we had a Christian background. We always celebrated Christmas."

Maria's eyes narrowed and I felt like I was losing points so I hastily added, "In our family, religion was mainly taking off your hat when you found yourself in a beautiful place, like the redwood forests or a sunrise."

Eva and her mother exchanged a glance. The van hit a bump and we all started.

"Sorry," Jaki said. Then he came to my rescue. "It's like that for us at Borobodur. Even though it's a Buddhist shrine, it has a special significance for our family."

Eva nodded and added, "My grandfather worked with the English on the restoration after the war, when the Japanese had left. He used to say that Gautama was the Buddha of wisdom and compassion while Jesus was the Buddha of love."

For the rest of the hour long ride out we shared stories of our families and ourselves. I learned that Eva's clan had a business in palm oil, with offices in both Jakarta and Singapore. English was important since it was the only language that they and their foreign business associates had in common.

"It is ironic," observed Jaki, "that while we were glad for the end of foreign domination, the language of our former masters is still the best way for nations across Asia to talk to each other. I hope that will change."

Borobodur was visible through the forest when we pulled off the main road and onto the dirt track leading towards the site. It was a huge layer cake of a place, surrounded by a wide dirt clearing that served as both a parking lot and a bazaar. Hawkers' stalls were right up against the monument and it looked to me like we'd have to climb over them to get access to the first level. Stepping out of the van, we were set upon by a throng of trinket sellers. They made the guys at Parangtritis beach look like amateurs. Boys and girls waving small Buddha statues, necklaces and framed photographs of the monument, their parents shoving bottled drinks and baskets of food at us. Jaki locked the van and had a brief conversation with two young men. They came to some agreement and set themselves beside the car and we made our way over to a set of stone steps. An aging wood shed with a corrugated steel roof flanked the steps, within a counter behind which sat a middle aged official in an olive green uniform. A printed sign read, "Kantor Pariwisata Entry 50 Rps." I stepped forward, paid for four tickets and we mounted the steps to the first terrace. The hawkers didn't follow, which was a blessing.

"Thank you, Vern," said Maria. "Jaki and I will have tea before we go up, but wait for us at the summit will you?"

To the left there were half a dozen small tables with chairs, shaded by large square umbrellas. Eva reached for my hand and led me towards the next upward staircase. We waved to her mother and brother and began our ascent to the next level.

"The custom," she explained, "is to keep your right shoulder pointed in towards the center as you walk around each level."

So we set off to the left, clockwise, and passed one headless Buddha after another. The figures were a bit larger than life size and set into alcoves in the wall. The bodies were seated in the classic lotus position with the arms and hands in a variety of positions. On statues where the arm and hand had been extended they had apparently been chopped off, leaving the forlorn stub of an elbow. The walls that defined the level were carved stone with figures in chariots, figures in robes walking with attendants who shaded them with large parasols. Wish someone was shading me with a parasol right now. A few stretches of scared stone where carvings had been cut out of the frieze. What was here was beautiful but the vandalism was also very much in evidence. A very few of the Buddhas did have heads, the ringlets of stone hair framing a serene face. I'd seen these faces before, on the Buddha heads displayed in the British Museum and the Louvre in Paris. As we continued our circumambulation I felt I was moving through a crime scene and I knew where the bodies were buried. Well, the heads at any rate.

All the way around the second level was further than I thought. The sun was brutal, heat radiating from the black stone of the monument. The prospect of four more circumambulations before we reached the top was unappealing. I could already feel the rivulets of sweat trickling down my back, causing my shirt to stick to my skin.

"Eva, could we just head for the top, would you mind?"

Her smooth forehead also glistened with moisture and she smiled wryly. "Do you want to go straight to desire?"

I must have had a humorous expression because she laughed and explained, "The top three levels are circles. You can't see them from here. Desire is the first, followed by form, and finally formlessness."

Got it. "Yes," I grinned, "let's head straight for desire." And we moved up the central staircase together.

Our effort was greeted with a delightfully cool breeze and a wonderful vista in all directions. Up here each circular platform was studded with bell shaped stone block enclosures, each of which housed a seated Buddha looking out through the checker board pattern of openings in the stone. More were intact than down below, but the vandals had been up here too.

I was sweating more profusely now from our climb and little trickles rolled down my brow and the sides of my face. Eva was moist as well but on her it looked erotic.

We sat on the lip of one of the stupas, looking out, the light breeze cooling us a bit. Eva's left hand rested on her knee and I placed my right over hers. She turned her face up to me, I leaned over, our lips meeting in a tentative, thrilling first kiss. Her palm turned up under mine and our fingers interlaced. She leaned her head against my shoulder. The earth perfume of her moist skin washed over me and for an instant I was flying above the tree tops that stretched out before us.

"Here," she said lightly and stood before me. She extracted a red and white bandana from her blouse side pocket. In my sitting position, she moved forward between my legs until we were very close. "Let's see if this helps," she whispered and placed the folded bandana across my forehead. She leaned into me to tie it behind my head, her breasts corralling my cheeks and I kissed the soft skin of her chest. The thin gold chain of the cross felt cool on my lips.

She leaned back then and made to admire her handiwork. My face was tingling where I had touched her.

"There," she smiled, "that looks good on you."

I reached out with both hands and held her trim waist, the skin warm through her thin blouse. I drew her towards me but felt her stiffen at the same instant I heard the voices coming up behind us. A father and his two young sons clambered up on to "desire" and I felt the moment slip away. Eva took my right arm and stepped back, inviting me to my feet. She slipped my arm around her waist and we walked towards form and on to formlessness.

On the ride back to Yogya, we were mostly quiet. Jaki had a decent collection of eight track tapes in the car and the tinkling Javanese classical music saw us home. Eva and I held hands and played some finger games but under Maria's watchful presence it was all promise.

"Do you have plans for tomorrow, Eva?" I tried to sound more casual than I felt. "I'd like to go out to that Hindu temple that Joko spoke of yesterday, Pramanan I think it was called."

"Prambanam," Eva corrected. "I have a class in the morning."

She glanced up front at her mother who was silent and looking ahead but clearly listening closely.

"Well, I'm meeting Luli at the Maliboro for dinner tonight. Yesterday, at the beach, we talked about going to the temple. We could all go together if your class finished early enough."

"That would be fun. I will see Luli tomorrow morning in class. Let me look at what I need to do and I will join you if I'm able."

That evening, over a small supper, Luli, Dani and I agreed to take the 11:30 am bus out to Prambanan. His class ended at 10:30 and that meant that Eva's class.

"In Indonesia, not like America," Luli explained. "Girls not go, do not go, alone with a boy. It is not a good, not proper."

So I was very pleasantly surprised when I met Luli the next morning at his student house and Eva was waiting there beside him.

"Dani cannot come," said Luli, "but we can go together."

Eva looked up at me with soft eyes and the hint of a smile. Her hair was pulled back and she wore blue jeans with a short-sleeved batik print of red butterflies on a crinkled sky blue background.

"Ready when you are," she smiled.

We walked together down to the main avenue. I hailed a trishaw and we all three piled onto the bench. Eva was in the middle and the driver looked doubtful as I wedged myself in. I was too wide to sit so I was sort of lying on my right side. The proximity was enjoyable as I was practically wrapped around Eva. We set off laughing and wiggling and trying to make it work. If we were all Luli's size, with his light build, it would have been fine. Finally I ended up sitting beside Luli and Eva was in my lap, legs stretched across me and using Luli as a backrest.

About half way to the bus station a rain shower started and quickly became a tropical downpour. Our driver lifted the buggy parasol into place and although our legs were getting a soaking, we were a cozy pile under the cover. Eva had her left arm around my neck, which turned out to be a good thing in more ways than one. We approached a railroad crossing where the asphalt had squished up into a small berm on each side of the sunken steel rail. Normally no real problem, but the three of us in the front of the trishaw was quite a bit of mass. Unexpectedly, as we hit the bump with the two front wheels, the entire contraption tilted violently forward. The wet ground came rushing up, Eva screamed and we unceremoniously tumbled out of the cab and sprawled into the street. Simultaneously a darkly clad body splashed to the ground just in front of where we landed. I looked back and saw the back wheel of the trishaw turning in the air, the driver's seat empty. He had been catapulted over the cab and now lay sprawled on the wet street a few feet in front of us! Automobile traffic flowed around our wreck while the rain continued to pound down. I'd been holding Eva when we flipped and only her pride was injured. Luli too looked to be alright and had stood up. I set

Eva on her feet and quickly went towards our driver who, I was relieved to see, was already getting to his feet as well. Everybody ok?

"OK?" I asked the driver. He shook his head vigorously in the affirmative and moved towards his toppled rig. Luli and I pushed down on the back bar and the little driver lifted the bench seat. The trishaw dropped back to the ground in proper position, it too apparently no worse for wear.

The squall was slacking off. We were all pretty soaked but I saw that Eva and Luli were talking and laughing. Adventures in rickshaw land. At the urging of our driver we all piled back in after hand pushing the little cab over the twin berms of the railroad track. By the time we arrived at the bus station the sun was out, not ten minutes later.

Eva and I sat together on the old school bus style bench seat. Luli was behind us and he leaned forward, his chin resting on the back of our seat. I liked him but his cheery presence was an impediment to the intimacy I was hoping for between Eva and me. Her blue jeans were still damp and sported a few mud soils from our spill onto the street. She sat with her back to the window, facing in towards me and Luli.

"Having a good time?" she smiled.

I returned her smile. "That was an interesting way to start the day." I leaned over and brushed at a smudge on her thigh. "Let's do it again on the way back."

"I think once was enough for me," she said, "but don't let me stop you."

She placed her hand lightly on mine. Her eyes were so inviting.

"There's Prambanan!" Luli injected into our moment.

He was pointing out through the dusty bus windows to our left. In the morning sunlight the temple towers were ornate, rose colored crowns above the trees. A few stalls were there, offering drinks and snacks where the bus stopped but nothing like the mess at Borobodur yesterday. We piled out with the other passengers and made our way to the little entry kiosk. Literally dozens of towers spread away from us. Their form reminded me of the drip castles we would build at the beach, allowing a slurry of sand to pour through our fingers. Ornate stone carvings that appeared as squat scepters standing on end defined the base of each massive structure, forming a small courtyard. The map on the entry path, a painted, flat metal plate, listed the names and dates of the larger temples in this section. The largest lay to our left, about two hundred yards away, labeled as the *"Shiva candi."* Eva pronounced it like "Chandee".

The sun was still the morning sun and the air relatively cool but I could feel that it was going to heat up. No trees meant little or no shade, except inside the temple chambers. I tapped the map, the Shiva temple, and said, "Let's walk to this one."

Luli and Eva nodded. They'd been here before. Luli suggested, "The big chamber in the *Shiva candi* is always cool. Everyone always goes there later, to get cooled off. Less people now." We made our way past a line of rubble, maybe the remains of an old wall. "We should also see the Slim Virgin before it gets too crowded," Eva added with a glance towards Luli. She was a few steps in front of me at that moment, her long black hair iridescent in the sun like the feathers of a raven. Slim virgin indeed.

The Shiva temple was huge. Standing at the base looking up, the imposing mass was daunting. We passed into the surrounding courtyard and entered a tall portal into the central chamber, suddenly alone in the cool, dim interior. A remarkable statue of a multi-armed deity, one foot braced on top of an unhappy looking creature, dominated the chamber. It was illuminated by the daylight that poured in through the tall rectangular entryway.

"Whoa!" I said, involuntarily. The word reverberated in the round chamber and gave me an idea. Feeling in my day sack, I pulled out a blues harp, key of G. I liked a good echo chamber. My first note gave Eva and Luli a start but they laughed. Eva encouraged me with, "Oooh, a concert," and took a seat on the base of the statue. I played for a while, long slow blues riffs, finding, using the reverb of the chamber to good advantage. It was a little like singing in the shower and I thought it sounded quite alright. To me, anyway. Eva and Luli clapped briefly when I paused.

"A doctor and a musician," she teased.

"Sorry to say, neither. But I do have fun." I held up my harmonica, "One thing is that they don't take up too much room."

We emerged, blinking into the sun. It seemed a lot brighter than when we went in but I supposed that was because I'd grown accustomed to the twilight in the Shiva chamber. Drifting towards other temples I caught Eva's hand and we walked along for a time in silence. Each of the *candi* had empty alcoves where I imagined carvings had once stood, now destroyed or hauled off for a collection somewhere. I found the museums of Europe to be wonderful when I traveled around last summer, but all the empty alcoves and headless

Buddhas gave rise to a sadness in me, especially seeing it with Luli and Eva. It was their heritage. I was walking around a house that had been robbed with the owners. They didn't appear saddened but I felt a guilt in myself, under the surface of my thought.

"There she is!" Eva interrupted my reverie and I looked up to see a rather beautiful woman, goddess like, in the alcove of the *candi* before us. Eva squeezed my hand and to my delight moved closer and slipped her arm around my waist. We stood facing the statue, Luli off to my right studiously not noticing us.

"The story I know is that she," Eva nodded towards the statue, "was the daughter of a vast and wealthy kingdom. But her father, the king, was defeated in battle by Prince Bandung. He had an eye for the princess and wished to marry her. She was afraid for her people if she refused him but also hated the man who had killed her father."

Eva looked up at me and I was very aware of the pressure and warmth of her fingers on my side, a caressing that was sending tingles up my spine. I slipped my arm around her waist and drew her a bit closer. A shadow of a smile on her full lips and she cast her eyes down demurely.

"The poor girl was in a fix," she said softly. "She resolved to set an impossible task for Prince Bandung. She would marry him only if he completed the building of a thousand *candi* in one night, to honor the gods and deities of the defeated land. Prince Bandung agreed and that evening, with the help of his priests and advisors, he summoned an army of demons to help him complete his task. It was not yet morning and the princess saw in desperation that the nine hundred and ninety ninth *candi* was nearing completion." Luli had wandered away, towards the other side of the temple. "So she gathered her attendants," Eva continued, "and together they built a great fire to the east. The light caused the roosters to crow and the demons, hearing the birds and seeing the glow to the east, feared the coming of the day and fled, leaving the thousandth *candi* unfinished. When Prince Bandung realized the trick he was angry beyond reason. He used his sorcery to change the princess into stone."

Eva detached herself and moved to face me, taking both of my hands in hers and smiled up at me, inviting me. "And now, here she is, the most beautiful of all the goddesses here, the Slender Virgin."

I pulled her to me and bent to her lips. We explored and embraced. The heady perfume of her skin, the warmth of the day was intoxicating. Sometimes a moment is all you ever get.

Eva separated herself from me as Luli reappeared around the corner of the temple. If he'd seen us kissing he made no sign of it and approached with two bottles of cool, sweet tea.

"*Panas?*" he asked, 'Hot?'

"*Ja, silakan,*" returned Eva and accepted one of the proffered bottles. She took the straw in her lips and gave it long pull, her eyes meeting mine in dancing laughter.

"Um, good," she said. "Thank you Luli." I was grinning involuntarily and added, "Yes, thank you," and enjoyed a long sip of the cool tea myself.

On the way back to Yogya, Eva spent a lot of time looking out the window.

"A penny for your thoughts," I murmured. Yes, ok, I was trying to act sexy.

"I'm sorry?" said Eva. She seemed startled.

I leaned back a bit and repeated tentatively, "A penny for your thoughts."

"Oh," she sighed, "not worth a penny, I'm afraid."

Suave me. I reached over to take her hand, "I'm willing to be overcharged." I'd heard that in a film.

Eva smiled wistfully. "I'm not looking forward to Jakarta. I've got a bit of packing and clean up to do and," she looked at Luli, "that essay for Jodo."

Was this really the crash and burn?

"When are you going?" I almost croaked.

"About four, I'm sorry to say. My mother wants to arrive home before it gets too late and it's a five hour drive."

I was more disappointed in that moment than I cared admit to myself. Time for my own stiff upper lip.

"Oh, I'm sorry to hear it. I had hopes we could get together this evening." I did a good job of sounding casual. Eva turned to me on the seat and grasped my right hand with hers.

"I'm sorry to disappoint you," she said gently. "This just came up last night. Family business."

My disappointment must have shown more than I knew. Not much of a poker player, me.

"Well, uh, when do you see yourself coming back? Is it just for the weekend?" I asked hopefully.

"No, probably all of next week. I'll have a lot of work to catch up, won't I Luli?"

Luli, who had been staring out the window, appeared surprised to hear his name. *"Permisi?"* he asked. He had not been following the conversation. Eva clarified in Indonesian, *"Minggu akan datang, banyak kerjia, Ja?"*

Luli nodded in the affirmative and replied in English, "Yes, a lot of work next week."

He looked a bit confused at the direction of the conversation. Eva saw that too and filled him in with a rapid burst of Indonesian. I couldn't follow at all, except for the word Jakarta. Luli nodded and cast me a glance.

The bus must have been a local because we entered Yogyakarta from the north after stopping at a few small villages on the periphery. As a result, I was surprised when Eva and Luli stood up to exit. I didn't see the bus station. Outside was the stop for the University and we descended not far from the road of student housing. We three walked the short distance to Luli's place. Eva had taken my hand, but the promise and magic of the touch had retreated. She said something to Luli who nodded and mounted the steps into his rooming house and disappeared. I followed him with my eyes but turned back to Eva when she said, "What are your plans?" Her downcast eyes made my chest tighten.

"Well," I began, "the next stop for me is Bali."

"It's a nice place, I hear," she murmured. "Wonderful art and dance, a form of Hindu like Prambanan. I'm sure you will enjoy your time there."

Luli emerged from the house now with a small notebook and a pen in hand.

"I'll probably take the night bus tomorrow. I'm paid up for tonight at the hotel and Luli," I nodded to him, "has agreed to show me some batik workshops he likes tomorrow morning."

Luli looked from Eva to me, then opened his small notebook and offered me the pen.

"Please give me your address in America. I give you mine here also. We can write if you like."

"That would be very good," I agreed and reached for the pen. I wrote my mom's address in Sherman Oaks because when I left I'd given up my stereo business and rental house to a friend and had no idea where I'd land after all this. "This is the house of my mother," I explained. "I don't know when I will be there again but she will always know how to find me. It's the best place to write for now."

I glanced at Eva. Her eyes were already a hundred miles away. I reached into my day sack and extracted my small notebook, leafing through it to a blank page.

"Here," I said, handing it to Luli, "give me a good address for you and I will write. I'll send you a post card from Kathmandu."

As he wrote, Luli commented, "I would like a post card from Kathmandu, Pak Bern." He returned my notebook with a smile.

"Eva," I ventured, "would you like a post card from Kathmandu?"

She turned to me with a simple, sweet smile. "I would prefer a card from London, to know you have arrived safely."

I offered her my notebook.

"You'll have it," I said, "and another one from Hollywood when I get home."

Her eyes appeared moist as we gazed at each other but she cheerfully responded, "I should love to hear from you in Hollywood."

The address she wrote was in Jakarta. Her handwriting was elegant, very easy to read. I folded my notebook and wedged it back into my sack.

A white Toyota van rounded the corner and Luli nodded towards it, "Jaki" he said simply. Eva turned and noted the approaching car, "Thank you for calling, Luli." Then she faced me and held both my hands. "I hope I shall see you again." She leaned up and kissed me lightly, chastely on the lips.

"I hope so too," then, "maybe in Hollywood."

She smiled at me, released my hands and touched Luli lightly on the shoulder, "*Selamat tinggal*," she said to us both. Luli touched his chest and returned, "*Selamat jalan*."

The van pulled up even with us, window half down and I made a little wave to Jaki, who was driving. He rolled the window down the rest of the way and gave me a little wave back. "*Bagus?*" to Eva. She nodded, "*Ja*," and without further ceremony moved around to the passenger door. One last look to me.

What was that? Regret? Relief? The door closed, another small wave from Jaki and Eva disappeared from my life.

Luli was looking at me with something like sympathy. His dark eyes were hard to read. I smiled at him and said, "I like her." Luli nodded and looked after the departing van. "She is *cantik*, very pretty," he said simply. We looked at each other for a moment and he seemed to read my mind.

"Maliboro?"

I laughed. "Sounds good to me," and we walked off to the restaurant for a late lunch.

There were four buses a day from Yogya to Bali. Including the ferry crossing from Java to Gilimanuk, the trip to Denpasar was a bit over fifteen hours. I hadn't pulled an all-nighter since the epic journey down through Sumatra, but I'd seen a few of the buses rumble past the porch of the Borobodur and they looked at least as good as the Greyhound buses back in the States. These were modern vehicles, large and roomy with reclining seats. So what the heck. From what I'd been hearing, towns in between like Surabaya were not places to spend time. I might as well hightail it all the way to Bali in one big push. The bus that left at 6 p.m. looked like my best bet, arriving in Denpasar about nine in the morning the next day.

After our lunch, I wished Luli well and a "see you tomorrow" and made my way to the big bus station. It was pretty far in the afternoon heat but I walked. I needed to do some walking.

So, here I was now with a bus ticket in my pocket walking back towards the hotel. The lights were coming on for my last night in Yogyakarta. Street stalls were already busy dishing up meals for hungry customers, the savory smells of barbequed satay and wood smoke. I felt a bit hollow, the way the thing with Eva had gone. But there was also the tingle of getting back on the road, of being on my own again. I mean, it was terrific, having connected with Luli and Dani and Sapon, to be accepted by locals and doing local things. Maybe because we were all students and so much of the music we listened to came from the same pot - Beatles and Rolling Stones, even Elvis, which was a bit before my time. It all was fun and familiar and shared. The language thing was sort of exhausting and at times, in a group, I felt like the "different kid" who had to keep performing. It was a mixed bag but there had been so much kindness and open, friendly interaction that I couldn't have asked for better. In a way I was a kind of ambassador for the USA and I wanted to meet their graciousness with my own.

It was full darkness by the time I arrived at the hotel. Owing to my late lunch with Luli I wasn't hungry enough for a big dinner, but the smells of the food stalls had got my juices flowing. I strolled across the veranda and took a seat overlooking the street. I ordered a large Bintang and a bowl of the spicy chicken soup, the *soto ayam,* a specialty of the little hotel restaurant. Having been here for three nights, I felt like an old hand. Funny how fast we can settle in to a place. There were new faces at a few of the tables. I noted Becky and David, the couple that Bernice implied were junkies. They looked better now than the first night I'd seen them, but were still pale and listless. We acknowledged each other with a small wave but that was it. Two tables away, a big man of maybe thirty was holding court with two surfer types who sounded like Australians. The other, with dark hair and a full-face beard had the accent of a non-English speaker.

"Well, it is wonderful there," he boomed. "Easy to travel and very cheap."

The two surfers shook their heads doubtfully, apparently unconvinced.

"But there's a war on, eh? How's that?" The blond one asked the question.

"It's not a war. The Royalists are from Vientiane south and the Pathet Lao are all up in the north, around Luang Prabang. I was there, man, no problems. And it's beautiful!"

This interested me. Where was he talking about? Vientiane rang a bell. I picked up my beer and wandered over to their table.

"Hello. Mind if I sit in?" I looked at the bearded man, "I heard what you were saying and it sounded interesting."

The two surfer guys looked up at me, a little vacant but not unfriendly. The blond one said, "Naw, no worries. Grab a seat, mate. Hank here is on about Laos."

"Thanks"

I pulled out the forth chair.

"I'm Vern. I'm heading towards Thailand and I like to hear what travelers coming from that direction are saying."

The big man grinned and said expansively. "A fabulous country. Beautiful women and wonderful food!"

The blond surfer said, "Russ," introducing himself, "and Henry," a nod towards the other, whose hair looked in need of a wash. Henry gave a little nod and looked back towards Hank. His lugubrious movements said this wasn't his first beer of the evening.

"And as you have heard, I am Hank."

He drained his beer and looked admiringly at the mug. "Such good beer they have, all over Southeast Asia."

He looked at us archly for a moment and added, "Such beer would be triple, quadruple the cost in Switzerland, you know."

The two large green Bintang bottles on the table were both empty. I motioned to the waitress, pointed at the beer bottles and held up one finger. She acknowledged and moved towards the cooler.

"Have you come down from Thailand recently?" I prompted Hank.

"All the way down," he replied.

The waitress placed the new beer on the table and I said, "My contribution."

"*Terima Kasih*," and Hank reached for the bottle and tipped himself half a mug.

"So you went to Laos?"

"Yes, a beautiful place. Beautiful people."

Hank looked into the distance, maybe a bit theatrical, and went on, "You can drink good French wine in Vientiane, and café au lait with fresh baked croissant. Real Croissant. The French, you know," he looked around at us, the professor, "they know how to live well in the tropics."

"Aw yeah," said Russ, "but you said the Pathet Lao were running the north. How are they?"

Hank shrugged and opened his right hand, palm up, "How are they? They are fine. They have won. In Luang Prabang, they now have a new money. Wait, here. Look."

He pulled a flat case from his pocket and removed two pressed notes that he unfolded on the table. One was toned in brown and rose, a graphic drawing of soldiers shooting upwards at a jet. The plane had a small stars and stripes on the tail and was going down in flames. The other note was easily three times as large, large as half a sheet of notebook paper. It had the number one hundred on each corner but the inner field was a florid painting, a Gauguin-like image of a beautiful Asian woman at ease in a garden overflowing with flowers.

"This," said Hank, touching the large note, "is the Royalist money, one hundred kip. This," tapping the smaller note, "is the Pathet Lao. They use both in the north but it is more difficult to find the new notes."

Hank admired the old, large note. "It doesn't matter. This is so much more lovely, like the old French money."

"So," Russ pressed, "there was no problem for you traveling in the north? No hassles?"

Hank did his shrug.

"Nothing more than the normal shit. It is not a war like you think of when somebody says war." He looked directly at me and gave a wink. "Now is the time to go, I think."

That night, as I packed up in my room, I wondered about Laos. Going into Laos never even occurred to me. I pulled out my Bartholomew map of Southeast Asia and spread it flat on the bed. Vientiane was over on the east side of Thailand, right on the Mekong River. Mekong. I'd heard that name on the TV so often as they talked about the war in Vietnam that just raged on and on. I followed a road on the map leading north past places with names like Vang Vien and Luang Prabang. Maybe, huh?

Check out time at the Borobodur was before twelve so after an omelette and some toast I finished my packing and hauled my pack down to the veranda, ready to head out. Luli had kindly offered to let me leave my backpack in his room while we went out to the batik workshops. Maybe it was a sheer coincidence, but I heard a friendly voice call out, "Pak Bern!" Out on the street sat Berdi in his trishaw, smiling over at me. I laughed and called back, "Hello Berdi. *Apa kabar?*"

Berdi climbed down from the passenger seat where he had been reclining. He looked at my pack hopefully.

"*Kemana pak?* Bus station?"

I shook my head. "*Tidak Berdi. Saya akan purgi ke rumah teman saya, dekat universitas.*"

If I'd said it correctly it meant that I was going to the house of a friend near the university. Luli had helped me tremendously with new words and phrases, but I had a long way to go. I'd heard it said Bahasa Indonesian was easy to learn a bit of but took a lifetime to speak well. When I listened to Luli and Dani talk, it blew me away how little I understood.

I'd intended to walk over to Luli's with my pack since it was less than a mile, but Berdi's eager energy was familiar and welcome and what the heck, I'd probably show up at Luli's house in a sweat and smell like a gym locker for the rest of the day. It was already warming up.

"We go?" asked Berdi.

"*Seratus rupiah,* ok?" I said, 'Hundred rupee.'

Berdi nodded his assent and reached for my pack. I was an old customer now. We rolled away from the hotel and I cast a look back over my shoulder but there was nobody familiar on the veranda. Berdi pedaled silently and I enjoyed the relaxing pace down to the university.

"Here," I said, pointing up the side street where Luli lived. We rolled to a stop in front of the house under the shade trees. Luli must have been waiting by the window. He was out the door and coming down the steps as I lifted my pack. His dark hair was slicked down and he wore the student's white shirt and sturdy olive green pants.

"*Selamat pagi,* Vern." He had heard Eva pronounce my name with the "vee" sound and now made the effort himself.

"*Selamat pagi,* Luli. Ready to go," I greeted him.

"Yes, yes. All set. Here, let me take this upstairs." He reached for my pack but I stayed his hand.

"No, no, I carry this everywhere. Thank you but please, let me."

The generosity towards guests in Indonesia still astounded me. I hoisted my pack and indicated the waiting trishaw.

"Luli, do you remember Berdi? From the day I met you?"

Luli glanced at Berdi, who smiled hopefully.

"How far to the batik workshops? Maybe we could go by trishaw."

Luli looked at me with an expression of mild amusement.

"Not far," he said, "Very near to the Taman Sari."

He turned to Berdi and they spoke rapidly together. It didn't sound like the Indonesian I was trying to learn.

"It's all set. He will take us to the batik village and wait, then return us to

The Appearance of Things

the Maliboro. A last supper." Luli smiled wryly at me, "We will get a Java price!"

I followed him up the wooden steps and into the entry hall. We passed the small sitting area and ascended the stairs to Luli's room on the second floor. He shared the small space with Dani, but just now the room was unoccupied.

"Where's Dani?" I asked.

"At the library working. He will join us this afternoon at the Maliboro."

I liked Dani too. He was quiet and earnest. We didn't speak together all that much since his English was not much better than my Bahasa but I felt a kinship with him from the times we had shared. I'd been very grateful for the use of his moto on the beach trip, and I liked it that we had made some music together, after Eva had left, me on a blues harp, him on guitar. He was a good enough musician to play in a key that worked with my "C" harp. The Jim Morrison poster on the wall was his.

I braced my pack against the wall and we went back down to the trishaw. Before starting off, I handed Berdi a ten rupee note. Luli looked distressed and protested, "No, no, I pay. You are *tamu*, my guest."

"Thank you Luli. This is from before. My debt."

He acquiesced and we climbed aboard the trishaw. Berdi gave us a running push then hopped into the driver's seat and began to pedal.

"Let's go over the railroad tracks again," I suggested. Luli laughed.

The batik village was a part of the same colony nestled around the Water Palace. I could see the poles with their bird cages in the distance, but we now approached from what I judged to be the eastern side. There were more flagpoles but these had colorful cloth banners flapping in the late morning breeze. Berdi pulled in under another spreading Banyan tree. He joked with a few of the other rickshaw drivers also relaxing in the shade.

"I wait here," he beamed and pulled out a packet of Gudang Garams, *kretek* cigarettes with filters that came in a fancy red and black box. I stayed with Luli as he made his way into the warren of workshops and small showrooms.

"Very famous batik here," he said, with a note of pride in his voice.

We entered a courtyard where a dozen women were working around a long suspended bolt of cloth. It was stretched on a frame from one side of the yard to the other, maybe forty feet in length. The artisans drifted along the length of the fabric, carrying small pots of dye and daubing at open spaces on the cloth. An intricate floral pattern was etched in wax that restrained the dye into defined areas.

"Here, look," Luli pointed at the repeating design. "Wax stops the color. Then it is boiled and new color can go."

Behind us a huge cauldron of steaming water had three men stirring what I took to be another bolt of cloth. We wandered back and now I saw what I'd missed going in, stacks of neatly folded cloth and brilliantly colored runners draped from the walls. Flower patterns, leaf patterns, whimsical and abstract, all in deep, rich blues and greens, vermilion and chartreuse, all the colors of the rainbow.

"Come," motioned Luli and we were back in the street. Fifty feet on, Luli turned into another shop and greeted a seated figure, *"A'salam malekum,"* hand to chest. The seated figure returned the *"malekum salam"* but the paint brush he held prevented the customary touch.

"This is my friend Pak Bontoom," Luli introduced me.

Pak Bontoom gave me an appraising glance and put down the tool he had been wielding. I saw it wasn't a brush after all, more of a stylus ending in a curved point with a tiny cup above it. It looked almost like a hash pipe. Now he touched his chest in greeting.

"Selamat datang," 'Welcome.'

"Selamat pagi, pak," I returned in kind.

Around us on the walls were paintings, or rather pictorial batiks: the stylized forms of the Javanese shadow puppets, the serene face of the Buddha, village scenes, a dynamic red, orange brown and yellow cockfight that reminded me of a satellite photo of a hurricane.

Pak Bontoom looked youngish, maybe in his mid-thirties. He had long black hair tied back in a ponytail and a thin goatee, the image of a scribe with his round wire rim glasses, but in place of a pen he used the melted wax tool, sketching out the lines that would resist the dye.

"Look," said Luli, motioning me near. I looked over Pak Bontoom's shoulder at the outline of a dancing Shiva. It was nearly identical to the statue I'd seen at Prambanan, minus the sad creature underfoot, yet the freedom of the drawing was more compelling, the swirls giving a lightness and motion.

"Cantik," I offered. 'Beautiful.'

Luli spoke with obvious admiration. "Pak will add the dye to make the color parts. It is boiled each time a new color. And the old color must be protected with more wax. A lot of work!"

It was impressive, original work and by the time we left I was the proud owner of the swirling cockfight. When I held it up to the outside light coming through the entry door, the piece positively glowed. I got the idea to take it home and stretch it over a frame, backlit from behind. I realized with a slight shock that this was my first souvenir, other than photos and memories. I liked that it folded up. There wasn't a lot of extra space in my pack.

The morning slipped into afternoon. So much beautiful work here. Luli and I drifted up one of the access stairs to the Water Palace perch and had a hot tea and smoked a clove *kretek*. The sky to the south, towards the beach, was purple with heavy rain clouds, boiling white columns above them climbing into the afternoon light. There were no buildings taller than two floors and the vast stretch of green jungle and palm tops spread away from us in all directions. It was like looking over an emerald sea from the bridge of a ship.

The sun was lowering towards the horizon as we approached the bus terminal. Berdi steered us towards the crowded entry but stopped short of the crush. Luli had insisted on paying Berdi after our time at the Water Castle so I insisted on paying for our last supper together. It all works out. I had not seen Luli or Dani drink beer before but this, as Luli said, was a special occasion. We were fast friends and I felt wistful, the fresh memory of them sitting there at the table. Good times and good food. Then a wave and I was gone. I reflected that I was also now stepping down from Berdi's rickshaw for the last time. We shook hands, Berdi and I. I gave him a hundred and fifty rupees even though we had agreed on only a hundred for the ride over from the Maliboro. I'm not an overly sentimental guy and I could see that Berdi was already scanning the crowd for his next fare.

"Selamat tinggal, Berdi."

A toothy grin, "Selamat jalan, pak Bern."

He hopped on his rig, I shouldered my pack and we went in opposite directions.

The bus actually had assigned seats, mine at a window on the left about half way along. My main gear was stowed under, but now I went through my day sack and extracted a new book. The Borobodur had a pretty good "take one, leave one" library shelf in the lobby, and I'd left *The Illustrated Man* and picked up a Penguin edition of *The Collected Short Stories of W. Somerset*

Maugham from what the book jacket called "The Malaysian Period." Last night I'd read one called "Rain", about an evangelist preacher trying to browbeat a sexy woman on a tropical island, the Reverend Mr. Davidson versus Sadie Thompson. It ended with Sadie loudly playing her Victrola record player, desire having derailed the preacher big time.

I found myself thinking about Eva. We'd gone up to desire together. Or had we? Was I somebody she actually wanted or just a few days' entertainment? I wanted to think she wanted me. How come? Would I be more or better somehow if she did? Did I want some story of her crying and wanting me to stay? "Joe, Joe, you promise me chewing gum." The thoughts about freedom came flooding back. The preacher was destroyed, destroyed himself, because his reality ran up against his illusion, his illusions about himself. Sadie seemed free to me. She knew who she was. There was a wisp of something here, just out of view, about illusion and freedom and…

"Hey!" a grinning jackanapes face leered down at me. Paul.

"Hey, it's Vern!'

Bernice peered around his shoulder. She giggled. Tipsy again.

"Hi Vern. I'd wondered where you'd got off to. We're heading for Bali!"

I felt a flash of irritation but then, what the hell.

"Hello Paul. Hello Bernice. Where're Franny and Alex?"

"Awww," droned Bernice and looked vaguely over her shoulder, as if she forgot something. Then she perked up and said brightly, "Here she is! Hey Frannie, it's Vern. We're all going to Bali."

Paul's meaty face was a bit flushed, but he looked cheerful enough.

"C'mon ladies. Time to take your seats." He smiled down at me and made a "Tsch" sound like a camera clicking, and winked.

"Catch ya later, mate." He fumbled on down the aisle.

I looked after Frannie as she passed and caught a glimpse of Alex at the far end. The gang's all here.

I was in luck. By the time we pulled out of the station, the seat beside me had remained vacant, so I crumpled my blue sarong into a ball to use for a headrest and stretched out over both seats. Luxurious! Even the little overhead reading lamp worked. I settled in with Mr. Somerset Maugham for the long ride. There were a few stops through the night that I half perceived from my slumber but at daybreak, when we finally arrived at the ferry port, everybody had to wake up and shuffle off the bus. I stuffed my well-used sarong back into the day sack and had a swish of water to get rid of the night mouth taste. In the grey light of dawn, I trailed along across the tarmac with my fellow passengers, stepped over the gap and on to the ferry. The cool morning air had a tang of salt and harbor. A flight of rust-stained white metal steps led us up to the passenger salon and a welcome set of sinks and toilets. The facilities were surprisingly well maintained and I made good use of them, emerging feeling fresh and rested. The little canteen at the far end of the salon had a stack of the banana leaf pyramids heaped on the counter. A young woman was fussing with a steaming pot and pouring hot tea into rows of laid out white cups. Breakfast.

I found a seat at one of the tables looking out over the slate grey sea and unfolded my banana leaf to form the disposable eating surface. As the eastern horizon began to glow orange for what looked to be a clear day I proceeded to moosh the contents together with my fingers - a generous portion of white rice and fine, spicy noodles, fried tempeh, green beans and some sprouts, chili with toasted coconut and small bits of cooked chicken. The savory aroma blossomed as I blended the ingredients together. I had a sip of the sweet, hot tea and popped a small handful of the rice mix into my mouth. Delicious. I was forming another bite sized ball when a female voice behind me said, "Vern, you've gone native on us!"

Bernice stood there with a cup of steaming tea looking amused. I smiled up at her.

"Good morning," I said and then bit into my formed rice ball and chewed happily. "Best fifty rupee breakfast I know."

Bernice smiled at that. "Too early for me, I'm afraid." She pulled out the chair beside me and settled gingerly into its embrace. She looked fatigued.

"God, I slept like shit last night," she lamented. "Haven't been up this early since the last boat ride, down from Padang." She took a sip of tea and stared out towards the sea. "But we'll be in Bali soon and that makes me almost home." There was a wistfulness in her voice.

"Is home a good thing?"

"Aw yeah," she sighed, "I reckon it's just about the best thing."

She turned towards me. "But you, you're just getting started aren't you? Heading all the way to London. Be some time before you get home, won't it?"

I nodded. "Yeah, I'm not really sure, even. I met a couple of guys in Europe last summer, a couple of Aussies. They came all the way in three months. I guess I could be there in April if I pushed it."

Bernice took another sip of her tea.

"Doesn't attract me. If I was going to London, I'd take a plane. Get to the main event and skip over woggieland."

"Brekkie?"

Frannie had come up from behind and now placed a friendly hand on Bernice's shoulder.

"Morning," I said. Frannie made eye contact, not unfriendly.

"Morning," she returned. Alex stood beside her and we said our "hi" to each other with a nod.

"No brekkie for me, thanks," Bernice responded, "but I'd fancy another tea."

She stood and addressed me, "Want another?"

"No thanks," I said, "I'm good."

She looked like she was going to say more then didn't. They moved off towards the canteen and I settled back to finishing up my rice. When I looked up Paul had joined then at the counter. I didn't feel left out when they seated themselves down at the far end of the salon.

The crossing and the remaining bus ride went pretty smoothly. Gilimanuk didn't look like much of a town, a big cement wharf complex surrounded by service buildings and in the distance, palm trees. There was a long line of trucks waiting to board. We were a caravan for a time, our bus and the trucks that off-loaded with us heading east along the coast road, but then the line began to thin out and I started to notice that I really was in a new place, a place that was "not Java." It was subtle at first. I'd grown accustomed to the woven bamboo walls and palm frond roofs that characterized rural Indonesia, the rice paddy stretching away into the distance and small hamlets flanking the road, but now we were passing ornately sculpted stone gates in every little village and the houses were often laid out in walled compounds. Each compound had multiple small shrines of gold and red carvings integrated into the yard entryway and topped by black thatched roofs. Many of the people we passed were beautifully dressed. In one village we needed to slow down to a crawl for a procession, and I found myself pressed against the glass of the window. The women wore lacy, colorful tops and on their heads they carried baskets piled high with carefully stacked fruits and flowers. Their batik sarongs tended to complement the crafted blouses and a glistening sash around the waist literally tied it all together. Even the older women looked gorgeous, and while the men were less colorful, tending towards short sleeved white shirts, they nearly all wore colorful cloth head pieces that reminded me of old photos of Indian soldiers in the British Raj. The men wore sarongs too, but in more sedate colors and plaid designs. Then it struck me that nearly every face I studied appeared both dignified and joyful. Unbidden, the scene from "South Pacific" when Bloody Mary sang 'Bali Hai' lept to mind. There was something beautiful going on here.

In that mind state I approached Denpasar. The increasing density of people and traffic and buildings told me we were coming into a town of some size. My fantasy of "Bali Hai" deflated as another hot, dusty, crowded tropical town closed in around us. The people we passed on these streets appeared just as harried as they had been in Jakarta.

The bus had been air conditioned, a fact I failed to appreciate until I stepped off into the humidity and scalding sunlight of the bus yard, a large, dirt lot crowded with all manner of transport. Scattered about were shade pavilions, cement pads covered by corrugated metal roofs. I stepped under the canopy that flanked our bus while the baggage men unloaded the gear. In this sun the corrugated metal roof gave a reasonable impression of an oven, as we stood below in the shade the heat radiating down on us was like being roasted alive. A tall thin westerner stood waiting beside me. Clean-shaven with ruddy blond hair that looked wilted in the heat, rumpled tan cotton vest that hung open, no shirt, draw string pants and sandals, he was smoking a *kretek* and looking into the distance as if he expected to see someone in the crowd.

My backpack appeared and before the attendant could drop it in the dust I stepped forward, grabbed it and retreated back into the shade. The four Aussies - Bernice, Frannie, Paul and Alex also took refuge with us under the canopy and brushed at their dusty bags. Bernice smiled up at me.

"Paul knows a good place in Kuta so we're heading over there in a taxi, if you want to come."

Hank, the big Swiss guy from the veranda at the Borobodur had been dismissive of Kuta. He'd recommended a place called "Losman Putu".

"Thanks for the offer Bernice. I got a recommendation for a place in Legian I want to check out first. Just in case though, what's the name of your place?"

She studied me for a moment, but I couldn't read anything in her expression.

"Hey Paul!" she called over. Paul looked up from his brushing, sweaty and a bit irritated.

"What's the name of the place we're going in Kuta?"

Paul shot me a "Don't come" glance but said, "It's called The Magic Mushroom," then returned to his clean-up work.

"Easy to remember," I said. "I wonder if it lives up to the name."

Bernice smiled easily. Even fatigued, she had that attractive Forget-me-not, blue-eyed twinkle. "I reckon we'll find out. Or at least, they will."

She cocked her head towards Paul and Alex. Her auburn red hair caught the sun just right.

It looked like Alex had found a *bemo*. She hoisted her bag and started to follow the others. A look back over her shoulder, "See ya in the surf," she called. I watched them trying to fit four people and their gear into the *bemo* for a moment.

"Excuse me, I heard you say you were going to Legian?" said the tall guy with the vest.

"Yeah," I found myself speaking a little cautiously, "I heard it was a better scene than Kuta."

He nodded, "Definitely. That's where I'm heading too. Share a *bemo*?"

"Sure. Great. I'm Vern."

"Graham," he replied and crushed out his *kretek* on the ground.

The dirt road to Legian was a rutted, sloppy mess. It must have rained heavily last night, to have so much standing water.

"Nice road," I observed to Graham. We hit another bump and a splash of mud and water sprayed back over us.

"It's good compared to upcountry," Graham shouted back over the roar of the little motor.

By the time we pulled up to the sign announcing "Losman Putu" both Graham and I had a new patina of mud splatters. A middle-aged man sat bare-chested on the floor of a small covered platform, watched Graham and I unload from the *bemo* and then called out, "Hello, you want room?"

"Losman Putu?" I asked.

"Yes, yes, I am Pak Putu."

He stood and stepped down to the ground in his coarse dark brown sarong, like a homemade blanket. His bald head was rimmed by a fringe of graying hair. With his round belly and bright-eyed smile, I felt like I was meeting the model for one of those Chinese good luck Buddhas.

"Muddy road," observed Pak Putu, who seemed amused by our mud splattered persons. Before I could speak he added, "All losman with private bath. You come." He whirled and set off down a path flanked by bush palms and hibiscus whose stark red flowers drooped out over the walkway. Graham and I looked at each other and followed. Pak Putu was waiting for us to catch up at the edge of a clearing, in the center of which sat an enormous bamboo pavilion. A scattering of travelers ate and chatted at tables beneath the palm frond roof that looked like a gigantic umbrella. Ganja perfumed the air. An elaborately carved wooden sign proclaimed the "Red Flower restaurant. Putu motioned for us to keep following and we set off down one of the paths leading away from the pavilion like the spokes of a wheel. The understory of hibiscus and bush palms was partially shaded by evenly spaced coconut palms, as if this was once a plantation. I was relieved to see that most of the towering palms were harvested and no heavy coconuts lay in wait overhead. The jokes about getting brained by a falling coconut weren't really jokes. Back on the beach at Lake Toba, a coconut had fallen near to where I was sitting with Mike and Tony. It literally made the ground shake when it hit. That baby would have meant sudden death by bashed in skull.

We followed Pak Putu past a number of bamboo cabins which looked spacious and comfortable, each with its own front porch and a couple of hammocks, some occupied.

"How far to the beach?" I shouted up to Pak Putu. He stopped in front of a cabin and obliquely replied, "You look?" He meant the cabin of course.

Graham and I hadn't spoken of sharing a place, but I was growing more accustomed to rolling with the unexpected. He seemed ok. On the bumpy ride out from Denpasar, I learned that he had been working for the last three years in New Zealand, North Island where his uncle owned a sheep operation. He said it had been good for the time he was there, but Graham was looking forward to getting back to civilization, meaning England. I spoke of my overland plans, and when I mentioned India his response was an enigmatic, "That's a very different place." It made me curious to hear more about his trip out from England. It said something that he intended to fly back from Singapore, skipping the return trip overland.

"You look?" repeated Pak Putu.

"We didn't talk about this, Graham. You want to share a place until your friends get here?" I asked.

Graham shrugged and replied, "Yeah, why not."

We followed Pak Putu through the little garden and up the wooden steps. Nice enough porch, not far from the restaurant, pretty garden, the cabin had two large beds with mosquito nets on opposite sides of the room. At the foot of each bed was a wide sort of bench seat. There was a simple wooden table and two chairs, while a single electric bulb was suspended in the middle of the room. The back door opened into a step down, enclosed toilet and shower area, the bamboo wall tall enough for privacy. It was all rather basic, but clean and apparently well cared for. Worked for me.

I tried again on the beach question. "Pak Putu, how far to the beach?"

"Very close, just hundred meter, over there," he replied, pointing away from the house.

"You like?" he asked, referring to the cabin.

"How much one night?" replied Graham.

"Two hundred rupee, *murah*, very cheap," grinned Pak Putu.

"Two hundred rupee, two people?" Graham continued.

Putu feigned shock and waved his hands, "No, no, two hundred rupee one person. Two person, four hundred rupee."

Graham and I exchanged a look and smiled. At four hundred fifteen rupees to the dollar, it was still *murah*, very cheap. We each dug out a two hundred rupee note and handed them over to Putu, who looked pleased and gave us a friendly nod.

"*Selamat datang*. Come to Red Flower later for register, OK?"

"OK," we agreed, and he was off. We dropped our gear inside and cleaned up a bit from the mud. My shirt and shorts were a mess, but a swim in the ocean sounded good to me. Cool off and wash up at the same time. Graham said he was hungry and headed off to the restaurant.

"Maybe I'll see you over there after I get in a swim."

"I'll likely be there. I need to catch up on some correspondence."

As I began to stroll through the forest of flowers in the general direction Pak Putu had indicated, I noted a large banyan tree at the trail fork that would be an easy landmark for finding my way back. The shade was pleasant and there was even a slight breeze that smelled of ocean. I rounded a corner and froze. The largest spider I have ever seen, bigger than my hand with outstretched fingers, waited on a simple web stretched right across the trail, maybe four feet off the ground. I could have walked right into it. The thought made my balls pull right up into my body, or at least it felt like that. I'm not crazy about spiders but I wouldn't say it crosses over into arachnophobia. But this guy! The main body was as large as my index finger, shiny and black with white and yellow markings on the abdomen. Perched in its web, the legs looked as thick as pencils, tapering at each joint until they were thin points hooked into the web strands. It stretched as wide as a dinner plate. The web wasn't much. These were just trip wires. This little beauty didn't want to entangle a prey in a sticky web. It just wanted to know you were there then, gotcha!

I had backed up a few steps and I looked around for something to shoo it away with, a stick maybe or some sand. I was walking on sand. I scooped up a handful and cast it medium hard directly at the creature, who reacted by shooting up her line to the right and disappearing into the leafy green wall. I was paranoid. I picked up a thin, dry branch and used it to break the trigger lines before passing through them. Nobody sprang out at me, no needle legs and fangs leaping for my moist eyes. Maybe a little more arachnophobic than I thought.

The payoff was in another fifty yards, a rather nice, white sand beach. The waves close in looked so-so. They were spending most of their force on the reef and the real break with the big rollers was three hundred yards further out. The turquoise blue, clear water was inviting and I was a pretty muddy guy. Two girls on towels looked over at me.

"Hi. Can I leave my stuff with you for a minute while I swim?" I asked.

The blond one said, "Yeah, no worries."

I stepped out of my sandals, put my wallet on top of them, and walked into the water with my muddy face, shirt and shorts. The water was excellent, cool enough to refresh but warm enough to stay comfortable. I stripped off my shirt and began to smack it down hard on the surface of the water. The explosive force of the impact tended to blast dirt out of the clothing. I had learned how to do a soap free laundry up at Lake Toba, but I'd still do laundry with soap when possible since the oils and grimes came out better. Still, this was good for mud removal, and I came out of the water feeling cleaner inside and out. What is it about water that makes my spirit feel so refreshed, beyond just clean, renewed somehow?

"Thanks again," I smiled down. The one with the dark hair never looked up, just kept reading the whole time.

"Welcome," said the blond and went back to her book. No interest there.

I didn't even have my trusty sarong to dry off with. It was in my day sack which was with my backpack which was all back with Graham at the *losman*. I felt a mild startle reflex to recognize that I just sort of trusted him, didn't I? The reflection on trust was still rolling around in my mind when I saw the tall landmark tree ahead, turned the corner and strolled over to the new digs. Graham was lounging back in the hammock and raised a hand in lazy greeting, the aroma of ganja in the air. Coming up onto the porch the Buddha sticks on the little table invited my attention as Graham relit a massive joint, took a hit and passed it to me. I had a long hit then passed it back. I was getting better at inhaling the ganja tobacco mix that most travelers favored, but on my own I still preferred my little pure pipe. "Thanks," I squeezed out. I went inside and dragged my pack over to the bench on the left side of the cabin.

Towel in one hand, dop kit in the other, I descended to our outdoor *mandi* and washed off the salt and the travel with soap and cool fresh water. There was a handy bucket so I also rinsed the salt out of my shirt and shorts and hung them on the little line to dry. Finishing off with a shave, I emerged feeling pretty high in all ways.

"That's pretty good Buddha stick."

Graham had a goofy smile, "Yes, very good really. From upcountry." We had a couple more hits each.

I pulled out my journal to bring things up to date, as I hadn't written anything since the parting with Eva back in Yogyakarta and that was beginning to feel like a long time ago. But instead of writing I found myself reading a lament from a guy who thought he was in love with an English girl he met coming out of the Goodge Street tube station in London. It depressed me to read about the same angst and yearning from six months ago that I was spinning for myself now around Eva, a melodramatic personal narrative in which the names changed but no insight emerged, an amnesia that doomed me to a repeating, gloomy loop of existence. I closed my journal, and returned it to the top of my pack. Suddenly exhausted I climbed on to the bed pushing the mosquito net aside, stretched out and closed my eyes.

A bright light made me squint when I tried to open my eyes, the bare bulb dangling from its wire in the middle of the room. A clunk, like a shoe being dropped, pulled my attention over to the left. Graham was shifting his pack around and now he collected the bag of toiletries that had fallen to the floor.

I sat up and swung my feet out from under the mosquito net and onto the floor. Graham glanced over, "Feel like going over to the restaurant for tea?"

Having grown accustomed to hearing dinner referred to a "tea" I answered, "Yeah, sure. I've got the munchies now." It was dark outside. "Graham, what time have you got?" He fumbled in his pocket and pulled out a wristwatch with one strap missing. "Going on seven. You had quite a lie in."

I tugged the mosquito net the rest of the way aside and stood up, a little unsteady. "Yeah, it was an all-nighter from Yogyakarta. I was catching up, I guess."

We walked together down the unlit path. Graham had a small flashlight, but the moon was about three quarters and we didn't need it really. Music drifted on the warm night air and I recognized "Hey Jude" from the Beatles. The big pavilion was attractively illumined inside with upturned spots on the ceiling and little kerosene lamps on the tables, sandalwood incense and ganja in the air. The place was about half full as we mounted the steps, and Graham hesitated at the landing, surveying the room. A wave from a table near the far edge and Graham smiled and waved back.

"My friends made it," he said and set off across the wooden floor towards their table. I followed along. It was not unlike the scene Pepy had managed at Lake Toba, except more of everything. There was a comfortable familiarity to "us", the other travelers, the music, the ganja. I felt relaxed and at home.

"Glad to see you made it!" Graham greeted the couple at the table. I'd come up behind and while Graham seated himself he introduced me.

"This is Vernon, from California. We arrived together. Vernon, this is Nick," indicating the dark haired young man, "and Nora."

Nora smiled at me, pretty.

Nick had very thick black eyebrows, longish hair and a goatee. He looked like Frank Zappa, the same always angry eyes, but his manner was friendly, charming even, when he said, "Welcome Vernon. Thanks for taking care of our Graham for us." Before I could respond, Nora added with a tease, "Somebody has to, don't they Grammaticus?"

Nora had very straight auburn hair, cut flat across just past her shoulders. In the light of the kerosene lamp I could make out her pale eyes, grey or maybe green. Her nose and lips were fine and delicate, the high cheekbones in this light lending a regal shadowing to her face. From someplace in my mind came "Cleopatra."

Graham bowed slightly towards her and said with a southern gentleman accent, "I've always depended on the kindness of strangers."

We all laughed at the Blanche DuBois reference. Increasingly, I found myself impressed with, and a little envious of, the erudition demonstrated by other travelers, especially those hailing from the UK or urbane Australians. Their banter was colorful, intelligent and amazingly wry, appearing unaffected and natural and I felt like a poorly educated cousin. In America, I was beginning to realize, we tended towards the monosyllabic banality of morons playing Scrabble. I had begun to make a conscious effort to dust off and expand my vocabulary, but you have to crawl before you can walk and I know I frequently came across clumsily, the Neanderthal at Cotillion. Still, most people aren't intrinsically cruel and I got points for trying. John and Louise back at Toba had been masters at teasing me about my process, but it was always tempered with an affection that invited me to drop my fears and defenses and take a chance. I liked them.

Graham addressed Nick, "I waited for you at the station for about as long as I could stand it, then Vernon and I found our way out here. When did you get in?"

"Oh, I'd say about four, late afternoon," replied Nick. "It was a hell of a mess on the road down, as you know. A lorry had lodged itself across the road near Batu Bulan and we were stuck for ages while they worked it out."

"But I found a beautiful sarong." Nora stood and stepped out from the table, showing off her prize. She was taller than I thought, and the sarong was indeed a beauty, ruby colored diamonds edged with yellows and blues, a hand woven look. She caught my eye and smiled, "Do you like sarongs, Vernon?"

"Well, that one's really lovely," I offered. "I've got two so far, a long Sumatran I like a lot, but it's a bit too warm for down here, then there's my cheap and cheerful everyday traveler's friend."

Nick laughed, "Towel cum hankie."

"Precisely," I returned.

It was a pleasant evening, good food, good smoke, good drink and engaging conversation. The area up towards Lake Batur sounded interesting but the muddy roads made it a real slog. At the end of what would be my last smoke for the evening, I stood and wished everyone a good night. "It's been a long one for me. I'm going to try some snorkel diving tomorrow if anyone is interested."

"I don't want to think about tomorrow yet," mused Nora, "I don't suppose I'll want to be swimming in the morning though." She spoke dreamily and I took that as my cue to leave.

"Good to have met you all. I imagine I'll see you around at some point." I held up a hand in farewell and made my exit.

The moon was considerably lower in the sky now and the path back in deep shadow. The thought bubbled up in my stoned mind, "I should have brought my flashlight" and scrolled across my consciousness: No Flashlight. Oh well, no worries, it was basically straight out the path I was on, fourth cabin on the right. The conversations and music of the pavilion fell behind and I could hear the scrunch of my sandals on the sand.

It was a soft, warm night and I stopped, looking up at the brilliant star washed sky. Through the palms, at about forty five degrees, I could see the Southern Cross. I started walking again when it felt like someone had placed their palm on my chest. Then the palm suddenly scampered up and over my right shoulder, brushing my cheek in its passing, and disappeared. I had a delayed motion convulsion and swatted at the empty space on my shoulder, an involuntary "uunngh" bursting from my throat. I didn't see it but I could see it, the huge spider in the middle of my chest, running up my shoulder and leaping for safety in the bush. I stood frozen, my heart sounding way too loud in my ears, and another involuntary shudder coursed through me. How many more of those between me and home? I didn't like the idea of feeling around for a stick, so I pulled out my trusty blue sarong and stretched it out full length. Tying a large double knot in the end, I began to swing it in a vertical circle before me. Road clearance. I moved down the path with my whirling sarong until I arrived at our cabin, glad that we'd left the porch light on. Back home safe, I made to untie the knot and was startled to see how many silk treads it was trailing.

In the bright sober light of the morning the world was fresh and inviting.

Graham was crashed out, sleeping naked on his back. He must be having good dreams judging from the size of his erection. I quietly pulled out my mask and snorkel, bathing suit and t-shirt and let myself out. I had hopes the sea would be clearer this morning than it had been yesterday, in the afternoon. Fins would have been nice, but they take up too much room in a backpack. I made my way down to the beach, this time spider free. I guess I paid my dues last night. It was early enough that the beach was deserted. The slanting light of the morning sun had the soft sand glowing orange gold. The surf had abated, even out by the reef and the calm water was actually a bit warmer than the air. I put on my mask and slipped under the water. Once out past the sandy edge, the water cleared up a bit and small coral mounds came into view. Yellow and black miniature Angel Fish were poking around the mounds and were undisturbed as I passed above them. By the time I was a hundred yards from shore, the water was about eight feet deep but it was disappointing to find the visibility not much improved. I could see clearly straight down but not much else, a circle of vision twenty feet in diameter. The corals I could see were mostly the small tuft formations and pretty beat up. It was just "OK" and I swam back to the beach feeling rather let down. I told myself there would be other places, away from the break that would be better. It was pretty and the beach was lovely, but not the South Seas paradise I was hoping for.

Back at the cabin Graham was still knocked out. He stirred when I passed on the way down to the *mandi*. I used the dipper and soap to good effect and, freshly bathed, I was ready for some breakfast. Climbing up the three steps into the main room I found Graham had rolled over and was snoring. Must have been a later night than I thought.

The Red Flower was open and the aromas of coffee and toasted bread met me coming up the path. There were a dozen others already engaged with their food and each other. No familiar faces so I pulled out a chair at a small table facing out into the garden. A worn folder on the table displayed a drawing of a red hibiscus, the word *"Daftar"* above the flower and the word "Menu" below. I thumbed it open and an attractive young woman in a flower print sarong approached, smiling.

"*Selamat pagi,*" she began, "you like Nescafe or *Kopi Bali*?"

"*Kopi Bali,*" I replied. Why drink instant when the real thing is available. She bowed ever so slightly and withdrew to a side table. A large glass jug held a brown powder and she opened the top and spooned two heaping tablespoons into a tall water glass. Placing the glass on my table she proceeded to pour hot water from a small pot until the glass was nearly full, stirring with a long handled silver spoon. It smelled like coffee. I bent forward and pulled a sip off the top. My mouth filled with muddy coffee grains and I made a face. The waitress giggled, "Wait a moment to go down." She pointed at the glass and a layer of mud was already beginning to settle to the bottom. My tongue felt like I had been licking beach sand. At a nearby table someone was drinking a glass of orange juice. That looked good.

"May I have an orange juice?" tilting my head towards the drinker. The girl smiled and turned to go but I caught at her hand and added, "Also, milk and sugar for the coffee, please."

"Yes, I bring."

She returned to the side table and lifted up a ceramic bowl in which nestled a can of sweetened condensed milk surrounded by a moat of water. Placing it on the table before me she cheerfully asked, "You would like breakfast too?"

"Please, yes, I would."

I lifted the can dripping from the bowl and peered at the two triangular punched openings. Hoping that only milk would come out when I poured, I tipped a good slug into my coffee glass. The heavy yellowish milk sank to the bottom, displacing the coffee mud. I stirred the whole concoction again and turned my attention to the menu while it settled. The first item was "Magic Mushroom Omelet" and it was bookended with the universal, round yellow smiling faces. Except these smiling faces had exes for eyes and a little tongue sticking up sideways from the smile. Goofy smiling faces. The image made me laugh.

"You like omelet?" the girl asked.

"Uh no, no thank you. Too early for me. I'll have the banana pancake with honey please."

She nodded and walked off towards the kitchen with a sort of sashay that held my attention. Her retreating figure with the long dark hair, tailored kelly green top and flowered sarong was very fetching. By now the kopi had settled and I ventured another sip. Tasty, better with the sweet milk, for sure. Just watch the last sip.

With breakfast under my belt, I set off along the beach road, walking towards Kuta. Might as well get to know the neighborhood. The sun was higher in the sky and I was grateful for the shade of the palms and my baseball cap. The jangly music I recognized as gamelan drifted towards me, getting louder as I walked. A man on a scooter passed me wearing the cloth headpiece, white shirt and sarong combo I'd observed yesterday on the way here. Perched gingerly sidesaddle behind him, a young woman balanced a basket of elaborately stacked fruit and flowers on her head. Her sanguine expression seemed to say "no problem" but I was impressed with her obvious poise and balance. Her lacy pink top, gold sash and batik sarong made a charming image as they passed.

In another hundred yards or so, a tall, carved double gate looking like two spread wings came into view. A large walled compound with multi-roofed shrines lay beyond the gate and the music I'd been hearing emanated from within. Dozens of beautifully attired men, women and children were flowing towards the portal. Once again, elegantly sculpted offerings of fruit and flowers, and in a couple of cases flattened cooked chickens, were balanced on the heads of the women as they mounted the stairs of the entryway. I was standing there gawking when a passerby stopped, smiled and with a gesture of his hand indicated I could enter. I felt suddenly embarrassed in my shabby shorts, t-shirt and baseball cap, surrounded as I was with such beauty and devotion. I placed my palms together as I'd seen others do and said, *"Terima Kasih, Pak."* I gestured down at my own poor clothes and added, *"Tidak bagus,"* 'Not good.' My would-be host nodded his understanding and proceeded into the temple. I suddenly wished I was better dressed.

Kuta and Legian were not all that far apart and by noon I found myself overlooking the attractive curve of a lovely beach. By California standards, it wasn't very crowded. With the shops and restaurants set back on the frontage road, the sunbathers stretched out on the sand, groups playing volleyball, shouting to each other in the surf and generally having a good time, it reminded me of Santa Monica in Los Angeles. It struck me as I walked along the beach, hearing snippets of conversation, that it was a mostly Australian crowd. Some surfer types had already overdone it with booze and dope and were busy boring the people around them. I recognized Paul in the group and found myself moving on. No sighting of Bernice or the others. I made my way off the sand to one of the little variety shops. I was parched and looking to refill my water bottle. The only thing I could turn up was a one liter bottle of Evian for a hundred rupees. Still, I gratefully opened the top and had a long cool drink. To the left, a pharmacy caught my eye. On a lark, I approached the back counter where a middle-aged man in a lab coat asked, "Can I help you?"

The Appearance of Things

"Yes" I said, "I have a very bad case of jet lag. Would you happen to have some benzedrine?"

He looked at me blandly.

"Benzedrine? No, no, I'm afraid not."

I shrugged. Nothing ventured. "Thank you," and turning to leave when he said, "This may be of some help, however."

He placed a small brown glass bottle on the counter that read, "Amphetamine Sulfate, 5.0 mg." Really?

I picked up the bottle. Twenty five tablets. "Good for jet lag?"

"Yes, yes," he replied, "like a benzedrine."

"How much?"

He put on a pair of reading glasses and I handed him the bottle. He turned the label this way and that and said finally, "Five hundred rupees."

Whoa! I tried to act calmly, responsibly.

"Very well," and handed over a five hundred rupee note.

Crossing back to the beach, I planted myself in the sand and opened the bottle. Let's start with four. I popped the pills into my mouth and washed them down with Evian. Pretty cool to be able to stroll into a pharmacy and buy some uppers. Back in high school, we'd buy cross-top whites from Bob Schwartz. Those were meant to be ten milligrams and you needed at least three to get a good buzz going.

I surveyed the beckoning water before me. There was a deep blue pool where the water was calmer and just then, a swim sounded very good indeed. Nearby, a group of six were yucking it up, sitting on a large blanket near the water's edge. There were four guys and two girls. Everybody had a can of Bintang beer and I could smell the joint that was going around. I walked the short distance over to them and squatted down near one of the guys wearing a palm leaf coolie hat.

"Beg pardon," I began. He was taking a hit on the joint and turned to me with a smile, offering the smoke. I laughed, had a good hit and passed it back.

"G'day," he said, "How you doin'?"

"Terrific. Thanks for the hit. I'm wondering if I can leave this," indicating my day sack, "with you while I go for a swim?" Blue eyes, pretty stoned.

"Sure mate. No worries. It'll be here."

"Thanks."

I stood and waved a hello to the seated group.

The water was very welcoming, not too cold, not too warm. I was already beginning to buzz a bit and the euphoria of the speed made the blue of the sky a little bluer, a little more electric. I floated on my back, eyes closed feeling the warmth of the sum and listening to all the clicks and cracks underwater, the seed gourd sound of a Latino rhythm. Rolling over I began a side stroke that took me down the beach a hundred feet and back. Up from where I came ashore was a fresh water beach shower and I let the cool water pour over me in a joyful rush. Dripping and glistening in the sun, I made my way back to the group on the beach. From my day sack, I pulled out my sarong and toweled off. The guy in the coolie hat looked up, squinting, and asked, "Fancy a cold beer?"

"Sure, that'd be much appreciated."

The others looked up at me and I introduced myself, "Hi, I'm Vern."

"I'm Jack," said the man with the hat as he reached over and into the bucket of ice and beer and pulled out a can.

"Here ya go, Vern."

He pointed at the semicircle of faces, "And that's Cameron, Julie, Ann, Franco and Neil."

Nods all around. I pulled the tab off the can and Julie said, "Give it here. We're keeping the beach clean."

Even though she had an Australian accent, her sun bleached hair and freckles looked straight out of California.

"Pull up a chair Vern," said Cameron. "Where are you from in America?"

I hadn't said I was from America but many people on the road possessed an uncanny nose for such things.

"Los Angeles, California," I replied. Then, "I'm guessing you all are from Australia?"

They were a group of school friends but just on a short holiday from university. I was feeling the buzz from the amphetamine sulfate already starting to slacken. It appeared that four were not quite the equivalent of one cross top, so call it five. If I wanted the equivalent of a three tab buzz I was going to need eleven more of these little babies. I spilled out eleven tablets then thought an even twelve sounded like a better number and washed them down with the last of my beer. An hour later my cottonmouth and conviction that really brilliant things were being discussed told me that amphetamine sulfate was ok.

I made my way over to the shop across the street and brought down ten more beers, as my contribution to the pot. Franco kept sending around cigar-sized joints and by late afternoon we were all hoarse from laughing and probably dehydration. Time to go.

I was walking back alone, passing the now empty temple, when the first bluesy rush hit me. One of the down sides to uppers is the crash. This one promised to be a doozey. My head already hurt. I refilled my water bottle at the Red Flower and dragged myself back to the cabin. My heart fell when I saw the scene there. Graham sat with the couple from last night, Nick and Nora. They had pulled the little table and chairs out from inside and even found extra chairs from somewhere. I felt done with socializing. Graham spotted me and gave a lazy wave, "Hello Vernon, how was the diving?"

I'd reached the bottom of the steps and was brushing at the sand clinging to my sandals and feet. "So so," I replied. "The water is lovely but the visibility left a lot to be desired. For that matter, there isn't a lot to see in close here."

"Care to join us?" said Nick mildly. He indicated the empty chair.

"Hello Nick, Hi Nora." I hesitated.

The bourbon sounded like a good mellowing agent just now. Bourbon and seven.

"Yes, thank you. That would be great. Let me just wash off the beach and I'll join you."

I pushed into the main room, picked up my dop kit and headed down to the *mandi*. The small bottle of aspirin I was looking for was in a side pocket and I gratefully opened the lid and poured out three tablets. I drank half my water bottle as I downed them. Stripping down and pouring the cool water over my head felt luxurious and seemed to release some of the tension I'd been holding in my shoulder blades. My face in the mirror looked toasted.

My real towel had a mildew odor and my blue sarong was too grotty to consider so I dried off with my t-shirt then threw all three into the wash bucket. I poured six or eight dippers of water over the mess and shook in a handful of "Rinso" from the little bag on the shelf, mashing the wet mass until I got some suds. Let it sit awhile.

Back upstairs I felt a bit more sociable and human. I pulled out my red and black long Sumatran sarong and tied it around me. It was heavier than the Javanese sarongs, but the soft, pliable material hung easily and it was comfortable. Stepping out on to the porch I found Nick busily chopping at something on a white plate with a wooden handled folding knife. Graham looked on with anticipation. Nora looked up and gave me her pretty smile, "You look cleaned up. Here." She pushed an empty glass towards me then reached down to a pot on the floor and pulled up a cold, dripping Seven-Up.

"Ice?" I nodded yes and she brought up three cubes with her wet hand and plopped them into my glass.

"Thanks." My mouth had a metallic taste and a quick sip of the soda from the bottle was delicious.

"Bourbon?" asked Graham and proffered the bottle of Jim Beam. "Another fine American product."

I poured in two fingers worth and followed it with the Seven.

"Cheers." My instant companions toasted me back. Nick kept chopping. The coolness of the drink followed by the warmth of the alcohol spread from my center out towards my limbs. That was good. I hadn't eaten anything since my breakfast.

Nick sat back from his labor where he had arranged the white powder into a dozen small lines on the plate. He grinned at us and rolled a hundred rupee note into a tube.

"Ladies first." Nora giggled and accepted the tube, lifted it to her delicate nose and inhaled one of the lines.

"Wooh!" she exclaimed and sat back rubbing the side of her nose with her index finger. Nick had a line, followed by Graham. He smiled over at me, offering the tube.

"Care for a toot?"

I reached for the rolled note, "Sure, where did you get coke out here?"

I had pulled the plate over towards me as I spoke and prepared to snort up a line.

"Coke?" said Graham. "No, no, this is triple nine!"

"Triple nine?"

"Yes, golden triangle. The best heroin in Southeast Asia."

"Oh" I said. "Sounds good," and snorted my line.

I'd never really understood the heroin thing. The few times I'd tried it in L.A. it was nothing special, nowhere as nice as good old Merck Cocaine Hydrochloride, a side benefit I had as the delivery boy for a large pharmacy in Van Nuys. It was my afterschool job in High School.

Heroin affected me about the same way prescription codeine cough syrup did, slow and dopey. Not my scene. But right now, after how many amphetamine sulfates, it felt like the right ticket. I could feel the bluesy, coming off speed feeling falling behind me. Another pull on the bourbon and seven, Yes, I can do this. This is fine.

A rooster screaming his brains out awakened me from a dream. I had been flying over a coastline, the waves crashing in. Just me, no airplane or contraption, not even a body. I blinked and turned over in my bed. The mosquito net was tangled around my legs and I shook free of it. That had been an interesting evening. I remember Nick and Nora and Graham wishing me a good night and them walking down the steps. I had laughed because both Nick and Graham were carrying chairs. It seemed funny at the time. I dragged my hand across my face and rolled my feet on to the wooden floor. Is this what it feels like to have a low IQ? Dull and heavy. I needed to urinate and found my way down to the toilet. After, I splashed water on my face and felt the tingle of wakefulness returning to my sodden mind. At the end of the day, I'm not for depressants. I did find out that triple nine referred to the nine hundred and ninety ninth Nationalist Chinese division that had taken refuge in the northern frontier area between Thailand, Burma and Laos when Mao and the communist army pushed Chang Kai Shek over to Formosa. They had the muscle to take over the lucrative opium trade and now made what was reputed to be the world's best heroin. The so-called Golden Triangle.

I cleaned myself up and rinsed out my towel, sarong and t-shirt from yesterday's laundry.

"Sorry Mr. Beetle," I apologized to the drowned bug in the rinse water. After hanging the stuff to dry on the little clothesline in our enclosure, I made my way over to the Red Flower. This time I had the Nescafe. The morning was beautiful, clear blue sky, the air perfumed by the frangipani in the garden. Out past the garden I heard a distant gamelan music being played. Maybe that temple from yesterday. But I felt a melancholy, a sense that while there was beauty here it was maybe a lost place. Maybe the stories of the magical, mystical Bali used to be true, fifty, a hundred years ago. Maybe it was like what happened in San Francisco, when Alan Watts would sit on his houseboat in Sausalito in the mid-sixties and speak to a gathering of people about waking up and how this is it. And the Haight Ashbury happened and Stan Owsley mixed up the best acid in the world and the Grateful Dead and Jefferson Airplane did free concerts in Golden Gate Park. And we could all touch the possibility of a magnificent now and tomorrow with peace, love and understanding. Then, somehow along the way, the monsters from the Id, the Blue Meanies, Altamont and the Hell's Angels beating that guy to death while Mick Jagger, up on stage mumbled in shock, "Hey people, come on now!"

Something that D.H. Lawrence said, how the human race never makes it to the butterfly in metamorphosis, how we crawl around as caterpillars chewing up everything we can find only to rot in our chrysalis. Sometimes, on the road, there was this searching for the Messiah, hearing that he was just ahead, just in the next village but when we arrive there we find we've just missed him. He has moved on. Maybe Bali was a bit like that. It was fun to get loaded and laugh and sing but I wasn't connecting with here. When you find paradise, stay awhile. But this wasn't seeming like paradise. Not really.

In a gloomy mood, I walked out to the main road and caught a *bemo* towards Denpasar. I wanted to give this place a chance. That ceremony yesterday, there was something here but hidden by a veil and I couldn't find my way behind. Well, ok, be honest, you made quite a veil for yourself yesterday, didn't you Mr. Castle? So, how about this, a plan of sorts, give myself a week here. I'll book a flight today back up to Singapore and start pushing north. If something really good turns up here I can cancel or reschedule the flight and stay awhile.

The *bemo* ended up in the dusty bus lot. According to the travelers' wall board at the Red Flower, I could book flights at the airline offices located in the Bali Beach Hotel. Across the dusty lot, a line of drink stalls caught my attention. Maybe before I start my trek to the hotel a cool drink would be in order. The heat and the humidity were unrelenting after the morning coolness disappeared. Leaving the bus station I walked the hundred yards over towards the market. I pushed by large inverted bamboo baskets from which multicolored roosters screeched at each other. Bushels heaped with mandarin oranges, the fuzzy red balls of the *rambutans*, bananas of all sizes arrayed up a wall, long bunches of green beans and onions, women with baskets on their heads pushing along with a red spittle of betel nut dripping out the sides of their mouths. Asian markets, they never failed to cheer me up.

I jostled through more chickens to a canvas covered stall where a few people sat with tall glasses of shaved ice and fruit juices. A robust man with thinning, dark hair and a thick black moustache was packing pineapple into a very large blender. A lower layer of mango glowed a bright orange yellow. With a roar, the machine pulverized the fruit. The chef poured in a cup of sweetened coconut milk. The tone of the machine shifted to a purr as the mix puréed to a creamy smoothness. He looked over at me and I held up one finger, pointing to the mixer. The chef nodded and shut off the blender. A Balinese man seated down the counter caught my eye and smiled, giving me a thumbs-up. Two large glasses were set out, partially filled with shaved ice. The juice master pulled the blender off its stand and deftly filled both glasses, giving each a stir with a long handled silver spoon. He poked a wide straw into each and placed one before me and one before the gentleman who'd given me the thumbs up.

The smoothie was frosty and deliciously, tropically sweet. The juice man looked over at me and raised his eyebrows, asking how it was. I raised the glass to him and said in English, "Delicious. Thank you." He grinned, gave me a slight bow and turned back to his prep counter.

"You an American?" It was a friendly inquiry, made in a friendly American accent.

I looked to my left, towards the speaker down the counter. "Yeah, California."

The stranger stood up with his drink and walked to where I was sitting.

"Mind if I join you? I'd like to hear a bit of English."

"No, sit down. I'm just sitting here enjoying my mango and pineapple smoothie."

"Rod McKinley," he said. "Out of Seattle." He extended his hand and as I took it I replied, "Vern Castle, out of L.A."

Chapter 4
Tanjung Benoa

"You only live once, but if you do it right, once is enough."

Mae West

Being a racing sloop, *Moonshiner* didn't have a lot of deck space devoted to leisure. Still, I made do with a folding deck chair and a straw hat. Rod came up from the galley and poured a bucket of rinse water over the stern.

"You look relaxed," he called.

I looked over and toasted him with my cold Bintang.

"Not so relaxed as all that," I replied. "Are we about set?"

Rod nodded, "Yep. Ready to head out."

I finished the last swig of beer, stood and folded up the chair.

"Ready or not, here we come," I laughed.

Since yesterday morning we'd watched the tenders hauling in visitors from the large cruise ship that lay offshore. The harbor at Tanjung wasn't deep enough for the big ships to enter, so they needed to use smaller boats as taxis. We'd asked one of the skippers, an official from the big boat, if we could come out for a visit. Rod and I had been returning from Denpasar on a supply run when one of the big tenders pulled into Benoa. We'd watched the mostly middle aged visitors shakily navigate the small pier and file past Cassie's on the way to a waiting bus.

"Lots of business for you," observed Rod.

"No business," Cassie sniffed. "They just come go. No buy."

The Appearance of Things

We were sitting on the coconut log benches having cold beers, our bare feet in the sand of the beach. The last of the visitors trooped past, a few curious looks towards Rod, Cassie and I. Cassie was a classic, maybe in her late fifties, she had a faded green turban from which a few salt and pepper wisps of hair strayed down her back. Her sun-wrinkled face could have been from a Navajo painting. She wore a dime store tan colored bra, the kind women usually used as underclothing, that had seen better days. It sort of fit with her ancient red and brown batik sarong. Her bare feet looked as though she'd never worn shoes. Standing in front of her little bamboo thatched shed at the water's edge, smoke from the cooking fire within drifting out the door and through the rafters, she was the picture of a South Seas Islander. Rod and I, barefoot, wearing frayed cut off shorts, open shirts and loose straw hats must have appeared as beach bums. It made me smile to think of the picture we three presented to the neatly dressed tourists filing past us.

The captain of the tender approached the table and sat down beside us. His neatly pressed white uniform with its black epaulets and gold buttons made him very official. His face was more Chinese than Southeast Asian but he was young and good looking with his dark cap.

"Hello," he greeted us, "is the beer cold?" Cassie was gawking at him.

"Hi. Yes, very cold," I responded. "Are you with the cruise ship that's laying off?" Sort of a dumb question.

"I am indeed," he said. "The *Rasa Sayang* out of Singapore." He spoke in unaccented American English.

Cassie came over to the table and looked down at him, "You want cold beer?"

He smiled at her, "Yes, *terima kasih*," and then to us, "Are you gentlemen living here?"

I laughed. "Thanks for the gentlemen part."

Rod jumped in then. "We're anchored over in Tanjung. If you had binocs you'd be able to see *Moonshiner* from here." He pointed out towards the harbor entry, "Just to the south of the entry channel, a yellow hulled sloop. You'll see her on the way out."

Cassie set the beer before him on the coconut log table and he nodded thanks to her.

"My name's Rod." He extended a hand towards the captain who smiled and said, "Larry," as they shook.

"Vern and I are staying awhile around Tanjung, getting some work done on my boat."

Larry looked over to me and I offered my hand as well, "Vern Castle, just passing through."

He did a sort of double take at that. I clarified, "Rod has been kind enough to offer me a berth for a while. I'm on my way back to Europe, through Asia."

Larry's eyebrows went up, "That's quite an undertaking!"

Rod put on his business face. "Vern's been a good hand, good to have him aboard."

I rather liked that about Rod. He was always the captain and master of his boat. I remembered when I first came aboard *Moonshiner* a bit over three weeks ago. The headman of the village had joined us. Wayan Krieg was a very likeable man and we were all on deck, enjoying some White Label scotch over ice at sunset. The language gap was there but we were working with it, and Wayan invited us to attend a temple ceremony in three days' time and to begin at his home with some special foods, a fish *satay* and *lawar*. When he stepped off *Moonshiner*, back into his dinghy and shoved off, there was a respectful farewell on both sides.

I asked Rod, "How did you and Wayan become friends? I mean, he's a nice guy and so are you but neither of you speak much of the other's language."

Rod nodded and looked thoughtful, then said, "Well, he's the captain of the village, of Tanjung. He's the chief. I'm the chief of *Moonshiner*. We're both chiefs, so we get along."

So, there at Cassie's, Captain Rod said to Captain Larry, "Any chance of coming aboard? I'd like to see your ship."

Larry broke into a wide grin. "That would be fine. You know, almost the entire passenger manifest is ashore for the next three days, exploring Bali. You'd both be welcome as guests."

It turned out that the *M.S. Rasa Sayang* was a new cruise ship and even though she had a twelve hundred passenger capacity they were out with fewer than four hundred. The crew compliment was three hundred and twenty seven so, as Larry said, a lot of folks without much to do.

We agreed to be here at Cassie's tomorrow at 2 p.m. when the tender would bring over another load of passengers headed for the upscale Sanur Beach.

On the little public motorboat back to Tanjung, Rod leaned over and said,

"You realize that we'll need to paddle over in my canoe tomorrow, right? Unless we want to get here at ten and wait around all day."

The man that served as the public link between Tanjung and Benoa with his boat had no particular schedule, but it was understood that during the slack time of midday no boat could be expected. He waited until there was enough of a load to make it worth his time. Basically he didn't go from late morning until early afternoon.

"That's fine by me," I said.

I enjoyed the elegant little canoe that Rod had brought down from the Solomon Islands. It was light as a feather, albeit a bit tippy if you weren't careful. We had become a good team in the last weeks and used the sleek little craft as our link with other boaties in the harbor as well as our ride into Tanjung. A few weeks back we had paddled over to Cassie's on a breezy day and had arrived soaked to the skin after a vigorous thirty minutes.

"We'll bag what we don't want to get wet," Rod advised.

So here we were, ready to go. We slipped the slim white canoe into the water at the stern of *Moonshiner*. I had my fancy clothes - long pants and a clean button-down shirt, carefully wrapped in a black plastic bag. I squatted down into the canoe and wedged the bag under my outstretched knees then steadied the boat while Rod dropped in and we set off. About half way across the bay, Rod called, "There she is!" and I turned to see the tender entering the channel out past the reef.

We arrived at Cassie's a few minutes before the tender, and with her permission Rod stored the canoe behind her shed.

"Time to suit up," he called.

By the time Captain Larry had disgorged his fifteen tourists, Rod and I were changed men, literally. I'd shaved in the morning and looking down at myself I couldn't remember the last time I'd been this dressed up. Maybe the flight out from London to Singapore? Cassie looked at us and began to cackle like some old parrot. The telltale stain of the red betel nut juice on the side of her mouth told me she was flying.

"All aboard!" Larry shouted. We walked out the narrow pier and greeted him.

"Well, you guys clean up pretty well," he laughed, and we stepped aboard.

The *Rasa Sayang* was a lot bigger close up and towered over the tender as we pulled alongside. A staircase with a landing had been lowered from amidships and we clambered out of the tender. "Permission to come aboard?" Rod to the uniformed attendant on the landing.

"Permission granted," he replied.

Larry came up behind us, joking with the officer who had met us on the landing and they shared a laugh together.

"Come this way," Larry directed and we followed him into a huge salon done in red velvet and dark brown leather. A very attractive girl behind the bar spoke to Larry in what I imagined was Chinese. He turned and introduced us.

"Soo Lin, please welcome my guests, Rod and Vern, to the *Rasa Sayang*."

A small crowd of staff was forming a semicircle around us at the bar, friendly and welcoming. Soo Lin placed her palms together and bowed slightly towards us.

"Welcome. You are our honored guests. May I offer you refreshment?" Her dark eyes and brilliant red lipstick were startling. I noticed that Rod was wide eyed with appreciation.

"Larry, what are you having?" I looked towards our host.

He smiled and bowed ever so slightly, "Nothing while on duty, thanks, but I'll join you tonight at dinner."

It took a moment to sink in and I stammered, "Tonight?" Rod and I looked at each other.

"Yes," Larry continued, "we've got staterooms all ready. You're able to spend the night, aren't you? Sorry if that wasn't clear."

Rod and I almost stumbled over each other as we simultaneously said, "Yes, of course!"

Whoa, very cool!

"Good then. Charlie here will get you settled in."

Another uniformed Asian man stepped forward and we shook hands all around.

"Hi," said Charlie, "Welcome aboard."

Most of the staff we met were apparently Singaporean or Malaysian, based on their nametags. Their physiognomy was marginally different from the Javanese and Balinese I'd grown accustomed to seeing, but the difference was subtle. The Javanese tended to be more delicate and small boned. Not everybody, just overall.

"Perhaps Champagne, to celebrate?"

I turned back to find Soo Lin presenting a chilled bottle of Dom Pérignon, 1969. Sixty nine was a good year for me.

"Yes, thank you!" Maybe a little too enthusiastic.

A small group settled around us and we had fun getting a little buzz going with good champagne. I was glad of the nametags around me and asked for two blanks, filling them in with our names so that our hosts would better know us.

I noticed in the stories we shared that Rod didn't mention the thing about the life insurance pay out and not being able to go home. Made sense to me. Still, I did hear some stories from him I didn't know, like trading big sticks of tobacco around the Solomons. A young woman about my age named Yan Li told us a story of when her parents fled a convulsion of anti-Chinese sentiment years before in Malaysia, losing everything but their lives and needing to start over in Singapore. She was the first person in her family to finish college and the *Rasa Sayang* was her first job out of school. Her degree was in Mathematics. On the *Rasa Sayang* she worked with the housekeeping staff.

"I hope one day to practice accounting," she confided, "but this allows me to get out of Singapore for a time. It is a very small place."

Charlie approached Rod and I, smiling, rubbing his hands together, a father about to spring a surprise on his children.

"The first dinner sitting begins at half past six. Let me show you to your rooms. You have a chance to get settled."

We followed Charlie to a broad central staircase. The walls were cream colored and gilded columns stretched between the two floors. Above, a huge domed skylight flooded the salon with light. We descended the wide, red carpeted treads into a casino space that was not currently in use, turned right and proceeded down a long, wide corridor.

"Here."

Charlie stopped and opened a carved wooden door with "117" in gold relief. We walked into the spacious living room, complete with a bank of windows facing the volcanoes of Bali across the sparkling blue water. A second door

Tanjung Benoa

opened into to a generous bedroom with a well-appointed private bath and walk in closet. Rod and I grinned at each other.

"God, Charlie, this is amazing. Thank you," I said.

"First class suites," lamented Charlie, "mostly unoccupied on this voyage. I'm personally happy to see you use them."

He opened up suite 119 next door. It had the same layout. I caught Rod's eye and grinned. Our own suites!

"Dinner in the Orchid Room, starting at six thirty. Follow the signs on the upper level. Larry and I will see you there. Enjoy."

As he was leaving, Charlie cocked his head sideways and said, "Confidentially, we're going nuts. There are as many staff as passengers. You guys are a welcome relief."

He padded off down the hall then stopped short and turned back.

"Oh, tonight there's no live entertainment since most guests are ashore but we are showing "The King and I" in the theater. Might be fun for you."

Then he was gone. In the theater? Amazing! Rod and I looked at each other and started laughing.

"This is pretty good!" gasped Rod.

"Are you kidding? This is great. I don't know about you but I'm going to enjoy getting cleaned up for dinner."

I went back to room 119. The bathroom had everything I could need - toothbrush, toothpaste, razor, shaving cream, cologne. I had a hot, fresh water shower, a luxury we didn't have aboard *Moonshiner*. I'd grown accustomed to soaping up with a bucket of cool salt water on the stern and just jumping in the ocean to rinse off.

By the time I heard a tap on my door, I was seated in front of the picture windows wearing a clean white bathrobe and enjoying a Chivas Regal from the mini bar.

"You look at home," observed Rod. "Ready for dinner?"

I rose and stretched.

"Yeah, that sounds like just the ticket."

Dressed in my finest once again, we headed up to the Orchid Room. There must have been multiple dining rooms aboard the ship because the Orchid Room was quite intimate, it couldn't have seated more than a hundred and fifty. The booths and layout reminded me of a Las Vegas supper club, complete with the solo piano player doing "dinner jazz" on the side away from the windows. A motion caught my eye and I spotted Larry and Charlie across the saloon in a large booth. We headed in that direction and I noticed that there were already a number of other guests enjoying their dinners. They impressed me as the older set who didn't want the adventure of taking the tender into Benoa. A bald man in a dark sports coat hunched over his plate, holding a knife in one hand and a fork in the other. A woman with short blue grey hair and a thin face looked on as he struggled with whatever he was cutting. She glanced up at our passing and gave a sort of weary "what can you do with this?" shrug.

The man, New York City accent said, "So who the hell does she think she is? The Queen of Sheba?" The clatter of the fork and knife drown out any response to the question we might have heard.

Larry rose in welcome as we arrived at the table. We shook hands all around and seated ourselves. "So now I can have that drink with you that I missed earlier," he confided. "How are the rooms?"

Both he and Charlie looked pleased and amused as we gushed our appreciation.

"I don't know if you like beef but the filet mignon is excellent."

Larry passed us the card of the evening fare. The only Asian thing on the menu was stir-fried rice noodle with duck and shitake mushrooms.

A server arrived smiling and expectant at the table. Larry greeted him by name then said, "For me Johnny Walker Black, ice, soda on the side."

Charlie held up two fingers. I followed suit and held up three. Rod made it unanimous.

A hand slammed down on a table, a raised voice, New York accent,

"I don't give a good god damn if she likes it or not!" Some shushing and a soothing female voice followed.

Charlie shook his head ruefully, "You always have a few that insist on being unhappy, no matter what."

Larry was right. The filet mignon was excellent and so was the Cabernet. Rod leaned back from his plate, obviously delighted and sated.

I grinned and teased him, "So, we'll be back to jaffles at this time tomorrow."

Tanjung Benoa

I was chief cook and bottle washer aboard *Moonshiner* and we managed some pretty good fare on the little kerosene stove in the galley. Jaffles were a favorite because we could load up the bread slices with anything, close the opposing cups, lay it on the flame for a few minutes and voilà, a grilled sandwich. Not bad on the clean-up either.

"Jaffles it will be," replied Rod, "but you have to admit this is a welcome departure."

It was indeed. Good food, drink and conversation. The word "departure" struck a chord inside though. I'd cancelled my original flight to Singapore when I came aboard *Moonshiner* and realized I'd found paradise in Tanjung, but the inexorable wheels of my visa limit kept turning and there was no way to renew in Bali. Two days prior I'd booked a ticket back to Singapore on the last possible day of my visa time. Now, only five days away, it felt too short and I was wrestling with scenarios of how to go out, renew and come back. Rod let me know I'd be welcome. I still had a little over two thousand dollars in traveler's cheques, but that wasn't much to get me all the way back to London. The flight to Singapore had sucked up almost two hundred. I couldn't really afford to go, come back and pay to go again. And there was more to see and know ahead of me, in Thailand and India and Nepal. Yet I loved it here. A scene from "Harold and Maude" came to mind, when Harold finally touched something real inside and declared to Maude in anguish, because she was dying, "Maude. You can't go. I love you!"

Maude had taken his hand and replied, "Oh Harold, that's wonderful. Now go out and love some more."

So it was that we wished Charlie and Larry a good evening and heartfelt thanks and headed down to the ship theater for "The King and I."

It was amusing to see the take on Thailand but I found myself watching the portrayal of love in the film critically. In my journal, I'd been reflecting on my yearnings for Camilla, the English girl of last summer, and for Eva, the Sumatran beauty of last month. I was starting to feel like a jerk that still believed in Santa Claus. The whole mythology of True Love was like a bad joke and I fell asleep on soft, clean sheets a bit angry with myself for being such a chump. What was this yearning to be in love anyway?

In the morning we sailed through the breakfast buffet like the proverbial kids in a candy store. Not from desperation of course, we were hardly starving, but with delight. I'd been fortunately raised with plenty. The first class experience, while not my everyday life, was neither strange nor unknown to me. My mother loved the Ahwahnee Hotel in Yosemite Valley, a grand old place from the turn of the century, and in my childhood, we'd often stayed there. I loved to roam the sensuous forests and the sculpted river valley while she played golf on the little nine hole course encircling the hotel. At nine in the evening we'd sit on the spacious veranda and watch the Fire Fall, when workers at the edge of Glacier Point, two thousand feet straight up, would push a mound of burning coals over the edge and we'd all "ooh" and "ahh" at the continuous stream of orange fire cascading down into the valley. I'd also come to know the elegant old lodges of Yellowstone and the Grand Canyon. Still, faced with the opulent offerings of the *Rasa Sayang*, it was difficult to resist the temptation to stuff our pockets with bacon and sausage croissants and other treats for later. I was glad we did resist though, especially when Larry met us at the tender for our departure with a going away bottle of Johnny Walker Black for each of us.

"Toast to our good times last night," he said. And we did.

Now paddling back across the water to Tanjung in the little canoe, I felt like I was awakening from a dream. Did that all really just happen?

"That was a trip, wasn't it Rod?" I asked between paddle strokes.

"Wouldn't have missed it," agreed Rod.

Our little anchorage at Tanjung was flaccid in the mid-afternoon sun. The air was still and the moment seemed frozen, holding its breath and waiting. We clunked into the stern of *Moonshiner* and offloaded our gear, leaving the little canoe floating and tethered. I stowed my dress clothes and the bottle of Johnny into the pack at the foot of my berth. The odors of salt on canvas and the slight kerosene tang felt like home and a maudlin rush engulfed me. I surveyed the little galley. Rod stepped down into the cabin. He looked a bit forlorn too. "Well, that was a time."

I'd been hatching an idea, a plan, and now presented it, ready or not.

"Rod, the rains have slacked way off and the roads are better, more passable, now. Would you be up for a trip up to the hot springs at Lake Batur? I'm flying out in five days and I'd like to do one tourist thing before I left. You know, see up country a bit?"

Rods face went through a couple of changes. Yeah, that would be fun. Oh, I'd be away from *Moonshiner* again.

"How many days are you thinking of?" he asked.

"Well," I began, "if the roads are ok, I hear we can get up to Penlokan, the town at the end of the lake, in around four hours. Then we take the boat to the village at the far end of the lake, where the hot springs are. There's meant to be a *losman* near the springs."

Rod was looking thoughtful. He ran his hand along the smooth wood of the galley table and came to a resolve.

"OK. What about the day after tomorrow, Wednesday. We go up early on Wednesday and come back on Thursday." Then he added, "When do you fly?"

"Saturday morning."

"That gives us some breathing room if we run into any problems," he reflected.

So it was decided. I could have just gone on my own if he didn't want to, but we'd been shipmates, even friends, for a month. I liked it that we'd be doing something a little more adventurous than the *Rasa Sayang* for our last days together. Wednesday at dawn we eased out into the rose light of the eastern sky. The little canoe cut through the glassy water, silent as an owl. As the orb of the morning sun began to creep over the distant horizon we pulled on to the beach at Cassie's. Balinese get up early and Cassie already had her cooking fire stoked. She eyed us from the door of her shed.

The early *bemo* into Denpasar was waiting, back up from the water's edge. Somehow, it was already almost full. Women in sarongs, chewing betel, with baskets at their feet on the way to the morning market. We stowed the canoe back behind Cassie's and climbed aboard the *bemo*. She watched passively as we pulled away, a little cloud of blue exhaust smoke in our wake. On the ride in, one of the old girls sitting near the front put her head out and spat a load of the red betel and tobacco juice. It blew back, spraying a couple of the other women and they made waving motions of disgust with their wizened old hands. Then everybody started laughing. Still, I was glad to be sitting on the other side.

The early morning scene at the Denpasar bus lot was a riot of comings and goings and dust and *kretek* smoke. There were no signs on any of the minibuses but everybody seemed to know that the blue one was going to Penlokan. We wedged ourselves in with six other passengers and I was glad I only had my day sack to worry about. It was tight but we pulled out of the station lot and began rolling along an already crowded corridor, in a generally northern direction. There was the luxury of a paved road until we reached the other side of a settlement called Batu Bulan, which literally translates as

The Appearance of Things

"Rock Moon." It's a stone carvers' town and the roadside was lined with the types of exotic images I'd seen on entry gates and temples - the fierce winged dragon bird called Garuda, snarling monkey images holding clubs, Buddhas, delicately carved women and panels of lotus flowers, all skillfully done in local stone. Then the paved road ended and we bounced up, we bounced left then right. By the time we reached the rim of the crater lake and deposited a few riders, my kidneys hurt.

"I guess they don't have shock absorbers in Indonesia."

Rod nodded and smiled, rubbing the small of his back.

"No, they have them, just don't put them on to save money."

Lake Batur spread out below us in the early afternoon sun. The left side, I'd say the north side, of the lake sloped up steeply into what looked to be an active volcano peak, a heavy cloud of steam was boiling up and spreading over the peak. To the south, there was a gentler lakeside terrain, even some forest about half way along. I followed the road down with my eye until it reached a small village hugging a strip of land that looked to be an alluvial plain. A miniature delta spread its fingers into the shallows of the lake. From up here it looked to be a lovely, tranquil place.

The ride down was surprisingly fast. The minibus deposited us in what passed for the public square, a rather threadbare park that had seen better days. Rod and I walked down to the water's edge and followed it along to the little pier. At first blush the place seemed abandoned, but within a few moments a young man appeared from a long shed, wiping his hands on a greasy towel.

"*Selamat siang,*" I greeted him. He smiled and returned the greeting. Then, "*Apa*" What you want? The word for boat was "*kapal*" so I tried to put together a sentence about "boat to hot water."

"*Kami mau purge ke air panas. Ada kapal?*"

He appeared amused and repeated back in English, "You want go with boat to hot water?"

I nodded yes. He tucked the towel into his waistband and pointed towards the far end of the lake, "Boat already go. Come back sore, afternoon."

Rod and I looked at each other. Shit!

"You want hotel?" he continued hopefully. We shook our heads "no" and said, "*Tidak, terima kasih.*" This is a lake. There can't just be one boat.

"Other boat?" I asked, "We rent, we *sewa kapal.*"

The boy shrugged, "My brother have canoe. He rent."

"Can we look?" I asked.

Without speaking, he turned and began to walk along the lakeshore. We followed and passed through a stand of thin trees and rivulets to another small beach. There, half in the water and half out, lay a roughly hollowed log. It looked like one of the fake fiberglass logs you'd see at an amusement park Log Flume ride. Rod started laughing. The hollowing job left a lot to be desired. The thing was about ten feet long and the sidewalls were easily three inches thick, the prow and the stern had been crudely rounded with an axe. It probably weighed four hundred pounds. While we stood looking at the so-called canoe the young man returned with his brother who was smiling broadly.

"Selamat siang," I repeated, You rent canoe?

"You want tour?" His eyes reminded me of slot machines, coming up dollar signs.

"No, no, *terima kasih*. We go to *air panas.*" I pointed across the lake. It wasn't a huge lake and we could easily see the little settlement at the far end.

"You go cemetery tour? I take you, there." He pointed towards the stand of trees on the south shore.

"Maybe," I said. "Maybe tomorrow, *munkin besok.*"

The brothers conferred together and our would-be guide returned, saying, "*Empat ribu rupiah*, four thousand rupee one day." We did a little obligatory dickering and settled on three thousand rupiah for two days.

With a bit of help from the two boys we pushed the massive canoe into the lake. Rod and I climbed in with the homemade paddles. They fit with the boat, being five foot long poles having a rectangle of flat wood lashed to the end, but we were away and the shoreline fell behind us. The canoe was so massive it required a serious effort to get going but once we were moving and settled into our paddling rhythm it actually went along quite smoothly and at a reasonable pace.

"It's not the shell," Rod grunted with the effort. He was referring to his beautiful, little light canoe from the Solomon Islands.

The day was blue and relatively comfortable. The altitude and the cool breeze over the lake kept the temperature reasonable, almost temperate. From out on the lake we could see the lava flow that must have poured out and down the volcano on a recent eruption. No greenery marred the black and grey slag sheet that had roiled all the way down and into the lake.

By the time we approached the village, it was late afternoon and the sun was approaching the western rim of the caldera. It had taken us nearly two hours to cross to the far end of the lake, in part due to the gentle headwind we faced along the way. We steered towards the village but caught sight of a large, white sign on the shore near the pier. An arrow pointing to the right said, "Batur Losman and Hot Springs, 0.5 km." A long, open boat with an outboard motor was tied up to the pier.

"Bet that's the public boat," observed Rod.

We continued along the shore for another fifteen minutes until thatched cabins and a small stream of steaming water flowing into the lake announced the guesthouse. Verdant grass grew all the way down to the abrupt rocky shore of the lake and there was no obvious place to pull out the canoe. We stepped out directly onto the soft turf and tied off the canoe to a small shrub growing a few feet back from the water line.

"G'day!" A smiling westerner in a sarong was moving down towards us from the largest cabin.

"When nobody came in on the boat, I reckoned we'd be having a quiet night."

Rod and I were unloading our small sacks from the canoe and I shouted over, "We like to do things the hard way."

He arrived beside us and extended a hand, "I'm Ned Trover. Welcome to Batur Hot Springs."

Ned was weather-beaten but fit, maybe in his fifties, shirtless with sun streaked blond hair and hazel eyes. A Balinese woman held herself back on the porch watching us.

"Thanks. Rod McKinley." Rod shook Ned's hand and I introduced myself.

"That must have taken some doing," said Ned, cocking a thumb towards our canoe.

"Not as bad as it probably looks," said Rod, "but I think a hot spring will be just what the doctor ordered." He rubbed his shoulder and smiled.

"Come on up to the house and we'll get you settled in."

We walked across the lush green meadow grass towards the house and the woman on the porch smiled pleasantly as we approached.

"Ayu, would you make sure number two has towels?" Then to us, "This is my wife, Ayu."

She was round faced and attractively plump with a full figure. Her dark hair was pinned up behind her head.

"*Selamat datang*," she greeted us and moved off towards the row of cabins to the right.

"Are you from Australia?" I asked Ned.

He motioned for us to sit at one of the tables on the porch and replied, "Aw yeah, born in Adelaide. Been awhile though. Ayu and I went for a visit about five years back and it wasn't for me. I reckon I'd say I'm from here now." He smiled broadly, gave us a wink then pulled a book off of a shelf and placed it on the table in front of us with a pen, "Government requires this."

Ned leafed through until he came to an open space. The names on the line above were "Thomas and Tina McFadden, Christchurch, New Zealand" with a sign in date four days earlier.

"Not very busy this time of year?" I asked.

Ned laughed, "Not very busy ever. People tend to take the boat over for the day and go back in the evening."

He looked out at Ayu, who was coming back up the steps, and smiled.

"Suits us though. A few nice folks like yourselves stay and it's all we really need."

I signed the book and passed it over to Rod who did likewise. Ned looked over our info, nodded and closed the book.

"A couple of weeks back the place was full, all seven rooms, with a German group. They were nice enough, with their hiking club, but I'll tell you I was glad to put 'em on the boat and send 'em packin'. We aren't here for that much work, all the time."

Ayu was leaning against Ned and they looked at each other softly.

"But you are in luck," Ned continued, "because tonight is a temple festival in the village. We have breakfast with your room, here in the morning, but in general our guests go to one of the *warungs* in the village for lunch and dinner. Tonight though there will be roast pig and chicken and music all around the *Pura*."

"That sounds good to me," I said. "We haven't talked about the price of the room though. What do we owe you?"

"Oh, sorry, yes. The double room is six hundred, including breakfast. That includes the use of the hot springs as well."

Not bad. I was intending to treat Rod and reached into my day sack for my wallet. Ned held up his hand, "Don't worry now. Pay tomorrow before you leave. We're walking over to the temple at about six if you want to join us." He hesitated and then added, "You'll need a sarong. I have some you can borrow, if need be."

"I'm good," I said. Rod nodded that he was too.

The cabin was comfortable and spacious with two twin beds. The thickness of the blankets caught my attention. Nights are way cooler up here. Our bathroom had a hot shower with gravity feed water pouring in from the hot springs up the hill. The front veranda had a terrific view out towards the lake. It was very cozy.

"I'm headed up to the hot spring," I informed Rod. "You want to come too?"

"I'll be along. I want to give the lake a try first."

Fair enough. I grabbed a towel and made my way up the path to the steaming baths on the hill. The natural pools had been edged with smooth, flat, grey stones and I lowered myself into the water. This pool had a little hanging thermometer that said "40" on one side and "104"on the other. I'd tried one a tad further up that said "45" but it was too much for me. Like Goldilocks, this one was just right. I heard a "whoop" and splash down towards the lake and imagined that Rod had just thrown himself into the cold water. Maybe when I got hot, I'd go in too. Five minutes later he came walking past the cabins and up the hill, a towel over his shoulders. On his way past me, I asked, "How was the lake?" He said it was great but I thought he looked slightly blue. The long "Aaahhh" as he settled into the water told me it must have been chilly.

I was enjoying some of my Johnny Walker Black on the veranda when Rod stepped out of the cabin, rubbing his head with a towel.

The glow of the setting sun was illuminating the eastern hills but it had sunk below the edge of the caldera behind us and we were in shadow. There was a freshness in the air we didn't get down at sea level.

"Ready to head over to the village?"

"Sure, off we go."

I finished my scotch and put the glass and bottle back on the sideboard in the room. I had on my short sleeved, button down, white shirt and old blue sarong and I wished I'd brought the Sumatran. It was cool enough for that one here and it was in a little better shape. Rod had on his old brown, black and white batik sarong and a grey t-shirt. We met Ned and Ayu out in front of their house and strolled together in the gathering darkness the short distance into the village. Ned, it turned out, had been in Indonesia for the better part of twenty years. He and Ayu had met when he worked in Denpasar, the manager for an Australian import-export company called Anchor Brands. Ayu had family in Penlokan. They'd come up here together over twelve years ago and built the little losman around one of the hot springs.

"Never looked back," smiled Ned.

I found myself thinking about recent ruminations on true love. A tiny voice was suggesting that maybe sometimes it wasn't such an illusion. I'd just met them, but Ned and Ayu touched a spot in my heart that still held out hope. I shoved it away. God, I'm such a sucker.

The Gamelan music from the temple was drifting out over the lake by the time we arrived. Darkness falls swiftly in the tropics and with the altitude and so few city lights, we found ourselves in a bowl of starlight. The still lake reflected the overhead stars and the glow of the Milky Way. Standing there on the edge of the lake I was floating in outer space, the velvet blackness below me and the multitude of stars above me. The lovely little temple lay at our end of town and we drifted into the music and the perfumes of incense and barbequed satay. People were moving in and out of the temple and in my sarong I felt free to join them. The colorful fruit and flower offering baskets were stacked on the edges of the shrines, people sat and talked and smoked. The eating was taking place outside of the inner temple, in the square that defined the entryway. Ned and Ayu drifted away, talking to friends. Rod and I found the lady with the roasted pig and held our banana leaf cones heaped with savory rice, jack fruit curry, sausage, lawar and tender pork. We sat on the stone edge of one of the little open gazebo platforms, eating our meal with our right hand as the people around us did, and just took in the night and the festival. That sense of being outside of time held me as surely as the air and the earth. The bittersweet knowledge that I'd be leaving all this in three short days added another layer of heart to the evening. My eyes burned and my throat felt dry.

Near the gate to the temple, a small group of older men stood laughing near a table upon which rested a very large clay jug. They had a rod with a small tube on the end and were dipping down into the jug, extracting some clear liquid. I watched as one old man tipped the rod and poured the liquid into a tiny clay cup the size of a shot glass. He raised the cup to his friends and knocked it back. They all snickered and hit their knees, for all the world like a bunch of kids who'd broken into daddy's hooch jug. Now this interested me. Sampling the different foods and drinks of a country impressed me as one of the delightful obligations a traveler had. Heretofore, the alcohols of Indonesia had been mainly European - Dutch Genéver, Dewars Scotch, Gordons Gin and various beers. Here it looked like something local was afloat and I gravitated towards the group of tasters.

"What do you suppose that is?" I asked Rod.

"Hmm, don't know. Maybe the local stuff they call arak?"

We hovered near the edge of the group. One of the old men, wearing a wilted looking turban, looked over and said something to me. It wasn't in Indonesian. The group turned, saw Rod and I, and made "come hither" gestures with their hands, their eyes merry. I moved forward. The old man in the turban dipped down into the huge jug and lifted out a tube full of the liquor and tipped it into one of the clay cups. He held it out to me. Cool! I took the cup and smelled it, an odor of herb and something musky. The man who had poured it made a "knock it back" gesture so I smiled, toasted them and knocked it back. It was very smooth going down and I felt the chemical warmth of the liquor, which seemed more like a thick brandy than anything else, begin to spread through me. The group looked at me expectantly so I smiled and lifted the empty cup to them. Two cackled and the old man with the turban put down the rod and reached into the jug with his bare arm. His eyes twinkled and as he raised his now wet and glistening arm from the jug, I saw his hand gripped an animal of some kind by the nape of its soaked little neck. He continued lifting until something that resembled a drowned cat hung in the air, a ribbon of liquid trickling back down into the pot.

My jaw must have dropped. Rod began howling and all the old men practically burst with rasping laughter, slapping their knees and elbowing each other. I was at a loss so I reached forward and held my finger into the thin viscous stream dripping off the whatever it was and put it in my mouth. "Umm, *bagus!*" I said and the old men roared some more. The cat holder let it drop back into the pot with a plop and said something to his friends. That set off another round of merriment. My buddy Rod stood behind me wiping at small tears in his eyes and hooting.

"Care to try one?" I asked Rod.

"No, but thanks," he gasped, "you can have mine."

Temple festivals tend to go late and Ned said we could expect to see some fire walking later, after midnight. I was feeling more tired than I should have but I chalked it up to the days travel and the Black Label. Hopefully nothing from the kitty pot. About eleven, I told Rod I was beat and heading back.

"Ok. I'll see you in a while. I want to wait for the fire walking though. How do you feel?" He looked a bit concerned.

"Pretty good," I allowed. "Why are you asking?"

"Because you look all red and your eyes are bloodshot."

My eyes were burning a bit. I felt it when we were paddling over but I put it down to the brightness and reflection off the lake.

"Maybe I got some bad kitty liquor," I said, and I hoped I was joking.

I don't know what time it was when I awakened. The night was still. Rod was snoring across the room. I was parched and my throat felt raw. The cool water from my bottle helped but I knew I had a fever. My forehead even felt hot to me. I made my way back to the bathroom and fished out my little bottle of aspirin. There was no nausea, which was good. I sneezed and it was like a dam broke. How did I get a cold? I blew my nose a few times and returned to my bed with a roll of toilet paper. Two aspirins, a shot of nose spray, more water, try to get back to sleep.

Dawn finally arrived. Rod had been sawing wood all night but was quiet now. I felt like crap but actually was sort of reassured that it was no worse and felt just like a regular cold or some kind of flu. My water bottle was empty so I dressed and quietly departed the room. Ned had a big bottle on the porch to refill guest water bottles and I made my way over. The sky was cloudless but appeared slate grey in the dawn. In my best stealth mode, I silently refilled my drinking bottle and strolled down to one of the lakeside benches to watch the sunrise. A movement to my right caught my attention. A young woman carrying a tray moved close by the water. She wore a white blouse and a patterned brown and white sarong with an extra pink sash around her waist. Placing the tray on the ground, she lifted out a small woven container about the size of a tea saucer heaped with red, orange and white flower blossoms. She laid the little basket gently on the soft green lakeshore. From the larger

The Appearance of Things

tray she now removed a small brass bowl the size of a teacup and a large, yellow frangipani flower. Dipping the flower into the bowl, she shook the now saturated petals over the flower offering, quietly uttering what I took to be a prayer. Then, from the tray again, a small bundle of incense was ignited and she laid two sticks on the flower basket and poked the rest into the grass beside the flowers. These simple acts of devotion held me like the last notes of a concerto and I remained motionless. She put her palms together, greeting the offering, then scooped some of the incense smoke out of the air and pulled it back over her head as if she was washing her hair. Even with my congested nose the sweet incense reached me. She stood and retrieved her tray. I sat quietly in the perfumed dawn watching her gentle withdrawal along the trail towards the village.

Back at the cabin, Rod was in the bathroom when I returned. I blew my nose again and heard a "good morning" from behind the closed door.

"How long you been up?" asked Rod as he exited the bathroom.

"Oh, pretty much since first light. How was the fire walking?"

Rod grinned, "The real deal. I saw something like it on the beach in the Solomons. How are you doing?"

I blew my nose again. "Well, I've been better. Just a cold but I wish I felt better."

We sauntered up to the porch of Ned and Ayu's house for breakfast. Ayu had a little table facing the lake already set with mandarin oranges and glasses of water.

"*Selamat pagi,*" she greeted us. "You like egg and toast?"

We both nodded and wished her good morning.

"Do you have coffee this morning?" asked Rod. Ayu returned, *"Ja. Ada. Dua?"* looking at me. I shook my head yes and added, "Ayu, *anda ada gula dan susu?*" 'Do you have sugar and milk?'

"*Ada,*" she affirmed with a smile, and went into the kitchen area.

"Think you ought to have milk with a cold?" asked Rod.

I shrugged. "Maybe not, but Kopi Bali without it doesn't taste good to me." I had a sip of water and began peeling my mandarin. "This should help, some vitamin C."

"Good morning." Ned appeared at the door wiping his hands on a towel.

"Been hearing some sneezing and nose blowing. Somebody under the weather?"

"That would be me. Good morning, Ned."

He looked at me from the doorframe with concern. "You ought to get that looked at before you head out. You look a bit flushed to me and it's a long paddle back."

"I took a couple of aspirins this morning, but thanks. Not much you can do about colds or flu. I'll be ok."

Ned stepped out on to the porch and looked more closely at me. "Fever?"

I nodded, "Yeah, the usual. Fever, headache, feeling a bit run over."

"Tell you what," said Ned. "I'll walk up the hill there and see if Ida Bagus can come over. He's good, the local *balian* and knows his stuff. You sit tight."

Before I could process or protest, Ned was off the porch and walking towards town. Ayu appeared with two coffee mugs and a large plate of toast. "Eggs come. How you like?" she asked cheerfully.

"Scrambled for me," said Rod.

"Me too." I wasn't too hungry but the mandarin was good. "Ayu, may I have another orange?"

She smiled but looked a little concerned herself. "Yes, I bring," and returned inside.

"What's a *balian*?" I looked at Rod, who shrugged.

"Probably the local medicine man. You never know. Sometimes they know best about what's around locally. Sometimes not. I met one in New Guinea who wanted to put cuts on my forearms to treat diarrhea."

"Maybe he just wanted your blood," I joked.

Rod didn't smile. He was looking off into the distance, "Yeah, maybe."

Ayu reappeared with two plates of scrambled eggs. Mine had another mandarin on the side. The eggs were delicious, with little flecks of chili and onions. They smelled like they'd been cooked in real butter.

I was finishing up my breakfast when Ned rounded the hillside trail, followed by a short, stocky man in a white sarong, long sleeved white jacket and a white head scarf.

Even though the breakfast was tasty and appreciated, the food in my stomach had brought on a bout of nausea. I was sitting quietly at the table trying to keep things down when they arrived at the foot of the steps and looked up at me. My brow and back were slick with sweat. Ned studied me for a moment and introduced the Balian,

"Vernon, this is *Pak Mangku Ida Bagus*."

I knew enough to recognize the designation *Mangku* was for the priest caste. I put my palms together and greeted him, *"Selamat pagi, bapak. Terima Kasih untuk datang Anda,"* which I hoped meant thank you for coming.

Ida Bagus gazed at me for a moment and then spoke to Ned. Ned nodded and the priest turned and walked toward the little covered platform near the lakeside.

"Pak Mangku asks you to come down to the Balé so he can look at you," explained Ned.

OK. I took a sip of water and got to my feet. I was still a little nauseous but just sitting there for a time had helped. It felt ok to walk down the steps and over to the little open gazebo.

Ida Bagus had the lightest colored eyes I'd encountered in a Balinese. They were almost grey save for the outer iris that formed a brown ring. Rod and Ned had stayed up on the porch and were now in a discussion, with Ned pointing and talking. I removed my shoes and crawled up on to the platform. Ida Bagus bade me sit facing him and he took my right hand in his and pressed his thumb into the center of my palm. He watched me intently and then reached into a small bag on his side and removed a glass tube with a wooden stopper. From the same bag, he withdrew a finger sized piece of wood that reminded me of a bit of driftwood, with its smooth, dark surface. He began to do a sort of mumbled hum and allowed a bit of liquid from the tube to fall on to the driftwood. Holding my open left hand in his he pressed in with his thumb again. With the other hand, he touched the moist bit of wood to my forehead and held it there for a few moments, then the right temple, then the left. All the time he maintained eye contact, and I felt the changing pressure of his thumb in my palm. Finally, he held the small piece of wood to my upper chest, just below the throat. His hum shifted into words but in no language I recognized. He let go of my left hand and reached to his side where a short kris, the Indonesian ceremonial knife, was sheathed. He lifted the knife halfway out of its hilt and took my left hand again in his. With this right hand firmly holding the little wood piece, he pressed it firmly into each fingertip of my left hand. Between each touch, he brought the wood piece into contact with the handle of the kris. This continued until he had "transferred" from all five digits. He repeated the process with my right hand. He pressed the little piece of wood into my fingertips hard, not hard enough to hurt, but almost. At last he pushed the kris back down into its sheath and replaced the smoothed wood stylus into his side pouch. Leaning forward, he reached out with both hands and squeezed my ear lobes between his thumbs and forefingers. His eyes twinkled and we both began to laugh. The process ended with him taking both of my hands in his and speaking to me as if I was a son about to leave on a long journey. I have no idea what he said but the tenor of the exchange was such. And it was an exchange, a subtle and conscious sharing.

Ida Bagus rolled his feet over the edge of the gazebo, slipped on his flip flops and stood. I followed suit and we walked together back up to the porch where Ned, Ayu and Rod sat sipping coffee. Ned and Ayu had wide grins while Rod was looking at me curiously, like something that had just wandered in from the desert.

"How are you feeling?" asked Rod. The question took me by surprise and I started to say "fine" reflexively. But like a bright light coming on in a darkened room, I realized that, in fact, I felt fine!

"I'm…." I looked at Ida Bagus who must have seen my eyes dilate in shock. He just nodded.

"I'm fine!" almost shouting. I put my hand on my forehead, no fever, no moisture. The nausea was gone, no headache, no body ache, no congestion. Just absolutely, completely normal.

I whirled and reached for the hands of Ida Bagus.

"*Terima Kasih, bapak!*" I couldn't remember any more Indonesian in that moment. I was excited. Magic had just happened and it was all so normal I'd practically missed it. How could a cold or a flu, whatever it was, just simply disappear? It was wild. I looked at Ida Bagus and felt such respect and awe at the mysterious thing that had just happened.

Ned said, "Well, you look a lot better than you did at breakfast," and gave Ayu a hug. She smiled at me, then up at Ned.

Rod looked confused and asked me again, "You really feel ok? Just like that?"

All I could do was shrug and laugh, "Yeah, just like that. What a mind blower!"

The Appearance of Things

I touched grateful, then almost an afterthought, "Ned, how much should I pay Pak Mangku?"

"Oh, you don't pay him. Not directly anyway. If you want to leave an offering, I'll see that it gets to the temple, then over to him."

Amazing was all I could think.

Ida Bagus and Ned walked back towards the village together after we'd made our farewells. I left a five hundred rupee note with Ayu as an offering. How do you pay for magic? Rod and I packed up our few things and walked down to our two ton canoe.

"That was a pretty incredible stay," I enthused.

Rod looked at me and said, "So, Mr. Science, how do you explain what happened?"

We shoved the log out into the cold water and hopped in. Ayu waved from the porch of the house and we began to paddle.

"Well Rod, sometimes in science the truth is 'don't know'. Sometimes that's how it is, like now. I do know that for all the symptoms to disappear like that, like I was never sick, well it seems like magic."

"So that's it? You've been talking science for a month and now it's like magic?" He sounded a little angry.

"Hey, I'm sorry. I'm not trying to piss you off or anything. You were there. I mean, when penicillin came out and people stopped dying from stupid, simple infections that probably seemed like magic too. I mean, maybe Ida Bagus is a healer, like for real, laying on of the hands and all that. Maybe the stuff with the wood stick was just show biz and it was him that did the healing. At UCLA I heard about research that was happening on spontaneous remission. People would be rotten with cancer or something, just about ready to die, then something would happen and it would all go away and they'd walk out of the hospital. There are reasons for stuff. We just don't know what they are."

Rod was quiet for a while and we paddled towards the far side of the lake, where the forest grew down to the water.

"I've seen a lot of strange stuff out there too," he reflected. "In New Guinea, you'd see these tribesmen who would pierce themselves with daggers and there wouldn't be any blood."

I heard him struggling so I said, "It may be that I had a bug which just passed through me, not a real cold or flu. Maybe if we'd done nothing I'd feel normal now too. Hell, it could have been a treat from my kitty punch!"

That got him laughing and things settled back. Made me wonder though. What was it in Rod's past that made the magic reference so loaded?

We were paddling now along the farther, southern shore and the going was easier. The slight breeze that opposed us yesterday was helping us along today. And the end point was known. Going home always seems faster that going out.

"The cemetery is supposed to be over there," Rod said, pointing towards what looked to be a clearing in the forest beside the lake. Something odd though, the movement in the trees as we drew closer. Like a group of kids trying to hide from us, too late, after already being spotted.

"It looks like some animals there," I called back to Rod.

He was focused forward and as we cleared a corner of the lakeside vegetation he said, "Monkeys."

That sounded charming, to see monkeys in the wild. How cool to come across a whole troop up here in the mountains.

"I'm not real happy to see them," said Rod. He had quit paddling but our forward momentum continued to carry us toward the shore. "They aren't the fun little guys from the cartoons."

There was a wariness in his voice I didn't like the sound of. A group of hunched forms with white faces were watching us silently from the shore.

"I'd say let's skip the cemetery."

Rod began to back paddle slightly, slowing our approach to the shore. One monkey was holding a stick with shreds of bark hanging from it. He was chewing on the stick. Hold on, that had meat on it. He was gnawing on a bone that had meat on it. Back behind the group on the shore, others were feeding on something as well. I felt Rod's uneasiness now myself.

"It looks like they've got a deer or something," I said.

A couple of the monkeys moved aside. A blackened and red rib cage could be seen laid out on the ground. I began to put a little energy into the back paddle too. Three of the larger monkeys down by the shore began yawning, as if they were sleepy or bored. The canines were huge, like photos of snarling baboons. A slight shift in the breeze and a stench washed over us.

"You know what," Rod quietly gave voice to an idea that was forming in my mind, "I think the cemetery is a charnel ground."

With the unspeakable expressed, the stick-bone that was being gnawed came into focus. It was a clearly a lower leg, a tibia, fibula and foot. Human. The monkeys facing us, now only about three canoe lengths away, seemed quite passive, but there was no mistaking the threat display yawns from the sentries.

"Yeah," I called back to Rod, "let's give it a miss!" and began to back paddle with greater vigor.

It's funny how an idea can change perception. Like one of those transparencies you lay over the drawing of a skeleton that shows you where the organ systems are, the dark lumps and piles and shreds of the charnel ground took on the reality of human remains, torn apart and consumed by a troop of wild mountain monkeys. Maybe I wasn't as cured as I thought, since the nausea of the morning seemed to be returning. A drop in the breeze didn't help either as the thick, putrid odor of corruption settled on us, a fog that I could taste in the still, oily air. Rod looked a little green around the gills so it wasn't just me.

We felt better as we pushed back out into the lake and the cool, welcome air over the water cleansed our nostrils. Away from it now, I could laugh a bit. "That was different. Not my idea of what I'd want to do with loved ones. Although, I could see Henry Kissinger there."

Rod snorted. "Naw, you'd poison the poor little buggers."

We both shared a laugh that released the tension of the horror.

"But really, can you imagine laying grandma out for those guys and just walking away?"

"Not me," said Rod.

I took a peek at him over my shoulder and he looked better than he had a few minutes ago.

The young man who had rented us the canoe must have seen us approaching and was waiting on the lakeshore beach. When we came in, he helped us pull the beast up on the shore.

"You like see the cemetery?" he asked eagerly.

"No, *tidak*, not like cemetery," Rod glowered and the boy's face fell.

"Tourists like," he replied, a little defensively.

Rod and I collected our plastic wrapped bags and began to walk up towards the town center. The boy ran up next to us and held out his hand. "You pay park money," he demanded.

Park money? We stopped and looked at him. We had paid the three thousand rupees for the canoe rental before we departed. What was this about?

"What park money?" I said.

"Tourist fee," replied the boy, keeping his hand out to be paid.

Here we go.

"How much is the tourist fee?"

"Five hundred rupiah. You pay now."

"Ok," I said, "we pay five hundred rupiah to the Penlokan Banjar. We go now."

The Banjar is like the community manager in all Balinese towns.

The boy looked surprised then his face hardened. "No Banjar! You pay tourist fee me."

Rod and I looked at each other and wordlessly picked up our bags and started walking. We'd gone maybe twenty feet when a spray of pebbles rained around us, a few bouncing off our backs. The kid was standing there defiantly and glaring at us. I found myself wanting to go back and smack him but decided that would probably make things escalate. We were the strangers. Rod must have had the same thought so we just turned and kept walking up through the brush towards town.

"Little asshole," hissed Rod.

The square where the minibus had dropped us yesterday was quiet. A few men appraised us from the tables of a *warung* facing the plaza. This place didn't have quite the happy-go-lucky feel of the Bali I'd grown accustomed to being in. The attempted extortion by the kid left a bad taste in my mouth. We went over to the *warung* and took seats at one of the empty tables.

"*Selamate pagi*," I said to the men who eyed us. One returned, "*Selamat siang*," meaning it was afternoon and I'd just been corrected. They went back to whatever it was they were doing before we showed up.

"Mountain people are different," Rod observed. "It's sort of like that in Washington too."

The Appearance of Things

Perhaps that was it, the dour energy of the place. An older woman came out from the kitchen area, followed by a man in a sarong.

"What time have you got?" I asked Rod, who glanced at his wristwatch. "Almost one thirty," he replied.

I addressed the couple from the kitchen in my best Indonesian. Admittedly, I'm nowhere near perfect but I'm pretty sure they could understand my question about what time the bus to Denpasar would come. Oddly, the couple just stood there looking at us, as if I'd said nothing. Just before it started to seem too weird one of the seated men said in English, "The bus come maybe two, two thirty." He smiled and I felt a sense of relief that we hadn't somehow wandered into the Twilight Zone.

"Terima Kasih, Pak," I thanked him.

That exchange broke the logjam the arrival of strangers had caused. It was as if things suddenly got normal. Some laughter at one of the tables, the old woman shuffled back into the kitchen, the man in the sarong put menus on our table that were in English and asked, *"Mau minum?"* 'Want a drink?'

Yes, I did. *"Ja, teh manis."* 'Yes, sweet tea.' Rod was looking at the menu and said in English, "Tea also, pak, and *bihun goering*." That sounded good so I piled on, *"Ja, dua bihun goering."* It was a fried noodle dish but the noodles were more like Italian spaghetti rather than the quick, curly Asian noodles. This one came with fried egg, spicy chicken and stir-fried vegetables. It was a tasty lunch, actually, and I was hungrier than I thought after the paddle trip back. I was finishing my second glass of tea when the minivan rattled into the square. The five passengers were apparently all locals and rapidly made their way out of the square carrying their bundles and baskets. Two of the men in the *warung* stood, one of them the helpful English speaker, and began walking towards the waiting van. He turned back to us and said helpfully, *"Denpasar.* Go now."

Rod and I had already paid up so I finished off my tea and we made it over to the van and climbed in. It was now two thirty.

"It's going to be dark when we get to Benoa," I observed.

Rod shrugged. We picked up a few more passengers on the ridge top and, fully loaded, bounced our way back to Denpasar. From the bus station, we had to hire a *bemo* down to Benoa because the regulars stopped running after dark. Rod and I were both pretty quiet on the ride, each wrapped in our own thoughts. By the time we got to Cassie's the dark sky was loaded with stars. A small open fire was burning on the little beach, near the table, cozy and familiar. Cassie came out of her shed at our arrival, a little bit of betel juice on her chin, eyes bright.

"Buy you a beer before we start back," I offered.

"Sounds good," agreed Rod. "That's a longer trip than you'd think."

We sat on the bench facing the fire, the table as our backrest. We'd both stripped out of our shorts and put on sarongs to help protect from the beach bugs that darted about in the light of the fire. I had a long sip of beer. This has been a great time. In twenty four hours I'll be in Singapore again and heading for parts north. Yet the excitement I felt about getting back on the road was tempered with a longing to not have this end. Even Cassie seemed to sense the ambivalence in my spirit and sat down beside me on the bench. I was tilting the bottle back for the last swig when a hand closed around my scrotum and penis. The surprise caused me to choke on the beer and I lurched forward.

"What's this?" cackled Cassie and gave my balls another squeeze. Rod burst out laughing and before I could further react, she released my privates and started slapping her knees and howling. They were both cackling like old women. At least Cassie has an excuse, I thought. Rod was rocking back and forth, a full-throated laughter shaking him. I began to laugh too and felt truly at home.

The little canoe was behind Cassie's shed and after the hilarity abated somewhat, Rod went around and pulled it out. Now, with our small amount of gear safely stowed in plastic bags, we pushed off into the quiet water. Cassie was standing on the sand, illuminated by the dying fire. The vision of her standing there grinning with a dribble of red betel juice on the side of her mouth, her old dime store bra and her ancient turban and sarong, lingered in my mind as we slipped silently away.

The stars reflected in the water reminded me of the bowl of Lake Batur last night, but now we were moving through them. Then I saw it, the light in the water. What I had taken for the stars being reflected was in fact bioluminescent life in the sea glowing a bluish purple. As we picked up speed with our paddling the bow wave glowed brilliantly and flowed away behind us, a shimmering con trail of our passing. With each dip of my paddle a sparkling lily pad of light sprang into existence. There were bright stars reflected on the water as well and our luminescent passage was another Milky Way in motion, swirling amongst the stars. We moved in silence and finally arrived at the stern of *Moonshiner*. I had just paddled across the universe.

The Appearance of Things

II
Back to Singapore

I'm not very good at leave taking, I've decided. Saying goodbye and knowing I'll likely never see that friend again is a little bit like death each time. It's one of the down sides to being on the road that I didn't plan for emotionally. Below the blue waters of the Java sea glimmered in the late afternoon sun. How placid it appears from thirty thousand feet. I'd spent yesterday closing up my life aboard *Moonshiner* and in Tanjung. We'd paddled over to the *Baroness* and Angel cooked us a wonderful Italian lunch of cannelloni and green salad that we'd washed down with good red wine. John had been very warm and when we departed he'd waved and called out, "On to the next adventure!"

I'd caught up with Wayan at the Chinaman's that night, over a light dinner. The conversation between him and Rod had been prosaic, kerosene and the like, and I could touch how life was going to go on as if I'd never been there at all. It was a river I'd dropped into, floated along with everybody for a while and now, having climbed out, watched the flow carry everybody and everything out of sight.

I'd given Rod a manly hug at Benoa before I boarded the *bemo*. We couldn't stay in touch because he needed to be dead for the next four years. No paper trail or it could get nasty. I gave him my mom's address and we left it at that. I gave old Cassie a hug too, which made her giggle and look a bit flustered. Inside I was still laughing about "what's that!"

My ears popped and the fasten seat belt sign had come on. Below I could see the dozens of islands and merchant ships in the waters around Singapore proper. I'd looked down at all this before, when I'd come out from London, a lifetime ago. The relativity of time. It made me smile now, the explanation Einstein offered when asked about relativity. "Well," he said, "relativity is like this - when you're talking with a pretty girl, an hour can seem like a minute. But if you're sitting on a hot stove, a minute can seem like an hour."

My months with the pretty girl of Indonesia were only a minute, after all.

Coming into a place for the second time is different. It's linguistically obvious that you can only go somewhere for the first time once. But the texture of returning has a richness too, an originality, and I departed the airport with a glow of confidence that had been lacking in my first hesitant steps into Asia. I decided to head down to the YMCA on the waterfront. It had been a recommendation in my Trailfinders guide when I first got off the plane and I still felt it was a good one. The rooms were clean, if plain, and the price was right. I had a plan. One night here then the night train up to Kuala Lumpur. From KL back to Penang. There was something I liked about Penang that made me want to go back and check it out. The one night I did spend there, out in Batu Ferringhi, had whet my appetite. This time, instead of hopping on the boat over to Sumatra, I'd take the time to get to know the island and Georgetown, which reminded me of San Francisco somehow.

The bus from the airport into downtown was short and sweet. I shouldered my backpack and walked the three blocks from the station down to the waterfront. The late afternoon sun still had plenty of punch and even though I knew where I was going, I felt dehydrated and slightly disoriented by the time I reached the YMCA. I enjoyed the luxury of having a bathroom en suite and the shower was much needed and appreciated. Standing at the window, looking out over the harbor and toweling myself off, the dream that was Bali felt very far away. I knocked back the liter of water that came with the room and still felt thirsty. When I'd finished drying off, I donned a clean pair of shorts and a batik flower shirt from Yogyakarta. Let's go see what Singapore has to offer a fellow. A little twinge of loneliness lurking there.

Mr. Somerset Maugham had written of the Raffles Hotel and the pleasure of a good Singapore Sling on the veranda. That impressed me as a good place to start. The lobby of the YMCA has all the charm of a hospital waiting room. The Chinese man on desk, however, spoke English with a British accent and informed me that if I exited to the right, crossed over the white bridge and went another four blocks I'd come to a park. The sea would be on my right and I'd find a collection of street food stalls the locals called The Satay Club. On my left, across the park, I'd find the Raffles Hotel. He hoped I'd have a pleasant evening.

Most of the old buildings along the street had a charming, somewhat tired colonial feel. The white facades had seen days of glory, it was clear. Singapore had a few skyscrapers in the downtown but out here, at the water's edge, it was still an exotic Asian seaport. The first bridge I came to spanned a wide waterway that penetrated towards the heart of the city. Its heavy, turn of the century steel superstructure reminded me of some of the older bridges over the Thames in London, albeit a bit worse for wear in the tropical heat and salt. To my right, the waterway opened into the harbor and a multitude of ships, anchored out or slowly slipping along. Down on the left side the channel narrowed and was crowded with wooden sampans and small junks. Huge bales of some yellow orange fiber were being wrestled on to carts by workers in coolie hats. Back from the docks, old trading houses with carved Chinese characters over their doors. Men wearing skullcaps and carrying notebooks were hurrying between off-loading boats and laborers, shouting directions. Further up the waterway precarious tenements cantilevered over the channel and laundry flapped on lines in the late afternoon light. There was a human scale to the whole enterprise that was reassuring, despite the noise and filthy water.

Four long blocks later the avenue opened up into a broad arc separating a seaside green from a more traditional English park. A pretty white Anglican church was situated back in the taller trees. Following the avenue into the distance, some rather uniform looking apartment complexes and more port facilities lay ahead

I crossed the street over to the park side and set off along a footpath that angled away from the water. Through the trees a Victorian gingerbread structure surrounded by manicured garden looked to be my destination. The Raffles Hotel, like so much of the British Colonial architecture, had a threadbare, tropical charm. As I drew near, a mixed crowd of Asians and Europeans were enjoying the wide, covered veranda. Old rattan fans whirred slowly overhead. Laughter from a group of officers in pressed white uniforms and dark hats over at a corner table punctuated the happy, genteel murmur and clinking glasses of the patrons. I immediately like the scene and bounded up the wooden steps into the ornate old lobby and reception. Access to the veranda was apparently through the restaurant and bar.

"Are you staying with us?" a young woman inquired. She stood behind a wooden lectern and eyed me in a less than welcoming manner.

"No, no, I'm not a guest in the hotel. I would however, like to enjoy a Singapore Sling out on the veranda." I smiled in what I hoped was a disarming manner.

Not disarming enough. "I'm sorry sir, there is a dress code and this section is reserved for guests of the hotel and clients with reservations."

She glanced down at my shorts and sandals, in case I hadn't got the message.

"However, if you'd like, please feel free to enter the snack bar area behind you. It is a more casual environment and open to the general public. You'll also find full bar services." She smiled perfunctorily and turned away to attend to a well-dressed couple who'd come up beside me.

"Thanks," I said but she was already engaged in seating the newcomers. Oh well. Dress code. Should have worn my tennis whites, old man.

The snack bar was pleasant enough, rattan chairs, white table clothes and the same overhead fans. I found one of the few empty tables out on the veranda and settled myself into a comfortable armchair. This was clearly the budget tourist side of things and I wasn't the only one with the idea for a Singapore Sling. Dozens of tall glasses of what looked like tropical punch dotted the tables around me. The crowd did look a lot less elegantly attired on this side. Older men in shorts and Hawaiian shirts with cameras slung around their necks, small groups of young sailors who were obviously not officers, tables full of office worker types, attractive young Asian women and men giggling, out on the town, and a few backpacker types like myself. Everybody seemed to be having a good time. What the heck.

"Are you ready to order?" A tall, young Asian man in long dark pants and a white shirt stood by my table.

"Well," I began, "I'd like to order a Singapore Sling. Is that what I'm seeing around me?" I nodded towards a nearby table where three young men in loose white shirts were smoking and laughing.

The waiter followed my nod and looked back to me, "Yes sir."

"Are they good here?"

The waiter looked a bit bored.

"They are famous here, sir."

"OK, I'll give one a try. And a snack, maybe. What's good?"

He shrugged. "The bowl of crisps is popular. Potato chips, banana chips, cassava and peanuts."

"Sounds good. Singapore Sling and crisps."

He turned and bumped into two men making their way along the veranda.

"Oops! Sorry mate," said the taller one.

They stood aside to let him pass. We made eye contact and I shrugged in a "what are you gonna do" sort of way. They stood for a moment looking around, trying to find somebody maybe. I picked up a card from between

The Appearance of Things

the sugar bowl and the salt shaker advertising something called the "World Famous Tiger Balm Gardens."

"Mind if we join you? Seems like there aren't any open tables."

The guy tall guy with the crooked nose who'd bumped into the waiter. Seemed like a friendly sort.

"Sure, pull up a seat." I nodded to his friend, who was apparently shy and hanging back.

Mack and Jimmy were on an eight day shore leave. Their cargo ship was offloading Australian wheat and picking up who knows what.

"It's a local run," grinned Mack, "Sydney to Singapore to Yokohama and back this time."

Mack was the affable one of the two, late twenties, reddish brown hair, goofy grin and a smashed nose.

"I tell people it was from a fight with Bruce Lee but in fact it was a hard how-do-ya-do from a sail boom."

The Singapore Slings were OK but a bit watery. Still, we were having a bit of fun and ordered a second round. I told Mack and Jimmy about the run-in with the pirates in Bali.

"We see those bastards out there," mused Mack. "If I had the helm I'd run 'em down, accident like."

Jimmy was friendly but taciturn, preferring to let Mack be center stage. He came alive, though, when he talked about Bangkok. Seemed that's where they were headed in the morning.

"You should see the beautiful gills, though" he enthused. He had a wholesome, blue eyed boyishness until you listened to his tales of "fukkin' the gills" up in Thailand. There was a slavering seaminess that made me glad I didn't have a daughter.

The second Singapore Sling tasted better than the first and I was beginning to feel the buzz. Out past the edge of the park the sky was glowing orange but the actual sunset was on the other side of the peninsula. Must have been a good one. Mack leaned forward with a sort of nudge and a wink.

"Tell you what, you don't know Singapore until you've been to Bugis Street, Vernon. It's a place that really starts rolling after dark."

He looked around the Raffles and added, "Quite a change from here." Jimmy snorted at the last bit.

"Sounds like a place to boogie," I said.

Mack grinned, "Yeah, it sounds like that doesn't it, boogie 'til dawn. But they spell it B-u-g-i-s, named after a tribe of boat people hereabouts."

I made a 'pay the check" hand signal to the waiter.

"What's there that you like?" I asked.

Mack and Jimmy looked at each other and started laughing.

"Well let's just say it's a unique entertainment here in town. You want to arrive after nine in the evening, after they pull out the tables and close off the street. We always go for a laugh, don't we Jimmy?"

Jimmy piled on, "It's like a night club see, except outside. Some of the local boys and gills dancin'. Got a wee twist since a lot of the gills aren't gills, if you follow my meaning." He winked at the last part.

"Hey, I'm from L.A. The female impersonation thing doesn't flip me out. We've got a club in North Hollywood called the Queen Mary. It's a date night thing."

Mack guffawed, "The Queen Mary! That's a good one. I reckon you'd feel right at home then."

"Maybe not right at home," I laughed, "but it sounds like a possibility for my last, hey, my only night in Singapore. Don't see myself staying here anyway."

We paid up and they headed off towards the downtown.

"Maybe see ya there," Mack shouted back over his shoulder.

I waved and meandered out across the park towards the Satay Club. The bowl of crisps was too meager to be supper. Darkness had fallen and the bright white gas lanterns across the way were like beacons to my lightly intoxicated senses. I crossed the avenue and walked over the grass to the collection of food stalls. Perfect place for a hungry guy who loves Asian cuisine - Indonesian BBQ satays, Indian Tandoori ovens with nans and kebabs, masala dosas, Malaysian murtabaks, wonton soups and savory pork stews with star anis. Heaven, in a word.

Mack and Jimmy seemed ok. The thought of being on a boat for ten or twelve weeks at sea then trying to cram in as much sex and drugs as possible on a shore leave had an edge to it that didn't attract me. I could see how it might skew the personality a bit. I imagine it could be fun for a young guy as long as he had plenty of penicillin near at hand. Seems like it would get old fast. Oh, what the hell do I know, maybe I should try it before I knock it.

"Taxi sir?"

The question popped me out of my reverie. I had been strolling slowly along the strand, feeling very well fed, headed generally back towards the YMCA. The glow from the two Singapore Slings had worn off. On reflection, not my drink.

"What time do you have?" I asked the driver. He seemed startled at the question but checked his dashboard clock and replied, "Eight forty five, sir."

"Do you know Bugis Street?"

A broad grin, "Yes sir, I know it. We go?"

"How much to Bugis Street?"

"Well, not extra far. We use meter. Maybe ten Singapore dollars from here."

The exchange was a little more than two to one, so less than five bucks. You know, one night in Singapore. I don't really want to just go back to the YMCA.

"OK, let's go."

I opened the cab door and hopped in. He flipped down the meter and we swung in an arc that took us back through the park.

"First time in Singapore?"

Dark eyes studying me in the rear view mirror.

"First time without jet lag," I replied.

"You like the girls at Bugis street, sir?"

"I've never been to Bugis Street. I'm meeting some friends there."

Appraising gaze from the mirror.

"You want girls, I take you to Little India. Beautiful girls. Dark skin. Light skin. What you like? Girl boys too."

"Thank you, but I think I'll stick to one adventure a night."

The eyes in the rear view mirror crinkled, "Where you from? Australie?"

"No, America. Los Angeles."

"You army man?"

"No, not army man. Just traveling. How about you? Are you a Singapore man?"

"Me? No, I'm Indian. From Malaysia."

"Malaysia? Are you here a long time?"

"Not extra-long. I go back to my family two days' time. Kuala Lumpur. Big festival of Thaipusam. Very beautiful for my family."

We had penetrated deeper into the center of the city and street illumination had increased. The card on the dashboard identified my driver as I. Rahul Gupta.

"Do you like Bugis street, Mr. Gupta?" I asked.

A slight surprise in the rear view mirror eyes.

"It is popular," he ventured. "Too expensive the beer I think."

A few minutes later, Mr. I. Rahul Gupta pulled to the side of the road and pointed ahead to the corner. "No cars, Bugis Street, we stop here."

The taxi meter read $8.40. I Pulled out a ten dollar note and handed it to him.

"No change," I said, "to help you on your way."

He swiveled in his seat and I saw the face that held the dark eyes in the mirror. I recognized the deep pock marks as the scars left by small pox.

"Namasté," he said, with palms placed together. "I wish you good fortune on your journey."

I placed my palms together, "And you on yours."

I rounded the corner and was confronted with wall-to-wall tables and chairs. People were swarming in the full city block that had been given over to creating an outdoor café atmosphere. Strolling the length of the block it was clear that many of the little cafes offering beer and plates of food served as other businesses during the daylight hours. A tailor's shop had two large coolers on the floor filled with beer and ice. At a side table within, a woman scooped full tea cups of cooked rice on to paper plates from a huge steamer while a little girl ladled on a dipper of some sort of stew. The clientele ran the gamut from well-dressed business men and their elegantly attired dates to the likes of me, western guys in shorts, sandals and shirts. I was even a rung up, since my shirt had a button down front. In my sweep of the street, I didn't see Mack or Jimmy so I picked an empty plastic table near the tailor's shop and seated myself in a folding chair. The little girl who'd been scooping stew came out and looked at me hesitantly. I smiled and said, "One beer, please." She returned my smile and almost skipped back into the shop, returning momentarily with a brown glass bottle labeled "Becks." The top was on but had been pried up and sat loosely.

"Eight dollar," she said.

I saw what Mr. Gupta meant - beer too expensive. I passed over exact change and she ran back inside.

In the middle of the block, an impromptu stage stood, only a foot higher than the street, flanked by a pair of speaker stands. Half a dozen women were dancing to music that sounded like a speeded up reggae track, trying to entice men standing nearby to join them. A few good sports had done so and looked ridiculously out of place. People were clapping and hooting, some standing beside their tables and carrying on a conversation with those still seated. I studied the girls on the stage and had to admit, if they were female impersonators, they were very, very good. No Adam's Apples, no beard stubble. I don't know what I expected, maybe like Los Angeles, a lot of old queens doing Ethyl Merman covers.

A truly gorgeous girl with waist length black hair, round breasts and a killer figure sidled up to my table. I looked up at her and smiled. She knelt down to eye level with me and began to run her index finger along the hair of my left forearm.

"You like a special time, big man?" she cooed.

She was very sexy, but with the eye make-up and the exaggerated moves I was suddenly struck with how she was merely the image of female sexuality, not the real thing. Maybe it was the smell of her skin as she leaned over me. She didn't smell like a girl. It was weird. Everything was right but it wasn't. Something of my thoughts must have shown through for she stood upright and looked down at me with a coldness in her eyes that wasn't there a second ago.

"No, thank you," I managed, "but you look great."

That won me a little smile and she moved on. I watched her glide away towards another table.

"Getting friendly with the natives, I see," Mack grinned down at me.

"Well, for the second time today, may we join you?"

Tanjung Benoa

I spread my hand at the other chairs around the table, "Here we are."

Jimmy was all agog, like he couldn't believe his luck to be around all these sex goddesses. It amused me to think what he'd do if one night, he ended up in bed with a girl who wasn't. Probably roll with it, I reckoned. From the looks on the faces of the men around me, it looked like rolling with it wouldn't be a big issue for most of these guys. What would I do?

We all sat there sipping our expensive beers and I heard a bit from Mack about some of the thrills to be had in the clubs of Bangkok. It occurred to me that a lot of sexuality is about the image of sexuality, not the reality. I looked around the Bugis Street scene. Many if these girls were "cover girl" pretty and that created a cognitive dissonance with the knowledge that they were male actors. It's an odd sensation.

One girl was over at a table, teasing a couple of sailors in white uniforms. As I watched, they stood up and walked together out of the illuminated area and disappeared down a narrow, dark pedestrian alley. Wonder who's getting what in where? The thought made me smile. I listened to a few more stories from Mack and then noticed two security types I'd have to call "plain clothes men" detach themselves from a shadow near the wall. They moved together down the little alley. It had been long enough to catch somebody "in flagrante delicto" I guess. I wonder who has to pay?

An angry scream erupted over towards the stage area, then an answering, even angrier cry. Suddenly people were on their feet to catch the fight, craning forward on their toes. I don't know why but instead of looking towards the screaming and banging, I looked away, at the faces of the people trying to catch the action. Nobody looked concerned. The expressions on the faces ranged from amusement to glowing eyed sadistic brutality. I felt I was watching the faces of a crowd at a circus the very moment a trapeze act went wrong and someone was falling to their death. My mild amusement with the evening evaporated. I was suddenly among the hungry and the angry and the hateful, looking for a fresh kill. It freaked me out and I dropped back into my seat. My comrades continued to savor the altercation, wearing amused expressions like people might have watching the clowns.

The ruckus died down and the clientele resumed their seats. I glanced over at the alley in time to see four plain clothes leading the two sailors away, their hands cuffed behind their backs. Everybody was having a good time.

"Well you guys, it's been a long one for me, all the way from Bali. I'm heading for dreamland. Hope you get all you want on your trip to Bangkok."

The Appearance of Things

"Well, good on ya', Vern. Safe travels yourself," said Mack.

"Nice to meet you," added Jimmy and tipped his beer to me.

I stood and pushed in my chair.

Mack added, "Quite a scene, isn't it?" He surveyed the neighborhood.

"That it is," I replied, and made my way out to the waiting taxis.

I felt deeply rested in the morning, rather a surprise with all the ups and downs of yesterday. In the lobby of the YMCA there was hot tea and some not very good Chinese sweetcakes wrapped in cellophane. I had some tea but tossed the cake into the rubbish bin after one bite. I needed to walk back uptown towards the bus station to arrive at the train station ticket office and I figured I'd find some good street food along the way. The morning was heating up even though it wasn't yet 9 a.m. It was time to get the show on the road.

A sleeper on the evening train to Kuala Lumpur was only about fifteen dollars more than a coach seat. I've enjoyed sleeping on trains, where I get to lie flat and stretch out. The rattle of the tracks and the gentle rocking is somehow incredibly cozy. The ticket seller assured me I was lucky to secure a sleeper, buying as I was on "the day of." The train departed Singapore at six in the evening and pulled into K.L. about thirteen hours later. It didn't look that far on a map, but that was the schedule.

I snagged a stool at a food cart in front of the station and had a delicious bowl of spicy chicken bits, scallions and noodles for breakfast. Now for a day exploring Singapore. The YMCA checkout was at eleven in the morning but for an extra ten Singapore dollars I could use the room until the train left at six. I liked having a refuge available if I needed it, not to mention a shower before the train trip. The plan I'd devised for myself was a walking tour around the city center, ending up at the Tiger Balm Gardens. I had no idea what to expect from the Tiger Balm Gardens but it sounded zany in the little folder yesterday at the Raffles.

Singapore downtown was relatively clean for an Asian city. The word from other travelers was that you could be fined for spitting on the street but I didn't test it. As I strolled among the high-rise buildings, an old quote from Calvin Coolidge came to mind - "The business of America is business." From where I stood it looked like the business of Singapore was business. The streets were mobbed with well-dressed men and women. Everybody seemed to be walking purposefully, checking wristwatches and gripping briefcases. Downtown Los Angeles was provincial by comparison. To my left, sandwiched between two tall buildings, was an anachronistic old Chinese temple. I poked around the front door and looked in. Huge spirals of incense looking like giant red mosquito coils hung from the ceiling, and men in business suits knelt on the altar, shaking bamboo tubes filled with sticks. They'd spill the sticks out and apparently read the result. It was fascinating to see modern suit and ancient practice fused into one person.

A signpost read, "Little India, 0.2 Km" - an arrow pointing in the direction I was going. Both L.A. and San Francisco had Chinatowns, yet since Singapore felt so Chinese overall, it was humorous to me that the local manifestation would be an "Indiatown." Why not? Go check it out.

After a few blocks, the taller buildings faded into older, two floored structures. The majority had shops on the ground floors and judging from the hanging laundry, residential flats on the second floors. Colorful saris draped in windows, posters of Hindu deities and little strings of lights, incense and exotic spices told me that I'd arrived. An ornate painted temple had the general outlines that reminded me of Prambanan, back in Java, but this one was stretched out, reminding me of a giant, box type cheese grater. Wearing flowing saris, dark haired women with dark skin, a red spot in the middle of their foreheads, carried trays of orange marigolds into the compound. Chains of the fragrant flowers dripped over their arms. Around both sides of the entry, shelves of stone were heaped with flower chains and burning white candles. Incense smoke whirled in the air. Shades of Bali - but not Bali. An old man wearing an ivory colored sarong, shirtless, his white hair pulled up into a top knot, stood by the temple door. I began to ascend the steps, as I had done at the Chinese temple but he raised an outstretched hand and fixed me with his eyes, clearly forbidding entry. A tan colored paste depicted a trident on his forehead, its shaft running down over his nose and chin, continuing down to his waist. In his left hand, he gripped a wooden staff easily a foot taller than his person. His grey eyes were not unfriendly but there was no mistaking his determination as gatekeeper of the temple. I used hand signals to ask his permission to walk in the grounds around the temple. He smiled, waggling his head back and forth in a way I understood to mean "yes, go ahead." I reckoned if I got that wrong, I'd find out about it in short order. I circumambulated the temple then, intrigued to see that there was something of Bali in the ritual around me, the incense and devotion but also that this Indian form of Hindu was very much its own thing.

The Tiger Balm Gardens, on the other hand, was an exercise in kitsch. An old friend in L.A. had introduced me to Tiger Balm back in the sixties, as an enhancement when smoking marijuana. "Put a little dab on each temple," he'd say, handing around the small, wide mouthed jar. "Don't get it in your eyes or it will burn." We dutifully put on our dab. "Now feel how it opens up your vision. It makes everything wide open."

If we got stoned enough it seemed to be true, and everybody would kick back listening to Santana, feeling the wide-open vision. I had my own jar of Tiger Balm in those days and felt it made me one of the cognoscenti. But the Tiger Balm Gardens! I guess growing up in L.A. with Disneyland and Knott's Berry Farm had jaded me. Those parks were works of art and they had good rides, something to do besides look at fairly cheesy painted cement sculptures of tigers and miniature Asian landscapes. After an hour of wandering around, I bought two jars of Tiger Balm and walked back to the park near the Satay Club to read and close out the day. Gazing out over the harbor, my mind settled. "I wonder what Rod and the other boaties were doing right now." I could picture the sun setting behind the volcano and the gentle rocking of *Moonshiner* and my heart ached for a moment. Then Dr. Seuss came to my rescue with a childhood memory of wise reflection: "Don't cry because it's over, smile because it happened."

Chapter 5
Thaipusam

> We live in illusion and
> the appearance of things.
> There is a reality.
> You are that reality.
> When you see this, you realize you are nothing
> And being nothing, you are everything.
> That is all.
>
> *Kalu Rinpoche*

I was at the train station a little early. The sleeper was a surprise, since even though there were assigned seats there were no compartments. An open corridor ran down the coach center, from one end to the other. The upper bunk was fixed in place, with little beige curtains that could be drawn for privacy. The lower bunk was, at present, two seats facing each other. When pulled out from the wall, the backrest collapsed down and the two seats would form a small, flat bed. As with those above, small beige privacy curtains attached to each side could be drawn. I was glad to have the lower bunk since it had the window.

On the other hand, I couldn't go to sleep until the person opposite decided to let me. In this case, the person opposite was a diminutive Indian man with glasses. He wore the extra-long shirt and loose pants I'd seen many citizens of Little India wearing today. My seat partner was dark skinned with short cut black hair and a thick moustache. I could imagine a young Mr. Gandhi.

"Hello. Where are you going?" he asked, in sweetly accented English. The mild, pleasant look he wore was very disarming.

"Well, of course, up to Kuala Lumpur tonight, but I'm heading to Penang."

He did the same head waggle as the old man in front of the Hindu temple.

"Yes, yes, Penang. Lovely place. I know it well."

He leaned forward, as if confiding something, "I am Patel. Hari Patel. Ginger candy?"

He extended a small square box that sat on the seat beside him and lifted off the lid. Several dozen small dark balls coated in sugar lay within.

"Thank you," I smiled, "that's very kind. My name is Vernon Castle. I come from America."

I reached into box and pulled out one of the little dark lumps.

"Where are you going, Mr. Patel?"

Mr. Patel selected a candy, popped it into his mouth and reclosed the box. He looked back at me with a twinkle in his eye.

"These are favorites for my nieces and nephews."

He placed the box back on the seat and patted the top.

"I am traveling to the home of my parents, outside of KL. A big family get-together, for the festival you know."

I didn't know. Then a flashback to the taxi driver of last night. He'd spoken of a festival called Thai something. Thaisam maybe?

"I just heard something of that, last night. It's called Thai something?"

"Thaipusam," he said helpfully. "Yes, yes, a very special festival in two days' time, especially in KL, at the Bat Cave. Biggest in the world," he said proudly.

"Well, I'm sorry I'll miss it," I responded, "It sounds like something worth seeing." I put the ginger candy in my mouth.

"Oh, if you are in Georgetown you can see it there too, although," he smiled sympathetically, "not nearly so fine as in KL."

The train jerked and we began to pull out of the station. Mr. Patel glanced at his wristwatch and announced, "Six oh two." He relaxed back into his seat and gazed out the window, hands folded in his lap.

"Very good candy, Mr. Patel!"

Thaipusam

The explosion of flavor had taken me by surprise, a strong, sweet aromatic ginger with a slow burn that kept going.

"Please, have another," reaching for the box by his side, but I held up my hand,

"No, no, thank you. Please save them for your family. I'm going to the dining car soon and I don't want to fill up on sweets. But they are delicious, the best I have had."

He nodded, satisfied with my response, and returned his gaze to the passing scene of industrial Singapore.

I pulled out my new Michener book, The Source, which I had traded for Somerset Maugham. Back on board the *Baroness*, John had a decent library and was glad to exchange books with me.

"The Malaysian period, huh? Haven't read any of these. Here, I liked this one a lot," and handed me The Source. I wasn't very far along in it yet, but I liked the concept of an archaeological excavation where objects on each level had a story to explore.

The clickity-clack of the rocking train was hypnotic and an hour had passed when I realized I was hungry. I closed my book, nodded to Mr. Patel and made my way two coaches forward to the dining car. The layout was elegant and friendly, with the front half being a cozy bar and lounge while the rear section boasted white table cloths, linen napkins, waiters and good looking fare. Although there was no door, the two sections were separated by a clear glass divider etched with lotus flowers. The steward looked up at me from his station as I entered.

"Good evening. How many?"

"Just one," I replied.

He surveyed the carriage. All the tables were occupied. One table that could have seated four had only a young couple seated beside each other.

"I could seat you now, if you like, or there is dining in the lounge."

The lounge looked crowded too and the tables were much smaller.

"Here, if the others at that table don't mind."

The steward walked down the aisle to the table with me following behind and stood back for me to seat myself.

"Sorry, do you mind if I join you? No tables for one I'm afraid."

It seemed polite to at least ask. Maybe they had a friend coming or something.

"No worries," the young man responded. His partner smiled a welcome.

Pat and Neil were on their honeymoon, out of Auckland, New Zealand, and on their way to Thailand.

"Some friends were on an island named Ko Samui last year and made it sound like paradise," said Neil.

Pat, petite and blond, added, "We've got good beaches on the North Island as well, but a tropical island paradise has my vote." She looked over at Neil and squeezed his arm, eyes glowing. They were clearly absorbed in each other and I busied myself with the menu.

A burst of noise when the carriage door opened and another group entered the dining car. I looked up to see three men and the woman who entered with them. She was beautiful, wavy blond hair cascading down past her shoulders from under a white, wide brimmed summer hat. Her companions were speaking German together and gesticulating with the carriage steward. She looked past them, a bit bored, when our eyes met and lingered. Tall, taller than her male companions, her lacey white blouse and loose skirt accented a wonderful, trim figure. Generous red lips and wide set cornflower blue eyes, almost Asian but with a weariness in them that made me sad for her. Veronica Lake leaped to mind.

The steward turned as he spoke, indicating the full dining room. One of the men pointed to the far end, towards the bar and the steward nodded. He collected four menus and led them down the aisle, past my table. A little smile played on her lips as she passed me. We'd had our eyes locked on each other since she entered and now, as her group passed, I smiled too. I couldn't help it. We were greeting and intending and when she glanced back at me over her shoulder I felt an electrical discharge flash between my brain and my genitals.

Now that she was seated behind me at one of the low bar tables I felt my neck burning. I swiveled for a peek back and she was looking right at me, her eyes merry, no sign of the earlier weariness.

Neil followed my gaze.

"Her name is Didi."

I turned back to our table. He and Pat were both grinning at me.

"They are in the same carriage as us," said Pat simply.

Neil looked at his bride and tried to tick off all four names, hesitatingly, struggling to remember.

"Didi, Rolf, Kurt and…"

"And Eric," provided Pat.

"That's right. Didi, Rolf, Kurt and Eric," confirmed Neil. "They're heading for Penang and then on to Bangkok."

"Who is Didi with?" I asked.

Neil and Pat grinned at each other again, as if the joke was just too good.

"They're just friends, all traveling together. College in Dusseldorf, I think."

He looked back to Pat for confirmation and she nodded affirmatively.

"Health sciences."

My fried rice with chili chicken arrived, along with a Heineken beer. I let the information sink in while I chewed, making small talk with Neil and Pat. When we'd all finished our meals, I suggested we all go down to the bar and that I buy us a "happy honeymoon" nightcap. I guess I'm about as subtle as a flash flood because Neil said, "That would be terrific, Vernon. Thanks a heap. I could introduce you to Didi, if you like."

I could feel the heat of my blush and Pat giggled when I murmured, "OK, yes, thanks. I'd like that."

We paid up and I followed Neil and Pat forward to the lounge area. We grabbed the little table across the aisle from Didi's group. For the second time in two days, I wished I'd dressed better.

"Ach! The honeymooners. How was your meal?"

Neil smiled, "Quite good really. Better than I would have thought on a train. How was yours Rolf?"

Rolf had a *burgermeister* jolliness, round faced, red cheeked, a bit heavy with straight auburn hair. "*Goot yeah, sehr goot also.*"

Neil, a man of his word, jumped in with the introduction.

"Rolf, this is Vernon, from America. He's heading to Penang as well."

"Hello," I said and offered a hand across the aisle. Didi was looking on in silent amusement.

The Appearance of Things

"And Kurt, Eric and Didi," Neil continued. Hellos and handshakes all around.

"Neil tells me you all come from Dusseldorf," I said, looking from face to face, stopping with Didi.

"*Ja, ja,*" answered Kurt. He was dark haired and rather slight. His thin moustache and goatee reminded me of the guy who was ill at the hotel in Yogyakarta, Matt I think it was. But Kurt had bright, healthy blue eyes and no pallor to his skin.

"We school in Dusseldorf. We three are born there," he said, indicating Rolf and Eric. "But our Didi is come from Wurzburg."

"Oh, I quite liked Wurzburg," I said, "Last summer I spent time in Deutschland, hitchhiking along the Romantischer Strasse."

"The Romantic Road," said Didi, "Pray tell, what were you doing on such a journey?"

Her voice was like a controlled growl, the English smoothed and rounded by her German inflection. Her eyes were playful in a way that meant business. A warning or maybe, an appeal, to not turn out to be a jerk.

"I love the altar carvings of Riemenschneider," I answered. It happens to be true. I had fallen in love with his exquisite lime wood alter carvings and had resolved to see all that I could find, from Würzburg to Füssen.

Didi's eyes grew a little wider and brighter.

"Riemenschneider, yes. We have wonderful works in Würzburg. You surprise me. Most of your countrymen do not know Riemenschneider, much less seek out his work."

"The main museum I went to in Würzburg had an amazing display of his work, both the wood and stone. The Adam and Eve is quite beautiful. Anyway, I found which villages still had his work and saw what I could."

We were so intently focused I was startled and somewhat embarrassed to have tuned out the other five so completely.

"Please excuse me," I said, turning to Neil and Pat, "I wanted to get you guys a honeymoon cocktail. What sounds good?"

Neil studied the rows of bottles on the shelf behind the bar and winked at me, "You might regret this Vernon."

I was not regretting anything at this moment.

"Neil, please," I assured him, "if it's there it's my pleasure to treat you." I turned to the others, "This round is on me. Would you join us?"

Neil conferred with Pat and said, "In celebration of Thailand, we'd like a Sang Thip, with ice and soda on the side."

The bartender, who was listening, reached on to the shelf and pulled out the bottle of Sang Thip and set up the glasses.

"It's a sort of Thai brandy," explained Neil, "but a few notches up from Mekong."

How about you guys?" I asked the German contingent.

Rolf, Eric and Kurt nodded to each other and Rolf said, "Three beers please and thank you very much."

I turned to Didi, "What can I get you?"

She gave me an appraising gaze and replied, "I'll have whatever you have."

The bar was reasonably well stocked. A familiar square bottle of golden liquid caught my attention. I pointed at the bottle and said, "Two shots of Cuervo Tequila, please, the reposado."

The barman looked where I was pointing and reached for the tall bottle.

"And slices of lime on the side."

I grabbed the salt shaker off the table and put it on the bar. "Some people like it with salt." That won me a smile.

Didi stood and came over to the bar to stand beside me. She was tall. When everybody had their drink, I proposed, "To Neil and Pat. And to the possibility of true love."

The last part surprised me because I hadn't planned on saying it. Didi looked at me curiously as she sipped her tequila.

Neil raised his glass to us all, "Thank you, Vernon. And to all of us, safe travels."

He and Pat sipped their brandy, then kissed.

Didi held her glass of tequila and looked at me lazily. I tapped her glass with mine, "Viva Mexico!"

We both laughed and finished off our shots.

First we lost Neil and Pat. They finished off their brandy, waved farewell and strolled together down the carriage and out. Didi and I had another pair of tequilas going when Rolf, Eric and Kurt stood and said, "Tschus!" and walked together down the carriage and departed.

"Well," mused Didi, "just us."

By now it must have been ten o'clock and the carriage was mostly empty. The steward glanced at us, but busied himself with removing the white table clothes and carrying them down the hall towards the kitchen area.

"Maybe we should let them go to sleep," I whispered into Didi's soft neck. The musky woman perfume of her skin and hair made me inhale, savoring her.

"Maybe we should," she whispered back. At that moment, we were alone in the coach and embraced. The kiss was long, our bodies fitting right into each other.

We passed down into the now dimly lit sleeper car. Nearly all the curtains were closed. When we came to my seat, Mr. Patel was obviously asleep above. The carriage steward had lowered the seats and made up the sleeping pad and sheets. A yellow nightlight glowed in the corner above the pillow.

Wordlessly, we sat on the little bed and removed our shoes then rolled in together, giggling a bit, and pulled the curtains closed. It was a small space. I reached in under her blouse as we kissed and unhooked her thin bra strap. The perfume of her excitement was intoxicating. Her soft breasts curved up, the nipples firm and sweet to my lips. Finally we were both unclothed and moist. I came into her as she knelt over me, both of us too long in the tiny bed for any other love shape. I think Mr. Patel must have been awakened when I thrust upward and Didi's firm back bumped the low ceiling that was his bed.

He was generous enough not to demand an explanation.

Given the space limitations, humor was a companion in our love making but we fell asleep delighting in the curve of each other. I have a vague memory of my naked bottom sticking out into the passageway between the split curtains, as Didi nestled in the spoon of my body. We awoke at the first lightening of the sky and lay together gazing out the window at the far eastern horizon. I had another erection feeling the warm curve of woman pressed up against me but she stroked my cheek and whispered, "Let's wait for tonight and a real bed." Those beautiful blue eyes gazed into mine and I could wait.

She dressed and returned to her carriage before the train began to stir. I felt good, better than I'd felt in a long time.

Thaipusam

Our layover in Kuala Lumpur was less than half an hour and at 8 a.m. the train to Thailand pulled out of the KL station with all of us aboard. The schedule said we'd arrive at Butterworth station, the mainland transfer point for the Georgetown ferry, at two fifteen in the afternoon. Didi and I were tired but felt goofy and were laughing a lot. I couldn't help but notice that Eric looked hang-dog while Rolf and Kurt chatted amiably. I caught a few dark looks from him, not hateful but he clearly wasn't delighted for Didi and I.

Neil and Pat, the honeymooners, gravitated towards our new lovers' energy, or so it seemed to me, and we were a pair of happy couples all on the same adventure. We four went up to the new dining car about half past eleven, leaving Rolf, Eric and Kurt reading in the coach section.

"I guess we'll be saying goodbye to you two at Butterworth," said Neil, smiling at Didi and I. Pat was studying Didi who sat by the window, placidly watching the mixed agricultural and jungle landscape slide by. Didi squeezed my hand lightly as she turned to answer Neil.

"Perhaps we should say *auf wiedersehen*. That really means until we see you again. You will come to Bangkok, after your island stay, yes?"

"That's right," confirmed Neil, "We're flying back to New Zealand from there in a fortnight."

Didi snuffed out the cigarette she had been holding and not smoking. She shrugged, "Well you never know then. We will be returning back to Frankfurt also from Bangkok."

It was clear to all of us that "we" meant Didi and her three friends. Pat saw the road hazard ahead and shifted direction.

"We've heard the Thaipusam festival is pretty spectacular. Lots of people though. Do you know where you'll be staying?"

Didi smiled then, her profile highlighted by the wavy blond hair. The way her lovely nose curved up slightly at the end reminded me of her breasts and I involuntarily gave her hand a squeeze. This morning, as she departed our nest, she'd said, "Let's wait for tonight and a real bed." I realized with a start that I hadn't given any thought as to where that real bed would be.

"Oh," she answered Pat, "Rolf has reserved a couple of rooms at a hotel he likes in Georgetown. A Chinese hotel, actually, called Tai An." She looked at me, her eyes suddenly playful, "So much more comfortable than the couchette. I'm sure you will approve."

"I'm sure I will," I smiled back but inside I was doing flips, to have a beautiful woman look at me like that, with such promise and mischief in her perfect blue eyes.

There was a graceful, de facto acceptance from Rolf and the others that we were now a group of five. Eric had regained his good cheer and we all stood together at the ferry railing, the cool breeze welcome, as the vessel pulled into the berth of the Georgetown terminal. My German was extremely limited and I appreciated that when we five spoke together it was mostly in English, for my benefit. Another plus for the people of Europe, in my book, that multilingual sophistication.

Didi had made it clear to me that there was not, nor had there ever been, a romantic connection with any of her travel companions. But it was also clear to me that Eric wished that wasn't the case. At that level, he had my sympathy. How painful to want and not be wanted in return. To his credit, he was gracious towards me, the interloper.

Rolf was our unofficial tour guide as he had explored Georgetown and Penang over several journeys in the last few years. Kurt, Eric and he were old school friends and they had that easy camaraderie that sometimes comes in a long relationship. The rickshaws of Penang were noticeably smaller than those I'd grown accustomed to in Indonesia and with each of us carrying baggage, the logical, workable choice was to hire five vehicles. Bringing up the rear, I laughed at the sight of our long queue of rickshaws with Rolf in the lead, winding through the streets, a Chinese dragon that had lost its skin. Near a small park, we turned up an alley that ran alongside a large, open pavilion. Half a dozen small kitchens were busily turning out soups and stir-fries, the clientele enjoying their meals overlooking the park and its pond. Before us, the sparkling white, Victorian style Tai An hotel awaited. Rolf led the way up the wide steps into the startlingly spacious, covered atrium that was both lobby and lounge. Three floors of guest rooms were organized around the central atrium with its spotless black and white tiled floor, large potted palms and seating areas. I looked up at the ceiling skylights and recognized the style of iron construction used at Victoria Station in London. This, however, was clean and white.

"*Gott in Himmel*," exclaimed Didi, taking in the white palace in which we stood. "Much more elegant than Rolf led me to believe."

Eric and Kurt were gawking, having much the same response. Rolf at that moment was speaking with the clerk at the front desk and I joined him there.

Thaipusam

"Rolf, this is wonderful! *Sehr schön*," I said. 'Very beautiful.'

"*Ja*, thank you. I stayed here last year and liked it very much. There is no lift, however, so we need to walk up."

Two wide white iron staircases on each side gave access to all three levels. The doors of all the rooms opened into the atrium and so I assumed, rightly it turned out, that the rooms had windows facing out.

"Would you like to register yourself and Didi?" he asked, a wry smile playing on his lips.

I nodded and dragged the register over. Didi's last name was Hauser but I didn't know her passport number so I beckoned her over and we signed in together. A thrill of pride and power lifted me. Here I was signing into a hotel with a beautiful woman I'd just met. The surge of feeling sophisticated and cosmopolitan made me stand a little taller and when we turned from the counter, I offered my arm. Didi giggled, slipped her arm through mine, and we made our way up to room three fifteen. Two porters followed with our bags.

When the porters departed and the door closed, we embraced and shared the clinging kiss we both longed for. Didi kept her arms around my waist, her hands interlaced in the small of my back.

"You could do with a shave, sir." She unlaced her hands and ran a palm under my chin. "And we both want a washing." With that, she tossed her hat on to the wide bed and stepped out of her dress and blouse. I appreciated her natural blond hair. "Me first," she laughed and strolled elegantly into the bathroom.

After I showered and shaved, I came into the room to find Didi sensuously reclined on the bed. I didn't have a full erection but I was glad I'd toyed with myself a bit while I was shaving. She lay on her side facing me, head propped up on an arm, a lazy smile playing on her lips. I was warmed and excited by the approval in her eyes and stretched out on the bed beside her.

"Much more spacious than the train," I teased.

I placed an arm over her trim waist and we came together in delight and greed. When we had spent ourselves, we lay entwined under the ceiling fan, wet again with our mingled sweat, her head resting on my chest. The scent of our two bodies together was heady, evocative, and I lay in the darkening room savoring the primal chemistry of our love making. A gentle purr from Didi alerted me she was sleeping and I allowed myself to drift into a dream.

The smell of cigarette smoke awakened me and I rubbed my face. Didi sat at the small vanity, with a desk light, wearing a long pink top and brushing her hair. Her eyes caught mine in the mirror and she smiled.

"Sweet dreams?" she asked.

"Not as sweet as being awake with you," I returned.

"Rolf put a note under the door inviting us to join them for supper."

She lifted the cigarette to her now red lips and its tip glowed orange. I couldn't read anything in her face or voice so I asked, "How does that sound to you?"

She shrugged.

"I'd like a bit to eat before we were back in bed again. I might wake up hungry and then I'd have to eat you." A sidelong look that made me laugh. I sat up on the bed and rubbed my eyes again. Out the window, it was completely dark.

"I suppose you'd want to start with the tender bits?"

She rose from the vanity and crossed the room to sit beside me on the bed. The filmy pink blouse accented, clung to, her lovely upturned nipples. We kissed and I didn't mind the tobacco taste that came with it. She caressed my ear with her lips and her fingers closed around my penis, "I'd save the best parts for last."

Her traveling companions were seated at the small bar in the atrium when we descended the stairs. Eric looked up and spotted us first. We waved and he held up a hand in greeting but looked melancholy. Rolf and Kurt followed his gaze and waved, then we were down, crossing the short distance to their table.

"Hello," greeted Rolf, "have a nice nap?"

Kurt grinned and had a sip of his beer.

"Ja," returned Didi, "and good dreams too."

It was almost 8 p.m.

"I think the pavilion would be best for now," Rolf said, "The food there is good and it is very close."

The food was good and as we sat with plates of pork sate dripping spicy peanut sauce, Chinese spring rolls and steaming chicken and shrimp chow fun, Rolf suggested we plan the next few days. Our unofficial tour guide was becoming official, but nobody minded.

Thaipusam

"The Thaipusam is the day after tomorrow and really, it's why I especially wanted to be here. You know that. Last year I missed it. I didn't know about it and came too late. That gives us tomorrow. I want to take you to that waterfall I told you about, if you like."

Kurt and Eric nodded "yes" and Eric, a little more enthusiastic added, "*Ja*, sure, the photos you show us look *schön*. I want to swim in a tropical pool."

Didi looked over to me and said mildly, "The waterfall would be nice, I think. What do you like?"

"I like to be with you while I can," I answered, "and swimming in a tropical pool sounds excellent."

But all this talk of the Thaipusam interested me. It sounded like a big deal.

"Rolf," I asked, "I'm just hearing about this Thaipusam festival since I arrived in Singapore. It must be good, for you all to come here especially to see it."

Kurt laughed. "He comes to study. We all do. A miracle of physiology."

I knew from our conversations that Rolf, Eric and Kurt were engaged in health service studies in Düsseldorf. Didi was studying for social service and many of their classes overlapped. When we'd talked about it, I felt again that twinge of having backed away from med school.

Rolf cleared his throat from a bite of Chow Fun.

"I haven't seen it for my own eyes," he said, "but in reputation people go into a trance state that prevents blood in the body piercing practices."

Body piercing practices? I thought back to the taxi driver in Singapore describing it as "very beautiful for my family" and I imagined colorful costumes and Hindu rituals and maybe dancing with music, like in Bali.

"Body piercing? You mean like how some Christians do the stigmata at Easter, the holes in the hands and all that?" I asked tentatively.

Rolf rolled his eyes and laughed.

"Really, a lot more than holes in hands." He warmed to his description and spoke quietly. We all leant in closer to hear.

"Last year there was a man who, the story goes, was out on the ocean fishing with his three sons. A big storm hit them and they were sure to sink and die. This old man prayed for their salvation and they somehow survived. He got what the people call a 'boon', a prayer answered. Now he must keep his promise and do the penance."

Rolf took a sip of his beer.

"His penance is to hang from a cross, upside down, like this."

Rolf moved his flat hand horizontally back and forth.

"You understand? The cross is above and he is hanging below. He is hanging from many big hooks in his body."

Rolf bent his index finger into a hook shape and tried to snag Kurt on his ribs. Kurt sputtered and shoved Rolf's hook finger away from his side.

"Stop that you!" Everyone laughed.

"So, he is hanging on the cross and it is itself on a cart with four wheels. His sons must pull the cart from the temple in town, through the streets and up to the Thannirmalai Temple on the hill over there." He pointed over his shoulder. I couldn't see anything in the dark but the huddled form of the mountain loomed behind us.

"Waah!" exclaimed Didi, "and why do they do this?"

Rolf turned to her, "Because he got his boon, his prayer answered. But you haven't heard the rest."

He paused for effect. Yes, he had us.

"Two of the sons are pulling the cart from the front with ropes. The ropes have great hooks on them and they are right into the back muscles of the two boys. They pull like horses with a carriage."

We looked around at each other.

"What about the third son?" I asked.

Rolf smiled. The *coup de grâce*.

"The third son also has the ropes and the hooks in his back. But he is tied to the other end and is pulling against them!"

Exclamations of disbelief erupted around the table followed by laughter and hooked fingers trying to snag each other. Rolf sat back, the amused professor.

"We shall see," he said.

In the morning, I stretched and felt Didi's warm body beside me. The glow from our love making in the night lingered as a soft laziness in the morning light. She stirred and opened her lovely eyes, then passed an arm over my chest.

"*Schönes nacht*," she murmured. I stroked the cascade of her soft hair and replied, "Yes, a beautiful night."

The waterfall was about halfway around the island and we needed to follow the small stream that flowed from it nearly a mile, up into the mountains from where the bus dropped us. The rich, fecund humidity of the jungle air was thick enough to swim through, or so it felt. Occasional breezes along the canyon caught the coolness of the water as it splashed over the smooth stones of the streambed. Rolf, our fearless leader, was out in front doing a running narrative about the insects and fungi and plants we were passing. Didi and I brought up the rear.

"He should probably become a professor, not a medic," she panted. "He likes so much to talk."

We were too far back to hear most of the details but I actually like to hear people who know what they're talking about go on about things that interest them. I've done my share of boring friends with paeans to mycorrhizal associations on walks through the Sierra, trying to explain how the trees can apparently grow right out of the solid rock or why we need a permanent presence on the moon.

Shouts ahead alerted us that we had arrived, and when Didi and I emerged into the clearing beside the pool the others were already whooping it up, leaping nude into the water. The ribbon of the waterfall cascaded freely down the pitted limestone wall. The cliff face reared up, white and sculpted, at least forty feet before receding out of view. The big pool was lovely, eroded out of the underlying limestone and spilling exuberantly into multiple smaller pools that constituted the streambed. The clear water was invitingly deep and we were both sweating from the exertion of the walk.

"In we go!" and I stripped out of my shirt and shorts and plunged into the cooling depths. Didi dropped her clothing and moved to the edge. Not only my eyes followed her graceful body into the water.

"Yumm," she cooed, swimming over to me and together we side stroked to where the cascade hit the surface of the pool.

By the time we arrived back at the shore, Rolf and the others had hauled themselves out and were lying naked on their backs, sprawled on the smooth, warm limestone. Stepping out dripping, I couldn't help noticing that the three were uncircumcised, the warmth of the sun reversing the cool water shrinking effect. From this aspect, they all looked well endowed. I looked down at my shrunken, circumcised member, which at this moment looked

The Appearance of Things

to me particularly white and withdrawn, and felt like the Peepee Weepy boy at the party. Eric lifted his head to check out Didi as she dried then over at me. The slight curl of his lips said he wasn't impressed, but maybe that's my fear talking. A friend once told me that Jews were the most optimistic people in the world. "What do you mean?" I asked and he said, "Well, we cut it off before we even know how long it will be."

The circle-the-island bus line ran about every thirty minutes. We hiked back down to the road and hit it pretty well with maybe a ten minute wait. By the time we returned to the Tai An Hotel, it was past three in the afternoon. "I'm hungry," announced Kurt, "who's with me?" Rolf and Eric signed up but Didi and I felt naptime coming on so we the sent "the boys", as Didi called them, off for a bite. We grabbed banana pineapple smoothies at the Pavilion for energy and retired to our lovely, welcoming bedroom. I could get used to this.

I awakened to Didi smoking a cigarette again. It was near sunset and she was seated in the white wicker lounge chair looking out the center window. A swirl of fork tailed swifts churned in the orange sky, their staccato calls sharp, like pebbles striking the glass.

"Hello," I gently called over. She looked over the cascade of blond waves covering her shoulder, a soft smile but sadness in her eyes. I could feel it, palpably. Rolling out of the covers I crossed to her and placed my hands on her shoulders. We stayed that way for a bit, watching the wheeling swifts and the deepening red orange sunset. She finished her cigarette and extinguished the stub in the ashtray on the windowsill. Her left hand found mine on her shoulder.

"I'll be back in Germany in six days," she sighed. "It will be very cold." She drew her open white blouse closed around her neck and added, "I don't like the cold."

I moved around and perched on the windowsill facing her. The gold light illumed her skin, sapphire-blue, almond eyes looked out at me and she was so beautiful in that moment I could scarcely breathe.

"Next stop for me is Phuket," I managed.

"Want to see a new island in the sun?"

Didi smiled her sad smile and looked down at her lap.

"I love the time we have together," she whispered. "Let me tell you when we get there."

"There" would be Thung Song, Thailand. Back a million years ago, we'd looked at the train schedules in Kuala Lumpur. There were four trains through Butterworth on the mainland that went daily to Bangkok. All of them, including the express train, stopped in Thung Song where major roads led east towards the Gulf of Siam and west towards Phuket. Maybe I should forget Phuket and follow this dream to Bangkok? I could follow her to the airport and get on the plane to Germany. We could get married and have children. What was I thinking?

There was nothing I could think to say except, "Yes. I understand."

I moved back into the room and headed into the shower. When I came out, Didi was at the vanity table writing what looked to be a letter.

"Are you interested in dinner?" I asked.

"No, no. You go ahead. Really I'd like some time alone anyway," she smiled, almost apologetically. "It has been a long time that I was with someone day and night."

I dressed and moved towards the door. Didi looked up from her writing, put down the pen and came to me. We held each other and kissed. I thought it a farewell but then, leaning back and smiling mischievously, she chucked me under the chin and lightly said, "Don't be out too late."

This afternoon, coming back on the bus, we'd passed an ornate Chinese restaurant that boasted, "The Best Peking Duck." I'd marked the location and now walked down the boulevard towards the harbor with duck on the brain. I was finding that Georgetown had many narrow streets that curved away. I always felt that where I was going was just around the corner. The duck place turned out to be more elusive than I thought and I finally stopped a rickshaw driver.

"You know Best Peking Duck restaurant, near here?"

"Yes, I know," the driver said brightly, "you come."

This pedicab had the driver in front so I climbed up into the rig, looking over his head, and we set off. The place was one block down and one block over. I couldn't figure how I'd got off track but there it was.

"Thanks," I said. "How much?"

He held up two fingers, "Dua." Two Malaysian dollars. Well it was worth a buck not to be wandering around lost, looking for dinner.

"Werner!" I recognized the voice and spotted Kurt, Rolf and Eric moving down the street in my direction. I waved a hello and waited for them to come up.

"Hello, I was just going in here for the duck. Have you had dinner yet?"

"*Ja, Ja,*" replied Rolf, "we ate. Now we go to Jimmy's."

The emphasis he put on "Jimmy's" reminded me a little of how Mack had said "Bugis Street" back in Singapore.

"Where is Didi?" asked Kurt.

"Oh, she was writing a letter and wanted some time alone."

A rather arch look passed between Eric and Kurt.

"She's a very private person," said Kurt.

"You're lucky you got so much time already," added Eric.

No doubt some history there.

"What's Jimmy's?" I asked Rolf.

Now it was his turn to look arch. He tapped his nostril with an index finger.

"Jimmy's is the best opium den in Penang," he confided. "Forget the duck. This is better. Come on," he encouraged.

I hadn't smoked opium in years, since the Beverly Glen Canyon days. It wasn't my favorite, but it wasn't bad. And going to a real O-den in Asia. That had to be cool.

"Let's go," I smiled to Rolf.

Jimmy's was just off one of the main streets, around the corner and a few doors down from the old P & O office. It wasn't particularly hidden or secretive, about as exclusive as a massage parlor. Yet, once we entered, it was different.

Ushered in by a quiet, small man, we four sat in a dimly lit lounge. An older Chinese woman sat behind a desk with a red light illuminating the ledger she was writing, transferring information from a pile of paper scraps. A hanging curtain led to a rear area and one by one we were collected by an older Chinese gentleman in a red robe and taken back. Rolf disappeared first, winking at us before the curtain fell back across the door. When I entered, it reminded me of the sleeper car from Singapore. The long room was wider but it had the same sleeper compartment layout. No curtains though. A series of oil lamps on small tables provided the only ambient light. When

Thaipusam

the old man led me down the aisle, I made eye contact with Eric who was nervously reclined in one of the little cubbies. He was trying to look blasé but the dilated pupils hinted at a more disturbing truth. My guide stopped beside an empty bunk. His clean-shaven face was orange in the light, placid features, the silken black skull cap and red robe very Chinese. With a wave of his open palm, he indicated I should recline in the bunk. In spite of the strangeness it didn't feel menacing here, more like bedtime in a less than wholesome summer camp. The gentleman who had shown me to the bunk now placed a small round table near the head of the bed with a tiny kerosene lamp burning in the center. The tall chimney of the lamp struck me as being an especially thick glass.

Another, older Chinese man, completely bald, arrived and seated himself on a short stool beside the table. He produced a long tube that could only be the opium pipe. It was of a singular design, reminding me of a bamboo flute, about two feet long and an inch in diameter. The inhalation end he directed towards me was plain, just the circular tube opening. The other end was the unusual portion, being a domed ceramic or stone, oblong bubble the size of a muffin.

The maestro, that's how I thought of him, held the pipe out to me with both hands, keeping the stone end in his left hand. It was heavier than it looked. When he felt assured I had a firm hold, he released the pipe and folded open a small brown packet on the table. It looked like a miniature tamale. Folding the leaf flat revealed a black mass about the size of a sugar cube but softer, rounded. From a sleeve, the maestro produced a long metal pin, the thickness of a pencil lead and pointed, maybe ten inches in length. Dipping the end of the pin into the opium tar he lifted free a small gob and held it carefully over the glass chimney of the kerosene lamp. The glob bubbled and expanded, a tiny black marshmallow roast. He withdrew the now swollen glob and skillfully began to roll it on the cool stone surface of the pipe, shaping and controlling as it cooled and hardened. A perfect little conical mass now on the end of the pin. Testing, he inserted the needle into the hole in the center of the stone bowl. From my close perspective, I saw that the conical plug of opium fit perfectly in the conical bowl of the pipe. Satisfied, the maestro withdrew the needle and gave it a last heating over the lamp, especially the bare, pointed end. Deftly he reinserted the needle back into the bowl, gave the needle a twist and withdrew it, leaving the opium plug with a hole through its center fixed in the bowl. Very cool.

He nodded to me and turned the bowl upside down and moved it over the hot chimney. I was meant to inhale when the opium was centered over the flame. I began to draw in slowly, watching the opium sputter and smoke. A warning glance from the maestro to draw harder, don't let it fall out, a balancing act. Then the sweet, pungent smoke reached my lungs and an involuntary semi cough sent pressure back through the pipe. The opium plug boiled outward and ejected down the chimney.

A look of annoyance spread over the maestro's face. I felt like a relay runner who had just fumbled the baton. I'd found Malaysian very close to Indonesian so I said, "*Ma'af. Lagi?*" sorry, try again?

The maestro studied me for a moment then re-dipped the needle into the packet and repeated the loading procedure. This time, I understood the process and successfully managed a good, long inhalation. I was rewarded with an approving nod from the old gentleman. I wasn't feeling anything after one pipe, of course, and I went through eight more before I caught a glimmer of changing consciousness. Rolf told us he usually took ten to twelve pipes so I went for two more. I figured the first one didn't count since I had coughed. The smoke was sweet and cloying. By the tenth pipe, my stomach was getting queasy and I was glad I hadn't had the duck dinner. If the maestro thought my first spill was annoying, what would he make of a pipe full of duck vomit. The thought made me giggle. Time to go.

The maestro rolled up his leaf of opium and moved on down the line. I rested my head on the block that substituted for a pillow, which I imagined to be more stable when lying prone and inhaling. The brief nausea had disappeared. I felt high but not even as strong as a joint. It was an "OK" feeling but not spectacular, the edges of consciousness a little softer. A few minutes later, Rolf passed my bunk and tapped me. "How are you doing?"

"Pretty good," I replied, "but not particularly high."

Rolf grinned. "It's not like a ganja high. You'll know better when you sleep. O is for sleep. We're going back to the hotel now. Do you stay or go?"

I roused myself to a sitting position. Yes, I was loaded, but less than I'd be on ten hits of ganja.

"Yes, I'll go too," and followed him back up the corridor.

There were quite a few people snoozing in the bunks, both Asian and Western. Why on earth would I want to stay here when I had a darling and a soft bed? Maybe they didn't.

We paid for our pipes with the woman at the front, hunched over her ongoing ledger. The cost was a reasonable one Malaysian dollar per pipe. I didn't mind being charged for the eleventh since I'd messed up on the first load. Still, a nice visit to an opium den for under five dollars. Asia on five dollars a day, eat your heart out Mr. Frommer.

Back at the hotel, I wished my o-den comrades a good evening and slipped into the room with Didi. The lights were out and she was silently asleep. She stirred as I slipped naked into the bed beside her and rolled towards me, sliding her warm arm across my stomach. I lay on my back and got lost running my fingers across the bare skin of her back. Her hand found its way down and the gentle caress lead to an erection that seemed to contain my whole being. She knelt over me and guided my upright self into her. Time was absorbed into our union and I crossed from this world into another and back. Moments when the points of contact of our bodies flowed into and out of each other, when we were one achingly beautiful organism. At one point I was sailing through the streets of Penang, four or five feet off the ground, my body trailing out behind me like the tail of a kite. The wind in my face as I flew along made me laugh aloud with joy.

I awoke to find the morning sun pouring into the room, Didi and I wrapped together like two drowned children after a flood. My waking movements stirred her back to life and we looked into each other's eyes across the pillow. I was simply and completely happy.

"Good morning," I whispered.

She smiled and stretched like a cat, "*Ja, gooten morgen.*"

We made our way through coffee and savory rice pudding in the atrium. Rolf, Eric and Kurt joined us about halfway through. Rolf caught my eye, "Interesting dreams?" he asked.

Eric and Kurt looked fuzzy but not a suffering sort of hangover.

"Yes. Some very interesting dreams. Didn't feel like dreams really. I remember it all as actual experience."

"So do I," added Didi and sipped her coffee with a Mona Lisa smile.

Ten o'clock in the morning found all five of us walking in the direction of the Lorong Kulit temple. Thaipusam had begun. Rolf had once again proved the astute professor and I understood the mounds of broken coconuts we were passing, tens of thousands of them, represented the "shattering of the ego in the pursuit of self-realization." While we had slept, a silver chariot bearing Lord Murga had its path washed clean by devotees smashing the coconuts ahead of its progress. What were they going to do with all these broken coconuts?

It was a festive atmosphere as we walked with hundreds of colorfully dressed locals, all filing along the street in the same direction. At each crossing, more joined. It was like the crowd moving in for a free rock concert in Golden Gate Park in San Francisco.

We approached an intersection ahead. The street was relatively open but it was cheek to jowl on the sidewalks. I was taller and could see over most of the crowd, at what they were witnessing.

Individuals and small groups were moving up the street in slow, deliberate steps. From my vantage there were women in saris carrying cloth covered metal pots on their heads and bare-chested men who appeared to be adorned with thin chains and green fruits, limes maybe. A hundred feet to the left, the courtyard of the temple. We made our way forward to the street and, keeping to the edge, worked our way down to the temple and through its wide-open gates into the courtyard. Within, a man and woman knelt on a stone slab, palms pressed together at chest height, eyes closed with incense smoke swirling around them. An older man dressed all in white circled them slowly, ringing a fist sized brass bell and chanting.

In a corner to the right, a shirtless man stood staring straight ahead, one arm balancing a brass pot on his head. Three women in red and orange saris were hanging fresh limes on his chest and back as if they were decorating a Christmas tree. The limes had large fish hooks protruding from them and it was with these hooks, pushed slowly into his flesh, that the limes were hung. A few feet further on, a man with multiple chains hooked into the skin of his temples stood with tongue protruding. A silver rod the size of a knitting needle with a Shiva trident on the end was pushed through his tongue by one of the priests. No way to pull that tongue back in to swallow.

I felt a hand on my arm.

"Look!" Didi gasped.

A young man wearing an orange sarong gathered up around his waist, like shorts, staggered forward at an impossible angle. Behind him another young Indian man held the reins of eight yellow polypropylene ropes that prevented the walker from pitching forward on to his face. Great silver meat hooks were buried into the muscles on each side of his spine and it was to these the yellow lines were fixed. These hooks were not superficially inserted but buried deep into the tissue. Holes gaped with the pressure on the lines.

Thaipusam

Rolf was no longer the professor. He moved jerkily with his camera, his eyes wide. He said something to Kurt and pointed, "*Kine blut,*" which I think meant "no blood." For some primal reason, we were all staying close together.

Rolf said to me, "We have capillary beds. You cut and it bleeds. Where is the blood here?"

Singularly and in small groups, penitents were moving out of the temple compound and into the street. Young women in elegant saris moved amongst the spiked and hooked trance walkers, talking and smiling to each other as though they were on a stroll in the park. I was looking at a Hieronymus Bosch painting come to life, Parade in Hell or something.

I took Didi by her hand, "Do you want to start walking up towards the other temple, the Thannirmalai?"

She looked back at me blankly, slightly dilated pupils. Shock? Then she came back into herself, "*Ja, ja.* That's good. We, we'll walk."

We came across Rolf photographing a man walking on the street with a metal plate nailed to his forehead and covering his eyes. He leaned forward, being directed by his handler who held the ropes issuing from the hooks in the man's back. "Go left" was the hooks on the left side of his spine being pulled harder. "Go right" the hooks on the right side were favored. To top it off the penitent had shoes made from nails being pounded through a flat piece of wood strapped to his feet. The nails were pointed up, into the bottom of his foot, so that every step was on to a bed of nails.

"Rolf," I said, "we're going to start walking towards the Thannirmalai temple, OK?"

Rolf couldn't get his eye away from the viewfinder and kept clicking. "*Ja, goot,* We'll see you up there. I want to catch up the hanging man."

Kurt stood nearby, focusing his small binoculars on something far up the hill. He looked over at Didi and I.

"You want to see the hanging man?"

Didi shook her head but I accepted the glasses and scanned the gradually rising road ahead. There he was! The cross was visible and I could make out the form of a man hanging below. There were three pullers in front though, no one behind.

"It looks like he needs all three sons going up the hill," and I returned the binoculars to Kurt. He nodded and said, "*Ja,* it's very steep I think."

Didi and I joined the growing flow of celebrants moving towards the hill temple. At every intersection, new penitents joined the procession. The trickle had become a torrent and we were swept along. New variations of puncture kept appearing. To our right, a man appeared encased in two thin rings of metal banding. He looked like the hub of giant bicycle wheels with the spokes protruding out of his flesh. The wheels supported an elaborate and colorful diorama of Hindu gods and Asuras, the demons. Pea sized brass beads on the spokes set the depth limit of how deeply they could penetrate his body, it looked to be about two inches.

The tropical sun blazed down on us and I had stupidly neglected to bring my cap. I pulled out my blue sarong and spun it around my head, turban style. Didi smiled at me from under her white hat and for an instant, she was the beautiful woman coming in the door of the dining car.

"Now you fit right in," she joked.

And we could joke. Amazingly, surrounded by what only a few hours ago was frightening and bizarre, we had evolved into connoisseurs of penance.

"Ooh, look at these."

Four young Indian men, each with six hooks in their back, pulled a flat wagon with a statue of the elephant god, Ganesha. Two women walked side by side, the kavadis balanced on their heads, with Shiva tridents as thick as pencils protruding through their cheeks on both sides.

Finally we arrived at the wide stone pathway leading up to the Thannirmalai Temple. A crowd milled about on the hilltop and witnessed the final steps of the penitents as they approached the altar. We crowded closer as one of the young men with eight great hooks in his back knelt and two attendants removed them. A few of the hooks were so deeply buried that they resisted being pulled out, the whole muscle group wanting to lift away with it. Watching that made my balls retract a little. Still, no sign of bleeding and I know Didi was dumbstruck.

As the man knelt, the priest reached into the deep tray of the huge incense burner and, while chanting, rubbed the ash down the penitent's brutal wounds. The priest then used a long handled dipper to lift water from a tank in the altar and wash the ash down, off the young man's back. Didi and I looked at each other in disbelief. The wounds were gone. A few shallow depressions marked some of the flesh but that was it.

"No way," I said. Didi just shook her head. We saw the same process for other back wounds, multiple puncture wounds, even the trident rods through the cheeks. Didi wanted to get close and try to examine one of the wounds afterward but it wasn't to be.

"Perhaps," she speculated, "the ash acts like the chemical stick men use when they cut themselves shaving?"

"Well," I said, "as you say, it's to stop the bleeding, close the capillaries. There's no bleeding here. Why is that?"

It was a mystery we weren't going to solve today. I thought back to Ida Bagus and his cure for the common cold at Lake Batur. Rod had grown angry when I called it magic. I didn't mean that there was no explanation, just that we might not always know the explanation for something. What is this? That's the key question in science. And I guess in religion too. What is this thing that knows, that was born and gets old and dies?

I glanced over at Didi, both of us gawking in incomprehension at the magic we are living in the midst of, right here and right now. I knew then I was getting off the train at Thung Song. I knew she wasn't. The magic and the mystery of finding each other, loving each other and then of letting go of each other. At this moment, life was infinitely richer and infinitely sadder. I reached over and closed my hand around hers. Those swirling blue pinwheels in her eyes. Kids sitting together on a precipice, our legs dangling over oblivion, mysteries swirling around us like incense.

Chapter 6
Phuket

*Whatever you think you can do or believe you can do, begin it.
Action has magic, grace and power in it.*

J.W. von Goethe

Haad Yai was the customs and immigration stop for our train as we entered Thailand. We were stopped on a siding while men in khaki uniforms patrolled the environs of our carriage. I had to wonder what they were looking for since there was a buzz of questionable activity going on all around us, barely concealed. Boys were busy sneaking bags of rice from the roof of the train stopped beside us on to the roof of our train. The boys would lay low every time an inspector strolled by on the ground. When he passed, they were up again and relaying bags to each other over the gap between the two carriages. Didi smiled and squeezed my hand at the clunking and thunking going on over our heads.

The express train north to Bangkok had appeared in Butterworth station right on time and by one o'clock we were rolling through the Malaysian countryside, bound for the frontier. At the ticket window, Rolf, Eric, Kurt and Didi had booked sleeper compartments to Bangkok, while I had booked only as far as Thung Song. Nothing had been said, but there was a subtle shift in the men's interactions with me, more of a "hail-fellow-well met" beer hall camaraderie. Didi was quiet beside me as we sat together in the dining car. The immigration police had moved through the coach moments earlier and we had both received our thirty day visitor's visa. What we needed to say had been said this morning, as we lay side by side in our bed at the Tai An. Our night together had been passionate and simply honest. The Thaipusam experience had blasted us open, our hearts and spirits raw like the wounds of the penitents as we loved each other. The healing ash of sleep sifted down through our dreams and at dawn, we held each other and whispered, *"auf wiedersehen."*

I couldn't pretend to know the driving forces at the core of this lovely woman. I was barely beginning to glimpse the constellation of desires and fears, hopes and aspirations that had landed me, alone, on the other side of the planet. In finding and connecting with Didi, and now in letting her go so as to go on alone, I could feel another tentative step taken in the direction in which I needed to go. How could letting go make me feel fuller? But it did.

"Aach! The farewell committee," said Didi.

Rolf, Eric and Kurt had entered the club car and were moving down the aisle towards us. Once we'd gotten underway from Haad Yai we were less than two hours from Thung Song, my departure point. They'd given us until this last hour but now it was late afternoon, time for a beer and a goodbye. And to reclaim their Didi.

"Hallo!" greeted Rolf, "I wanted to buy you a beer this time, before we went apart."

"Thanks," I responded. "That would be appreciated."

Didi and I were seated on an upholstered bench seat in a corner beside the window. A small table held the teapot and cups we'd been using. The adjacent bench seat was vacant and Rolf planted himself nearest me, joined by Kurt. Eric pulled up a chair from the next table over and we formed a little circle. Rolf waggled a finger at the carriage bartender, a dark young man wearing the gold and red tunic of the train staff. He looked up at us from behind the bar but didn't come over.

"Five Singha beer," Rolf called over.

"Four," Didi said, "I'm still drinking my tea."

The barman put four open Singha bottles on the counter, each with a glass inverted over the top. Eric did the honors and brought them back to the table. When everyone had a beer glass, except Didi who held her teacup, Rolf toasted, "To good luck and good fortune in our travels." We all tipped back our glasses and then looked around at each other. Before it grew awkward, Kurt broke the silence.

"Werner, how long do you stay at Phuket?"

I shrugged. "A few days at least. If I can find a beach that is good, maybe a week."

"I have heard very good things about Phuket," said Rolf, "especially on the south and west of the island. You like to snorkel dive, yes?"

I nodded, "Yes. I heard that a beach called Patong has a good reef and a few bungalow places to stay. I'll probably start there."

"Do you think you will come up to Bangkok before one week?" asked Eric.

It was a loaded question and we all knew it. Didi gave my hand another little squeeze and addressed Eric, "No, I don't think we'll see Vernon in Bangkok. He leaves me here in Thung Song. We will all be back in Deutschland before he is in Bangkok." She said it with an almost brutal finality. Rolf rescued the moment, "Well then, one more beer and we'll say *auf wiedersehen*."

He winked at Didi, who smiled. Kurt stood, walked over to the bar and said back to us, "This time me. Didi, *ein bier* now?"

She pushed out her lower lip and nodded, "*Ja*, my first Singha beer in Thailand."

We relaxed and told storied of Thaipusam, laughing and exclaiming at the wonders we'd seen yesterday.

"I caught up with the man on the cross," said Rolf. "All three sons had to pull on the uphill."

Nobody could offer a convincing reason for the absence of capillary bleeding. We were all scratching our heads about it when the train began to slow. Thung Song. We looked around at each other.

"Well, it looks like my stop."

I tried to make it sound light.

We stood and shook hands all around. Eric looked melancholy again, maybe a little beery.

"If you were with me," he moaned to Didi, "I wouldn't leave you."

Didi looked at him evenly. "And that's why I'm not with you."

Rolf and Kurt looked startled but quickly recovered. Rolf took Eric under the arm, "Hey, come on you," and smiled at him. Eric looked sheepish. The three men waved a last farewell and left Didi and me standing in the car.

Didi smiled up at me, "It's true, you know."

The Appearance of Things

We held each other and kissed, as if for the last time.

The open platform at Thung Song was hot and humid in the late afternoon sun. Sellers of bottled drinks and rice meals in banana leaves worked the sides of the second class carriages. The windows of the sleeper cars didn't open, to keep in the AC, I suppose. Before I exited the platform, I scanned back along the closed windows and found Didi's eyes watching me. We crooked a finger at each other then I turned and moved down the steps leading into the station hall. I felt hollow, as though I had just made a very bad choice that couldn't be undone.

My heart fell further when I looked out at Thung Song, a ramshackle collection of single floored wooden buildings with rusted, corrugated iron roofs and a sprinkling of forlorn palm trees, limp in the stinging sun. The road in front of the station was barely paved and dust swirled in billowing clouds behind each passing vehicle.

For the first time in months, I couldn't make out a word of what was being said around me. It all sounded like people were singing, "my, my, me, die, die, me, kap." More subtly disturbing, all the signage was in Thai script. There was nothing I could see that yielded the slightest clue as to its meaning. Finally, across the street, a yellow sign with an arrow pointing to the left. The top was written in Thai but under the arrow, in English, "Bus Station 0.1 Km." Thung Song didn't feel like a place I wanted to stay in for long so I hoisted my pack and set off down the road to the bus station. Maybe get a late afternoon bus to Phuket.

The five minute walk exhausted me. The heat and the humidity and noise and the dust of the road assaulted my senses. I began to mentally kick myself in the butt. I could be in an AC sleeper with a beautiful woman. I dragged myself into the station building, where, out of the sun, the overhead fans twirling, I began to feel back in myself. A long drink of water from my bottle, even warm, was a lifesaver. Thankfully the ticket windows had Roman scrip below the Thai script. Bangkok, Surat Thani were there, as was Phuket. When I reached the window and asked, "Phuket?" the pleasant woman behind the counter said, "Tomorrow," and tapped the schedule taped to the wall beside her. It read, "Phuket 9:00, 12:00, 15:00." Ok, missed it for today. I guess it's one night in Thung Song.

"One ticket, nine o'clock, tomorrow. Ok?" She looked at me quizzically from behind her glasses, smiling all the time. I reached in past her and tapped the nine o'clock on her schedule. "Tomorrow."

Grinning cheerfully, she nodded her understanding and prepared a small paper stub that she slid forward to me.

"*See sip hah baht.*"

In Singapore and Malaysia, with all the English being spoken, I'd grown lazy with language. Indonesian had served well in Malaysia because they were so close, closer than say, Spanish and Italian. Now, the reality of Thai and a whole different culture brought me up short. Seeing my confusion, the ticket seller flipped over the ticket and wrote "45" on the back. I nodded my thanks to her and pulled out a fifty baht note. The moneychanger in Butterworth had given me the so-called official rate of twenty baht to a dollar. I'd cashed in twenty dollars on the principle that it's good to arrive in a new country with at least a little cash in my pocket. Now that I was here, I needed to find a bank.

The ticket seller gave me my five baht change and when I said, "Thank you," she responded by putting her palms together and bowing slightly. She said, "*Kah,*" which I took to mean, "You're welcome."

Crossing the hall, I looked for something that might be a tourist information kiosk. How do I find a hotel when I can't read the signs? How do you say hotel in Thai? A load of passengers spilled into the hall from a bus that had just arrived. One of them, a westerner, was speaking animatedly to a small group of Thais who laughed appreciatively at whatever it was he was saying. He bid them farewell, picked up an old brown suitcase that had been handed down from the bus, and began walking in my direction.

"Excuse me," I began as he passed. "Do you speak English?"

He stopped and looked at me, apparently startled to hear himself addressed in English. The confusion passed quickly, replaced by a wide smile.

"Yes! Yes I do. Sorry, it's been awhile. What do you need?"

"Sorry to bother you. I just got off the train and it looks like there's no bus to Phuket until tomorrow. Can you recommend a hotel? I can't read any of the signs."

The young man laughed. He was very thin, I noticed.

"Not many hotels in Thung Song. It's not what you'd call a tourist destination." He hesitated, "I'll tell you what, I'm going over to a guest house near here and that would probably be your best bet. It's where I always stay."

Gratefully, I shouldered my pack and followed along.

Jay was a Peace Corps volunteer, based in an agricultural area called Huai Yot, about forty miles south of here.

"It makes Thung Song look like the big city," he grinned.

He looked taller than he was, in part because he was so emaciated and in part because the local Thais were all a head shorter. Jay's short, dark hair was tightly curled, the kind that if he let it grow would look like an Afro.

"I'm going up to Bangkok for a check-in with my administrators," he explained. "Also, to get myself checked out. I think I've picked up a parasite of some kind, I just keep getting thinner and thinner no matter how much rice I eat." Jay looked down at his own frail form. His dark eyes looked tired as he surveyed the thin forearms and calves. "You'd never know I was junior varsity now," he said wistfully.

"How long have you been here?" I asked. In the light of what he was saying, his thin face and hollow cheeks were alarming.

"Coming up on two years. It's been great though. I love what I've been doing, what I've been learning. The Thais are a wonderful people."

The two-story building we stood before gave no indication of being a lodging. I followed Jay on to the narrow stoop. He pushed open the door and we entered a sparsely furnished, stuffy lobby. A young woman, long hair extravagantly coiffed atop her head, beamed when she saw Jay. She stood, giving us the both the pressed palms greeting, "*Sawadee Kah.*"

Jay pressed his palms together and returned, "*Sawadee, Cup,*" and they immediately launched into a conversation in Thai. To my unpracticed ear it sounded like they were singing a duet. Two very attractive women smiled at us from around the hallway doorjamb. At a pause in their dialogue, I commented, "You've really got the language down, Jay."

"Well," he returned modestly, "if you were a native speaker you'd hear that I speak like a child with a foreign accent." He smiled at the girl and then to me, "I'll share some basics with you later, if you want."

The young lady at the counter said something, pulling Jay's attention back to her. He nodded and looked over to me.

"The rate for the whole night is thirty baht."

The whole night?

"I always stay here coming and going," he added, "You get a private bath

Phuket

and the rooms are clean." He looked back at the desk girl and grinned at her, "And they are very nice here. I like it a lot."

"Sure," I said, "that sounds good to me. Thanks for your help. Say, where is the bank here? I need to change some money."

Jay grimaced, "No exchange bank in Thung Song, sorry to say."

He spoke to the girl behind the counter, who listened and bobbed her head. "*Nung dollar yee sip baht,*" she said.

"She can give you twenty baht to the dollar if you have cash," said Jay. "That's a bit less than you'd get in Phuket, but they're set up for tourists. It's pretty good for Thung Song."

I nodded and went into the small cash stash in my side pouch, extracting a twenty dollar note. I passed it over and the young lady gave me back three hundred and seventy baht, deducting the thirty for the room.

"How do I say "thank you" in Thai?"

"*Cup koon, cup,*" replied Jay.

I repeated it to the girl and she gave me a wide grin, dipped her head slightly and placing her palms together said, "*Kah,*" then started to giggle.

We went up to the second floor and got settled in, a welcome bath to wash off the sweat and grime. The little window in my room faced east and as I toweled off I looked over the rolling hills of tall green palms, stark against the blue sky in the late afternoon sunlight. There was a little tap on my door. Jay stood there holding a small, worn, yellow pamphlet.

"Here. This is what they start you off with in the Peace Corps. It's basic, but probably all you need for a short visit. Up north, and in tourist areas, it seems like a lot of Thais have pretty good English skills so I'm sure you'll do fine."

"Thanks!" I said, "I can't guarantee you'll put on any weight but I'd be glad to buy you dinner."

Jay smiled, "Dinner would be great. Tell you what. Just make it a large beer with dinner. That would be a luxury outside my Peace Corps pay scale."

Darkness had fallen and the night market of Thung Song was alive with music and laughter. It had transformed from the sad, dusty little town of the afternoon to a festive, open-air community gathering. Jay and I wandered amongst the rows of tables and stalls. Baby clothes sellers beside agricultural tool booths, trays of Zippo lighters and costume jewelry displays competed with blaring cassettes of Thai pop music. We followed our noses to a small central zone of tables and chairs surrounded by the ubiquitous food stalls I was coming to love.

I was drawn to a woman grinding chilies, cilantro and garlic in a mortar. Jay looked over my shoulder, "Oh, green papaya salad. That's wonderful but you'd better be ready for hot."

Jay wandered down a few stalls and waved me over.

"Here," he enthused, "you've got to try Mieng Kham. It's a southern Thai dish that I don't think you'll see in Bangkok or further north. I love it."

We ordered two large Singha beers and sat down at a table opposite the Mieng Kham lady. She placed a wide, round metal tray on the table that had multiple depressions filled with dried shrimp, chopped ginger, fresh cut lime bits, peanuts, minced scallions, toasted coconut and a dark, sweet sauce with little spoon sticking out. In the center, a pile of leathery green leaves.

"Now here's the trick," said Jay. "Take a wild tea leaf and fold it into a cone like this." He demonstrated and I followed suit. "So now you take a pinch of everything and throw it in, coconut and sauce last."

In a moment, he held out a small green cone topped with toasted coconut and the sweet palm syrup. He folded the top of the packet shut and popped the whole thing into his mouth and began chewing. A look of religious ecstasy spread across his face, "*A loy mah*! Delicious!"

And it was. The night market was a gustatory revelation, an incredible variety of new and surprising tastes and combinations. Growing up in North Hollywood in the 1950s, Asian food was basically Chinese, Cantonese Chinese. Nothing had prepared me for the startling diversity of Indonesian and Malaysian, Szechwan, Nyonya and Haklo and now Thai. We had a rich, heavy coconut based hot curry called "Pah-nang" loaded with succulent strips of pork and a spicy, garlic fried thin eggplant that literally melted in my mouth. Jay was right about the green papaya salad being hot, and the intensity of the flavor blew the top off on my head. I grew up with the heat of Mexican cuisine but this stuff was a whole new order.

We headed back towards the hotel at about ten o'clock. I was tired but excited by what I had tasted. "That was incredible food!" I raved to Jay.

He smiled and nodded, "For me, some of the best food in the world. When you go further north, there are some really outstanding things too. It's kind of like Chinese, where different regions have different dishes. Thailand is like that too."

Phuket

In Singapore and Penang, I'd had an inkling as to what Jay was talking about. All the regional specialties at the Satay Club or the Pavilion in Georgetown. I just hadn't articulated it to myself. To me, like a lot of Americans, Mexican food was Mexican food, Chinese was Chinese.

"I like coming up here," continued Jay, "Down in Huai Yot, it's a much more simple diet. We don't get the meats and fish you see here. And Bangkok!" He looked at me, "Bangkok will blow your mind. Thais love good food."

Our guesthouse looked dark when we approached the door but I could hear what I imagined was Thai pop music coming from a tinny radio. The lobby was dimly lit with strings of tiny, multicolored Christmas lights and a new young woman was sitting behind the desk. She nodded to us as we entered. Her heavy eye make-up reminded me a little of Bugis Street. Jay went up the stairs, but I was curious. I walked over to the hallway and looked down the corridor, lit dimly orange red with a few bare bulbs protruding from the wall. A few women in halter-tops and very short shorts stood in doorways, looking back at me, smiling. The music I'd heard emanated from behind one of the closed doors, near to where I stood. I recognized the woman nearest as one of the girls who'd been watching us from behind the doorjamb when we checked in. She smiled and gave me a coy wave, then stepped back to the door of her room, as if she was holding it open for me. Unbidden, a vision of Didi gazing at me from our bed this morning. I wasn't ready to go down that hall just yet, so I held my palms together and bowed slightly to the ladies, then went upstairs to bed.

I met Jay briefly in the morning as he ran out to catch an eight a.m. train up to Bangkok.

"How'd you sleep?" he asked with a grin.

"Good thanks. Dinner last night was fantastic but it burned on its way out this morning."

Jay laughed. "It'll do that. The secret is more rice. Think of the other dishes as just condiments for the rice and you'll be good."

I wished him well and he was off. Over tea, I wondered about the Peace Corps. What would it be like to be pretty much on your own in a small village for three years? I wonder if they'd think a guy with a degree in Zoology was a good applicant? Jay had a B.S. in Agricultural Science from the university in Illinois, but they had him teaching maths and English to adolescents. Something to consider when I get back. I wonder if he had malaria?

It was on the ride down from Thung Song to Phuket that I saw my first *kharst* formations. We came over a rise and were suddenly driving through gigantic white icebergs that rose vertically from the flat green rice paddy and palm jungle. They were so unlikely, as though some huge hand had stabbed the earth with limestone icicles, the mythical landscape of Chinese paintings but for real. The upper reaches of the icebergs were topped with greenery, vines dangling down the sheer sidewalls. Great alcoves in the stone were adorned with stalactites, the sort I'd only ever seen in deep limestone caves. I don't know why I found open-air stalactites startling but I did. They ringed the massive stone towers.

The air heated up and grew heavier as we descended towards the plain leading to the sea. Rice paddy and green fields rolled away from the road on both sides, and children riding water buffalos waved to us as we passed. Another Buddhist temple came into view, its red and green roof tiles and golden ridgeline reflecting the early afternoon sun like sparkling water. On the grounds, a group of boys with shaved heads and orange robes were playing a game of football. A few smiled widely and waved as the bus passed. The countryside had been dotted with small and large temples. When our bus had departed Thung Song at nine, we passed a long procession of monks in orange robes walking silently, single file along the roadside. Each carried a bowl with both hands held about waist height. From my vantage point on the bus, I could see meager portions of rice, vegetables and fruit in the bowls. Some had what looked like meat or curry in small plastic bags on one side of their bowl. I thought back to the night market. Not much in those bowls.

The bus stopped on a sandy turnout to allow a string of cars to cross a spindly one-lane bridge. At first I thought it was a wide river, but the open sea to the right and the wide channel to our left suggested more. The Thai man seated beside me must have noticed my extra attention to the goings on.

"Phuket," he said and made a hand motion towards the bridge.

Somehow, perhaps owing to my recent Penang experience, I had expected that we'd be taking a ferry to the island.

A few of the other passengers were apprehensive as our driver pulled out on to the bridge. They crowded forward, looking out the front window. The bridge was more of a catwalk, two strips of wide boards laid flat on the supporting superstructure with an opening straight down to the water in between. The crowd in front was saying things to the driver who, thankfully, ignored them and focused on the task at hand. I looked straight down into the clear blue water and made a quick evacuation plan. Straight out the window. Probably everybody else's plan too. The crossing was only a few hundred yards and in less than three minutes we were back on land. Some of my fellow passengers burst out with the nervous laughter that can follow close calls.

Rumbling into Phuket town, the sun at its zenith, I found myself squinting in the harsh light that poured in the open window. Except for the temples, which my seat passenger explained were called *"Wats"*, Phuket town had the same unremarkable architecture as Thung Song. Shabby buildings of basic wood plank siding, weathered grey and with corrugated iron roofing, made up the bulk of the village. The bus rolled to a stop on what was apparently a main street. A few two storied cement buildings, one with a sign that read Bank of Siam in English. That was a relief and I determined to make it my first order of business. But my spirit felt low and the unremarkable, hot, humid little town didn't help matters.

I wished my seat partner goodbye with the palms-pressed-together greeting that was so much a part of every interaction here. According to Jay and his Peace Corps pamphlet "getting to know you" section, the gesture is called a *"wye"* and is the starting point and ending point of every exchange. As a guy, I needed to say, *"Sawasdee, Cup,"* while a woman would say, *"Sawasdee, Kah."* I'd read and re-read the introduction on Thai culture, something I was grateful for, especially the "Do's and Don'ts." One of the important "Do's", when doing the *wye*, was to give it with full attention. It isn't a casual wave hello, something slovenly that is tossed out before the really important stuff of getting what you want. It sets the stage for further respectful interaction. Some of the "don'ts" were a surprise, like not pointing my feet at someone I was sitting with or talking to. Women were not ever, never, supposed to touch monks. Don't pet children on the head. Don't have my head higher when speaking to an elder. It was quite a list.

So, on into the bank I went. The office was air-conditioned and I gratefully removed my pack and stowed it against the wall, inside the front door. I wyed to the guard and to the girl sitting at the desk with the "Exchange" sign. She bade me to sit and I handed over a one hundred dollar traveler's cheque from my wallet. She studied the check earnestly and looked up with startlingly beautiful eyes.

"US dollar ok. You have passport, please."

I dug into my stupid side pouch, as I now thought of it, and extracted my document folder and from that, my passport. She opened the cover and carefully compared the signatures, looking back and forth between

The Appearance of Things

me and the paperwork. A man approached from behind her, looked over her shoulder and then at me. I wyed and said, *"Sawadee, cup,"* to which he responded formally. He said something to the girl, looked back at me once and withdrew.

"You sign here please," she said, pushing the check back across the desk. Another careful comparison of signatures then she nodded, "One minute, please," stood, and retreated behind the teller counter.

I looked around the room. An elderly Buddhist monk in worn saffron robes sat quietly on a bench beside a somewhat anxious younger man in a white shirt. Three young women standing behind a counter at the far end were surreptitiously casting glances towards me and then silently giggling and nudging each other.

"Here you are," she smiled.

I turned back to the desk and received my money. After a thirty baht service fee, I ended up with two thousand one hundred seventy baht, a tad better than the money changers. Every little bit counts. I stood, and so did she, and we wyed each other.

"Cup koon, cup," I said and that got me a pretty smile. I grabbed my pack and the guard opened the door for me, the whole thing like a dance with everyone aware of the part they were playing. The formality was new. People were courteous and the interactions respectful everywhere I'd been thus far in Asia, with a few exceptions, but this was more ritualized that anything I'd yet encountered. Last night at the market with Jay, he'd said something unexpected. "Thailand is a Buddhist culture. I think it's the most civilized place on Earth." When he'd said that, I just accepted it as a general statement from someone I was having a beer with, but it keeps ticking in my mind. I think of civilization in the USA and what comes up is a sort of check list - clean drinking water, clean food, good medical care, modern conveniences like cars and electricity and telephones, good quality roads and safe building construction, vibrant arts and music and literature and universities. But then, last summer in Europe, I saw that real civilization had to include how people lived and how they treated each other. The civility of a shared meal in Italy, seated comfortably outside in the shade of an orchard with rough bread, good wine and singing. Making the time to enjoy life, not just consume it and rush on to the next obligation. It was a Zen koan, to ask, "How is Thailand the most civilized place on Earth?"

After leaving the bank I made my way back towards the bus area, thinking to find a ride out to Patong beach. The main road through Phuket town was flanked with deep cement culverts on both sides to handle runoff from the monsoon rains. The de facto sidewalk in front of all the little businesses lining the street had narrow cement ramps over the culvert every twenty or thirty feet. It was while crossing over one of these, heading towards the bus stand, that I heard my name called.

"Vernon! Hello."

Behind me, in the shadow of an arcade, stood John and Louise, from my time at Lake Toba. They were smiling broadly. I felt delighted, and I turned too quickly for a guy wearing a pack. The momentum caused me to lose my balance atop the small cement ramp. I saw the expressions on their faces shift suddenly from greeting to surprise as I nearly toppled into the culvert below. Doing the best I could with a bad situation I leapt sideways and barely made the lip of the ditch, staggering forward. John and Louise had also jumped forward to catch me. We bowled into each other, stumbled and began laughing.

"Steady on!" shouted John.

Louise, with her red haired, blue eyed sardonic smile, said, "Find you and lose you in the same moment!"

It was more than good to see them.

"God, I'm so surprised to see you guys! I thought you'd be on to India."

"Mighta' been," replied John, "but since Toba we're moving a bit slower that we planned."

They were both holding woven shopping bags stuffed full of fresh vegetables and dried noodles.

"Are you opening a restaurant?" I asked, looking into one of the bags.

"Oh, some things for tea," smiled Louise, "We've taken a tiny house on the beach with some others. Do you recall Nick and Maura?"

"He wouldn't," John noted. "They came after the New Year."

"I was just going to find a bus down to Patong beach. Know anything about it? I heard it was good."

Louise looked at John, who said, "Well Vernon, you can follow along with us. That's where we're bound. I reckon it's the best beach on the island."

We found a beat up, blue panel van parked in the bus area. The paper sign in the front window read "Patong". "Here we are," breathed John. He heaved his bags on to the bench seat and climbed in. Louise passed in her bag and joined him while I sat one row up. The driver put my backpack in the wire roof rack, along with two fighting cocks in bell shaped bamboo cages. On the bumpy ride over to the southwest side of the island John told how they had left Toba and made their way over to Singapore. A cousin of Louise's worked there in shipping and had his holiday planned to include them. John described how they'd explored the east coast of Malaysia and the mountain area called the Cameron Highlands. "Beautiful country, that," praised John, "After Neville went back to Singapore we wandered out to Tioman Island. I thought that was the ultimate fantastic until we got here."

"You're the connoisseur, aren't you Mr. Nelson?" teased Louise.

"I am that, Miss Cottrell," he answered with a grin.

The beach appeared suddenly when we turned a jungle corner and the road cut gave us a panoramic view. Gentle surf massaged the whitest sand I've ever seen. There was a reef break out about a hundred yards, tall palms and a few small buildings at the south end. We wound down the hill and further down the beach, to the north, stood three more substantial structures.

"The one at the far end is called Loy's. The best seafood around," said John.

The little bus skidded to a halt on the gravel behind a two-storied yellow building.

"This is Poon's place. There's a restaurant here," John cocked a thumb at the weathered yellow structure, "and they've got some rooms. Noisy though. It's where we stayed the first night."

His short laugh said one night was enough.

"Better," Louise weighed in, "is the Patong Guest House, over there."

She pointed down the beach to a set of low-slung buildings set back in the palm grove.

"That's where Carrie and Clare are staying."

She looked at me thoughtfully, "Get yourself settled in and then come down and see us. We're in the second bamboo hut at the end there. It's the one with the hammocks in front."

"Thanks for the invite," I said, "and for noticing me in town. It's a great and good surprise to see you here."

Phuket

I looked down the wide open beach. A few small groups sat on the sand, a few others were splashing about in the amazingly clear water. "I've got camping gear with me. Maybe I'll just set up the tent on the beach."

My words caused John to look up from the shopping bags he was arranging, there on the ground. "We had a couple from New Zealand camped out last week. They had some things taken, when they were away from their campsite. I reckon it'd be smart to check your goods with Lake at the guest house if you're going to sleep out."

"Don't want to lose your passport," added Louise. "It's not so easy to get it replaced out here. She's got all of ours and some other things as well."

John nodded in agreement.

"You're in Asia, mate. Don't leave it lying about if you want to keep it."

We all walked together down to the guesthouse. I carried the shopping bag for Louise, which made John smile. I felt a bit like a kid carrying books home for the pretty girl in school.

The Patong Guest House was really three interconnected buildings arranged like three sides of a hexagon, facing the sea. There were wide, covered decks in front of all the rooms, with the buildings connected by a roofed walkway. In the rear, a separate bath and toilet house.

Walking up the central garden path, towards the middle bungalow, a woman came out the door and leaned on the rail, watching us approach. John waved and called out, "Hello Lake." Her dark hair had a few streaks of grey and was gathered in a ponytail. Maybe she was in her mid-forties, crow's feet on the sides of her dark eyes. She came down off the porch as we neared, a huge searchlight of a smile.

We all stopped and formally wyed. On the way over, I'd decided to spend at least one night at the guesthouse until I knew the lay of the land better.

"Hello John, you bring me business?" Her voice was smoker rough.

"Hi Lake. Yeah. This is our friend Vernon, from California. He's just arrived. Have you got a room for him?"

Lake looked me up and down, sizing me up with a professional eye.

"Yeah. Got room," she growled. "Bring bag." She turned and walked towards the low-slung building on our right. John and Louise were grinning at me.

"I think she likes you, Vernon. You'd better watch yourself." Louise looked at me archly.

I grinned and against my will, felt myself blushing. John saw my flush and piled on, "Lake's quite a girl, Vernon. She usually gets what she wants, so I hear." He winked at Louise.

The room was basic, but felt clean and airy and with the front window shutters pushed open a cool breeze came through from the sea. Under the shade from the surrounding coconut palms, the place was very welcoming. We settled on a price of twenty five baht per night and, while I got settled in, John and Lou picked up their supplies and headed out.

"Come on down before sunset," Louise called back.

Following John's suggestion, I entrusted Lake with my pouch of travel documents and extra money, which she locked into a large cupboard in her apartment.

The sea was far too appealing and I felt way too road weary to do anything else before jumping in. I padded across the fine, white sand towards the water. It is a remarkable sand. Even in the fierce heat of the tropical afternoon, it was comfortable to walk across, down to the lapping clear blue waters. How is that even possible? I swam out fifty yards into the deliciously cool water. Below me, canary yellow Angel fish and turquoise blue parrot fish swam about. Next time, bring the mask. The view back to the shore revealed a perfect, gently curved crescent of beach, fringed with palms. The emerald green of the jungle rising up behind made the blue of the sky pop with an electrical intensity. I could stay here awhile. The cloud of doubt that had colored my perspective since getting off the train in Thung Song evaporated into the clear blue sky. My spirits were also buoyed by having reconnected with John and Louise. They were a notch above most of the travelers I'd met, and a kind of wisdom emanated from them that I found very attractive.

I swam back to shore and walked straight back towards the bathhouse to rinse off. Lake was standing in her doorway watching me as I made my way through the garden up to a well-made wooden model of a house sitting atop a post. A small offering of flowers on its miniature porch reminded me of Bali. I stopped and studied the model, with its intricate wood shingles and rails.

"Spirit House." Lake had moved out on to her porch and leaned on its railing with both hands.

"Is it like a shrine?" I asked.

She shrugged and smiled warmly at me, "Like a shrine, yes. To give the spirits of this place a home."

Phuket

I'd noticed that the majority of the houses I'd seen thus far in Thailand had a cement post somewhere near the front topped with a birdhouse sized model of a temple. Often there were flowers or other offerings to be seen, but this Spirit House was much more elaborate and detailed, a real house in miniature.

"Beautiful," I said and walked on back to the bathhouse. I'll confess that I liked the way Lake looked at me as I passed.

It was only a five minute walk down to the south end of the beach, if I stayed to the hard ground path above the sand that ended about a fifty feet short of the hut. Rather than trying to push through the fallen palm fronds and coconut husks at the rear I went out on to the beach in front and walked in the sand. A small yard was defined by three foot tall bamboo posts interlaced with dry palm fronds to make a fence. Half a dozen coconut palms swayed inside the fenced area with two worn hammocks stretched between the three palms in front. There were also a couple of woven bamboo platforms, about the size of a twin bed, for sitting outside. Tropical cozy.

I liked the sound of music and laughter emanating from their little house. Through the open front door, I saw Louise walk past in a red sarong, holding a large aluminum teakettle. There was a loud, metallic clank as she set it down, out of sight. "Hello?" I called in. John appeared at the door, no shirt, wearing a brown and black sarong. With his past shoulder length, brown hair and mouth framing thick moustache, he always reminded me of a rock star. I guess it was the way the hair was trimmed, shorter on top, making it look more like a headdress than a haircut. Sort of like one of the musicians from Three Dog Night, but his bright, intelligent brown eyes and ready smile cut through that image and were a saving grace. John was physically slight and only of medium height, but he carried himself like a big man and I never really thought of him as small.

"Vernon! Come in. You made it."

I followed him into the dirt-floored room. Louise looked up from the stove area, a rectangular cement brick counter. There was one missing brick in the surface that formed a channel and Louise had the big kettle straddling the opening. A small cooking fire burned below and she was fanning it with a woven palm disk.

"Hello Vernon. Fancy a cup of tea when the water boils?"

My first thought was that I should loan them my camping stove, a gasoline powered SVEA that did a great job of pots of water.

"Sure, thanks. That's quite an operation you've got going there," I replied.

The smoke from the fire rose up behind the counter and exited through holes in the roof. I looked up and around. This was a pretty rude little construction. The walls were loosely interlaced bamboo strips, loose enough that I could see right through them to the outside. Both the doors and the windows were simply bamboo frames sheeted with more interlaced bamboo and tied to their frames with lengths of rope. The roof had a thicker bamboo ridge beam and slimmer rafters slanting down to the walls. A large sheet of silvery, plastic tarp covered the whole thing, held down by the palm fronds laying on top outside. A good wind would probably knock the place down. It was a shed, not a house. John followed my visual inspection and read my mind.

"It's a fishermen's hut. Belongs to one of the families that bring fish in here." He grinned, "It's not where I'd want to be in a typhoon, but we had a rain last week and it kept us dry."

"Home sweet home for now," Louise was philosophical. "And I think we're nearly ready for a homemade cuppa." She poked in a few more twigs and fanned the fire to an orange flame.

There was a dividing wall with a door, bisecting the room we stood in, and through that door, another space of about the same size. A figure looked around the door and smiled, "Did I hear cuppa?"

Nick had dark, very curly hair, wet and dangly looking. His thin face was well formed, Mediterranean I thought, with dark eyes and a thin moustache. Several days of beard growth gave him a rugged look, but he was about John's stature. Behind him, literally in his shadow, lurked a thin, shorter woman with red henna hair. Maura was attractive the way nearly all twenty four year old girls are, but I could see the bitter older woman with disappointed, thin lips just beneath the surface. These were going to be her best years, right now.

"You did indeed," Louise replied to Nick's inquiry. She fanned the glowing embers till they glowed brightly. She continued, "Nick, meet Vernon. I told you we met at Toba? He left for Bali before you and Maura arrived."

I stepped forward and put out a hand, "Hi. I guess John and Lou told you they just found me wandering around in Phuket."

Nick took my hand and smiled with his mouth, but not with his eyes.

"Hello. Welcome to Patong." He drew Maura out into the light. "This is Maura. Maura, Vernon."

She smiled and nodded and I said, "Hi." There was suddenly the oddest sensation of mistrust in the air. John picked up on it and cheerfully informed Nick and Maura that I was staying down at Lake's with Clare and Carrie. That somehow changed the atmosphere back. I got it then. Nick and Maura didn't want another person moving in here. So I took it a step further, "Yeah, for at least a couple of nights, anyway. I have some camping gear and I'm thinking of pitching out on the beach. Wanted to check out the scene first, though. John tells me there was a theft last week."

"That's a problem, that," Nick agreed. He looked around the room and smiled ruefully, "For that matter, it wouldn't take much to break in here either. We've all got what we can't afford to lose locked up with Lake. You're smart to do it too."

"Hot water," announced Louise and pulled the steaming kettle off the fire. Five drinking glasses were laid out on the cement counter. She held out a wide mouthed glass jar filled with white liquid, "Who's for cream and sugar?" "Me." "Me." And all hands went up. Louise pried the top off the sugar can and scooped a spoonful into each glass. She resealed the can carefully, then unscrewed the jar and poured milk into each glass. John came over and stirred with a spoon while Louise shook loose tea into a fine strainer from a foil packet. They were a good team, with John pouring the hot water from the heavy kettle and Louise moving the strainer back and forth over the glasses. The steaming tea's aroma was lovely.

The dining table was a large cable spool and the rough bamboo lounges around it made up the sitting area. "Here we are," said John, placing the five steaming glasses on the table. "To the best cup of tea on Patong Beach and the most beautiful cook." Louise smiled at him and curtsied to us, engendering a laugh. While we gabbed about where we'd all been and where we thought to go, John joined five cigarette papers together and crumbled a pile of ganja and Drum tobacco into a uniform mix. Tearing a strip off the rolling paper packet, he fashioned a paper tube filter and deftly rolled the whole mess into a passable, cone shaped joint. It went very nicely with the tea.

"What say we all go out for the sunset?" Nick suggested.

The ganja was very good and we all staggered out of the semi-dark house squinting against the bright sunlight. I delighted in the soft texture of the sand as we trooped down towards the water's edge, all together. Patong

The Appearance of Things

Beach faced almost directly west, but the sun was setting off to our right, a bit to the north. Time of year, I guess. Thin clouds over the sea were catching and reflecting the slanting sunlight and the colors seemed to swirl together. John sighed, "The three best sunsets of my life have all been right here." One of the things I appreciate about getting high in a group is that, mostly, people are content to relax into things and just dig it. So we five sat quietly, even reverently, as the multi-hued parade of the sunset revealed itself, mutated, grew impossibly intense in tones of orange and red and green and blue, then faded to dark.

We walked slowly back towards the beach cabin, now pitch black within. John lit three of the candles they had placed around and the place looked positively cheery and welcoming. Still, I felt it was time to move along. In this case, five's a crowd.

"I'm going to head back down the beach," I announced. "Are you guys coming down that way later, dinner or something?"

Louise nodded, "We're meeting Clare and Carrie and going down to Loy's for tea. Join us if you want."

"Thanks, that sounds good. I haven't met Clare or Carrie, but I guess that's not a big problem, eh?"

"No worries, Vernon," said John. "It's open tables all the way 'round here. Have a rave with Clare about your pirate ship in Bali. I reckon she'd get a good laugh on that one."

It was really very dark walking back down the beach. I was glad I'd come along in the daylight and knew there were no obstructions in the sand to collide with. It was as though I was walking along with my eyes shut, except for the yellow lights in the distance that had to be the restaurant places. I glanced up at the velvet black sky. The stars were beginning to shine but not enough to light the way. What phase was the moon in now?

After a long five minutes of walking, I recognized a dimly lit horseshoe of buildings up to my right as the Patong Beach Guest House. Low light orange bulbs burned over the patios of each building. There were two women at the end of my building, smoking and sharing a large bottle of Singha beer on their little patio. I waved down to them as I fumbled in my day sack for the key to the door padlock. "Evening," I called down. I located the key and popped the lock open. The door swung in of its own accord and I felt on the wall for a switch.

"Are you John and Lou's friend?" asked one of the women.

Phuket

I hesitated in front of my open door and dark room, "That's right. My name's Vernon. Might you be Clare and Carrie?"

The speaker giggled, "No, I'm only Clare. This is Carrie."

In the dim light from forty feet away I could see they both had light colored hair, orange yellow in this light, and big smiles.

"Are they coming down here?" asked Clare, "We're going over to Loy's for dinner."

"Yeah, I'm sure they're coming down. We were just enjoying the sunset and it got a bit late. I think they're just getting ready." I hesitated then asked, "Where did you get the beer?"

"Lake's got a bunch. Just knock on her door."

I reached into the room again and slid my hand along the wall, located the switch and flipped on the dim overhead. I stepped into the room then leaned back out, "I'm going to get one. Can I bring you anything?"

The two girls conferred a moment then Clare called back, "We'll split a large one with you, if you want. They get warm fast just sitting around."

Lake looked at my bloodshot eyes and smiled, handing me the beer and a glass, "Having a good time?"

I know she was older, but she had a way of making me feel flustered, as if I was trying to impress a date and not succeeding. I didn't see her as a potential sex partner. Did I? I passed over the twenty baht note for the beer and not very smoothly stammered, "Yes, thanks, a very good time." She bowed her head slightly and gave me a look that seemed to say, "I know you," and then shut the door. I hesitated for a moment, then, looking blankly at the unfinished wood, walked back towards my patio.

Clare, Carrie and I worked through two more large Singha beers. They had arrived at Toba just after I'd left, before New Year. Carrie knew Louise from Sydney and although they hadn't planned specifically to meet up, the general outline of the Sumatra trip was known to both. Meeting up on Samosir Island was a nice surprise, at least as far as Carrie was concerned.

A crunch on the gravel announced John and Louise.

"Hello 'ello, I see you've found each other," grinned John.

Louise stood back with her arms folded across her chest, that thin, amused smile she did so well playing on her lips. The long, turquoise blue dress she wore set off her pale skin and long red hair.

255

"Good evening. Are Nick and Maura with you?" I asked.

"They're having an evening in," replied Louise. "A bit of alone time before Michael and Tony arrive."

That was news to me and I perked up, "Do you mean Mike and Tony from Lake Toba?"

"Well, they're from Sydney, actually," teased John, "but, yeah, the same. We got a letter from them Poste Restante last week. They're coming up from Malaysia. Actually, I half expected to see them in Phuket today, when we found you."

The prospect of a reunion cheered me. I held the time we were all together at Christmas on Samosir Island as a very meaningful part of my journey. It was the first time I felt like a member of the community of travelers, and the power of all of us, on the road together.

"I hope they get here before we have to bugger off," said Carrie. She looked pouty at the prospect and I had the impression she meant Mike when she said "they".

Clare and Carrie, were both tall and well built. There was a sweetness in Clare's eyes I found appealing. Carrie had good surfer girl looks with tanned skin, blue eyes and full lips. There was a toughness in her speech and manner I'd experienced in some of the other Australian women I'd met on the road. She and Clare could have been sisters, with Clare being the softer, more feminine of the two. She had a delicacy to her lips and nose that was at once more refined and more vulnerable.

Carrie stood and knocked back her remaining beer. "I'm for dinner. Are we set?"

General agreement, and we moved off as a hungry, happy mob walking down to Loy's. I strolled beside Clare, "I heard Carrie say you needed to head out. When is that happening?"

"Aw, in five days' time. Well, four now. We've got a flight out of Singapore, back to Sydney. Must get back to work, I'm afraid." She smiled at me rather wistfully. "Not like you lot, off all the way to London."

From our patio conversation I knew that they both worked in the administration of the university and enjoyed the long Australian summer break along with the students. But I experienced an "aw shucks" feeling at her news. My connection with Didi had opened some gates of desire and Clare was an appealing woman. I had to admit to myself that I liked the idea of finding a woman to travel on with. Not desperate, just open to the possibility.

Loy's was terrific. Or maybe it's more accurate to say that a couple of large fish, cut cross hatched, deep fried and served with hot, sweet, Thai chili sauce is terrific. I also discovered Mekong and soda more profoundly. We sat at an outside table under the stars, all well fed and sassy. A small silver bucket of ice in the center of the table, multiple bottles of soda water, a plate of sliced limes and a large, now nearly empty bottle of Mekong Thai Brandy is an excellent way to end a fine meal. Another ice cream cone sized joint was going around too. I felt like I had found paradise, again.

"Vernon, do you have your harmonica with you?" John looked at me quizzically, bright eyed.

I was off somewhere in dream world and his question pulled me back to the table. I looked around at a few pairs of expectant eyes.

"Umm, yes. I mean, no, I don't. Not right here right now. Back at the room though, yes." That was about as clear as mud. John shot Louise an amused glace but ignored my confused response. "We need some music," he pronounced and began to tap the side of the ice bucket with the handle of his fork. Clare laughed and said, "Here we go," and using a spoon began to tap a counter rhythm on her glass. A memory surfaced in me of Seville, Spain, walking down narrow stone streets behind groups of students who were joyfully clapping out complex rhythms. I began to clap out a compatible cadence and John looked up at me in surprise, then his eyes twinkled and he shifted tempo. Clare and I followed right along and the others jumped in. Louise put a handful of pebbles into an empty Coke can and began to shake along with her improvised maraca. Carrie turned out to have a lovely singing voice and layered in a chant that curled like smoke around the growing rhythm. Being a little high helped, I guess, but it sounded great to me. Loy looked out the open door of the restaurant, smiled and waved to us.

Michael and Tony arrived two days later. Stretched out in a hammock, I was settling into Patong and had almost finished <u>The Source</u>. John and I had been out to the reef snorkeling earlier in the day, when the water is clearest. Perhaps it was an effect of growing up with Disneyland but I loved rides. Our nature ride at Patong consisted of walking up to the point with our mask and snorkel, having a good smoke and then allowing the current to carry us along over the brilliant corals, psychedelic tropical fish and other creatures of the reef. I feel like I am flying over an alien planet. I'd taken to wearing my baseball cap backwards to shade my neck, as well as a t-shirt, after getting a good sunburn the first day. I probably looked like an alien to the fish.

Lying there in the hammock, reading in the early afternoon, I felt the luxurious softness of a siesta coming on. I didn't have a care in the world, unlike the girls. In the last two days, both Carrie and Clare had told me privately that each thought herself to be pregnant. It wasn't an appeal for help but each, in their turn, had asked me to keep it confidential. I don't think they had even told each other. Why they told me, I've no idea. Maybe it was a little like how people share intimate things with the unknown person beside them on a plane, someone they'd likely never meet again.

John and Louise were stretched out in the shade on one of the bamboo bed frames from the house. Louise rested her head on his abdomen as he read. Nick and Maura had gone off to Phuket town to get supplies and change some money. The beach was medium crowded with day-trippers and I caught snatches of music and laughter drifting down from Poon's.

A string of firecrackers popping on the beach in front of Poon's caused me to gaze down the beach and I saw them. Mike had a distinctive look when walking with his pack. He held the shoulder straps with both hands, like a banker surveying the room holding his lapels, and he took wide, loping strides that caused his long hair to rock forward and back. I could make out the neck of a guitar sticking up in the air behind his pack. Tony, more compact, looked to be taking two steps for each one of Mike's, even though he wasn't that much shorter. He rocked from side to side when he walked and his forward lean gave the impression he was walking uphill even when going along the flat. I sat up in the hammock and waved my arm. They had no idea I was here, but cheerfully returned the wave. I called over to John and Lou, "Hey, I think that's Mike and Tony coming down the beach."

Louise started, as if she'd been asleep, and sat up rubbing her eyes. John folded his book and swung his feet to the ground. We all looked down the beach at the approaching figures and John grinned, "That's them, alright." I got out of the hammock and we stood, and watching them walk the last hundred yards along the beach front dirt path.

"Hello cobbers," John shouted. "Found your way down here, did ya"?"

Everyone had big grins.

"That we did," Mike called back.

They came up to us with handshakes all around and hugs from Louise. She held Mike's shoulders a moment and they smiled broadly at each other.

"Well Vernon," said Mike. "I didn't expect you as well. Good to see you."

I liked his Australian twang, the way it colored his otherwise cultured English.

"G'day mate," added Tony and shook my hand once more. "Glad to see you again up this way."

We moved back towards the cabin and they leant their backpacks against the outside wall.

"I see you've found another palace," Mike commented.

Louise laughed, "Home sweet home, for now at any rate. Come on then, don't leave your gear out here." She turned and walked into the cabin.

Mike and Tony looked at John, who shrugged, "Your home now too, I reckon."

I felt a twinge of envy that they were in while I was out, but my rational mind told me it was pre-planned and don't be a sap. I wondered, briefly, how it would go with Nick and Maura when they got back, but it wasn't my problem.

John lifted the cracked top of the old Styrofoam cooler on the floor and lifted out dripping bottles of Singha beer.

"Not as cold as last night," he winked, "but still wet and wild."

He handed the cool bottles around, "Here's a proper welcome. Glad to see you made it."

The beer tasted good and my spirits were high. Mike wiped a bit of beer foam delicately from his thin moustache with an index finger.

"We saw Clare and Carrie on the way here. They pointed the way," said Mike. A look passed between John and he.

"I reckon they're glad to see you," said John. "I know Carrie was afraid they'd miss you."

Mike nodded, taking in that bit of information, "That was quite a time we all had, back on Samosir."

Louise sipped her beer and gave Mike one of her feline, sardonic smiles, "I reckon you three have some catching up to do."

Mike smiled thinly, "I reckon we all do, don't we?"

I felt unseen animals scurrying between them and the pregnancy conversations with Carrie and Clare did a flip-flop in my mind.

We took our beers out to the beach and settled down on a shaded bit of white sand. Mike and Tony had gone further north in Sumatra and also out to a surfing spot on the west coast, after leaving Samosir. I was surprised to learn that they were in Penang for Thaipusam too.

"Wasn't that incredible," I gushed. "Did you see the guy hanging upside down from the cross?"

Louise looked repelled by the image.

"Ah yeah," replied Tony enthusiastically, "I couldn't believe that one. What a thing!"

Focused elsewhere, John said, "Still have some Drum, I see."

He looked almost hungrily at the blue pouch of tobacco that lay casually in Mike's lap. Mike finished rolling a smoke, licked the paper and sealed it with a final twirl. He grinned, "We found a shop in Penang with imports. I bought all they had. There're three inside for you."

"Did you now! You little beauty."

John stood up and drew out a crumpled blue pack of Drum from his shorts pocket. He folded it open and looked in, smiling, "Fuck me. In the nick of time too."

He extracted a pre-rolled joint from the bag, "I'm saving this one for when you arrive and now's the time."

I'm discovering that I'm more sentimental than I realized. The afternoon unfolded, there in the shade of the tall palms, and we talked and shared, swam in the blue sea, laughed, smoked, and talked some more. Our shared Thaipusam stories made me feel like we'd done something incredible together and it seemed to have the same effect on Mike and Tony. In the dazzling stream of new faces and places over the past months, I realized the thing I missed most was old friends. It was odd how that door opened a feeling that Mike and Tony might be new friends. I'm not a rock or an island, I guess. Weird song, anyway.

Mike reminded me of a young David Niven with dirty blond, long hair. He was elegant without seeming prissy, a good guitarist and singer, as he demonstrated again on the beach later in the afternoon.

"I like that song," I said, "It's familiar, but I can't place where I know it from. Did you play it back at Toba?"

"Might have. It's J.J. Cale, 'After Midnight,'" Mike replied.

"He's a Yank, very popular back home. I've got the album <u>Naturally</u> with me on cassette."

He looked over at John, "Do you still have the tape player, John?"

"I do," he replied, "but the batteries are shit here. We've got to get some more."

Nick and Maura showed up late afternoon and settled right in. And they'd brought six batteries from town, a welcome addition to our moveable feast. Towards sunset Clare and Carrie wandered down for their extended reunion with Mike. We were really quite a mob, sitting there on the beach. I touched the edges of the insight I'd had in Toba at Christmas, how we were citizens of a borderless country, knitted together by whatever that thing is that calls you out on the road. Looking out at the sea, the peaks and troughs of the choppy water would catch a ray of sunlight and just for a moment reflect it, creating a flash, a sparkle. I could see the physics of the random forces summing together to produce that tiny peak on the surface of the water, how it reflected and shone for a moment, before collapsing back into the whole. It was like that with people on the road, the random forces bringing us together for a moment that would sparkle, then we'd all drop back into the vast whole of existence, until the next moment, and the next. Sentimental. I looked around me at the faces glowing in the orange light of the sunset. You could really see people, all the warts, all the imperfections, and yet still come together in brilliant peaks that reflected the light. It wasn't our light. It was just the light.

I took another hit of the ganja and passed it along to Tony. He was smoking a straight Drum cigarette and for a moment sat holding both, looking confused.

I laughed, "Well Mr. Regan, take a hit on one and pass the other along."

Tony cracked up in his good natured, sheep dog sort of way, handed me the Drum cigarette and took a hit of the ganja. The Drum had a seductive aroma that smelled good at this moment, so I took a hit. I didn't smoke normally, but with all the tobacco they mixed into the ganja I felt like I was getting plenty of both. Strangely, and not so pleasantly, the pure tobacco set off a rush of dizziness. I handed it back to Tony and steadied myself on the sand, struggling within a swirl of nausea. The straight stuff was more of a kick in the head than I expected. It reminded me of how I felt with betel nut, which I'd tried and not liked back in Bali. Another one of those things that seemed like a good idea at the time.

I'd given up whatever hope I might have been nurturing about striking up something with Clare. That first night at Loy's had been such fun, making music together and walking back under the stars, that anything seemed possible. She'd taken me into her confidence then, with her suspicion about being pregnant, and that had changed the dynamic. I still found her engaging, intelligent and attractive. We had a nice relationship "in passing." Now though, sitting by our small beach fire after the sunset, it was obvious that both she and Carrie were in orbit around Mike. They were continuing whatever dance it was they'd begun back on Samosir Island and Mike glowed in their attention. He and Nick shared the guitar. I added a few harmonica riffs from time to time but mostly it was their show. At one point, as the evening wore on, Tony looked over at me and shrugged. I saw what he meant, the happy couples and us, the odd bachelors on the fringe.

Tony's upper front teeth were set at odd angles to each other and when he smiled it reminded me of Alfred E. Newman of MAD magazine fame. His happy-go-lucky, sidekick energy was an enjoyable counterpoint to Mike's smooth and charming civility. Now it felt like we might as well head out for a bit of dinner and let the couples thing run its course.

"Hey, Tony, I'm going down to the place called Poon's, where your bus came in, for some dinner. Want to join me?"

John was staring into the small fire with Louise relaxing in his arms. Nick and Maura were lying side by side on their stomachs, looking into the fire and talking, Clare and Cassie were adoring Mike as he strummed an instrumental piece.

"Aw yeah, I could do with some tucker," he said.

Everybody got it and when we stood up to head out, Mike called over, "We'll see you down there in a bit."

I doubted that we would. And we didn't.

The next morning, after a bite of breakfast, I set off back down the beach to the "club house", as I was coming to think of John and Lou's cabin. I'd introduced Tony to the Mekong custom and felt a little fuzzy. We'd had a good dinner at Poon's of chili chicken with basil and rice. I hadn't had a bad meal in Thailand yet. After, when Tony headed back down to the cabin, we could still see their fire on the beach.

I'd made the choice to stay on at the guesthouse instead of camping. The number of day visitors to the beach made it a little too busy for me to comfortably set up a camp. John and Louise had graciously offered to let me pitch my tent in the yard of the clubhouse, but I actually liked having a more private place of my own. Still, my loan of the camp stove and solar hot water bag made our semi communal clubhouse more comfortable and I was glad to share.

I found the four of them, Mike, Tony, John and Louise, sitting in front of the cabin with glasses of steaming tea, enjoying the morning. I liked the fresh, cool air of the beach at this earlier hour. The day always seemed so full of possibility before the heat and humidity of the afternoon suggested a siesta.

John smiled a welcome, "Morning Vernon. Fancy a cuppa?"

"No, I'm good, thanks. Lake has good tea for us every morning," I replied.

Mike and Tony looked rather bleary, especially Tony, but they nodded a good morning. Both had cigarettes burning that they were enjoying with their tea. I had the oddest sensation of wanting a hit when I smelled the smoke and sat down on the bamboo platform beside Tony.

"Hey Tony, can I get a hit of that?"

Tony looked at his cigarette, rolled as a long cone, thicker at the burning end.

"Aw yeah," he said and passed it over.

The memory of the near nausea last night asked me what I thought I was doing but something else, something like an itch inside of my mind, wanted a puff of the aromatic smoke. I took a puff into my mouth then inhaled it with air. Something remarkable happened. The itch, the vague, uncomfortable in my own skin sensation, disappeared after that first puff. It was replaced by something relaxed, something at ease. I took a second hit, this one deeper, and was flooded by a sense of well-being. Some part of me that had been unconsciously tense let go, replaced by a deep satisfaction. I realized with a shock what it meant to be addicted to cigarettes! A story from my childhood reared up and swept me into a maelstrom of memory.

Cigarettes

Post-war Los Angeles in the early 1950s was alive with home construction. Not only post-World War II but post-Korea had unleashed an unprecedented demand for housing and LA had a lot of room to spread out into.

I was born in July of 1951, at St. Joseph's Hospital in Burbank, a little town at the east end of the San Fernando Valley. The Valley was a sylvan refuge of walnut and orange groves, small ranchettes with left over Victory Gardens that continued to flourish in the warm Southern California climate.

Mine was an old ranching family that had homesteaded an area about 30 miles to the north, strangely named Castaic. My mother, Vi Netta, was the second youngest of nine children and was born in a mortared stone ranch house with a corrugated metal roof situated in the center of a 2000 acre rancho. Growing up, she'd ride her horse bareback to the little one room school, hop off, and let the horse find its way back home without her. Everybody knew their jobs.

Vi Netta had the soul of an artist and an adventurer, so when she was of age for high school she moved in with her older sister Lorraine in Long Beach. Lorraine, who was twelve years older and married, had a wonderful old Spanish style mansion and it served as an elegant base from which to attend a big city High School along with the resources to support her artistic ambitions. Along the way, impressed by a barnstormer in a biplane who had landed on the ranch when she was 9 and given rides to all the kids, she became the youngest woman pilot in the United States for a time. My father was a pilot too. A family of pilots. She smoked Viceroy cigarettes and the air in our house would often have an inversion layer of cigarette smoke at just about the height of my head. I'd put my arms back and pretend I was a jet flying through a thin cloud cover. I knew that when I grew up I'd smoke Viceroys too.

Cigarettes. Then I found out what they were. Our modest home in Sherman Oaks was in one of the new neighborhoods that were spreading across the San Fernando Valley. We had about half an acre of property with a line of four big beautiful walnut trees along the north side. Across the street, Mr. Martin had his home-cum-workshop-cum wrecking yard. In my youthful eye, it was a paradise of possibility. I loved to wander amongst the rows of car parts and machines, torches and wrenches and hummingbird feeders.

His place occupied two big lots. Away from the house and workshop was a well-tended Victory garden, a wandering flock of goats and several huge pepper trees. They were easy climbing with their knobby trunks and inviting clefts. I was transported by the spicy smell of the leaves and the red pepper corns when I crushed them between my fingers. I pulled myself into the upper branches, out on an adventure.

One of my favorite things to do was to take my red Flexy Racer wagon and pull it behind me as I made my way to the market and corner drug store. It was a circuitous route, winding along the grid of the new neighborhood streets for about three quarters of a mile. The Victory gardens and walnut trees were being replaced by small family homes and, nearer the main drags, two story apartment buildings. The pace of change was astonishing, even to my youthful eyes, when a month could seem like forever. All this construction opened up a business opportunity for an enterprising nine year old like me. I could pass many building sites and collect the glass soda pop bottles the workmen left lying around. Nobody minded, and I enjoyed the smell of the fresh fir timbers being used to build the homes. It was the resin smell, a volatile rich thickening of the air that reminded me of walking in a forest. Southern California was dry but we'd often drive to Northern California, where the big family ranch near Laytonville stretched from Highway 101 all the way over to the Eel River. Southern Oregon was another sweet forest smell, and I anxiously anticipated our trips up to Kirby and Cave Junction, where my Aunt Irene was the school teacher and my uncle Arthur was the Forest Ranger. Being raised in the near desert of Southern California, the moist northern forests exerted an almost irresistible pull on my spirit.

I'd collect empty bottles in the sweet wood smell, loading my wagon with ten or fifteen pieces of booty on the way to the market. At three cents per bottle on the return deposit, I'd soon have thirty or forty cents burning a hole in my pocket and all the wonderful sweets of that time calling to me - Hostess cupcakes for twelve cents, an RC cola for a dime, a Snickers for a nickel. The market was pretty good, but the drug store on the corner, the Monterey Pharmacy, had the crown jewels of candy racks.

I found myself perusing the Big Hunks and the Abba Zabbas on those vast racks when Fate entered the store in the form of a shabby stranger. It wasn't unusual for a stranger to enter the store. I certainly didn't know everybody. But this stranger was different. His gait was hesitant, almost a shuffle. As I peeked around the candy rack his ancient hands appeared as claws extending out from the sleeves of the nearly floor length, unkempt canvas raincoat.

Even to my young eyes he was a filthy mess. His unshaven face and too long dirty hair surprised me. This was, I knew, a hobo. My mother had pointed a few out to me during one of our rare excursions into the downtown of Los Angeles, not with derision but more with a note of sympathy in her voice. "That poor soul…" she might say.

The last time I'd seen a hobo was on a visit to Olvera Street. We loved to visit Olvera Street, a little slice of Mexico in LA, not far from the art deco Union Station. It offered intriguing street wares, restaurants, and had a magnificent candle making shop where I spent hours dipping and re-dipping long tapered candles in huge cauldrons of colored wax. In her younger days my mother and some of her Gypsy Moth friends would fly their small planes down to Ensenada, Mexico. They'd land on the beach and spend the weekend drinking and dancing. She loved the gay, warm, multihued heart of Mexico and reached back to it all of her life.

So this apparition, this hobo, had my full albeit surreptitious attention as he shambled down the drug store aisle towards my candy land. His eyes moved furtively along the rows of cans and bottles lining the shelves. Stopping, he reached out and extracted a round, white can and twisted open its cap. With his left hand, he reached up, grasped his upper teeth and removed a full dental plate from his wizened old mouth. With his right claw hand, he began to shake a white powder from the can into the concave depression that formed the top of his dentures. I thought to myself, with a small shock, "That man is stealing!"

He replaced his dentures and bit down, settling the plate back into place with a clacking wet smacking. Then he closed the can and returned it to the shelf.

I'd never seen anything like this and stared openly, not knowing how to react. I was not well concealed however, for suddenly he turned and found my wide eyes with his. The whites of his eyes were blood shot and yellowish, but from the iris blazed an almost golden intensity, a maniacal brilliance. He approached me.

I took an involuntary step back and he struck, "Little boy," he snarled, his lips pulled back in a rictus, the dentures clacking, "do you know what cigarettes are?"

I was taken aback, steadying myself on the candy rack. He held my eyes and I was frozen in something like terror.

I whispered, "No."

Phuket

He leaned toward me, the grimace becoming a leer, eyes on fire,

"They're the devil's penis!"

I gasped and nearly fell backwards, then scrambled out the nearby side door, my heart beating in my ears, his mad countenance filling my mind's eye. I didn't know what had happened, but it was wrong somehow and threatening. Everything in me shouted: "Danger. Run away!"

I circled around to the front of the market, grabbed my wagon and fled back to the safety of home, my unspent thirty-nine cents jangling in my pocket. I burst in the front door. My mother looked up from the table where she was reading the paper, having a cup of coffee, smoke curling from the Viceroy, and smiled at me. My eyes went to the cigarette, with the deep red lipstick on the speckled brown filter. The devil's penis!

Memory lane, one ambush after another.

I handed the smoke back to Tony who was looking at me oddly. "I didn't know you smoked," he said.

"Neither did I," I replied.

The next surprise of the morning came when Nick and Maura emerged from the cabin and announced that they were moving on. "We've decided to head over to the other side," said Nick, "to Koh Samui."

"There's a bus from Phuket straight up to Surat Thani," explained Maura.

I think it was the first time I'd seen her looking enthusiastic about anything, poor girl. Louise wore her enigmatic smile.

John stood, "You're the man of action," he grinned at Nick.

He and Nick shook hands and Nick said, "So, probably see you next in Bangkok. What do you reckon, maybe a fortnight?"

"Aw yeah, thereabouts. Three weeks maybe?"

John looked questioningly at Louise who nodded, "Yes."

"I'll leave a letter at Poste Restante. We'll probably base ourselves at The Malaysia or The Atlantis, but I'll let you know," said Nick.

The third surprise of the morning arrived when Mike stood up and grabbed his day sack off the bench.

"I'm off for a walkabout with the ladies. There's meant to be another beach beyond that point there," he indicated the northern limit of the beach, "and they wanted to see it before they left."

The Appearance of Things

As he departed, John called out, "Don't stay out too late."

Louise giggled and added, "Have the car home by ten."

Mike smiled patiently back at us over his shoulder and gave a thumbs up.

John looked over at Louise, "I reckon they've got a few things to rave about."

"I reckon they do," agreed Louise, watching Mike's back recede into the distance.

Tony and I looked at each other.

"I'm going out with my snorkel stuff to the reef. Feel like a swim?" I asked.

"Aw yeah," replied Tony. "Let's do it."

Later that afternoon we were pulled out of siesta time by the arrival of a blue, red and white fisherman's boat. They hauled out of the water, up on to the beach and we all walked over to examine the catch.

"Beautiful prawns!"

Louise peered into the bamboo basket of huge blue shrimp resting on the bottom of the boat. It didn't take much urging. We dug into our pockets and walked away with two kilograms of fresh shrimp. John was almost dancing a jig singing a "shrimp on the Barbie" jingle from somewhere.

"Nick and Maura don't know what they missed," mused Louise.

Our beach feast took shape. Lou made up a good sized pot of rice while John, Tony and I stripped the shells off the shrimp and rolled them in a sweet Thai chili sauce loaded with thinly sliced shallots. Mike showed up about four thirty with Carrie and Clare in tow. When they saw the bounty, Mike and Carrie walked back to Poon's and returned with beers, ice, soda and Mekong. Clare, Tony and I very carefully gathered up a good load of dry firewood from above the high tide line. I hadn't seen any but I knew there were cobras about and preferred not meeting them.

By the time the multihued sunset was underway, we were all seated around the cooking fire, delighting in our beach picnic.

"These are the best prawns I've ever tasted," raved Clare. "Better than lobster, I'd say."

Another fine night of music, laughter, good smoke and Mekong. I could get used to this. I was used to this! It was late, near to eleven, when I roused myself from a nod. We were all contemplating the red coals and flickering flames of the dying fire.

"Good night all," I said to the group. I noticed that Carrie and Clare were seated back to back, literally using the other for support. Mike lay sprawled nearby on the sand, his head resting on his arm.

I walked back to our clubhouse where I'd left my day bag. A chill went through me. The bag was lying in the dirt beside the front door and I hadn't left it there. My heart sank when I picked it up - much too light. I'd taken my small flashlight down to the beach and now saw the top of the bag was unzipped. Shit! They'd left my book and water bottle, but the camera and small film bag were gone, along with my travel clock and wallet. I shined my light into the cabin and nothing seemed more amiss than usual. Even the old tape player still lay on the cable spool table. I felt kicked in the stomach. All the photos of Bali and Penang, gone, just like that. The other stuff was a pain in the neck, but there wasn't much in my wallet, a few hundred baht, and I could get a new driver's license when I got back to California. But my camera and my photos! I felt ill.

I dragged myself back down to the beach and told everybody the news. There was a childish fear in me that it was my fault and people wouldn't like me now. My grown up mind told me that was irrational.

"Bloody hell," spat John. "We were all right here. Bastards!"

He stood up, along with everybody else, and we returned to the cabin. What else might have disappeared? Mike had his guitar in hand, I had my harmonicas in my pocket, Tony had his day pack with him. He'd taken some photos of our picnic.

John and Lou went into the back room and poked around in their bags and on the shelves. "Looks ok in here," John called out. In the front room though, where my bag had been, Mike found his backpack had been gone through as well.

"The bloody bastards got my wallet and knife," he cursed.

Not a very jolly ending to our lovely picnic.

I walked back to the Patong Guest House with Clare and Carrie. At that moment none of us felt great about the pitch black of the night outside the beam of my little flashlight.

"Probably the same ones who robbed the Kiwis a few weeks back," suggested Clare.

I was glad I'd parked my pouch with Lake. At least I hadn't lost my passport and major funds. Losing the wallet and money it contained was a violation and inconvenience. But it made my teeth hurt, losing the irreplaceable photos that would mean nothing to the thieves - Rod and Didi, *Moonshiner* and Bali and Thaipusam. I went to bed angry. I could get another camera and film in Bangkok, but those dear parts of this marvelous journey now only existed in my memory and my journal. I wanted to kick myself in the head for not taking better care.

Over the next five days my spirits recovered. I grabbed some money from my stash with Lake and went up to Phuket town where I found a decent wind up clock and a new Thai leather billfold. Maybe having the Buddhist eight spoke wheel embossed on it would deter the next thief, but I doubted it.

The camera would have to wait until Bangkok, but Tony was great about taking pictures and even lent me his camera when I felt I needed a shot of something. We agreed to stay in touch and he'd send me the photos of our Patong times when they were finally developed.

Mike too recovered his good cheer, after a period of grieving. "That pocket knife was from my father, twenty first birthday," he ruefully said on the night of the theft.

The day after Clare and Carrie left, Mike looked like a weight had been lifted from his shoulders. In the morning he'd been playing his guitar, sitting out in the hammock. He and Tony were laughing and smoking. Music was also coming out of the cabin where John and Lou were cooking up a pot of porridge. In a funny way it was "back to normal" to have it be just us five. The unspoken tension between Mike and the girls had always been in the background. I figured it had to do with the pregnancies both women hid but I didn't feel like poking my nose where it didn't belong. Still, the new, light Mike was once again the old, light Mike I remembered from Toba. "Tell you what," he said, "that beach I walked to with Carrie and Clare was fantastic. You gents feel like giving it a look today?"

I'd been on Patong beach for ten days now. On my last trip into Phuket town, I'd booked on the big tourist bus up to Bangkok and was leaving to go north in three days. The notion of a little exploration appealed to me at that moment.

"Sure, I always like to see what's over the next hill."

I looked at Tony and he had his goofy grin on, "Aw yeah," he said, "let's have an explore."

John and Louise stayed behind, grateful for some privacy. We three strolled down the beach past Poon's and Loy's to where the jungle spilled down the hillside and on to the beach. A path wide enough for a jeep but deeply rutted led up the red clay hillside. For a couple of smokers, they charged up the slope and I found myself panting to keep up. It was a surprise for me when we reached the ridge top. The ground leveled off and there was no new beach in sight ahead. The trail began to descend down into another jungle canyon. Our path narrowed in with trees and understory shrubs and quickly became a descending switchback. Below I could hear what sounded like running water.

We emerged beside a wide, shallow stream shaded by a canopy of tall, broadleaf trees growing on each side. Fifty feet upstream a man stood unmoving in a pool of water that was up to his waist, holding a throw net and studying the surface. He didn't look up at us. A little boy squatted on the shore watching him, turned briefly to glance at us but immediately refocused on the man in the water. The fisherman skillfully threw the net, giving it a spin. The small, lead weights along its perimeter pulled the airborne net into a ten foot wide circle that slashed down and disappeared into the water. He slowly pulled a line attached to the center of the net and moved forward in the water. The boy stood from his squat and slipped along the bank parallel to the fisherman. He unfurled a long net bag, the sort that might have previously held onions in the market, and stood ready while the fisherman gathered in the line. The surface of the water was disturbed around him, as if by a swarm of tiny fish. As we three watched, the fisherman moved towards the shore. His legs were covered with what appeared to be black macaroni. Leeches. He seemed unconcerned and tugged the net into the near edge of the pool. Two largish, white fish struggled in the tangle and the boy waded in, removing them from the net and depositing them into his waiting sack. Emerging from the water, his spindly brown legs were now spotted with the black leeches. He picked up a smooth, flat stone and scrubbed off the parasites, and a dozen thin trickles of blood sprouted and began oozing down towards his bare feet. The fisherman refolded his net for throwing and moved back into the pool.

"Did you ever see African Queen with Humphrey Bogart?" I asked.

"The leech scene," Mike nodded his head.

Tony now looked at the stream we needed to cross, a mild revulsion on his usually good-natured face.

"You can see the little buggers swimming between the rocks," he observed.

We all stood there, staring down into the water, a multitude of undulating black forms beneath the surface.

"How did Clare and Carrie like this part?" I asked.

Mike made a face.

"There weren't any when we came. I mean, I didn't see any and we crossed here. Jesus, look at them!"

Downstream, just below us, the rocks were close enough together that we could cross by hopping one to the other. And really, it wasn't like a pit of crocodiles or some other unpleasant sudden death. Just the same, we were all laughing nervously as we crossed.

"Made it," Tony called triumphantly. He was the point man while Michael and I followed behind.

One more ridge and we descended to a small, perfectly white crescent beach, a mini-Patong, but with no development and no people.

"Crikey!" exclaimed Tony, "This is something."

We set up on the grassy edge, under a clump of coconut palms for shade, and piled into the blue, refreshing sea. Both Tony and I had masks and we paddled out to the reef, which was more colorful and intact than the one near in to Patong. Great stuff.

In the early afternoon, an open boat with four Thai fishermen landed on the beach and immediately set about building a fire and offloading some good sized fish. They spotted us and waved us over. With a lot of laughter and sign language, we ended up drinking beer and tearing off handfuls of fresh barbequed fish. We joined in a game of netless volleyball with a woven rattan sphere they'd brought. It was tougher on the head and hands than a regular ball, but these guys were used to it. I was blown away how they could spike it with their feet, doing a sort of flying kick. These men were all lean and fit, unbelievably skillful. They had it all over anything I'd even seen on a football field.

The following two days had me wondering why I was about to move on from paradise. Following my own advice, I had found a paradise and I had stayed awhile, but knowing when it was time to move on was an edge I hadn't yet got around.

I had been meditating, off and on, over my days here. When I was at UCLA the Maharishi Mahesh Yogi had been popular, setting up centers teaching his Transcendental Meditation. I was drawn to try it after spending most of the summer of '69 on LSD, body surfing at Santa Monica and wandering around in the Yosemite High Sierra mountains of California. I'd gone on a couple of their retreats and found that when I really gave myself over, remarkable things happened. But it was tough, here on the beach. Smoking ganja and drinking Mekong weren't a hundred percent compatible with Transcendental Meditation and I didn't find myself experiencing any great clarity of mind when I'd sit.

There was a growing faith, however, that I could trust life. That the universe was not a hostile place and that I could let go of a good thing and another good thing would come along, maybe not immediately, but it would come. Watching other travelers was instructive. One thing I could see in operation - that to move through the world with an open hand was better than moving through with a closed fist.

That afternoon we figured out how to use our growing collection of old "D" cell batteries to run the cassette player by cutting a piece of bamboo in half, lengthwise and making a stack of all the old cells in series. Four new "D" cells provided the six volts to run the player, but if we stacked twelve old ones, at about half a volt each, we got the same power and the machine ran like a top. We got up to sixteen, but after that it became difficult to keep them all touching properly, end to end.

Louise didn't keep a daily journal like me, but she did collect her thoughts in a notebook and from time to time, the odd quote. She clapped at our collective cleverness and said, "I have a quote for the occasion." She pulled out her notebook and read: "From the Scottish Himalayan Expedition. Until one is committed, there is hesitancy, the chance to draw back, always ineffectiveness. Concerning all acts of initiative or creation, there is one elementary truth….. that the moment one definitely commits oneself, Providence moves too. All sorts of things occur to help one that would otherwise have not occurred. A whole stream of events issues from the decision, raising in one's favor all manner of incidents and meetings and material assistance which no man would have believed would come his way. Whatever you think you can do or believe you can do, begin it. Action has magic, grace and power in it." She snapped the book shut, "From W.H. Murray."

The words, or maybe really the sentiment of the words, stayed with me. I wished everyone well that departure morning and we agreed to try and link up in Kathmandu, via Poste Restante. Maybe we'd see each other again. I hoped so. Now, on to Bangkok!

Chapter 7
Thai Time

"I have been and still am a seeker, but I have ceased to question stars and books; I have begun to listen to the teaching my blood whispers to me."

Hermann Hesse

I

Bangkok. Even the name feels pointed and curved up at the ends, like one of the temple roofs we were passing. The tourist bus from Phuket was completely full. Another all-nighter, sitting up.

"We're coming in to Sukumvit Station," said Todd, my seat partner. In the way of things, I'd learned he was from Oklahoma and was living here in Bangkok where he worked for the heavy equipment company Caterpillar. His specialty, he confided conspiratorially, was military support, but the work was secret and he couldn't talk about it. He was in his late thirties and had the personality of a used car salesman. Maybe it was the flat top haircut, combed back on the sides and the serious tan. He reminded me of a character named Kookie from an old LA television series called "77 Sunset Strip". He was the comic relief in the crime drama and was constantly whipping out his comb to slick back the hair on the sides of his head.

"The Malaysia is good. I stayed there when I first came to Bangkok. Close to a lot of the action."

He winked at me, "Bangkok is the place for a single guy, I'll tell ya."

With a bump our bus pulled off the wide street into a passable bus station. I was pretty beat and it wasn't even noon yet. As we stepped down off the bus the humidity and the heat were heavy as a blanket, much heavier than Phuket.

I shook hands with Todd, "Thanks for all the stories and info about Bangkok. I hope your deal on the beach place works out for you. Sounds like it would be fun." He'd been going on about a beach south of the city, on the Gulf of Siam, where he and some friends were using their Caterpillar connections to push construction of a luxury hotel.

"Thanks. Yeah, Pattaya is up and coming. You should go down that way and check it out. Oh, just over there you can get a *tuk-tuk*. They all know The Malaysia."

I looked where he pointed. Lined up along the wall of the station waited dozens of the little golf cart taxis we called "*bemos*" in Indonesia. Maybe these *tuk-tuks* had been upgraded with Porsche motors or maybe the drivers were simply nuts. My driver hunched over the wheel, swerving and accelerating through the dense traffic, a suicidal bat out of hell. I gripped the roof to resist being thrown out into traffic by the radical stops, starts and right-angled turns. The unexpected madness of it all got me laughing. The driver grinned and gave me a thumbs up.

When we whipped on to the side street of The Malaysia, I expected him to slide in to home like some baseball star. I wyed upon my departure from the little cab, a motion he returned with a wide smile. A tall, lanky blond guy pushed past me and jumped into the back of the *tuk-tuk*. They sped away as he barked directions to the driver. Bangkok was a place on speed.

The lobby of The Malaysia had the same hustle as the streets. I wanted to give it a look since it has almost legendary status with the travelers I'd met in Asia. But after two slow weeks on the beach at Patong and a lousy sleep on the bus, the jackhammer energy around me was daunting.

"Two hundred baht," the clerk behind registration looked at me with a take-it-or-leave-it matter-of-factness. It was only ten dollars, but I'd been spoiled by the more reasonable rates in the south.

"OK," I said and he passed me the registration document. One or two nights wouldn't break the bank, but it was a big city and I felt like I'd be able to find something better tomorrow or the next day.

My room, up on the fifth floor overlooked the largest Asian metropolis I'd seen and it had a background noise that was kind of a growl, low and throaty. I gazed down on the swimming pool. A swim sounded good and it looked like I could get a poolside lunch as well. Breakfast had been a banana, a cup of tea and a long time ago.

The poolside area had an affable, threadbare quality that I liked. I put my towel over a chair at an empty table and pulled off my shirt.

"Going for a swim?" a male voice from the next table. I turned to see a round faced guy with a narrow rim straw hat and a Hawaiian shirt, hula dancers and outrigger canoes.

"Uh, yeah. Would you mind keeping an eye on my stuff here?"

I hadn't brought down my wallet, but I had a hundred baht note and the room key in my shirt pocket.

"Yeah, sure, no problem," he said, "but I ask since the pool has a reputation of never having had the water changed."

He grinned and I had the hit of a joker.

"Really?"

There were half a dozen westerners splashing at one end, laughing and speaking German. The water looked clear and I got the mild chlorine perfume in the air. It was very hot, even though the tall hotel shaded this side of the pool patio.

I grinned at the gentleman, "I guess we're lucky that urine is a sterile solution."

He laughed and I jumped in. The water was cool and I floated on my back, gazing up at the clear, blue sky. The Malaysia was about six floors high and boxy. As I floated, I saw a window open high up and something black flew out. It drifted lazily down, like a handkerchief or a stocking, and landed on the water nearby. A pair of ladies panties. I guess they weren't needed.

I felt a bit guilty using the poolside shower when I came out, as if I was betraying the spirit of The Malaysia Hotel swimming pool, but it felt good to get the chorine smell off my skin. On the way back to my table I stopped at the grill. They had a cheeseburger and fries for eighty baht. I couldn't remember the last time I'd had a cheeseburger and fries so that's what I ordered. I also picked up a small, cold Singha beer for twenty baht. Easy to spend a hundred baht in Bangkok. A sign on the wall read, "Bar girls may not use the pool."

Back at my table, I grabbed my towel off the back of the seat and gave my hair a better drying. The guy who was being funny about the pool looked up with a grin.

"Thanks for keeping an eye on my stuff," I said.

"No problem. Just arrived?"

"Yeah, I've been down on Phuket for two weeks and took the overnight bus up here."

"Steve Munroe," he said, extending his hand. I introduced myself and, in the easy way of the road, joined Steve at his table.

"Did you like Phuket?" he asked.

"Well, the town's not much but there are some great beach scenes. I reconnected with friends I met in Sumatra and we all had a brilliant time down on a beach called Patong. Best sunsets I've ever seen."

Steve was thirty three and teaching at the American School in Bangkok.

"Are there a lot of American children in Bangkok?" The idea that there would be surprised me.

"Quite a few. More than you'd think, I'd bet. There's a big military presence here with the war going on next door. A lot of the families have come over. But there's a big expat community here as well - Europeans, Australians, Indians. Lot of business done here."

He looked towards the lobby doors, shading his eyes.

"Wealthy Thais want their kids to learn English and go to American universities, so we get them too. Why, are you interested in teaching?" He turned his attention back to the table and lifted the iced drink he had to his lips.

"Maybe, someday. I've got my degree in Zoology from UCLA, pre-med. But for now, I'm out on the road, heading back to Europe overland."

Steve whistled, "Wow, that's some trip. How long do you plan on spending here in the kingdom?"

Good question. "Well, I got a thirty day visa when I came in two weeks ago so two weeks more, at any rate. Can I renew a visa here?"

Steve shook his head, "Not if it's the "on entry" kind. I had to get a special work visa outside the country and I needed the school to sponsor me on that one. You'll need to be out of Thailand in two weeks."

An idea occurred to me in that moment, "Could I go into Laos, then come back in?"

"Laos?" Steve looked startled, "I would have said take the night train down to Penang and come back. That's what most people do. Laos could work, I guess." He looked at me doubtfully. "There's a war on there, you know."

I told him the story about Hank, the Swiss guy, how he'd been there with no problems.

Steve steepled his finger. "Yeah. Well, for one thing he's Swiss. You're an American. They aren't at war with the Swiss."

"Hello Steven!" An attractive young woman was crossing the patio towards us. Steve smiled broadly and stood up.

"Ah, Marisa. Bon jour."

Introductions all around. Marisa was the reason Steve was sitting by the pool at The Malaysia. She lived up in Chang Mai, teaching and helping out at an orphanage. Steve had met her on a trip he took up to Chang Mai over the Christmas break and hoped to help her secure a teaching position here at the American School.

"Are you all checked in?" he asked with a smile.

"Yes, yes, thank you." She looked around at the hotel, "Same old Malaysia."

Steve chuckled, "The old girl is an institution all to herself. A lot of people's first and last introduction to Bangkok."

My cheeseburger and fries arrived. Marisa looked at the plate and then wryly at me, "A very American meal, Mr. Vernon."

She pronounced my name in the French way so it came out "Vair Nogn."

I blushed and stammered, "My first burger since leaving California. My usual is whatever's local."

"Well," she offered, "a taste of home. I would love a good Pinot Noir but alas, we are not in France."

A light bulb seemed to go on in Steve's eyes, "Say, Marisa, you went to Vientiane didn't you? Vernon here was just talking about going into Laos for a visa renewal. How did coming back into Thailand go for you?"

She shrugged, "Going out, coming in. You just do it."

From her purse, she produced a light blue packet of Gauloises cigarettes and lit one. The scent was like burned coffee.

Marisa continued, "It's nothing for me to go into Laos, the French are welcome. I think you would need a visa. I'm sure you would. I met Americans in Vientiane and they got a visa here in Bangkok."

This was good news. If there were other American travelers in Vientiane, it was probably a good bet I could go in un-hassled. I leaned forward on my seat, "Did you go outside of Vientiane, to other towns like Luang Prabang?"

"No, but I wasn't interested. I like the old French feel in Vientiane," she smiled prettily. "Café au lait, a fresh croissant or baguette, good cheese. These are not things we have in Thailand."

"Or good Pinot Noir," chimed in Steve.

Marisa smiled at him, "Or good Pinot Noir, that's right. But," she looked at me, "I understand your question. Many people go up the road to the north. I heard many good things. It's ok I think."

I had a bite of cheeseburger while Steve and Marisa talked about the school job. The flirty way he was teasing her along said his efforts at helping her to find employment were not purely altruistic, but she apparently liked him back and her easy, gracious manner seemed natural.

Steve removed his hat and ran his fingers back through thick, wavy, dark hair. If you could ignore the shirt, he turned out to be a rather handsome man - dark eyes, good chin. Sort of a slightly pudgy Tyrone Powers look.

"Man, it's hot this time of year, isn't it?" he said. "Well, if you're about ready, we can keep the four o'clock appointment with Carl."

The cheeseburger had been good and I was still picking at the fries. Marisa glanced over, "Those are *pommes frites*. I've never understood why Americans call them French fries. What is French about them?"

We laughed and Marisa added, "If you go Vientiane, there you will find good food of France. And also good wine. Try the *pommes frites* at La Paix restaurant and you won't be sorry."

She stood and both Steve and I got to our feet. He was shorter than me and I thought I picked up some proprietary movement in the direction of the woman. Maybe just my imagination.

"Here. Give me a call. Bangkok is a big place and I'd be glad to see you again."

He handed me a card that read: "Steve Monroe, Bangkok American School", with a phone number.

Marisa smiled at me and said, "I'm sure I'll see you again too. I'm here for at least two days," she hesitated and looked at Steve, "unless I get the job, eh? Then I will need a better place to live."

I can't help doing movies. She looked like Audrey Hepburn in "Breakfast at Tiffany's", very cute and wide eyed.

A plan was forming in my mind. Tomorrow, I'd find the Laos embassy and get an entry visa. I could do an arc of travel up towards Chang Mai and then across to Laos before my Thai visa expired. I dipped my last *pomme frite* in red ketchup and popped it into my mouth. I could already taste that fine French food in Vientiane.

I headed back into the lobby, on my way up to my room, feeling a bit blue to have no particular plans for my first night in Bangkok. The thought arose to call Steve, but was immediately dismissed. He was going to be busy showing Marisa a good time. Who could blame him?

A group of men, jock types, were gathered around an attractive blond who was seated in front of a wall mounted TV. They were gripping glasses and a bottle of Mekong sat half full on the low, lounge table. One guy, flushed and grinning, leaned towards the woman: "Say squirrel again, Natasha."

She was a tough cookie and very much in control. She looked coolly at the drunk, "Why you want me say it again, Bob?"

Russian accent, I think.

"Because honey, it's so good when you say it," Bob replied, weaving slightly.

It was weird. Then I saw that the program on the TV was a cartoon show I recognized, the Rocky and Bullwinkle Show, and understood the Natasha thing. She was the dark haired Russian spy with her cloak and dagger partner Boris. They were forever trying to get the best of Rocky and Bullwinkle. Bullwinkle was a moose and Rocky was a flying squirrel. When cartoon Natasha said "squirrel" it came out in a trill of r's and did sound amusing. Making fun of Boris and Natasha's Russian accent was part of the humor.

A ping on the elevator door and it opened. A balding, white haired older man, big Texas moustache, cream colored rayon shirt and slacks, stepped out with an arm around a happy, laughing Thai girl in very short shorts. They pushed out and through the front doors. He was two feet taller than she.

I stepped into the elevator, which smelled like an ashtray. I went up, showered and shaved. The face looking back at me in the mirror did not look amused. Should I go back down to the lobby and watch TV? The absurdity of the question made me smile.

"OK, Vern," I said to the image, "let's take you out to see the town." For

The Appearance of Things

a fleeting instant I was talking to someone else, a not-me in the mirror, someone I didn't really know. I thought about that feeling all the way back down to the lobby, where the jocks were still at it and the Mekong bottle was empty. Natasha had escaped, but they were now having fun with the waitress from the snack bar, who was trying to clean up the chips wrappers scattered on the floor. I left that scene behind and stepped down on to the street. The air had cooled somewhat and in the gathering dusk, lights were coming on. I could hear music over a fence and smelled a barbeque going on somewhere. Todd, the guy on the bus, had described Sukumvit Road in glowing terms, a place where the action was. He had also grinned and said it was "different" with a sort of nod and a wink. Not having a better idea, I walked down the block to the big road that was Rama IV and caught a *tuk-tuk* .

"Sukumvit," was all I said and the driver gave me a knowing look.

"What you want? Party?" he asked.

"No. I want good Thai food," I replied. He laughed and we sped off into the city.

Different. It's an interesting word and not my first choice. The human current in which I found myself was a frantic swirling down a sidewalk loaded with hawkers' stalls and wild characters. It put me in mind of one of those psychological tests, where they show you a picture and you say the first thing that comes into your head. "Yikes!" "Whoa!" "Are you kidding me?" "Jesus Christ!" "Muslim woman." "Cowgirl." "Ghost." "Creep." "Holy shit!" and so on. It was like being on Hollywood Boulevard near Vine, peaking on acid. The ramped up, noisy, hungry, desperate flow surged toward me and around me. It was fun.

The little side streets that ran off Sukumvit at right angles were called Soi. They were numbered so it was easy to navigate. On this side of the street, after Soi 9 came Soi 7, if I was heading towards downtown. I wondered how high the numbers went in the opposite direction. Soi 1001? Sukumvit itself was wild on the sidewalks, but as I walked and explored I began to get the flavor of the little side streets. The clubs and restaurants and food stalls crowded together festively and the aromatic smoke from a row of barbeques grabbed my attention, even though I told myself I wasn't hungry. Two women worked a set of huge woks fired by what looked like rocket engines, complete with the throaty roar. A dipper of chili oil thrown in volatilized, releasing a cloud of vapor that set me off on a coughing fit and made my lungs hurt, but also made the air into something I could taste. A nearby stall with hot trays loaded with curries and vegetables said I needed to stop and try this.

The cook put a scoop of rice in the center of the plate and looked at me expectantly. Something coffee colored and lumpy reminded me of the coconut curry called Panang that I'd loved in Thung Song. It called out and I pointed. She ladled a portion onto the side. Then a tray of stir-fry green beans and red chilies and finally a yellow sauce that had something leathery, like thin fried tofu and mushrooms. I pulled out a stool at a small communal table and seated myself across from a man eating what looked like a plate of fleshy red chili peppers with bits of meat. He looked up at me with merry, crinkled eyes. Saint Chile maybe. I followed the example of the people around me and ate with a spoon as my primary utensil, using a fork as a push tool.

"Drink?" a grinning woman knelt beside me, presenting an ice chest of cold beers and soft drinks. I bought a cold Singha that was just right. The rich flavors and outrageous spice combinations continued to blow my mind.

Three tall westerners were coming towards me down the Soi, part of the flow of humanity surging past. The one on the end looked up and caught my eye. Todd! Out on a prowl with two buddies. A rush of conflicting emotion coursed through me - pleasure to see a face I recognized, caution, not really who I wanted to hang out with, resignation, here they come.

"Hello Vern. Fancy seeing you here! How's the curry? Oh, my friends Ernie and Pete," he turned, indicating his companions. I nodded to all three but I had a mouthful and couldn't speak. Didn't have to, apparently. "We're heading down to the Plum. Come down and join us when you finish." He pointed further down the Soi to what looked like a neon apple sign hanging out from the wall. After he'd said it, I could make out the swirl that spelled "Plum."

I swallowed, "OK, great, Thanks. What's there?"

Todd was clearly loaded and gave me an exaggerated, good old boy wink. "Beautiful girls is what's there. Come on down, bye!"

He moved off with Pete and Ernie. They were vaguely reptilian, but not in a creepy way, more like a group of stoned geckos out for a good time. Steve had informed me the Thais referred to westerners as "farang", which sounded like the word "foreign" but had a meaning something like "over ripe jack fruit", whitish and fleshy. Watching the three heads bobbing down the alley I had to admit we did look sort of ripe and fleshy.

A sudden press in the Soi as more people poured in off of Sukumvit. The speediness of this place is incredible. I had the impression that things were just getting started, and I had to admit there were beautiful women here. Not just the girls in shorts hanging around the jocks in The Malaysia lobby.

The Appearance of Things

In shops, walking down the street, serving curry, in passing cars, a refined beauty all around me. Finely sculpted, delicate noses, perfect cheek bones, and exquisite laughing eyes, the Thais are a uniquely handsome people. The change had been subtle as I traveled, from the attractive Pacific Islander wide foreheads and flattened noses of the Indonesian archipelago, to the rounder, warm Malaysian and elegant Indian/Chinese descendants to these wonderful Thai beauties. So much human beauty in Asia. I felt a bit of a pink lump. Am I beautiful to anybody like this? At the moment, I couldn't see how I would be.

The last sip of the Singha beer to follow off the last bite of brilliant curry. "*Krup coon, krup,*" I wyed the cook. She smiled and wyed back.

I decided to look into the Plum and check out the scene. The wide double doors reminded me of the last time I'd gone into a club, at New Year's. The memory of poor Matt up on the stage made me laugh again. This room was smoky and noisy and dark, with spotlights illuminating the dance floor. Scattered silver poles stretched floor to ceiling. Hanging on to the poles, completely nude women were doing dance routines in time to the music. Well, music is a generous description of the repetitious, downbeat sound, but it was easy to bounce to.

Todd and company were sitting at a table over to the left, each with a nude woman hanging on them or, in Todd's case, sitting across his lap. I didn't feel like joining them. A soft but possessive hand snaked around my upper right arm. A very attractive woman smiled up at me, "Hello, you like sit and have a drink with me?"

She was pretty in the way that would command my full attention had I seen her walking down the street, very beautiful really. But here and now, she was completely naked with firm breasts pressing into me. She came around, facing me, her skin erotically anointed with what my medulla recognized as her vaginal moisture. I was stunned, and allowed myself to be drawn down into a nearby, wide, padded leather armchair.

Beautiful smile, coy, teasing eyes, "My name is Suzie. What yours?" Cheerful, perky delivery, like meeting someone at a party. At this point I was sitting and she sat on my knees, straddling me, arms around my neck. Everything was revealed, body hair almost non-existent. I told her my name and added, "Suzie, you are very beautiful but not tonight for me, ok?"

Another nude woman, taller, appeared at the table holding a tray and they made a brief eye contact.

"Ok, not tonight," she said brightly. "What you drink? We have fun anyway!"

My wisdom mind told me to get going. Another mind I scarcely knew was enthralled by the naked beauty and the sexual perfume and the soft, alluring lovely straddling me. A third woman had come up on my left and seated herself on the armrest. The heat from her bare abdomen radiated on to the side of my face. She smiled down at me and began to run her hand through my hair, her dark, perfect nipples at eye level. The waitress eased up on my right, pressing her bare thigh into my shoulder, her eyes, too, ripe with promise. I was in a steam bath of female sexuality. A hand printed sign over the bar across the room read, Best Margarita in Bangkok.

"Margarita," I said, holding up one finger. Susie leaned forward. "Me too?" she asked. I nodded and held up two fingers. A look of satisfaction crossed her face.

"Where you from, Von?" Susie asked.

The waitress walked away with the order and Susie hissed something at the girl on the armrest who left off playing with my hair and drifted away. Susie deftly slipped from straddling me to both legs across my lap and wedged into the leather seat beside me. She giggled and grinned at me, her playfulness a complete and charming surprise.

California," I managed. "America."

"I like America," she said, then added, "You like Thailand?"

"Yes, I like Thailand. Very lovely place.... and people."

It was a novel experience, to be having a mundane conversation with a beautiful naked woman lounging in my lap. The tall waitress returned with two, fish bowl sized glasses of what looked like lemonade over ice. She settled them on the small table and handed me a slip of paper that read, "2 Margarita - 100 baht, Bar Girl Fee - 50 baht."

I sighed and laid out the cash.

"You give my fren twenty baht tip, ok," said Susie, smiling at me and nodding her head up and down.

Well, I was getting an education for a lot less than I paid at UCLA. The waitress accepted the twenty baht with a seductive smile at me and said something to Susie in Thai, who covered her mouth and laughed delightedly.

"She say you look like a big man!" which made me blush and Susie laugh some more.

The margarita impressed me as alcohol free and when Susie tasted hers she said, "We trade," and shifted the position of the glasses on the table.

And we talked, in a warm and human way. Susie was from the northeast of the country, the mountainous land east from Chang Rai. Her family was very poor and she sent money home to help support everybody.

"I tell my mother I work in hospital," she giggled.

I was enjoying sitting with Susie, her soft sexy womanness pressed up against me, talking like a pair of students in the cafeteria at school. She was a nursing student, and proved it with a good knowledge of physiology. I finished my margarita and felt a tiny buzz. Susie had sipped maybe a quarter of her lemonade.

"Susie, I liked meeting you. I'm going to go now but thank you."

She smiled brightly, "You pay bar fine. I go with you!"

She squeezed my thigh in a "we're going to have such fun" sort of way.

"What's a bar fine?" I asked stupidly.

She probably couldn't imagine somebody not knowing what a bar fine was and answered simply, "Three hundred baht."

Seeing my confusion, she pointed to a Thai man at the end of the bar wearing dark glasses and a sports shirt. He looked over at us, unsmiling.

"You pay him my bar fine, three hundred baht. We go, ok?"

I got it.

"Oh, I understand. Sorry, not tonight. Sorry," I stammered.

A shadow of disappointment crossed her face for a moment, then the light returned, "You come back tomorrow. We go. I show you Bangkok." She smiled demurely and ran her fingers along my inner thigh, "We have fun. I like you, ok?"

There was a sweetness and innocence about her that surprised and touched my heart.

"OK. Maybe. Maybe I'll come back tomorrow."

I was not being truthful and her eyes told me she knew it. When I got to the door I looked back for her, but she had disappeared in the writhing mass of people moving in the smoke, under the lights. I hadn't noticed how much more crowded the place had become until that moment. Out in the starkness of the night lit street I felt I was awakening from a dream, the erotic scent of Susie still clinging to me the only evidence that I wasn't.

The Malaysia was like what they say about New York, the city that never sleeps. There was a thrumming, restless intrusion into my sleep all night long, as if the entire place was on wheels. Through the walls and the ceilings and the floors came bangs and screams and moans. The wall behind my bed became a sounding board for the athletic thumping of my neighbors. Somebody was having fun. By the time the sky began to lighten, I'd resolved to move on from The Malaysia.

The Embassy of Laos was in a neighborhood bordering a spacious, green park. From the array of national flags I spotted as we passed in the *tuk-tuk*, a large number of countries had their embassies around here. I had hoped to get the visa and go, but the uniformed clerk took my passport, two hundred baht and told me, "Come back on Thursday, after noon, for your passport and visa." That was two full days from now. I stood on the front stoop of the old colonial building, blinking in the late morning sunlight. It occurred to me that this pleasant neighborhood of tree lined streets felt better than the busy Sukumvit area. I began to walk in the dappled shade of the flowering jacarandas, their cheerful blue blossoms scattered on the sidewalk. Soon I found myself beside a tree-lined canal with grassy strips on both sides, the aroma of garlic and lemongrass in the clouds of vapor rising from a small boat ahead. There, on the shore, two Thais sat on woven mats eating steaming bowls of noodles. A woman wearing a black headscarf squatted in the open boat, fanning a charcoal brazier. She glanced up at me with a smile and nodded towards the mats spread on the bank. One of the seated Thais smiled too and shifted to make more room.

The savory noodles with bits of pork and leafy greens and chilies were unlike anything I had yet tasted - spicy and richly toasted sesame. Sitting there under the trees on the grass, eating exquisite food from the tiny floating kitchen, the pleasant company of welcoming strangers, I got a sense of what Jay the Peace Corps guy had meant about civilization and Thailand. I nodded appreciatively at the cook and gave her a thumbs-up. She laughed gaily, pleasing like a glass wind chime, and returned my gesture.

Following my small lunch, my stroll ended at the edge of a wide river. Bunches of glossy water hyacinth drifted past on the coffee-with-cream colored water, while tugs pulled loaded barges in both directions. A man roared past in what looked to be a supersized canoe. A gimbal mounted automobile motor in the rear sprouted a long stinger with a prop that tore at the water, driving the boat forward. The driver sat in front of the motor, steering with an attached pole that extended forward from the roaring motor. He looked like he was hanging on to the front of a rocket, barely in control! The boat must have been doing fifty miles an hour, almost out of the water. Below, in front of me, the near water churned with the black bodies of huge catfish. What were they fighting over? Downriver, on the other side, a tall stone obelisk loomed, a temple of some kind. It had a Hindu look, solid and imposing. I could make out visitors moving up and down the broad stone steps that led to the river and a set of docks.

A long, narrow torpedo of a boat sped by, heaped with passengers. It reminded me of the water taxis in Venice with dozens of people sitting just above the water line. It roared up to a small dock about a hundred feet further on and the small crew secured it, tweeting instructions to the skipper with bosun's whistles. Passengers piled off and on and then they were away, tearing off to the next stop. It was a taxi! I liked the idea of exploring along the river, so I walked toward the unloading pier. A map on the wall of the terminal was helpfully written in both Thai and English and showed the various taxi stops. There must have been at least forty of them. The river, called the Chao Phraya, described a huge arc around the center of the city. I had arrived at a stop called Thewet.

A man who'd been talking loudly on a nearby payphone hung up and walked away. That gave me an idea. I pulled out the card from Steve Monroe, deposited a five baht coin and called the number.

"Hello, Steve Munroe," a voice answered.

"Hi Steve, this is Vern Castle, the guy you met yesterday at The Malaysia Hotel."

There was a brief hesitation, then, "Oh, yes! Hello. How are you doing? Did you get your visa for Laos?"

"Sort of. They said two days. That's why I'm bothering you. I'm down at the Chao Phraya river right now, at a dock called Thewet. I'm wondering if you've got any suggestions for a place to stay around here. The Malaysia is not where I want to be."

I heard laughter at the other end.

"Well, it's a slice, that's for sure. It's funny you'd call right now. Marisa feels the same way about The Malaysia and has moved to a place I like called Shanti Riverside, not too far from where you are."

He hesitated and went on, with something arch in the tone of his voice. "Things went well for her on the interview and she's going to be doing orientation at the school for most of the rest of this week."

"So she got the job?" I asked.

"Yup. Marisa is now officially our new French teacher. Congratulate her if you see her. I'm meeting her over there later and we're going out to celebrate." It was clear from the way he said it that I wasn't being invited along, not that I expected to be.

"Well good news for both of you then, huh?" I replied. Then, "So, this Shanti Riverside is close to Thewet?"

"Yeah," said Steve, "two stops south of you. Go down to Phra Athit. When you come out on the street, turn to your right. It's down about a hundred yards. Good location. It's a few more baht than the Malaysia but you won't have panties floating in the pool."

I heard his chuckling at the other end.

The river taxi thundered away from the dock at Thewet. I stayed on the back of the boat in the open air, and got an eyeful of the river life and the skyline of golden towers. The air was muddy smelling, humid but with spicy undertones. It was speedy on the river too but so wide open it didn't matter much. The traffic and exhaust and exotics in the Sukumvit area were kind of oppressive once I got past the adrenalin rush of the *tuk-tuk* suicide derby. I actually felt a tingle of relief when the clerk at The Shanti handed me a key. The room was a bit smaller than the one at The Malaysia, but it looked out over the river and the guesthouse itself was like a garden - a little bar and restaurant around a pond, isolated from the street noise.

I popped for another *tuk-tuk* to haul me across town and wait while I gathered up my gear at The Malaysia. It was slow going coming back, interspersed with moments of terror as we dashed opportunistically toward every opening in the traffic flow. The street grit filled my pores and even though I soaped up and scrubbed my face when I got to my new room the towel came away with dark smudges. Going for a total clean up sounded like a good idea so I made my laundry pile and gave myself a head to toe scrubbing with a rough wash cloth and a new bar of Dial soap, followed by a shave. This time, the new side of the towel stayed white.

With the laundry dropped off at the front desk I slipped over to the garden bar. Not too surprisingly, there sat Marisa and Steve. Steve looked up, spotted me and grinned, "I see you found the place."

Marisa had her back to me, but turned and smiled prettily, "Hello. Too much Malaysia for you as well, eh?"

"Maybe just enough," I returned with a wink. "*Bonjour* Marisa. Congratulations on the teaching job. Hi Steve, thanks for the recommendation and the directions. This place is great."

"You're welcome. Join us, if you like. We're heading out soon and then the table will be all yours."

I looked around and saw what he meant. It wasn't quite five in the afternoon, yet the bar was fully occupied. I eased myself into the extra chair. Why did I feel stiff? The waitress came over and I ordered a small bottle of Sang Thip with soda and ice on the side. The honeymooners from the Penang train were right - Sang Thip was a few cuts above Mekong.

"So when do you start?" I asked Marisa.

"Oh, officially next week but I don't begin my classes until the new semester, in about two weeks."

She turned and impetuously took both of Steve's hands in hers, which seemed to both surprise and please him.

"I'm so grateful for your help! Also, to be helping me find a place here. It is very handsome of you," she gushed.

Steve did a pretty good "aw shucks-little old me" shake of the head, "It's enlightened self-interest. We needed a good French teacher and I personally think you are terrific... in all ways." Marisa was demure and very attractive, in that self-effacing moment. "You'll be able to go up to Chang Mai on Friday," Steve continued, "to start packing up for the move down here. The faculty meeting on Thursday is all you've got until then."

"Well," she shrugged, "maybe it's best I spend the time looking for a flat, I think."

Steve nodded and then said, "Yeah. That's probably good. I don't know how much you have in Chang Mai, but you can leave things with me until you find something. But you know," he paused for effect, "I'm pretty sure there's a flat available where I'm living, if you're interested. I like the place a lot - good neighbors, close to the school, a pool."

Marisa lit up and clapped, "Oh, that would be very good, if it was not too expensive."

Steve was reassuring, "My rent is about five thousand baht a month, including the utilities. I think the place that's available is the same, which is good for that part of Bangkok. Nice kitchen and living room, one bedroom and bath, view out over the park. Even a little private balcony."

It was clear to me that he was steering her into proximity. There was no overt pressure, he came across as the gallant knight, and Marisa impressed me as being completely aware of herself in the world. If she was going along with this, then it had to be to her liking as well, didn't it?

A little voice in the back of my mind was saying, "Not necessarily," and I flashed on Susie from last night, doing what she had to do so as to be able to send money home. That freedom thing again. They were worlds apart, Marisa and Susie and yet... what did I know, really, about either of their circumstances. A scene from "To Have and Have Not" reeled across my mind. Lauren Bacall pulls out some cash and offers it to Humphrey Bogart in the hotel room and he says, "Wait a minute. And you said you didn't have the money for a ticket back home. You're good." She fixes him with a look and says, "It's not enough to get home on. Just enough to be able to say no, if I want to."

This was all unfolding between Steve and Marisa. All the causes and conditions in each of their lives were unknowns for me. I was just a guy passing through.

"When can I get a look at it?" Marisa asked Steve.

"Let me talk to the manager in the morning. If it's still available, I could try to get him to show it to you tomorrow."

She nodded and seemed to decide something, "*Bon.* You call me here tomorrow then?"

"Yes, as soon as I know something," he said and lifted his cocktail for a long sip.

His head was tilted back when Marisa made eye contact with me and gave a kind of "What's this shit?" look, with a roll of her eyes. It was such a surprise I almost choked on my Sang Thip. In that moment, in my mind anyway, the entire complexion of the exchange shifted. I must have looked funny because she giggled. Steve put his now empty glass down on the table with an air of finality.

"So my dear, shall we move towards that celebratory dinner?"

He stood and offered his arm. As she stood, Marisa glanced at me and then back to Steve. What did I think I was seeing? My initial impression was that they liked each other and that this was a deal of mutual benefit. But there at the table, in that last moment, her eyes held a resigned "time to pay the piper" sadness, behind the gracious smile. It wasn't the first time that I'd felt insight walking hand in hand with paranoia in my perception of things. Am I really seeing what I think I'm seeing?

I watched them leave, gripping my drink, and felt the cool wet condensation in my palm. Behind my eyes, loneliness sat at a darkened table and raised his drink to me.

The nightlife near the river had a very different flavor than the Sukumvit neighborhood. Not far from the guesthouse was Khosan Road. If Sukumvit catered to the businessman crowd, Khosan was for the hippie traveler crowd, at once more familiar and less interesting. There was something comfortable about the bootleg cassettes and Ray-Ban sunglasses for sale in the sidewalk stalls. Mobs of young travelers, some wearing their backpacks, roamed the ganja perfumed neighborhood in search of cheap food, cheap beer and cheap lodging.

I could relate to it but was pulled towards the illuminated golden temple roofs I could see in the distance. Twenty minutes of walking, the last part across a huge park, brought me to the wall of a castle. At least, it looked like a castle. Approaching through the park, I could make out a fantasy of ornate rooflines and golden spires. Now, at the base of the wall, there was no hint of what lay within. A queue of monks in their ochre robes filed solemnly past me and, curious, I followed behind them as they rounded a corner of the castle wall. One by one, they entered a small, guarded portico and disappeared through the wall. A sign on the wall in English read, "Royal Palace. Open 9:00-16:00. Admission 50 baht." This was a come-back for tomorrow, for sure.

A burst of laughter emanated from a plaza across the street, light bulbs strung in the trees illuminating dozens of tables. People sat under the trees, eating and socializing. Around the perimeter, well-established food stalls with aromas like beckoning fingers for my suddenly hungry self. The crowd was mostly Thai, mostly young, and dressed lightly on this warm, humid evening.

"Hello. You, come look."

A woman stood smiling behind a counter with about twenty, deep trays of curries and meats and noodles. She made "come hither" motions with her hand, her dark eyes sparkling from the overhead lights. I went, looked and ordered by pointing while she chatted away in Thai, laughing at her own jokes. It was only when I went to pay that I realized she was male. I wondered in passing if I would meet women in the roles of men. Human sexuality was a lot more open and varied here. Things are not always as they seem, I was learning.

Enjoying the last bite of my BBQ pork sate with peanut sauce I noticed a burst of people pouring out of a passageway between the buildings, towards the river. Tossing my litter into a nearby can and waving to the cook, I threaded my way through the other diners and down the passageway. I had a hunch that I'd find a pier on the river and sure enough, there it was. The route map on the wall identified it as Tha Chang, the boat stop for the Royal Palace. I needed to go up river two stops to get to my hotel. The comfort of familiarity was beginning. Bangkok was starting to open up.

In the morning, while I was sitting in the little hotel garden sipping tea and enjoying a breakfast of spicy chicken bits with fried rice, Marisa appeared. She scanned the tables and caught my eye, resulting in her pretty smile of greeting. I waved and indicated the empty seat at my table.

"Good morning. How was your celebratory dinner?"

She blinked, "Oh. We had a good time. Steve is a very nice friend to me."

She looked over my shoulder and pointed at my cup of tea. The approaching waitress stopped and returned to the kitchen to get a cup.

"I'm very excited to have been selected for the school job," she continued, "and it will be good to have some money again. Also to know better the life of Bangkok. It is exciting, like Paris."

The waitress returned with her cup of tea and Marisa engaged her in what sounded like very competent Thai. When she left, Marisa turned back to me.

"I hope that the flat is nice. It would be the first time in a year I have someplace just for me."

"What do you do today," I asked.

Marisa shrugged, "In the afternoon, after the school, we will go to see the flat, maybe. I must call at two. Until then," she smiled, "I am free like a bird. What shall we do?"

The Appearance of Things

A small electrical ripple zapped through me.

"I have an idea," I said.

The ferry roared as it slid into the wharf, sharp forwards and reverses of the motor inserting us skillfully up against the old tires that served as bumpers. The quick tie-and-hold as we scrambled off and flowed with the crowd, out towards the street and the Royal Palace.

"This is where you ate your supper last night?" Marisa asked, passing the food stalls, now open for the day. "It all looks wonderful. Don't you love the Thai food?" she enthused.

Standing on the sidewalk, we waited for a break in the traffic to cross. When it came, Marisa took my hand, "Ok, let's go." I liked the feel of her cool, delicate hand in mine and when we reached the other side she didn't let go. We walked hand in hand around to the entry.

"Let me take you to the palace," I said and laid a hundred baht note on the ticket counter. She grinned at me and pushed her ready fifty baht note into my hand, "I already owe too many favors around this town. But thank you. You are really very sweet."

Her wide, blue-green eyes looked at me warmly. I wasn't sure how long her dark brown hair was since it was piled and pinned atop her head whenever we met. Made sense in the tropical heat but I found myself wondering what she'd look like with her hair down, the elegant line of her neck hidden.

The Royal Palace is a gigantic jewel box of mosaic mirrors and gem-like tiles, golden Buddhas and wandering monks, yet what commanded most of my attention was the feel of her hand holding my upper arm or the soft stroking in the middle of my back when we stood taking in the sights. Later, we went together to the train station to book sleeper seats on the Friday night train up to Chang Mai. It put me in mind of my last sleeper coach ride, but I already knew I'd be sleeping alone. The man she called "my whole love", some lucky guy named Jean Claude, was finishing up a project in Paris. He had already applied for the transfer with his architectural firm and would be joining her, here in Bangkok, in the not too distant future. That bit of information had come up after she kissed me lightly in the hall of the Emerald Buddha. I responded by pulling her closer in embrace, but she pushed back gently and looked into my eyes, "Do you have anyone special, back home?" she asked. The question made my heart contract.

"I did. But we lost each other and couldn't find our way back."

Thai Time

I was putting some time and space between me and that loss. It startled my new world to be reminded, here and now, of my old world.

Marisa told me of Jean Claude before I could get too ramped up over what some gentle touch and flirtation might mean. I didn't ask if she'd told Steve about Jean Claude, but I thought not. Maybe she had, and he was just going about showing her who was the better man. Or maybe he wouldn't have been quite so helpful in jobs and apartments and she knew it. People are complex.

Friday evening, before the train left, we three had dinner at a roof top restaurant overlooking the Chao Phraya. Steve was a bit annoyed, I think, that Marisa had suggested that we all dine together. She had signed the papers on the apartment and he was ready for another celebratory dinner. She and I were both sitting in the garden bar, having checked out, when he walked into the lounge.

"Hello," he greeted us as he crossed the room, "I wanted to see you off." He nodded an acknowledgement to me, but was focused on Marisa.

"Please sit," she said, "My treat, what will you have?"

Steve looked at our Singha beers and said, "Thanks. I'll join you." He caught the bartender's eye and held up a bottle. The man nodded and Steve turned back to us.

"Your train leaves at seven. How about having dinner before?"

Marisa smiled, "That would be lovely," and then turned to me. "You'll join us, won't you? We're taking the same train and it only makes sense." She covered my hand with hers and added, "You've been my tour guide and *confidante*. You simply must come!"

At that moment, the waitress set down the bottle of cold Singha in front of Steve. He looked like he was winding up to say something about Marisa inviting me along, but checked himself. Instead, lifting his beer bottle, he toasted, "Ok then, to the journey ahead. Safe travels for all and a prompt return, Marisa."

The dinner went off pretty well. I didn't mind being Marisa's foil for an evening and Steve recovered his humor. He spent a lot of conversational energy on what they'd need to do when she got back. To his credit, by the end of the evening and a bottle of Sang Thip, he was gregarious and generous. Both Marisa and I had to insist on paying for our share of the dinner.

"Well, there'll be other times," he said, giving her hand a pat.

II

The sleeper was more comfortable that the one I'd taken from Singapore to KL, but memories made it lonelier too. Yet I did sleep deeply, the gentle rocking of the coach a physical lullaby. Marisa and I wished each other farewell outside the station, she heading towards the orphanage to close up her life there, me walking along the riverside towards a guest house she recommended called "Je t'aime". It was outside the old walled part of Chang Mai. According to my Trailfinders guide, the preferred area of the city was within the walls, but I liked the quiet, riverside location and the old part of the city was a mere ten minutes' walk across the bridge. Since it was only for this one night, I preferred the more natural setting.

The town was much smaller than I expected. I found the guesthouse and dropped off my gear, then walked the perimeter of the old wall, where it still existed. Along the way, I visited the five "must see" wats in Chang Mai. At one, on a hill, pilgrims bought postage stamp sized pieces of gold leaf and pressed them on to a stone image of the Buddha. It had received so many gold leaves that it looked encased, like a full body cast after an accident, except made of gold. After the plainness of Thung Song and Phuket, the small towns in the south, Chang Mai impressed me as ancient and filled with spirits. I pressed my hand against a stone rampart, as though feeling for a heartbeat. I felt this in Europe too, the humility of time stretching behind me and in front of me.

Back at Je t'aime, I joined a few other travelers watching the sunset over the river. Some good ganja was going around when a guy with a dark beard sat down at the table. We nodded a hello to each other then both did a double take. Where did I know him from? He spoke first, his dark eyes crinkling into a smile.

"Hi. I think I recognize you from Samosir Island, just this last Christmas. Were you there?"

"I was," I confirmed, "and I recognize you too. I'm Vern." I put out my hand.

"Alan Firestone," he said and we shook hands.

"You didn't have a beard then, did you?" I asked.

He ran his hand under his chin and grinned, "No, that's right. And you played harmonica on the walk back that night from Mongoloy's. We were behind you."

Why this all made me feel so delighted I can't say, but it did. As we talked I recalled Alan balanced on the log in Lake Toba and joking around the table at Pepy's.

"You were traveling with two other guys, um...."

"Yeah - Michael and Jeff. They flew back to New Zealand last week from Bangkok."

While we caught up, two French guys at the table rolled a large, European style joint and sprinkled a line of heroin into the mix. Alan looked admiringly at their effort then back to me, "The Golden Triangle is pretty amazing. Been up there?"

"No, but I'm heading north tomorrow, to a place called Taton," I said.

"What's in Taton?" Alan asked.

"According to what I've heard, you can take a boat down the river from there, pretty much all the way to Chang Rai. It's meant to be really good. A guy I met in Bangkok, who's a teacher there, did it in December. It's not the Mekong, smaller. He said it's good when there's enough water. I guess if you keep going, it flows into the Mekong."

Alan looked thoughtful. One of the French guys lit up their joint. He was wearing a long sleeved white shirt that seemed incongruous. The smoke had an acrid smell I didn't like.

"This river looks full," he nodded down towards the water, which did look high. The trunks of small trees along the edge were out in the flow of the stream. There must have been rain up country, pushing the level higher than usual.

"Yeah," I agreed, looking out at the river, "so maybe it will be good up that way."

"You want a hit?" Heavily accented English. One of the French guys held out the heroin laced joint.

"*Merci*," Alan said and reached out, took the joint and had a long deep hit. He started to pass it to me but I shook my head. It smelled like the old pesticide called Malathion. Alan looked at me questioningly then shrugged and passed it back. The French guy with the black jacket and long hair was already rolling another.

The Appearance of Things

Henri, the owner of Je t'aime, and his Thai wife offered a *prix fixe* dinner of spring rolls, pad thai, spicy vegetables and rice for fifty baht. The smells drifting out over us from the kitchen were tantalizing. I was feeling a little slow from the ganja earlier that afternoon so I signed up. Alan was starting to nod from the heroin laced smoke and was tuned out when I got up and went to take a shower.

The next morning, I was out early to get the little, northbound minibus. No sign of Alan around the guesthouse so I wrote a note wishing him well and gave it to Henri to pass along. Not much of a reunion but that's the way it went sometimes, on the road.

The hills and valleys of northern Thailand rolled by. Children guided mud splattered water buffalo in the flooded paddy. They dragged a heavy, thick section of banana tree behind them to smooth the mud for planting. A man standing astride the log held the reins and tapped the animals with a slender wand of bamboo to urge them along. Ochre robed queues of thin monks mindfully carried their bowls along the sides of the road, not looking up as we passed. Most village dwellings were held aloft on stilts, almost high enough off the ground to walk under. Built from the forest materials of palm frond, bamboo and wood, very few seemed prosperous enough to have the corrugated metal roofs I'd seen further south. The only buildings of substance were the Wats and they glowed with care - clean and ordered. Most had groups of robed children with shaved heads playing somewhere on the grounds.

Fang, our destination, was larger and by comparison relatively well off. Our battered minibus wheezed into what must be the center of town. Several two story buildings with thick, corrugated asbestos roofs loomed up around us. Spreading away from our stop were a number of narrow, unpaved lanes.

I stepped off the bus and stretched, relieved to be out of the confining vehicle. The late afternoon sun still had plenty of punch and I moved into the shadow of the nearest building while they pulled the various bundles and packs off the roof, settling it all on the boardwalk beside me.

The boat down the Kok River left daily at 10:00 am from Taton, another two hours north. Our minibus driver had some English skills, certainly more than my Thai at this point.

"*Kor toad, Kuhn,*" I began, "Excuse me sir, bus to Taton, what time?" I asked. He grinned at me and rubbed the top of his close cropped hair cut.

"Taton? Yes, tomorrow, seven morning," he shrugged good-naturedly.

So, a night in Fang. The other passengers were collecting their belongings and scuttling in different directions. The driver was smiling at me, apparently wondering what I was going to do, which made two of us.

"Where is the hotel, *krup*?" I ventured. He kept smiling but looked at me quizzically. Great. I extracted the Peace Corps book and looked up the word for hotel. I knew that *"yoo tee nai"* meant "where is" so I linked it up and said, *"Rhonegram, yoo tee nai?"*

He kept looking at me and smiling, but either I wasn't pronouncing it correctly or what I was saying was nonsense to him. New approach. I put my hands together and laid my head against them, like a pillow, closed my eyes and made a snoring sound.

"Yoo tee nai?" I repeated.

He nodded and laughed, then, shook his head, *"Mai mee,* no have hotel." I knew *"Mai mee,"* when it turned down sadly in tone at the end. No have got.

The driver saw my predicament and pointed up the hill, towards the local wat.

"Sleep there. No problem, ok?" He smiled and nodded affirmatively, again reassuring me, "No problem, sleep there."

I thanked him and picked up my backpack. He took my elbow and walked me across and down the street to a path leading up the hill. On each side of the entry stood the Singha, stone lions I knew were symbols of protection. I wyed the driver and started up the path through the forest. I had my sleeping bag and rainfly. Camping out was an option, but I still stung from the theft on Patong beach when I lost my camera. Also, though it seemed like a good low weight alternative when I bought it, a rainfly didn't afford much protection from cobras and such. Maybe I could rig up my small mosquito net in some way.

Such were my musings as I reached the temple. The wat grounds were extensive, spread out over a natural shelf on the side of the mountain. The actual temple, with a statue of the Buddha at the front altar, was modest in size and ornamentation. I'd guess it could hold forty people, seated on the floor. It was dim within the sanctuary and the Buddha statue was illuminated by an electrical footlight. The light cast an elongated shadow on the wall behind, creating an imposing outline of the little Buddha.

Away to my left a large open platform I knew to be the Dharma hall. On

The Appearance of Things

Phuket, we had seen large community gatherings taking place at the local wat, usually led by the senior monks or even the abbot. In Thailand, I'd observed, the wats and the community flowed into each other. Steve had said that outside the big cities, the wats were essentially the schools and that most young Thai men spent a period as monks. John and Louise used to kick a soccer ball around with the children at the Phuket wat. John referred to them as monkeys.

"The monkeys have it better than we did at the boarding school. No sour old nuns whacking yer knuckles left, right and center."

"Not the girls," Louise had observed wryly.

At the time, I'd assumed the girls went to another school but Steve's comment made me wonder what happened up country.

On the far side of the temple, a larger building made from dark, polished wood with a covered veranda drew my attention. This would likely be the housing area, the *vihara*, for the resident monks so I made my way in that direction. Rounding the corner of the temple a group of boys with shaved heads and ochre robes came into view, walking in the garden in front of the broad wooded steps leading up to the veranda. A small group of boys lounged on the deck, talking and laughing. Then a shout went up and multiple faces turned my way, followed by a mad scramble. In moments, I was surrounded by a knot of giggling, smiling faces. I wyed the group and many wyed me back. More than a few of them jostled and elbowed each other, giggling, in orbit around the newest diversion.

An adult monk appeared on the veranda and the kids scattered. He descended the steps and calmly strode over to where I was standing with a few of the remaining boys. We wyed and greeted each other. Now what? I smiled and extracted my Peace Corps Thai book. There wasn't anything I could find for, "Hi, can I sleep here? There's no hotel in town." I had a few phrases marked and the first one was, "Sorry, I can't speak Thai." I gave the phonetics a try.

"Kor tod, pom mai pu pasa Thai, krup."

The monk looked at me smiling, touched his eye with a forefinger and nodded to the book. The phrase was written in Thai and I held the page for him indicating the passage. He nodded and said, "Sorry, my Ingris not good."

Better than my Thai, at any rate. I tapped my chest and tried to read the introduction phrase - <u>my name is.</u>

Thai Time

"Ching kong chan kur Vern, krup."

He peered at me for a moment then said, "Von."

I nodded affirmatively and took a shot at <u>What's your name.</u>

"Ching kong kuhn chew a-rai, krup?"

The monk now grinned, understanding my butchered effort and touched his chest, *"Aachan Mee."*

So his name was Aachan Mee. Making progress. Now the sixty four thousand dollar question. I found the dictionary words for "sleep" and "here" and tried to link them together.

"Pom nang chini, krup?"

I pressed my palms together and rested my head on them, trying to do a charades version of the question. Aachan Mee dipped his head, struggling to formulate a response, then said, "You want sleep here?"

I nodded affirmatively, "Yes, if I may."

He seemed relieved somehow, and responded, "No problem. *Mai pen rai, krup,*" and moved towards the wooden steps, beckoning me to follow. The mob of little boys was back, giggling and following him up the steps. I slipped out of my sandals and left them besides others on the stoop. Aachan Mee's approving glance told me I was at least doing something right.

We walked together down the wide veranda. About half way along, Aachan Mee stopped and indicated with his open palm, "You can sleep here." Open air, nice view out over the forest into the valley. What's not to like.

"Thank you. *Krup koon, krup,*" I managed.

Leaning my backpack against the wall of the building, I asked another important question – where is the bathroom. I'd got pretty good with that one, *"Hong nam, yoo tee nai, Krup?"*

Aachan Mee said something to one of the boys who wyed to him and then reached for my hand. Better to show than try to explain, and my bladder was grateful. He led me back down the steps and around to the far side of the *vihara* building. A chattering group of young monks surged along with us, also vying to take my other hand and pull me along too.

It was a clean, simple bathhouse with five squat toilet stalls along one side and five dipper style washrooms opposite. My guides milled about outside while I relieved myself and then we flowed back and up on to the veranda.

The Appearance of Things

As we walked, I told them my name was Vern and that I was from America. This got a laugh, but I'm not sure why. The tonal nature of the language probably made for some amusing mistakes by farang like me. Maybe I just told them my name is Mud or something.

Aachan Mee was waiting beside my pack when we returned. He'd brought a clay water jug topped with a glass and set it beside my gear, on the floor.

"Kuhn Von, you like food now?"

He looked at me with such kindness and concern. It was certainly the case that I was hungry and thirsty. One of the phrases I'd memorized, because it was so true, was, "I like Thai food." It seemed appropriate right now so I nodded and replied, *"Pom chop a-han Thai, Krup."* That got Aachan Mee laughing. He turned to a tall, young monk standing nearby, older than the boys, and said something. The young man wyed and departed, gliding down the path towards town.

It was dusk now and a few lights glimmered below in the town, a few others in the distance across the valley. A temple bell had rung earlier and one by one the boys had drifted away toward the Buddha hall. I was alone now on the veranda and in the fading light, unpacked a few things to make my impromptu camp comfortable for the night. The air was warm enough that I could make do with just my tropical sleep sack, but I pulled out the down sleeping bag as well to use for padding between me and the wooden floor. I smoothed the fabric and stretched out, feeling the luxury of lying down, my head braced on the side of my pack. The night sounds of crickets and frogs drifted up from the forest below as well as a hint of jasmine incense from somewhere. I listened and drifted, images of the past few days like lucid dreams - Marisa's pretty smile when she waved, children riding a water buffalo, saffron robed monks walking beside the road.

A light tapping came from the steps area and, sitting up, I saw the young monk who had earlier gone down the hill towards town. He made "come hither" motions with his hand so I stood and walked down the stairs to join him. We wyed to each other then he turned, indicating I should follow.

At the Dharma hall a young woman knelt facing one of the Buddha statues at the front. She finished her prayer or whatever it was and bowed when we approached.

The young monk said something, indicating the woman. I caught the word *"a-hahn,"* meaning "food" and nodded. She and I wyed to each other then she opened a plastic bag, extracting a square, folded banana leaf package and a little, hammered aluminum rice pot. As we sat together on the edge of the platform she spread the banana leaf open to reveal a steaming stir-fry of vegetables and meat bits, probably chicken. A generous scoop of the cooked white rice was laid in beside the vegetables. Lastly, she pulled out a metal spoon and fork, wrapped in a white cloth, and rested the service on the leaf. It looked and smelled terrific and my stomach betrayed me with a growl. A shy smile and she withdrew back to the front with the Buddha statues, her back to me, a long black ponytail extending to her waist.

It was not yet fully dark but candlelight was emanating from the temple. I could see the backs of a dozen children and hear their evening chanting, their young voices like children singing anywhere. The meal was in fact quite delicious, with piquant basil and four alarm hot chilies. I ate in silence, basking in the quiet beauty of the place. Finishing, I rolled up the utensils in the white cloth and the banana leaf in itself. My rustling of the plastic bag putting away the utensils alerted the young woman who stood and recollected the rice pot.

I didn't know how much to pay for the meal but when I removed a fifty baht note from my wallet, her lovely face recoiled in shock and she waved her hands in a "no, no, no!" gesture.

"Mai pen rai," she said, no problem.

I understood it then, as an offering to the temple, and returned the note to my wallet, somewhat abashed with my clumsiness.

I wyed to her.

"Krup koon, Krup," in thanks. Such a sweet smile and lovely eyes. She could have been thirteen or thirty, I couldn't tell. One last *"sawasdee"* and she was off down the trail.

Walking over to the temple, I looked inside. Aachan Mee and the other young monk were moving around the room distributing small, white candles to each child. He spotted me at the door and indicated I should enter and sit, which I did. A young monk shyly passed me a candle as well, and returned to the front, facing the Buddha image. Aachan Mee tapped a dark, bowl-like bell on a cushion and led the group in a simple chant I'd heard before. It began *"Buddang saranang kechami"* and cycled through three repetitions, three times. At the end, he rang the bell three more times and we all bowed a wye towards the Buddha statues.

He stood and exited the temple, lighting his candle from one of the large, burning candles that flanked the doorway. Following his lead, we all exited, igniting our own candles on the way out and in single file walked three times around the temple. We ended by placing our still burning candles on the layer cake ledges of a bell shaped monument in the garden. In the simple, charming ritual, I harkened back to that first night at the temple in Tanjung, Bali, when a beautiful young woman named Kadek tied a cloth around my head so I could enter the temple.

Such a contrast with last night, sitting by the river in Chang Mai with Alan and the two French guys nodding on heroin. It made me smile. The whiplash of being on the road, hurtling between the ridiculous and the sublime.

Back on the veranda, before I crashed out, I extracted my little wooden recorder. I needed more practice, but simple melodies, with no sharps or flats, were within my grasp. In this quite setting a harmonica riff would be jarring but the soft, wooden flute struck me as just right. There was a little, mediaeval riff I was working on, from the album "The Lady and the Unicorn" by John Renbourn. As I quietly played, a few of the children emerged from the *vihara* and sat near me. We smiled at each other, but nobody spoke. They drifted away after a few minutes and I was left alone on the deck. The soft jungle night hummed with light and I fell asleep gazing at stars and fireflies.

I awoke at dawn in the glow of a clear morning. There was a distinct sensation of feeling safe and protected even before I recollected where I was. Maybe the lingering flavor of a dream. Aachan Mee found me as I finished rolling up my sleeping gear, and I thanked him for his kindness. There was a small offering box in the Dharma hall and, as I departed, I slipped the fifty baht note through the slot. I almost tipped my hat to the Buddha image at the front of the hall, but the gesture suddenly seemed cocky and ungracious. Instead, I turned and bowed to the statue, my palms pressed together. It wasn't a bow to a deity. More of a grateful acknowledgement for this place.

Walking down the hill it felt like an important discovery - that I could count on simple but reliable accommodation at rural wats. There was always a wat not too far away in Thailand. Wouldn't work for female travelers though, something to reckon with if I did hook up with a travel partner.

The little minibus got me to Taton just past nine. Taton wasn't a town, really, but there was a little café near the boat area where I enjoyed two fried eggs on rice swimming in a savory green curry sauce. I eyed the boat as I chewed. It was about the same width as a rowboat, but maybe three times as long. It looked like I'd be the only passenger, along with the three boatmen and a cargo of plump burlap bags they were loading in the front. The bags were squishy and changed shape as they fell and settled. Maybe rice or some other seed?

Fifteen minutes before we were to leave, a green Toyota Landcruiser slid to a dusty halt and three people stepped out - a Thai man and woman and Alan Firestone! He grinned and waved when he saw me.

"Hello! We made it," he declared self-evidently. He introduced his travel companions as Tam and Prong. Tam was a pilot for Thai Airways and spoke excellent English. His very beautiful wife spoke less well, but was comfortable to let Tam do the talking. They'd both lived in the States while he trained on the big Boeing jets.

"Alan joined us on the drive up this morning," Tam explained. "After last night we didn't expect to see him awake," he added with a laugh.

They'd left Chang Mai before five in the morning. Alan had connected with them at Je t'aime and when he learned they'd set up a car and driver he volunteered to contribute to the costs and come along.

"So you knew about the river trip already?" I asked Tam.

"Oh yes. Two years ago I made this trip with some school friends. I talked about it so much that Prong wanted to come and see for herself."

He squeezed her hand and they beamed at each other.

One of the boatmen said something and Tam nodded, "Time to get aboard."

I handed my pack over, and saw it wedged in between the sidewall of the boat and a couple of the burlap bags. It was already getting warm and I pulled on my baseball cap and settled on a bench seat. The water felt cool on my hand as I trailed it in the current. Alan sat beside me while Tam and Prong were forward.

"I'm glad you told me about this," Alan said. "Yesterday, when I was talking with Tam in the garden, he mentioned a river trip they were taking this morning. When I heard Taton, I figured it had to be the same one as you." I was pleased to see Alan. When he wasn't nodding on heroin, he was engaging and funny.

The boatmen shoved us out into the current and we were off. The Kok River wasn't very wide or deep. It reminded me of the Merced River, flowing through the magnificent Yosemite Valley in California. Cool, clear water, mostly about waist deep and about forty feet across.

Alan was sporting a woven palm coolie hat. With his dark beard and open shirt he could have been a stand-in on a "Robinson Crusoe" film set. His nose, in profile, was startlingly straight and pointed at the end. As we drifted with the current, I told him about my experience at the Wat and he nodded, "Yeah, Wats are great. I stayed at one down in Surat Thani, in the south. They had pilgrim rooms, so I wasn't out on a deck or anything. It was what the Thais call a "practice monastery", where monks and lay people can go to learn deep meditation. You were in a regular one, I think. Mostly just kids, huh?"

"Yeah, that's right. I only saw two adults the whole time. The rest were like little boys in grammar school."

"Wah! Look at that!" Alan pointed.

A hatless, balding fisherman ahead on the opposite bank was pulling in a hand line. He held two, silvery white fish by the tail with his teeth. They draped down his bare chest. The impression was of a walrus with large tusks. He gazed at us passively as we floated by him.

An hour or so into the journey the boatman in the prow made his way back to Tam and said something. Tam nodded and turned back to us, "We are going to hit the first set of rapids in a couple of minutes. He wants us to get down low, sitting on the floor of the boat."

At the same moment, the motor picked up speed. We had been idling along, going just a bit faster than the flow for steering control. Now, the skipper gripped the motor control post and seemed to be looking ahead at something none of us could see. I hadn't heard about the rapids, but since boats went up and down the river, how bad could they be? Tam and Prong settled themselves on the bottom of the boat, using their bench seat as a backrest. They gripped the sides of the boat, talking and laughing. Alan and I looked at each other and did the same, settling ourselves down just as we rounded a bend in the river.

Ahead, boulders the size of Volkswagens dotted the suddenly roaring river. They looked to be dangerously jagged, not something I'd want to hit in any sort of boat. We dropped into a slot of white water and a bow wave broke back over us. Prong screamed and buried her head into Tam's chest. He held her close with his free arm and shouted, "Yahoo!"

The turbulence went on for the better part of mile. Twice our little boat scraped along the side of a boulder, but the skipper minimized the impact and kept us in the center of the flow. The third boatman was hunkered down behind us and looked terrified, a vision that was not reassuring.

At last, we sailed out into a wide, calm area, soaked but exhilarated. The skipper slowed the motor back to the cruising speed and the other two boatmen used scoops made from cut-out bleach bottles to bail water out of the boat. I looked back at the captain and he was smoking and laughing. He pointed to the man who had looked afraid, "No swim!" and laughed some more. It wasn't the first time I'd heard the paradox of people who earned their living on the water being unable to swim. To my western mind this sounded like bad planning.

The midday sun was intense and the cooling effect of our wet clothing was very welcome. Alan pulled out a blue packet of Drum tobacco and extracted a pre-rolled joint.

"How about an afternoon smoke on the river," he grinned.

Tam and Prong waved the joint away, but the thin skipper took a long hit and cackled when he handed it back. We were pleasantly high when the boat pulled over to a settlement on the opposite side of the river. While one of our crew stood on the shore holding the bowline, the non-swimmer began to pass burlap bags to the men filing down the river bank. They didn't look Thai to me. Three other men standing back on the bank holding the reins of horses wore robes. They had wary eyes with Fu Manchu type moustaches and wispy beards. They looked like photos I'd seen of Mongolian shepherds, but what were they doing here?

Tam was holding Prong's hand and they gazed placidly back out over the river. Their silence felt strange to me. Two of the men who had carried burlap bags away now returned, carrying watermelon sized black plastic bags that were tightly wrapped with electrical tape. Our boatman received these new bags and buried them beneath the burlap at the front of the boat.

The three horsemen gazed down at us and I had a flash of how the pirate crew had looked at Rod and I, that day back in Tanjung. I glanced back at the skipper. He was studying Alan and me. There was a smile on his face, but his eyes looked hard. Not dead, like shark eyes. More like the guys I'd seen collecting the bar fines for the girls in Bangkok. I guess we all understood each other. Maybe the ganja was making me a little paranoid. Maybe not. The way Tam was looking at his fingernails suggested that it was probably best not to appear too interested.

We made the rest of the journey in a tranquil, late afternoon somnambulance.

The Appearance of Things

There had been two more sets of rapids, but not nearly so harrowing as the first set. By the time our little boat pulled into the landing at Maesai, we were moderately toasted by the sun and another of Alan's joints.

Tam and Prong actually had a car and driver waiting for them. Tam explained, "I have a flight out the day after tomorrow. We have to be back in Bangkok tomorrow night, I'm afraid. But that was quite a trip, wasn't it?"

He put his arm around Prong and she smiled at us, "It was very good to meeting you. Did you enjoy?"

Behind us, the boat had pulled back out on to the Kok Rover. I looked at the skipper. He wasn't smiling, but he held up an open palm that impressed me as a sort of universal "go in peace" signal. I wyed back to him and turned to Prong.

"Yes," I answered her inquiry, "especially the first set of rapids. Were you frightened?"

She turned to Tam who said something in Thai and she laughed, "Oh yes! Very big fear, but no problem."

Alan and I wished them well and waved as their car retreated.

"Well, this is the real Golden Triangle," said Alan. "Sort of the Wild West. Man, those guys back at the horse station. Where did they come in from, huh? And those two bags we picked up." Alan looked at me archly, "What do you imagine was in those?"

The two French guys back in Chang Mai had suggested another guesthouse to Alan, here in Maesai, called "La Vigne". There was a wooden signpost at the end of the little dock that said just that, with an arrow pointing to the right. Not having a better suggestion myself, I figured "why not?" We hefted our backpacks and walked along the tree-lined street. Some of the buildings we passed had a European air, although rather worn, and I imagined how they might have appeared during the French colonial times. Not as pronounced as the English in Singapore, but something apart from Asia nonetheless.

"So what do you think was in the bags?" I asked Alan.

"Oh, I'd say about a hundred thousand dollars' worth of the best heroin in the world," he replied and smacked his lips.

La Vigne was quite similar in layout to Je t'aime in Chang Mai. Picnic tables and benches under the trees along a small stream, an overgrown but lovely garden, bungalows built off the garden and a main, older house in the front.

Thai Time

It looked ok and it was just for one night. I wasn't sure about Alan, but I had five days left on my Thai visa and needed to make the leap across the border to Laos at Vientiane. On my map it had looked possible to go straight in from Chang Rai. There were roads that snaked across the mountains, following the Mekong, all the way to the border crossing at Nong Kai. But Marisa had been adamant about not going that way.

"It's too uncertain," she had said, "and you could be stuck for days and not make Vientiane on time."

There were other places to enter Laos along the Mekong, but as she had said, "The war isn't over yet." I had to bite the bullet – go back south to Bangkok and then take the train east to Nong Kai.

We split a room and Alan wandered out to the green while I cleaned up. When I caught up with him he was seated at one of the picnic tables. I strolled up in my cheerful, American mind-state and stopped dead. These guys looked like they all had a bad case of the flu - dark circles under the eyes, lethargic, unkempt, an air of unhealthiness hanging over them like circling birds. Alan was his usual beaming self, chatting away and apparently oblivious to the droopy reception he was getting.

He looked up and smiled at my approach, "Hey, you clean up well! Grab a seat."

His three companions nodded acknowledgement when I took a seat at the table but didn't introduce themselves. The guy in the middle, with stringy, dirty blond hair, had a porcelain plate before him that held a heaping teaspoon of pearly white powder in the center. He was focused on making a series of little piles around the plate using the tip of a long, pointed knife. The two on either side looked on with a grim, black haired intensity. The image conjured, unbidden, the vision of a Rembrandt painting I'd seen in the Rijksmuseum in Amsterdam, of burghers measuring out gold in a dimly lit trading house. Except that the burghers had seemed more alive than this crew.

"Dom says this is triple nine, straight out of Burma," Alan seemed elated.

Dom finished his chopping and mounding and picked up a short length of cut plastic soda straw. He snorted one pile in his left nostril then one more in his right. It was the first and only time I saw him smile. The plate went around, Alan eagerly awaiting his portion. It came to me, "Well, here I am in the Golden Triangle. Let's try the local stuff."

I snorted both little piles. Unlike cocaine, there was not the immediate feedback from my body. Within a few minutes, however, I felt the mentally sticky haze descending and simultaneously remembered why I didn't like this feeling. I guess other people have a positive effect from heroin. I find it more akin to pouring airplane glue into the workings of a pocket watch. I sat nodding with the best of them, thinking, "This is not my drug."

Maybe it's the opium roots of the stuff, but I slept until mid-morning. It was after ten when I wandered out into the garden and found Alan hard at it with his newfound friends. Two more had joined them and all six were sailing high, smoking cigarettes and staring off into space. I wondered how long the others had been here. For an instant, I wondered if we'd been killed in the rapids and the Christians were right and this was hell. It passed, but I did want to get going.

"Alan?" A bleary eyed, upturned head then a light of recognition in the eyes.

"Vern? Hey, how ya doin'?" he mumbled.

"Pretty good. I'm going down to Chang Rai now, see if I can get a bus down to Bangkok today."

Too many words, I guess. His eyes lost focus and he seemed to be looking over my shoulder. I surveyed the group and frankly wondered if heroin was really anybody's drug.

Alan and I had spoken of Laos. He'd said going to at least Vientiane intrigued him but not just now. He didn't have a long-range plan other than to stay in Southeast Asia for an undefined amount of time. He hinted at someone special in Bangkok but never went further into it with me. I had to wonder, looking at him here in the humid light of late morning, if that special someone was heroin.

I wanted to turn and go but my feet stayed rooted, the feeling that I was failing a friend. I mean, I'd stopped a complete stranger from stepping in front of a bus last summer in London. He looked left and started to launch out into the street, the bus coming from the right. My left arm shot up across his chest and restrained him and I think the side of the bus grazed his nose. We'd looked at each other for a moment, stunned, and he'd mumbled, "Thanks," and was gone. Now, here was a guy I scarcely knew making some choices that appeared dubious, but he was an adult and I wasn't his fucking mother. What do you do?

I rested a hand on his shoulder, "So Alan, I hope you make it over to Vientiane. Maybe I'll see you there, huh?"

The touch on his shoulder brought him back and he made contact again.

"Vientiane? Yeah, probably. That was good times yesterday, huh?" he grinned, then spied the plate and slid it gingerly across the table towards us. "How about one for the road?"

His face struggled with the effort to look arch, then crumpled, like an unhappy thought.

"No, I'm good. Ok, well, hope I see you down the road."

Before I headed out, I left a note stuck to his pack, wishing him well and saying I hoped I'd see him in Vientiane. Walking down the road from La Vigne, I had the overwhelming sense I was abandoning someone in need. It was not a good feeling.

I flagged down a supersized *tuk-tuk* on the Chang Rai road and hopped aboard. Face to face with a grinning monk. A-wise, as he introduced himself, was on his way down to a wat in Bangkok. His English was very accomplished, and he immediately started drilling into me.

"America is a long distance to come, isn't it? Why are you here in Thailand?"

There was an appealing, open sincerity in his manner that was very inviting. I launched into my story of being on the road "to find out." He listened and nodded.

"It's wisdom that seeks wisdom," he said with a smile.

The storefront that served as a bus station in Chang Rai had a forlorn air, as though the bus had stopped running years ago. When A-wise and I entered the empty office, the only action was a slowly creaking ceiling fan. A moment later, an anxious looking man in rumpled khaki entered and wyed to A-wise and then to me. He spoke briefly with A-wise then slipped behind the desk and seated himself. He had large, soulful eyes that appeared wet, the whites yellowish and bloodshot.

"Bangkok?" he said, looking at me.

I nodded affirmatively and said, "*Krup*" which sort of means "yes" in this context. While he prepared the two tickets, another man drifted into the room and leaned against a sidewall, supervising the proceedings.

"*Roy hah sip baht,*" a hundred fifty baht, he said, and I pulled out my bill fold to pay. A-wise reached inside of his orange robe and removed a plastic sandwich bag containing money. When he opened the bag and extracted a few bank notes, the man leaning against the wall startled forward, his eyes wide. The seated ticket seller also looked concerned and watched the small plastic bag and the monk's hands as if a venomous snake had suddenly appeared. A-wise took note of their consternation and said something in Thai. The supervisor and the clerk looked guardedly at each other but seemed to relax. A-wise looked over to me wryly. "Monks are not supposed to handle money. I have special permission from the abbot since I am traveling alone."

We collected our tickets and exited out on to the street. It was now about twelve noon and the bus didn't depart for Bangkok until four. It was going to be another all-nighter, but at least I didn't have to worry where I was going to sleep tonight.

"I must go to the main wat here, to bring a message to the abbot. It is a place you can rest until the time to depart. Will you come with me?"

A-wise was not physically large yet his clear, calm gaze made him seem present in a big way. It's funny how, sometimes, trust is immediate.

"Yes. Thank you."

We walked in silence away from the office, down a side turning and toward the temple whose green, red and gold roof tiles stood out against the blue of the sky.

Entering the compound of the wat, A-wise was greeted by two monks, one of whom retreated back towards the *vihara*. I guessed he was going to inform the abbot and sure enough, a few minutes later he re-appeared followed by a very much older man. The robes were the same, the plain burnt orange cloth, but he was accorded a deference I hadn't seen before. A-wise wyed then knelt and bowed to him three times, touching his forehead to the earth. Well, not quite into the dirt. With each bow he placed his palms on the ground and it was the back of his hands that touched his forehead. I had wyed the old monk as he approached and now he looked squarely at me with what I took to be interest and amusement. There was a youthful light in his eyes that conferred agelessness to his countenance. He was somehow old and not old, at the same time.

A-wise arose from his final obeisance and the old monk motioned towards me. A-wise glanced my way and spoke quietly to the abbot. During this exchange the old man continued to gaze at me, a physician listening to a professional opinion. There was nothing I could discern as critical or judgmental in his eyes. He looked at me in a kindly manner and we smiled at each other. Then it was over and he turned and walked back the way he had come. I was aware of a wish in myself that he not go, which surprised me.

A-wise said, "I will leave you here. Please be comfortable. There is water," he indicated a clay jar in the nearby Dharma hall, "and I will see you on the bus." He turned to go then stopped and looked back at me, "It is a long journey. If you wish to bathe you are welcome to use the bath house there," inclining his head toward a long, low building across from the open platform of the Dharma hall.

"Thank you, A-wise. *Krup coon Krup*. See you on the bus."

We wyed and he disappeared along the same path the abbot had taken.

I dragged my backpack and day sack over into the shade afforded by the roof of the Dharma hall, extracted my copy of the Somerset Maugham short stories I'd bought on Khosan Road, and settled back for a read. I was alone with the Buddha statue at the front of the hall. The statue's right arm presented an open palm, held aloft and I recollected yesterday's boatman as he departed, how very much he resembled the impassive form before me.

A memory of Alan's face this morning, at the table, the anguish crouching in the dark, dilated pupils. When do I get involved and when do I walk away? I was getting pretty good at walking away.

There was a physical discomfort in me and I felt suddenly restless. I put the book down. Pulling my pack down flat, I seated myself and folded my legs Indian fashion. I felt self-conscious and looked around, half expecting to see some monks laughing and pointing, but I was still alone. Why should I feel weird trying to meditate in a Buddhist temple? My chest felt tight and my brain was still a bit gummy from yesterday's libations, but I took a deep breath and settled down with my Transcendental Meditation mantra. I needed to smooth out some of the wrinkles.

After about twenty minutes, I had to admit to myself that my thoughts were all over the place. I wasn't blissful and calm, nor did I feel any better about leaving Alan at La Vigne this morning. A quick peek around and I unfolded. Maybe I wasn't cut out to be a meditator type, so I picked up the book again and read a story called "The Pool", about a Scottish man who falls in love with a half-caste Samoan girl in the South Seas. Like so many tales of Westerners in Asia, it ended tragically. As much as anything, the tragic events center around cultural differences and misunderstandings. In "Lord Jim" Conrad had his hapless hero take a bullet in the chest to pay for his culturally conditioned errors of judgment. Maugham had his character,

The Appearance of Things

Lawson, living in his Scottish reality. The girl, Ellen, was living in her Samoan reality. Even though they experienced the same world together, each saw a different world.

I closed the book and looked up. It seemed the expression on the face of the Buddha statue was more amused than when I sat down. I smiled back and thought about a comment Art had made, sitting at the Chinaman's back in Tanjung. We'd been talking about the travelers' scene over at Kuta Beach.

"A lot of people hold the world at arm's length. You can travel all around but never really let anything in, not let it touch you. Hell, I guess that's what a tourist is, somebody who goes around being an inspector, collecting experiences like they were postage stamps."

He'd laughed then and winked at me, "This is the school. Take the curriculum."

Chapter 8
Laos

> The subject tonight is Love
> And for tomorrow night as well,
> As a matter of fact
> I know of no better topic
> For us to discuss
> Until we all
> Die!
>
> *Hafiz*

I

The all-nighter bus from Chang Rai to Bangkok was comfortable enough, but I rolled out into the early afternoon light of Bangkok feeling bleary and rumpled. Twenty hours of driving with a few stops for food and toileting will do that to you. A-wise sat quietly for most of the journey and when he bid me farewell at the station he looked no more the worse for wear than when we'd met. My stubble of beard growth felt sweaty and gritty. A-wise didn't seem to have any facial hair. In the humid heat, I envied him.

The second all-nighter was going to be better as I was able to book a sleeper from Bangkok to Nong Kai. The train didn't depart until nearly nine o'clock at night, so I rented a cheap room near to the Hua Lamphong train station to rest and refresh. The oddly named Jasmine Seedy Hotel lived up to the seedy part, but I had the pleasure of a bath and getting off the street for a while before the train left. The laughter of two Australian men shooting pool with some of the girls from the lobby rang through the thin walled building and added a homey feel to the place. Stretching out on the simple bed felt luxurious. I relaxed back and let my eyes rest for a moment.

I awoke with a start and had a momentary flash of paranoia. It had become instantly dark outside my window, in the blink of an eye. The brain kicked in. I'd stretched out on the bed and closed my eyes to rest them. It was as if somebody turned out the lights. I reached out and fumbled the switch of the bed lamp. What time was it? I grabbed my day sack and fished out my watch. A reassuring seven thirty. I hadn't missed my train, but it was time to go.

Crossing over to the station from the hotel plunged me into the swarm of humanity that is Bangkok at night. Hua Lamphong station glowed with a golden light, while crowds surged through banks of open doors. Once inside, I studied the departure board and found my platform, number six.

The great hall was lined with eateries and the cornucopia of alluring aromas reminded my empty stomach to growl at me. Near the entry gate, an enterprising cook had set up a dozen small tables and twice that many folding metal chairs. I ordered a plate of chicken sate with peanut sauce and a pad thai, my favorite stir-fried noodle dish so far. Settling my pack beside the small table, I sat down and tucked in. A young woman shyly brought my Thai iced tea to me and gently positioned it on the rickety little table. I passed her a couple of one baht coins and she giggled when she accepted them, then quickly retreated.

"You don't have to tip them, you know," said an accented English voice to my left. He had a blond, layered "rock star" haircut and an incongruous thick, dark moustache under equally dark eyes, but his good-natured smile caused me to smile back. As I was about to find out, Peter Dugoslav was a mechanic from Dusseldorf, Germany, on holiday in Thailand.

"So I've been told," I replied, "but I like to offer a little something when I get good service."

"Or when the girl is cute, huh?"

That made me laugh and we fell into easy conversation. It turned out that Peter was also headed to Vientiane on the same train.

"*Ja, ja*, I have three weeks left on my holiday. I will go up all the way to Luang Prabang. This last year I was in Vientiane, such a *schöne platz*, a beautiful place. But this year I will go up the road and know more of Laos."

When we stood up to walk for the gate, I was surprised that Peter was a head shorter. His eyes widened slightly as he too noted the difference but said nothing.

Once aboard the train, I stowed my pack on my top bunk and pulled the little set of curtains closed. Peter was four seats forward and also on an upper bunk. He stored his pack likewise and turned to me, "So, I think a Mekong in the club car, yes?"

That beatific, wide smile. This seemed to be a man who loved life and it was catching. "Sounds good. Maybe they have Sang Thip!" and off we went.

Our train had departed the station at exactly 8:45 pm and now the lights of the city sparkled in the windows as we clicky-clacked our way out of Bangkok. The lounge car was daunting and somewhat disappointing. Right up until the moment I pushed the door open and entered, the notion of going to Laos had been exotic and daring. I felt myself to be a bit of the adventurer. That tenuous self-image evaporated when I entered the lounge and was faced with a coach full of Europeans, Canadians, Australians and even a few other Americans. It was a cattle car of tourists, all heading the same way. I swallowed and waded in. Peter immediately found a table of fellow Germans and motioned for me to join him. He really was full of beans, what the Germans call *"gemütlichkeit"*. It was one of those useful words I learned last summer and Peter was its embodiment. In short order, everybody was high and laughing their heads off.

Slowly and to my relief, as the evening unfurled in the gently rocking coach, I discovered that not everybody was heading for Laos after all. One large group of Australians planned to attend a famous Issan Elephant festival, north of Nong Kai and still in Thailand. More than a few of the others were planning on crossing over to Vientiane for a few days only for visa renewal purposes and quickly returning to Thailand. A Canadian couple, blond haired, blue eyed Christy and her darker boyfriend Paul, were planning on going up as far as Vang Vien. Personally, I was open to going further north, but I wanted to test the waters in Vientiane for a while. Once I got settled, I'd ask around and see what I could find out.

Our train pulled into Nong Kai almost twelve hours later, a little before nine in the morning. Peter, myself, another German guy named Klaus, Christy and Paul were all heading the twenty or so miles to the international bridge over to Vientiane. The largest taxi we could find, an old Mercedes, was still a tight fit for the five of us with all our gear, but we made it work and by ten in the morning we were in line at the Thai border station. The crossing was quite a racket. After we checked out of Thailand, we hoisted our packs and began walking towards the bridge that was about a hundred feet away. An official little man in control of the turn-style informed us that foreigners were not allowed to walk across the bridge and we would need to take a taxi to the Laos side, about a thousand feet away. We were eyed by a small group of men, laughing and smoking beside a three car fleet of old Chevrolets. Paul was inclined to argue the point, but in the end we all put in our twenty baht and piled in on top of each other to make the crossing. The Laotian border guards watched us silently as we unloaded and headed towards their station. Inside, a mirthless official examined each of our passports in turn, looking us over and stamping the visa page. When he got to mine, he flipped through my passport, as if searching my travel history then looked up at me. "American," he said. It was an observation, not a question and I felt uneasy that I was the only person so singled out. He said no more, stamped my Laos visa and returned my papers. We filed out of the other side of the office into the tree-shaded lanes of Vientiane.

It was only a thousand feet across the Mekong but the charming riverside walk, the horse drawn carriages, the French colonial mansards on many of the grand old buildings - all spoke to the fact that I really was in another country, almost in another century. Peter said he was heading for the place he stayed and liked last year, called the Saylom Hotel. Paul and Christy had a recommendation for a place called The Constellation Hotel, but they trailed along with us to see the Saylom, just in case. In the lobby, Klaus, who'd been quite taciturn, told Peter in German that he'd see him later at the German café. He passed his bag off to Peter, bowed slightly to the rest of us and left. He appeared to have business to attend to and as I watched his departing back, I wondered what sort of business that was. Peter shrugged and arranged a shared room for the two of them. I secured a single room and dropped off my gear.

The Saylom was fine for me, but the Canadian couple were a bit sniffy about the place and chose to push on to The Constellation. I liked the Saylom, with its powder blue, wooden siding and its sleepy, topical ambience of ceiling fans and potted palms. The bare wooden floor had once been decoratively painted and in the less used corners the hint of elegant swirls and lines could still be seen. My simple room was tidy and looked out into the trees shading the avenue below.

The first order of business was to get set up with a pocket full of the local currency. I'd paid my first night in Thai baht, a remarkably cheap ten Thai baht. I already liked the place. In Thailand, ten baht got you nothing. Here, I had a decent, clean hotel room for less than fifty cents!

Stashing my remaining Thai baht in my passport folder, which I knew I'd need on the return, I prepared to find a moneychanger. By then, Peter was back down in the lobby, as we had agreed, and we headed out on to the street. Up on the next block was La Banque Royale du Laos and we queued up at the foreign exchange window. The little sign stating today's exchange rate did not prepare me for what happened next.

I pulled out a fifty dollar traveler's cheque. The exchange rate was two thousand two hundred kip to the dollar. The largest denomination note they had was a hundred kip note - and what a note it was! In the old French style, the note was large - maybe five inches wide and nine inches long. One side had a florid Gauguin-like painting of an Asian woman surrounded by opulent flowers. The reverse side had a prosaic picture of the king and the Lao script, similar to the Thai style of writing. Within a few moments I had before me eleven piles, each the size of a good paperback book! The sheer volume of the notes required me to zip open my day sack, transfer the water bottle and reading book to the front compartment, then stuff the rear chamber full of bank notes. I couldn't believe it! My day sack was literally stuffed with money, eleven hundred large bank notes. The teller looked on impassively during this operation, but I thought I detected a hint of amusement in her dark eyes.

I glanced over to Peter and saw him involved in the same stand-up comedy routine, stuffing notes into a side pouch that most definitely was not up to the task.

"It looks like we just robbed the bank," I observed. Peter was shaking his head, "Last year it was nine hundred to the dollar. That was bad enough. *Mein gott,* all this money now!"

We found our way back out on to the street. Peter was grinning, his little side pouch and both of his button-down pants pockets brimming with bank notes. He clapped his hands together and rubbed them, "So, the German café is this way," he nodded up the street, "and I will show you where the market is as we go along."

Peter enjoyed playing the tour guide and I was happy to let him, being the new kid in town. Again, I was struck with the wide, tree-lined boulevards, how "French" it all seemed. As we strolled, I imagined that it could have been

Paris of the 1890s, except for the cars and the odd garrison building with sand bags in front of the door.

"Pathet Lao headquarters," Peter observed.

We passed The Constellation Hotel, three stories high and looking like a Mississippi River steamboat. The Victorian wood filigree accents on the white verandas had red and pink bougainvilleas intermittently entwined and the entire structure sagged a bit in the middle, just like the old steam boats. A bit further on we passed La Paix, the restaurant Marisa had mentioned back in Bangkok.

"Peter, have you tried that one, La Paix," I asked, pointing.

"Oh *ja*, it's good I think. I had the steak and chips plate last year. It was good. Buffalo steak. A little tough," he smiled, "and a little expensive. Come, you will like the German café and a cold beer."

He marched on and I followed, a bit behind. From the rear, his broad shoulders and shorter legs reminded me of a bulldog. A nice bulldog with strong arms and a determined pace.

In the next block we turned right, on to another wide boulevard. I was surprised to see ahead what appeared to be a copy of the Arc de Triomphe, poking up above the trees. Peter noticed my gaze, "The king had that built three years back. The Americans gave him cement to build a new runway at the airport," Peter laughed at this little joke. "Instead, they built this. It's pretty good I think." His blue eyes twinkled with merriment. "It's, how they say, making ploughs out of cannons."

We proceeded towards the monument down the avenue until we came to the first cross street. Peter pointed across the avenue, down the smaller street, "The big market is that way, about a hundred meter. It's very good. Better in the morning, I think. Tomorrow we will go early for soup." He held up a hand with the index finger touching the thumb and mimed the classic pose of a French chef, kissing his fingers, "The best soups in Asia."

We turned right on to the little side street ourselves, going away from the market, and after a dozen paces we arrived at his "German Café". The wrought iron sign over the entry read simply "Biergarten" and Peter led the way through a small bar room. In fact, with the dark wood and long bar it reminded me more of an English pub than it did a German restaurant. Out the wide backdoor, however, was a large atrium in which two tall, flowering trees provided shade over groups of tables and benches. Much more "Biergarten" like. Dozens of bulbous, red clay pots lined the base of the enclosing walls and from them burst forth hibiscus flowers in reds and whites and variegated yellow-golds. There was music in the background, Strauss, I think, quietly playing. The air felt cool and the space was charming, another world from the street we had just quit.

"There is Klaus," said Peter, and then I saw him too, sitting alone at one of the smaller metal tables near to the trunk of the tree. His face was transformed, happy and open. With his shoulder length, curly blond hair he looked quite cherubic, transformed from the dour Deutscher of earlier in the day. A near empty glass beer stein sat before him on the table.

"Hallo Peter," he waved.

We joined him at the table and as he pulled out a chair, Peter asked in German, "*Habt du die medizin bekam?*" To me, it sounded as if Peter was asking Klaus if he had the medicine. Sure enough, Klaus nodded and produced a small, paper carton that he pushed over to Peter. I'm nosy and couldn't help trying to read the top of the box. Peter held it up so I could clearly read the penicillin label. "For the gonorrhea," he explained, "I think from Bangkok; or maybe Pattaya." He shrugged good-naturedly and slipped the box into his shirt pocket. We ordered cold bottles of Spaten beer and toasted each other. Klaus and Peter spoke English for my benefit since my German was rudimentary at best.

"To being back in Vientiane," they said and we tucked into a much too heavy lunch of sauerbraten and spaetzle. I was hungry, but in the warm, humid tropics, this was like dropping anchor, especially combined with the beer. Klaus was also interested in going north and he fell into conversation with Peter. I pushed at my half eaten plate with my fork and decided to strike out on my own. I motioned to the waiter to bring me my check. My total came to four thousand kip, in part because of the imported beer. I counted out forty of the florid bank notes and as I did so realized that it was still less than two dollars. This was going to take some getting used to.

I pushed back from the table and stood up, wishing my luncheon companions well. Peter eyed my unfinished plate and asked with some disappointment, "You didn't like the food?"

"No, no. It is delicious. I just can't eat too much when it's hot like this. The food was really good and so was the beer. Thank you for bringing me here."

Peter nodded and without comment speared the piece of untouched sauerbraten on my plate and pulled it on to his.

"I think it's good," he mumbled.

Klaus caught my eye and grinned. I almost laughed, but Peter's determination as he cut into the meat stopped me. I liked him and didn't want to hurt his feelings.

Back on the street, I made my way across the wide boulevard with the Arc de Triomphe and walked towards the public market. I knew Peter was right, that it would be better in the mornings, but I wanted to poke around on my own. About five minutes' walk down the lane there it was, hundreds of canopies supported by rope and bamboo poles. There were still plenty of people moving up and down the long, covered aisles and I plunged into the heart of the place. Passing the low platforms covered with shoes and sandals, I came to the area of meat sellers. The tables were being washed down, the area cleaned up as they were done for the day, but, just beyond, locals were milling about, bargaining for dried fish and piles of potatoes.

The aisles were apparently organized by type of merchants, greens here, root vegetables there, fruit beyond. As I wandered about I happened on the tobacco sellers section. Huge piles of shredded tobacco of different hues - cinnamon, blond and almost black. One pile completely covered the platform, maybe six feet long and two feet high and it smelled, remarkably, like Drum tobacco. It even had the same stringy, fine cut - what the Drum package called "half zware shag". I picked up a pinch under the watchful gaze of an old woman in a coolie hat. It really did smell like Drum but the texture was a little dryer. She passed me a clear plastic bag and indicated I should load it up with what I wanted. What the heck. I reached into the pile and grabbed a good handful, stuffed it into the sack and handed it over.

Her skin was chestnut brown and the flesh around her eyes crinkled when she laughed at my purchase. An old balance beam scale in front of where she squatted on the platform remained motionless when she placed my bag on the weigh plate. She leaned over and grabbed another handful of the tobacco and shoved it into the bag. The scale moved slightly. It must have been a pound or more. I started to protest but stopped. I could give it away, probably, so never mind. Squinting at me, she said something I couldn't make out and held up five fingers. Five what? Five hundred? Five thousand? From an old biscuit tin, she held up five, one hundred kip notes. Got it! I pulled out my roll of notes, peeled off five and handed them over. She nodded and handed me the bag, grinning. Papers. How do I ask for papers? I mimed rolling a cigarette, putting it in my mouth and lighting it. She watched me carefully and then began to cackle. Great. I looked around but tobacco road didn't seem to have anybody selling papers. Nobody even pipes for sale, that I could see. How did they smoke it?

The old lady tapped my forearm and pointed down the aisle, as if she had suddenly understood my want. I wyed to her and said thank you in Thai, *"Krup coon. Krup,"* and moved off down the aisle in the direction she had pointed. To my astonishment, tobacco gave way to ganja and not a little. It made Amsterdam look penny ante. Row after row of long, pressed buds. Pre-rolled joints the size of mini cigars and mountains of high quality Thai stick. The air was perfumed like I was inside a hashish storage locker. I couldn't believe it. I walked for maybe fifty feet, stunned by the quality and the quantity and the openness with which it was being sold. Ok, get serious. Standing before a mountain of Thai stick, brownish green choice buds wrapped on a thin bamboo stick and held in place by a silken thread, I inhaled the aromatic perfume. It was like holding a large chunk of fresh Red Lebanese under my nose back at Melkweg in Amsterdam. I began to select a good handful. The merchant, a younger man in dark slacks and a red Izod knockoff sports shirt said, "Hey man, you like the best, huh?" He smiled in a genuine way, not the least bit "too cool."

"Yeah," I replied, "this is amazing."

"First time in Vientiane, huh?"

I nodded and he went on, "The Thai stick are one hundred kip each. The loose ganja, on the branch, is by the kilo, two thousand kip."

He held up a pack of the pre-rolled joints, bound together by a thin strip of palm leaf tie, "These are one thousand kip. You get twelve. Good quality."

"Do you have cigarette papers," I asked, holding up my plastic bag of tobacco.

He blinked at the bag and reached under his counter, pulling out what looked to be a small notepad with the picture of a pink flower and Chinese calligraphy.

"I have Peony, rice paper," he offered.

I took the pad and leafed through it, thin rice papers, each about the size of a three by five card. Good for rolling the giant European joints, but no glue. A pain in the ass.

"Do you have any European papers, like Rizla or ZigZag?"

He nodded and said, "Yes, I have. But expensive. Two thousand kip one pack."

From under the counter he lifted what looked like a shoe box and opened it to reveal cellophane wrapped packets of Rizla papers and even a couple of rolling machines. It made me smile, to have the papers more expensive than the ganja. I didn't want to be greedy so I grabbed out two packs of papers and put them with the fifteen Thai sticks I'd chosen. Still, I felt like a bandit. In Phuket we were paying a hundred baht for five Thai sticks, about a dollar each, which seemed cheap at the time. In Los Angeles you'd pay twenty dollars for each stick and that was if you were lucky enough to even find them. Now I was buying fifteen for seventy cents.

I paid up, wished the merchant well and moved down the aisle, already feeling high even though I hadn't smoked a thing. At a stall selling hair brushes and pins, a tall woman in an ivory colored, long sleeved dress was fitting a comb into her hair, studying the effect in a mirror attached to the canopy post. The dress had a sheen and cling to it that accented her figure, at least from behind. Exquisite silky black hair draped down her back and past her waist, held in a loose braid with a whimsical yellow butterfly at the end. As I passed her, our eyes met in the mirror. There was a sweetness mixed with interest in her open gaze that induced a mild electrical shock down my spine and I blurted out, "Very pretty" and smiled.

She turned from the mirror then and faced me. I froze, suddenly self-conscious and wishing I'd kept my mouth shut. She was beautiful. We studied each other for a moment, then she smiled with her whole being and simply said, "Thank you."

I fumbled around for something more to say, rooted, my feet unwilling to move. Her dark eyes seemed to sparkle as she waited.

"It goes well with the other one," I managed. The clip she was considering had a butterfly motif as well, but this one glinted with rhinestones set on a tortoise shell base.

She laughed then and pulled around her braid. The little yellow butterfly dangled between us.

"I enjoy butterflies," she said, in such warm a way that I felt less of a clod. We were nearly eye to eye, standing there. She was perhaps three inches shorter but that still made her over six feet tall. Turning back to the merchant she spoke briefly then extracted a clip purse.

"May I buy that for you," I wanted to be gallant. I wanted to not let her go.

Her lips curved up in the slightest way and she looked over at me. Something dark and deep in the back of her eyes studied me for a moment, an almost imperceptible nod and she said quietly, "If you wish. Mercí. Thank you."

The merchant, a thin faced middle aged woman with salt and pepper hair, must have followed the conversation for when I stepped forward she said, "*Sam sip*," literally "thirty." I was learning that locally, people simply said how many hundred notes and left off the hundred or thousand part. I stripped off the thirty notes, aware of the eyes of the girl beside me, not on my billfold but on my face.

I hoped she wouldn't just say goodbye and disappear. But, we turned away from the merchant and began to walk down the aisle together. She reached out and touched the goulimine bead necklace I was wearing, "What are these?"

Last year, in Morocco, I'd come down with cholera in Marrakech, probably from eating a bowl of soup from a huge cauldron at the gates of the medina. Later, I told myself that cauldron had likely been dishing out soup since the Crusades. They never washed it, just kept a constant stream of ingredients flowing into it. Maybe it hadn't reached a boil since the last infusion of water. At any rate, what did I expect. You pays your money and you takes your chances. I had slowly recovered, living in a hole I'd dug on the beach at Taghazout, near Agadir, with my traveling companion Mike. We had both come down with the cholera, but luckily we weren't usually delirious at the same time. One of us would crawl out and bring back water and soup for rehydration. As we healed, we came to know an old Englishman living on the beach in a beat-up caravan who was a merchant in African beads. These glass tubes, these goulimine beads, could be ancient. He claimed many in his collection came out of the 16th and 17th centuries, used as trade items across the Sahara. I'd poured over his piles and actually found two that were the same, cobalt blue bodies with red, five pointed stars surrounded by a thin white line. The stars appeared to be emerging from the blue depths when you looked at them. I also found one larger piece, twice as long the as the star beads and a bit thicker. It was the color of old bone and was studded with brownish red circles having clear, dark centers you could look inside of. They looked like the iris of an eye, hypnotic to gaze into. That marvelous piece was bookended by the blue beads on my cord.

Now, I fingered the necklace, my travel talisman, as I had come to think of it. In a real way, it was the first outward sign of a new self that was growing stronger within me. Even beginning to wear it was a little victory, like overcoming a fear of dancing.

"What are these?"

"They are ancient African trade beads," I replied, "to remind me of things I don't want to forget. And," I said a bit sheepishly, "maybe a bit for good luck."

The last part brought another smile from her and I rushed in, "My name is Vern."

Her eyes lost their playfulness for a moment and she wyed to me, "*Sabaidee baw*, Vern. Welcome to my country. My name is Hom."

"*Sabaidee*, Hom. Thank you. How is it you speak English so well?"

Hom touched the thin gold chain that graced her shapely neck, drawing out a small, golden cross as she spoke.

"I am from Vientiane. Before the war I was in a church school here. My parents wanted me to learn both French and English, for my future. But...," she trailed off.

"But the war ?" I offered.

She nodded and said no more. By this time we were walking together out of the market. As we strolled I told her a little of myself, of growing up in Los Angeles, of going to the university. At one point she asked, "Do you regret your decision to not become a doctor?"

It must come across like that, the way I tell it and I replied, a little defensively, "No, I wouldn't have been a good doctor. Not then. I don't know. Maybe I'll go back to school after this, after this trip."

Hom was twenty. Her Buddhist parents had owned a small farm and duck breeding operation, north of Vientiane. The fighting between the Pathet Lao and the Royalists had driven them east. The last she knew of them was via a hand carried letter, from a town called Phonsavon. Very difficult to get to, these days.

"That was more than two years ago," she shrugged, "and I am here."

We had stopped in front of the Hotel Continental.

"You live here, at the hotel?" I asked.

"I am here now," she replied, "there!" and she pointed to the upper right side of the building.

Laos

I liked everything about her, this Hom.

"Will you join me for dinner tonight?" I suddenly felt about twelve years old, asking out a girl whom I had a crush on in school. "I mean, if you don't have other plans."

She smiled ruefully but said, "No, no other plans. Yes, I should like that, Vern." Her dark eyes held me and now I really felt about twelve years old.

"Oh, great. That's terrific, Hom! I'll come by, what time, uh, how about at seven?"

Hom looked down for a moment, the shadow of a smile on her lips,

"Yes. *Bon.* Seven." She hesitated and then added, "I am in room 312."

I floated back to the Saylom hotel in the late afternoon heat but the air felt soft somehow, tender. How could she look so cool and fresh in long sleeves? So beautiful. The oddest sensation of being brand new in the world enveloped me. For a very long instant, there was no past or future, just a scintillating now, now, now, whispering ecstatically from my chest out through my limbs.

After a shower, I pulled the tobacco and ganja out of my day sack. Maybe it was crap but there was a lot of it. Give it a try. Using a single Rizla paper I rolled up a tapering pure tobacco cigarette and fired it up. It wasn't Drum but it was a smooth smoke. This wouldn't go to waste, at any rate. I next unwrapped one of the Thai sticks and rubbed down four of the little buds to smoking texture. The burst of hashish aroma was promising. I rolled up a second smoke of mixed ganja and tobacco and went down the hall to Peter's door and knocked. Getting stoned is pretty much a social thing for me and I was feeling celebratory. Nobody answered but I heard laughter from within so I rapped again. This time, the door opened and Peter stood there in a towel, a glass of beer and a cigarette in the same hand, grinning broadly.

"Werner!" He stood to one side and bade me enter like the maître d' at a restaurant. Klaus was there and another guy I recognized from the train. The air in the room was redolent with beer, tobacco and ganja, in spite of the open window. I took a seat on the edge of a bed and held up my joint.

"I brought a little something, but it looks like you are ahead of me."

"Würdest du ein bier?" asked Peter and held out a bottle of Stella Artois.

"Ja, vielen dank," I replied and accepted the proffered bottle.

"Werner, this *ist* Werner," Peter introduced me to the newcomer, laughing at his own joke. Everybody was pretty high so I fired up my own ganja, took

The Appearance of Things

a good hit and passed it around. I imagine if a non-stoned person recorded our next few hours it would not sound overly hilarious, but I thought it was great fun. I've heard that if you learn something when you are stoned, you recall it well when you get stoned again. My German is rudimentary but I spent a lot of time high in Deutschland last summer and it all seemed to come back to me that afternoon. On the wall above Peter's bed, someone had scrawled, "Vientiane is dead." I didn't think so.

I'm always surprised how quickly darkness falls in the tropics and the twilight outside the window said it was time to go get myself together. I had a date with a beautiful woman.

The beer and the ganja had mostly worn off by the time I presented myself at The Continental Hotel. The evening had cooled as well and my long pants and button down shirt were relatively comfortable. Corny though it may be, I'd stopped at a flower seller on the way up the street and I held a small bouquet of six red roses. They looked a wee bit tired but the tropics will do that to you. Still, they had a great perfume and I thought them pretty.

Hom's room was near the end of the upper balcony, facing out on to the street below. The third floor of The Continental didn't seem quite as kept up as the first two floors and dried bougainvillea leaves crunched underfoot as I made my way along. I knocked on 312 and again felt the giddy schoolboy tingle under my skin. No answer. My heart dropped a little and I knocked again, a rhythm of what I hoped was a cheerful little "shave and a haircut" tattoo. I waited.

The door opened tentatively and Hom peered out through the opening. "I thought you would not come," she whispered.

I held aloft the bouquet and smiled, "A gentleman does not forget a lady."

She opened her door wide. Her knee length, short-sleeved dress had a print of red hibiscus flowers scattered on a white background. Hom's long hair was straight down over her shoulders and framed her perfect oval face. The hint of cleavage was more revealing than her dress of this afternoon and I appreciated her figure from the front. She really was striking.

"Come in. Here," she reached for the flowers, "let's get them into water. They are very thoughtful."

She turned towards a set of shelves on the rear wall and selected a small white vase. While she filled it with water at the sink of her tiny kitchenette, I looked about her flat and felt touched by the homey details. It was larger than my hotel room and besides the countertop cooking area, there was a separate bedroom and bathroom. She had made paper chains, using strips of colored paper to make interlocking rings that hung from the doorway and divided the bedroom area from the little salon. A pair of photos sat on the shelf. One was a sepia photo of what must have been her parents, looking severe and turn of the century; the other was of a group of schoolgirls smiling. Hom returned with the flowers and set them on a little coffee table. None of the furniture matched but she bade me sit on a serviceable sofa covered with red and yellow brocade. The low table also held a bottle of wine and two glasses.

"Thank you for the flowers. It is a beautiful idea," she said. Now she seemed a bit nervous and reached for the wine bottle, "Do you like wine?" She tentatively passed me the bottle.

"I do, and this looks lovely. Thank you for having it for us. Shall I open it?"

She smiled now and said, "I have made us a dinner here. Please, yes, open the wine and I will set out plates."

The surprise must have shown on my face for she added, "Restaurant is not my custom. I hope you will like Lao food."

She looked down, as if she had made an error. I reached out and took her hands in mine and she looked up at me earnestly.

"I love Lao food and Thai food and Indonesian food. I love food too much!" and I patted my own stomach.

Hom laughed and threw her arms around my neck, "We'll have fun here," and kissed me.

What had been smoldering in me erupted and I put my arms around her, pulling her to me. My hand ran down her firm back to the top of her hips and somewhere in my brain registered "no under garments."

Hom stood and pulled me up with her, dancing eyes, the swirling dark silk of her hair cascading around me. We kissed again, long and lingering and exploring. She took my hands and we grinned at each other, carefully passing through the paper chains into the bed room and down on to the covers. We didn't speak as we undressed each other, except a small gasp from me when my searching hands found no pubic hair. The soft, sensuous curves of her body thrilled a man in me I'd never met and I lost myself in the erotic perfume of her skin. At one point in our union she huddled over me, the only points of contact our genitals and her hair across my chest. Never had I known this commanding love-making and when I came, my arched back felt close to snapping.

After, we lay in each other's arms as lovers do, and with my fingertips I traced the delicate vertebra, from her neck down to her warm and clinging waist, and beyond.

That night, I never knew what was for dinner or what the 1973 Côtes du Rhone tasted like. Instead, we moved in and out of sleep and love making until the sky lightened with the next wonderful day.

I think over the next five days I saw Peter once, when I was back at the Saylom picking up fresh clothing and making sure they knew I hadn't abandoned my room or belongings. I came out of my room into the hall at the same moment he did and we waved to each other. It was about eleven in the morning and Hom was at the Ministry of Commerce, where her language skills earned her a small salary as a document translator.

"Hallo Peter," I called. "How is Vientiane for you this time?"

I felt abnormally cheerful and it showed.

"Hello Werner. I'm good to see you. After four days I was wondering what happened to you. Disappear or something."

The concern on his face both surprised and touched me, that he had cared enough to notice.

"I met a beautiful girl," I blurted out. "Can't get enough of her."

Peter broke out in a Cheshire Cat smile and stroked the ends of his thick, dark moustache.

"*Ach so,*" he responded, "you have a *leibling* now. No wonder we don't see you!"

I think I must have been blushing because my face felt hot but the words tumbled out, "Her name is Hom. We met in the market, that day after I left the German café. I bought her a hair clip."

The last part sounded a little lame after I'd said it, but I didn't care.

"Hair clip?" said Peter. "So you don't pay a bar fine?"

I blinked, taking in what he'd just said.

"No, no bar fine. She's not a working girl, like you mean."

Peter gave me a knowing wink, "They're all working girls. You just have tee-loc. Lucky!"

"What's tee-loc?" I said stupidly.

"It's a Thai thing. Here too, I guess. When a girl takes a fancy to you and she doan charge anything. Like girlfriend, travel friend. You pay the bills. That's good enough."

I felt stunned. Yesterday, I'd finally convinced Hom to let me take her to La Paix. "I really want to take you, Hom. It's very lovely there. White tablecloths, music, good food and wine. I know you said, "Not my custom," but it's mine, to share with you."

She had agreed, reluctantly, but I think we both looked beautiful when we entered and were seated by the maître d'. And the food was delicious, even Hom thought so. She isn't much of a wine drinker, as I found out when we finally got around to opening that Côtes du Rhone at her flat, but we shared some this night. I felt so happy and content, as we toasted each other. On our way out though, we passed a table at which sat Christy and Paul, from the train. They didn't look up and I paused beside their table.

"Hey Paul, Christy. Good evening. This is my friend Hom." I turned to present her and she was inspecting the floor.

"Hom, this is Paul and Christy. We all came on the train from Bangkok."

The exchange was suddenly very awkward, Christy and Paul making quick eye contact with Hom and nodding perfunctorily. Hom nodded back and was silent. She looked very uncomfortable and I felt it was time to move on. It was weird.

"Night then, enjoy your meal."

Hom and I moved towards the door. When I looked back over my shoulder, Paul and Christy were watching us with stern expressions on their faces. At that moment, I chalked it up to some form of racism or maybe they saw me as one of those old guys in Bangkok harvesting maidens.

There hadn't been any talk of money between Hom and I. It was true that I'd pay when we did things together, like the boat ride along the Mekong the other day or when we'd stop at street stalls for spring rolls or soup or something. That just impressed me as the natural order of things. Mostly we'd simply have fun together, Hom showing me "her" Vientiane. All of our exchanges with Laotian people were filled with laughter and warmth.

So I said to Peter, "I don't think Hom is a working girl. At least, not the kind you mean. She works alright, but at the commerce ministry or whatever they call it."

Peter saw my defensiveness and held up his open hands, "Sorry, sorry. I don't mean to offend. For me it's not a problem. Regular here, that's all." He hesitated and then asked, "Before, we talked about going north, up to Luang Prabang. Klaus and I will go to Vang Vien on Monday. Do you come or," he winked, "do you continue to enjoy Vientiane?"

That made me grin too. I was head over heels for Hom, lost in the exquisite mystery of her eyes, the perfume of her sex that bathed me and led to places in myself of wanting and desire I'd never known, never even suspected. I felt proud of myself as a man when we were together and I liked it.

"Monday, huh?" It seemed too soon. Leaving Vientiane and Hom in just three more days made my head hurt.

That evening she and I walked together along the riverside again. It was a sweet aspect of being beside the Mekong. The life moving up and down the muddy waters, the park and the wide promenade always filled with people in the early evening, lovers, or so I fancied. That stroll had quickly become one of the things Hom and I cherished together. The canopy of the trees and the antique street lamps, we could have been walking beside the Seine in Paris, in some past, romantic time. On this night, our conversation as we drifted along turned on a comment I'd made to Hom about her neck cross and her Buddhist parents.

"They believed the church school would help me more than the government school," she reflected. "In Buddhism, it is not a conflict with Christian. There is kindness and generosity and love. Wisdom is wisdom," she said simply.

It surprised me, her ease with having a foot in each world. I knew the Thais didn't worship Buddha the way certain schools of Christianity worship Jesus and a father-god entity, something outside of and superior to themselves.

Growing up in my predominantly Jewish neighborhood of Southern California, friends would attend Hebrew school after regular school and I attended my share of Bar Mitzvahs. My family wasn't Christian or Jewish, more like vague pantheists, ranchers who took their hats off when in the presence of beauty. I think my earliest inkling of the sky god concept came from my mother. She told me that my dead father was with god. The way she said it, it sounded nice, like he still really was somewhere, up there, and could look down and love me. The god thing wasn't important. What mattered to my young mind was that my father, my real father, still cared for me and was watching over me. It was reassuring. Later, when I was nine years old, we went to see Charlton Heston in "The Ten Commandments" which was very impressive, the burning bush and all that. In the autumn of that year, we met

Laos

Mr. Heston at a dude ranch outside of LA, the Kemper Campbell Ranch. He was trying to pick up my mother and, being nice to the kid, bought me my first slingshot. It was cool to have Moses give me a slingshot.

I asked Hom, "Didn't the church school try to persuade you that the Christian religion was more true than the Buddhist religion?"

We had stopped walking and leaned together on a stone railing, overlooking the Mekong. It was a warm night and below us, on the wide riverbank, fireflies danced their zigzag flight paths in the inky darkness. I had my arm wrapped around her slim waist and she leaned closer into me before she answered.

"Long ago, in a village to the north, there was a very wise teacher. He had the reputation of being an arahant, an awakened one. A man came to him and asked, "Oh wise one. Please tell me if there is a life after this one, so that I shall know how to live."" Hom turned to me and took both my hands in hers, holding me with her earnest dark eyes before she continued. "The wise man asked him, "If I told you that there was a god who judges you and when you die, you will be rewarded or punished, according to the life you have lived, how then would you live?" The man considered for a long moment then answered, "Well, I would live with love so that in the next life, I would know the love I have given. And I would live with kindness, that I might receive kindness in turn. And I would live with generosity, because god would smile on the generosity and I would be rewarded in the afterlife." The old man nodded, then asked, "And if I told you there was nothing beyond this life, that you live just this short time and die into non-existence, how then would you live?" The questioner again considered and slowly replied, "Well, I suppose I would live with love, since this would be the only chance I will ever have to love and it feels correct and good. And I should live with kindness, since this life is so short, that I should be remembered as kind, and because when I am kind, it feels correct and good. And I would be generous, since if this is all there is, of what benefit is there in clinging to great wealth." "Just so," said the wise man and the questioner departed, feeling satisfied."

Hom looked up at me, her eyes luminous with a hint of mischief, "Does that satisfy you?" she asked with a smile.

It made me laugh and I wyed to her, "I am satisfied and grateful for your wisdom."

Before we returned to her room, we shared a bowl of coconut ice cream. It was delicious.

II

On Sunday morning, as Hom and I shared a croissant and café au lait on the veranda of The Constellation, Peter and Klaus passed below on the street. We spotted each other at the same moment and Peter waved. He said something to Klaus who also waved, then proceeded up the street while Peter mounted the front steps and approached our table. He grinned at Hom and I and made a slightly theatrical bow, "Peter Dugoslav at your service."

I smiled and Hom looked back and forth at the two of us.

"Peter," I said, "I would like you to meet my friend, Hom Kham Dao." Then to Hom, "Peter and I met on the Bangkok train."

Hom indicated a chair at the table and coolly said, "Hello Peter. Would you care to join us?"

Neither of us wanted another "La Paix moment" but it was instantly clear that Peter was taken with Hom and more than happy to join us. He plopped himself into the proffered chair, eyes sparkling.

"*Ja*, thank you. We are just going to the market for morning soup. You are very welcome to join us but I think you are already eating, yes?"

Before I could answer, the waitress brought the banana crepes we had ordered and set them before us. She looked at Peter for an order but he waved his hand.

"*Ach zo!* That looks very good too. Well, I will not interrupt your breakfast any more."

He placed his hands on the arm rests of the chair and made to rise, then hesitated, "Werner, the bus to Vang Vien leaves tomorrow at nine. Should we save a place for you?"

Hom was cutting her crepe with a fork at that moment and I saw the briefest hesitation in her hand before she continued, eyes cast down on her plate. Lifting the bite to her mouth, we touched each other's eyes.

"I don't know Peter. Maybe I'll join you later. How long will you be in Vang Vien?"

Peter pushed out his lower lip and raised his shoulders in a shrug.

"How long? I don't know. If it's good, maybe a few days. I want to be in

Luang Prabang by Friday though, spend a week around there before I go back to Bangkok."

He rose to go and I also stood. We shook hands, "I imagine I'll see you along the way," I said, "but don't hold the bus for me tomorrow, OK?"

Peter grinned and he bowed again to Hom, "I'm pleased to have met you," he said. She smiled back at him and there wasn't a trace of anything but kindness in her eyes.

After Peter departed, there was a pregnant silence as we ate our crepes. Hom set things moving again. "Your friend wants you to come along, I think." She took a bite of her crepe and studied my face. I wasn't ready to go where I needed to go. My heart felt it was being twisted like a dish rag.

"Have you been to Vang Vien?" I asked.

I felt a fountain of hope gushing up from my core. Yes! That's it. We could travel together around Laos. It would be great! She speaks the language, we'd have a terrific time of it.

It was as though Hom could read my mind. Her eyes held such a tenderness and she touched my hand, "No, I have not."

Then the story crashed.

"From here, from Vientiane, the Pathet Lao are in control. I cannot go north or east. I, we, are called "enemies of the people." Outside of Vientiane is very perilous. I must be here."

I had passed the Pathet Lao headquarters here in Vientiane nearly every day. They lounged in front, wearing dark glasses and looking more like street thugs than soldiers. Their compound lay between the Saylom and The Constellation. When Hom and I walked down the avenue, she always guided us to the opposite side of the street. Even then, we'd had a couple of shouts from the jerks in front.

Not far from La Paix, there was a nightclub called "Cocos" that the Pathet Lao leadership favored. We'd see them pull up in Mercedes sedans, piling out with cigarettes and laughing girls. The majority wore black suits with mandarin collars and wrap around dark glasses. Who wears dark glasses at night, really. Here in Vientiane at any rate, the Pathet Lao appeared as mafia hoodlums. I recalled the money they had printed that the Swiss guy had shown me in Jogyakarta. Scenes of noble communist fighters shooting down jets with American flags on their tails. If these creeps were going to be the new rulers, I reckon Laos would be better off with the old king and his cronies. Changing times.

"Vern," Hom pulled me out of my story, "you want to go and see the north. Please, please do it. It is why you have come. I am very sorry I cannot go with you. Really very sorry." Her voice trailed off with the last words and she looked away, down the tree-lined street.

The unspoken truth lay between us for the rest of the day and into our last night together. It was not the morose truth of a coming execution. Instead, we walked hand in hand around Vientiane, touching a few favorite places like the temple grounds, with the fanciful dragon sculptures and the impressive King cobra, its open hood shading a serene Buddha. Our smiles and laughter came easily, naturally. I knew I would see her again, when I came back from the north, so it wasn't the big farewell in my mind. I told myself it was just a, "See you later" sort of parting. But a twinge in my heart asked honestly, "Then what?"

We went past the Saylom. I picked up my gear and settled the bill. I also left a note for Peter that read, "See you at the bus station tomorrow. I'll be there before nine. Vern."

That evening, I gave Hom the small box as we sat facing each other on her bed. We favored candlelight and had lit a dozen new tapers around the small bedroom. The soft, golden light played on our naked bodies. I loved her sweet smile as she touched the ribbon butterfly on the top.

"I hope this will be something you like," I said quietly.

She stroked the back of my hand, "It already is."

Hom unwrapped and opened my gift. The thin silver chain held three goulimine beads I had chosen for her before we ever met. The central had multicolored rings that reminded me of her paper chains. It was flanked by two, nearly identical beads of a marbled lime green with finely detailed yellow hourglass shapes that looked like butterflies.

Her eyes were shining, "So beautiful. Will you help me?" and she drew closer, holding up her hair that I might slip the necklace about her sculpted neck. Our love making that night had a tenderness and a ferocity. It made me feel eternal - that we had been, that we are, that we always will be. I wondered if all real lovers felt this way.

In the morning, Hom stayed in her room. I walked down the stairs of The Constellation wearing my backpack and stepped out onto the street, enveloped in a wordless, hollow sense of loss. I began my walk towards the bus station, but couldn't stop myself from gazing up towards Hom's corner room. There she was, on the balcony, in the long sleeved ivory dress I'd first seen her wearing. She was smiling down at me, her finger lifting the silver chain out free from her neck. I could see the golden butterflies and the colored rings. I smiled back up at her and our eyes lingered. I touched my heart and she nodded, then disappeared from sight as I moved down the morning street.

"Hallo Werner!" Peter called from the waiting bus. It reminded me of the Sumatra bus, from Lake Toba, but with open sides. Peter and Klaus sat on the bench behind the driver and I could make out their packs in the growing pile on the roof. "Come on. We have a seat for you. Get a ticket there," Peter pointed to a shack with a corrugated metal roof a few yards away. I passed my backpack to the roof man, secured my ticket and made to swing on to the bench seat beside Klaus. On the way up, I must have lurched forward because my face slammed into the side view mirror, cracking it in the center.

"Ohh," moaned Peter, "Seven years bad luck" and he slapped me on the back then peered at my nose. "Looks like the mirror got the worst of it from you!"

My nose was tender but when I touched it, no blood came away on my fingers. Sort of lucky, I guess.

"Good morning," I said to Klaus and Peter, both of whom were grinning broadly.

Peter leaned forward, past Klaus, "I did not think to see you today. Your girl is very beautiful. Maybe you don't say goodbye, eh?"

"Well, in German you say *auf wiedersehen*, see you again, right? I'll see her again when I come back this way," I said, "so I don't say goodbye."

Peter said something to Klaus. He laughed and then slapped me on the knee, "*Ja, auf wiedersehen* is good."

We rolled out of Vientiane, passed the Arc du Triomphe, and were soon passing rice paddy and small farming hamlets. The road was newly paved for about the first thirty minutes, but as we approached the hills it reverted to a graded gravel highway. As we wound upward, occasional openings in the forest yielded glimpses of the sort of limestone cliffs I'd first seen in the south of Thailand, the Kharst formations. We stopped periodically to allow passengers to get off or sometimes to pick up someone new. The further we got from Vientiane, the more frequently the newcomers were dressed in the traditional tribal clothing. The men tended to have a folded black cloth hat with red or yellow embroidery, baggy trousers and a kind of burlap or rough cotton jacket. The women impressed me as almost "Asian gypsy", having headpieces adorned with many small shining coins and colorful dresses done in a multilayer style that looked Eastern European. One of the western passengers, an Israeli guy named Anon, described them as "hill tribe people" and tried to come across as an old hand in these matters. It sounded like he was bullshitting a bit, but I learn by listening and right now I was listening.

"Yeah," Anon continued, "I was south and a lot crossed over the river to get away from the fighting. The Thais don't like them, down there. They call them aborigines and make them stay out of town."

Anon had been for two years previously in the Israeli army and had been on the road now for more than six months, off to see the world.

"I flew to Bangkok. Not so good crossing Arabia with an Israeli passport," he laughed.

About noon, we descended into a river valley. The tall limestone pillars were more pronounced here, their jagged, broken escarpments encased in tangles of vines and snake-rooted tropical broadleaf trees. The forest had given way to farms again and we passed a wat having a distinctly different roof style from the Thai temples - more of a wide, graceful sweep with detailed woodwork under the eaves. A road sign announced Vang Vien and we ground to a dusty halt in the middle of a one lane, wooden framed village. Vang Vien consisted of a few dozen houses scattered along both sides of the road. On the south side the houses were backed up with rice paddy stretching back a few hundred yards before the jungle took over and ended the view. The north side, behind the houses, had a few paddy as well, but the show-stopper was a wide vista with a lovely, clear river meandering around sculpted limestone boulders while tall, majestic limestone columns marched off into the distance. After the muddy Mekong, the clear blue water spoke to me and I took a deep breath of the cooler, clean air. We must have gained more altitude than I realized. This place was dramatically beautiful.

Apparently there was only one place for visitors to stay, a rambling hostel-like affair with two floors, a great room and an outside deck restaurant. Peter, Klaus and I strolled in and propped our packs against the little pony wall that separated the front desk from the great room. While we waited for the desk clerk to help the first arrivals, I noticed a very attractive blond woman sitting back in one of the easy chairs. Her long, shapely legs stretched out in front of a fellow sitting on a stool, talking animatedly to her. I got the image of a shoe salesman trying to make a sale to a disinterested client. Peter and Klaus were handling the room stuff so I drifted over to a signpost that held the restaurant menu and began to study the offerings. It also put me closer to the shoe salesman and his mark, where I could hear the conversation. I'm not usually an eavesdropper but there was a compelling feline quality about this woman, in her repose a kind of lazy calculation, a flickering in her clear blue eyes.

"Oh yes," he said, "I agree completely. Reporting can be a very dangerous game. Last year I was in Saigon when a barrage of mortar shells came in outta nowhere. One moment, we were in the garden of the restaurant enjoying dinner, the next everybody was diving for cover."

"Was anyone hurt?" the reclining beauty asked.

"Not on that one, thank goodness. But," he hesitated and leaned in towards her, "I have seen men killed. Been very close to it myself."

The journalist, if that's what he was, had an unfortunate bald patch that stretched back from his forehead to his crown. His somewhat disheveled, limp hair was a bit too long and hung listlessly on each side of his ears. I'd guess he was in his mid-thirties, but maybe older with those creases in his gaunt face and thin frame. He reminded me of the character Ichabod Crane in "The Legend of Sleepy Hollow" and I found myself sympathetic to him and his efforts to pick up this long stemmed rose. I was missing Hom.

A high sign from Peter, that we were all set, put me back in motion and we trudged upstairs to our room with our packs. Room three had four beds, one of which was apparently already occupied. A safari hat and a small knapsack lay on the thin mattress, proclaiming "mine."

"I want to go over for the cave swim," said Peter. "Will you come?"

Klaus and I looked at each other and shrugged, why not. We settled our gear and I produced a good-sized joint and held it up.

"Feel like a smoke before the swim?" I asked.

Klaus and Peter grinned and Klaus said, "*Ja, ja,* it is a good idea." We fired up and began to pass it when the door opened and the journalist stood in the doorway.

"Hey, it smells good in here. I guess we're sharing," he said, and crossed the room to the occupied bed. He plopped down and for some reason put on his hat.

"Nick Stevens," he said, and tapped the brim of his hat. We introduced ourselves and passed him the joint.

"You gotta love Southeast Asia," Nick said and took a deep hit on the smoke. He informed us that he was a freelance journalist out of Toronto, Canada. "I'm doing a series on the road between Vientiane and Luang Prabang that's been picked up by The Star," he confided.

"I saw you doing research downstairs," I kidded him a bit.

Nick held out his two palms, open and upturned, "Hope springs eternal from a young man's heart. Diana is traveling with her brother and was, alas, unable to join me for dinner tonight." He laughed, and it was a young, almost adolescent, giggle.

One of the big draws in Vang Vien is the river. The hostel had a dozen or so inner tubes that guests used to float downstream, along the curving watercourse of the river. At one point, the river flowed into the mouth of a vast cavern and disappeared into the blackness. In theory, a person could float through the cavern and come out some two kilometers away, where the river re-emerged and continued its flow through and out of the valley.

A small sign on the wall at the front desk read, "Guide Service Here." Peter had asked when we checked in, about a guide through the cavern but the desk man had shaken his head "no'" and said, "No guide now. Water high." He had ducked his head down and feigned banging it on the bottom of his hand, "Hit head. No good." I wasn't disappointed since I had no expectation but I saw that Peter felt a little let down.

We all took one last hit of the joint and Peter said, "I want to go in to the cave with a light. Maybe it's possible to go and they just don't want to do it."

"I wouldn't do it," offered Nick. "When I got here last week, there were two Australian guys freaking out because their friend had taken a torch and gone in on a tube. He said he was just going to check it out a bit." Nick looked meaningfully at Peter and went on, "When he didn't come out in half an hour, one of the other guys got a torch and went in. He came swimming out without the tube and without the torch. Said there was a place where it went down under and it was like a suction pump. He lost the tube and the light and had to pull himself back against the current. His hands were all bandaged up from the cuts he got off the limestone snags in the darkness."

We were all gaping at Nick and the story. He looked around at us and went on, "They kept going out to the place where the river comes back out, even camped there for the first two days, looking for their friend. Gave it up after three days. Went down to the Australian consulate to report it on Friday."

Nick shook his head and I felt, in my rather stoned mind and in my stomach, the horror of dying in the darkness, in the swirling, airless cold.

So as we trooped out the back of the hostel and towards the river, I wasn't feeling as light as I had the hour before. Life can turn on a dime and there aren't any guarantees out there.

The afternoon was warm and the clear waters of the river still beckoned but I felt a second rush of trepidation when we rounded a bend and there, a few hundred meters ahead, the gaping maw of the cavern. Stalactites, some the size of trees, extended down from the arching roof and for an instant I was staring into the terrible jaws of some ancient sea monster. Yet the flow of the river was gentle and we saw people in the water, easily swimming both upstream and downstream. I knew that could be misleading since the rate of flow increases when the channel narrows and I could imagine it got pretty narrow under the ground, in the darkness.

We were parallel with a hemi-lemniscate island that lay mid channel. Its teardrop shape had allowed a sandy beach and a deep blue swimming hole to form along the downstream edge. It was connected to our side of the riverbank via a large, fallen log. Peter was already stripping off his shirt as he charged across with Klaus, Nick and I following behind. I really was pretty high and nearly lost my balance in the crossing. Some hindbrain survival instinct kicked in when I saw the wicked limestone points in the water below and I twirled, recovered and went on. Nobody saw it but an inner voice said, "Maybe getting stoned less would be a good idea." Jumping down off the log to the sandy beach, in this lovely spot, I felt ill at ease. I turned to survey the beach and a huge blast of cold water struck me in the face and chest. I gasped.

"Hey, it's good. Come on!" Peter laughed and scooped another wave towards me with his powerful hands.

The shock of the water and his crazy, good-natured laugh completely altered my reality. I stripped off my shirt and sandals and leapt into the welcoming, cool water. I floated on my back for a moment and the chill water was a magnet, drawing the iron filings of fear and anxiety out through my skin, cleansing my whole being from the core on out. An involuntary "Aaah" escaped my lips and a deep sense of having arrived enveloped me. So delightful.

The Appearance of Things

As the afternoon wore on the ganja wore off and we made a few swimming forays down towards the entrance to the cavern. The sharp limestone protrusions below the surface, the result of the rivers flowing erosion, needed care. More than a few visitors at the hostel were sporting tape and gauze bandages on a leg or a foot and I could see why. Still, in the warmth of the day, it was just magnificent to swim and dive in the clear, sweet water. The river was about forty feet wide, a little more than 12 meters, where it entered the cave and about ten feet deep. I was trying to think more in metric units because it was easier to talk with people when I didn't have to explain arcane units of measure. At any rate, our forays into the cavern had Nick's cautionary tale in the background and none of us seemed terribly keen on going too far in. It certainly kept me from pushing my luck.

In the late afternoon, back at the hostel, sunburned and lazy, I was enjoying a cold beer on the back deck. Nick was holding court at the next table, going on with his war correspondent stories, and a couple of new arrivals were listening in rapt silence. The English beauty, Diana, was reading on a lounge, keeping to herself but within earshot. Her brother, a slim, sandy haired fellow with freckles and buckteeth, had just brought her an iced tea. He seemed more her manservant than her brother but it wasn't my lookout. There was something unsavory about him, the way he hovered around the various men trying to engage his sister, exulting when she sent them off with a flea in their ear. Nick had made another attempt with her and after he had described a daring exploit near Danang, she had blandly asked at what age he had started to go bald. The question brought him up short, poor guy, and the brother, Thomas, had sniggered. In spite of her obvious outward beauty, I began to see them as an ugly little team.

"What do you think, Vern?" Nick was looking over to me from the other table, smiling broadly.

"Umm, sorry, I was off on a daydream. What do I think of what?"

"Of putting together a walk out to the waterfall tomorrow. What we talked about down on the river," Nick replied.

"Sure. Yes. Sounds good to me. Did you find the guide?"

In our riverside conversation, Nick had offered to Peter, Klaus and I to locate a guide for the walk, if we were interested.

"*Ja* sure," Peter had said, "let's go. I like to see more around here."

Klaus and I had agreed and Nick had been good to his word.

Nick went on, "Yup. He's the cousin of the manager here. He'll take us out tomorrow, all the way to the fall and back for twenty thousand kip. He said it's a two hour walk out from here and wants to leave at eight in the morning."

Nick looked at me for confirmation and I nodded "ok."

"The waterfalls here are really brilliant," one of the newcomers at the table with Nick chimed in. He had short, chopped looking blond hair and spoke with what I thought was a New Zealand accent. "We made a trek out to the Kwang See fall, outside of Luang Prabang. Really a beaut, that one."

"The snakes and bugs were a bit dodgy," his darker friend added, "but yeah, well worth a visit."

"Have you just come down then, from Luang Prabang?" I asked.

"We have," the blond one answered, "it's really good there. Right on the Mekong River."

"Were there a lot of other travelers there?" I continued.

The pair looked at each other and shrugged. The dark one answered, "Aw yeah, there's a fair number, I reckon. Not too many Americans though, if that's what you mean."

It wasn't precisely what I meant but it was good information. Also, not much of a surprise. I'd met very few American travelers in Asia thus far. Mostly they were European, Australian or out of New Zealand.

"Did you see much military activity?" asked Nick.

The two were suddenly the center of attention and they adjusted themselves to sit a little taller and segued into a more serious demeanor. Here we go, I thought.

"There were a few groups of soldiers, Pathet Lao soldiers, that we saw on the way down here. Two big check points. And in Luang Prabang, they've got a machine gun post in the street, near to the government house," the blond one answered.

"Were there any aircraft?" Nick pursued.

They exchanged a look that reminded me of a couple of carnival men deciding how far to string along the rube.

"Aircraft. Well the airport there is open. There were a couple of planes a day when we were there. I know it's possible to fly to and from Vientiane 'cause that's how we did it, got to Luang Prabang. And some people we met

The Appearance of Things

flew down to Vientiane yesterday. But that's about all. Nothing military, I don't think. No jets or anything. Is this for your story?"

It was Nick's turn to preen.

"I'm not sure what will make it into the final series but it's good information. Thanks for that."

He cast a surreptitious glace towards Diana, who at that moment was waving a handkerchief in front of her face to dispel the clouds of insects that were gathering around us as dusk approached. Her brother, Thomas, perched on a stool near her feet reading a paperback book whose title I couldn't make out. It was odd, how they were both there and not there.

Peter and Klaus emerged from the great room clutching bottles of beer and joined me at my table.

"Nick found us the guide for the waterfall tomorrow," I said casually.

"*Sehr gut!*" exclaimed Peter and turned towards Nick with his beer raised, "Thank you Nick. What time do we go?"

"We need to be ready before eight," Nick replied, "and bring water. It's a two hour walk in the heat each way."

"But with a swim in the middle, yes?" asked Klaus, hopefully.

I was growing to like Klaus, as we spent time together. Today on the river we'd talked about school and the choices we make in life and I'd found him very thoughtful, if a little fatalistic.

"We have an abitur in Germany, a test that decides if you go to university or technical. That's why I am become an electrical worker. I don't mind. My brother goes to university. He wants medical, like you. Like you did. But I think he's not so happy now. I have more freedom."

The next morning found all of us in the great room, waiting for the cousin. My feet felt odd, to be encased in shoes again after so many months in sandals. But shoes were strongly suggested for our jungle walk, especially by Nick, who went on about snakes and biting ants and leeches. A little before eight, a Laotian man entered the hostel and greeted the desk clerk. The cousin. He was short, maybe five feet tall and lightly built. When the deskman pointed us out to him I saw his shrewd eyes take us in, his smooth face impassive and opaque. He approached and wyed to us, which we returned.

"I am Lan. Thank you. We go now?"

We followed Lan out of the hostel and along the road leading out of the village towards Luang Prabang. Lan walked beside Nick.

"Those good boot. Where you get?" he asked Nick, nodding towards his shoes.

"In Saigon," Nick answered, "Army PX."

Lan peered at him silently for a moment then asked, "You American GI?"

"No, no," responded Nick, waving his hands, "Canada. I am a journalist for a newspaper."

Lan nodded, as if that bit of information put him at ease. "You write my country?" he asked.

Nick nodded, "I write about the travel, from Vientiane to Luang Prabang."

Lan nodded again and came to an abrupt halt. He pointed at a raised path to our right, one person wide, that led out across the rice paddy and disappeared into the jungle in the distance. "We go this way," he said and unceremoniously launched himself down the path. For a little guy he was very fast and we found ourselves stumbling behind him on the muddy, pitted path. At one point, Peter miss-stepped and sunk up to his right knee in the rice paddy. When he heaved his mud covered leg out of the mire it made a comical sucking sound.

Peter shouted, "*Scheise!*" and Klaus started laughing. Lan stopped and surveyed us. His face betrayed nothing of what he must have been thinking. I imagined that he felt he was out on a walk with the four stooges.

The jungle was not solid or impenetrable. Once we got in under the tall tree canopy the path opened wide enough for a cart and the understory was sparse such that one could easily walk in any direction. Scattered pools of standing water reminded me of the quicksand scenes in the old Tarzan movies. Small palms and bushy broadleaf plants dominated, all under a cathedral-like canopy of tall hardwoods that grew maybe fifty feet apart. Periodically, we passed fields and small houses and about one hour out, a complete village. It impressed me that the little settlement was rudely constructed, comparatively, as if done in a hurry. The inhabitants wore the colorful clothing I'd seen earlier, after leaving Vientiane. They eyed us suspiciously as we passed.

"Hmong," Lan had said, "refugee from American war."

Perhaps I imagined it but he sounded slightly contemptuous, not of the American War but of the people, of the Hmong. Still, he spoke to some of the inhabitants we passed and gave the impression of being involved with this village. At one point, he stopped and shared cigarettes with a group of men and there was some laughter.

The day was heating up as we entered a valley flanked by low limestone cliffs and I could hear the flow of a stream off to my left. A flying insect buzzed past my face. It was about the size of a golf ball and I felt the whoosh of air as it sped by. Klaus smacked the back of his neck and his hand came away bloody. As we moved on, the trail began climbing and the understory grew increasingly dense. I began to wonder what would happen if we met a bear. Or a tiger. The tiger thought gave me pause. Right up until that moment I hadn't considered wild animals. There really were tigers in the forests of Southeast Asia. I found myself studying the undergrowth more carefully as we passed.

We climbed slowly and finally, Lan said, "Waterfall down here" and we turned off the main path and descended into a vine draped basin. Monkeys moved above us in the trees, screeching warning of our approach. Birds at different levels in the forest added their voices and our quiet walk now had quite the jungle soundtrack. Through the jungle canopy, I caught glimpses of the limestone cliff face we were approaching and sure enough, we reached the wide stream and followed it another hundred meters to the turquoise pools at the base of the fall. It was an enchanting spot, a multitude of colorful birds and butterflies swirled in the air with the mist-created rainbow arc from the waterfall as a backdrop. The steady roaring voice of the fall made conversation difficult but few words were needed. Everyone but Lan stripped off and waded into the inviting water. Minerals, over the years, had formed a series of swimming pools below the fall with white, sandy bottoms. It felt luxurious to fall back and wash off the mud and sweat and bug bites, then to float and relax, looking up at the spectacularly blue sky, fringed by palms and tall trees. I'd guess the fall was fifty meters tall. It wasn't the biggest and best but it was pristine, tropical and perfect. A heart twinge, wishing I was there with Hom, just the two of us. Still, with the instant camaraderie of the road, I was with friends and we had all come together in this moment, celebrants in this great river of time.

"That was good," declared Nick, toweling himself off. I removed my little packet of rice and fish from the hotel restaurant and tucked in. I wanted to eat before I started smearing on the insect repellent, a war surplus DEET that tended to dissolve plastics. It seemed like a good idea to not eat anything that could dissolve plastic.

Lan again led us on the way out, which was good. It's odd how, in the jungle, it all looks so different on the return trip. Perhaps it is the effect of the changing angle of the sunlight on the leaves, as the sun makes its passage overhead.

Finally I spied a round stone on the path that I remembered and beside it, the reassuring footprint of Nick's boot. At the Hmong village we got a mild surprise. Lan stopped, saying, "I will stay this village. You know the path, there," he pointed and we all nodded.

In the distance we could see some of the limestone pillars looming behind the village of Vang Vien, above the forest canopy. It seemed a simple matter to find our way back.

We thanked Lan and set out, back down the path we had walked this morning. Peter and Klaus strolled side by side ahead, the angle of the afternoon light gave the overhead leaves a cheerful backlighting and all was right with the world. The smell of ganja drifted back to Nick and I and we increased our pace to catch up and be part of the party.

"Werner, do you have some repellent I can use," asked Peter, slapping the side of his neck. We stopped and passed around the DEET and the joint.

"Agg! Tastes like shit on the joint," Nick observed and we all laughed in agreement.

Twenty minutes later our sylvan hike through the forest came to an abrupt halt. Ahead, a series of rapid-fire reports thundered through the jungle.

"What the hell is that," said Peter, apprehensively.

As if in answer, another series of blasts erupted ahead, but more to the left from the first bunch. We stood frozen as the shots increased in both volume and intensity. Who could be shooting? A particularly loud set of reports now came from ahead and to our right. Nick had reflexively ducked and squatted down.

"There's a firefight ahead. We had this in Vietnam, when a unit would surprise a group of Viet Cong on patrol in the forest."

A firefight? The war had come home and suddenly was very real. The firing raged between us and Vang Vien, maybe forty minutes away if we went straight.

" Maybe we can go around," offered Klaus. At that moment a furious round rocked the forest and we all dropped to a squat.

Nick nodded knowledgeably, "Maybe, but if we get off the path we'll really be out in the jungle."

We all looked out at the forest that had seemed so sanguine and benign a few minutes before. As if in some divine warning, a large lizard burst from cover , running panicked to our right. From out of nowhere a very large black snake in hot pursuit. I'd never seen a lizard being chased by a high speed snake and the vision startled me. In an instant it was over, the snake launching itself through the air and clamping its jaws over the lizards head. The churning black ball rolled out of sight in the undergrowth, the lizard legs flailing uselessly at the air from between the coils.

Nobody said a thing. Then I suggested, "What if we backtrack, towards the Hmong village?"

There were a few nods of assent. Moments later, another burst of gunfire, this time almost behind us followed by more off to the left.

"It sounds like the fight is moving around us, that way," Nick pointed to the left. Wordlessly, we all began to move cautiously forward, the way we had been going and that now seemed to be opening up.

"Quiet as we can," whispered Nick. The smell of wild fire reached us. I said nothing but tried to gauge the direction of the air movement. The breeze, if there was one, was not sufficient to move the leaves of the canopy in any way I could track. That was good in a sense. Who needs to be fleeing a wind driven wild fire as well as a bunch of armed fighters.

The reports were now coming in mostly from our left and behind us and we all picked up the pace in an unspoken agreement. It appeared we were putting the conflict behind us when a rush of smoke moved through the canopy and a burst of machine gun erupted almost on top of us, flames licking around a stand of giant bamboo less than a hundred feet away. Nick transformed into a sprinter and began to tear down the trail but Peter and Klaus didn't move, staring at the fire almost in disbelief. I followed their gaze to the flaming bamboo and flinched when one of the green chambers exploded from the heat, followed by another and then another. Nick looked back from his sprint and stopped, gawking at the little farmer who was using a back mounted tank of flammable liquid to keep the green bamboo blazing. He saw us standing there, staring at him and gave us a little wave, before returning to his chore. In the distance, another set of reports arose from the jungle.

The farmers were burning off jungle to create more fields! The dawning realization that we had not been in any danger, other than smoke inhalation. Life turns on a dime. In one moment, we were running for our lives from a war that was engulfing us. In the next, we were four moderately stoned guys walking past an agricultural burn. We didn't quite fall down laughing, but nearly. Nick waited as we walked down the path to join him. He looked at us a bit sheepishly, "The firefights in Vietnam sounded just like that. It's so freaky!"

Back in Vang Vien, it was down to the river for another swim, in part to wash off the stink of fear in our sweat. I bought our little group cold beers, back on the rear deck of the hostel and we toasted our narrow escape in the late afternoon warmth. This wasn't an exploit Nick was inclined to pontificate about but word got around anyway, via Peter and Klaus who were laughing and chatting with a newly arrived pair of German travelers. Diana was in her lounger, now being entertained by a ruggedly handsome Frenchman whose name I didn't know. Judging from the sour expression on her brothers face, he was having more success than poor old Nick. Her tinkling laughter rang out more than once, as we sat nursing our beers.

Vang Vien seemed like a place a person could stay for a while and a fair number were doing just that. I noticed, in the hotel register, that Paul and Christy had been here for three days, before we arrived. They were likely here when the Australian boy went missing in the cavern. The awful suddenness of that life being snuffed out chilled me. Here we all were, out on the road to have fun and open our horizons. Who among us expected death?

At dinner, Peter, Klaus and I decided we'd take the transport truck to Luang Prabang in the morning. While we were at the front desk, buying our passage, Nick came up.

"So, I guess we're all heading north tomorrow, huh?"

"*Ja*," agreed Peter, "it's very good here but I'm with six days to spend and I think it's good in Luang Prabang also."

When he said that, I touched the brilliant, wide-open world of possibility that lay before me, with no time limit and the allure of India and Nepal ahead. A pragmatic voice reminded me that my traveler's cheque packet was not as thick as it had been. But like death, the end for me seemed very far away.

Our transport turned out to be a small Toyota truck with bench seats on each side facing each other. Open-air up to a sturdy metal lid that served as both a cargo carrier and extra passenger space. My fellow passengers included Anon, the Israeli, Nick, Klaus, Peter, English Diana and her troll of a brother, Thomas and two Laotian women in traditional clothing. Anon and I had helped hand up the luggage and when we looked into the cramped interior we both opted to start off on the roof.

It was the best seat in the house, as far as I was concerned, and I leaned into the breeze with the luggage as my backrest. We wound our way up and out of the valley under the high canopy of broadleaf hardwoods. I had pre-rolled some cigarettes with my Vientiane tobacco and a wee line of ganja in the core. Anon and I shared a couple and wordlessly enjoyed the open-air vistas of the passing forest.

One hour out, we had to stop and unload at a Pathet Lao checkpoint. Nervous looking soldiers, now in plain khaki uniforms and what appeared to be French gendarme hats, looked over our baggage and our persons. Comrades held machine guns at the ready during this, looking on humorlessly as we shuffled off and back on to the truck. Anon inclined his head towards the gunmen when we were back aboard and quietly informed me, "AK 47's. Russian," in reference to the weapons.

Another hour on and we stopped again, this time for a pee break and Peter called up, "Hey Werner, how about a trade?"

I climbed down, as did Anon, and we traded with Klaus and Peter. It was cramped but Diana was easy on the eyes, at least. We hadn't been underway more than half an hour when we stopped fast, enough to skid a bit on gravel road. I looked forward through the driver's window and saw a line of soldiers across the road, the officer in front with his hand held up in a "halt" signal. Four of them came around towards the back of the truck while one spoke sharply to the driver, who then got out of the truck cab looking humble and stood with his eyes cast down. All the soldiers were holding AK-47's, not pointing at us but casually at the ready. The soldier who had barked at the driver came around to stand squarely at the rear and peered in at us. In a crisp English, he growled, "All Americans out!"

An electric chill ran through me. I was the only American. Before anyone could react further, he laughed and they all climbed aboard, acting like school kids who had just pulled a joke on the teacher. Two climbed into the passenger compartment, laughing and chatting with the Lao women, who answered tentatively and shyly. One went to the roof and the other two stood on the back bumper outside, holding on as we began to drive again. Diana and I were on opposite sides and she mouthed the word, "Lucky" and I nodded in agreement.

We drove for maybe four or five miles and one of the soldiers on the back slapped the side of the metal roof a couple of times. The driver came to a halt. They all dismounted and wyed to us, then disappeared into the undergrowth at the side of the road.

"That was exciting," sneered Thomas, "did you soil your britches?"

There was something rat-like in his face and for an instant I wanted to hurt him. Diana was watching me coolly and even though I wasn't trying to have her, I didn't want to appear ungallant. Habit.

"I had a moment," I replied thinly.

Thomas apparently wanted more so he continued, " You can't really blame them, the way your lot has been bombing the place. I think…,"

He was cut off by Diana putting a hand on his knee, "We know what you think, Thomas, and I for one don't care to hear it again."

Thomas' eyes darted towards Nick, who was considering him with a sardonic expression, then to the floor.

"I only…" he began, then went silent.

III

Luang Prabang lies at the confluence of the Khan River and the vast Mekong. Coming down from the hills to the flood plain, I caught glimpses of the Mekong, reflecting silver gold, and some of the spread of the city. It looked to be mostly single level, wood frame buildings with red brown rusting corrugated metal roofing. A scattering of palms and broad leaf trees filled in between the buildings. Before the bridge to the airport, that crosses the Khan, we turned left on to a road that paralleled the river and followed it to the base of a rocky hill. The way led around the base of the hill to the right, very close to the river and into what I supposed was the center of town. There was no station to speak of but we offloaded in front of a very solid, two floored stone building with a restaurant on the ground floor. Across the street, the wide, sweeping roof of a Lao style wat rose above the thick, green hedge flanking the sidewalk.

"Darling! You are a sight for these eyes!"

A clean-shaven man slammed the door of a black Land Rover parked nearby and walked towards us. I noticed that the car had British plates.

"Really just more of a sight after that ride, I'm afraid."

Diana brushed a loose strand of blond hair back from her forehead and gave the approaching fellow a dazzling smile. He caught her up, hands around her torso, but no kiss, I noticed.

"Well, no matter," he replied smoothly, "we'll get you settled in at the compound and have lots to talk about."

He turned towards Thomas, who now had both of their cases in hand, "And you Thomas, not looking too much the worse for wear."

Thomas gave a perfunctory smile, "Hello Alex, kind of you to meet us."

Alex was mid to late thirties, suave tennis pro looks with a leading man sort of chin.

"Here, let me help you with those," and he relieved Thomas of the smaller of the two cases. He moved off towards the car and Diana looked back at us, her former traveling companions, "I hope you'll enjoy your stay. Behind you is Phou Si Hill, not a bad climb and really the best place to see the layout of town. TTFN."

She turned, entered the waiting car and they drove away. Thomas' face in the rear window looked very smug.

"TTFN?" said Anon, "What is TTFN?"

A memory surfaced in me from a cartoon, a Winnie the Pooh cartoon I'd seen as a "date movie" back in high school. Date movies were the one's you'd take a girl to see, to show her you were sensitive. I remember that everybody had to see <u>Elvira Madigan</u> to show they were both sensitive and deep.

"Tah-tah for now," I blurted out.

Anon, Peter, Klaus and Nick looked at me.

"TTFN. It stands for tah-tah for now, sort of a see-you-later."

Peter snorted, "I think our Diana is a government worker."

"Or connected to one," Nick added thoughtfully. He looked after the departing Land Rover and I wondered what his journalist mind was turning over.

It seemed we were now a group of five. That's the way it went on the road and I was growing accustomed to the little constellations that formed, had a life, then dissipated. In a sense, we were all alone, all the time, but occasionally clumped together as a colonial organism, a Volvox of human cells rolling through the pond of life. Hell, a degree in Zoology has to be good for something.

The Golden River, a guest house beside the Khan about two blocks down had a room for two and a room for three. Peter, Klaus and I signed up for the triple while Nick and Anon took the double. After we'd settled ourselves, we sat together in the small hotel restaurant that had a nice deck overlooking the river and toasted to our journey with bottles of *Bière Lao*, the local brew. It wasn't too late and I felt like exploring.

"Anybody up for following Diana's advice on a walk to the top of the hill?" I asked.

Underwhelming response.

"Naw, I've got to organize my notes and get my thoughts on paper," Nick said. "I'd be up for dinner later, though."

Peter and Klaus were into their beers and Peter said, "Tomorrow for me. I'm hungry now." Klaus nodded his agreement so I turned to Anon. He shrugged and gave a wide jawed grin, "Sure, why not. Let's go."

Anon reminded me of some of my friends back in L.A. Dark, wavy hair, brown eyes, straight Roman nose and a square jaw. I liked his quick wit and the dry humor.

We had passed what appeared to be a stairway going up Phou Si Hill on the way in so Anon and I hiked back along the river and rounded the base of the stone mountain. A few hundred meters from the corner, we found the white entry kiosk and paid our thousand kip entry fee. Apparently, Phou Si Hill was considered a temple and the new government was now charging admission. It was a pretty rigorous hike, even on the paved path. We passed a series of painted cement dragons and Buddhas in nooks. A couple dioramas reminded me of the Tiger Balm Gardens in Singapore. There were numerous small shrines that sprouted burning incense and fresh flowers, a testament to frequent visitation yet we didn't see anyone around. When we finally reached the top, it was a stony ridge that ran gradually uphill to our left. The view in front was the Mekong River and below, what they called the "old" part of town, with its tree lined waterfront. Over to the right, you could see how the old town was actually on a peninsula formed by the curve of the Khan River, where it doubled back and joined the Mekong. Numerous wats dotted the townscape. Red flowered, African Tulip trees and blooming purple Jacarandas grew abundantly between the houses and along the lanes. Behind us, the way we'd come into town, I could see the bridge over the Khan River and, in the distance, the little airport.

Anon and I began to make our way along the ridge, toward a white temple that seemed to be the highest point. We hadn't gone fifty feet when the trail put us abreast of a sandbag wall and a very good sized gun emplacement, loosely covered by a roof of camouflage netting. Within a young man in the Pathet Lao uniform, wearing a floppy Khaki cloth hat, sat beside a stack of artillery shells. He looked up and smiled when we appeared and beckoned us over. Holding up the stub of a cigarette, he mimed lighting a match and said, "*Khun, mee fai?*" which I took to mean "got a light?" I took out my BIC lighter and passed it over. He tried to light the stub, which was good for one hit.

The site was perfectly situated, overlooking the airport and the river. Anything that came in by boat or plane would be literally under the gun.

I pulled out a bag of my Vientiane tobacco and said in broken Thai, "*Khun, tan khan buree, Krup?*" which meant "do you want a cigarette?"

The young soldier nodded emphatically and bade us sit with him on the sand bags. He studied our clothes and shoes, chatting amiably, as I rolled first one, then two and finally three cigarettes and handed them around. The soldier lit his and passed back the lighter, holding up his cigarette and nodding appreciatively. He continued to speak to us as we lit up, pointing at the airport and a couple of times at the artillery piece, that I now saw was mounted on a six foot wide circular metal disk. Wheels and gears could be operated when seated in what looked like a wide, metal tractor seat. I was glad we had bought a couple of bottles of the sweet, green tea before starting the climb and I extracted two from my daysack and offered one to the soldier.

So there we were, an American, an Israeli and a Lao, sitting on sand bags in a gun emplacement overlooking the airport of Luang Prabang, smoking cigarettes, sipping green tea and laughing as we tried to use my Peace Corps Thai book to talk to each other. Lao is close enough to Thai that it actually worked pretty well and we learned that Pom was a farmer from a place to the west called Luang Nam Tha, conscripted by the Pathet Lao. Basically, they told him, "now you work for us."

One odd moment came when he asked us where we were from. Anon said he was Israeli, which didn't register at all. He could have said he was from Mars. When I said I was from America, Pom's eyes showed nothing

Laos

but delight and interest. He had heard of America, that it was very far away. There wasn't a shred of animosity or change in his demeanor that I could discern. We finished our cigarettes and tea. I rolled Pom half a dozen more and left him with a small box of matches. We all wyed to each other and Anon and I walked on to the temple where we sat shaking our heads and laughing as the sun settled below the western horizon. A magnificent sunset over the Mekong, the misty river valley glowing a golden orange.

Another set of stairs below the temple led down the mountain, on the Mekong side of Phou Si Hill. Descending, an ornate compound came in to view across the street below us. I guessed it was a government building but in Vientiane the Lao flag was all red with a white figure of a three headed elephant in the center. The flags hanging from the eves of this building had a white circle on a dark blue middle strip with red strips on each side. I hadn't seen a Pathet Lao flag but maybe this was it. Red, white and blue. Sounds familiar.

We spilled out on to the street after passing through a narrow park and down a wide set of stone steps. Diana had been right about the view from the top. I felt oriented. This was the same street our hotel was on, about a kilometer further down.

Darkness wasn't far off and both Anon and I were thinking dinner. We began walking towards the hotel, checking out the offerings on the way. Ahead, music that sounded live drew us both to a garden archway. A carved wooden sign spelled out The Four Seas and across an open patio, we saw a young woman kneeling on a dais playing a long stringed instrument with little sticks, sort of a hammer dulcimer. She was against the far wall in a very beautiful old teak house that had been converted into a restaurant with two levels. A burst of laughter from upstairs and glasses clinking. The patio was set up to be an outdoor dining area, separated from the street by a low wall and a vine covered trellis.

Not for the first time since entering Laos, I felt an appreciation for the civility of the place. I wished I was in this romantic setting with Hom, both of us standing there clean and well dressed. I had to settle for slightly grubby and Anon, but so it goes. He was ok. On the way down the hill, he'd spoken of some of his exploits in the Israeli army, having been ambushed on patrol and losing friends. He made Tel Aviv sound like a great place to visit, with good music and beautiful "sabras." The army life, not so good.

"So, what do you think? Hungry?" I asked.

The Appearance of Things

"Yeah, sure, looks ok for a try."

I had the local specialty, a slow cooked spicy fish in a banana leaf. The chat at the table wasn't typical traveler BS that night. We'd been talking about the 1967 war and the attack on the Israeli athletes at the 1972 Munich Olympics. I guess the gun emplacement up top had added a certain gravity to our spirits.

"I have Arab friends. We grew up together, our lives. I can't see it only the Zionist way. But when I traveled in Europe, Spanish girls called me "baby killer" and spit at me because I am Israeli. Like what happens to US soldiers when they come home from Vietnam."

Anon took a long sip of his beer and looked up at me, "I don't know the answer. But I like Hillel, who said, If I am not for myself, who will be for me? But if I'm only for myself, what am I? And if not now, when? That's what it's like to be an Israeli."

IV

Limestone is a wonderful mineral. It can be dissolved by water and yet, reform itself in water. We sat in awe at the base of Kwang Si Falls, the rock before us a landscaped stairway to heaven of brilliant blue-green pools with white sandy bottoms. Vines and orchids graced many of the small terraces leading up to the base of the main fall. Flanking the great flow in the center, dozens of garden pools formed an interconnected staircase up and up to the jungle canopy, more than fifty meters above us. The cacophony of singing rivulets and cascading splashes combined to produce a quiet roar, the omnipresent background of a thousand watery voices.

I was sprawled on the yellow orange lip of a deep pool, gazing at the refractive ripples in the water, created by the gentle current curling around my slack fingers. The way the ripples reflected the light of the sky sent an electrical tingle through my eyes. A golden butterfly with black dots on its wings flitted between me and the falls and I laughed out loud at the vibrating trail of its flight path, that hung in the air like a maroon colored smoke then curled away into non-existence.

It had been quite a while since I had dropped acid and was more than a little surprised when Klaus produced a handful of bright orange tablets this morning.

"Anyone for tripping at the falls?" he had asked.

Of course, everyone had said "yeah" and now here we were, an hour out of Luang Prabang, up in the mountains, each discovering the jungle paradise in which we found ourselves.

It's funny, dropping acid with a group of friends. Tim Leary had spoken of "set and setting" meaning the mind-set of the person and the setting in which the trip took place. Our group mindset over these last days in Luang Prabang had been most definitely mellow, smoking ganja and reading in lounge chairs beside the Khan, wonderful food for the munchies, sunsets from the top of Phou Si Hill, even the silly journey over to the so called Famous Pak Ou Caves.

The walk up to the caves from the boat stop was lined with children holding delicate bamboo cages with small birds for sale. It was a pilgrimage spot, visited by Buddhists from all over Southeast Asia. At least it was before the war. I had liked the idea of buying the bird and setting it free, not because it would bring me great good fortune, as the child seller insisted, but because it just seemed the right thing to do. To set free that which is caged. So, between the boat ramp and the cave entry, I must have bought half a dozen birds and felt my own heart soar as I popped open the cage door. The little soul would sit for a moment, seemingly uncertain as to its freedom, then launch out into the air and flutter away. It was the children, laughing on the hill, that made me turn and follow the flight path of my sixth release. It fluttered away but at a downward angle, following the slope down to the river. He landed ungracefully in a patch of dry leaves about forty meters down and sat chirping, looking about. A mob of children moved along the bank holding little cages and, I saw, methodically recollected the birds to be sold again to the next passers-by. I felt momentarily offended but then had to laugh at the interaction. The tourist gets his liberation moment, the child gets his thousand kip and the bird? I guess the bird gets some bugs while he waits for the next customer.

The cave was really more of a long overhang stuffed with hundreds of Buddha statues. Surveying the unremarkable collection put me in mind of the road side attractions along the California coast, when we'd drive all the way up to my Uncle Art and Aunt Irene in Southern Oregon. There was the World Famous Drive-through Tree, a huge redwood that somebody had cut a car sized hole for people to drive through. And the World Famous Log House, a hollowed out length of redwood tree that someone had made into a single wide trailer sort of dwelling. Not to forget the Snake Pit or the Trees of Mystery. So the World Famous Pak Ou Cave was the Laotian version of another roadside attraction. I promised myself I'd look for the bumper sticker when the boat got back to Luang Prabang.

A splash got my attention and I saw Anon standing nude, up to his waist in a pool, eyes closed and face upturned towards the sun. He was rhythmically bending and splashing both hands down into the water. He was tripping! Across the way, Nick had climbed up to one of the hanging basket pools on the wall and was facing out, moving his hands like the conductor of an orchestra. Peter was floating on his back and Klaus was absorbed by a patch of yellow flowers, growing mid-stream in one of the multiple rivulets.

My eyes followed the hanging basket pools on the left side of the main fall, first to one, then to the next. A clear way to the top revealed itself! The falls and the jungle were extending me a physical invitation and I accepted. Raising myself from the pool to a standing position, a wave of dizziness engulfed me but then passed through and out into the earth. I began to move like the water, flowing up to the first platform.

I had kept my black Jockey underwear on when we arrived. Not having fully come on to the acid, a little voice within whispered "keep your balls covered." Now I reached the second pool, then the third. Something slipped away from the fourth pool, back into the undergrowth but I knew it was safe. I was a balloon, light, light as a feather and I floated effortlessly from pool to pool to pool. All of a sudden, or so it seemed, a flat sheet of water lay before me. To my right it cascaded over a clean limestone lip and fell beautifully through the air. Way down below I could see my fellows. Anon looked up and waved both hands. He looked small and shouted something I couldn't hear. I waved down and turned. The cool, dark stream led into the forest and a great spirit of exploration filled me. I began to follow the dark water, flowing shallow on the vast limestone sheet that formed the bottom of the stream. Indeed, it was the underlayment of the whole forest. The dark mystery of the jungle surrounded and supported me. Light ahead, a clearing! I stepped lightly out of the stream and up the sloped bank into a harvested field. Small, dry tufts of what had once been rice plants protruded from the cracked earth of the paddy and I stepped delicately between them. The blue of the sky was an electric turquoise.

Bonk! Bonk! Bonk! In the distance a rhythmic drum was sounding and it called me towards it. Thatched roofs and the woven bamboo walls of a farming village across the field. I floated across the field, a cloud of awareness drifting toward the bonk, bonk. Emerging from the dry paddy, up the gently sloping pathway into this beautiful, welcoming place. Two children playing a stick game continued as I passed. Bonk. Bonk. Ahead three women in the psychedelic, multihued hill clothing. Two worked in tandem, wielding long wooden poles with a thickened end, that they plunged into the hole of a short , thick log set upright in the soil. Bonk. A third woman squatted beside a pile of dry husks, gently scooping them into a palm leaf tray. She tossed the husks into the air with small up flips of the tray, allowing the breeze to blow away the dry chafe and leave the rice grains behind. She knelt and tossed and I squatted before her, enamored with the rice cleaning and the breeze and this wonderful place.

Something, some call, and I stood and withdrew from the village. I had looked into no one's eyes and no eyes had been turned on me. I was invisible somehow and I drifted, a cloud, back across the paddy, back down into the stream, over the edge of the falls and my stairway back.

The "peaking" part of the trip was getting behind me and I was beginning to reform as a Vernon. The Vernon looked down the stairway and had a vertiginous chill. This was very high up. You'd better take it carefully, he counseled. I knew that and I was careful. At the third pool from the bottom I stopped. The falls were no longer in sunlight! What had happened to the day? Odd, how time just passes. I recalled tripping up in the High Sierra, how we'd just sit out on a granite slab and watch the whole world of shadows and colors swirl around us as the sun made its overhead passage.

Movement, a red swirl, caught my eye and I looked down into the clear water and white sand. A tiny string of red from my left ankle. I touched it, under the water, and watched the little red streamer follow my finger out and away from the ankle. It didn't hurt.

Klaus, Peter, Nick and Anon were talking and laughing out in the sun, away from the cliff face. They sat in a semi-circle around a little pool, their feet in the water, smoking. A whiff of ganja reached me as I approached.

"Hello Werner, what did you discover?" Peter asked and held the joint out to me.

"*Danker*," I said, accepting the joint with my mostly dry left hand. I took a hit and it felt like a wind tunnel of cinnamon spice and dry leaves. The cough was spontaneous and it made my vision go to flashes and explosions of light. Sitting down seemed like a good idea. I plopped on to the pool edge beside Peter.

"There's a beautiful village at the top of the falls," I managed, "I watched a woman use the wind to clean rice."

"Bwah!" Nick exclaimed, " You walked into a Laotian village on acid? Like that?"

Like what, I thought for a moment. I looked down. I'm a six foot three white man in black underwear with acid eyes. I suddenly saw his point and laughed, "Yes, yes, I guess I did."

Acid has a way of making me feel like a depth charge went off in the middle of my identity, blowing it in all directions so there isn't any "me" anymore, just a point of awareness. As the trip begins to come to an end, all the little pieces that I guess have been in some kind of orbit begin to coalesce again as "planet me." It never seems to come back together exactly as it was before but, hey, that's why acid will always have my respect. Not for everybody and that's for sure.

I was coming back together now with a bit of a headache. My face was hot and my ever increasing self was aware of being pretty darned sun burned and needing some shade.

"I need to get something to drink and out of the sun," I said and stood up to go back where we'd left our day sacks, under a tree below.

"*Ich auch*," Klaus added. I could see his burned eyes and chapped lips needed out of the sun too.

We made our way to the lower falls area and found our taxi driver lounging in the cab, his bare feet sticking out the driver's door. He sat up and rubbed his eyes, looking out of the cab at us while we rummaged around getting water bottles.

"*Sabaidee baw*," I said and he waved back.

"Go now?" he asked.

I looked back up towards the falls and saw the other three making their way down towards us and nodded, "Yes, go now."

The ride back to Luang Prabang was curiously but comfortably silent. Except for Anon, we were all glowing with sunburned faces and lips. It had been exhausting to be out in the elements all day but satisfying too with the sense of camaraderie that comes from a shared adventure.

The next day, Peter, Klaus and I went out to the airport to arrange a flight back to Vientiane. What had been two full days of ground transport coming here was reduced to little more than an hour by air. I found myself cataloguing stories I wanted to share with Hom, when I saw her tomorrow. The visceral yearning for her had been with me since departing Vientiane but it had a new urgency, now that I was literally holding my return ticket. I didn't know what the future held for us but I felt open to anything and everything. There was euphoria in the realization of that fact.

It had become an instant tradition for us to climb Phou Si Hill for the sunset over the Mekong. On this last evening in Luang Prabang, I sat with my traveling companions on the lip of the little white temple, facing west. The ganja was good and I touched again that wistfulness of the hello-goodbye nature of making friends on the road. Nick was planning on staying on for a time in Luang Prabang while he worked on his series for The Toronto Star.

"It's just a more authentic read when I can see and smell and touch what I'm writing about," he explained.

Anon had met another Israeli here in Luang Prabang. Her name was Bat-el and we hadn't seen much of him since she arrived on the Vientiane plane, two days back. Nobody could blame him. Bat-el was gorgeous, with tight, blond ringlets, kaleidoscope blue eyes and an extremely voluptuous figure. She was smart and funny in our conversations and Anon was already head over heels. I could relate to it. They planned to travel back down to Vang Vien together, with Anon playing the tour guide. We all had a good laugh when Anon described our "fire fight" out on the waterfall walk. Bat-el put her arm around Nick and said, "You were right. I'm glad these jokers had you there. Best to be careful when bullets could be flying."

She leaned over and kissed his bald head, her ample breasts bookending his face. His look of shock and delight set us all to laughing again.

So there was the old wistfulness when we descended the steps of Phou Si Hill and made our way down to the Four Seas for dinner. It had been a brilliant orange and blue sunset and we were all mildly toasted. Entering the garden area, we made our way towards one of the longer tables that could seat six, passing a table where four guys were talking and eating.

"Aw yeah, Phuket was really brilliant."

It was a voice I recognized and I backtracked to the table and said, "Did I hear Phuket?"

The two diners with their backs to me turned simultaneously and I was grinning at Mike and Tony!

"Vernon!" cried Mike and both he and Tony stood up and we hugged hello. It wasn't as if we were long lost relatives but in the surprise and delight of abruptly finding each other here, it's as if we were.

"Are John and Louise here?" I asked hopefully.

"Naw, they're back in Bangkok," Tony replied, "getting their India and Nepal visas. We're meeting up in Kathmandu."

"Wow. Ok, so eat up and let me buy you a beer. We're over there," I indicated the table where Peter, Nick, Klause, Anon and Bat-el were smiling at our reunion.

"It's amazing," I explained back at our table, " I met Mike and Tony at Lake Toba, in Sumatra, back around Christmas time. Then we hooked up again on Phuket in Thailand, along with a couple from Toba as well, John and Louise. I'm floored to see them here."

So it was quite an evening of hello-goodbye. Mike and Tony had flown in from Vientiane and were planning on the overland return, via Vang Vien. I noticed a few glances between Bat-el and Mike and wondered where that was going. Probably nowhere, I told myself.

We talked about trekking in Nepal and it sounded terrific. Klaus and a guy named Tim, who'd been sitting at the other table, had both hiked up to a place called the Annapurna Sanctuary, something they both agreed was awesome. Then Bat-el said something that made sense to me.

" I think I liked it better out of Pokara to walk in a loop. You can hike big circle trips and go through villages. The teahouses are like little hotels and you can get food and everything. It's good to see the village life more for me."

By the end of the evening, we were all pretty loaded on the local alcohol called "Lao-Lao." The restaurant had a huge clay jug with a tap that was dangerous and the lao-lao tasted better and better as we went along. I had the skeleton of a plan with Mike and Tony to try and reconnect in Kathmandu. They had a direct flight from Bangkok to Kathmandu in a little over three weeks' time. John and Louise were aiming at being there too, at about the same time, but were working on a scheme in Bangkok to buy electronics they could sell for a profit in India.

"In India," Mike had said, "it's easy to sell a few things, like a camera. Earn quite a bit of the ready."

It was a new and interesting consideration. Even my slightly inebriated mind could appreciate that I might be able to supplement my dwindling travel funds with a simple purchase in one place that I could sell for more in another place. Good idea, really. I immediately thought of the camera shop in Bangkok where I'd bought the Ricoh camera to replace my stolen Olympus.

Mike, Tony and I left it that we'd try to reconnect in Nepal via a note at the Poste Restante in Kathmandu. I liked the idea of going on a trek all together, if it could happen. This meeting was unexpected and I was touched how glad we were to see one another again. Maybe. Maybe it would happen. But first, Vientiane!

V

Three steps down, from our plane on to the sweltering tarmac. The heat in Vientiane was intense after the cool uplands. It was high noon and the sun actually stung my skin. I hurried across the scalding asphalt to the terminal building. The lao-lao from last night had left me a little headache this morning and I felt dehydrated, in spite of having consumed more than two liters of water since breakfast.

Peter, Klaus and I piled into a taxi and headed straight to the Saylom Hotel. I thought of going directly to the Constellation but didn't. For one thing, at midday, Hom would likely still be at her ministry job. I wanted to surprise her with a clean me and fresh flowers. If she wanted to invite me to stay with her, more's the better, but it felt pushy to assume too much.

But also, there were my travel companions. I'd only known Peter since we met at the train station in Bangkok, about three weeks ago, nearly. We'd liked each other and it had been a hell of a ride. It's not everybody you can ask, "Is your gonorrhea cured yet?" and have it be a source of laughter. I'd grown to like and enjoy Klaus as well and now another diaspora was at hand. Tomorrow, Klaus and Peter would be bound for Bangkok on the evening train out of Nong Kai. Peter returning to work in Germany and Klaus pushing south. He wanted to check out Phuket after hearing stories from me, amplified last night by Mike and Tony. And me. Where was I going? In the short term, this evening to Hom and the Constellation. Somehow I couldn't feel into any reality that went beyond that, not just now.

So as the afternoon slid towards evening, Peter and Klaus headed out to, of course, the German Café. Peter asked half-heartedly if I wanted to join

The Appearance of Things

them but then grinned and simply said, "Say hello to your girl for me. *Auf wiedersehen.*"

Cleaned up and carrying a fresh little bouquet of six red roses, that looked better this time, I mounted the entry steps at the Constellation and passed the front desk. The clerk looked up at me, then back to his paperwork. I know he recognized me since I recognized him but we had the habit of minding our own business.

The few dry bougainvillea leaves on the third floor balcony seemed to me a red carpet strewn with rose petals. I took a deep breath and knocked on 312 , then waited. I didn't hear any movement within, so I knocked again. Wait. Still nothing. No rustling inside, no opening door, no Hom smiling in welcome. My heart dropped a little and the arm holding up the cheerful flowers slowly lowered to my side. Was she not yet home? Maybe she was out. I mean, it's not like I'd called and we had a date. OK, so what now. I slipped off my daypack and tore out a sheet from my small note pad and wrote:

"Dear Hom, I am back from Luang Prabang and looking forward to seeing you soon. I hope you like the flowers. I will go to La Paix and have a small dinner. If you will come, I will be so happy. If you do not come, I will return here after to find you. With love, Vern"

When I wrote the last, I realized it was true. With love. I tagged the note to her door and slipped the bouquet between the door handle and the doorframe, where she'd find it when she came home. On the way out, the clerk made brief eye contact before looking down. I don't know what was in it, but that quick look seemed ominous.

La Paix was wonderful, as usual. I enjoyed a lovely Bordeaux red and a superior chicken cooked in wine. But I sat facing the entry, looking up every time the door opened, hoping to see my raven-haired beauty entering the room. By ten o'clock though, I'd had enough of waiting and began to walk back towards the Constellation. From the street, I looked up and my heart fell the rest of the way. The red roses were still in the doorframe, the little note on the door folded and untouched. My mind was a trapped animal, barging into bars of thought I didn't want to look at. Was she with someone else? Maybe she's walking hand in hand with another man, along the riverside park. Well, ok, maybe she is. You left, didn't you? By what right do you command her loyalty?

I walked back to the Saylom, up to my room and lay down on the bed in my clothes. It was only when Peter and Klaus burst in that I awakened.

"Oh, Werner! Sorry we're so noisy. I didn't know you were here," Peter said in a stage whisper. He and Klaus were high enough to be weaving and unsteady but Peter looked at me with clear eyes, "Missed your girl, yes?"

"Yes. Missed her. She's not at home."

Peter nodded sympathetically, "Oh well, sometimes it's that way, *ja*?"

"Ja," I answered, "sometimes like that."

In the morning, both Klaus and Peter were cheerful and upbeat.

"*Zo!* Thailand tonight, eh? But *viel spass* in Lao. I like it very much."

Peter rubbed his hands together and grinned over at me, "A good coffee and the world looks better."

I was grateful for his good cheer and needed it right now. Turning the story over and over in my head, in my dreams and lying awake. That's what it was, a story I invented in my head. I remembered the monk, A-wise. He'd told me a story on the bus, of an old monk who was meditating in a cave, high up in the mountains. As part of his meditation, he used his skills as an artist to draw, on the wall of the cave, a tiger in exquisite detail. One night, he awakened and, seeing the tiger, was terrified. I felt like that monk right now, with my painting of love on the wall and awakening to find it was only an illusion.

But it's tough to let the story go. After coffee, I made the walk back to the Constellation. I'd written another note to Hom, telling her I was sorry to be such a fool, thanking her for the way she shared herself with me, blah, blah, blah.

From down on the street, I could still see the roses in the doorframe, their sad little heads bowed down, limp from lack of water. "Like me," I thought.

I made my way up the entry steps and was passing the desk when the little clerk actually spoke to me by name.

"Mr. Vernon, you will not find Hom there."

I was rooted in place and all I could do was stare at him.

He continued, "Last week, letter come from Hom parents, from Phonsavan. She must go. No come back, I think."

"Her parents?" I stammered, "Phonsavan?" I was like an idiot.

"Phonsavan in east Lao. Very danger with war. Bombs. She go," he ended simply.

My face must have been a wreck because he looked at me with shining eyes himself then handed me a small tissue ball, tied with a ribbon.

"She leave. Say for Vernon."

I reached out and received the small packet and I already knew what it was. The round, glass marble that had rested on Hom's little table, the one with the golden butterfly within. I didn't open it but placed it wordlessly in my chest pocket.

I looked up at the young man behind the desk and felt I was seeing him for the first time.

"Thank you," I said, "*Krup coon, krup.*"

"*Mai pen rai,*" he answered and looked back down at the papers on his desk.

I walked towards the market. I don't know why. Maybe because of the memories of Hom and I meeting there. The photograph of a train in a shop window caught my eye and I stared into the little office of a travel agent. He saw me, standing there in his doorway, and stood up from his desk," Come in. Come in. How can I help you?"

He was Lao but also had European facial features, dark hair parted in the middle and round glasses. I made a decision.

"Can I book a ticket on tonight's train from Nong Kai to Bangkok with you?"

He smiled and indicated the chair in front of his desk, "Yes, of course. We can book the train or the bus. Please, sit down."

I asked about a sleeper on tonight's train and after two phone calls he assured me that a ticket was available but I would need to pay in Thai baht. He'd have the ticket for me here at three o'clock. That was cutting it pretty close as Peter had said the train left at eight that night and I would need to go through the whole border crossing hassle and get transport the twenty or so miles into Nong Kai. It would be far easier if we could all go together.

"I'm afraid that might be too late. If you can have the ticket here at two, that would be better for the border crossing."

He nodded and said, "If you have the Thai baht with you right now, I can send my assistant and have the ticket here for you before two."

Maybe it was a set up but he seemed straight and I wasn't caring very much about caution at that moment. I extracted the money from my stash and handed it over. He made another phone call and when he hung up, closed with "See you at two."

Out on the street, it was as if things had come back into focus. I took a chance that Peter and Klaus would be at the German Café and walked purposefully in that direction. At the corner, we nearly plowed into each other. They were heading down to the market.

"I must buy some gifts for friends back in Germany. How's with you?" Peter asked.

I told them, as we walked towards the market, how things were with me and that we'd be on the same train back to Bangkok.

"*Schöne*," said Peter, "so we'll have a good ride back to Bangkok together."

He looked at me thoughtfully and patted my shoulder. "Maybe it's good this way, eh?"

I smiled at him and shrugged, "Yeah, maybe."

There was a rendezvous in Kathmandu in three weeks and I wanted to be there.

Chapter 9
Calcutta!

There is no illusion greater than fear.

Lao Tzu

I

"Tell you what mate, you want to see how bad it can get on earth, cross the bridge over the Hooghly and walk around in Howrah."

Those words from an Australian traveler, when he heard where I was bound for, were rolling around in my head. They frightened me.

Now I was on Sudder Street, in Calcutta, the location of the Salvation Army Hotel. It was a recommended place in my little Trailfinders Guide. I stood on the street in front of the blue-green dilapidated building, looking at the red "Full" sign prominently displayed on the closed front gates. Just getting here had been a marathon event.

At six that morning a taxi driver had honked for me in front of Somboon's little house, along a klong in South Bangkok. I'd reconnected with Somboon the night before at the Grace, a club that Peter and Klaus had insisted we visit for their last night in Bangkok. Now, four days later, it was my last night in Bangkok.

She was petite, beautiful and very Thai. When Peter and Klaus had been juggling beauties at this Patpong night club, Somboon stood back and observed our table. We noticed each other.

Now I was back. She came around, behind the booth I was sitting in, and ran her finger around the inside of my collar. I knew she was checking to see

The Appearance of Things

if my shirt and I were clean. It made me glad I'd put on a fresh shirt for this last night on the town.

Somboon and I had taken the taxi past my guesthouse, where I'd collected my things and checked out. Then she directed the driver to her place. It struck me as pretty far out of the center and before the driver left, with Somboon's help, he agreed to return at six in the morning to get me out to the airport in time for my Calcutta flight.

Our lovemaking had been a delight. Somboon was skilled and gorgeous. With her tenderness and ferocity, a passionate end to my time in Thailand. Later, as we lay side by side, she flipped on a small, bed stand light and pulled out a short stack of letters.

"These letters from my friend, John. He works on a big oil platform and love me. Here, you read."

She was playful and light, soft and so very human. In America, the seamy urban subculture of drugs and prostitution was so poisoned with self-loathing that it held no attraction. I found the red light district in Amsterdam more fun and engaging, but still, it had an off-putting edge with a "made for tourists" bawdiness that didn't ring true. In Thailand sexuality was so above board and friendly and fun. I'd needed a long time to recalibrate my attitude. I was adjusted now, just in time to be leaving. I took the letter that was offered and read as Somboon stirred tea and poured us little steaming cups, her dark eyes open and proud.

Dear Somboon,

I sure do miss you down here. I put that picture you gave me right on the mirror and I look at it every day. The other fellas on the rig here tell me I am a lucky man and I sure do think so too. I love you honey and I will be back to see you as soon as I can. Sometimes the thought that you are there waiting for me is the only good thing I have going for me in this whole darned life.

You take care and I love you a lot.

xxx John"

Calcutta!

I put the letter down and met Somboon's shining eyes.

"It's a nice letter," I said.

Somboon nodded and replaced it in the envelope after carefully refolding the paper.

"John good man. Maybe I marry him. I don't know," and she laughed with such childlike merriment that I envied John for an instant. But the night had passed in her tender embrace and the taxi had roused me. Somboon shifted, but made it clear she was going to remain asleep. I kissed her sweet forehead and her lips formed a small smile, then she snuggled herself into the pillow and was silent.

The taxi driver looked at me a few times in the rear view mirror on the way out to the airport but we didn't talk much. I wyed to him when I left the taxi and he returned the gesture.

The flight to Calcutta was via Rangoon, but not for long enough to go out and poke around. With the time difference, we were on the ground in India at eleven in the morning, local time. I'd heard things about Calcutta over the years and most recently some pretty good earfuls from other travelers. Images of the dead lying on the streets and horrific poverty were common themes. A group of Austrian girls in Bangkok had sounded almost hysterical and I got the impression of "bats out of hell" as their experience of leaving India.

Calcutta. I walked out of the terminal to hail a taxi. What was that smell? Woody and mildly spicy, muddy sage. Familiar somehow. I got a driver's attention and he roared up to the curb. We tossed my backpack into the back seat and I clambered in beside it. I noticed virtually all of the passenger cars on the road were the same model, something called an Ambassador. It had a boxy, late 40s English feel and Mr. Singh, my driver, proudly explained, "Built in India. After independence, we got the whole Morris factory out of England."

Mr. Singh had a white turban, a very impressive grey beard and moustaches that were rolled somehow into a curve that pulled down under his chin and then disappeared under his turban in the rear. His hazel eyes studied me through the round frames of his glasses.

"Where are you from?" he asked in a crisp, clipped English.

"I'm from America, the USA," I answered.

He nodded, as if that was significant, and continued, "Are you married?"

I shook my head and smiled, "No. Not married. Not yet."

"How old are you then?"

"I'm twenty-three. Twenty-four at the end of July, actually."

"Where are your mother and father?"

"Well, my father is dead. He died in an airplane crash when I was one. My mother lives in Los Angeles, in California."

"Do you have brothers and sisters?"

"No, sorry to say. Just me."

I looked out the window at what I thought was a pile of rags beside a small fire until the pile turned and dark eyes looked out at me.

"Who is taking care of your mother?"

"Well, she works. She takes care of herself."

"In India, we say the child has a great debt to the parent," he eyed me critically in the rear view mirror.

The road in to Calcutta from the airport had a forlorn, post-apocalyptic tenor. While we had been talking, or really, while I was being interrogated, we had been passing crushed hovels with small groups of people in rags huddled around numerous cooking fires. The air was smoky, like a fog, and had that curious odor I couldn't immediately place, familiar but new. I was beginning to see cows moving undisturbed amongst the ruins and out in the road, chewing mouthfuls of garbage.

"The cows are holy in India, I am told," changing the direction of the conversation, I hoped.

Mr. Singh waggled his head from side to side and I was reminded of those silly, rear-window ceramic dogs some people had in their cars, the head bobbing on a spring.

"The cow is like the mother of India. Would you eat your mother?"

The proposal startled me and I said, "No, not likely," then added with an intention of humor: "She's a tough old bird."

The eyes in the rearview mirror were not amused, so I tried another tack. When we departed the airport we had agreed on a price of fifty rupees, about six dollars, to take me to the Salvation Army Hotel.

"Do you know the Salvation Army Hotel?" I asked hopefully.

"Oh yes, the Salvation Army Hotel. Very Popular. Very nice too, I think."

We turned onto a busy boulevard and circulated in a round-about. Outside the window of the cab there were parks and trees and quite a few flower gardens. It was starkly different from the outskirts with wide lanes and well-tended monuments. It had a regal quality. One particularly grand, white building, surrounded by a vast lawn, stood out.

"What's that?" I asked.

"Ah, the Victoria Memorial. A very special place in Calcutta," he replied.

The cab bore to the left and we plunged back into the tight packed buildings of the city, albeit a more cared for looking neighborhood, with tree lined streets and a few modern, multistory structures. Suddenly, we came to an abrupt halt in front of a pile of paving stones. Ahead the street was torn up and dozens of men and women scurried about, hefting stones over to the squatting masons.

"Well, this way is buggered up," observed Mr. Singh, "I'll tell you what you do. Can you see that red tower, there, beyond those trees?"

I looked and saw what he was pointing at, across a small park.

"Yes, I see it. Why?"

"That is the start of Sudder Street, where you will find the Salvation Army Hotel. You can walk from here in one minute. It will take quite a long while to drive around this," he gestured at the roadworks.

A shrill whistle in front of us and a policeman waving for us to turn left and follow the traffic, the wrong direction. I paid Mr. Singh the agreed-on fifty rupees and waved farewell as he edged off into the detour flow. A short walk later I found Sudder Street, but no Salvation Army.

"Where do you go, sir?" queried a voice from behind me.

A thin man with great dark eyes and a loin cloth stood facing me, his head slightly tilted to the right. He was barefoot and his head was shaven.

"To the Salvation Army Hotel," I replied.

The little man nodded and said, "Come. I take you," and indicated what appeared to be a wooden chariot, with a single bench seat fit between two huge wooden wheels. A pair of long poles extended forward, attached to the chariot, their distal ends resting on the earth. I realized it was a rickshaw, a real rickshaw.

The Appearance of Things

"How much to the Salvation Army?" I asked. He smiled and held up both hands, ten fingers extended. "Ten Rupee," he said. The official exchange rate was a bit over eight to the dollar. I determined to bargain and held up five fingers, "Five rupee," I replied. He did that odd head waggle and indicated I should climb aboard. I hefted my pack up to the bench seat and then hauled myself up. My driver moved to stand between the two poles, his thin, bare back to me, and bent to the poles. With a quivering tug, he lifted them and I rocked back slightly. He tugged at the whole rig and we began to creak forward. As he got it moving, he began to trot, pulling us along at a speed not much faster than a brisk walk. I could hear the plap, plap, plap of his bare feet on the stone of the street. His breath was coming in gasps and I suddenly felt like a cruel colonial baron with my TB ridden slave dragging my privileged ass through the streets. Mentally it was a very uncomfortable ten minute ride. He stopped on the street before the front of the Salvation Army Hotel, looking exhausted and winded. How much is it worth to have a human pull you down the avenue? I stepped down and felt ashamed. He pointed to the Salvation Army sign, smiling. There were perhaps six teeth left in that smile.

I passed him a ten rupee bill. "All for you," I said. He steepled his palms and bowed slightly. "Namasté," he said simply, then picked up his posts and trotted off down the street with his rickshaw. I was standing there, stunned by what had just happened.

So, here I was, on Sudder Street, looking at the red "Full" sign on the grey-green gates of the Salvation Army. At first, I thought to ring the buzzer and say, "Really?" but gave it up. Now what?

A few passersby looked at me curiously. A woman in a red sari with sparkling gold threads interwoven in the cloth and a gold ring in her nose studied me briefly and smiled. She too was barefoot. Then a man wearing what appeared to be white pajamas, a dark linen vest and a black Nehru hat stopped. In very clear English he said, "If you're searching for a hotel, I can recommend that one."

He pointed up the street, on the other side of the roadway, a garden wall with a light green entryway. The sign read "Fairview Guest House."

"Thank you," I said, "you're kind to take an interest."

"You are a visitor to my country. I'm certain you would do the same, were I a visitor in yours," and with that he moved briskly on down the street.

The Fairview Guest House had a room for me, a garden room in fact, and five dollars got me the room as well as both breakfast and lunch, which was still being served. It looked and smelled delicious. Mrs. Patel, the apparent Grande Dame of the place, also spoke cultured English and informed me, "You are more than welcome to dine with us today, but I'm afraid we would need to charge you ten rupee for the extra meal." Looking at the bowls of curried vegetables, lentil stew, rice and flatbreads on one of the nearby tables, I nodded my head emphatically and said, "Yes, please, Mrs. Patel. It has been a very long day of travel for me." I'd eaten a spring roll at the airport in Bangkok and that was now about twelve hours ago.

I pulled out one of the white, wire backed chairs and seated myself at a table beside a flowerbed. Movement and a high squeaking in the shrubbery and suddenly two tiny grey shrews spilled out on to the stone terrace, engaged in a tiny shrew battle. I shifted my chair to see them as they rolled under my table and the noise of the chair leg on the stone startled them. For a fleeting instant we looked at each other, then they fled for the cover of the flowerbed. Their little, black bead eyes and twitching noses made me smile.

Three young men at the table beside mine had also watched the show and one of them said, "Got yourself a ringside seat, mate."

I laughed, "My first shrew fight."

Clive was Australian and he introduced his table partners, Brian and Peter Gregory, also from Australia. Peter Gregory had the appearance and energy of a jock and bristled at Clive, "Pete, please."

Clive smiled thinly at Pete but said nothing. He had slicked down dark hair, intelligent eyes and thin, pencil moustache. Clive went on say they were all from Sydney, making a point of specifying Paddington, a part of the city he implied was cooler than the rest. It reminded me a bit of myself specifying North Hollywood instead of just saying LA.

Brian's head was covered with large, blond curls framing a cherubic round face and moist, guileless, blue eyes. His hands fluttered when he spoke and there was a sort of breathless enthusiasm about everything, until Pete shut him down. With his size too small T-shirt, bulging biceps and short cropped sandy hair, Pete was the image of the athlete. They were odd characters, almost theatrical, but also engaging and informative. Clive was holding forth on why and where I should go to secure my student rail discount.

"The trains here are brilliant and really, the best way to go if you've got a choice," he explained, "and students get a fifty percent discount. But you must have the national card from the train admin office. They won't accept just a school ID."

I still had my International Student ID from last summer in Europe but Clive insisted that was a no-go. "You can use that I.D. to get the national card at the railways' office," he said.

"But it's for second class only," added Brian, "which can be rather intimate."

I noticed that when Brian spoke, Pete would often have a proprietary hand on his thigh and give him a little squeeze of approval from time to time.

They had finished their lunch and Clive slid his chair back, wiping his mouth with the linen napkin, "We're heading over to the zoo shortly if you'd care to come along. I can point out the train office on the way."

Going to the zoo in Calcutta was something I had never considered. It sounded just bizarre enough to be interesting and it seemed fun to hang out with these characters for the afternoon.

"Sure, that sounds like a slice. Let me finish up here and I'll meet you at the front gate in five minutes?"

The three exited the patio and went off towards what I supposed was their room to get ready. I took a forkful of rice and curry and made haste to finish up.

"Going off with the poofters, eh?" a voice from the table behind me.

I turned and found two meaty faces set in what I'd have to call aggressive countenance, jaws jutting out, fork and knife poised over their plates.

"What?" I asked.

"Heading out with the poofters to the zoo," said the one on the left, a twinkle of challenge in his small eyes.

It took a moment to translate then I realized these guys were referring to Clive, Brian and Pete as homosexuals in Australian slang.

"Yeah," I replied, "been there?"

"Where d'ya mean, the zoo?" said the one on the left, a bit of curry spittle on the side of his mouth.

"Yeah, that's what you asked about isn't it?" I found there was irritation creeping into my voice. I immediately didn't like the piggy boys.

"I wouldn't go with poofters anywhere," burbled the one on the right.

These guys reminded me of fireplugs and I was glad at that moment to be six foot three. I stood up suddenly, looming over them and they gave a start and then just gawked at me, wary.

"I guess they don't scare me. Enjoy your meal."

I walked off towards my room and didn't bother looking back. Couple of jerks. Not everybody you meet on the road is destined to be your new best friend.

Growing up, my mother's vocation as an interior designer had brought me into frequent contact with homosexual men in Los Angeles. I was just a little boy and these acquaintances, often referred to as bachelors or uncles, were to a person always kind and gracious to me and my mom. In her circle of close friends there was a couple named Burt and Bob who designed and made beautiful drop curtains and lampshades from rattan strips and thick yarns in their small factory in Sherman Oaks. I loved watching Burt run the big loom. They were frequent guests at our home and we at theirs for fun, bohemian parties.

Another male pair, Herb and Alan, had been her clients and became friends. They had a beautiful home up in the Bel Air hills, above UCLA. We enjoyed their wonderful pool and I loved the sunny afternoons swimming while they and my mom delighted in each other's creative company. In those days, it seemed like everybody smoked tobacco and enjoyed alcohol and thinking back on the elegant evening parties we attended, I was a privileged child. They moved away after the big Bel Air fire, in 1961, destroyed everything they had built. For a ten year old, helping Herb fish silverware and art pieces from their ash swamp of a pool where they had thrown them before fleeing that terrible inferno, the sadness and loss was wrenching to witness. Alan held Herb in his arms, weeping in the ashes of their lovely home, and we all felt devastated.

Waiting for Clive, Brian and Pete at the front gate, it occurred to me that I'd never met a homosexual couple my own age, at least not consciously. I didn't even really know if Pete and Brian were a couple. Maybe that was just the fantasy of the piggy boys. So in the late afternoon, there we were beside the Hooghly River, strolling in the Calcutta Zoo which was better than I'd expected. Many of the enclosures looked nicer than how some of the people were living on the way into the city.

On the way over, Clive had pointed out a red stone, colonial vestige: "That's the train office. Give yourself plenty of time."

Pete and Brian had laughed at this advice, not in derision, but in agreement.

The most remarkable thing about the Calcutta zoo is that more animals were roaming about outside than in the zoo. They seemed to be visiting as well, the way the outsiders looked in at the zoo animals. A line of vultures sat on a fence looking down on a pair of monkeys grooming each other in their dry compound while other, larger monkeys bounced around in the trees outside the fence. A camel stood chewing placidly in his enclosure while outside a large, black bull strolled past in the middle of the street, followed by a thin man in a dirty, white turban leading two camels and a donkey. Behind him a pack of three dog-like animals, like coyotes, slinked warily along.

"Eh, look there," said Clive. "A sadhu among us."

Walking nonchalantly, a wide smile on his face, came a near naked man in a loincloth, his body smeared with yellow mud. He carried a trident spear and his apparently long black hair was arranged in a bun atop his head. One hand was held up in a benediction to a peacock walking towards us, intermingled with the visiting families holding their children's hands. Calcutta was a Buñuel film!

Determined to secure my student rail status, the next morning, after a breakfast of sweet milky tea, porridge and fruit, I set out for the train office. The office itself had very high, yellowed ceilings. Ancient fans, suspended on long extensions, swayed gently as they spun. Below them, nine men in turbans sat scattered about at desks piled high with papers, earnestly focused on writing and occasionally smacking an ink stamp down on one of the sheets. I stood quietly at the counter and waited.

At a nearby desk an elderly man with his grey beard tied around and under his chin, thick glasses and a reddish brown turban, stamped another piece of paper and glanced up at me. We made eye contact and he held up his hand in a "just a moment" gesture and took another sheet off the stack covering the corner of his desk. The stack was at least a foot high, the papers yellowed with age, and was duplicated on the other side of his desk. I got the impression the papers had been there awaiting attention since independence. Finally, he adjusted his glasses, rose and moved to the counter at which I waited, and peered at me over the tops of his glasses, "How may I be of service, young sir?"

I was ready with my International Student ID card and pushed it across the counter to him, "I'd like to apply for the student discount rail card, please sir."

He waggled his head, "Yes, yes. Do you have your applications completed?"

"No, I haven't received any applications, sir."

He put out his lower lip and reached under the counter, extracting a packet of papers then passed them over to me. "Well my little lollypop, you'll need to fill these out before we can proceed."

I gasped a short laugh, having never been addressed as "my little lollypop" before. But his friendly, no nonsense expression checked me and I replied, "Thank you."

He indicated an empty desk, "You can take a seat there. Come back when you've completed all questions and made your signature."

It was a three page form with two duplicates. After I completed the first page, I used it as a template for the other two and was soon back at the counter. The little clerk looked up and I thought I saw a twinkle of amusement in his bright eyes. He held up his hand with another "just a moment" signal and worked through three more documents while I stood. Finally, he came over to the counter and looked over my paperwork, nodding.

"Alright. Very nice," with the head waggle. He turned, returned to his desk and, for a moment, I thought he was going to put my application at the bottom of one of those piles. Instead, he placed the packet in his work area and seated himself.

"Come back in one hour. I will prepare your document. There will be a fifty rupee processing charge." He looked at me over his glasses and I nodded assent.

Along one side of the building was a canvas canopy and I'd smelled good things on the way in. The tea sellers or "chai wallas" were a ubiquitous feature on the streets around town. Some had sit down areas like this one, others were just a fellow walking about with a stack of clay cups and a great, steaming kettle shouting, "Chai." I passed in under the canopy and took a seat on the rough wooden bench, shiny with long use, and inspected the offerings. This was a two-man operation with a deep fry wok steaming at the rear. The cook, a large, healthy looking man, stirred a batch of cooking samosas. His partner squatted on a platform near a glass case in which a dozen clay bowls of curd rested. Beside the case was the steaming kettle of chai.

The Appearance of Things

The samosas smelled great, but I started with a chai and a curd. The chai walla lifted a medium sized, obviously handmade red clay cup from his stack and poured in the sweet, milky chai. The bowl of curd was served with a metal spoon and a container of sugar on the side. Clive had said the curd was from buffalo milk and I liked the thick, tangy stuff immediately. In short order the samosas were out and cooling, so I ordered three, along with helpings of the mint sauce and coconut sauce.

A striking thing for me was that after I paid, the chai walla just tossed my used clay cup and bowl into a scrap pile where they shattered into shards. It wasn't high fire clay and I imagined that the broken bits just melted back into the earth. Disposable without pollution. The same for my banana leaf samosa plate, and a cow further up the passage was munching contentedly on all the old plates. From the earth and back to the earth without a lot of fuss.

Back into the office and back to the counter, another head waggle and "just a moment" signal. Finally, the little old clerk shambled over and said, "Have you the receipt?"

"What receipt?"

"The receipt showing your payment of fifty rupee, as I told you."

"I thought you meant I would pay here, in one hour."

He gazed placidly at me with something like sympathy.

"You must go to the office of payment, second floor, my little lollypop. But," he glanced up at the antique clock on the wall, "you may be missing them. Go quickly!"

I nodded thanks, exited the office and hurtled up the stairs. A glass pane on the door to my left read "Payments" and I reached for the doorknob. Locked. Shit! A click behind me as a young woman exited from the room opposite. She was wearing a purple sari and carrying a stack of shiny metal containers. "Payment?" I said hopefully, in English. She studied me for a moment then re-opened the door she had just exited and said something to an unseen listener. The answer from within was a hopeful, "Well, send him in."

A name plate, white letters emblazoned on a shiny black background displayed on the desk, introducing Mr. Rajiv Coomarary. He had apparently just finished his lunch and the close air in the small room was redolent with curry and basmati rice. A wide clean-shaven face beneath a receding hairline, generous lips and puffy eyes turned up to me.

He smiled, "So you need to make a payment?"

I nodded affirmatively, "Yes, fifty rupees for a student rail discount pass."

"Ah, yes. I can help with that," and he slid open a top drawer on his right, extracting what appeared to be a generic receipt book.

"Sit down there. I'll just be a tick," and he indicated a dark wooden chair against the wall.

I seated myself and scanned the sparse room. It felt institutional, painted the indeterminate shade of pale blue green I associate with hospital hallways. The orange, white and green flag of India hung limply in the corner beside worn looking photos of Nehru and Indira Gandhi. The opposite wall had an ornate little suspended shrine with a picture frame holding a photo of a man with bright eyes and dark, curly, wet looking long hair. The sudden report of a stamp slamming down pulled my attention back to the desk.

"Here you are," he said, sliding the small paper across his desk. "That will be one hundred rupees."

"One hundred? I thought the pass was fifty rupees." I picked up the receipt and looked at the fifty rupees written in the paid box.

"Fifty rupees for the rail pass and fifty rupees processing fee," he said blandly.

With that, he leaned back in his chair, folded his hands across his ample stomach and simply smiled at me. All was right with the world.

"Thank you," I responded. I paid and departed without further comment. What are you gonna say? I felt a little older and wiser.

Back below, I presented the receipt to my little lollypop and observed, "Payment charged me a hundred rupees for a fifty rupee receipt."

The little man did the head waggle as he took the paper and handed over my cellophane covered rail pass. "Bakshish," is all he said. Then he smiled in the same beatific manner as his confederate upstairs. I guess we were all happy.

II

The Victorian steel bridge over the Hooghli River led into the Howrah. The taxi driver had dropped me on the Calcutta side and now I stood blinking in the midday heat, contemplating the pedestrian path across the bridge.

There were two reasons to keep going. First, the Howrah station was the departure point for the night train to Silaguri, a place I would need to go to catch the narrow gauge rail up to Darjeeling. Second, I felt a sort of visceral challenge to cross and walk around the Howrah itself. When that Aussie guy in Bangkok had hissed it was, "the worst you can get on Planet Earth" I'd felt a stab of fear run through me. Why go there? But Calcutta had disarmed me. Certainly, there was a grinding poverty much in evidence. You didn't need to look very far to touch that. But there was also a lighthearted happiness to be seen, in the eyes of passersby and in so many of my interactions. There was a real, ineffable beauty to India that was growing on me. In the last few days the jarring juxtaposition of the horror and the sublime had begun to resolve itself inside me, with a growing affection for the place. A walk down the avenue brought the odors of incense and faeces, visions of cavernous eyes and outstretched bony hands alongside beautiful girls in brilliantly colored saris, their dark eyes shining and smiles mysterious, legless beggars and brimming food stalls laden with delightful sweets like *gulab jamin* and *halwa* and the oddly named milk bars called *Barfie*. I began to see the pain and the joy, the hunger and the plenty, the breathtaking loveliness and abject horror, almost like a swirling kaleidoscope. India was everything, all at once. It invited me. So I stepped out on to the wide wooden planks that formed the pedestrian gangway across the bridge and began to flow with the mass of people moving across towards Howrah. Across the river to my left the vast cavern of the Howrah Station brooded, smoke from the departing steam locomotives silhouetting the ochre toned arched roof of the place. From this distance it reminded me of Victoria Station in London, but somehow Indian flavored with the crowding and water stains.

Slowly, to the right side of the bridge, across the stream of taxis, bicycles and motor rickshaws, the sprawl of the Howrah came into view. With an odd mix of trepidation and elation I moved down the access road at the other end of the bridge, around and under the elevated main road, and into a warren of narrow streets and mud brick dwellings. That smell again! I'd noticed it on the taxi ride in from the airport, but it was more present here, the air had a vague haze of white smoke. Cooking fires I imagined, but not the familiar wood or grass smoke odor.

Moving down a lane, not more than six feet wide, children wearing tattered shorts or nothing at all began to tag along with me, laughing and smiling and pointing. Their great dark eyes looked at me wonderingly. The streetside walls of many dwellings appeared decorated with pancake sized wafers with a hand print in the center. The polka dot effect of the tan mud walls speckled by the dark discs struck me as a good photo so I stopped, extracted my camera, and sighted through the rangefinder. A smiling face appeared replaced by another, then another and I laughed as the little mob of children jockeyed for position in front of the camera. I got all seven of them posed in front of the wall, took the shot and they seemed delighted, except for one little naked boy who was holding his penis and crying. An older boy put an arm over his shoulder and he suddenly burst into a broad smile, his face still wet with tears. I took another shot for good measure. We moved on, some of the children running ahead.

Rounding a corner, we came upon an ancient woman squatting before a small cooking fire in front of an open door. A spittoon shaped aluminum jug was balanced on a tripod of two rocks and a piece of broken brick. Beside her lay a stack of the fibrous, brownish grey pancakes. She broke one in half and fed it into the small fire under the pot then gazed up at me. Her rheumy eyes were almost blue. In a minor revelation, I realized the pancakes were dried cow manure, and even though we had seen numerous bovines roaming about the warren, there was little or no manure on the cobbled street. It all ended up as fuel! The omnipresent incense-like odor now made perfect sense. I flashed back to Jakarta and the notion of niche, how kids would earn money selling little bags of tobacco they collected from discarded cigarette butts. It seems like nothing goes to waste in Asia.

My wanderings continued for another hour, the contingent of child followers shrank and swelled, some content to just walk along, others with outstretched hands chanting, "Paisa, Paisa." Paisa were the aluminum coins that were fractions of a rupee, not much in the scheme of things, but experience in Indonesia taught me the hard way. Better not to hand out any "Paisa." What begins as a small gesture of good will soon becomes the center of a demanding mob as the word spreads.

I began working my way back uphill, away from the river and towards what I hoped was Howrah Station. A winding sound from within a small shop drew my attention. The sound came from a hand turned bellow looking a bit like a hair dryer. An iron with an open back, filled with hot coals was being fanned to a higher temperature and as I watched, the clerk put down the bellow, flipped the tiny door of the iron closed and proceeded to press a white shirt laid out on the ironing board before him. I wanted one of those irons!

Further on, a man, or what I assumed was a man, passed me. His head was shrouded in a dirty white cloth and our eyes met as he passed. Intelligent, gentle eyes. Then the glimpse of the open nose bones, missing lips and exposed maxilla, the leprosy created Golgatha visage, sent an electrical recoil through me. And he was gone. A chill, as though I had just been passed by a medieval vision of death.

The blare of automobile horns and motors told me I was nearing the bridge road and one turn later there it was, with its flow of humanity. Howrah. If that Australian guy thought that this was as bad as it gets on earth, he obviously hasn't been to Morocco, from where some of the nightmare scenes when I was lost in the medina of Fez, feverish with cholera and stumbling into a tannery, screamed back from my memory. No, Howrah was definitely not as bad as it gets on earth, not by a long shot. I crossed the trunk road and made my way towards the train station.

Clive had been a wealth of information and I was intrigued with his description of getting to Kathmandu overland from the east, from Darjeeling. The name, Darjeeling, had a kind of romance for me and I loved the tea. He described a route from Calcutta that involved going north by rail, including what he reckoned was a very scenic narrow gauge line up from Siliguri. So, step one was getting to Siliguri. There was a night train that arrived early enough to pick up the narrow gauge morning departure. As luck would have it, a second class sleeper was available this very night and with my new 50% discount student rail card I was able to book the berth for a mere fifty seven rupees. I wouldn't have minded another night in Calcutta but Clive, Brian and Pete had moved on and at five days residency I was now a senior guest at the Fairlawn. Was it really just five days ago that I had stood looking at the Salvation Army Hotel, wondering, "Now what?"

There had been some fear in coming here, to Calcutta, to India. More than I thought or had allowed myself to notice, because now that it was gone I felt a spacious ease, sort of like holding my breath without knowing I was doing it. Now I could breathe again. I'd grown accustomed to Southeast Asia and crossing over to India, I realized now, had held a dread of the unknown. I sat on the veranda of the Fairlawn on this late afternoon, enjoying my supper and a cold beer, feeling something I wasn't accustomed to - proud of myself.

Chapter 10
Darjeeling

> Life is like riding a bicycle.
> To keep your balance, you must keep moving.
>
> *Albert Einstein*

The aptly named Mountain View Inn had a long bank of windows facing out towards the Himalaya. A steaming cup of top-rated Darjeeling tea with cream and sugar sat before me. It's a special taste, Darjeeling, and the thin cup warmed my hands on this chill morning.

"I think the one on the left is Kanchenjunga," said Frank, who I'd met on the waiting platform in Siliguri for what they called the Toy Train, the narrow gauge rail up to Darjeeling. Frank hailed from Dusseldorf, like Peter, my former traveling friend in Thailand and Laos. Unlike Peter, however, Frank was slight and rather withdrawn. Straight dark hair framed his pale face, the thinness of which betrayed the malaria he'd been suffering from in the lowlands.

"The one on the left? It looks lower than the one beside it," I observed.

"Well, there are five peaks together and I think the one that's back a little is the highest, even if it looks lower from our angle here." He sipped at his tea and had a bite of the scone he'd ordered.

The ride up from Siliguri had been spectacular. Clive got that one right. The diminutive steam train had seesawed up the steep mountainsides. It was incredible engineering. The train would go up a modest grade for about 300 meters, pass an intersecting track, and stop on the angle. Next, a trainman would dismount and throw a lever at the intersection, putting us on the line for the next rise. We'd back up the next section, climbing another elevation and passing a higher intersecting track. This process was repeated maybe twenty five times until the train had surmounted the incredibly steep face of the mountain.

Looking out toward the green valley as we gained elevation was like going up in a balloon. I'd purchased a bag of ripe mangos from a platform vendor at one of the stops, and had shared them with some of my fellow passengers. I have to admit I love eating delicious things while traveling on a small train with open windows and beautiful vistas. The open windows did have one downside - cinders the size of sesame seeds caught in the hair of my forearm resting on the carriage sill. I'd never thought about the rain of particles that followed the belching smoke of a steam train.

We rolled slowly through small mountain towns built on both sides of the track, a track that also served as the main street when there were no trains. The tolerances were very close and we would pass by people sitting on their porches or in their living rooms, eating supper five feet away. We could look into each other's eyes. It was like a living diorama, and I wondered if they covered their plates from the cinders as we passed.

With the peaked metal roofs and tall evergreens, Darjeeling itself had an attractive alpine ambience that I welcomed after so many months in the tropics. The air at 2100 meters had a dry crispness that reminded me a bit of the High Sierra in California, the pine scent comfortably familiar. Although in the Sierra we didn't have exotic Tibetan beauties strolling through the streets, laughing and joking with one another.

Frank and I had taken a room together down the lane at a place called The Timber Lodge. It was homey and adequate. The English doctor he'd seen in Calcutta had recommended Darjeeling as a good spot to convalesce after the bout of malaria. It was hard to get rid of, if not impossible, once it was well established in the body. Frank was taking a quinine-based medicine, but it only reduced the symptoms. He planned to stay until he was well enough to get back to Bangkok and then home to Germany. In the three days we had been here he had scouted around and found a small guesthouse with a lovely vista out over a tea plantation, the Himalaya in the distance. When we got back from the government guest house up on Tiger Hill, he'd move over there and I'd start making my way towards Kathmandu.

"That's where you're heading," said Frank and cocked a thumb towards Kanchenjunga. "It's really where India and Nepal meet. Tallest mountain in India, but third tallest in Nepal."

It was literally awe inspiring to gaze across the distance separating us from the snow-covered peaks. They had to be a hundred miles away, but on this clear day the impression was that they were just the other side of the valley. I didn't mind Frank going on about the Himalaya. He'd studied Geology back in Germany and knew what he was talking about. That was a nice change from some of the bilge I'd heard on the road.

Tiger Hill, behind Darjeeling and about two thousand feet higher, had a government guesthouse that was locally famous as the place to spend the night to see sunrise over Kanchenjunga. Technically, it wasn't going to be sunrise over the mountain since it was northwest of us, but as the highest thing around it was meant to be pretty spectacular, picking up the light of the rising sun and glowing against the dark night sky. In the late afternoon, we caught the local bus up to Tiger Hill. I liked the old guesthouse right away. Being up where there was seasonal snowfall, the solid construction reminded me of the antique lodges in the national parks of western America.

The Ahwahnee Hotel in Yosemite Valley, with its hewn granite block walls and whole tree trunk framing was a favorite haunt of my childhood. The grand lodge occupies a choice spot in a wide meadow, down in the valley below Glacier Point. It was well over two thousand feet straight down from the cliff edge to the valley. In the summers, at sunset, they would build a huge fire on the edge, mostly from chunks of pine bark, and we would gather in the meadow below. Then came the call: "Is the fire fall ready?" bellowed by a ranger standing among us. The response came from the top, more faintly: "The fire fall is ready." Our shouter would then cry out, "Let the fire fall!" The crew on the top would begin to shovel the red coals over the edge, forming a beautiful orange red ribbon of light that cascaded down the cliff into a cleared area at the base. It was the kind of zany thing the Park Service would allow in the 1950s. The rising environmental consciousness of the late 1960s ended the show and in the summer of 1968 I watched the last fire fall. In remembering it now, the vast Himalaya stretched out before me, I felt a poignancy, not homesickness but sort of a temporal longing. I'm way too young to be nostalgic for the old days but that's what it was.

Frank and I tossed our minimal gear into the simple room at the guesthouse. It was bare bones with wood plank floors, two narrow cots and a small table and chair. I didn't see any evidence of electrical lights so I knew the kerosene lamp on the table was it. Glad I brought my flashlight.

Back downstairs, the other guests had already gathered and sat eating the communal meal being served. It was lumber camp rules apparently, so I

The Appearance of Things

grabbed the little buckets of rice and dahl before the French people could empty them out in a second large portion for themselves. Some guy with a black beard and moustache glared at me for a moment but I just said, "Mercí," and put the pots in front of Frank and myself. It wasn't a gourmet feast but the mountains make everything taste good.

The large fireplace and sitting area were comfortable and after dinner I settled in with my flashlight, reading Breakfast of Champions. I like Kurt Vonnegut as a writer and this book was ok, but just ok. Cat's Cradle was far superior but never mind, the book exchange shelf back at the Fairlawn in Calcutta was rather sparse and I was grateful just to find something that was a "maybe".

Frank had left the table immediately after the meal, looking stricken. I had the uncharitable hope that he didn't vomit in the room. I guess malaria hit different people in different ways, or maybe he had some sort of intestinal thing on top of it. I'd been up and down with the old guts since hitting India, but, so far, nothing a Lomotil couldn't stop.

A loud clanging in the hallway jolted me awake, out of a deep sleep. Where was I? It sounded like an old fashioned metal triangle from a cattle drive Western. Consciousness returned and I remembered I was in the lodge and this had to be the wakeup call for the sunrise viewing. I fumbled for my flashlight and thumbed it on. What is it with 5 am? It was cold, but we'd made the effort to get up here for the early morning show. I hauled out of bed and began to dress. Frank wasn't moving. I had a moment when my light caught his open eyes staring straight up, his mouth flaccid.

"You ok?" I asked tentatively.

He started slightly and replied slowly, "*Ja. Ja,* all ok. Time to go to the mountain, yes?"

We shuffled out in the darkness and found that the French people had already packed the old Land Rover . The driver leaned out the right window and shouted back to us, "Grab on the back. We need to go." There was a shelf, about a foot wide, that ran along the back of the vehicle with a metal ladder leading to the roof. Frank climbed up and took hold of the ladder rails, I joined him on the other side and we were off. The old Rover needed new shocks I'd say, since every bump and bang translated through my legs and spine to my teeth. I bent my knees slightly to get some damping. We were ascending a steep, rugged road behind the hotel but I couldn't see ahead to what was coming. Frank looked petrified and on one big bump nearly lost his hold on the ladder rail. He swung back in, clinging to the ladder like a man might cling to a tree while being lashed. I just reacted and reached around him and held both sides of the ladder too, my body pressed against him and he pressed against the ladder. My hands felt numb from hanging on, and I really began to wonder if we were going to get thrown off and left lying in the road. A face in the back of the Land Rover was illuminated red by the taillights, pressed against the rear window and sneering out at us, little piggy eyes and a dark goatee. He was enjoying our discomfort, or so it appeared, and a wish to smash the window and grab him by the throat washed over me. Anger added strength to my grip on the ladder railing.

Then we were there. In the spreading glow from the eastern sky we stepped off the back and made our way round to the front of the car. Frank was rubbing his hands and looked over to me in a way that said it all. The other passengers piled out and I noticed that Goatee was helping a woman extricate herself from the rear seat. Frank was seized by a coughing fit and nearly doubled over, but I caught him up, "Whoa! Steady on. Are you alright?"

He smiled wanly and held up an "I'm ok" palm, straightening himself. The French people were talking and pointing, getting their cameras out and at the ready. Goatee and the woman moved forward and I heard her speak in Australian accented English, "I'm fine, James. Really. Don't fuss so."

They stood apart and didn't look in our direction. I resolved that "James" would be hanging on the back for the ride back down. Just wouldn't be room for him inside with us already in, poor chap, but you understand.

Now the mountain peaks to the north and west were definitely lightening up. Even though some of the brighter stars were still visible above us in the night sky, the peaks had a grey, metallic radiance. Slowly, the grey shifted to white and their tips began to glow a reddish orange. To the east, the sun was still way below the horizon. As we stood, the orange-pink light began to bathe the snowy peaks, working down their slopes, a black and white picture fading into Technicolor. I had my little Olympus rangefinder out but I slipped it back into my pocket and simply watched. That's where I was heading tomorrow and the future looked bright and beautiful.

As it happened, Goatee and the lady had small rucksacks and chose to walk down the mountain path, down Tiger Hill and back to Darjeeling on their own. I took my angry fantasy of elbowing him out of the way and tucked it into the little bag of impotent revenge stories in the back of my mind. Let it go.

When we returned to the Timber Lodge in Darjeeling it was past midday. I helped Frank carry this gear down to the guesthouse that was to be his convalescence retreat.

"You're going to Nepal then, tomorrow?" he asked.

"I am. You think you'll be ok here?"

Frank smiled, "*Ach ja,* I'm good. *Scheisse!* Tell you, don't get malaria, ok? You don't know it but in Germany I'm like your Superman." He laughed thinly and it turned into a cough.

"Well, Superman, get better then," and we gave each other a hug. "I'm not sure when but I think I'll be in Germany in the autumn. I've got a friend to see in Dusseldorf." I'd told him about Peter.

"You've got two friends to see in Dusseldorf."

Walking up the hill, I looked back down at Frank sitting on the open patio of the guesthouse. A very pretty Tibetan girl was pouring him a cup of tea, smiling and chatting. He was in good hands.

Chapter 11
Kathmandu

> Do the right thing. It will gratify some people
> and astonish the rest.
>
> *Mark Twain*

I was drenched with dye for the umpteenth time. This one, delivered by water balloon, was a lovely shade of blue and tickled as it ran down my neck and into my T-shirt. My T-shirt that had not long ago been a rather nice powder blue. Now a pair of black handprints graced my chest and the shirt looked like a bad tie-dye job done with me inside. I looked like a bad tie-dye job.

This morning I had awakened in a small border town called Baratnagar. There was not much to recommend in Baratnagar, being a motley collection of mud huts and dusty streets, but it was across the border, inside Nepal, and boasted a thrice weekly, very reasonably priced, flight into Kathmandu. The bus ride down from Darjeeling had convinced me to forego the pleasure of another fourteen hours of winding roads and motion sick passengers. I was fortunate enough to not be seated beside a sprayer, one of those people who desperately try to cover their mouth when they vomit only to have it forcefully spray sideways over all and sundry. I knew there were bound to be more bus rides in my future, but the flight was less than twenty dollars and I had decided to treat myself.

The view of Mount Everest was spectacular, flying by at twenty thousand feet and the mountain rising another two miles above us. Rugged glaciers on the southern flank, cracked and deep blue within, were straight out from my window seat. Everest was surrounded by dozens of other peaks that, from my perspective, looked to be just as high, but the little Nepali stewardess assured me that the one we were passing was indeed Everest.

I caught a taxi into the center from the airport and landed at a recommended spot called the Oriental Lodge, not far from the center of things at Durbar Square.

"You have arrived on a very auspicious day," my driver remarked. Outside the cab the surging crowds on the streets verged on mayhem, but of a very joy-filled type. My driver had instructed me to roll up the window and when the first water balloon of green dye hit the car, I was grateful to have listened.

"What is going on?" I asked, almost in awe.

"It is Holi, our great festival of color," grinned the driver, a young man with slicked back, short dark hair and very dark skin. "A festival of love and beginning again. When the Lord Krishna colored Radha's face." He said this last part tentatively and looked back at me in his rear view mirror. Didn't everybody know about Krishna putting color on Radha's face?

We ground to a halt in front of the Oriental Lodge and I looked about warily as I paid the fare. A group of drummers and dancers at the far corner had drawn a crowd and I made my way out of the taxi and into the lobby of the hotel without attracting attention. The young man at the desk clasped his hands together in the traditional "Namasté" greeting then offered a small bowl of brilliant pink powder.

"Welcome," he smiled and touched his index finger into the powder and extended his arm towards me. He was clearly asking permission to recreate on me the dab adorning his own forehead. I smiled and bent forward over the desk towards him. He drew a line down my forehead, all the way to between my eyebrows, and beamed at me. I bowed back to him and asked, "Do you have a room available?"

He nodded vigorously, "Oh yes sir! This is a very auspicious day."

He turned to the key rack behind him and handed me a key, "Very good room. You can see the stupa."

The Oriental Lodge was three floors high. The old post and beam construction lent it an ancient, solid feel, and the slightly musty odor of the place took me back to last summer in England, a historical village in the Lake District by the name of Keswick. Just like here, the ceilings in the old inns were very low and I had to bow to enter my room. The clerk was right about the view though. The room had two little balconies that jutted out over the street below. To my left, the street rose gradually uphill towards a vast white dome. A pair of beautiful painted eyes looked back at me from a golden structure atop the dome, and long strings of multicolored flags fluttered in the breeze, draping down out of sight from the upper most point.

Laughter erupted from the street below and a plume of multicolored dust swirled in the air. People were pelting each other with hands full of paint or dye powder, carried in small sacks. I noticed that the throwers were respectful of eyes and that there was an atmosphere of good cheer, like rice tossing at a wedding. Well, when in Rome, or in this case, Kathmandu, do as the Kathman-du. I fished out my powder blue T-shirt, spoilt a bit by a bleach stain near the pocket, and headed out into the street. If I was going to get doused, this was the shirt to do it in. I couldn't do much about my old jeans but it didn't seem to matter much. Two young men and a young woman spotted me and loped over, each with their right hand in a sack of colored powder. Here was an untouched canvas! They didn't just blast me though, which is what I expected. Instead there was a shy reserve and one of the men asked in English, "Will you join us, sir?"

With three gentle, smiling and multihued faces shining on me, what could I do? I held out my arms to my side, palms up and smiled back, "Thank you, I would be happy to join you."

A handful of magenta powder was applied by the male speaker to the right side of my head, starting with my hair. Then the girl, whose laughing eyes seemed coy and promising, carefully did my entire moustache in brilliant purple and stood back to admire her work. A last smear of fluorescent orange from the top of my head, down the left side of my face to my shoulder and I was on my way. My artists parted, giggling and waving, and I moved on down the street, looking at least in my own mind very much a part of the action.

Passing the entry door of a two-tiered restaurant with an upper balcony and the inviting name, The Pleasure Room, I stopped and peered into the dim interior. Half a dozen westerners, some daubed in colors like myself, relaxed at low tables. The air was redolent with hashish and steaming mint tea. My gaze focused on a woman nearby, taking a long draw on a chillum, lit by the man sitting beside her. As she exhaled, her ice blue eyes met mine and she held the chillum out to me with a grin. I was relatively new to the chillum but understood the basics of holding the cone shaped pipe between my left thumb and forefinger while cupping my right hand around the cone from behind. This allowed me to draw on the pipe without actually touching the pipe stem with my mouth. I'd had enough sloppy, wet joints passed to me in my lifetime to appreciate the hygienic aspects of this method. Sometimes in Europe people would prepare multi-paper joints with little, rolled cardboard filters and we'd pass them the same way. It was understood that one didn't foul up the mouthpiece with saliva.

Stepping across the veranda, I seated myself on the bench beside the pair and accepted the chillum. The woman, pretty long blond hair and high cheekbones, nodded to the lighter in her friend's hand and said something that sounded like *"foyergebst"*. He had stringy, long brown hair, and a thin but pleasant face with deep-set dark eyes. He smiled a little dreamily and inclined his head to me, passing the lighter as he did so. I didn't expect the hit of pure hashish and almost coughed it out. They both looked amused as I held it in and my eyes started watering.

"Thanks," I managed.

This was my first hit of Nepalese hash since leaving Amsterdam and the sly, opiated sweetness of the smoke was like being greeted by an old friend. When I exhaled, there was that distinctive aftertaste one didn't get from Red Lebanese or the Egyptian stuff. Having explored pure opium in Southeast Asia, I knew the backtaste and also knew it wasn't the main component of this hash. It was there, though.

The single sheet menu on the table was in English and I noticed that nearly every item, except for the curd, had "hash" or "bhang" as the title ingredient. I dipped my head in thanks to the pair and sort of walk-floated to the back counter and ordered the mint tea. I returned to the bench and re-seated myself.

"Can I get you a tea?" The thin faced man said in accented English, "We like the chocolate cake very much," and inclined his head toward a plate on the table, "but that's enough for now."

The girl smiled at me, "Another time, perhaps. I like you color schema."

We began to laugh, as one does. Dieter and Inga were from Hannover, Germany, and had been in Kathmandu for over two months.

"It was very fucking cold in Februar, *ja*?" he said, looking to Inga.

She rolled her eyes and nodded agreement. "Like ice," she said, not losing any of the smoke from her chillum hit.

We talked about where we had been and where we were going. Then Dieter said something surprising. "You were smart to come west. We spend too much time in Iran and Afghan. India and Nepal, fantastic!"

My face must have said something because Inga immediately added, "It's not bad, that way. Only it's better here, better for us." She looked down, as if remembering, and went on, "If we did it over, we would fly to Bombay or Kathmandu from Europe. For us, it is much more the culture and people we like."

Dieter put a hand on her leg and they smiled at each other.

That was food for thought. I finished up my hash mint tea. Drumming in the street drew all of our heads towards the door and the festival of love and life.

"You should walk towards Durbar Square," Dieter suggested, "It's like going in a time machine."

I roused myself and stood up, "Ok, and thanks for the good taste. See you again, I think."

"Tschüss," Dieter smiled, and Inga just gazed at me with sleepy, lovely eyes.

Moments later I was back in the sunlight and the noise and the swirl. The colors were so much brighter, coming out of the darker Pleasure Room with unaccustomed eyes. I swayed slightly and looked left then right. Which way was Durbar Square? At that moment, a water balloon loaded with magenta dye appeared out of nowhere and drenched me. A boy who couldn't have been more than twelve or thirteen then stopped before me and placed a bucket of what looked like black paint on the ground. Both of his hands were jet black up past his wrists and he held them up, fingers spread wide. I saw that he'd used his hands to make a visually striking pattern on his own body, like a mini zebra. He was offering me a set of handprints! I touched my chest and he nodded emphatically, dipped his hands into the pot and planted them in middle of my shirt. He stood back to inspect his handiwork. An older woman was squatting against the wall nearby and began to cackle, holding out a small tray with sacks of colored powder. I selected a wonderful fluorescent lime green and handed over the rupee.

"Thank you," I said to the boy and I placed a smear of my powder in the center of his chest. We gave each other the Namasté bow and I asked, "Durbar Square?" He pointed to my right, towards the musicians, and motioned I should accompany him. He bent, collected his pot and wordlessly began walking.

The hashish tea and the chillum loads did not leave me in the most cogent condition. After a rather psychedelic period of wandering, my young guide pointed to a multileveled brick platform with tiled roofs that was reminiscent of Bali but also uniquely of here. He climbed to the second level, and I followed. From that higher vantage point we were clearly in a huge square with half a dozen similar platforms, surrounded by medieval walls studded with ornately carved windows and topped with dark, sculpted wooden mansards. I walked around towards what offered a better vista towards the center, overlooking the swirling crowds. The boy with the pot of black dye had disappeared. I sat back on to a pile of large bags that must have been filled with some grain or seed, giant beanbag chairs! The vision before me, of people and color and movement, was like an exotic aquarium with schools of tropical fish. An overwhelming sense of grace and beauty arose and time passed, not passed and I felt so at home, at peace. It was as if the moment had a texture and existence outside of time.

At some point, the fading of the light lifted me out of my reverie. The plaza was still packed but an exodus was clearly underway, not as a torrent but as a trickle. I joined the flow heading back down the street, toward where I thought was my hotel. It wasn't nearly as far as it seemed in getting here. There it was and I found my way up the stairs. After a hot shower, a deep, dreamless sleep.

Next morning I strolled down the street in the opposite direction, away from the Durbar. Another traveler at the hotel had suggested the oddly named Aunt Jane's as a good place for breakfast or dinner. The splotches of red and yellow spread on the cobblestones were familiar and harkened back to the mad exuberance of yesterday's festival. The cool morning air was tinged with wood smoke and incense, at once homely and exotic. I felt high but not hung over. Holi really was a joy filled memory and I found myself wrapped around it and protective, a tender shoot needing care.

Aunt Jane's smelled like apple pie and cinnamon. I found an empty table near the front windows and ordered a chai and what they called their Famous Banana Pancake. A whiff of hashish told me somebody was already hard at it. I didn't bother looking around to see who because a tall woman with long, curly, auburn hair had just walked in and she had all of my attention.

In my heart I was hoping to find a woman to travel with from here on to Europe. All the women travelers I had found attractive and interesting since leaving Southeast Asia were either already attached, going in a different direction or, truth be told, not interested in me. I felt like my radar about people was improving, though. Louise had told me in Phuket, with her wry grin, "Just be yourself Vernon. Everyone else is already taken." I found out later she was quoting Oscar Wilde, but at the time I was very much taken with her and her apparent sagacity. Again, the sense of being a citizen of a floating country, the country of travelers that sloshed between Europe and Asia and a relaxed feeling of belonging I'd not known before. Either I'd meet somebody or I wouldn't.

The girl at the door looked my way, lovely face, wide set eyes with an appealing sparkle. "Hi, got room at your table?" Husky, confident voice, Australian accent.

"I think I was waiting for you," I replied, shooting for casually charming.

She grinned, then introduced herself with a generous smile. "Margaret," she said, pulling out the chair.

"Vernon," I returned and couldn't help smiling back.

"American or Canadian?"

"American," I said, "California."

My famous banana pancake arrived at that moment, steaming and aromatic.

"Mmm, that looks like the ticket," and she held up one finger to the dark haired girl server, "Me too and… how's the chai?" I nodded approvingly. She turned back to the waitress, "And a chai."

Margaret hailed from Melbourne. I'd never been to Australia, but I'd met so many travelers from there on the road in the last six months that I was getting a feeling about the place. Melbourne people gave the impression that their city was a bit more formal than Sydney but rather more sophisticated fun was to be had as well. A little like how in California LA was bold and brassy where San Francisco was the very hip grande dame.

As we talked, doing the get-to-know-you dance, the shoe never dropped about "my boyfriend" this or "my husband" that. I liked the way she played with her green blue eyes. She'd crinkle her nose a bit like a rabbit and had a robust laugh I immediately took to. When we both stood to leave, it was apparent that we'd be a good fit physically as well.

Margaret reached out to collect her small day sack off the chair and I saw her wince with pain. "Crikey," she exclaimed, "I must've strained a shoulder yesterday." Then added with a radiant smile, "That was quite a show, wasn't it, all the colors?"

I agreed that it was and as we began to walk towards the post office together I was glad to have someone who knew the way.

"I check Poste Restante about every three days. Me mum's got a worry with me out here," she explained, "and the family in England writes too. Want to know when I'm showing up."

Our breakfast discussion had touched on trekking out of Pokhara. It seemed to me we were moving towards an informal alliance with each other, at least on the trekking idea. Going out alone, especially as a woman, was a bad idea and we both knew it. We were testing the water with each other, her more than me in this regard. All the "getting to know you" stuff did seem to be going in the right direction. I wanted to check Poste Restante too since I'd written everybody from Bangkok that this would be my next mail stop. Then the oddest sense of time engulfed me. I'd written those letters before heading out to Laos, before finding and losing Hom, before that amazing trip to Vang Vien and Luang Prabang, and the acid trip of trips out at Kwang See falls. It was so long ago, a lifetime ago, hardly even me. But it was. The stunning relativity of time passing on the road had me shaking my head in wonder when Margaret announced: "OK, here we go."

Half a dozen steps led up to the portico of a solid, colonial style brick building. I followed her up and into the surprisingly vast interior, ceiling fans whirring far above our heads. The Poste Restante was at the far end of the hall and a small queue of westerners shuffled towards a pair of grated windows that looked like a bank teller's station.

Margaret looked at me sideways, "Expecting anything?"

I realized with a small shock that she was looking for the other shoe to drop too. A warm flush ran through me that maybe this lovely woman and I might be heading to Europe together, And out of nowhere it was like my nuts pulled up into my body and the old fear of not being enough engulfed me. It had been so long since this particular demon had beset me that, for an instant, I was disoriented. There I was feeling cool, confident, proud - a worldly traveler and a man. Next moment touching the weak and inadequate, an ugly impotence pulling my heart and spirit into a black tar, threatening to drown me. I don't know what my facial expression was, but Margaret's expression shifted from flirty amusement to something like alarm.

"You ok?" she asked, placing a warm hand on my forearm.

Kathmandu

I glanced at her. An anger exploded in the middle of my chest, directed inward at the weak one that was trying to come into existence. Like opening the door of a blast furnace, the withering fire of the rage hit the impotent one and I felt it scream as it died. It all happened in an instant. I looked at Margaret, found a sheepish smile and winked.

"Maybe a little superstitious, like getting a telegram. You never know what the news might be in a letter." I shrugged, "Mostly I just hear from friends and, like you, my mom. That's all."

I forced a smile but she seemed reassured.

"Aw yeah, nobody likes bad news, eh. Well, hope you don't get any," she grinned and gave my arm a friendly squeeze.

And it was all good news. Two letters from friends in LA, two from my mom, one of which had a cashier's check for a hundred dollars marked "Merry Christmas". A twinge of guilt that she was still working and I was out having the time of my life. And, surprise, a note from Mike Cassoway.

We went outside and sat on the ledge of the building, reading and re-reading our mail. The note from Mike said he and Tony planned on being in Kathmandu the first week of April, and here it was, April 5th. Maybe they were already here. "This is good news," I said to Margaret, holding out the letter. "It's from a couple of Australian guys I've been running into off and on since Lake Toba, in Sumatra. We all hooked up in Thailand, on Phuket, and then I saw them up in Laos. Mike said they'd be coming this way. Incredible!"

Margaret reflected for a moment, "Well, it sounds like our little expedition is beginning to form up, eh?" She smiled her pretty smile and a twinge of jealousy stabbed through me. Mike was a handsome guy. She'll like him better. I tamped the fear back down. What was the matter with me?

"Yeah," I nodded, "I reckon you'll get a kick out of them. Maybe some others too, John and Louise. We might end up as quite a mob roaming through the Himalaya."

In the way that odd, unlikely and entirely surprising events arise when traveling, Mike and Tony turned the corner of the building and began walking towards us, chatting animatedly together. They drew abreast of us, not yet noticing me sitting there with Margaret.

In my best fake Australian accent I said, "G'day mate, spare a fag?"

Mike looked up at me and froze, then burst into laughter.

"Bloody hell! Small miracles. Vernon, we were really just talking about you!"

Tony held back, surprised and grinning self-consciously, looking over to Margaret and back to me.

"Margaret, meet Mike Cassoway and Tony Regan. Mike, Tony, meet Margaret McGrath from Melbourne."

They flopped down on the ledge with us and we all had smiles a mile wide.

"When d'you get here?" asked Mike.

"Well, literally yesterday, just in time to fall into the middle of the Holi Festival. Were you guys here for that?"

"We were here," proclaimed Tony and lifted up his T-shirt, displaying a large swath of purple stain across his belly. "Some of it don't wash off so easy."

Margaret's robust laugh rang out and Tony quickly lowered his shirt, looking a bit caught out but showing his bucktoothed smile nonetheless.

Mike eyed Margaret appreciatively for a moment then said, "Tell you what, we're going to go check for mail. John and Lou should have a note here by now as to where they are." He shook his head, "We come around the corner and here you sit. Don't go off - we'll be quick."

"She'll be right," added Tony and they shot up the steps.

Margaret was looking at me, quite amused.

"So your friends seem very glad to see you. What are the chances, do y'think?"

"What, you mean that we'd be sitting here and they'd come round the corner, out here in Kathmandu?"

"Jeez, I guess the chances are about a hundred percent." We laughed at the absurdity of it.

And there had been a sort of plan but I felt too delighted to bring that up. Mike and Tony had been staying at the locally famous Camp Hotel but were ready for a change. As Mike said, "The place was built for hobbits. I can't stand up straight in any of the rooms and the beds are so close to the ceiling that I crack my skull if I sit up in the night." They had been in Kathmandu for the better part of a week and were planning on heading out to Pokhara in a few days. "Best place to start a trek from, we hear," explained Mike.

I had wanted to spend more time exploring the Kathmandu valley but figured I'd be back this way after the trek. And the expected letter from John and Louise had arrived. They weren't leaving Bangkok for another two weeks.

"We'll meet them up in Pokhara but they'll miss the trek," Mike reflected.

"Lou wan't too keen on it anyway," Tony said with a shrug.

Mike shot him a glance that made me wonder what wasn't being said.

They moved over to the Oriental Lodge and we three got a larger room together. Margaret was there as well, sharing with a woman she had met here named Frannie. She was also from Melbourne and they seemed to be fast friends. So now we five sat in the Pleasure Room, sipping minty hash tea and getting serious about doing a trek together. Things between Margaret and I felt stalled, but Frannie had immediately warmed to Mike. Tony seemed to be perpetually the odd man out but he didn't mind the role. He'd had a snort of his heroin before we left the room and was nodding pleasantly.

Mike tapped the map before us on the table. "It's basically a one day walk from Pokhara to Naudanda. Then we can go in about three different directions."

"I like a loop, so we're seeing new territory for most of the trek," I added.

Mike and Margaret nodded and she traced a dotted loop with her finger. "This one, that goes out to the Ghandrung place, has a good loop but there is backtracking from Biritanti, back to Naudanda and Pokhara."

Frannie sipped her tea, "I heard from some people who did the Annapurna Sanctuary that it was fantastic, but it's pretty much up and back the same canyon."

The map didn't really give us the topography, but high peaks were marked and the rivers obviously traced canyons. The tenor of the conversation was "no problem" and the plan was made to push out to Ghandrung. We'd need to visit the government trekking office in Pokhara for the permit but other than that, and collecting some cooking gear, it was good to go. I looked across the table at Mike and noticed him smiling wryly at Frannie. She was attractive, oval faced with henna red, longish hair that was naturally wavy. Her dark eyes had a seductive depth to them at this moment as she returned his gaze. Some guys just seem to have that appeal for women. I admired and even envied that quality. I caught Margaret's eye and she smiled, but there was a fatigue in her face and not much sparkle in her eyes.

"Are you ok?" I asked.

She seemed startled and I saw her rally herself, sitting up a bit straighter and brushing a few strands of auburn hair back over an ear, "Aw yeah, never better, just a bit of a headache."

There was a jolly huskiness in her voice, the good sport, but I was getting to know her better and this felt forced. Maybe it was just the smoke and the hash tea kicking in. We weren't yet lovers but there was the quick bond of friendship that can form on the road when people are a long way from home.

Back at the Oriental Lodge, Tony looked a little shaky when I came into the room. He was seated on his bed and hunched over a cloth spread across his lap. He looked up, "Hey Vernon, tell you what. I need you to keep this away from me." He held out a medium sized tin of Tiger Balm and pressed it into my hand. But I knew inside wasn't Tiger Balm. He'd opened it earlier in the evening and dipped out a penknife blade of pearly white powder.

"Keep it away from you? You mean don't let you have any?"

Tony nodded sincerely, a pleading quality of suffering in his eyes, "Even if I beg you, ok?"

I guess we both knew that if he really wanted and demanded the tin, I'd pass it over. "OK," I said, accepting the container and slipping it into my jeans pocket. Tony sniffed and rubbed his nose, looking a little ashamed. He wordlessly left the room, heading down the hall towards the water closet. Extracting the tin from my pocket, I stared down at the yellow tiger on the red background. What the hell should I do with this? A beam in the low ceiling caught my eye, a decent gap halfway long between the wood and the plaster ceiling. I wedged the tin in so that it was invisible unless you got right up and peered into the opening. It was a good hiding place and at least I wasn't holding the stuff. Getting caught with it here probably wouldn't be a good thing.

Next day we all set out in different directions. Cashing the check my mom had sent me required hours at the bank, with copies of my passport needed and endless clerks looking at the check and looking at me. And that was for the official exchange rate, about twenty five percent less than the street rate. What are you gonna do? I was grateful to have the cash. Margaret, Frannie and I met at the tourist office and booked on the minibus to Pokhara. Mike and Tony had decided to save about six dollars and take the regular bus. It was another curvy road between Kathmandu and Pokhara. Enough said.

Late in the afternoon, Frannie and Mike announced they were off to take in the sunset from Swayambunath, the big stupa on the hill about two kilometers outside the city center. The way they said it didn't invite us to come along. Margaret and I smiled at each other and Tony studied his very interesting fingernails.

"Sounds like a good Kathmandu night out," I offered, then to Margaret, "And what d'you fancy, Miss McGrath?"

She glanced over at Tony and said, "I think we three should head out for some tucker at Aunt Jane's."

Tony looked up then, and his face said, "Thanks."

I bobbed my head in agreement, "Sounds good to me. I've got the munchies." Lunch had been a bowl of curd and honey at Himalaya Cold Drinks, tasty but not much of a meal. "I'm going to treat myself to a buff steak and anyone else who'll join me." Both Tony and Margaret raised their hands and we all headed out.

About five minutes later, walking up the hill towards Aunt Jane's, Margaret stopped and placed a palm on her forehead. "I don't know what's the matter with me," she gasped, "I feel weak as a kitten." I offered my arm and she leaned on it, as we continued walking. A pang of real worry crept from the back of my mind into the present, but I said, "Well, maybe a good dinner will put you right. We did a lot of walking today." She nodded and smiled wanly. We walked the rest of the way a little more slowly. Tony shot me a look of concern but kept to his silent self.

On the way home Margaret seemed more herself. She took both my arm and Tony's arm as we walked down the hill, Dorothy approaching Oz with the Cowardly Lion and the Scarecrow. The suave Tin Man was out with Frannie.

The minibus had a seven a.m. departure and I left Mike and Tony snoozing in their beds at first light. They were awake enough when I finished packing to wave goodbye. "See you in Pokhara," managed Mike. We had agreed I'd leave a note as to where we were staying on the message board at the trekking permit office. The local bus was cheaper than the mini, but it also took three hours longer.

Frannie had a dark look about her as we sat three across in the back of the minivan, me on the far left, Margaret in the middle seat. "How was the sunset?" I asked cheerfully.

Margaret cast me a glance that said, "Leave it alone," so I did.

Kathmandu was just waking up. The air was glowing pink as dawn light caught the smoke of the cooking fires and incense. We were virtually the only vehicle on the road and the ornate stupas and huddled villages were coming to life in the light of the sunrise, quietly beautiful. In the center of many villages a huge tree had been transformed into a temple, festooned with prayer flags and small shrines. I also knew the burned dung smell and had begun to love it, the way it spoke to the heart with an ancient tenderness.

I was glad of the left seat for several reasons. The unencumbered view out over the mountains was stunning. The hills we drove through were mostly bare of trees and the flower studded green slopes reminded me of parts of Switzerland, but on a larger scale. The second reason was I didn't have to see all the near misses with oncoming trucks and busses. Frannie yelped more than once and finally put her jacket against the window, faking sleep.

I leaned over to Margaret and whispered, "What happened?"

She cleared her throat gently and leaned closer to my ear, "Let's just say that if Mike is going on the trek, Frannie isn't."

I felt surprised and wanted to ask "What happened" again, but Frannie stirred and began to fumble for her water container, looking out the window with a set, grim expression.

Pokhara has an oddly rural feel to it, open lanes and lots of trees. There wasn't anything like what I'd call a downtown, except maybe the tourist office and the trekking permit government buildings, where the minibus ended its run. It was more like being in a large neighborhood, separate one and two story houses connected by gardens and tree shaded passages. Looming behind a set of wooded foothills, the snowy peaks of the high Himalaya were an impressive backdrop. It was exciting and a bit daunting to think that's where we were headed.

Margaret, Franni and I found rooms at Green Acres, a rambling Victorian villa, two floors high and surrounded by loosely tended gardens and a few fruit trees. Near the entry path, a magnificent lemon tree dominated the grounds. With spring making itself felt, the buds of the coming flowers on the tree saturated the warm air with a lemon perfume. I stopped and just inhaled. I love springtime.

The owner, Hamid, a small-boned man with tender, dark eyes produced a pitcher of lemonade and three small glasses and bade us sit at one of the small garden tables. "The lemon drink of my home," he proclaimed and filled each of our cups. "Welcome, please enjoy your complimentary first glass as my guests."

Mostly, I had learned, water needed to show some sign of having been boiled before being consumed. This was most often accomplished with the presence of a small tea leaf, giving the water a slightly orange or brown tint. Hamid noted our hesitation and offered immediate assurance. "Made with our own boiled well water. Very clean, no worries." He said this last part with a hint of Australian twang and a head waggle. His manner was so sweet and charming. I liked him immediately. We tipped our glasses to him and offered thanks. And it was delicious, not too sweet but wet, cool and refreshing. "Two rupee per glass or a pitcher for ten rupees," he added.

When we signed in, I noticed a guest list of some fifteen or twenty people. Everyone I could see, either on the classical veranda or out at the garden tables, was a westerner. This really was trekking central but what the hell, that's why we were here. I could see the charm though, of setting up a household in this lovely valley and staying for a while, like we did in Phuket. There was meant to be a lake nearby with good swimming.

A few miles away to the north, a long ridge extended itself into the valley from the far foothills, the great foot of a giant. I could make out, even from this distance, the zig-zag route of a switchback ascending the flank of the ridge, leading to the top. A gradual climb along the ridge led to the wings of the foothills, extending back in both directions, roughly northeast to southwest. Beyond them the spiky, snow covered peaks jutted into the electric blue sky. A few thunderheads had boiled up between the foothills and the higher mountains beyond. In the fading afternoon light they glowed, golden pillows.

Nightfall came, but the ambient light lingered, reflecting down into the valley from the white peaks. No Mike and Tony. Frannie appeared less tense than in the morning but said nothing about what might have gone down to end her participation in the trek. We three ate our chicken curry dinner quietly, making small talk about the day and refreshing ourselves with the lemonade.

Margaret was worrying me more. Since we'd arrived she had been listless and almost like a rag doll. "Do you have any fever?' I asked and uninvited, placed my palm on her forehead. It was cool, almost clammy, the opposite of fever.

"No," she sighed, "just this horrid headache and feeling like I've popped a cork and everything is running out. Took a couple of aspirin and that's helped a bit." She lifted her right arm and looked at it like a stranger, "I don't know what it is. I can scarcely lift my arm."

She gazed over to Frannie, who was watching her intently and looking alarmed. "Look Maggie, sorry to ask but have you got the shits?" She leaned over and placed a hand on Margaret's forearm.

Margaret looked at her kindly and shook her head "no."

"I know what you're thinking Fran, but no, it isn't dysentery or any sort of tummy wog I know about. Don't know what it is. I feel so strange, like my body is leaving me."

I was growing alarmed as well. So far, on the road, I'd met malaria, Bali belly, all manner of gut problems, people yellowed with hepatitis, even wasted with leprosy. This seemed more neurological and I was picking back at some UCLA pre-med thinking. She was acting a bit like loss of electrolytes. I felt that way in Morocco when we got the cholera, but I know she's been eating and drinking enough. If she hasn't got the shits, what else? Some kind of parasite or virus?

"There's a clinic we passed coming into town. You saw it, yeah? If you're not feeling better in the morning, let's get you over there for a check-up, ok?"

Margaret smiled at me, "You are a dear. I'm so sorry to be a bother. I'll be right as rain in the morning," she said, forcing the perky tone. "You'll see."

I awakened in my room at first light. The dream, I didn't remember, but the feeling it left in my body was light and happy, like a flying dream does.

The two empty beds in the room reminded me that all was not right with the world. Where the hell were Mike and Tony? And how was Margaret this morning? It didn't appear that we were headed towards being lovers but I liked her a lot. It was fun to meet a woman with such pluck. Maybe it was something that Australia did to women? They pick it up as sort of an armoring since so many of the Australian guys I've met are a rough lot. Margaret had that audacity in her laugh and in her self-assured firm voice.

I went downstairs and had a chai and porridge. I was finishing up and enjoying a mandarin orange when Frannie appeared beside my table looking distraught.

"Vernon, you need to come up. Maggie is seeing double and can't stand on her own to get to the loo."

I felt my heart drop and something I didn't like, a voice inside saying, "Oh shit, here we go." It was the tinny, selfish voice of someone who didn't want to be bothered. That's not who I am, is it? I followed Frannie upstairs and found Margaret looking at me with wide, fatigued, fear filled eyes.

"I…can't move," she whispered and her pretty face collapsed in tears. Frannie and I both quickly sat on the bed beside her, Frannie taking her hand and squeezing it. I really didn't know what to do.

"Here, let me help you sit up," and I reached around her back and cradled her head in my hand. She wasn't quite a dead weight and I could feel the muscles of her abdomen tighten with effort, trying to help.

"I'm so sorry," she murmured and her head nearly fell forward.

"We'll take you down to the loo, alright Maggie?" Frannie was gentle and solicitous.

Pulling her up on each side, Margaret seemed to find her footing and supported herself. We slow walked down the hall and I was grateful Green Acres had an actual European style sit down toilet and not a squatter. When she'd finished, we walked her back to the bed. Frannie agreed to stay while I set up a taxi to get us to the hospital clinic.

Hamid had no telephone, but he sent a boy running and within fifteen minutes a rattling old London black cab pulled up at the bottom of the path. Between Frannie and I we got Margaret dressed and helped her down the stairs to the waiting cab. She seemed stronger and said the double vision thing had abated, but her arm was shaking as she reached into the cab to steady herself and was obviously a long way from "right as rain".

The clinic was a single story complex of three buildings connected by covered walkways, its plain tan exterior streaked but not in disrepair. I went in and told the nurse at the desk we needed a wheel chair or a gurney. She spoke cultured English and told me to promptly return to the car and wait with the patient, then disappeared through a door behind her. In less than a minute two orderlies arrived pushing a gurney and brought it alongside the car. Between myself, Frannie and one orderly, we got Margaret out of the cab and stretched out on the wheeled, flat bed. Margaret looked up at us silently but mouthed the words, "Thank you."

We wheeled her over the threshold and into a side examination room. On a side table I noticed what appeared to be injectables of saline and glucose solutions but they were in old Coca Cola bottles. A small hole in the cap gave access for a syringe needle, but where was sterile protocol? Before I could think too much about it the doctor entered the room - a young, good looking Nepali man. He was neatly dressed in clean whites and set straight into examining Margaret.

"Good morning," he smiled, "I'm Doctor Kavini and I'm going to need to check your vitals, for the record."

He nodded towards the clipboard being held by the orderly. I don't know why, prejudice I suppose, but his clipped, educated English accent put me at ease. Margaret too, I think. She nodded assent and he began to unbutton her blouse. I made eye contact with Frannie, who understood, and excused myself from the room. The hallway was a bit littered near the edges and what I took to be paint splotches on the walls, on closer inspection were dried blood. They were just at the right height for a gurney and the unpleasant image of the bed hitting the wall with a bleeding patient leapt to mind. The staff seemed competent, but the facility sure needed some care.

I wandered out an inner door, into a small courtyard containing a bench and a shade tree. A few tired flowering plants were scattered about near the walls of the building. Settling on the bench I reflected on what I would want for myself, if I were Maggie.

The hum of bees in the tree and the warmth of the sun were hypnotic and after what seemed a very long time, movement down the hall caught my attention. Frannie had come out of the exam room, looking left and right, finally spotting me through the window. I stood as she opened the door.

"We need you to go back to the hotel and collect Maggie's things." She looked very stressed out. "It's not conclusive but Dr. Kavini says her symptoms are consistent with tuberculus meningitis. They want to send her to the big hospital in Kathmandu, by air, today." Frannie looked back down the hall and added, "I'm going with her. Look, if you'll bring my bag too that will really help. My passport pouch is under the pillow. Grab that too, alright?"

"Yeah, sure, of course," I stammered, "What can I do for Margaret?"

Frannie looked a little exasperated, then her face relaxed. "If you'll just bring the gear, it will be loads of help. I'm going to stay here with her."

In the taxi I felt stunned at the speed with which things had altered. The trekking trip with Margaret and Frannie had completely blown up, my new friend Margaret had gone from robust to bed-ridden in four days, Tony and

Mike had disappeared and who the hell knows what happened between Mike and Frannie. How did everything get so screwed up?

The taxi rounded a corner, heading down the lane towards Green Acres when a pair of walkers on the side of the road came into view. I recognized the pair from the back - tall, long-haired Mike and shorter, thicker Tony. I knew their backpacks and could see Mike's guitar as we passed.

"Stop! Stop here, them!" I shouted to the driver.

Stepping out of the cab, I waved and yelled back, "Looking for a ride?"

They recognized me and shouted, "Hallo Vernon. We're a bit late, I'm afraid."

Mike was wearing a white headband that was certainly a bandage of some kind. As they drew up, I saw that Tony too was a walking wounded having a bandaged left forearm and his face splotchy with bruises.

"What happened to you guys!" I gasped.

Tony shrugged and looked upward, as if appealing to a deity to witness for him. Mike spoke, "Bloody bus went off the road. It was a near miss. Rolled over four or five times. We wedged in a rock fall and that's the only thing that prevented us from going all the way down!"

"Dead," added Tony dryly.

He looked pretty beat up.

"Come on then. Put your packs in here. I'm going back to the Green Acres hotel, where we're staying."

"Yeah, got your note at the trekking office when we got in. That's where we were heading," Mike said. Then he asked rather cautiously, "Is Frannie there?"

Where to begin. "God, it's been pretty weird here too. Yes, Margaret and Frannie are there, eh, were there. They're both flying back to Kathmandu this afternoon. I'm on my way back to collect their gear and return it to the hospital."

"Hospital?" asked Mike, "What happened? Did you lot crash as well?"

"No. No, Margaret got sick last night. I mean, she was really sick this morning, double vision, bad headache, couldn't stand up." Mike's eyes grew larger as he listened. Tony was staring out the window of the cab, shaking his head, I guess in disbelief. "The doctor at the hospital here thinks it's some kind of bacterial meningitis, but they've got to get her back to Kathmandu for some kind of spinal tap to be certain. Frannie is going with her."

At this last point, Mike visibly relaxed but his face was still showing concern when he asked, "Is Maggie... well I mean, is she going to be ok?"

I shrugged. "Honestly don't know. People die from meningitis, if that's what it is."

"Crikey," Mike mused, "came on just like that, eh?"

We were all quiet when the taxi pulled into Green Acres. Mike and Tony went in to register, happy that I'd set up the room for three. I went into Maggie's room and gathered up her and Frannie's rucksacks, stuffing whatever I found lying around into the bags as well. I guess if it were the wrong underwear, they'd get it figured out. I found Frannie's passport case under her pillow, as well as a surprisingly long and pointed knife. Both of those things went back into her bag.

On the way out, I stuck my head into my room. Mike was standing in front of the small wall mirror, his bandage off, gently touching a pretty bad smash on his forehead.

"I'll be back in a bit. I'm bringing their luggage back over to the hospital."

Mike nodded and Tony said, "No worries. See you back."

"Try the lemonade, when you get settled in. It's pretty good. See you soon."

I felt truly glad to be able to do something to help Margaret. There was a lingering back taste of shame, though. I was grateful that Frannie had decided to take on the responsibility of getting her back to Kathmandu. I knew myself well enough to know that had Frannie not been a part of the picture, I would have been there for Margaret and seen to it that she got the help and care she needed. But I also knew that I was relieved not to be the one and was still looking forward to the trek with Tony and Mike. That's where the shame came in.

Back at the infirmary, I lugged the rucksacks into Margaret's room and set them at the end of the bed. She looked better, eyes clearer. Dr. Kavini had apparently acted on his instincts and given her an injection of the antibiotic cocktail they usually used for this condition. The tuberculosis was apparently all too common in the Kathmandu valley.

"So sorry to be such a mess, Vernon. I was looking forward to our trek,"

Maggie's voice was ragged, she gazed at me from the bed and I nodded in agreement.

"Me too."

It's such a helpless and frustrating feeling when someone you like is ill. We visited a bit then Frannie suggested maybe it was time for us to let her rest. "I'll send a telegram to the Green Acres, when we know something," she said.

I gave Margaret a hug as I left. The taste of the salt of her tears lingered on my lips as the taxi took me back to Green Acres. Our only real moment of physical intimacy had been to kiss the tears on her cheek as we said goodbye. Life is so weird sometimes.

The telegram had confirmed the meningitis and added she and Maggie were flying back to Australia together. Frannie confirmed Maggie had responded well to the antibiotics but just wanted to go back home. I couldn't blame her. It felt like a near thing and it was sobering to realize that any of us could get knocked down. At least she was near help, not out on the trek in East Jesus somewhere. May we all be so lucky!

Four days later, Mike, Tony and I were stuffing our backpacks, making ready to head out on the first leg of the trek up to Naudanda. A few of us were headed out this morning, including a couple from New Zealand named Tim and Katie as well as a guy named Mathias, from Western Canada. We weren't officially traveling together but there was only one trail and there we were.

Before departure I headed to the toilet facility for the third time that morning. Nice to be headed out on a hike when you've got the shits. I ate two Lomotils early on and things were slowing down. One more before we started walking. At least it wasn't one of those wogs that makes the guts feel like they're being twisted into knots. Not yet anyway.

Walking up the switchback was brutal. We'd started later than we should have and the south facing slope was in full-on morning sun. I finished my first bottle of water much too soon. Mike and Tony chatted as they walked and to my astonishment, smoked Drum tobacco all the way up. They just went along as if they were out for a stroll in the park.

"How can you guys smoke while you're hiking?" I croaked. They looked at each other and shrugged.

"Dunno," Tony said simply, "doesn't seem to make a difference."

The Appearance of Things

I was passed by a slight Nepali man, walking shoeless on the worn rocks of the trail. His hard, calloused feet appeared immune to the uneven, pointed stones. The fact that he was also carrying four wooden cases of Coca Cola in glass bottles, using the Nepali head strap method, made me feel very out of shape and hopeless. "You'd be moving along fine if you didn't have the shits," I told myself but wondered if it was true.

Six hours later, we pulled into Naudanda. To be fair, Mike and Tony strolled in, I dragged in. The village was literally a wide spot in the trail with wood and stone dwellings scattered along both sides. Looking back I could see Pokhara and the lake and the green valley perhaps a kilometer lower than we were. It was a lovely view but I was too thirsty to appreciate it just then. Flopping down on the wooden bench of the Machapuchari Guest House I asked for water. I had tried to slake my thirst on the trail with a warm Coco Cola but that was a bad idea. I felt ill and the warm, foamy burps didn't help anything.

The guesthouse owner came back smiling with a clay jar topped with a clay mug. It was heaven, and the cool water had the reassuring flatness that tasted boiled. I hoped so, anyway. My guts didn't feel any better. I decided to pull out my stash of Tetracycline and do the old "one capsule every twelve hours for five days" treatment. It wasn't something I did lightly. Temporary bouts of diarrhea were common to all of us traveling and you couldn't pull out the big guns for every little thing. On the other hand, two weeks of crawling along feeling like this sounded terrible. And a bad idea too. In my reading was the strange little fact that most of the deaths on Himalayan climbing expeditions were not from falls or altitude but from diarrhea. People lost all their sodium and potassium and calcium and things just stopped working. Things like nerves and muscles.

The smell of Drum pulled me back and I looked up at Mike and Tony, sitting on the other side of the little table with their backs to me. Out in front of us rose a series of massive, snow covered peaks. One right in the center looked like the Matterhorn in Switzerland, but giant sized. We could see these mountains from Pokhara, but only the tops. Now the immense scale of the place began to dawn on me. I traced the slope of the hillside leading down into the valley before us. Far below, the rushing white water of a large river. It had to be eight or ten miles just down to there. The base of the Matterhorn-like peak started down there, on the other side of the river. I visually followed a line up the broad face of the mountain, past the green belt near the river, up through the band of trees into the alpine region of grasses and finally on to the sheer face of stone and glacier, up and up. What must have been a huge blast of wind lifted a small cloud of loose snow on the upper slope and moved it like drifting cotton candy in slow motion. This was the biggest single thing I'd ever seen on earth, an apparent pyramid twenty miles wide at the base. And right in front of us!

A worn card on the table had a panoramic photo of the peaks. The Matterhorn shaped one was called Machapuchari or "Fish Tail" mountain. I couldn't see where the fishtail idea came from but it was almost twenty three thousand feet tall. In California, the highest mountain we've got is in the Sierras, Mount Whitney, at about fourteen thousand five hundred. To the left there was an arrow pointing to a peak called Dhaulagiri that was almost twenty seven thousand feet and beyond that the whole Annapurna Complex. The river canyon wound up to our left and disappeared around the toe of "Fish Tail".

We were on the coat tails of foothills that kept going up too, on this side of the river. It was daunting. Even the foothills of the Himalaya were taller than the tallest peaks in the USA! I knew they were big, but knowing the altitudes of the peaks hadn't prepared me for the awesome grandeur, impossible, untouchable, like gods.

That evening Mike and Tony stayed up smoking hashish with Mathias but I was zonked out. I paid for a bucket of warm water, washed the dust of the trail off and crawled into my sleeping sack. For now, the shits were under control. It would be better tomorrow and I was asleep in minutes.

Biritanti is a village straight out of Tolkien. Its location at the intersections of two rivers, numerous small rivulets running in and through the town, the slate and thatch roofed buildings helter-skelter up the hillside all combined in charming harmony. The narrow streets were essentially wide, stone staircases. The wheel was definitely of little use here. We walked slowly uphill, the smaller of the two rivers on our left. There was the rush of water but not as a roar. More like the continuous whisper of breakers on a near seacoast. From here I could see the Fish Tail aspect of Machapuchari, how what had appeared as the peak from down canyon was in fact the forward facing of twin peaks, connected by a concave stone ridge. It clearly did look like the caudal fin of some great sea creature.

Tim and Kate, the couple from New Zealand, shouted, "Hello!" down to us from the wide, covered balcony of a building we were passing. Mathias looked up and waved, "Hey, there you are. Where are you staying?"

The Appearance of Things

Tim looked a bit like Cat Stevens, with dark, curly hair and a thin black beard. He was wearing one of the Nepalese flannel shirts, with the wrap around front and Mandarin collar. Red was a good color for him and he smiled roguishly down upon us.

"You're looking at it," he indicated, with a steaming cup of something in his hand. "The entry is right over there, up the stairs. Come on up and check it out. It's a good place," he laughed.

Kate rested her chin on her arm and smiled down at us too. She looked sleepy. Her short-cropped blond hair was pressed down on the left side of her head and looked damp. She wiggled a finger in greeting.

The very cozy teahouse, simply named Good Place, had comfortable lodging, great views and a kitchen producing some delicious aromas. Two days of solid hiking had brought us into the mountains and a thousand years away.

"We've been up the canyon a bit," Tim explained. "There's a brilliant waterfall and pool for bathing. Cool but not too bad while there's sun."

We were all drinking the locally made beer called Chang. It was milky and semi-sweet, made from barley and fermented at room temperature. It had slight carbonation and an earthy, citrus sort of flavor. The owner of Good Place, a warm and friendly man with a haircut that reminded me of Moe from the Three Stooges, made his own and was proud of the product.

"Well," I said, "I'm up for a swim. How about you guys?"

Mike and Tony nodded and we made to stand up.

"I'm going to settle here a bit," Mathias said, "but tell me how it is." He grinned and toasted us with his Chang. "This is really pretty good, once you get used to it."

We found the first pool after a moderate uphill, about fifteen minutes' walk from the village. Tim had soft-pedaled the beauty of the place. The angle of the sun slanting into the canyon caught the red, purple and pink flowers of the rhododendron trees lining the edge of the deep, cobalt blue pool. The ribbon of the waterfall was shimmering silver. The warm air was filled with a vast number and variety of butterflies, more than I've ever seen in one place.

"Crykie!" exclaimed Tony, eyes wide.

Mike sighed and sat on a stone, beginning to untie his shoes. "I reckon we've found a little bit of Paradise." He looked up then and I think it was one of the first times I recall him looking unconditionally happy.

We all stripped down and piled into cool the water, whooping and laughing. I was so tempted to drink some, as I would have in the California Sierra but here, who the hell knew what was upstream from us. Fastidious personal hygiene was not a local trait, given the piles of shit we passed on the trail.

Lying on warm, flat sheets of stone in the afternoon sun, drying off and drifting, I actually fell asleep. A scuff on the surface of the rock awakened me, Mike looking down with a grin.

"Well Vernon, sorry to disturb you but Tony and I are headed back."

I started up and was surprised to see the waterfall now in deep shadow.

"Whoa! I guess I needed a nap. Hold on then, I'll come along with you."

A movement by the side of the big pool, still in the late afternoon golden light. The long blond hair of a naked woman, standing up to her waist in the in the sparkling water, her back to me. I gazed appreciatively for a moment and turned back to Mike and Tony, "When you find paradise, stay awhile."

"Amen to that," returned Mike. Tony just grinned.

For having had a nap, I certainly slept deeply enough that night. Mathias and Tim provided a number of chillums with the sweet Nepali hash, the opium content helping both my guts and my head. Over the next five days, a happy haze of contentment settled over us. We developed a routine of small explorations up the canyon, discovering new and exquisite pools and cascades surrounded by their natural Zen gardens. I loved the little horse trains that made their way past us on the wide stone stairways that served as roads and trails. The Nepalis decorated the smallish animals with henna patterns and colorful woven blankets and often they sported a headdress that looked like a feather duster. They reminded me of the dressed up ponies in the circus ring when I was a kid.

At this moment, there were about forty trekkers scattered about the village in various teahouses. It was a population in flux as people arrived and departed daily. The general feeling was that we had found Rivendell, the Elven dwelling in the Misty Mountains of Tolkien fame. On our seventh night, though, that reverie was rudely interrupted with panicked screams.

We were into our usual chillum passing at Good Place, after dinner and pre-crashing out. Mike was playing some J.J. Cale guitar licks and I fumbled along with some harmonica harmony. A guy named Elias, who had earlier introduced himself as a group therapist from Vermont, had eschewed the hash but was enjoying some Chang with another couple from New England. When the screaming started, we all sat up and tried to figure out where it was coming from. Then we smelled the smoke. Everyone in the little restaurant piled down the stairs and into the cobbled street. Up the hill, maybe two hundred feet beyond us, flames were beginning to engulf one of the stable structures. The dry hay stacked against the wooden sidewall burned a furious yellow orange and embers rocketed up into the dark night sky. More than a dozen of the villagers were whacking ineffectively at the growing conflagration with blankets and wooden rakes. The screaming was coming from the little ponies trapped within. It was terrified and human.

The fire was out of control and I stood there, paralyzed. A voice inside told me there was nothing I could do and I listened to it. All of us standing there gaping seemed to be hearing the same voice and we just stared at the enveloping inferno. Then, breaking the spell that held us, Elias called out, "Come on. Let's make a bucket brigade!"

A bucket brigade? The river was below us, down a steep embankment maybe a hundred feet away. A few of the villagers had buckets and were filling them in painfully slow fashion. It was worse than useless. There was no way. But a few began to search out and bring buckets from nearby houses, starting down the hill toward the flowing river. And just standing here, watching it burn like it was somebody else's problem, was also worse than useless. I loped over to one of the Nepali's who was slowly filling a bucket at a tiny rivulet and tapped my chest, pointing to the others moving down the stream embankment. The man's face was wet with tears but we locked eyes and he understood, handing me the bucket. In a short space of time a line of twenty or more westerners were handing full buckets up the hill and empty ones back down. But we were too far apart for it to really be working. When the first two buckets reached the fire and were thrown at the flames, the villagers noticed what we were doing and a shout went up. Some ran over to join the line, other in search of more buckets. Within moments, dozens of new hands joined and additional buckets appeared. Amazingly, we began to win. One bucket after another quenched the burning walls and the thatch roofing. The conflagration stopped its advance. In the end, we stood together in front of the smoking ruins, trekkers and villagers. We weren't celebrating or laughing. Two of the beautiful little horses lay dead and burned within. There were several other bodies of what must have been goats or thin sheep crumpled in the wet, glistening blackness. A villager was moaning with the burns he had received leading the other three horses to safety through a burning wall. A group of women were gathered around him, anointing the charred flesh on the sides of his face and arms with some oily ointment.

I happened to glance over at the same time Elias looked my way. His clean-shaven face was gleaming with sweat from the exertion and I realized that mine was too. I was suddenly flooded with respect for the man and more than a little ashamed of myself. He read my expression and leaned over, "Thanks for your help. We made a difference."

I was grateful for the bone.

"You made a difference, Elias," I replied.

I'd been disappointed in myself before. It's not a nice feeling.

Now, in the cool morning, I gazed out over the river in the early light, sipping a hot Milo. It reminded me of the Ovaltine, from when I was a kid. Mike and Tony were talking about last night and how great it was that everybody had pitched in and how maybe we'd saved the village. I didn't feel much like a hero though. More like a soldier who hid during the big battle. I could feel the queasiness in my guts, partly the uncured bacterial thing, partly the knowledge that, without Elias leading the charge, I would have just stood by.

"You guys about ready to head for Ghandrung?" I asked.

Mike looked up, his face questioning, "Aw yeah, that's a possibility isn't it?"

Tony seemed, like me, a bit introverted this morning. He thoughtfully spooned in another mouthful of porridge, then said, "Good by me. A change wouldn't hurt."

The fire, apparently, was an event that triggered a "time-to-go" response in many of the trekkers and there was a flurry of leave taking going on around the village. By ten thirty we were packed up, paid up and moving towards the exit.

Mathias was beginning to look pretty scruffy with his new dark beard and stringy hair. He'd not shaved since we left Pokhara and kept smoothing down his new chin growth with his left thumb and forefinger. I think he was trying to train it into a Van Dyck style, but it wasn't long enough yet.

We began the trek up the wide steps, passing the burned out barn. The bodies of the poor horses and goats were gone, except for one burned hoof and foreleg that had been left behind by the renders.

The Appearance of Things

"I guess that bit was too far gone for anybody," I observed.

"I'm glad they didn't let them go to waste," Mathias joined in.

He had a good profile, straight well-formed nose and forehead. His coffee-brown eyes shone sadly when he turned to me and continued, "I lived for a while in Quesnel. It's a little town in central B.C. We had a barn burn there a few years back. Killed over thirty horses. They used a bulldozer to make a deep trench, pushed all the bodies in and then covered it up. I remember the smell." He shook his head, remembering, and we walked on in silence.

As the river valley continued to climb the view began to open up and with it our spirits. Mike and Tony were on ahead smoking as they hiked, as usual. Down the canyon behind us I could make out Kate, Tim and several others. The goal for today was a spot called Ghoripani as there was meant to be a decent tea house for food and lodging. We'd been told that the big deal in Ghoripani was to climb up something called Poon Hill to see the sunrise on Annapurna.

We four pulled into the little settlement very late in the afternoon. We had climbed for most of the day and the air had a high altitude chill. The teahouse, Poon's, had a hand painted sign over the door that read, "Welcome Poon Lodge, elevation 11,742 foot." Pretty high. The lodge itself was very simple, basically a great room with an open fire burning in a central, shallow pit. A cupola-like vent at the peak allowed the exhaust to pass out, but the place still had a friendly, wood smoke atmosphere. A few other groups had staked out floor space already so we explored around and picked a spot for ourselves, rolling out our claims with our sleeping bags. Poon and his wife served a barley, dahl and potato plate with a chapatti from their little kitchen. Trekkers sat eating in the far corner at a set of rough tables with benches.

"I like it," announced Mathias.

Mike and Tony smiled at him and Mike chided, "A bit like Canada, eh."

Mathias grinned back, "In BC we've got a terrific network of hostels along routes in the mountains. Usually not so grand as this," he indicated our surroundings with an open hand, "but cozy and dry in a storm."

I liked Poon's too. After supper and a chillum, we sat in our sleeping bags and it felt like a group of kids near the fireplace on a Christmas Eve sleepover.

I awoke in complete darkness with my guts giving me notice that they were about to blow. The fire pit had burned down to red coals and the floor between me and the outside was chockablock with sleeping trekkers. I wiggled out of my sleeping bag and thumbed on my light. I had on a T-shirt and underwear and no time for anything except to bolt across the room and try to get out before I couldn't hold it anymore. I trod on an outstretched hand along the way and heard a distress cry of "Ahhh!" The outside air hit me like liquid nitrogen, shocking, stinging, and I stumbled across the stone littered earth away from the building. It had to be now and I tore my underwear down to my knees and squatted in the dark, steadying myself on a large boulder. The warm splash on the back of my legs and heels was disappointing but at least the pressure was released. My guts cramped up and I just stayed where I was, almost literally frozen in place. Before the sun had set, I'd poked around a bit and knew that off to my right, about fifty feet, there was a watering trough for horses. I worked off my underwear, trying to not get too much shit on them and managed to scrape loose soil and gravel over the mess I'd made. "Make it better in the morning," I promised myself. Now, gripping my shorts and wearing a T-shirt I made my way gingerly over the rough ground to the trough. A thin layer of ice on the surface broke when I put my hand in and began to splash water over my backside. A thin stream fed the horse trough and I stood with my back to the trough, straddling the outflow, trying to get the water to not bounce back into the tank. The freezing water ran down my legs and over my feet, draining away with the outflow. I was gripped with an urge to laugh. A few days before I didn't drink the water in the big pool at Biritanti since I didn't know what might be going on upstream. Turns out that I was what was going on upstream, a possible definition of ironic. I wished I had a bar of soap but rubbing would have to do for now.

Back inside, I dried and warmed my shivering calves and hindside by the glowing coals and crept back to bed. I'd rinsed my soiled underwear and spread them over the top of my pack to dry. Donning a dry set of underwear, just in case, I went back to sleep and the rest of the night passed without incident.

"Hey Vernon, waykie, waykie."

I opened my eyes to find Mike grinning down at me, dressed and looking ready to go. "We're heading up to Poon Hill for the sunrise. I guess you had a hard night," he said, nodding towards my still drying underwear, "but Tony and I thought you might like to join the fun. Mathias has the shits and is staying here."

"Yeah, I do," I managed. "Give me a couple of minutes to get dressed, ok?"

"Ah yeah, no worries. We'll be outside," and he strode across the room, followed by Tony.

The Appearance of Things

Somebody had built the fire back up and I got myself dressed in the flickering yellow light. I downed a quick cup of the hot chai Poon and his wife had ready for us early risers. Outside, the stars were still visible but the eastern horizon was lightening.

"Ok," I gulped in the frigid air, coming up alongside Tony.

"Saw you go out last night," Tony mumbled. "Doin' ok?"

"Aw, a bout of the shits. You know how that goes."

I was nonchalant but I knew the Tetracycline should have knocked out anything bacterial by now. Have to get checked when we get back to Kathmandu.

Standing atop Poon Hill, Annapurna was already glowing orange. Tony cupped his hand under his folded arms, "It's bloody cold. How high are we?"

A guy with what sounded like a French accent looked over and said, "About five thousand meter."

That didn't sound right since we hadn't climbed higher than another fifteen hundred feet on the way up here. We could make out the teahouse below in the growing light, which was almost twelve thousand. Still, thirteen thousand five hundred feet is pretty damn high. In the clear, cold air, Annapurna looked very close, the multiple peaks illuminated by the rising sun. In my mind, I could hear the opening chords of Also Sprach Zarathustra, like in Kubrick's 2001.

On the way back down, there was a conversation about the Manali to Leh passage that intrigued me. "Manali was great. I wish we had those hot springs here. We wanted to go on to Leh but it was too early in the year and no way past the snow until late April or May." The speaker was addressing his trekking partners. I didn't know anybody's name but I'd seen their group down at Poon's. The word amongst travelers was that Leh is a miniature version of Tibet with high monasteries and a living Tibetan culture. If you couldn't get into Tibet, this was the next closest thing.

"What's transport like when the road is open?" I asked.

The speaker, a tall blond Australian or New Zealander with a wide, goofy smile and hazel blue eyes looked back at me. "Aw, there's a bus that goes but a lot of people walk it. It's high, higher than this," he pointed around at Poon Hill, "and I reckon it's about a hundred and fifty kilometers, right over the mountains. Then you drop down into Kashmir."

It was something to think about. I'd also heard the houseboats on Dal Lake near Srinagar were a trip. Maybe my next loop. Mike had been listening in too.

"What do you think?" I asked him.

"It's funny but when we saw John and Lou, they were talking about that route. Maybe that'll be the trek they do make. Dunno, let's see when we get back down."

Getting to Ghandrung took the balance of the day. I'd downed a couple more Lomotil and only ate a banana so my guts were quiet. We walked for miles through actual forests of rhododendron trees, their brilliant red, white and pink flowers forming a canopy twenty feet over our heads. I had no idea that rhododendrons could be actual trees but here they were.

We rounded a bend and laid out before us was the Annapurna complex. Strangely enough, since leaving Ghoripani the general lay of the trail had been mostly level or even downhill. The air felt thicker and more humid. The river canyon between us and Annapurna was the same river that came in from the other side of Biritanti. We had come through a pass and were now walking around the hip of the mountain. I could see that our return loop would have both Annapurna and Machapuchari on our left, straight across the vast valley, all the way back to Biritanti and beyond.

Ghandrung was like the best seating at an amphitheater of the Himalaya. There was a remarkable consistency to the structures, as though they had all been built by the same hand. Cream colored stone walls with some dark timbers, two floors high and slate roofs was the main theme. The village followed the contours of the mountain, interspersed with farming terraces lush with brilliant green spring barley. Like Biritanti, the lanes were essentially broad cobbled staircases. There was a compact neatness to be place I liked. We walked through, following the hand painted signs to the Poppy tea house and lodging, people smiled and stopped in their work to give us a "Namaste" welcome.

The Poppy had a wide covered porch facing the mountains with lots of comfortable places to sit and read or just gaze into the distance. Ghandrung wasn't quite as attractive to us as Biritanti had been, with the canyon swimming pools and innumerable butterflies, but it had an ancient quality that was unique from anyplace else we'd seen on the trek. More than back in Pokhara or Kathmandu, the people living up in these mountains seemed ageless. I had asked a few how old they were and was shocked that the "little old lady" was actually only thirty. It was as though anyone over twenty looked really old but not wizened. Maybe it's the result of the high, dry climate and really hard work but unless a person was a young girl or a child I really couldn't gauge their age.

The problem arose on our third day. Mike had gone off on a walk with a woman from Denmark named Caia. I was kicked back, reading <u>The Magus</u> by John Fowles, on the porch of the teahouse. Tony came around the corner and sat down near me on a stool. He was sniffling and seemed a bit shaky.

"Hey Tony. What's going on? You pick up a cold?"

Tony smiled his sheepish smile and rubbed at his nose. His movements were sort of jerky and I put the book down and focused on him.

"Aw, no, just, uh, a bit sniffly," he replied.

Then he leaned towards me and did a sort of stage whisper. His eyes looked moist and nervous.

"Hey Vernon, I'd like to get that can. The one I gave you in Kathmandu, ok?"

The image of my hand slipping the can into a crack in the rafters at the Oriental Lodge burst into my mind. Tony misread the revelation on my face and hurriedly added, "I know, I know. I said keep it away. But I really need to get it now, ok?"

"Oh shit, Tony," I exclaimed, "I forgot completely about that. I hid the can in our room in Kathmandu. It's probably…"

"You what!" he almost screamed and jumped up. The stool crashed down behind him. His eyes were filled with panic, looking left and right, a cornered animal. I'd never seen a more bereft expression on another human. He had just been sentenced to death, to be carried out immediately.

"God Tony, I'm sorry," I stammered. "I completely overlooked having stashed it when we were leaving and packing up."

There was a flash of rage in his normally gentle eyes but it died out immediately and he began to walk away saying, "That's alright. It's ok. It'll be ok."

I felt really bad to have let him down but somehow also ok about it. The heroin thing was tough. A strong whiff of hashish and I knew Tony was going for the next best thing, the opiated Nepalese hash. I briefly wondered if I was addicted to getting stoned and decided I wasn't. If it wasn't available, no big problem. I could drink.

We were able to make good use of our cook gear on the way back down to Biritanti. Mostly it had been just to boil water for drinking or the occasional cup of Milo, the Ovaltine stuff. But it was two full days of walking back to Biritanti this direction and no little settlement or tea houses along the way. There was meant to be a sort of shelter about half way along, a basic stone hut with a wooden door and no windows.

It was growing late when we found it, relieved that it was not already occupied. Sleeping outside would have been ok as it was warmer as we descended, but it's cozy to have a roof overhead in new territory. We cooked up our own rice and dahl as well as a pretty darn good sauté of baby fern fiddle heads with marsala powder and ghee.

In the late night, Mathias nudged me awake, "Hey, do you hear that?"

I pulled myself out of sleep and listened, the alarm in his voice sobering. There was the crunch of gravel outside of our little hut and a sort of throaty rumble. Bear, I thought, as if I was in the Sierra, then paused. Do they have bears in the Himalaya? It sounded too noisy to be one of the large cats but what did I know. Maybe top predators don't have to be quiet in these parts. Something was sniffing at the bottom of the door, that was for sure.

"Yeti?" I suggested and Mathias snorted, "Yeah, right."

But neither of us moved to open the door and whatever it was receded.

"Gone now," Mathias whispered.

We both lay back and next thing I knew morning light was coming in under the portal. Mathias was up and cautiously opened the door. The dawn flooded into the room like a cool breath. "No tracks," he said, studying the gravel just beyond the door. The comment was mostly to himself, but I knew he was talking to me.

"Whadda'ya mean?" Tony asked, sitting up in his sleep sack.

"Something sniffing around last night," Mathias returned, "Vernon heard it too."

Tony glanced over to me and I nodded my confirmation, "Something big," I added.

"Crykie! What do you think it was?"

"No tracks I can read in the gravel here," Mathias said, indicating the patch in front of the door, "but I think I'll have a little walkabout and look for some prints."

Nothing turned up, though, and we enjoyed speculating in the warm sunlight during the walk down to Biritanti.

The swim in the pool after the long two days of walking was like a nice "welcome home." It was still fine there in Biritanti yet we were all in agreement about trying to make it all the way to Pokhara in the morning. The way was mostly downhill and the weeks of hiking had hardened us.

"I think John and Louise will be there," Mike commented.

We'd been out for fifteen days and, charming as Biritanti was, I was ready to get back down to Pokhara. The fruit trees would be blooming and spring in full swing. I think spring is my favorite season. I wanted a little more time in the area before heading back to Kathmandu and then back down into India.

Mike, Tony and I had decided over the trekking trip to hang together for a while in India. It was a mixed blessing for me. We enjoyed each other's company and it would be good to face who-knows-what with friends. On the other hand, there was much to recommend in traveling alone. I liked the independence of movement and choice I had in Southeast Asia. In a very real way, it was easier to meet people being alone. If John and Louise joined up, we'd be five, a rather daunting pack to break into for any stranger. We'll see. If it's not to my liking I can always wish everybody farewell and go back to freelance.

We got up early and by first light were heading down the valley towards Naudanda. In the distance, the valley of Pokhara was not yet visible but I recognized the contours of the hills behind the lake. Coming back from the unknown and moving towards the familiar felt good. I caught up to Mike, "Do you think that John and Louise will be at Green Acres?"

Mike shrugged, "If they got my note at the trekking office, yeah, maybe. At least, we'll probably have a note where they are, if they aren't there."

Naudanda was much closer going down, or really just felt closer. The unrelenting uphill coming in combined with not feeling tip-top in my guts had left me with a memory of it being quite far away. Yet we found ourselves walking down the ridge and through the little town by noon.

There was a rumble of thunder. Looking back, a huge, boiling cloud front looming up behind Machapuchare, still far up the valley but moving our way. We'd been lucky so far on the trek with the weather.

"Looks like we might get some rain before Pokhara," I observed.

Tony looked back up the valley at the churning, massive, dark thunderheads, "Yeah. Comin' this way. You might get that shower you've been on about sooner than you planned."

He grinned at me and I felt reassured that there was no lingering animosity about me losing his heroin. He was much lighter and happier since we left Ghandrung, with clear eyes and a sort of humorous delivery that reminded me of the Tony I'd met at Lake Toba. He was very much a "take life as it comes" sort of person and his kind nature didn't begrudge much, or so it seemed to me.

The rumbling, however, grew more ominous and I noticed we all picked up our pace a bit heading down the switchback off the Naudanda ridge. It was just rain, but the Himalaya seemed to do everything on a grand scale. Getting caught out in the open with lightning, soaked to the skin, was not my first choice in entertainment. I was relieved when we made the last descent off the ridge into the valley. Walking across the plain of orchards, the air was sweet with the bloom of a thousand fruit trees.

"Take a look at that!" Tony exclaimed and we stopped, looking back the way we had come. A towering wall of cumulonimbus had cast Naudanda into shadow and as we watched, a grey veil descended from the dark, flat base of the clouds and the little village disappeared. Flashes of lightning punctuated the veil, beautiful but I was glad to be off the ridge. The storm could stay in the mountains. We made haste in the warm sun the rest of the way to Green Acres and all breathed a sigh of relief when we settled our packs in the lobby.

Hamid greeted us with his warm smile, "I'm so very glad to see you! Was your trekking experience a good one, I hope?"

"Brilliant, yes," Mike smiled, "but I'm ready for a pitcher of your famous Green Acres lemonade. I think I could drink one by myself after that walk today."

Tony, Mathias and I nodded our agreement.

Hamid beamed, "Oh, that would be most welcome. Plenty for all and more to come," and he hurried off.

The sun in the garden was beguiling and we grabbed a little table in the garden beside the lush lemon tree that was the source of so much pride for Hamid. In the two weeks of our absence, the tree had come into full and exuberant bloom. The gentle hum of the bees working the sweet flowers, the warmth of the afternoon sun in the garden and our well-earned fatigue from the walk all combined in this moment.

Mike held up a glass of lemonade to us, "Well cobbers, job well done!" and took a long pull of the cool drink. We followed suit and soon it was Drum hand-rolls all around. Mike had found a supply of the tobacco in Bangkok and generously shared from his dwindling supply. I didn't want to get back into tobacco but this was a moment of fellowship.

A crash of thunder startled us. The sun disappeared and a sudden cool breeze said the storm wasn't going to stay up in the mountains. A few scattered drops of rain said the party had to move up on to the veranda so we picked up and headed under cover. I looked out through the trees towards the mountains. The vast grey veil that had eaten Naudanda was crossing the plain and was nearly upon us.

"That's going to be quite a downpour," Mathias noted.

Then came the clinking sound, like somebody tossing small gravel on to the corrugated roof of the building. Hailstones. The hail began to fall viciously, ice balls the size of small grapes, and the clinking on the roof became a deafening roar. Hamid appeared at the door, his face a mask of desperation and pain. I followed his gaze and understood. The lemon tree was being beaten as if by an avalanche, the leaves tearing and the blossoms ripped away. Hamid cried out and ran towards the tree, desperately trying to shield some of the blossoms from the savage onslaught with his own body, hunched protectively over a lower limb. Some of the guests standing on the veranda were laughing and pointing at him, but Biritanti had taught us four something.

"Come on," I shouted over the din.

No further explanation was needed. We snatched up several of the tablecloths from around us and launched ourselves out in to the hail, towards Hamid and his tree. By now Hamid was tearing at his hair and wailing, his efforts to save the blossoms hopeless. The hail was already inches deep on the ground and when the stones hit our heads and hands it was painful. Mike and I stretched a tablecloth over some lower branches that had been partially protected by those above. Hamid joined Tony and Mathias to cover another section, but his movements were of a broken hearted man going through the motions. The bombardment was already slackening, but the three minute downfall had left the beautiful tree torn and bedraggled. I couldn't tell if we'd saved anything. I didn't really think so. The wet table clothes weren't much easier on the tender blossoms than the hailstones.

Almost as quickly as it began, the hail stopped, the grey veil moving on. Hamid stood before his ruined tree, weeping. Mike, Mathias, Tony and I were soaked to the skin, but the discomfort of the wet clothes and hailstone bruises were minor compared to the devastated man before us. Helpers from the house came out and Hamid rested his hand on the forearm of a woman who led him silently back inside. One of the workers, a tall, balding Nepali, did the head waggle as he and Mike gingerly removed the tablecloths, trying to not damage any of the few remaining blossoms. He studied the destruction and glanced over to us, his eyes sad: "It is the will of God. We are left to clean up."

We all understood that the famous lemonade of Green Acres was likely to be in short supply in the coming season. A random event can so drastically change the life and prospects of a person. Maybe it seemed more so here in Asia, where so many lived so close to the edge. The "will of God" thing rankled me. What kind of god pulls this sort of crap on Hamid? On anyone, really. The memory of agonized young faces in the childhood bone cancer unit at UCLA leaped to mind.

No John and Louise at Green Acres but they are here in Pokhara. When we checked back in, Hamid had passed a note to Mike, before the lemon tree disaster. Seems that they had rented a little house that the note described as, "Overlooking the lake and snow-capped big boys," and the note included a map, but it was late, we were beat. Another two mile walk didn't sound attractive.

"Let's go over in the morning," Tony suggested, "I've done my bit today and I'm ready for some good tucker."

It was agreed. We had a sumptuous dinner, compared to our teahouse fare. But we didn't see the once cheerful Hamid for the rest of the evening.

Next morning, John and Louise waved down to us from the porch of their little house.

"Hello Cobbers!" John shouted. Louise struck me as prettier than the last time I saw her, leaving Phuket. Her wavy red hair was longer and fuller. Same sardonic smile but with a lightness around her cornflower blue eyes, as if an anxiety had been vanquished. John looked good too although a bit thinner than I remembered. His bright, animated face glowed with welcome and good cheer. Maybe they were both just happier, and it showed.

We spent the afternoon on the porch with its view out over the lake raving about our trek. The white peaks of Annapurna and Machapuchari reflected in the still water, the electric blue sky washed clean after yesterday's storm. After a few chillums, the conversation turned on the Manali to Leh route.

"But I think Lou and I would do the bus, eh?" John looked over to Louise who nodded. "A hundred and thirty kilometers with backpacks and freezing nights is something I could miss," she smiled.

John pulled out a medium sized aluminum suitcase from inside and lay it on the porch. "Here, look at this. Straight out of Bangkok" he grinned and thumbed open the case. Within nestled a serious looking Sony videocassette recorder, complete with battery packs and six video tapes. "This'll bring big bikkies in India. Pay for the rest of the trip back to England, I reckon."

"If they don't pinch it in Indian customs," Louise added soberly.

I liked the idea of bringing something to sell. I was thinking more of Europe when I ordered a load of silk, drawstring bags in Kathmandu. They were little beauties with colorful Tibetan symbols. I felt sure I could flog them at street markets and do ok. A hundred of them cost me forty dollars but I reckoned I'd be able to get four or five dollars each in Europe. It was a risk but they compressed well and didn't take up too much space in my pack.

The next five days passed gently, with swims in the lake, music, singing and numerous chillums. Mike, Tony and I, by invitation, had set up at the little house in the second bedroom. Mathias had bid us farewell and headed back to Kathmandu, "I'll look for you in Leh at the end of the month. Who knows?"

It was a lovely few days, our Phuket reunion in the Himalaya.

The plan was to head back to Kathmandu on the coming Friday and fly down to Patna, in India on Tuesday. That gave me enough time to get checked out for amoebas in the hospital and see more of the Kathmandu valley. After Mike and Tony's adventure on the regular bus it wasn't a hard sell to get everybody on the minibus for the return. So it came to pass that on Friday afternoon we pulled into Kathmandu and made a beeline to the Oriental Lodge. I knew Tony was thinking about his Tiger Balm tin and his face lit up when the desk clerk recognized us and offered the same room. He bounded up the stairs and we found him sitting glumly on a bunk when we entered.

"Any luck?" I inquired.

Tony shook his head, "Naw. Maybe you'd have a look?"

I walked to the beam and peered in but knew before I looked that it was gone. I could see the ceiling all the way through. Mike knew the story and said nothing, busying himself with pulling a few things out of his pack. I started to offer another apology but Tony waved it off, "Don't worry. Better not, anyways. It was time to give it a rest." Mike shot me a look that seemed to say, "Amen to that."

Louise had been feeling off as well so she, John and I made our way to the Royal Hospital. After I described my symptoms, the nurse gave me a little clay cup with a lid and requested a stool sample. When I did my business and delivered it back to her, she carefully placed the little pot wrapped in gauze in a metal tin and labeled it with my information.

"Come back on Monday and we will have the results," she smiled, then added, "the doctor will most likely give the disinfectant even if the results are negative, because of your symptoms."

Amoebic dysentery was nothing to be slack about. I was still having bouts of intestinal cramps and frankly some pretty bloody episodes. The "on again-off again" nature of it was pretty typical of the amoebic type. The Tetracycline had helped, but my guts told me I needed to take care of this with a bigger stick. That's the thing about having studied pre-med. I could imagine some pretty bad stuff.

I met John and Louise in the lobby. She was holding a cotton wad in the crook of her arm, where they had taken the blood. They both looked glum.

"Hey, what's up?" I asked, concerned.

Louise looked up at me blandly and shrugged, "I'm pregnant."

I guess one is meant to say "Congratulations!" at hearing that news, but neither of them looked like they wanted to be congratulated. John broke the silence that followed, "Looks like we'll be giving Leh a miss on this trip," he smiled ruefully.

Louise giggled then and poked him in the side with her finger, "That's good then. You've had all the lays you need for a while."

John laughed out loud at that one and in our new reality, we headed off to the travel office near Durbar Square.

Chapter 12
Back to Mother India

> The world is full of magical things patiently waiting for our wits to grow sharper.
>
> *Bertrand Russell*

I

"Excuse me please, sir. Can I ask you to keep an eye on my things while I go to collect my baggage. I'm afraid it will be stolen if I leave it alone."

The guard stood a little straighter, his old bolt-action carbine at the ready. He held the muzzle like a walking stick. "Yes sir," he said crisply, "your things will be safe here with me. Do not worry."

I was grateful to the man for his willingness to help. He was guarding the exit door of the baggage and customs hall at the Patna airport, where we had just arrived on the short flight from Kathmandu. His carefully wrapped khaki turban had a red cone in the center, something I hadn't seen before, and his neat khaki uniform looked fresh even in the heat and humidity of the terminal. He reminded me of Omar Sharif with his deep-set dark eyes and neat moustache. Dr. Zhivago in the flesh.

I strode over to the lined up baggage that was coming in off the flight. Mike, Tony, John and Louise were busy sorting through to locate their various bags. John was already gripping the aluminum suitcase with the video camera. A set of long tables was manned by half a dozen officials, randomly requiring new arrivals to lay out their bags for inspection. Some passengers, mostly older foreigners, were just waved through. They were particularly attentive to younger Indian and Nepali arrivals however and I didn't observe even one to get the wave on.

John and Louise, chatting nonchalantly together, began to pass by the line when an official looked up from the bag he was poking through, "Hello? Excuse me please."

John's face froze in midsentence. Louise turned to the officer and gave him a dazzling smile, "Oh, hello. Can you help me, please. I'm in desperate need of a WC. Is one nearby?"

I couldn't tell from my angle if she was batting her eyes, but the man looked flustered for a moment, then stammered, "In the arrivals hall."

John had put the case down and Louise now picked it up, "Thank you very much," she replied and walked towards the exit door.

John, now holding his and Louise's pack, looked at the officer questioningly. He shrugged and did the head waggle, making a little "move along" gesture with his fingers and went back to the bag open before him on the table. John nodded and shouldered his pack, hand carrying Louise's out the door. My guard nodded to him as he exited. There was look of relief on John's face and why not. He had done it!

Mike and Tony got a pretty good going over, with one official shining a light into the body of the guitar. The inspector I got ignored my backpack but peered into my day sack, lifting out the bottle of Johnny Walker Red and the carton of State Express 555 cigarettes. "Ah," he mused, "Johnny Walker. Very good scotch." He smiled wryly and returned the bottle and cigarettes to my bag. I was then waved on. We were allowed one liter of spirits and one carton of cigarettes duty free. The high importation duties in place in India just about guaranteed that one could sell purchases for a significant profit, enough, we were told, to pay the cost of the flight down.

As I exited I saluted the guard and picked up my bag, "Thank you so very much for your help," I said. He nodded but maintained his posture.

I met Mike and Tony in the hall. John and Louise were out front arranging for a cab to get us all to the train station. The plan was to make it to Benares by this evening. Tony looked at my airport carry bag, "How did you get everything through?" he asked. When I'd purchased three bottles of Johnny Walker and three cartons of cigarettes, Mike had raised his eyebrows. "How do you plan to get all that through?"

The truth is I wasn't sure. One thought was to ask a fellow passenger to carry some if they weren't full up, for a share in the action. But it turned out that everybody was in on the deal and they all had their own action. We'd also heard that the customs at Patna were pretty reasonable and I considered that if they found it, maybe a little baksheesh could be paid instead of the full duty. I guess I just really hoped I'd be lucky and not get the big search. It was a very impromptu thing, to ask the guard to watch the bag but it had worked! I wouldn't want to do it twice, but now I stood to make almost three hundred dollars. That wasn't a fortune but easily enough for a month in India, maybe more if I was careful. My traveler's cheque folder was getting a bit slim and this would help.

I felt a little guilty for pulling the white sahib thing, though. A hangover from the British Colonial times was the sense of privilege Indians extended to white Europeans. It was a kind of reverse prejudice and it went up my nose when I saw people really working it, being condescending to Indians just because they could. Yet as I'd just demonstrated to myself, I wasn't above enjoying some of the benefits of that privilege. Is accepting my own hypocrisy hypocritical?

After more than a month in the high Himalaya, the heat and the humidity of the Ganges valley was a direct frontal assault. By the time we reached the Patna train station, my shirt was soaked in my own sweat and my shorts looked like I'd sat in a puddle. The streets were quiet for an Indian city. It was early afternoon and the temperature was well over forty three Celsius, about a hundred and ten Fahrenheit. People were just staying inside. Even on the moving train, with open windows, it was like being blown down with a hair dryer from on high.

Benares. The city appears suddenly when the train leaves the fertile plain and begins a clickity-clack crossing on a long Victorian steel bridge over the Ganges. The flood plain was wide here and the river bent towards us, then away. The city tumbles down the far bank, built on the high ground. The late light accentuated the oranges and ochers and maroons of the stone walls, a sandcastle fantasy of towers and domes, temples that looked unearthly, built by aliens from another world. Bursting out between the ancient buildings' wide sets of steps cascaded down to the river. Thousands of small boats, dazzling in their variety and color, hummed along the edge. Scores of people stood waist deep in the river, pouring water over their heads and there, the smoke rising from a flaming log pile, a shrouded figure resting, burning, in the midst of the orange inferno. Our train passed over and went slowly into the dense mass of the city.

The Appearance of Things

Varanasi Junction, massive and teeming was our introduction. Dozens of train platforms stretched away in both directions, literally thousands of people milling around us. A huge, white Brahma bull wandered placidly, stopping to browse on bits of banana leaf refuse. Combined with the heat and the dust and the cacophony I felt like I was being tumbled in a cement mixer. But it was India. Incense and marigolds danced with the open sewer of the train tracks. We pushed out to the front of the station. Mercifully, the sun had set, but the heat radiating off the stones was not quick to dissipate.

I looked around at my comrades. We were all frazzled. John and Lou had a card for a hotel near the river recommended by a pair of travelers we met at The Pleasure Room back in Kathmandu. "Taxi! Taxi, sir!" We were surrounded by a sea of bright eyes and smiling dark faces. For some reason, everybody's teeth looked perfect and brilliant white.

A large Sikh in a red turban pushed forward and spoke authoritatively, "Here, you come. We all go." Helpful hands were snatching at our baggage but we clung to our belongings and waded down to his waiting car. It was a tight squeeze with five, but John handed over the card for the Birat Guest House and we were away.

Well, sort of away. Anyone who has heard the phrase "the streets were teeming with people" should be in Benares at sunset, after a brutally hot day, to gain a real appreciation of the experience. Our car had people walking in front, walking wall to wall on both sides, and filling in behind us as we passed. We drove at the velocity of the surging crowds.

A million different stalls offered what looked like an infinite variety of goods and baubles, spices, snakes in jars, batteries and toothpaste, jewelry and tandoori, naked light bulbs hanging from trees illuminating the endless bazaar. A wall of stalls offering the exquisite silk brocades the city was famous for. Sitar and tabla music drifting out from a second story window. I felt like I was stoned.

Finally we sat in the relative quiet of the Birat Guest House roof garden, showered and unwinding. The cool lassies, a sweet yogurt drink with ice we all hoped was ok, tasted especially delicious tonight. I was on the second day of the intestinal disinfectant they gave me in Kathmandu and for a change didn't feel the mild nausea in the background. Funny what you can get accustomed to. The beds of the guesthouse were exactly right for the weather. Thin, soft rope formed a tight net over a sturdy wooden frame, with just a sarong below and one above to discourage the mosquitoes. I got the full benefit of the overhead fan circulating the air, cooled top and bottom. It was hot and humid, but bearable.

Next morning Tony and I headed out early to beat the heat of the day. Mike stayed back with John and Louise, who were having some sort of pow-wow about selling the camera and our other goods. Tony and I wended our way through ancient stone streets, narrow and shadowed, down towards the river. Along the way, we passed near-naked, docile beggars huddled against the walls. They silently watched our downward progress toward the *ghats*. Many had a small bowl before them on the ground to receive any offering, and a fist sized leather bag suspended around their necks by a thin leather cord. The most striking thing was their eyes. I'd seen beggars all over Asia and the usual pleading or abject expression in the face was absent here. There was the odd sense of being looked upon with the kindest indulgence, of a grandfather or grandmother fondly gazing at grandchildren. Both Tony and I dropped a few paisa coins in the bowls as we passed, receiving a quiet and gentle nod of acknowledgement in return.

Ahead, the Ganges glistened through a gap in the buildings. We made our way down on a wide stone staircase that led directly onto the river. At this early hour the sun was scarcely above the eastern horizon yet the riverbank was already lined with bathers standing up to their waists, some up to their necks. All were absorbed in prayer, facing the rising sun. The water sparkled gold and the air had a tinge of coolness. If it hadn't been for people obviously defecating along the bank in both directions I would have probably taken a dip in the holy river myself.

We strolled along the stairs to our left. They interconnected with other steps coming down to the river. All along the way bathers in prayer, people washing clothes, small boats coming and going, the air perfumed with incense and feces and river mud. Smoke ahead told us we were approaching a burning *ghat*. Rounding the base of what appeared to be a castle turret the scene opened up on to a broad, flat terrace with piles of wood heaped near the back wall. Men with shaved heads, dressed in white, moved solemnly between the woodpiles and the fires, tending, poking. We walked closer. Tony reached out his arm across my chest then, holding me back. He inclined his head towards the rear of the woodpile.

"Vernon, hold on. Look here," he said quietly.

The priests were bent over the wizened corpse of an old man. They had him laid out on a sheet of while muslin and were dripping a clear, yellow liquid over his body and chanting. One of the priests bent down and removed the little leather sack from the dead man's neck and suspended it from a branch in the nearby woodpile. As we watched they folded the muslin, gently enshrouding the old man. Ten feet away another enshrouded figure was lifted and carried toward the river by a group of four and laid out on a pyre of logs. More of the yellow liquid was ladled over the body and a flaming torch placed under the pile. The flames began to spread and where the liquid had splashed the logs the fire leaped up, brightly, intensely.

A westerner, tall, middle aged looking, wearing a straw fedora and wielding an expensive looking camera was moving around the *ghat* snapping photos. It struck me as disrespectful but no one paid him any notice.

"Come on then," I said back to Tony.

He was watching the flames grow on the pyre near to us. A pair of human feet were showing amidst the flames at the end of the pyre, where the muslin had burned off. The day was heating up and we could feel the radiant energy from the fires on our faces. The wood smoke had an incongruous butter smell and for some reason I thought about pancakes. I didn't feel hungry though, especially after we passed a more burned down pile and saw a head, the upper section of the skull blown off by the boiling brain within.

"Crykie," mumbled Tony and we both made our way up the next flight of steps, away from the river and the heat and the greasy smoke.

Back at the guesthouse by midmorning, we found everybody else up in the roof garden, under the canopy. From here we could see how the river curved around the nose of the old city, the vast flood plain on the other side. It was beginning to get really hot again and the still air over the plain rippled like it was made from some transparent gelatin.

"John and Lou are leaving for Delhi on the train tonight," Mike announced. "With a stop in Agra for the Taj Mahal," Louise added.

Their morning had been spent trying to line up a buyer for the video camera, but it seemed that Benares was not the market we hoped it would be for our contraband.

"Guy in the market offered me almost exactly what I paid for the scotch in Kathmandu," Mike groused.

"Delhi is where we'll be able to sell the camera," John assured himself, "not the kind of money around here to get a good price."

I had purchased a *lungi* on the morning expedition with Tony. A *lungi* was like a sarong but thinner. My cotton sarong from Bali was actually too warm to use for a top sheet here but I needed something for the mosquitoes. I liked the tan, green and white plaid of the light fabric. The few gold threads running through the weave marked it as Indian and it made a nice addition to my two other Southeast Asian sarongs. Souvenirs had to be useful to make carrying them around worth the space, and this was immediately useful. In the heat of the day, we soaked our sarongs in water and laid them over us on the rope beds, under the ceiling fan. My personal swamp cooler. I spent the afternoon reading *The Book of Skulls* by Robert Silverberg, in under my damp tent. Every time I ventured out, to re-soak my *lungi* or get a drink of water, the daunting heat was breathtaking. I didn't know it could get this hot on earth - and people lived here! My *lungi* went from dripping wet to completely dry every half hour.

Not long after sunset, we saw John and Louise off to the Varanasi Junction. It was agreed we would meet them in Delhi in four days' time. Mike had the address of the Moti Mahal Guesthouse, near Connaught Circus in mid-Delhi, another traveler recommendation. There was the back-up plan of Poste Restante if we missed each other.

Then to food! We were actually famished, once it began to cool off. And so was every other person in Benares. We wandered out and found the street food scene rivaled the best of Bangkok. I found a stall with a delicious *tamatar chaat*, a sort of chickpea tomato stew. We all piled into another little stall for a rich vegetarian *thali*. I'd grown to like the *thali* style tray. It reminded me a bit of the TV dinner trays from the 1950s, with the little aluminum depressions for each item. In India, the *thali* varied daily and from place to place. At a minimum there would be a bread such as a puri or a chapatti, a spicy vegetable curry of some sort, dhal and basmati rice, always cheap and cheerful. The secret was to look for a cook who was fat and happy.

Here in Varanasi, the variety of sweets was also outstanding. Warm, round *gulab jamin*, a deep fried sweet cheese ball in syrup and the carrot-based *halwa* became instant favorites. A new twist was a drink similar to a lassie called a *thandi*, milk based but with ground almonds and spices like cardamom. Here we could get a *thandi bhang*, a regular *thandi* loaded with ganja paste. It made sleeping the night away no problem. We became nocturnal creatures, active after the sun had set, hibernating beneath our wet *lungis* through the heat of the day. But on our third morning I awoke at dawn. It was to be our last day in Benares and I wanted to go out on the river and take some photographs. Mike and Tony were literally bhang-out, so I left a note and worked my way down to the *ghats*. An Indian man in a straw hat,

The Appearance of Things

his sleeves rolled up, sat in his turquoise boat smoking a beedi. He smiled welcomingly when I approached.

"Good morning, sir. Are you interested in a boat tour?"

"I am. Not extra-long, but I would like to move along the shore for a time," I replied, "perhaps one hour. What would you charge me?"

He stood then and said expansively, "What you like. I am at your service," and indicated the bench seat forward.

"I will pay you twenty rupees for one hour, if we are agreed."

He did the head waggle and again pointed at the seat, "We go."

We started off going upstream, to the right. That was fine with me as I had not been along the *ghats* in that direction and I wanted to photograph the Maharaja's palace, a fantasy of orange brick towers and domes, rising almost vertically from the river's edge where the whole of life was on display. Worshippers scooped the waters up and over their heads, women smacked laundry on flat rocks at the water's edge, a small procession pushed a miniature reed-raft bearing a papier-mâché Ganesha out into the slow current, the elephant god bedecked with a mountain of orange marigolds. I'd heard the early morning light described as golden light by people who were very engaged in photography and here at least that was certainly the case. The current was not strong near the shore and we traversed quite a distance, passing both the palace and a temple that recalled the ancient Prambanan temple in Java. The day there with Eva had been on my mind since I sent her and Luli the promised post cards from Kathmandu. Message in a bottle. I wondered if I would ever see them again but in memory.

We passed another set of burning *ghats*. My boatman, Kashore, rowed quietly. He didn't appear terribly strong yet his strokes in the flat water were solid and powerful. I felt the little boat surge forward with each pass as we accelerated, then slowed.

"What is the little leather bag around the neck?" I asked.

Kashore glanced to his left, towards the burning *ghat* where a priest was removing the thong from around the neck of a new corpse.

"That is wood money," he replied, "Varanasi is the beating heart of India. To die here is the greatest blessing. That man," he nodded towards the corpse, "could have been a banker or a rickshaw driver. He gave his possessions to his sons and journeyed to Benares to pray and await moksha."

Back to Mother India

I thought back to the beggars I had passed on my walks around the city. Kashore was suggesting they were happy with their condition.

"Kashore, when I see these people on the street, I feel sorry for them - for their poverty and pain. So many are suffering."

Kashore waggled his head, "Karma, young sir." He stopped rowing and leaned towards me, his eyes serious but his countenance gentle, "They will die in Benares and be freed. You will not. It is they who feel sorry for you."

I was startled by the proposition and simply nodded, rather dumbly.

We had gone quite some distance up the river and now Kashore turned the boat and put us a bit further out where the swifter current would help to carry us back. A lump in the water a dozen yards ahead resolved into a dark, naked back. A man with dark hair floated face down. Passing, I could see the darting movements of small fish near the face, picking at the whitening, water logged tissue.

"Kashore, why is this man floating in the river? Why hasn't he been cremated?"

The boatman shrugged, "Perhaps he died from cholera or some other disease. If a man dies from disease, the body is put directly into the river for purification."

The biology student in me almost shrieked "What!" but I held steady, "So the diseased are not cremated?" I ventured. "Nor are holy men or children," Kashore added.

He put in a deep stroke to head us back towards the river's edge. Somehow we were back in line with our starting point. I rested my hand on the rim of the boat as we turned towards the shore. A small splash of the river water hit my left hand and I involuntarily wiped it on my trouser leg. If Kashore noticed my recoil, he said nothing.

The day was warming. I moved up the steps, away from the river. There was the oddest sense of displacement, as if I had just discovered I was adopted or something. It wasn't the same world I had awakened to this morning. Moving through the narrow street, I found myself at the end of a queue of people filing into the door of a temple. Most were carrying marigold garlands or small orange candles. Without thinking I followed the woman in front of me and found myself in a stone corridor, drifting towards the inner sanctum. The bright, pure tone of a small brass bell being rung reverberated through the passage. An elderly woman, head wrapped in a shawl, held up a marigold chain to me, one finger held aloft. I passed her a one rupee coin and continued into the domed chamber, the flowers dangling from my hand. At floor level, a round stone bowl, maybe a meter across with a tall ovoid stone erect in the center, occupied the middle of the candlelit room. We circulated around the stone to the right, moving clockwise. It reminded me of a huge mortar and pestle. A priest with plastered down silver grey hair and a great grey moustache, a yellow paste line down the center of his forehead and wearing only a loin cloth, was ringing the bell and pouring water from a brass pitcher over the top of the obelisk. I placed my garland of marigolds around the edge, as I saw others doing, and was slowly swept from the room by the soft surge of the crowd. Moments later I was back outside, on a different street. Awakening from a dream. I had no idea what I just did or why. I took a deep breath and realized with a start that I couldn't recall the last time I had inhaled. Maybe the bhang was having a second go in my brain!

By the time I returned to the Birat Guesthouse the heat was upon us.

"So Vernon, how was your river trip," Mike inquired with a grin.

"Really amazing," I replied, shaking my head. "I'll tell you about it but I have to write it down right now, while it's still up here."

I tapped my forehead.

"Ah yeah, good on ya' then. Care for a toke?" Mike asked.

It was only then that I even noticed the chillum.

"We found the government hash and bhang shop this morning after brekkie," Tony grinned, a bit red eyed.

Mike held up what looked like half of a thick milk chocolate bar.

"Ten rupees for a *tola*."

We'd learned that the unit of measure for hash here was the *tola*, about twelve grams or a bit less than half an ounce. It wasn't the home-run quality of Nepalese but was certainly on par with Red Lebanese.

I held up my hand, "No thanks, not just yet anyway. The bhang from last night is still kicking. I feel weird enough right now."

They shrugged and went back to the chillum. I pulled out my travel journal and tried to make sense out of this morning.

Our last night in Varanasi was more of a half night. We'd booked a second class sleeper to Agra that departed from Varanasi Junction just past midnight. It would be hot, but not the torture of doing it midday.

Now, waiting on the platform, sitting on top of my pack, I looked around at the crowd. This place apparently never slept. A shout of consternation from the next platform over. A large black bull was nosing into a woman's wicker basket and she had leaped up, trying to shoo it away in a non-violent manner with her shawl. The bull, however, was unaffected and proceeded to untuck the cover of her basket and pull out papadams, the large Indian cracker. He was obviously enjoying them and the nonplussed woman shouted at her cowering husband and children.

Flying insects orbited the large bare bulbs far above us in the station rafters. The air was still and humid, the odor of burning coal predominant with undertones of curry and unwashed human bodies.

When our train chugged to a stop beside the platform pandemonium erupted. People were suddenly on their feet, pushing, shoving, trying to squeeze through the narrow carriage doors with all of their possessions. Windows were thrown open and the first aboard waved to their families. Baggage began to be shoved up and in through the openings.

We looked at each other, half amused, half in shock.

"Crykie!" Tony blurted. "It's bloody mayhem."

Our carriage was meant to be number 9 so we hefted our gear and began a walk down the platform, searching the numbers. The carriages were not in order and we walked quite some distance down the platform in search of the right car. The outside roof of the train was increasingly loaded with people who appeared out of the dark yard and scampered up maintenance ladders between the carriages. The dimly lit interiors of the cars were a riot of suitcases being passed, people squeezing past each other, shouting and laughter.

"There she is!" Mike announced with some relief. We clambered aboard and found that our second-class sleepers were wooden slat affairs, stacked three high on each side of the carriage. Mine was occupied by a rather chubby Indian man, a diminutive woman in a blue sari and a girl child with large dark eyes that looked made up. Mike and Tony found similar arrangements.

"Look here," I said to the chubby man and showed him my ticket. I tapped the number 27 on the frame and pointed to myself. He looked annoyed and slid down, crushing the woman and child against the end wall of the sleeper shelf. Sigh. I shoved my pack in beside the man and shoehorned myself into the remaining four foot wide cubby hole, my head resting on the side of my pack. It was going to be an interesting night.

I awakened at a stop a few hours down the road, when my bunkmates departed, and quickly stretched out to fully occupy the bench. The gentle swaying of the carriage and the regular clicking and clacking faded into the night. It felt a bit cooler. The mountains reminded me a little of the Himalaya. My mind told me they were the Himalaya and I saw no reason to argue. Ahead, the one I had come to see waited. He was old, older than anyone I'd ever met. White hair and beard cascaded down over his grey blue robe and he smiled patiently as I clambered over the last stones and stood before him.

"Sit down," he nodded to a carpet on the earth beside him, "and tell me what it is that you seek."

I had come a long way to find him, this man I already knew was wise. I felt a little embarrassed to be doing the "come to India and find your guru" thing but this had just happened, like an accident that was meant to happen and I didn't question it.

"I want to be happy," I said, simply, and knew it was true when I said it.

He gazed at me and his eyes were my mother's eyes, that light shade of hazel blue with the little gold ring around the iris. I felt love and loved in return.

My reality jerked to a halt at Agra station and the odd dream retreated as consciousness of my surroundings rippled into clarity, the need to act asserting itself. The hustle of people pushing by in the corridor, luggage banging, calls and a train whistle. It was maybe seven in the morning. I couldn't really say how much sleep I'd had. In my mind's eye I looked over my shoulder at that last, retreating dream. It felt reassuring somehow but of what? The night had passed in a semi-awareness of shakes and rattles, snatches of dreams and a hard wooden bed. I'd had better nights.

The train wasn't staying in Agra. Only moments after we had stepped down on the platform and set about collecting ourselves, it jerked and slowly slid out of the station. Mike, Tony and I just stood there. We all looked like rumpled beds, I thought. My mouth tasted dirty and I waved to a passing chai walla. We sat down on our packs, there in the open station, and silently drank our clay cups of hot, sweet, milky India tea and shared a packet of biscuits that tasted like Animal Crackers.

"What do you imagine third class is like?" Mike asked rhetorically.

But here we were in Agra, a small town grown up outside the gates and grounds of the Taj Mahal. We found a little cheap and cheerful called The

Taj Palace, checked in and set to washing off the night. Thankfully, it wasn't as hot here as Benares, at least not at ten in the morning. I felt better after another cup of tea and a rather good *thali*, served up just beyond the front door of our lodging.

"Who's for it?" Mike stood and stretched, ready to head for the main event.

"Hang on," Tony replied, "I want to get my camera," and he disappeared back in towards our room. I went as well and picked up not only my camera but my G harmonica. And we walked down the lane to the entry gate of the Taj Mahal.

In some respects, first impressions and all that, it looked just like the photos I'd seen all my life. Then details began to emerge. The long pool of water, or what should have been the long pool of reflecting water, was dry and dusty. This was, after all, the hot time of the year, and the gardens looked as tired and wilted as I felt walking in the full sun. The lawns were as parched as the fountains. Yet the Taj Mahal itself had a magnificent energy that only grew stronger as we approached. My childhood photographic impressions had not prepared me for the exquisite inlay work in the white marble. Drawing closer, until I could reach out and touch the cool, smooth stone, the marvelous and intricate twining vines, fruits and flowers, I felt no seam or flaw in the surface. Colored marbles and semi-precious minerals like lapis lazuli and turquoise and cat's eye, reds and greens of agate and translucents like onyx made the rock hound in me drool. Pick any square meter of wall, inside or out, and the inlay work would make it a masterpiece.

"I can't believe the whole place is like this, inside and out, all the way up!" I spoke to Mike and Tony but they were so enthralled it was as if I was talking to myself.

Perhaps because it was approaching midday the site was virtually deserted, except for two sleepy guards near the front entrance. Now was the time. I went into the main room of the tomb, extracted my harmonica and tried a long, low note. The reverb was extraordinary. The space wasn't so large that it was echo, the sound delayed then returning. The note was picked up, expanded and deepened. I began a very slow, bluesy riff and the building played back, the sound warping and wrapping around me. This wasn't original. I was harkening back to 1968 when Paul Horn came out with an album called "Inside the Taj Mahal." Still, it was more than a little thrilling to have my music bouncing around in here. Mike and Tony came across the entryway, grinning. "Don't stop," Mike said, "it sounds fantastic."

We sat and I played, maybe fifteen minutes. When a few other tourists entered, though, I felt the moment break. I self-consciously shook out my harp and slipped it back into my pocket. Playing harp in the Taj Mahal was not something I always wanted to do until I got there. God, that was fun!

"I've a proposal," Mike stood up, "Tonight is a full moon. How about we come back after tucker, break out the chillum and watch the moon rise over the Taj Mahal? I'll bring my guitar, you Vernon, bring your harp and we'll have a time of it." It sounded like fun. We'd all seen the government hash and bhang shop near the entrance. It was also curiously romantic, something I might suggest to my lover, rather than a couple of stiffs like Tony and me. But Mike had that romantic streak, a poet for poetry's sake. We'd get high and play music to the full moon in the gardens of the Taj Mahal and that's pretty good.

Five hours later, with darkness approaching, Mike, Tony and I were walking back towards the Taj, our pockets stuffed with cash, our stomachs stuffed with fine Indian food and our heads on their way to being stuffed with good Indian hash. "That was really brilliant," enthused Tony, "the best feed I've had in a long time."

A few hours earlier, I'd had the really pretty good idea of taking our whiskey and cigarettes up to the fancy Holiday Inn hotel. "Tell you what," I suggested, "this is a tourist place and I'll bet we could make a deal with the manager of the hotel to buy our goods."

"You reckon?" Mike asked, "Yeah, I mean, ok, why not. Let's give it a go."

We cleaned ourselves up so as to look at least presentable and entered the posh lobby of the Taj Holiday Inn. All in all, I think we still looked pretty scruffy and it wasn't a surprise when we were intercepted by a well-dressed concierge twenty feet into the lobby.

"Good evening. May I help you?"

He was smooth and reminded me of an Italian tenor, hair slicked back, nice suit. "May I help you" translated to "what the hell are you doing walking in here, hippy scum."

"I'd like to speak with the manager," I replied, "We have a proposal I think he would find of interest."

The concierge hesitated and appeared to be about ready to show us the door so I opened my day sack and revealed the three bottles of Johnny Walker

Red. A carton of cigarettes also peeked out. Understanding washed over the man's smooth face and his posture relaxed.

"Please, gentlemen, take a seat over there and I'll return shortly."

He strode across the lobby to a door on the left side of the reception counter and disappeared within. A very attractive, raven haired woman in a yellow and gold sari behind the counter smiled over at us, her bright red lipstick almost startling.

"What do you reckon this place costs for a night?" Tony asked, somewhat awed.

The concierge reappeared at the door and motioned for us to join him. We passed into an office suite and another well-dressed Indian man, who could have passed for Errol Flynn, stood to greet us. His shrewd eyes sized us up.

"I understand you have goods we may wish to purchase. Please, sit down," indicating the chairs in from of his desk.

Before I sat, I extracted the three bottles of scotch and three cartons of cigarettes and arranged them on the desk between us. Mike and Tony followed suit. It was quite a haul and I noted the glint of pleasure and desire in his eyes.

The deal was short and sweet. We dickered a bit, including a dinner for the three of us in the hotel restaurant, just to see what fancy food tasted like.

"I'll have Paul take you over," he said, nodding at the concierge.

"Tell chef our guests are here for the Raja dinner. Pleasure doing business with you. I hope you will enjoy the rest of your stay in Agra." And we were dismissed. I glanced back as we were departing the office. He was already holding one of the bottles and smiling at it.

"They treated us right," Tony patted his stomach, "That was a bit up from a *thali*, eh?" Mike and I laughed in agreement. Meat wasn't something I particularly missed but tonight, the lamb and the chicken and the fish were a high protein extravaganza. "The vindaloo was brilliant. We've got top lamb and Indian restaurants by the dozen in Sydney but I've never had better than that."

Mike picked his teeth as we walked back, "Good on ya, Vernon. You Americans have a sense for business."

I bristled inside around the "you Americans" language but knew he didn't mean any harm. I was beginning to feel pretty cool and international. Didn't want to be any particular brand of person. I believed in America, though, in a kind of Jimmy Stewart Mr. Smith Goes to Washington sort of way. But I wasn't one of the mad dog nationalists that had "love it or leave it" on a bumper sticker. Last summer, back in Europe, the two friends I was travelling with had purchased Canadian Flag patches up in Vancouver when we flew out. They sewed them on their packs and were pretending to be Canadian with people we met in England, our first stop. I thought it was sort of lame and I'm not sure if they were really fooling anyone. When asked, I just said I was American. One night, we were in a London pub and this big blowhard was going on, an expert in everything. He'd ordered beers for my friends when they "confessed" to being Canadian. Then he turned to me, "How about you, mate? Hail from Canada too, do you?" I smiled and shook my head no, "Nope. America. Los Angeles." He made a sour face and did a theatrical turn back to the bar, shunning me. I said to my friends, "Enjoy yourselves. I'm heading back to the hotel." They had enough grace to at least look chagrined.

So the full moon illuminated the Taj Mahal and a few good chillums illuminated my brain. Mike was a good guitarist and his voice had an appealing lilt. I added in when I could on the harp and a few other travelers joined us. A pair of Australian girls knew the lyrics to Mike's "We had a chicken, no eggs did she lay" and they joined in. It was a sweet-hearted evening.

The next day started off normally enough. We had our bit of breakfast and caught a second class express toward Delhi. It was close to eleven in the morning when the shit hit the fan.

Mike, Tony and I occupied a little four passenger open cubby. The carriage was arranged so groups sat facing each other on each side of the aisle. One by one, we took turns going down to the loo to have a chillum in the disgusting privacy of the little chamber. The toilet was an empty compartment roughly the size of a large telephone booth. A tiny window looked out over the passing farms and mud brick villages. Near to the floor a thin brass faucet protruded from the wall and provided a dribble of water to wash your bum or your hands. The toilet wasn't even a squatter. A raw hole in the floor, centered, was the facility. The hole, large enough to drop a cantaloupe though and ringed with different grades of shit, went directly down on to the passing ties and gravel.

It was necessary to stand with my back against the wall to keep from soiling my flip-flops while I loaded and lit the chillum. We were smoking in the bathroom because, even though our stash was from the government hash

Back to Mother India

and bhang shop, we'd noticed that the only people who smoked openly were the sadhus, the eccentric, traveling holy men of India.

So I'm back in my seat, sanguinely gazing out the window at the passing countryside when the train slows and stops at a country station. People get off, people get on, we start moving again. Next thing I know, there's a presence in the aisle behind me and Tony is looking up, petrified.

"Excise Tax check, stand up please."

Turning, I'm facing a group of characters from a Gunga Din casting call. They're all in tired looking khaki uniforms and eyeing me. The speaker is a short Indian man with a wide forehead that stretches up to his balding pate. He's squinting at me through a pair of small, dark eyes, over a sharp nose and a pencil thin moustache. Thin colored bars on his shirt pocket marking rank are prominently displayed. Immediately behind him is the tallest man I have seen in India. His head nearly hits the top of the carriage while his frumpy uniform bears no rank whatsoever. He looks like Lurch, the huge cadaverous butler from the Addams Family sitcom. His face is a molten mask of flaccid malice and he's gripping an old carbine at the ready. I think without the gun he would appear bovine. The other two are standard issue army guys who appear a little seedier than usual. They too are gripping carbines, their eyes moving nervously from side to side.

"Stand up please," the commander repeated, "this is an Excise Tax search."

He's speaking to me. I cast a look at Mike and Tony sitting opposite, who are stoned on their asses and looking like rabbits in a headlight. I raise myself to a standing position, facing the little man and I can see from his expression that he is surprised at my size. He takes a step back, but recovers himself and reaches forward. Sticking out of my shirt pocket is the top of the Government Hash and Bhang wrapper. Plucking the packet out of my pocket, he stares at it a moment, in triumph.

"You! You are in possession of hashish and I place you under arrest. You'll go to jail. And you'll rot in jail!" he states with some finality.

Having just done a massive chillum load not long before, my mind was not very nimble on this point. From the look of frozen horror on Mike and Tony's faces I knew I was on my own for now.

"What on earth are you talking about," I stammered, "I bought that hashish at a legal government hash and bhang shop in Agra, just yesterday."

A look of smug satisfaction crossed the little man's face, "Agra is Uttar

Pradesh state. It is forbidden to bring hashish across the state lines into Delhi."

"That's crazy," I almost shouted, 'I buy this legally and now you…'"

"You will come with us," he sneered, "and you'll go to jail. You'll rot in jail!"

I sat back down, feeling stunned. This has got to be a scam somehow. It was then I noticed that in the entire carriage nobody was looking our way. People looked down, out the window, feigned sleep, the works. Across the aisle an old man was looking straight ahead, his hands resting in his lap. He looked over at me and I realized he had been watching the whole proceeding. His expression was not one of particular concern, especially compared to my frozen seatmates. I looked back at the little officer and thought I detected a note of theatricality in his eyes. The humorless Lurch looked on, eyes hooded, mouth a straight line.

I stood up then. "Excuse me," I said to my inquisitor and moved to kneel nearby the old man, who continued to regard me dispassionately. "Are these men for real?" I asked him. He showed no comprehension at my question, his wrinkled old hands folded in his lap.

"He doesn't speak English," a young fellow beside him offered.

I looked at the old man, his rugged face reminding me of photos I'd seen of a Navajo elder. I don't know why, maybe just my stoned brain, but I wanted his advice.

"Would you explain to the gentleman my question, please?"

The young man nodded and began to speak at length to the elder. When he was done the man looked at me and unclasped his hands. He pointed at the standing soldiers, then clamped his right hand over his left wrist and made a brief pantomime of being led away. Then he opened the palm of his left hand and acted like he was dealing cards out of it with his right.

I nodded. I got it. If they take you away it's going to cost a lot. He watched me and, I fancy, saw that I understood. Then he pointed at the floor and lowered his gaze archly. He did the card dealing motion again, only less so. Fewer.

So if I let then take me away it going to cost more than if I pay right now. That was the solution! Baksheesh right now! Duh, ok, it's sort of obvious but not to my freaked out and stoned out mind. I was glad I had stashed all my hard earned contraband money at the bottom of my sleep sack. I had a wallet with only traveling rupees. Maybe.

I stood and faced the officer, "Sir, there appears to be some grave misunderstanding. Please, I need to speak to you in private," and without waiting I moved off towards the latrine at the end of the carriage. He followed me, and Lurch followed him and the other two brought up the rear. Opening the latrine door, I stepped inside and beckoned him to follow. He barked something at Lurch, who gave me a mean eye, then entered the latrine accompanied by the smaller of the two regulars.

We stood for a moment, our faces rather close together because we were all with our heels against the walls and leaning in. Looking down at the ties and gravel going by beneath us, an idea popped into my head.

"Sir, give me my hashish please."

The officer looked surprised then suddenly curious. He extracted my hash packet from his pocket and passed it over to me. I held it in front of my face and said, "Thank you." Then I dropped it. Our three heads nearly collided as we watched the packet sail down through the latrine hole and disappear sideways in the slipstream of the rushing train.

The soldier looked shocked, the officer looked furious and I grinned. In a split second, the expression of anger on the small officer's face slipped into amusement. He reached into his other shirt pocket and produced another, different packet, "Now, this is your hashish!"

He burst from the latrine, "You had your chance. Now you'll go to jail and you'll rot in jail," he glared back at me.

Nuts. That wasn't such a good idea after all. But the situation had shifted. Now, Lurch and the two soldiers huddled with their officer, his back to me, their vaguely hostile yet worried faces looking my way now and again. The adrenaline had done a moderately good job of clearing my brain. Mike and Tony sat on the opposite bench facing me.

"Crykie," Tony whispered, "What are we gonna do?" He nodded at the huddle, "These guys seem serious. What did you do?"

At that moment, the officer looked over at me, his confederates behind him. He said nothing but I swear, his face had the expression of a kid whose feelings I'd hurt - sulky and wounded.

New idea. I stood and approached him. He glared at me sullenly, like I had betrayed his confidence during the shake down in the latrine and now we weren't friends anymore.

"Come on. I have an idea," I said and jerked my thumb towards the latrine

The Appearance of Things

door. He looked down and crossed his arms on his chest, silent. I took a chance, reached down and pinched him on his tummy. He looked up, surprised.

"Let's go. We can fix this, you and I," and he allowed me to gently tug him down the hall and back into the latrine. This time, it was just he and I. He peered at me in the close confines with a wounded suspicion.

"Sir, I have come from across the world to see your wonderful country. You must not penalize me for being ignorant of some of your customs. Please..." and I pulled out my wallet and lay it open between us.

"This is all the money I have available, my traveling money. If you will accompany me to a bank when we reach Delhi, I should be able to change a travel check."

Extracting the six ten rupee notes and two green five rupee notes, I offered them. His eyes moved from the wallet to my face then back to the proffered cash.

"I apologize to you for breaking the law. I made my purchase at your government's shop. How should I know that the law would change a few miles down the line?" I asked, reasonably. "Please accept this fine and let us let bygones be bygones."

A jolt in the carriage told us both we were stopping at a village station. He looked again at the money and pursed his lips. I followed my hunch and pinched him gently again on the tummy.

"Sir, I am a visitor to your country. Let this be my lesson."

I saw his eyes decide. He grabbed the money and shoved it into his pants pocket, did the head waggle and almost smiled, "Now, you know the law."

He exited the latrine and, with the train stopping, signaled to his confederates. They all piled off on to the station platform and disappeared into the crowd.

I flopped back on to the seat. The old man opposite held up his left hand and nodded slightly. I think he approved. His old head swiveled to the scene outside the window and no more was said.

"Christ, Vernon!" Mike gasped, as if he had been holding his breath, "What was that about?"

Tony was gazing out the train window, over the platform. "They just hopped on to the train over there, going back the other way." He looked over to me, "You reckon they were real coppers?" his hazel eyes curious.

"It was worth seventy rupees to not find out," I replied.

Mike was still recovering and I leaned forward, "Mike, you'll be going to jail. And you'll rot in jail!" He blinked and we all burst out laughing.

Just past noon we arrived in New Delhi and caught a taxi over to the Moti Mahal Guest House. Again, it was hot, but still nothing like the deadly atmosphere of Varanasi. We found John and Louise eating lunch in the shaded garden of the hotel. Fans with rattan blades whirred overhead.

"Ah, the wayfarers arrive," John smiled. He and Lou were seated at a white metal table enjoying a *thali* plate. Also at their table was a handsome Indian man, light skinned, western looking in hair and dress. He scrutinized us with blue green eyes as we spread ourselves around the table without taking seats. Louise did the introductions.

"Douglas, these are the friends we spoke of – Mike, Tony and Vernon, there." She said the last as though I was subtly a different animal, maybe a bit suspect. I liked the way her eyes twinkled when she teased me. It was flirting of a sort, I guess, but there was a level of warmth under it. "And this is Douglas Chaudhry, with whom we are all sharing the dormitory." Sharing?

Douglas wiped his mouth with a white cloth napkin and stood to greet us.

"Hello. Very pleased to meet you. Have you had your tea?" His accent was London English, educated.

Tony grinned, "I could do with some tucker," and plopped down into the chair beside John.

Mike looked at him briefly then extended a hand across the table to Douglas and said in his own cultured English, "Pleased to make your acquaintance. Are you here long?"

"Only school holidays, I'm afraid," Douglas replied and motioned for Mike and I to sit as he settled back into his chair. A young woman hovered near the table, her blue and red sari rippling from the slight air movement of the fan. John looked around at us, "Fancy the *thali*? They do a good job with it here." We three nodded. She favored Mike with a charmingly shy smile and departed for the kitchen.

"Douglas thinks he may have a buyer for the video camera," John went on, "so we're off to the old city after lunch to meet him."

Douglas nodded agreement, "This is the uncle of a friend at school. He has very good contacts locally." His clean-shaven face, movie star quality jaw and hair were like one of the leads on a Hindi film poster. Why do we tend to trust attractive people?

John and Louise were highly amused by the tale of the hashish encounter on the train.

"So Vernon, we might have been bringing you tea and bikkies at the local slammer," John grinned.

"Not likely," Douglas, an edge of seriousness in his voice, "the name of the game was always baksheesh. You did well."

The compliment pleased me.

"I wasn't certain they were really police, you know. But the old man, showing me the image of being led away, it seemed the best course of action.

"They scared the hell out of me," Tony added and gave me a wink.

After we dropped our gear off in the surprisingly large upper floor room, Mike and Tony joined John and Lou on their expedition to sell the camera. My choice was to strike out on my own and get a taste of the city.

Connaught Circus was a central roundabout with a smallish park in its center. A few of the old Ambassador cars circulated freely around the circle along with assorted *bemos* and cycles and street carts. I relaxed on a shady bench, a brief respite from the heat of the sidewalk, and listened to the birds and cars and motorcycles buzzing around me.

"Sir, I can offer you a top job in ear cleaning."

A little man with a shaved head and large round glasses had taken a seat beside me. Between us, he opened a wooden box filled with carefully stored, small brass tools and ointments.

"Very clean. No problem," he coaxed with a head waggle.

"I don't think so. Sorry."

"Sir, I can tell you I have looked. Your ear canals are in need of a good cleaning."

His short grey bristle of a moustache and bright, earnest eyes were disarming. He removed a small brass rod, about the thickness of a pencil lead. It terminated in a tiny spoon shape.

"Allow me to show you," and he used a cotton swab reeking of alcohol to clean his device. He appeared tidy and intelligent. Don't put anything larger than your elbow in your ear, my mom had said. Take a chance, whispered my inner adventurer.

"Well then, let's give it a go," I allowed.

He perked up and moved behind me. He pressed back my left ear and I felt the little tool move smoothly and gently in my ear canal, tracing out a full circle sweep.

"There, you see."

He held the small rod before my eyes. Sure enough, a dark brown glob decorated the end of the spoon.

"How much for a cleaning?" I asked.

The head waggle, "One rupee for each ear," he replied.

Three minutes later I held a small tissue dotted with dabs of earwax and paid my two rupees. I didn't notice any improvement in my hearing but I was impressed with his skill. Ear cleaning in Connaught Circus was pretty close to the last thing I expected.

Departing the small park and crossing back into the maze of the city, my wanderings led me into a warren of alleys shaded by colorful muslin canopies. Fresh fruit and vegetables vied with kitchen wares and crafts for my attention. At one stall, I stopped to examine a set of woven lamps constructed on concentric hoops that accordioned down. Maybe a gift for mom?

"Begging your pardon, sir. I will tell you your fortune for ten rupees, a very good fortune."

An older man in a soiled white turban grinned up at me. With his long, thin grey beard and mischievous eyes, he seemed to be saying that we were sharing a fine joke together.

"I'm not really interested in having my fortune told but if you can tell me the name of the girl I went out with in high school, I'll give you ten rupees."

That would stump him and send him on his way. Or so I thought. Instead, his gleeful eyes lit up. I had just made him a winning proposition.

From a small pouch on his side he produced a sheet of paper about the size of a post car and the stub of a pencil, handing both things to me. What's this? "Write her name on the paper," he smiled.

OK, it's a scam. I looked around for a confederate or a mirror. How was he going to spy on what I was writing? I intentionally moved a few steps away and cupped my left hand around the paper. Satisfied he couldn't spy on me from where he was, I used the pencil and carefully wrote "Nancy Dupres" on the paper, taking care that neither he or anyone else in the vicinity could even see the movements of the top of the pencil. I then folded the paper in half and then again and crossed back over to the fortune teller. Without even looking at the paper he said, "Fold it two times more," so I did. Now it was a very tight little packet about one inch square. "Hold it in your two closed hands," he instructed.

To be on the safe side I actually placed the wad in my left hand, sandwiched between my index finger and middle finger, where I could feel it securely held. I cupped my right hand around my closed left fist. He reached out and placed his old hands on my wrists and closed his eyes, his face upturned towards the light. He released me and smiled knowingly, extracting another small piece of paper from his pouch and slowly printed something. He folded his piece and cupped it in his right hand, now grinning at me joyfully.

"Open your paper!" he commanded. I extracted my small wad, now slightly moist from the sweat of my hands on this warm day. I folded it open and displayed to him "Nancy Dupres." He laughed aloud and passed his paper to me for opening.

"Nancy Dupres"!

I burst out laughing and so did he. Blown away, I gladly handed over a ten rupee note.

He bowed to me, turned and wandered off into the market crowd. I watched his speckled robe and turban disappear into the shadows.

That evening, I related the tale to the group. Tony thought it was terrific.

"Bloody hell," he enthused, "the guy must have been a mind reader."

"Are you certain there was no way for him to have seen you writing?" Mike asked.

Douglas smiled and said nothing.

The sale of the camera had been delayed. Apparently the uncle needed a day to collect the eleven hundred US dollars they had agreed upon. John hoped to conclude the deal tomorrow afternoon.

"We'll fly back to England at week's end if it all comes off well," he explained.

It was, I could see, something of a disappointment for Mike and Tony to have them bailing out early. In my heart of hearts I was sad about it too. I liked them a lot. But Mike had more of an interest in the Manali to Leh journey with them than I realized. I think he was rather in love with Louise. For that matter, I guess we all were, a bit. I enjoyed it hugely when she teased and poked gentle holes in my illusions about myself. It was never mean spirited. But, according to the clinic in Kathmandu, she was almost three months along. A long, hard trip across the Middle East with morning sickness and who knows what else had no appeal. Time to get back to the arms of the family.

Douglas had offered to show us his favorite restaurant in Delhi. "We have better food in Bombay, I think, but for Delhi, the Braxton is really quite good." And it was. Comparable to the feast we had at the Agra Holiday Inn but with more variety of dishes and flavors. We'd traded for the dinner in Agra but the menu prices there were three or four times higher than the Braxton. We all rolled back to the Moti Mahal feeling superbly fed and rather "in the know" about Delhi.

As was my habit, I tucked my passport and money pouch under my head in bed, sandwiched between the mattress and the bed frame. The large family room on the upper level of the Moti Mahal slept all six of us comfortably. Yet, if I were John, I'd have wanted more privacy with my sweetheart. The other guest rooms had been full when they arrived and I imagine they just accommodated to what was available. We'd all done that, of course. And it wasn't my call. They were very focused on saving money at this point and the clubhouse atmosphere with all of us together was fun. After the last chillum was passed around, I hit the sack and slept very deeply.

"Bloody fucking hell!"

A shouted curse is not the nicest way to be awakened but there was an edge of panic in the voice that pulled me rapidly out of sleep into alertness.

"That bloody bastard!" John hissed through clenched teeth.

I sat up and saw Louise upright in bed, alarm spread over her normally lovely face. Mike and Tony had been likewise startled awake. John stood in the middle of the room in boxer shorts, the aluminum suitcase with its careful foam pockets for the camera and accessories hung empty from his hand. He dropped the case and it clattered on the tile floor. He strode about the room, lifting up clothing and packs, searching. No camera. No Douglas. His bed was empty and he was gone from the room.

"What is it?" Mike asked, a shaken look in his eyes. He already knew what it was.

"That bastard nicked the camera and who knows what else, is what it is." John spat the words out, his angry voice tight and monotone.

"Whaa..t?" Tony cried, rolling his feet out of the bed and onto the floor.

John looked round at all of us, his eyes furious but his stance despairing. He bent to the case and lifted it again for a moment, then placed it gently on the side table.

"Douglas. He's gone, the camera's gone and my wallet isn't in my pants." John's voice was shaking now.

Mike lifted his pants off the end of the bed and squeezed around the pockets, "Mine too. The bloody little bastard! This is the second time my wallet's gone missing." He was thinking back to when we got hit on Patong Beach.

"He woke me up at five and asked to borrow my watch," Tony reflected, "Said he needed to do some early business and would see us later. I told him no, that I needed it and went back to sleep."

John shot Tony a look, as if he was about to berate him for not sounding the alarm when Tony exclaimed, "Crikey, the money from my shirt pocket is gone!"

I rolled out of bed and pulled back the mattress. My goods were all there and I breathed a little sigh of relief. Tony saw me and said, "When I saw you put your bag away there last night, Vernon, I thought you were being a bit excessive. Now... crikey."

Louise had sat silently through the discovery and the ensuing fulminations.

"It's gone," she said calmly, "and there's nothing for it."

She stood up then, her sheer cobalt nightgown clinging to her. She moved to where John was standing and embraced him. He went stiff but she held him closer. "It was always a chance we'd lose it, to customs or thieves or some other way. You know that. We talked about it in Bangkok when we bought the bloody thing." John relaxed then and put his arms around her. For a moment, they just stood there, as if they were all alone, clinging to each other. Louise was starting to look pregnant.

She leaned back, her face tender looking into John's wounded eyes.

"We'll be ok. I know Nicholas will cover us on the tickets back to London. We'll ring him today and he'll swing into action."

John shrugged, "Yeah, I know Lou. I know."

He took a deep breath and stood a little taller, "Well, so much for my fine business plans, eh?"

Mike's face was a dark thundercloud, "He got our trust, didn't he. All of it a fucking set up."

Tony nodded in agreement.

Confusion distilled into anger towards Douglas and towards India in general. You tell your story and it seems like every other traveler tells you his. India is quite unforgiving to us "smart guys." Our seasoned travelers' image of ourselves had been kicked in the crotch. For a time, we were silent, sitting with our own thoughts.

John went down and told Mrs. Patel, the owner, what had occurred in the night. Did she know any more about Douglas Chaudhry. Both Mrs. Patel and her husband followed John back upstairs. They stood at the door, round faced and wringing their hands, looking very disturbed and upset.

"I am so sorry this happened to you in our home. Nothing like this has ever happened before." The poor woman pulled at her sleeves, as though trying to hide her hands. "We are very upset as I am sure, so are you."

Nobody suggested calling the police. We all knew that would be a fruitless avenue to pursue, as would going back to the teashop to find the uncle, if that's who he really was.

Over breakfast, an idea occurred to me. Of course I wanted to help if I could. As the one who didn't lose anything on this robbery, I was touching a sort of survivor's guilt.

"You know, this might be useless but I'll go over to the market area I found yesterday and see if I can dig up the fortune-teller walla. Just maybe he can give me something on how to find this Douglas creep before he flogs the camera."

John looked up and managed a tired smile, "Ah yeah, why not. Nothing to lose."

Mike and Tony came along as well since we all needed to change money and get the Pakistan and Afghanistan visas before heading out of Delhi.

The Appearance of Things

"At least the filthy bugger didn't get our passports or travel checks," Mike reflected.

"Wouldn'ta got much from me if he had," Tony said, "Still have my Agra money though. He didn't get that."

A short search of the market area turned up my fortune-teller. I explained to him what had happened and he listened with a sympathetic countenance.

"Can you help us?" I asked, hopefully.

He shrugged, a head waggle and an apologetic smile, "No, no. I'm sorry but this is not something I am able to help with."

There was a rueful cast to his expression, perhaps touched that anyone might actually believe in him. He held my gaze for a moment, as if to say, "You and I both know there is no magic here. How could I possibly help you as you ask?" I rather hoped he could give us a lead where Douglas might be trying to sell the camera based on his prosaic worldly experience. My sense that street people always knew what was going on in the black market had been confirmed over and over again. But even if he knew, there was nothing in it for him to tell.

Most of my US dollar cash was used up. I kept two one hundred dollar bills in reserve for "just in case" money. We'd received a better rate on the black market than the bank gave for cash, but travel checks needed to go for the official rate. That meant the Bank of India and that meant another hour of fussing around. So, it was late in the afternoon when we finally made it to the Afghanistan Embassy.

We filled out our forms, passed over the thirty seven rupee fee and were told, "Come back tomorrow after two o'clock to collect your passports." With any luck, we'd then make it over to the Pakistanis. We needed to have all our paperwork set up before we left for Manali. The buzz in traveler world was that things were getting weird in the Kashmir area around Srinagar and we shouldn't count on getting visas or money changed near the frontiers.

It felt good, especially now, to have friends with whom I could travel all the way back to Europe. The Pakistan news was not good. Foreigners, particularly Americans were treated with suspicion and hostility. Mr. Nixon had put an arms embargo on Pakistan during their 1971 war with India and the emergence of Bangladesh. Now, with India having just set off an atomic bomb, the Pakistani government was looking at cutting off all links with the USA. If that happened, I'd have to go over or around and both of those options were pricy.

Politics. It wasn't the first time on this journey that I'd hit travel problems. Last summer in Greece, the military junta that had been running the show collapsed and Turkey invaded Cyprus. They were burning American flags in Athens and for a while it looked like we were going to be in the middle of a shooting war.

That evening our hosts the Patels cooked a special Indian meal for all of us, an effort I think to apologize for the theft. John and Louise had recovered their spirits and the evening had sweet melancholy as we prepared to go our separate ways in just a few days.

"We'll be back in London before you lot get up to Manali," John reflected.

The reality that the oft discussed Manali to Leh journey together is now a dead letter was sinking in. John and Lou were already scheduled to fly out in three days' time. Louise's brother Nicholas had acted immediately to get his little sister home to England. Mike, Tony and I had decided to beat the heat and go up to Manali anyways.

"Not certain if we'll go the whole way around to Leh," Mike said. He scooped up the last bit of dahl and curry with a piece of chapatti and glanced at Louise, who was smiling at him.

"Well, we'll expect to see you, all of you, when you get to England," she said warmly.

Not all adventures end with sliding into home, the crowd cheering. Sometimes it's just a last look around, turning off the light and closing the door.

II

The train to Chandigarh departed from Old Delhi Station right on time. John and Louise saw us off and when they waved at our departing coach I had such a hollow feeling. Something exceptional had come to an end and flashes of Lake Toba, our Christmas Eve and the walk back with the fireflies and singing and music. I felt almost like weeping. Mike and Tony sat in the gently rocking carriage, silent and thoughtful. We all felt it, whatever "it" was. And yet, I felt also more open and deeply happy. An odd juxtaposition of emotions.

Outside, the near barren plains began to give way to small groves of trees and finally to forest. We were heading back up into the high country, up and out of the oppressive heat and humidity. Mike was clearly still roiled by the robbery, in large part because, as he said, "I liked him and trusted him."

Our so-called express train made frequent stops and it was late afternoon when we finally arrived in Chandigarh.

"Nice with all the trees," Tony observed.

The wide boulevards were clean, but at this hour the heat was still oppressive. We found a cheap government guesthouse, nearby the bus station, and purchased our tickets for the early bus to Manali. None of us felt much like exploring and after a light meal and a couple of chillums we were all grateful for the oblivion of sleep.

Something healed in the night. I awakened at first light with a tingling sense of delight for no reason. Morning cook-fire smoke laced the air, an ox cart slowly passed, birds called and I fell in love with India again. The day itself felt newly born, and the corny bumper sticker sentiment, "This is the first day of the rest of your life" popped into my mind and I laughed out loud. Mike, startled awake from my outburst, looked at me hazily, "You seem chipper." Slightly sour edge to the comment.

"Yeah, I don't know. Maybe it's that we're going back to the mountains today."

But it was more than that. It was as though I'd awakened in a much larger house and was running wild and free through its unexplored halls. An experience of spaciousness that was literally filled with joy. No explanation but I'll take it.

On and on we climbed. Our ornately decorated bus, little red Christmas lights glowing around the front window, entered the foothills shortly after leaving Chandigarh on the road to Simla. Cascades of white water rushed down the frequent valleys and occasionally we caught a view back out over the plains, dimmed by the dust and humidity. Evergreens began to intersperse with the broadleaf forest and the air had a fresh tang. I leaned out the window and inhaled. A memory of leaving Los Angeles as a kid, crossing the hot central valley of California and beginning to climb into the High Sierra, towards Yosemite. There was such a gracious innocence in going to the mountains. I was coming home, again.

The air was cool in Simla. The entry board for the town stated we were now at two thousand, two hundred meters, over seven thousand feet. Simla was still a living memory of the Raj. The old colonial era wooden buildings crowded the ridge and there was an air of charming dignity about the place. The bus continued deeper into the mountains, dropping down off the ridge to follow a river course. The water roiled and roared its way down the canyon. Our little two-lane road was at times dangerously narrow with a harrowing drop into the river, should a mistake be made. Yet my spirits continued to rise. I began to catch glimpses of high, snowy peaks in the distance. Heading out on backpacking trips always had this taste of euphoria. I'd plan all year for those trips to the very high country. They became the healing I didn't consciously recognize that I needed.

When our bus entered the lower reaches of the Kulu Valley we were flanked by apple orchards. Solid stone and timber dwellings were scattered about between the flowering trees. The signature U-shaped glacial valley was studded with pines and cedars. They marched up the steep slopes until the bare stone of the peaks marked the tree line. I had been in the heat of the plains for what seemed like ages and now, my heart was emerging from shadow.

Manali is reminiscent of an Austrian or Italian Swiss mountain village but with a distinctly mediaeval Asian tone. Not exactly the solid beam and half-timbered fortresses of Kathmandu, more the clean, straight lines of the Alps with hot curry influences. Clearly this place is built for snow loads and, since form follows function, some similarities in design were inevitable. The peaked roofs and the great, meter-in-diameter evergreens stretching up the hill were familiar and welcoming.

We set up in a little hotel not too far from the central square. For Tony, one of the first orders of business was to score some of the famous local hashish, an endeavor that got Mike animated as well. In the time it took me to go through my pack and pull a load of laundry together, they were back, grinning like the proverbial cat that ate the canary.

"Hey Vernon, look at this," Tony enthused. "Two *tolas* for fifteen roops!"

He held out his open palm. This wasn't the almost powdery hash of Agra. In Manali it was a rich, solid chunk that appeared as deep brown clay. He heated the edge of the block with a lighter and crumbled off a fluffy teaspoon for the chillum. The citrus sweetness billowed out into the air, suggestions of mint with a heady background of vanilla earth. Mike, his depression apparently behind him for now, pulled out a packet of Drum and rubbed a pinch into the hash pile, now a full chillum load. We passed it around and its contents surpassed the best I'd had at Melkweg in Amsterdam. There went the afternoon.

The Appearance of Things

Outside of town, further up the valley, were the locally renowned Vashishti Baths, a temple hot spring complex. The next morning, relatively recovered from the hammer blow of hash at high altitude, we resolved to take our towels and swimsuits and explore them. The way led further up the valley, following the single lane road leaving Manali and over the ridge on which the town was built. As we topped the ridge, the Kulu Valley opened before us, its vast u-shape speaking to an ancient, immense glacier that bulldozed this canyon. The cut was perhaps two miles across, bisected by the blue white rapids of the river. The entire town of Manali occupied a small corner of the terminal moraine, the material the glacier left behind in its final retreat. The river had cut through the far side of the moraine, a rough scar in the loose rock and gravel. From where we stood, atop the ridge, it was downhill into the valley, the base of which was a grassy and uncultivated flood plain. Upsweeping valley walls had clefts through which poured multiple waterfalls, careening down from the higher snowcapped Himalaya that reared up behind. Ahead and to the left, across the valley, a long ridge extended out from the canyon wall towards the river. The ridge was contoured with agricultural terraces and, along the top, a Nepalese or Tibetan style village. From this distance we could make out the solid walls and thick slate roofs that spoke of the winter snow load. I recognized the swept areas on both sides of the ridge as avalanche scarring.

"Hey, you guys. See those sweep marks on each side of the ridge there?" I asked.

Tony held his hand to shade his eyes, "Aw yeah, look at that. No wonder they're out on the ridge. They must get some incredible avalanches around here, I reckon."

"Leh is that way," Mike said, pointing up the canyon, "It'd be one hell of a walk from here."

The broad canyon slowly curved round to the left. In the distance a solitary truck or bus was picking its way along the gravel road, moving towards us. From our vantage point it appeared smaller than a sesame seed, underlining the vastness of the space and reminding us again of how huge are the Himalaya.

Walking on down the road, there was steam rising from within and around a set of rough looking wooden buildings ahead. It was late morning and cool. The prospect of a natural hot spring in this setting was appealing in the extreme.

Fifteen more minutes of walking brought us to the Vashishti temple complex. On the right, a massive stone wall with a single wide portico surrounded the steaming baths. The temple itself had the filigree of a gingerbread house, albeit made from thick, blond pine - heavy and charmingly solid. Only when we were this close did I really get the slate roof. These were not cute little Swiss village tiles. Each piece was a meter square and three fingers thick. The weight of the roof alone would be staggering.

"I don't get any sulfur," I sniffed, surprised because most of the hot springs I knew in California had the volcanic rotten eggs smell to contend with. I'd seen people freak out when their silver jewelry went black from the sulfides.

There were few people about and soon after changing we three sat in beautiful, clear, hot water. A small sign in English explained that these baths had been in continuous use for over four thousand years.

"Pretty clean for all that," Tony grinned.

"John and Lou would've loved this, I reckon." Mike was circling the melancholy drain again. "Only thing I'd change is having it out in the open. I'd like to be looking at the mountains instead of these granite walls."

I tried to keep it light and kind of upbeat. Why, I wonder? Am I concerned for Mike or just trying to keep him from bringing me down? In zoology, it's suggested that altruistic behaviors in animals are ultimately self-serving - you just have to look for the hidden gain that might not be apparent when a rabbit stamps his foot to warn others of the intruder.

Back in town, I was feeling relaxed enough that I eschewed the evening chillum. The steaming purity, with no odor other than wet granite and wood, had left me feeling cleansed, physically and mentally, yet somehow exhausted. Sleep came early and easy.

In what I imagined would become our daily ritual, we marched back to the hot spring the next day and enjoyed a good soak.

"I'm thinking to explore some the trails into the hills today. Anybody feel like a good hike in the mountains?" I asked.

Both of my confederates looked at me with slightly bloodshot eyes. Mike had worked a bit of hash into a piece of milk fudge this morning. He and Tony were pretty zapped and it took them a moment to process my proposal. Then Mike drawled, "Uh, no, no thanks for me today. I'm feeling like I'm doing everything I want to do right now. Maybe head back in a bit and have a sandwich at Yoli's."

The Appearance of Things

Tony offered his goofy grin, "Yeah, me too I think. Sandwich sounds good."

So we headed in different directions. They were laughing and rolling up the road towards town when Mike turned and called, "If you're not back by nightfall, we'll call out the dogs!"

I set out on a narrow footpath, away from the temple towards the opposite canyon wall. The path slowly climbed through a meadow of long grasses and tiny yellow flowers. Before I reached the trees however, about twelve people emerged and trooped down the trail towards me in single file. I stopped to catch my breath and watch them descend. At this distance they appeared to be European and were following a figure with a shaved head in orange robes. All were walking very carefully, delicately, as though they were trying to avoid slipping on loose gravel or something.

I recognized the robes, the ochre robes of the monks in Thailand. A Thai monk here? As this curious looking crew drew closer, it was apparent that the monk was not Thai, but also of European descent. His ears extended out from his head at right angles and seemed too big. He was, like Tony, wearing a grin I could only call goofy. The day was warm and sunny and as they drew closer his shaved head reflected the bright ambient light. I found myself planted in place on the narrow path watching their approach, unintentionally blocking the way.

I wyed to the monk, "Sawasdee, cup," and bowed.

He smiled at me, came to a halt and bowed back. In a comical chain reaction everybody behind him stopped too, and just stood there, grinning and looking about, a few glances towards me. They were a ragtag lot.

"What are you doing here?" I asked incredulously.

"Oh, well, we're having a meditation retreat," the monk smiled. English accent, hard to place what part, sort of sing-song. "I'm called Luang Pee Kitti Subho."

Usually I'm a reasonably courteous person, but I was virtually unconscious about having blocked their progress towards the hot spring. A few members of the queue, clutching towels, looked me over, curious.

"My name's Vernon. Vernon Castle. May I join the retreat?"

This had come out of nowhere and Luang Pee appeared startled at the request.

In the early seventies I had been initiated and done Transcendental Meditation practice when I was at UCLA, even attending a couple of TM retreats, so it wasn't a complete cold call. There was a connection I felt with the monks in Thailand and Laos and now with this odd English monk.

"Oh well, I'm afraid we're just ending the first ten day period," he waggled his head Indian style, "and, um, I'm afraid we're full up in the house for the next one." He was sympathetic but his stance shifted and it came through that he felt done and was preparing to move on. No room.

"I have a tent with me," I offered, "I could sleep outside."

His eyes softened then and I had the sense of being really seen, in that moment. "Look here," he said gently, "we're all off to a much needed hot spring visit. Why don't you come around tomorrow and we can speak about it. Ask people where Leah's house is - you'll find it easily enough."

With that, I had enough sense to step off the trail and said self-consciously, "Thank you. Please excuse me for just stopping you like this. I was so surprised to see Thai robes here in the mountains, I...."

"Not to worry," Luang Pee said with a grin. "See you tomorrow."

The group proceeded down the hill past me, a few making friendly eye contact. Their group gestalt was one of intoxication, not unlike Mike and Tony as they headed back up the hill to Manali. I recalled from the TM retreats I'd done that by the end of five days we were all smiling oddly and feeling a bit loopy. The monk had said ten days! The prospect cheered me.

Returning back to the hotel in town, late afternoon, I found Mike and Tony well and truly stoned. A Dutch couple, Marjo and Dirk, sat on my bed passing a chillum. Mike was playing some J.J. Cale and singing "After Midnight." I related my encounter with the monk and that there was a chance we might be able to join the next retreat. I fudged a little with the "we" part.

Tony looked pained but said, "Aw yeah, I guess we could take a look, eh?"

He glanced over at Mike, who was busy studying his fingering on the guitar strings. Mike looked up, "Wha...? Um, yeah, ok, why not." He found the fingering he was looking for and sang out:

"We're gonna cause talk and suspicion,

give an exhibition

find out what it's all about.

After midnight, we're gonna let it all hang out."

Marjo and Dirk were nodding appreciatively. Tony started laughing then handed me the chillum.

"Why don't we walk up there tomorrow, to this Leah's house and check it out?" I encouraged. It was pushing them a little bit, but I had a feeling this could be a good thing. I didn't think of myself as pushy.

Tony shrugged, "Well, I know you Americans all like that sort of stuff. Yeah, ok, I'll go up with you. Let's see what's going on."

Mike sang another verse of "After Midnight" and we all settled in.

Next day, in the late morning, I spoke to the hotel manager about Leah's house. "Oh yes, the yoga retreat," he responded with a head waggle, "Well, you must take the central road, just out and to the right. That will lead you up there."

"Is it far?"

"No, not so far. If you began walking now, maybe you'll be there before the hour."

It was almost ten thirty, so maybe a half hour's walk.

Mike had decided to join us and we three set out on the gently sloping, narrow road. The path led up through a few houses then into a lovely open forest of pines and cedars. I was impressed with some of the larger trees, a sort of Sugar Pine I imagined from the needle length and cluster. Some of these were certainly old growth, tall, many of them more than a meter in diameter. Some twenty minutes of walking brought us to the top of the ridge and a vista of the broad valley opened between the trees. The pine scented air was cool and wonderfully low in humidity. Out to our left the long ridge with the Tibetan village straddling it was maybe a kilometer away as the crow flies. Smoke was rising from a few of the stone chimneys and the chime of distant bells blended with the soft rustle of the breeze in the pine needles above us. I could make out strings of prayer flags, draped from a tall pine at the lower end of the village. They fluttered gracefully and a sense of gazing at Shangri'la enveloped the three of us.

"Too far away for a good photo with my camera," Tony mumbled, "I reckon with a telephoto lens, if I had one...," he trailed off.

A smallish man, barefoot and bearing a huge bundle of sticks braced on his bent back, rounded the road, coming uphill towards us. The Nepali style sling supporting the load off his forehead caused him to be looking downward. He had not noticed us. A little boy walking beside him was also barefoot, wearing dirty shorts and a tattered brown T-shirt. He spotted us immediately and his dark eyes were both curious and fearful. He spoke to the old man who then looked up and saw us. There were very few teeth remaining in that smile but his was a sweet and open face.

"Leah's house?" I asked tentatively.

The little boy pointed back the way they had come and over to the left. The undergrowth was dense but we could make out a dirt path leading up and away from the road, well-tended, perhaps five feet wide.

"*Danyahvad*," I said, probably mangling "thank you" in Hindi. It was odd that after so many months of trying to learn the local language wherever I was, I'd mostly given it up in India and Nepal. The national language in India was apparently English and whatever was local changed every hundred miles. It made my head hurt. Add to that the fact that nearly everyone wanted to practice their English with a foreigner and it became quite difficult to learn. I couldn't even count yet in Hindi.

We turned on to the path, and after walking a hundred yards up the gentle rise the understory gave way into a small apple orchard. The green grass between the trees was trimmed, not like a lawn but probably with a hand scythe for forage. Following the contoured terrace a two story wooden house came into view, rustic but cozy looking. The front yard was a spacious, stone slab deck, perhaps thirty feet wide and sixty feet long. Bounding the downhill slope was a short, broad stone wall. The orchard terrace we were walking along led straight on to the stone patio. Emerging from the trees, we found eight or nine young men and women sitting relaxed on the wall. They all swiveled their gaze on to us as we approached. Their expressions ranged from friendly smiles to casual curiosity.

It was funny, how we all looked like members of the same tribe. After being in India for some time, we had our loose shirts, baggy drawstring pants, wool Nehru vests, a *lungi* over the shoulder along with various beads and necklaces and sandals. Should any of us be suddenly transported to Trafalgar Square, an observer would likely observe, "Hmm, just in from India, are you?"

At the far end of the patio a low cookhouse squatted. An outdoor Indian clay stove was burning, flames roiling under an enormous aluminum pot. Under the overhang, three more women and a man were engaged cutting carrots, onions and cabbages into cubes on a long table and scooping them into the pot. Nobody spoke, but there were snatches of laughter from within the big house. We three smiled and nodded our way across the deck, finding a place to sit on the low, stone wall. I wasn't quite certain what to do, but it didn't appear that I needed to be in a hurry to do anything.

"Quite a view from the living room," Mike quietly confided.

The wide-open vista of the Kulu Valley from the vantage point of the stone patio, unobscured by trees, was brilliant. The apple orchard fell away down the slope and the white peaks in the far distance looked close enough to reach out and touch. I knew it was more than fifteen miles to where the valley bent around to the left and disappeared from sight. Today, the cloudless sky was that crystalline, electric blue of the high country and everything seemed possible. The Tibetan village on the ridge appeared closer too and I could hear the flapping of prayer flags on the wind from time to time. From this lofty viewpoint, the dozen waterfalls cascading into the valley were straight out in front of me. I touched how the spirit of the Yosemite infused this beautiful valley, at least in my heart.

"Yeah, "I responded to Mike, "it's pretty nice."

On the far side of the house an old waterwheel turned slowly, driven by a small channel of water flowing from up the hill. The axle of the wheel entered a shed opposite the house and I imagined it was, or had once been, a mill of sorts. The effect was of an exquisite fountain and waterfall. The gurgling, clear flow spilled into a small pool at the base of the wheel and then following a stone channel away under the patio, re-emerged to cascade down the granite face beyond the sitting wall, on into the lower orchard. The homesteader in me wondered if the flow would be sufficient to drive a small hydroelectric generator. It was a good flow turning the waterwheel.

With its steep, brown, corrugated roof, a wide front porch shaded by the overhanging upper story and bare wood battens silver with age and weather, the house had an Old West feel to it. The lower floor consisted of one great room that occupied nearly two thirds of the floor space and a second, smaller room with its own entry. The monk emerged from an upper room and descended down a flight of exterior steps to the patio. Mike and Tony were looking around, clearly impressed with the setting but perhaps somewhat uncomfortable with the silence. People were nice, they just weren't chatty.

The monk disappeared into the kitchen shed without noticing, or at least acknowledging, us sitting there with the others. A burst of laughter rang out from within the kitchen shed.

"Hello!"

A big, lanky, curly haired blond guy wearing a green *lungi* stuck out his hand. His eyes were intense blue pinwheels and he appeared on the verge of being a wild man.

"I'm Mac!" he declared. I reached out and took the proffered hand, delighted with the zany, friendly energy.

"I'm Vern. These are my friends, Mike and Tony," I said, pumping his large hand and nodding towards the others.

Hello's and wha-da-ya-knows all around, as Mac was from Australia too and bubbling over with a grinning enthusiasm. "Queensland," he replied to Tony's inquiry about where.

A gong was sounded and the apparent motion of the people around us revealed itself to be a slow motion queuing up. It continued until everyone, including ourselves at Mac's insistence, was lined up and facing the cookhouse door. A young blond woman, short, maybe five foot two, held a Tibetan gong bowl on a pillow and proceeded to ring it three times. The line began to file past the kitchen door with people collecting an enameled plate, fork and spoon off the table as they passed.

Mac grinned broadly at us, "Lunch time. Grab a plate!" and moved forward. Mike, Tony and I looked at each other and did as Mac suggested. The food smelled delicious and it was - basmati rice with dhal ladled over the top by a beautiful woman with fine, porcelain features, straight long blond hair and huge, smiling green eyes. Beside her, a young man with a dark brown beard added a green, leafy vegetable, some potato curry and a chapatti. We sat on the little wall overlooking the valley, quietly as the others were doing, and savored the simple fare.

"Are you going to come for the second retreat?"

I turned and was looking at Mac's toothy grin. "I'd like to, if there's room."

He laughed, "There's always room - men downstairs, women upstairs."

After we'd cleaned our plates and utensils at the big, soapy basin and replaced then on the drying table, I noticed the monk speaking with a small, rapt group over by the millwheel pond. I approached and sat on the pond wall ledge, awaiting my audience, because that's what it felt like. I'd read accounts from Zen literature, how young men would sit in the snow outside of the monastery, sometimes for long periods, to demonstrate their determination for entry. Sitting there in the warm sunlight, listening to the laughing water, was not hardship of the Zen order but I knew I was determined to get on the retreat somehow.

"Well," the monk in his funny, lilting English voice, "you notice what's happening, don't you? And note it to yourself. Yet there's no need to act on or chase after every stray impulse that drifts across the consciousness."

I listened to what was apparently a question and answer session. It sounded rather familiar, not unlike the TM retreat discussions.

"My legs and knees ache so much sometimes Luang Pee." The speaker, a young man with a whispy beard and thin face, shrugged and went on, "I feel like I'll never be able to stand. Then you ring the bell and it all goes away just because I know the sitting is over!"

Mike and Tony had come up beside me and we listened to the give and take of the conversation. Tony leaned forward, his eyes sharp, and seemed intensely engaged. I noticed that his hands were clenched fists atop his knees, his chest pressing down on them. Mike kept an eye on the girl who had been ladling out the dhal at lunch.

After about twenty minutes, the monk turned to me and with friendly, shrewd eyes asked, "So Vernon, why do you seem so keen to join us here?"

His use of my name startled me for a moment. I guess I'd introduced myself on the trail yesterday but he'd remembered. I nearly always need to ask a couple of times when I meet new people. I'm good with faces but names, for some reason, flee rapidly from my memory.

"Well," I began, "in the late sixties I used a fair amount of LSD." A few people giggled knowingly. I grinned and went on, "But it always seemed, at best, like a brief look in a window, or maybe out of a window. Remember the lyric, Turn off your mind, relax and float downstream, this is not dying.... Well, I started reading people like Alan Watts and Ram Dass and doing some yoga. I don't know exactly. But in 1970, there was a Transcendental Meditation center that opened in Westwood, near UCLA where I was studying. I got my mantra and began meditating. I liked it, but I like getting stoned too." A few more giggles. "Anyway, in '72 I went on two retreats of five days each and it was really pretty good, a lot better than just the half an hour a day."

"Were the retreats done in silence?" the monk asked.

"We talked at meal times and when we weren't meditating, except for one day," I reflected, "in the middle, when nobody was supposed to talk at all."

Luang Pee nodded, "Here we take the five precepts, that is to say we keep the noble silence throughout the retreat. We agree to not harm living things, to not use intoxicants or engage in sexual misconduct. Lastly, we agree to not take that which is not freely given."

He had spoken all the words gravely, seriously and slowly, then waited for me to respond, keeping his eyes on mine.

"That sounds good to me," I affirmed.

Luang Pee looked questioningly at Mike and Tony, who were sitting beside me and had followed every word. They nodded but, I thought, in a somewhat resigned way. No intoxicants. Well, it was only for ten days.

The monk went on, "The problem of course, as I mentioned to you, is space. We are rather full up and I don't think there will be adequate room for all of you."

I jumped in, "Look, I've a decent little tent with me and sleeping gear. I'm quite fine outside, up there in the orchard on the grass." I pointed back the way we had entered from.

Luang Pee ran a hand over his smooth head and grinned, "Well then, if you'd like to join us for the next retreat, we can see how it goes. The bell rings at five thirty tomorrow morning and we will take the refuges together in the meditation hall at six. Best you collect yourselves and return here before darkness falls."

I felt elated. Mike and Tony smiled weakly and we took our leave.

"Crikey," Tony moaned, "Five thirty wakey wakey. That's been awhile."

Mike said nothing.

Walking back down to Manali, I was feeling on top of the world. It wasn't quite the case for my friends but they were being good sports. I was grateful and we did feel like rather good friends by now. They were humoring me, but I thought they'd probably like it and be glad we all did it together. This time it would be a trek into the heart.

III

The word "retreat" evokes something like a getaway or a pulling back, maybe visions of relaxing with a cool drink and gazing at passing clouds without a care in the world. It turns out that spending every waking moment focusing on what is happening in the here and now, training my mind not to create stories about what is happening, is a real challenge. Try looking over your own shoulder and busting yourself, over and over.

The first day went well enough. Mike and Tony found sleeping spots in the men's dorm room while I set up my little camp on the soft grass of the apple orchard. Sleeping outside with the cool mountain air washing over me was deep and dreamless.

How do we know when we've had a really good night's sleep? I noticed that my body tells me. There's no memory of having an experience, yet there is a direct sort of knowing that emanates from a center within me. Odd.

The basics were simple enough. Sit comfortably, give very careful attention to the tactile sensation of the air entering and leaving my nostrils. When the mind drifts away, bring it back without kicking off a new discourse about having drifted off. Over and over.

Piece of cake, right? God, my knees are killing me. Whoops, bring it back. When's lunch? Whoops, bring it back. Her breasts are so... Whoops, bring it back.

After an hour of sitting still, we would then do walking meditation. Stand up, paying attention to all the intentional movements in the process, left foot lifts, moves, places back on the earth. Balance shifts. Right foot lifts, moves and places. Making my way up to one of the orchard terraces, walk forty feet, stop, turn around, walk back, over and over. Left foot lifts, moves, comes back to earth, intention to shift weight on to left, shift, right foot lifts, moves, comes back to earth. Staying completely focused on the lifting, moving, wow, that bird has such brilliant blue.... Whoops, lifting, moving, placing.

It's sort of like extreme boredom training, but I'm determined to stick with it. In the hours and the days I come through to the fascination with the air moving in and out, focusing like a watchmaker, carefully, slowly, smoothly placing each tiny gear, each tiny spring, focused, absorbed. Gong! The bell rings and it's time for another walking period, lifting, moving, placing.

Unbidden, the poetry of an old Ken Nordine riff from *Word Jazz*, classic beat from 1957:

"He stood there, up on the stage,

We waited in the dark.

Then from out of his tallness came the chanting,

At first, like a whisper, we could barely hear it,

The fliberty jib bob, the bippity bop.

We were caught up in something we didn't understand

He had trapped us.

Slowly he moved us through the land of hush,

Through incessant, savage, throbbing crescendos of ecstasy,

As if it was the only thing we could do, we began to chant,

The fliberty jib bob, the bipitty bop,

And he joined in, and the magic was with us,

He was up on the stage, laughing with all his might

Shouting Yes! Yes!"

Whoops, well, maybe not, but it was compelling nonetheless.

After three days I wasn't drifting away so much. After five days, a direct knowing of deep quiet and spaciousness. It's sort of like my head had been crammed with bees, buzzing and caroming off my skull and that was regular mind. Over five days, the bees slowed, then went to sleep, then disappeared. Empty, but not lonely, because the emptiness was so full of presence. Remarkable.

The memory of the oppressive heat of the Ganges valley faded. Going into the meditation hall began to feel thrilling. Like the rest from the deepest of sleeps, my body felt and knew presence even though there weren't any mental souvenirs to bring home. It was the breathlessness of freefall.

I was trying to stay focused on my own practice, as per the instructions, but I couldn't help from cocking an eye at Mike and Tony sometimes. The first few days they both seemed as delighted as I felt. While Mike's roving eye dwelt appreciatively on some of the ladies, he carried himself well in the walking meditation and I had the notion he was strutting his stuff for the opposite sex. Tony looked mostly uncomfortable and fidgety during sitting times but he simple glowed with pleasure when doing the walking practice.

Despite appearances all was not well. As Tony grew more quiet and open it was as if the floodgates of repressed anxiety began to also crack open. On the sixth night, I later discovered, he awakened in a sweat, shaking like he was going through a withdrawal. It was as if the meditation practice had allowed out what he used drugs and alcohol to keep contained. In my "ignorance is bliss" state, I had no idea this was happening for him.

I was surprised then, when I stood in line for breakfast on the seventh day, to see Mike and Tony sitting on their gear near my tent in the orchard. I'd wondered why they weren't at the early morning meditation. I walked over and Mike indicated with a nod of his head towards the path out that we needed to talk, away from the silence of the retreat house.

"Vernon, Tony and I are pretty done with this. We're going back down to the village. You're obviously really liking it, so no worries. We'll be down at the same hotel so when it wraps up here, come on down."

Tony looked wan and shaken.

"I really feel like shit," he confessed. "It was like I was coming off of a run last night." He looked down at the ground. I could see he felt bad at a bunch of different levels.

"Are you guys ok with waiting for me?" I asked.

"Aw yeah, we're mates," Mike smiled, "There's enough to do hereabouts for four more days, so, yeah, no worries."

I was saddened to see them walk off down the path and a little envious. They'd be having beer tonight and some of that fine hash we'd found.

I loved the retreat though. Sometimes I'd make my walking meditation back into the hills, following ancient footpaths and laughing, bubbling little water courses. In the evenings, after a hot drink and our last sitting, Luang Pee would light a candle on the little, low table at the front of the hall and tell us stories of the Buddha and the heart of the teachings. We leant in and crowded closer, a crew of pirates around a treasure chest as it was opened, the golden light glinting off our eager faces. It was the joy of setting out on an adventure.

The tenth day arrived all too soon. All good things come to an end, yet I felt I had hit a sweet spot and was reluctant to disengage from the process. The alchemy of "yes" was undeniable. There was to be one-day break including a visit to the hot spring. I felt gladdened that this time, I'd be one of the goofies float walking down to the baths.

That afternoon, after a lovely hot soak, I sat in repose on the ledge, overlooking the magical valley. In a shift that caught me by surprise, my body, my heart decided to stay on, to do the next ten day session.

"What about Mike and Tony. They waited for you!" shouted my rational mind. I didn't have an answer near at hand.

It was choiceless, a falling in love. From deep within, a middle of me, I knew I was on to something true. More than once, I'd reflected back on that dream, on the Agra train, about connecting with an old wise man up in the mountains. Luang Pee wasn't old, scarcely in his early thirties, but I felt in him a conduit to the purist water I'd ever known, a human invitation to a truth that was as old as time itself. Outside of time, really.

Nobody was selling anything. The cost of the retreat was just the cost of the food, about ten dollars for the whole time. I understood now the monks and the sangha, the keeping of the flame over thousands of years. My travel hardened cynicism cracked open and I wanted to keep going.

I found my friends at the hotel when, in the late afternoon, I walked down from Leah's house. They had a celebratory chillum loaded up and were anxious to get back on the road again. Mike noticed I wasn't carrying my backpack and looked at me questioningly but said nothing to dampen our reunion. We had some deep tokes and I felt the familiar tingle of great hash.

Both friendship and honesty demanded that I be straight up about my decision. Maybe not the best idea when stoned, but I owed it to Mike and Tony to lay it out.

"Hey you guys, I gotta talk to you about the retreat. It's really cool, what's going on for me up there. There's one more ten day session, then everybody is heading for Dharamsala. I need to keep going with this."

Mike looked pained, "Aw well, look Vernon, we've been hanging out here for the last four days. And it's been good. But neither Tony or I want to be here another ten days."

He looked over to Tony who was taking it in. He nodded agreement, "Yeah, that's it. I'm ready to keep going."

"Look," Mike said, "Maybe we can plan to meet up somewhere ahead. Maybe Dharamsala and Mcleod Ganj. Since we aren't going to do the Leh trek, that could give us the little taste of Tibet we were talking about."

"Yeah," added Tony, "We've only got sixteen days left on the Indian visa. That would be in the right direction."

We'd talked about the Manali to Leh option in Delhi but decided against. When we secured our Pakistani visas, the warning was we couldn't cross in from Kashmir. The border was closed to Islamabad, the Indians and the Pakistanis both laying claim to Kashmir with a lot of war talk. The visa officer told us we'd have to cross much further south, at Lahore. To get from Leh to there was a mess. Other travelers had said it was a real pain in the ass with all the checkpoints and delays.

It was a genuine regret to miss Kashmir. I'd heard about the opulent house boats for rent on Dal Lake, around Srinagar, all the way back in Sumatra and it sounded fantastic. Why is just getting along so damn hard for the human race?

So it was decided and I was grateful to my friends for sticking with me. We'd meet in Dharamsala in twelve days' time, then head for Amritsar and the Pakistan crossing. Dharamsala had a reputation on the travelers' circuit as being a really good stop if you were at all interested in the Tibetan Buddhist lineage. The Dalai Lama had his monastery there and the area was meant to be beautiful, a little like Tibet.

"There's a lot between here and Dharamsala," Mike had the map out and we looked at the route, back through Simla and then northwest through a number of hill towns. He and Tony agreed there was more than enough to keep them happy exploring along the way.

"OK, that seems pretty good."

Mike looked at his little calendar, "Eleven days from now, that'd be April twenty first. Let's connect where the bus comes in. We'll get a place set up and you join us there."

A flood of relief poured through me. I had enjoyed solo travel, but it was a fine feeling to have friends and be on an adventure together. Not to mention that other travelers coming from Europe had painted a pretty hairy picture of their travails crossing Afghanistan and Pakistan.

The day was fading. We wished each other, "Good travels and see you in Dharamsala!" and I was off, back up the hill. In the gathering darkness the hash played with my mind, with my "now." On the lovely walk down through the trees, I'd felt on top of the world, throwing off sparks, tingling with cellular joy. But the walk back, stoned out, the deepening shadows hissed lurking danger. I felt like a dog with his ruff up. I am afraid and the fear is palpable, a fog, a coffin coming up behind me. I tell myself everything is fine and I have to resist the impulse to whirl and confront whatever is closing in on me. I am whistling in the dark, minus the whistle.

Almost complete darkness now. The turn off for the trail to Leah's house is barely visible, I'm walking carefully forward. A surge of relief, there is my tent, the house illuminated from within by candle light, a few people quietly gazing out towards the early stars over the valley, a few others reading by kerosene lamp or chatting quietly. I move forward and wonder why I am so shaken, what happened to the balance and serenity so painstakingly cultivated over the last ten days? I pass a lovely, slight, German girl from Heidelberg swinging gaily beneath a tree branch. She smiles at me. The storm of fear and dread passes. So strange.

The five-thirty morning gong signaled the start of the next retreat. We all shuffle into the cozy meditation hall, some of us wrapped in blankets against the morning chill. The welcoming burble of the little brook splashing into the millpond outside the window is familiar and sweet. There is no incense burning but the old cedar walls still softly perfume the air of the room. I settle in, gladly.

Within fifteen minutes my legs and knees began to burn and my heart dropped. I had been through the hell that comes from sitting still for extended periods of time, at least in my own mind. I had paid my dues. In my sweet spot, the last two and a half days of the retreat, it was as if my body had finally settled and opened. The pain had subsided to a small whisper of ache in the background, scarcely noticeable. I had the thought at the time, "This is it!" and settled into a thought free deep blue.

Now, as though none of that settling had ever occurred, the large, rusty nails were once again being slowly, excruciatingly pushed through my knees. I felt my commitment to the next ten days suddenly leap out of my aching body and bolt for the exit. This was not what I expected.

"If you are experiencing discomfort," Luang Pee had said mildly, on the last retreat, "notice the manner in which it arises, stays awhile, then passes. Allow yourself to move if you must, but try to make it through at least two waves before you do. Then, move mindfully."

Those words came back to me this morning. My sitting cushion was my crumpled up sleeping bag. The "happy seat" had become my tormentor. I felt for all the world like Humphrey Bogart in The African Queen, when he forced himself back into the leech ridden swamp and continued to pull that old boat forward, lost and uncertain.

That morning at breakfast, the joy I expected to reconnect with and continue nurturing was nowhere in sight. I ate mindfully in silence, alone with my disappointment and frustration. During the sitting, I had peeked around a few times. I was surrounded by comfortable, happy yogis. Vernon was the fraud in their midst. No enlightened Buddha was shining out of me.

I took refuge in the lifting, moving, placing of the walking meditation. At

The Appearance of Things

least that didn't hurt. When the gong sounded and it was time to return to the hall, I felt heavy, a guy who had failed himself. What was I thinking? I should have gone with Mike and Tony.

On the fifth day, we settled down for the hour long sitting that preceded lunch. It began for me as virtually every sitting had since we started back. There was no position that didn't ache - crossed legs, kneeling, legs out in front - no respite. I re-bundled my sleeping bag, now stuffed with my towel and sweat shirt, and tried to go for the most comfortable cross-legged position I could muster - the sort of half lotus they called Burmese Style. It was comfortable for nearly a minute, then I began to contract. I sighed inside and tried to open up to the feeling, "and this too." In my mind, the pain had me folding into myself, like a spider sprayed with poison, legs curling under in an agony of death. Nothing but to go into it.

The waterfall was not the waterfall. I was the water falling, directly, timelessly. Light poured into room. I was the light and the dust motes swirling in the rays of the sun, the Tibetan village was not a thing out there. I was the village and the smoke and the bells ringing on the cool air. I was the cool air that was rising now, eternally, timelessly, all that is, I am that.

What! What?

I was a body. I was this body. There was no pain but a knowing, a rapidly fading burst, the sun going behind a cloud, I was nothing and being nothing, I was everything.

I snapped straight up and stared out of eyes. My eyes. The room was the room, filled with yogis, Luang Pee, eyes closed at the front. The waterfall was again the waterfall and the "me" was behind my eyes and between my ears, this fathom long body. But not. Through the closing rip in the sky everything I knew to be true was smoke and mirrors.

"We live in illusion, the appearance of things

There is a reality

You are that reality

When this is seen you know that you are nothing

And being nothing, everything

That is all."

That isn't some old Tibetan being poetic. That is a description of reality and he's up ahead, shouting back over his shoulder what he sees, what he knows.

The gong sounded. That was an hour? I was stunned and motionless. My fellows rose and quietly departed the room. I felt as some ancient tree, rooted in place on this earth. No need to move.

Everything changed and nothing changed. After some time, I did rise and mounted the stairs up to Luang Pee's room where I begged an audience. He looked at me and held the door open. We sat down and looked at the pinwheels of eternity spinning in each other's eyes.

I stammered what had happened. I was awestruck, my words tumbled out and barely made sense to me. A phrase from the Psalms came boiling up in my consciousness and into the air between us, "And I shall dwell in the house of the lord forever."

Luang Pee smiled at that.

"Is that it?" I asked.

It was Luang Pee's moment to be without words and we stared across the distance at each other. Then he collected himself and managed, "It isn't yours."

My mind reached out, trying to wrap around, trying to grasp the fading inner light, trying to own it. Fruitless. It's nothing I can hold. It's never mine. My world-weary twenty four year old cocky know-it-all was revealed as… nothing.

But then, what?

I spent the remainder of the retreat in a zone something like shock. I sat in meditation. Sometimes the body ached. Sometimes it thrilled with electrical discharge, sometimes a deep cobalt blue to rest within, neither seeking nor avoiding. Knowing now was, always has been, ever will be the fabric of consciousness, outside of time. The profundity of the Dharma talks hammered me, hot iron being struck on an anvil. Sparks flying. Dukkha, annica, anata. Nothing to do but bow.

When the retreat ended it was as though it didn't end. The continuity of here and now was a glowing campfire at which I sat warming myself, absorbed by the dancing flames.

IV

Now, a group of us on the bus bound for Dharamsala, careening down the river valley, breathtaking drops plunging into the roaring white water. It swirled around boulders the size of sedans. Our wheels at times inches away from a precipitate drop into the depths of the canyon. An ongoing knowledge that this moment, this right now, was a silky perfection that embraced me as a deep feather bed.

The mind's eye reflects back over the last days at Leah's house. Some surreptitious glances from other yogis, Maria from Heidelberg in the swing, her joy-filled surrender to the motion, blond hair flowing back in the wind touches my heart and I feel love for her. I pick some small yellow flowers and hand them to her when she comes to rest. Our eyes find each other and the pinwheels pull us in.

"Oh well.... we're here to be meditating, aren't we now," the voice dripping with sarcasm and near rage.

I look up and meet the eyes of her nominal boyfriend, Irish Edgar. His pupils are pin holes, willing me away. In his hurt, in his rage, I touch the truth of his words. Yes, I wanted her and yes, I was reaching out with desire. A bolt of pain and regret flash through me. An understanding that I was not wise. I was not enlightened. I felt more ignorant now than before. The Buddha is meant to have said, "Sometimes, the closest you can get to the truth is in the knowing of what is not true."

I pulled out my journal on that last day. It was like a dream and I had to write the dream down before it faded and I lost it. So I wrote:

"When people believed the sun and the stars circled the earth, that was the reality in which they lived and loved and died. The sun rose in the east and went down in the west. At night, the stars swirled overhead, pivoting around a central point in the night sky. The reality of a geocentric universe was observable and confirmed by experience every day. Except it was wrong. When Copernicus sent us towards the heliocentric truth of our solar system, everything and nothing changed. The person I was on Monday in the geocentric reality is the same person I am on Tuesday in the heliocentric reality. And yet the reality has shifted. Geocentric is the illusion and appearance of things. Heliocentric is the actual reality, stripped of our stories and relationships."

I read it over and felt dissatisfied. That wasn't the heart of it. The camel had got his nose under the tent of my reality and now I knew directly that the Vernon story was just a story, that what I really was, what all this is, can't be summed up. It would be like trying to cram the ocean into a shot glass. There wasn't a concept because we can hold concepts in our minds, rolling them over, evaluating them. Perhaps it's poetry that comes closest.

The bus arrived in Dharamsala in the late afternoon and I was gladdened to see Mike and Tony standing off to the side.

"Hey, you silly bugger," Mike grinned. "Back from your mountain cave?"

Tony's broad smile was illuminated from within, eye's dancing.

"Good on ya, Vernon. I'm really glad you made it. We've got a little hut at Mcleod Ganj. You're going to like it, I reckon. It's in the forest."

I felt more happy and free in that moment than I ever had in my life.

"God, I feel like it's been a lifetime since I've seen your mugs. It is really good to see you guys."

We smiled goofily at each other for a moment then looked over at a commotion beside the bus. The baggage was beginning to be handed down.

"Hold on, I'll get my gear and we can head out."

When my pack came down, I was standing beside my seatmate from the bus and fellow yogi, Georgina.

"Where will you all be going?" I asked her, nodding towards our little mob picking up their gear.

Nearly all of the people from the retreat had come on the bus. Luang Pee had arrived yesterday and the conversation on the trip was about the next retreat, a big one up at Dalhousie. It was what Luang Pee called a Rains Retreat and was planned to go on for three months. Three months!

Georgina gave me a luminous, promising smile. Her long, curly auburn hair fell on both sides of her face and heaped up on her generous breasts. Extra-large deep brown eyes with a very sexy tilt, almost Asian.

"The Cedar Lodge for now," she said, "it's up in Mcleod Ganj. Come on up." She looked at Mike, "And bring your friends."

Here we go.

"We'll see you there. They tell me we're already set up with a cabin in the woods but I expect we'll be around."

The Appearance of Things

Mac leaned out the side door of the small bus preparing to make the three mile trip to Mcleod and shouted over.

"Georgina, we're going up now. Are you coming? Vernon, you too."

He recognized Mike and Tony and added, "Hey, g'day. Didn't know what became of you two. Glad to see you here. Going up?"

The bus was filling fast so we quickly jumped on. There wasn't any roof baggage so I sat with my pack in my lap, as did most of the others. Tony was beside me and Mike somehow ended up beside Georgina.

"I wondered where you disappeared to," she said to Mike. "What happened?"

"Aw well, I reckon we got what we could use in those first six days. Not my thing, really. But, you've got to take a chance sometimes on something new, right?" He winked at Georgina and she laughed.

The switch back up the mountain to Mcleod Ganj allowed some grand vistas out over the smoky plains below. All too soon, we'd be back down there, in the dust and the heat, making the push over the Khyber Pass into Afghanistan. Strangely though, a shift had occurred. Heading back to the west wasn't heading for home. I was as "at home" as I would ever be, right here, right now.

Luang Pee had read aloud from *The Four Quartets* of T.S. Eliot one evening, and now the words came back to me, gazing out over Mother India.

> *Love is most nearly itself*
> *When here and now cease to matter.*
> *Old men ought to be explorers*
> *Here or there does not matter*
> *We must be still and still moving*
> *Into another intensity*
> *For a further union, a deeper communion*
> *Through the dark cold and the empty desolation,*
> *The wave cry, the wind cry, the vast waters*
> *Of the petrel and the porpoise. In my end is my beginning.*

Chapter 13
Afghanistan

The only way to make sense out of change is to plunge into it, move with it, and join the dance.

Alan Watts

I

"Don't just do something. The Buddha said sit there."

The inscription made me laugh. I had climbed up the inner passages of the huge Buddha, carved one thousand five hundred years ago into this sandstone cliff. Now, sitting here on top of his head, the valley of Bamyan stretching out below me, I traced the words with my finger. Somebody had taken the time to scratch the joke into the brownish red sandstone. It was relatively flat up here on the top of the head, a platform that was maybe fifteen feet on a side, covered by the arching rock of the alcove. I could imagine the inscription would still be here in another fifteen hundred years, some future archaeologist thinking, "Hmm, Buddhist humor."

The cliff face was an ancient Buddhist monastery, honeycombed with interconnecting chambers. Many of the chambers gave access to different levels of the Buddha statue. The arms were gone now, but a thousand years ago monks would works ropes and levers within, and both forearms would be raised in benediction over the valley. His face must have been wonderful as well, painted and inlaid with sandalwood.

When the armies of Islamic expansion swarmed over this valley about seven hundred years ago they slaughtered all the monks and cut the face off the Buddha, leaving a flat, blank wall where serene eyes and a gentle smile once graced the green valley. It didn't endear Islam to me. What a bunch of dicks. Right up there with the Inquisition and Crusades. All the sky god religions have violence in common. God's will, I suppose.

The same mob moved on to India and overwhelmed the brilliant cultures of the north to form the Moghul Empire. While the Taj Mahal is an incredible monument and artistic achievement, the kingdom of Asoka was more to my liking. After he converted to Buddhism about twenty two hundred years ago there was a flowering of peace and justice in India, like no other place in the world at that time. I'd seen some of his stone markers in Delhi, setting out the laws of the kingdom, including rights for women and animal welfare. But that was all a long time ago and right now I was sitting on some of the ruins of that flowering in Northeastern Afghanistan. The last six days were a kaleidoscope of rapid-fire impressions. We had burst out of the Himalayas, crossed Pakistan in two days, over the Khyber Pass and into Kabul.

I had to laugh at myself a little. We had all allowed the traveler buzz to infect us about Pakistan and it was only the last night, roaming in the bazaar at Peshawar, that it dawned on me how fun and zany the place was. The border crossing at Lahore had been a pain in the ass, that was for sure. Mike and Tony crossed easily, but my American passport marked me for special treatment. I was nearly blocked from entry for lacking a cholera vaccination. There is no vaccination for cholera, but they put a special note in my passport requiring me to go to a government ministry of health to be "certified." That had taken the rest of my afternoon in Lahore while Mike and Tony explored the old town market. "Very cool," was Mike's assessment of the bazaar, but from that point on, Lahore to Rawalpindi to Peshawar, it was as though we'd dropped into a party that was ongoing since 1947. The old buses were decorated to the hilt with murals and sculptures and electric lights. Adrenaline pounding percussion in the omnipresent music, surging and joyful, was the background to the smiling laughter of the people we encountered. The entire nation was young and alive and celebrating.

Leaving Peshawar and Pakistan, our bus had screamed down the huge set of switchbacks from the top of the Khyber into the valley of Kabul. That night I found myself at a garden restaurant called Sigi's in the new part of Kabul, the Shar-i-now, three chillums to the wind, playing chess with meter tall pieces on a huge outdoor chessboard.

The well-known Chicken Street, lined with American and European style shops, full of young westerners, could have been a trendy anywhere. Kabul felt like being back in the west and I already missed Asia. I needed this rural time in Bamyan to let myself catch up with myself. So there I sat and meditated, on the head of the Buddha. Things were moving way too fast.

Our time in Dharamsala and Mcleod Ganj had been a fine reunion. Mike and Tony secured a sweet little cabin in the forest, and we spent three days together in the Tibetan community. We were above one of the main temples and the misty view out through the trees was a window back in time.

"God you guys! You found another good one."

We were sitting on the porch, enjoying Drum cigarettes and Indian beer. Below us, maybe a hundred meters down through the forest, a continuous line of Tibetan monks in their burgundy and yellow robes filed past the prayer wheel temple. Bronze cylinders, each about the size of a roll of paper towels, were mounted vertically on a rectangular frame. The cylinders had inscriptions of Tibetan prayers on the surface. The thing to do was walk slowly around the temple, clockwise, keeping your right shoulder towards the center, and spin each cylinder as you passed. This was meant to send the energy of the prayer out into the world, or so it was explained to me.

Other monks were doing prostrations around the plaza of the temple complex. They had homemade pads on their hands and knees, so when they knelt and stretched out there was a bit of protection. They needed to lie completely flat on the ground, belly down, for the prostration to count.

"We've been here for five days now," Tony said, nodding towards the temple, "and it's been like that every day from morning 'til night."

The Dalai Lama was up the hill at his temple complex. On my second night, he offered teachings in English for westerners in the area. Most of my fellow retreatants were there as well as dozens of others. He spoke to us of living with kindness and not clinging to past hurts. Pretty amazing for a man who barely escaped with his life when the Chinese invaded and destroyed Tibet. Practice what you preach, in action.

"Are you coming to Dalhousie?"

I looked into Georgina's lovely eyes and shook my head.

"No. I mean, it sounds great, a three month retreat, but we've only got five days left on our visa and my friends are anxious to get on to Europe." I smiled.

Georgina's brow furrowed, "You can get an extension down at Chandigarh, you know."

The Appearance of Things

I did know. But something had happened to me back in Manali. Right now, I needed to get out and wrestle with the world, to "take the bull by the horns," as Luang Pee said in his talk on the ten Zen ox herding pictures. The universe had opened up and I was holding a personal invitation to step out and really meet life. For now, my next retreat was out there in front of me, moment to moment.

"Yes, I know about the extension. But in truth, I think where I need to go right now is towards Europe. Something happened, Georgina, you know? I need to follow that."

"But...." she started, then stopped. We looked into each other's eyes and her face softened. She looked down for a moment then took my hand in hers.

"You have my address in London," she said warmly. "Keep in touch, will you?"

It felt thrilling to have a beautiful woman say that to me.

Outside the temple complex, we watched a group of monks involved in what was described as "dialectic". I couldn't understand the Tibetan, of course, but it was oddly alarming to witness the group of monks aggressively shouting at a solitary young monk sitting on a stone. It was as though he was being admonished for some wrongdoing. Some of the speakers would slap their hands together and roar into the young man's face. He looked miserable.

"That what happened to you up at the retreat?" Mike asked, grinning.

"No, no it didn't," I grinned back. "But I don't really know what we're seeing here. It's pretty weird, huh?"

The truth is, based on what I'd learned about the teachings of the Buddha, not a lot of what was called "practice" in Mcleod Ganj made sense to me. Turning prayer wheels? Ok, nice idea. Prostrations? Well, I guess you could get rather quiet inside with that sort of repetitive activity, like the slow walking practice maybe. They said a typical practice was one hundred thousand repetitions that might require a few years to complete.

I had to conclude that the Tibetan style of Buddhism wasn't for me. But since I hadn't really tried it, my view was based in ignorance. On the other hand, I hadn't tried the hooks in my back at Thaipusam either. One of the central lessons in the life of the Buddha was that self-mortification is not the way, any more than a life of self-indulgence. The notion of the Middle Path wasn't a compromise, a half-way point between the two poles. It was a stepping out of the duality of the poles entirely.

Afghanistan

So we departed Mcleod Ganj and began the big push west. It was also suddenly clear that we had a financial incentive to get moving. "I'm down to four hundred and fifty dollars," Mike announced on the last evening at the cabin, where we'd been sitting out on the deck with beers and going over our goods. Always a bad feeling to get down the road and not feel your passport or bill fold where it should be.

I went over my now thin traveler's cheque packet. The sale of the whiskey and cigarettes had helped, but that cash was now long gone and I had to start drawing down my cheques again.

"I'm at six hundred and twenty," I said, "but I've got two one hundred dollar notes hidden in case of emergency."

Tony looked into his passport case and then sheepishly up at Mike and me.

"Aw well, I reckon this is the time to ask. I thought I'd have something waiting for me at Poste Restante in Delhi but it wasn't there. After what happened to John and Lou, I didn't want worry about it. I can get money sent when we get to Germany. My uncle is holding it for me, from the aluminum mine job up in Gove." Mike nodded. Both he and Tony had spent time up in the Northern Territory working before departing for Indonesia. Tony went on, "I was gonna ask if you could spot me something along the way. I'm down to two hundred and a bit."

Mike looked surprised and then over to me, "Yeah, we can get there I reckon. I'm meant to have five hundred waiting for me in Tehran."

I nodded in agreement. "Between us, we'll be ok. When you're close to tapping out, I can give you a hundred in cash. Pay me back in Germany."

"That's right," Mike added, "I can do you another two hundred in Tehran. She'll be right, mate."

Tony looked both relieved and a bit chagrined. "Sorry to have to ask. Bad planning."

I had an uncharitable thought about heroin consumption but let it slide.

The bus to Pathankot and the train from there to Amritsar consumed most of the day. We set up in a clean little Indian hotel near the Golden Temple then walked on over. Part of the travelers' ritual in Amritsar was the Sikh Golden Temple daily meal. Despite the saying, sometimes there is a free lunch. Strangers were welcomed for the simple fare of potato curry, dhal and chapatti. It also got us inside the temple complex for a look around.

"Last smoke?" Mike asked.

We stood outside studying the rules board for visitors, including no alcohol, no meat and no smoking. I declined, but Mike and Tony lit up. I strolled to the edge of the lake and looked out towards the actual temple site. The Golden Temple was in the middle of this rather large, man-made reservoir. A wide causeway led from where we were standing out across the water to the building. It really was covered in gold, at least the upper two floors. Across the lake stood two, red brick minarets. The map in front called that the Langar kitchen and it was where we were heading after the temple walk for the famous meal.

"Right then."

Mike smiled and tied his yellow *lungi* in place as a head covering.

Tony and I followed suit. A shallow trough needed to be walked through barefoot, to ensure all visitors washed their feet before entering. We deposited our shoes in what must have been the world's largest shoe rack and shuffled along with the crowd and out to the temple.

"What do you reckon he's doing?" Tony meant one of the massive Sikh guards, ornately dressed and swinging a wide sword through the air before a group of applauding children.

"Maybe showing them what they do if you get caught smoking," Mike suggested.

The lake cooled the air a bit. A gentle breeze over the water kept our slow pilgrimage across the causeway bearable. From within we could hear the reader, his solemn voice reverberating. The inside of the temple was so mobbed we simply circumambulated the structure, looking through the open windows at the artistry within.

At the vast, open, Langar kitchen we sat on the floor with hundreds of others and received the delicious food offering. It was a sweet and fitting end to our time in India.

II

It was on that memory that I opened my eyes and looked out on the rows of poplar trees, their green leaves quivering in the late afternoon breeze. My vantage point on the Buddha's head was perhaps two hundred feet above the little stream draining through the valley. It was striking, the fertile green valleys surrounded by the desolate, dry mountains. The agriculture of Afghanistan, from what I'd seen this far, was restricted to the narrow bands of these small river valleys. There were meant to be broad swaths of grasslands further north, towards the horse country of Mazar-i-Sharif. But here, straight west of Kabul, it was essentially a desert.

Smoke off the cooking fire was curling up from the main building at our hotel, the Marco Polo. This morning a homemade flatbread with honey, hot from the oven, was a nice treat. I knew the cook was working on a sort of mutton casserole for the supper tonight. The thought cheered me and I rose to begin making my way back down.

The salon of the Marco Polo was striking. From outside it appeared to be the same modest, mud brick construction, a single story affair that constituted most of the rural buildings we'd come across. Yet, upon entering, it revealed an Arabian Nights' fantasy of rich, hand woven carpets, wall hangings on every surface and surprising framed paintings. At the far end of the salon a high shelf held the kerosene pressure lanterns for nightfall. Classic bowls with red glaze and traditional Islamic geometric designs hung on the wall and various drums rested in the corners. The paintings were a surprise because they depicted people, mostly women in coy poses. Not pornographic in any way but old fashioned, figure concealing swimwear from the turn of the century.

When I entered, Mike and Tony were seated in the far corner reading. A metal tray on the floor in front of them held a yellow teapot and cups. A few others looked up then went back to their own tea and conversation. One guy I hadn't seen before, wearing a black and white checkered headscarf, had a hawk-like countenance. His sharp eyes followed me across the room.

"Hey Vernon," Tony smiled up, "Fancy a cuppa and a bikkie? How was the Buddha?"

"Yes on the cuppa. I need some water too. It's dry out there."

I lifted the curtain to the back and Pani, the cook, greeted me with a nod.

"*Asalam malekum*, Pani."

"*Malekum Salam*," he replied, touching his chest.

"May I have a bottle of water, please, Pani?"

He smiled then, "Dry work climbing the Buddha, yes. Tonight, as I promised, *Qabili Pilau*."

The Appearance of Things

The aroma of the lamb and other ingredients permeated the small space.

"It smells like cinnamon a bit," I ventured.

"Raisins and orange."

He filled a clay jug with water from the big vat in the corner, passing it and a teacup to me.

I nodded thanks and withdrew back to the salon.

"I'll have some of that water too." Tony held out his empty teacup and I poured him a full one.

"I know you'll be pleased Vernon. We've got an early departure tomorrow." Mike grinned. He'd heard me gripe often enough about the penchant for pre-dawn departures. Yes, it was cooler in the pre-dawn, but the day came anyway and we'd always end up both hot and fatigued.

To the northwest, about four hours by rough dirt road, lay Band-e Amir - the high desert lakes district. We didn't know a thing about them when we arrived in Kabul but the buzz in the local travelers' scene cast them as one of the natural wonders of Afghanistan.

Our travelers' hotel, the amusingly named Holiday Inn, had an information board describing various excursions. Many were in and around Kabul but a few were further afield. The five day loop we were on had us in Bamyan for two nights, one night out to Band-e Amir and back to Bamyan for a last night before returning to Kabul. A pair of enterprising Afghanis with jeeps managed the transport and were, as best we could figure, the only way to get out and back from these isolated sites.

"How early is early?" I asked Mike.

"Omar said five thirty departure. That's not too bad. We'll be halfway there before it starts to warm up. Arrive early enough for a good look about as well, I reckon."

I sighed. He was right of course. In truth, I loved being outside when dawn was breaking, just listening.

A group of three Afghans in traditional hill clothing pushed into the salon and settled against the far wall. The loose pants and rough woolen vests were a look I liked. They wore knit style tube hats rather than the more urban turban, rolled up all around the edges. The top was flat and drooped slightly over the roll. Looked a bit like a pie.

I was growing accustomed to the fierce stare ritual. For reasons you'd have to be an Afghan to understand, the default facial countenance is a fierce stare. When we first arrived here it made me wonder, "What are you so pissed off about?" After a few days in Kabul it became clear that the answer was, "Nothing," or maybe "Everything." It wasn't personal. When I'd look back it was like watching a TV with no reception. Just a gray fuzz. Everybody walking around looking fierce at each other. I've heard people talk about their 'City Armor' in places like New York. It's a "don't mess with me" grim determination that does not invite contact.

The owner of our hotel in Kabul was Badi, who had lived for many years in England. When I mentioned the stare, he confided to me, "Oh well, it's harmless enough. If it bothers you just blink. The one who blinks loses. It's as simple as that." Normally, I blink regularly so this wasn't a problem. I tried it and magically the fierce stare found something else to stare at.

The group of Afghans across from us looked over. Here came the stare. I lifted my teacup to them, said *"Asalam Malekum,"* and blinked. They returned the greeting and set to muttering between themselves.

At five thirty the next morning Mike, Tony and I were seated in the back of Abdulla's jeep with the two German guys and the couple from Amsterdam. Omar's jeep held the three Afghani guys, a pair of Frenchmen and the hawk faced guy I'd seen last evening. He was a question mark, not in attendance at Pani's wonderful feast of lamb and sweet rice last night. There was an odd, furtive quality about him. He seemed a hunted thing and I wondered what his story was.

If a person is a desert lover, they feel right at home in Afghanistan. Our drive out through parched yellow-white hills and red rock canyons reminded me very much of southern Utah, in the desert southwest of the USA. Except that area was green compared to here.

We crossed a small mountain range and the topography shifted to wind sculpted mesas with snow-capped higher peaks in the distance. Band-e Amir was a flat arroyo, maybe three hundred meters wide, between two yellow mesas. The little settlement was an oasis with numerous mud-banked fields that could have been rice paddy but instead were growing wheat or barley. The golden heads of mature grain were nearly the color of the surrounding mesa walls. A natural, mineral dam further up the canyon formed a wide arc, like a curtain, from wall to wall. It was an odd, cumulus looking thing, rather like an ochre cauliflower in texture, about four meters in height. Straight back from the village, a metal floodgate had been set into a cut in the stone.

A cascade poured down the face into a small channel running past us and out into the fields.

"Well it's bloody hot," Mike wiped at his brow. "Let's go up for a swim."

We'd stashed our gear at the guesthouse and it was not quite noon.

"Swim sounds good by me."

Tony had his *lungi* draped around his shoulders and was smoking a Drum.

"Where do you reckon they're going?" I asked. The three Afghans were continuing on foot, away from the settlement and through the fields. Roughly woven sacks with added rope straps served as backpacks. The bags were bulging with something.

"Maybe taking seed out to wherever their village is," Mike guessed.

Omar and Abdulla relaxed on the veranda of the guesthouse, drinking tea and chatting with the owner. The Dutch couple were already climbing the metal steps beside the floodgate, towards the top of the dam. We followed suit. None of us were prepared for the sudden vista of the wide, crystal clear lake beyond the dam, jarring in this dry, desolate space. This was a limestone accretion wall, similar to the pools I'd seen at Kwang See falls in Laos, but on a vast scale. How many tens of thousands of years for this sort of build-up?

"Crikey! Look at the fish!"

I walked along the rim to where Tony stood, peering down into the transparent water. Chubby blue fish swirled in the depths beside the nearly vertical inner wall of the dam.

"Wonder if that's what's on the menu for tonight. Are you going to jump in?" Tony looked at me with something like trepidation. "It's really cold," he said, "put your hand in."

I knelt and put my arm in up to the elbow. It was cold but doable on a hot day like this. I smiled over to Tony, "Aw, it'll feel good once you're in."

Water dripped off my arm on to a worn knob of the limestone and it was transformed. Lighter, cream colored concentric rings defined caramel colored, translucent interiors, tree rings made of precious stone.

"Whoa, Tony, check this out."

He looked over my shoulder and whistled, "Yeah, that's good, isn't it." I thought it was marvelous but there's no accounting for taste.

We worked our way around towards the canyon wall on the left. The intrepid Hollanders were nearly to the far end of the lake and making their way up over the stone to the next level. A small cataract on the wall above them marked the next lake in the series. There were meant to be five lakes going up the canyon and it was only from the uppermost that one could see the whole complex.

"If we're going all the way up, I'm for a plunge right now to cool off a bit."

Mike put his day sack down and stripped off his shirt.

The water did look inviting so Tony and I followed his example.

Mike made quite a splash going in and came up moments later spluttering, "Christ! It's like ice."

Tony and I jumped in and had to agree. The lake felt a lot colder than it did on my arm, sort of in the realm of an ice cream headache.

"How could it be so bloody hot and have the water this cold?"

Mike hauled himself out and stood shivering, followed by Tony and myself. It felt good but one minute was enough.

By two in the afternoon we'd reached the uppermost level and were rewarded with the panorama of the stacked, cobalt blue lakes in the barren yellow and ochre desert. It was daunting. As far as we could see in any direction appeared lunar and lifeless.

"Tough place to make a living," I observed. Enough to give anyone a fierce stare.

That night, while we read on the porch after our fish supper, a few snatches of the conversation beside us drifted over. The hawk faced guy and the French men were in a discussion that had some of the passionate overtones of a political discussion. It was in French, though, so the content went past me. The little bit I did get told me that the mystery guy was a Palestinian named Fouzi. On our ride back to Bamyan, I learned a lot more.

There were ten of us going back. Mike was enjoying the Dutch couple who were entertaining him with tales of Amsterdam. He joined them and the French guys in the rear jeep. Tony and I, the German guys and Fouzi were with Omar in the front jeep. For a time we all rode silently along, enjoying the dawn vistas and cool morning air. The two German guys, Wolfgang and Karl, spoke good English. About two hours out, Fouzi joined the four of us in friendly banter about the trip and the more general conversation about who we were and where we were going in our travels. People usually didn't do canned presentations about themselves, but within a short time I knew that Karl and Wolfgang were friends from Stuttgart and had come overland to Kabul from Europe. Kabul was their last stop and they were flying back in four days.

Tony and I raved about our journey west, thus far, and how we knew each other. Fouzi described himself as a student pursuing political studies and international finance in Beirut, Lebanon. He held out his black and white headscarf.

"This is called a *kufiyah*. You are from Europe or America or Australia. I am Palestinian. This," he held the scarf up to flap in the wind, "is my country."

Later, it was Wolfgang's comment about working in a bank that gave Fouzi the opening he must have been waiting for.

"A bank! It must be a lot of work in Germany, with so much money!"

Wolfgang smiled at that.

"I would like it better if it were all mine, but that was not to be."

Fouzi's eyes took on an intense glimmer, focused on Wolfgang.

"Maybe you should have been born a Jew, yes? They have all the money, don't they."

Wolfgang's smile evaporated.

"The money is international," he began evenly, "most of it held by international business, by corporations."

"Yes," replied Fouzi, warming to his subject. "International. It's that way isn't it, all over the world. The Jews behind the scenes, controlling, directing corporations with non-Jewish names, but you look at their names and you know. Controlling the money everywhere."

Karl was ignoring the conversation, looking out over the desert. Wolfgang shifted uncomfortably. Fouzi was enjoying himself.

"Wherever there is money, or pornography, you find the Jews, don't you. Like termites."

Fouzi turned to me, seeking agreement in the eye contact.

"You should read Mein Kampf," I suggested.

The dark, intense eyes flickered with confusion but remained challenging.

"Eh?" he responded.

"Mein Kampf. It's got a lot in it like what you're saying."

I held his questioning gaze neutrally. Fouzi appeared momentarily bewildered and tilted his head.

"Mein...what?"

"*Mein Kampf*," Wolfgang blurted out, "It's a book by Adolf Hitler."

He turned then, and joined Karl in looking out over the desert.

Fouzi's face migrated from bemusement to understanding and his penetrating eyes gleamed as he tried to drill into me. I decided not to blink and regarded him pleasantly. Then he smiled.

"I understand. You are an American. Your Hollywood and government is run by Jews. You live in a soup of Jews and think the flavor is natural."

His eyes flashed, challenging. I spoke mildly and held his gaze.

"I'm a Jew."

I couldn't see Tony's face but I imagined it looked similar to what he wore for the Indian train hashish bust.

Fouzi snorted and looked down at his hands then back to me, less challenging but still intense.

"Jews took away my homeland. They made my father die. I have this! I wear this!"

He shook the balled up *kufiyah*.

"One day we will take back our homeland. Jews like money. Maybe one day we will buy it back and show them what human beings are like."

A silence settled over the jeep. Fouzi withdrew and leaned over the back corner, searching the horizon. His words had been so filled with hate and contempt. Now I looked at the man, his thin face and sharp nose, and felt nearly overwhelmed by his aloneness. A voice within me had needed to confront him, but now, looking at him in profile staring grimly out over the desert, I could see the burning coal of pain at the center of him. Gandhi's words came to me - "It's an eye for an eye until we are all blind with hate."

Back in Bamyan, departing the jeep, I put a hand on his shoulder.

"Fouzi?"

He stopped walking and gazed at me without warmth.

The Appearance of Things

"I want to know more. Would you eat with us tonight?"

His eyes widened slightly and he tilted his head to one side, regarding me.

"Why would you want to do that?" he asked simply.

"Some words from Gandhi came to mind on the way here."

I told him the quote and he nodded.

"Yes. Gandhi, the guru of non-violence."

Fouzi was silent for a moment, collecting his thoughts. Then he looked up, "One of your teachers, Hillel, said something I admire very much. *"If I am not for myself, who will be for me? If I am only for myself, what am I? And if not now, when?"* We stood for a moment in the late afternoon, a warm breeze in the popular trees causing a sound like sand sliding down paper. "It is good that we should eat together. I will join you."

He turned, took a few paces towards the hotel then stopped and turned back, eyes intelligent and calm.

"*Asalam malekum*," he touched the center of his chest.

"*Malekum salam*," I returned, and touched my own.

I sat with Mike and Tony in the salon. We'd washed off the dust from the jeep ride and were quietly enjoying sweet tea. Aromas from Pani's kitchen were sneaking out into the room. I'd asked earlier and had been told, "Kababs."

"I didn't know you were Jewish," Tony said.

We'd been talking about the trip, filling Mike in on the conversation with Fouzi.

"Well, not officially. A lot of people I love are though, and it just sort of popped out. When people try to get me to go along hating with a nod and a wink, it's kind of a reflex. Sometimes in the States you'll hit some cracker who wants to call blacks "niggers." You're supposed to keep your mouth shut and go along. I think from now on, I'll say my mother is black."

Mike laughed, "Aw yeah, I can see that."

We all looked up at the rumble of a large vehicle passing. Except it didn't pass. A squeal of metal on metal, slamming doors and a commotion outside. Pani appeared from behind the kitchen curtain holding a pot he was stirring. He looked towards the entry door with concern.

A pugnacious army officer pushed abruptly into the salon and surveyed our little gathering of travelers. All appeared startled at his sudden and incongruous appearance. He spotted Pani and barked something. Pani jumped slightly and raised his shoulders, replying in the same language. It looked like, "Hey, you!" and "Who, me?" but must have been more because the officer seemed satisfied. He nodded and withdrew from the room.

The alarm on Pani's face brought me to my feet. I went to the still open door and looked out. A big troop transport truck and heavy duty enclosed jeep occupied the entire road in front of the Marco Polo. There was a commotion out back where the sleeping quarters were. Quite a few of us stepped outside to see what was going on.

The answer came moments later. A phalanx of uniformed soldiers appeared from around the corner of the building. Between them was Fouzi, hands cuffed behind his back, being led towards the big jeep. His face was resigned but not fearful. Forced inside he was seated by the rear window. Our eyes met and his lips tightened ruefully. Then he turned to face forward and did not look back.

The convoy rumbled out of town towards Kabul leaving us standing outside in the fading light. The dust of their departure swirled in the dry air.

Mike shook his head.

"I reckon he's in for it."

III

Upon returning to Kabul we found our way back to Cable Hogue, the best restaurant we'd found since leaving Delhi. Their pies rivaled Aunt Jane's in Kathmandu and that's saying something. I had the rice stuffed pumpkin then felt like one myself.

"So, tomorrow I reckon we take a *bemo* to the Iranian Embassy and get the visa going."

Mike looked at Tony and I for agreement, and we nodded pleasantly. The first chillum of the evening had been a potent one.

"Sounds right," I agreed, "I want to also go past the silversmith and see how the work is going. He's got to be almost finished."

I'd purchased two black star sapphires in Bangkok. At the time I wasn't certain what I'd do with them, but they were lovely stones and easy to carry.

The Appearance of Things

Encountering the jewelers and silver filigree workers here on one of our explorations gave me the idea to have a charm made for my mom and a ring for me. Mohammad, the guy I'd settled on, told me "one week" and took my drawings as well as the measurement of my ring finger. With our time out to Bamyan and back, one week would be tomorrow.

The trajectory back to Europe was going to be direct and speedy. Kabul was pretty much our last big stop before the Greek islands. We could make it in one go to Herat, the Afghani town before the Iranian frontier. A night there and then across to Tehran.

Mike had called Australia via the long distance line at the post office in Kabul. His father had assured him that his five hundred dollars were awaiting him at the American Express office in Tehran.

"Load off the mind," he said, after the call.

Tony had called home as well, but it was too late to get a letter and money order out to Iran. His uncle told him to look for it in Athens. That reassured us all since it was still quite a jump up to Germany and Tony was going to need the first hundred from me, probably by Tehran.

"Good news all around, I reckon," he'd said with a grin.

This wasn't my first experience with short funds. I had no doubt we'd muddle through and have a good time of it. Back in 1971, the Greek islands had saved my ass, financially speaking, and I figured they would again.

My friend Sam Littleman and I had taken a charter flight from Los Angeles to London. That charter returned to Los Angeles from Amsterdam three months later. At two hundred and seventy three dollars for a roundtrip, we couldn't do better. Sam and I were a year out of high school, in our first year at college. We were nineteen, pretty wet behind the ears when it came to foreign travel. A guidebook from Harvard press called "Let's Go- Europe" made Europe on five dollars a day sound plausible. That meant for three months we'd need about four hundred and fifty dollars. To be on the safe side we'd both saved up six hundred dollars each. On top of that, we'd purchased the marvelous Student Rail Pass. It allowed unlimited second-class travel all over Europe for two months, starting from the day we first used it. Wasn't good in England but we figured on hitch-hiking there. What's not to like? Except by the time we arrived in Amsterdam, after three weeks banging around in England and Scotland, only about three hundred and fifty dollars remained in each of our pockets. And that was living on the cheap - hostels, camping, one beer a day, thumbing rides. At that rate we were screwed.

Afghanistan

"Sam, I think we'd better punch the ticket and head south."

The word was that life in Greece was a lot cheaper. We needed cheaper and soon. Sam had agreed and that was how we ended up on the ferry from Brindisi, Italy to Corfu, Greece. That was a turning point in more ways than one. On a beautiful deserted beach called Glyfada we set up a large, orange plastic tarp and made camp. This beach had everything. A sweet water spring poured right out from a rock ledge on to the soft sand, the water cold and pure. It was both our shower and drinking supply. Up the beach a few hundred yards, the two-room hut of a local farmer served as a taverna. Grape vines cascaded down the hill behind and half a dozen fig trees, loaded with ripening fruit. The farmer and his wife made the most delicious red wine I'd ever tasted and would fill our liter bottles from the big tank for less than twenty cents. The farmer's brother, Mario, was home from the merchant marine and served as chief cook and maître d'. He was chatty and funny, a terrific source of local lore.

We found ourselves living like kings on less than a dollar a day. Half a dozen other wanderers had also made the beach their refuge, including a pair of pretty women from Canada, Rhoda and Helene. We four fell in together and had nearly a month of friendship and adventure, exploring Corfu from our home base. I learned to love Greece in that blush of discovery.

"So you reckon it's still like that, eh Vernon?"

Mike had been listening to me waxing poetic about Greece since we'd left India.

"Yeah, well it's been three years but I'm pretty sure we'll find something good. I was in Yugoslavia, on my way down there in '74 when all hell broke loose in Athens. Turkey had just invaded Cyprus and we almost got trampled by people getting out. That all settled down pretty quick. I felt pretty dumb for not going on."

"I remember that," Tony said, "It sounded bad in the papers."

"Aw yeah, but I think if we can get across Turkey and jump into the islands, we'll be right. Nobody's said any different that we've heard."

Greece was a topic of conversation for travelers in Kabul. The general tone was mellow, especially out on the islands.

We had the map spread on the table. Our little Holiday Inn had an inner courtyard shaded by an old, gnarled fig tree. Lamps suspended in the branches overhead afforded enough light to sit outside in the cool of the evening reading the fine print.

"Right here, this place called Kuşadası." I tapped the southwest corner of Turkey. "We can get the ferry over to Samos and check it out. If it's not the place, there are still dozens of islands between Samos and Athens. I know the ferries are cheap and run often. We'll find someplace good for a little hang out time before going up into northern Europe."

At least I hoped so. We were moving into a part of the world I'd known in the past. But Asia had shaken up the works. The one who banged around with friends on a summer vacation didn't exist anymore, the memories from another lifetime.

"What do you know about these islands?"

Tony pointed to a group southwest from Samos. The big one was called Naxos. Above it, a name I recognized.

"Mykonos. Yeah, I've heard of this one. Did you ever see the movie Zorba the Greek?"

Tony nodded, "Yeah, a while back though."

"I think this place is famous for the Greek style windmills, like they showed around the countryside in Zorba. Remember the big white cylinders with black tops? The blades were like sails, made out of cloth."

Tony looked up uncertainly, "Yeah, I think I know the ones you mean."

"Well, it's sort of dry there. I can remember photos of it being dry and rocky. If we go up that way, I'd be willing to give it a look."

I was really looking forward to the Mediterranean. The last time I'd been by the sea was Phuket. God, that was a long time ago. I'd never really missed the ocean until it wasn't around. The more we talked about it, the more ready I was to get out of the desert.

Three days later and another five a.m. departure. The bus to Herat was via Kandahar. By two o'clock, we were in the center of that dour metropolis. I was glad we'd decided to push on through. The town had a forlorn quality. In Kabul, it was rare but not impossible to see a smile or hear laughter. Kandahar was unrelentingly grim. The hour-long stop for eating and toileting was more than enough.

"Quite a place," I said to Mike. We had walked down the main bazaar street from the bus halt, seeking some food stalls or even a little restaurant. Herat was another sixteen hours away and we needed something. The sun was blazing overhead. Afghanis sitting in the shadows of shop awnings glowered at us in passing. A few food vendors along the route had nothing remotely appetizing. Stripped scapula bones and shanks hung from the carts. They had left a coarse little goat tail attached to a femur head via a strip of skin, proof that it wasn't a dog's leg. The almost omnipresent drone of the flies made my skin crawl.

At the sad little public market, we found some fresh Afghani flatbreads, a few cucumbers and some oranges. It would have to do.

"Bread's good."

Tony tore off another piece and put a strip of the cucumber on top. It was modest fare but it did the trick. We climbed back aboard, ready for the all night run to Herat.

The desert between Kandahar and Herat was strangely familiar to all of us.

"This looks a bit like the Nullarbor Plain," Mike gazed out the window towards the sparse scrub and desert.

"Yeah," agreed Tony, "a lot like Western Australia."

To me it was reminiscent of the Owens Valley and Mojave Desert, northeast of Los Angeles but without the saving grace of snow-capped mountains on each side. "A whole lotta nothing" would be accurate. And yet, the setting sun was a deep orange, filtered by the dust in the desert air, magnificently huge on the western horizon. There's nearly always something beautiful in the heart of things.

Herat was marginally better than Kandahar. At least there were thin trees providing some semblance of shade on the dusty streets and a few rose gardens around the tan, mud brick dwellings. In the morning light, the town even looked welcoming. It had been a long twenty seven hours from Kabul. After settling ourselves in a decent guesthouse and a needed bath, we all crashed out until nearly noon.

Mike had been up and out first, gathering information from some of the other travelers in residence. Now, sitting in the little courtyard garden, we shared a large plate of goat bits and biryani rice.

"The bus to the frontier is another early one," Mike said between mouthfuls. "Just talked with a guy who came across yesterday. There's no place to change money at the border so I reckon we'd better take care of business here."

"I didn't see anything that looked like a bank coming in, did you?"

I agreed that we needed to show up in Iran with enough Riales to get us to Mashed. We also had to dump our Afghanis before crossing. Apparently, you couldn't change them outside of Afghanistan. Cross the border and the money became an expensive souvenir.

Mike grinned and ran a hand through his hair.

"No, not a one. But there are a few shops on the main street to do money changing so that's our choice."

We set to work, spending as many of our "Afs" as we could. The guesthouse for the night, pay off the lunch, pre-pay dinner, get the ticket for the bus to the border. It went fast.

Gathering back in the room we lay our remaining cash on the bed. An equivalent of sixty three dollars in Afghanis between us. Tony tossed in forty dollars US cash as well, "That's all in for me." It was a nice gesture. We all knew what it meant.

The Iranian Embassy had told us the "official" exchange rate was fourteen and a half riales to a dollar. That made our cash total worth just about one thousand five hundred riales.

"Did you find out how much the bus from the border to Mashed is going to be?" I asked Mike.

He nodded, "Aw yeah - eighty riales."

"There's a night train to Tehran from Mashed as well," he added,

"That's meant to be another two hundred and fifteen riales."

So it looked like we'd have enough to get us to Tehran with about two hundred riales each to spare. That was good.

The main street of Herat was paved. The ribbon of road stretching from Kabul to the Persian border had been an international aid project back in the sixties. The section through Herat itself was crumbling cement. The cracks and potholes weren't too bad, but cars dodged around them like some road test obstacle course.

"There's one."

Tony pointed across and up the street a bit toward a worn looking storefront. It appeared to be a tourist shop with ornate wooden boxes, Afghani shirts and swords displayed in the window. A sign in the corner of the window, red block letters on a white background, proclaimed Change Money.

We waited while a huge double trailer truck rumbled past then crossed through the dust cloud over to the shop. A dangling brass bell tinkled when Tony pushed open the door. We stepped inside. Across the cluttered room behind a narrow, glass case, the proprietor sat writing in an open ledger book. He wore no hat or turban and his black hair had a greasy sheen. He glanced up when we entered and stood.

"Welcome. Please come in."

He moved around the corner of the counter to greet us. His grey robe was of thin linen and he was tall for an Afghan. His shaded, dark eyes were too close together for my taste. In concert with his short, black beard they gave him a feral look when he smiled, like now.

"How I can help you?"

Mike cleared his throat, "G'day. We need to do money change for Iran."

His eyes narrowed slightly, almost suspicious.

"No travel cheque. Only cash."

Mike nodded and he moved back around behind the counter, closing the ledger book.

"How much riales?"

By gesture he invited Mike to lay out the cash on the counter.

I bent over to look within the display. Mike was engaged pulling out his wallet and laying down the money.

I was pleased with the charm I'd designed and had made for my mom. A silver pentagram with the black star sapphire set in the center surrounded by a flat silver disk. The engraving work of intertwined vines and leaves was very good and matched that on the ring I now wore. The ring caught the proprietor's eye.

"You ring. From where you get?"

The black star sapphire and lustrous silver looked great together. Other than my goulimine bead necklace, it was the first piece of jewelry I'd ever worn.

"From Kabul," I replied.

He peered intently at the sapphire.

"Where stone?"

"From Bangkok."

He nodded and turned his attention to the cash Mike was counting out on the counter.

On a scrap of paper, he did a tote then reached under the counter, extracting a metal box with a hinged lid. From that box he began counting out Iranian riales in notes of ten and twenty.

"There," and reached for our cash.

"Hold on," I said.

I had placed my hand on his as he reached for the money and now he quickly retracted it. What was that look on his face?

"How much in riales?" I asked.

He turned his tote toward us so we could read his figures.

"One thousand eighty riales," he said.

Mike and I exchanged a glance.

"That's not right," Mike said. "The official rate is fourteen and a half to the dollar."

He tapped the two US twenty's and the stack of Afghanis.

"This is equal to a hundred and three dollars."

The shopkeeper's face expressed consternation.

"No, no," he replied, growing flustered.

"No official rate. Official rate ten riales to dollar."

I looked over to Mike.

"Let's try another place, Mike. I don't think this man wants to do business."

Mike nodded and made to pick up our cash off the counter. The shopkeeper tried to stay his hand, tapping his tote paper and shouting, "No, no. This official rate."

"Not official rate." I spoke calmly but a little more loudly.

He whirled at me.

"You don't know," he hissed, doing the fierce face.

Afghanistan

I held his stare, "No. I do know. Official rate fourteen fifty. Don't talk stupid."

At the utterance "stupid" he exploded across the narrow counter, eyes flashing, grabbing me with both hands by the front of my shirt. I simply reacted and brought both my arms straight up between us, breaking his hold, and pushed him back, hard, with both hands.

He slammed into the wall behind the counter. A clattering rang out when a couple of display items hit the floor. The look of surprise on his face mutated into ugly malice, his eyes on mine. Reaching behind, he withdrew a good-sized dagger and moved around the counter toward me.

Mike and Tony had jumped back at his explosion and now stood rooted in shock.

He moved now, holding the knife up between us at eye level. I looked back directly into his eyes, not at the knife. Something shifted. He wasn't so sure anymore and the doubt showed in his eyes. He came at me slowly, the knife blade up and poised for poking. It wasn't a lunge, it was a dance. We kept our eyes locked on each other.

When he was an arm's length away, he suddenly stabbed at my face. I'd kept my hands loosely hanging at my sides and was relieved when the point stopped inches short of my right eye.

I didn't blink but suddenly it was all clear to me. Afghanistan! I blinked, both eyes, casually, giving him the signal. The twinkle of triumph glistened in his dark face and the knife lowered. He slowly backed up, returning to his side of the counter. Our eyes never left each other.

"Crikey!" Tony sighed.

It was the first utterance since the explosion and the spell was broken. I stepped forward and picked up our money off the counter. The shopkeeper watched me, dagger at the ready, but made no effort to stop me. I glanced at him briefly then turned my back and moved toward the door.

"Let's try another shop," I said.

Mike and Tony followed me out and we moved down the street.

"What in the bloody Christ was that?" Mike exclaimed. "It happened so fast."

It hadn't seemed fast to me, but I knew what he meant.

"I think when I said - don't talk stupid - he thought I was calling him stupid and flipped out."

"Crikey," Tony breathed, "when he pulled out that knife I thought we was done for."

He looked sideways at me.

"Did you know it was a bluff?"

I laughed.

"Tony, I didn't know shit. It just happened."

I reflected a moment and added, "Remember when we were in Kabul, the manager, Badi, at the Holiday Inn?"

Tony nodded.

"He and I had a chat about the fierce Afghani stare. It's sort of a kid's game of whoever blinks first is the looser."

Mike shook his head, "So you knew to blink."

He smiled then, "I was getting ready to jump in. We're mates. But it looked like you had it handled, just standing there like you were waiting for a bus. I could see it on his face."

"Yeah. Well, it freaked me out. It was sort of like, Stupid! I'll show you who's Stupid."

We all laughed.

Tony hadn't said anything and I looked over to him. He appeared a bit dazed but when our eyes met he focused in and said with a wink, "Good on 'ya Vernon."

So, on we went. The best we could get in Herat was just a tad over thirteen riales to the dollar. The Afghanis didn't seem to want their own currency back and gave us a heavy discount.

Walking across the militarized border, I was glad to have Afghanistan behind me. No doubt we had met some wonderful people and it was a pretty good time. The hash was tasty, Kabul was ok, the journey out to Bamyan had been cool. I wondered where Fouzi was, what they'd done with him. But I also knew for a fact that the world is full of wonderful places and peoples and cultures. I'd met travelers in Kabul who has been there for months, in a couple of cases for years. It was a place and a culture they loved. Mark Twain said, "It's a difference of opinion that makes a horserace." It wasn't my place, but it was theirs.

I stepped across the frontier into Persia and the words of Rumi made more sense to me than ever before:

These spiritual window-shoppers,
who idly ask, "How much is that? Oh, I'm just looking."
They handle a hundred items and put them down,
shadows with no capital.

What is spent is love and two eyes wet with weeping.
But these walk into a shop,
and their whole lives pass suddenly in that moment,
in that shop.

Where did you go? "Nowhere."
What did you have to eat? "Nothing much."

Even if you don't know what you want,
buy something, to be part of the exchanging flow.

Start a huge, foolish project,
like Noah.

It makes absolutely no difference
what people think of you.

Chapter 14
On to Greece

We shall not cease from exploration
And the end of all our exploring
Will be to arrive where we started
And know the place for the first time.

T.S. Eliot

"Hey, look at this!"

Mike was squinting at an old photograph in the display box. We were awaiting our turn in the Iranian customs and immigration shed at the border.

Sepia photographs of unhappy hippies, held at machine gun point by scowling soldiers. Their old Volkswagen van peeled open, revealing stacked blocks of poorly concealed hashish within. There were hookahs and opium pipes in another nearby display cabinet, as well as more photos of opium poppies growing. More soldiers held farmers, their thin arms crossed over their heads in surrender. Posters in English and German and Farsi declared that drugs were illegal in Iran and attempts to smuggle would be dealt with severely.

One large, striking photo showed seven men, their hands tied behind their backs, hanging from a beam with ropes around their necks. That said it all.

Tony was peering at the hanged men.

"Hope you're not holding anything," I said, gently kidding him.

He looked up at me, startled, pupils contracted to pin points.

"No," he said unsteadily. Then again, as if trying to reassure himself, "Not a thing."

I had an "Uh-oh" moment but we made it through and joined a dozen others on the bus to Mashed.

As fate would have it, we were in time for the train to Tehran, but it was sold out. We'd gone in on a taxi to get to the train station with a Danish couple, Martin and Susan. Now we stood outside the station under a tree.

"I guess we could get a place here for the night and try for the train tomorrow," I offered.

Mashed was the Emerald City compared with Herat. The vast majority of citizens were in European clothing - button down shirts and trousers. Strikingly, there were women strolling on the street in dresses and pants, many of them wearing make-up. Everybody was so covered up in Afghanistan that it was a bit of a shock to see the casual attire around us.

"I'd rather do the bus," Mike said. "I know it's another all-nighter but I'd like to get to Teheran and get the money sorted out."

My heart dropped at the thought of another all-nighter but there's a certain level of exhaustion you hit, when sleeping all crumpled up feels normal. There was a general consensus to press on. We took the taxi back to the bus station and signed up for the night bus to Tehran.

Our first Persian dinner was just outside the bus station and it was superb. They had a cylinder of seasoned lamb, arranged in layers on a vertical spit. The spit rotated in front of a gas flame on one side, sizzling and smoking. The cook used a long, thin carving knife to cut roasted meat into a plate and served it up with a delicate flatbread, spicy yogurt and a wonderful coriander sauce. I felt full and happy when we bumped off into the night.

Tehran is a big, modern, European style city beautifully situated on a wide plain at the foot of the Alborz Mountains. When our bus arrived at three in the afternoon the snowcapped peaks were glowing in the late light of the day. They reared up directly from the plain, many over four thousand meters high. I knew from the map that the Caspian Sea lay on the other side of this daunting range.

"These are some high mountains," I observed.

"Aw yeah, almost like back in Kathmandu," Tony agreed.

We both had our faces pressed up against the window of the bus, craning to see the tops of the mountains. There is delight in the unexpected, sometimes.

Mike, in conversation with the Danes, looked over to us.

"Martin and Susan are going to the Amir Kabir. Should we go along?" "Good by me," Tony said. I nodded a "yes" as well. They had been through here a couple of months back and knew the town a bit. "It's the best hotel we found in the center. Not cheap but better than the others we saw," Martin had assured us.

A short taxi ride later we stood in shock at the reception desk.

"Yes, that's correct. The triple room is nine hundred riales, the double room eight hundred riales."

The desk clerk looked disdainfully at our backpacks and rumpled clothes. His face said "take or leave it and stop wasting my time."

"There are other places around here you could see. When we were here, this was the best price we found."

Martin registered the impact on our faces but shrugged and began counting out the eight hundred riales. Susan leaned behind him and confided to us with a sympathetic smile.

"You know, in Europe you'll pay more. Big cities are expensive. This would be more in Copenhagen."

Mike, Tony and I looked at each other. Between us, we didn't have nine hundred riales.

"What do you reckon?" Mike asked.

Tony shrugged. It was up to Mike and I since we were paying.

"Well, one night won't kill us. Let's get you to the mail call and then to a bank."

It was left unspoken what we'd do if Mike's money hadn't come in. Hope for the best.

After we agreed to the room and paid a three hundred riales deposit, the manager allowed us to store out bags. We wished the Danes well and set off to improve our fortunes.

I was glad and grateful to open a letter from my mom and find, along with her note, a cashier's cheque for two hundred dollars. I'd written a description to my friend Avi from Kathmandu, detailing the fun I'd been having with amoebic dysentery. He was a medical guy and I knew he'd be amused. He'd talked to my mom and she'd sent the money here, along with a sweet plea that I take care of myself.

Gratitude and humility are profound emotions. Standing here on the street in Tehran I was connected to people who loved me across time and space. My story of being "alone and on the road" had truth in it. But at this moment, I was powerfully reminded of all the shoulders I stood on to be here now. The Buddha taught wise attitude and livelihood, to move through the world with love and compassion and earn your way without doing harm. How then will I live? How do I help?

Luang Pee had said as much when I wished him farewell in Mcleod Ganj. I had found him in the little study of the *vihara* and bowed. When I looked up, his eyes held the wordless, wide open luminous space I felt in myself.

"Luang Pee, thank you for sharing the Dharma. It is a gift beyond all gifts. I am grateful to you."

We gazed at each other for a moment.

"Well Vernon, it's a different chap I see than the one who walked into Manali." He hesitated, then added, "It's humility."

Luang Pee ran a hand over his shaved head and smiled his odd, crooked smile. We both burst into laughter.

"So, off with you," he said, "Safe travels. We'll meet again."

I left him sitting on the floor beside the small writing table, illumined by a single bright candle. Behind him, the image of Avalokiteshvara, the embodiment of compassion, looked serenely down on us both.

Mike received his five hundred dollars and we both turned our cashier's cheques into traveler's cheques plus enough rials to cover our time here.

The AmEx office was close to the impressive Shahyad Monument. It loomed up before us with the mountains behind. Now, approaching sunset, the snow and the white marble of the monument glowed a reddish orange. It was really quite lovely.

"I guess that's the Shah's answer to the Arc de Triomphe in Paris."

I was sort of joking. Tony surprised me when he replied with some gravity, "The double arch is more graceful but, yeah, I see your point."

Both Mike and I fronted Tony a hundred dollars each. He surprised me a second time with a defensive, "This'll be coming back to you straight away when we get to Athens."

He was angry and it showed. Mike looked over at me and we both decided to let it go without comment. I'd always heard the best way to lose a friend is to loan him money. Hope that wasn't going to be the case between us.

Tehran prices were a cold bath after Southeast Asia and India. We'd unconsciously grown accustomed to fine meals for a dollar and decent lodging for two dollars. While it was marginally more expensive in Afghanistan, the tenfold jump here was terrifying. Five hundred dollars suddenly felt wholly inadequate.

The wonders of the Persian Empire would have to wait. Before returning to the Amir Kabir, we booked the morning bus to Tabriz and the Turkish border. Martin had assured us that Turkey was significantly less dear than Iran, "half of what you pay here."

Fifteen hours later, aboard a clean and comfortable super bus, we watched the outskirts of Tehran thin out into a gentle, rolling countryside. The hills were arid but the green valleys between them were well irrigated and cultivated.

Our evening in the city had been instructive. After darkness fell, the streets belonged to young men. There was an edgy undertone I didn't much enjoy, a sneering condescension. It may have been intended as playful but came across as hostile. Like talking with hustlers who looked upon us as rubes to be toyed with. Maybe it was the part of town we were in, the urban center of a huge metropolis. Downtown Los Angeles wasn't all that different at night.

Mike summed it up.

"What a mob of cunts!"

We were on a mission now, however. Except for a two day stop in Ergut, Turkey, to play tourists around the ancient underground cities of Goreme, we pushed west across Turkey to Alanya, on the south coast.

The near constant motion since departing Kabul had a life of its own. The Greek islands had become our Holy Grail. To our collective great relief, rural Turkey was very inexpensive. Transportation costs were the big deal. Now, here in Alanya, the goal was in sight, literally.

"It looks like an ocean to me."

Tony was squinting over the bright blue Mediterranean. We stood above the beach, the sand wheat gold, water clear as azure glass. Small waves lapped the shore but it was calm as a lake.

"I'm ready for a swim," Mike grinned, "Who's for it?"

The sea was cool but not too cool, silky and fresh. Tony lost some of the tension that had clouded his face since Tehran, genuinely enjoying himself. We all leapt together off the low cliffs into the water, welcome laughter after the pressure cooker of intensive travel.

That evening, sitting on the open patio of our Pensione, we relaxed with red wine after a fine meal of moussaka. The sky still smoldered orange with sunset and lights were coming on around the arc of the harbor.

"I'll tell you what, we're in Europe now. We have arrived!"

I smiled over at Mike and Tony and we toasted to each other.

"It's different. You can feel it."

Tony's voice was soft, the tension of recent days erased from his face. It had been quite some time since I'd felt the warm glow of good wine.

The Pensione was affordable and the food was great. We'd decided on three nights here to let our bodies catch up with our brains. The Greek islands were still ahead, but seeing the Mediterranean, swimming in the sea, the familiarity of Alanya, all subtly whispered we had made it. We could slow down.

The southern coastal road of Turkey was popular. Many of the European guests at our hostel had come across from Greece.

"Kos? Too built up for me. If you blokes are wanting free camping, it's not your place."

We'd met the speaker, David, on our first night. He was a freelance travel correspondent from Devon, England and literally a fountain of information.

"Since the blow-up in Cyprus, your only way over to the islands from this part of the world is Kuşadası to Samos."

That had been our original plan but Mike had a conversation with a woman on the bus who suggested Bodrum, Turkey and the ferry over to Kos. That had led us to the coastal road and to Alanya. It looked good on the map. The travel restrictions were something we were only now discovering.

On this third night David had joined us for dinner. We were sharing a baklava with pistachio nuts and some strong Turkish coffee. The openheartedness of the Turkish people had been a welcome surprise. We had been allowed to pay for our own coffee only once since crossing the frontier from Persia. The welcome mat was out and the Turks loved their country. I found myself loving it too.

"Samos is really lovely," David continued, "Very Greek with everyone walking the promenade around the harbor in the evening. Grandmothers chaperoning their granddaughters, families, young men." His eyes always lit up when he talked about young men and had said straight out, "Turkey is a wonderful place if one happens to be homosexual."

"But I was thinking - if you want free camping Rhodes and Lesbos, like Kos, are off the menu. There are some places, no doubt, but I rather think they'd be cheek-to-jowl. Like one of those French campgrounds."

He looked at us over the top of his glasses in a way that left no doubt about French campgrounds.

"Crete is a possibility, along the southern coast. But I think if I were you," he leaned in, not wanting to be heard passing the secret, "I'd go to Ios."

Later we pulled out the map.

"That's where you were talking about, Tony," Mike recalled.

We found Ios in an island group called the Cyclades, collected around the large island of Naxos, Mykonos further to the north.

"We can check out Samos and these other places along the way."

I felt encouraged. We'd find something good.

II

The harbor of Ios lay tucked in on the southern coast of the island. Getting here had consumed two days from Samos as there was no direct ferry service. This morning we'd awakened on the island of Syros, a little place that was all business. They did have a bank so we each loaded up with a hundred dollars in Drachmas.

"So when this is near gone, we head for Athens and I can pay you back."

Tony had recovered his good spirits since we hit the Mediterranean. We were three friends again, journeying toward the heart of Europe.

Samos was a beautiful place, green and verdant. They were justifiably proud of their wines and we enjoyed a few evenings drinking them in one of the tavernas facing out on to the promenade. David had been spot-on about the island. We joined in the flow of the walk on our warm evenings, appreciating the slow, civil life of the inhabitants. Two days of exploring the island turned up quite a number of beautiful beaches. Unfortunately, if the beach was more than ten feet wide, somebody had a house or a hotel planted nearby.

So it was with some trepidation that we rounded the southern point of Ios and began making our way towards the anchorage.

"That's a good looking beach up that canyon there."

We stood together along the railing of the ferry studying the coastline. The island group was dryer than Samos, green but more of a chaparral than a forest bio system. The canyon Mike was looking at did appear promising. There was a wide beach, cobalt blue water, no houses or hotels, some agricultural development rolling up the canyon away from the shoreline.

"Hold on."

Tony saw it first. A hillside above the left end of the beach was coming into view. That aspect had been blocked by a small island between us and the shore. My heart fell a click. It was loaded with tents of various shapes and colors. Now that we were closer, quite a few people were swimming and sunning on the sand below the tent area.

"Well it looks pretty good from here," I offered.

"Maybe we could pitch our camp toward the other end, toward those trees there."

I felt annoyed with myself. Yes, I wanted a repeat of the time on Corfu. I wanted a deserted beach with good water, good wine and food and pretty girls.

"A cause of suffering is attachment to outcome." I could see Luang Pee's face as he intoned those words during an evening talk. I knew it was true but I still wanted what I wanted. I could do "acceptance of what is" if I didn't have any choice. But I don't think the Buddha would sit on a sharp rock if a smooth seat is available nearby. Maybe something like, "follow your dreams but don't get too crazy about it." There were a lot of Greek islands out there. We couldn't check them all. I felt the pain of hope.

Our ferry tied up at the concrete pier extending out into the small harbor from the beach area. The big beach and valley we'd seen was to the east, over a modest ridge. Directly behind the harbor, a blue and white village climbed the hill, to a summit dominated by a white domed church.

"There are your windmills, Tony."

Around to the left, on the slope of the village hill, a set of five white cylinders defined the horizon, their cloth blades turning gently in the light breeze.

The boat crowd offloaded and moved down the pier, toward the cobblestone street leading up the hill. A few horse carts met groups of laughing tourists. They piled in and set off to the upper reaches of the village.

"What's Chora?" Tony asked, looking at a signpost.

"It means the Old Town," I said.

One of my lessons on Corfu was the fact that what we thought was the town name was actually just a description. There were a lot of towns called Chora.

"I wonder who the patron saint of Ios is?"

Mike laughed. I'd told him and Tony about Saint Spiro, the patron saint of Corfu. It seemed like half the population had Spiro as part of their name. If, on the street, you shouted out, "Hey! Spiro!" a couple of dozen people would turn around.

The signpost Tony was inspecting pointed up the hill for Chora. Another arrow indicated a footpath leading up and over the ridge, toward the beach we saw coming in. Milipotas Beach. I guess that was where we were heading.

Mike shrugged, shouldered his pack and started walking. It was not yet noon but the day was warming up. A swim would be a good welcome to Ios. We followed him up the ridge and within fifteen minutes found ourselves on the downslope to the lovely beach below.

Two tavernas we hadn't seen from the boat were tucked in at the bottom of the hill. It wasn't a bad scene, really. There were toilets, water and food available. No huge hotel dominated the scene. The tent area wasn't that appealing. Campsites were cleared spots in the scrubby growth and didn't have much to recommend them. Down on the sand looked a lot better.

We walked past the tavernas and over to the water's edge. Resting our packs in the sand, we stripped down to our underwear and jumped in the sea. The clear, turquoise water and white sand were beautiful. I left Mike and Tony floating on their backs and walked along the shore to the eastern end of the beach. A few groups sitting on towels nodded greeting in passing.

It seemed strange that with all this space, everyone would be clumped together at the west end.

The "why" became clear when I walked up toward the trees. Multiple "No Camping" and "No Nudity" signs protruded from the edge where the sand met the soil of the valley. Looking west, a dozen placards marching back to the tavernas. Definitely not what we had in mind.

I came back as Mike and Tony were emerging from the water.

"There's no camping down at that end," I explained.

"Aw well, it'll be alright, Vernon. The water is really good and the camping isn't the worst I've see."

Mike was eyeing a pair of long legged blond women who had come down to the beach wearing scant swimsuits.

"Tell you what," I offered. "If you guys'll stay with the gear, I dunno, maybe have some lunch at the taverna up there, I'll go have a look about on the other side of the harbor. I saw a footpath when we came in. Maybe there's something good on the other side."

Back at the seaport, I followed the little cobbled street around toward the windmills. A footpath led up in the direction of the mills then forked. I made my way along, up the ridge that formed the western side of the harbor. Near to the top, a sign reading, "Taverna 0.7 km" with an arrow pointing along through the scrub and stunted little trees. The air had a sweet herbal aroma. Pulling off a handful of tough leaves from a nearby scrub, I rubbed my hands together and was rewarded with a burst of highly charged oregano. Around me I recognized thyme and some plants that could have been sage and mint. It was a wild Greek herb garden.

Where Milipotas had been a sheltered valley, this side of the island was more exposed and noticeably dryer. The land narrowed to an isthmus a thousand feet wide before rearing up again into a smaller mountain that stretched off to the northwest. Its sheer sides plunged directly into the sea.

The tavern lay at the start of the isthmus and clearly had a water source. Tough oleander, decked in red and white and pink flowers, flanked the tavern on both sides as well as the few bungalows behind. Half a dozen trees, Cyprus family, grew in proximity and the bright green arbor over the outdoor patio looked to be a grape vine. Out in front of the tavern, facing southwest, a sheltered bay with a deep cobalt sea beyond.

Drawing closer, the sheltered front patio looked to have seven or eight

On to Greece

tables. The arbor was most definitely a grape with bunches of unripe fruit visible. Seven patrons at the lunch hour, sunburned young Europeans, occupied a few of the tables. The red and white checked tablecloths were a nice touch. I heard snatches of German and English.

When I entered the tavern proper, I burst out laughing. I couldn't help it. The largest wine barrel I'd ever seen occupied the rear of the room. It was floor to ceiling, maybe ten feet wide. How the hell did they get it in here? Then it dawned on me, studying the framing of the building. They hadn't brought it in. Obviously, the building had come second and was built around the wine barrel. Somebody was serious about their wine.

"*Kalispera!*" a friendly salutation from behind the bar. "Hallo. Welcome."

The speaker came around into the room and thrust out his hand. I met his dancing, dark eyes.

"I am Nikko."

"*Yassou*, Nikko. I'm Vern."

We shook hands, firmly but friendly. Two men meeting.

"That's quite a wine barrel," I smiled.

Nikko followed my gaze and his face glowed with pride, "Naxos retsina. The very best. Will you try?"

How could I say no? Why would I want to?

"Yes, please Nikko. *Nai afetistou.*"

Hello, thank you and please had come back to me quickly when we arrived in Samos. So had the memory that shaking my head "no" was "yes" in Greece. It was a bit counterintuitive for an English speaker. Up and done head movement and saying "*óchi*" meant "no." Shaking my head side-to-side and saying "*nai*" meant "yes."

Nikko returned to the bar and picked out two small glass tumblers and a half-liter carafe. He was compact but clearly fit. His thick, black moustache reminded me of India but his fine nose, lean face and dark, curly hair were pure Greek. He bent to the spigot at the base of the barrel face, filling the bottle. At his invitation we both pulled out chairs at a nearby table and he filled the tumblers.

"*Yamas,*" he said with a wink.

The honey colored wine was cool and quite delicious. He had said it was a retsina but the pine sap taste was subtle, almost invisible. With the slight citrus aroma it had strains of the good Chenin Blanc I'd had in France last year. Nikko saw my delight with satisfaction.

"This is great wine. *Afetastou!*"

"*Perikalo,* from my family," he replied and refilled out glasses.

The walls of the room were adorned with sepia photographs of people in traditional Greek costume, horses, windmills and more than a few ships. On the right side of the room, opposite the bar, a solid stone fireplace said it gets cold around here in the winter.

An attractive young woman, dark hair braided down her back, emerged from a door on the bar side of the huge barrel. She carried two plates I recognized as classic Greek salad - fresh tomatoes, some thin sliced onion and pepper, a big slice of feta. With good olive oil, a crush of oregano and some Kalamata olives, it was a bit of food heaven.

Nikko followed my gaze and said something to the girl in Greek. She gave me a nice smile and returned to the kitchen.

"Where you from? Australia?"

I had to smile at that. Being around Mike and Tony for these long months had rubbed off a bit on me, language wise. I didn't speak like an Aussie but some of the inflection was creeping in.

"No, *óchi,* America, California."

That news seemed to delight Nikko and he beamed, "America. I love America. My brother in Long Beach. You know Long Beach?"

"Long Beach near Los Angeles?" I asked.

He laughed and clapped his hands.

"Yes! Near Los Angeles. How many Long Beach you got?"

The wine was good and we both started laughing.

At that moment, the girl from the kitchen reappeared, carrying another Greek salad and a plate of thick bread slices. She set it before me.

"Please. Not good to have wine and no food. You are my guest. Eat!"

Nikko wouldn't let me pay for a thing. I felt abashed and protested.

"You come back. Bring friends, ok?"

OK. Before I went back over the hill, Nikko showed me the four guest rooms out back and the nearby spring. It had been bricked to form a small reservoir, but the outflow spout produced a decent flow of cool, delicious water.

"*Nero*," Nikko said simply, "Please drink when you like."

The isthmus was dramatic. The north facing side had a curved sandy beach with some rough rock outcroppings. Small waves slapped up white fountains of foam. The breeze was up and white caps extended to the horizon. The south side, facing out toward the bay, was sheltered by a cliff face maybe twenty five feet in height. From the tavern you'd never know the fine sand beach at the foot of the cliff existed. It ran for hundreds of yards along the base of the cliff and varied in width, maybe forty feet wide at the most. A unique feature that had me ready to run back to Milipotas beach screaming "Eureka!" was the set of eroded overhangs, almost caves, that ran along the cliff face. Most of these alcoves were slightly above the sand line, probably the high water mark for winter storms. Many extended into the rock face for one or two meters, some even more, and were spacious enough for a person to stand upright. We wouldn't even need the tent! There were a couple of alcoves with groups of two or three already camping. I wasn't a nudist particularly, but it was clearly a clothing optional scene. A well-tanned couple were laughing and splashing in the sea when I passed. It was very relaxed.

My hike back over the hill to Mike and Tony was a magic carpet ride. It wasn't the Corfu camp of memory, but all the elements were there. All the cells in my body felt like they were singing. The tension of hope and expectation I didn't know I was holding had evaporated.

The guys were sitting at the first tavern on Milipotas, smoking Drum hand rolls and sipping beers when I appeared on the beach. Mike perked up when he read the look on my face.

"You look happy. What'd you find?"

I could barely contain myself, but I took a deep breath and became the meditator.

"Well, I think you'll both be pleased with the other side. Quite nice actually."

I was a model of reserve. And it was worth it. The dumbfounded look on Tony's face when he saw the wine barrel at Nikko's was a real Kodak moment.

We filled our canteens at the spring, drinking our fill of the sweet, cool water. It had been a hot hike in the warm afternoon.

The Appearance of Things

"I reckon good water is the best thing in the world," Mike reflected.

And I loved his eye popping "Bloody hell" when we dropped down to the cliff beach and into a group kicking around a football in the nude.

We hauled our gear down to the lower beach and set up camp in a pair of alcoves. Neither was big enough for three so I set up on my own. In a way, it was my monastic cell. It had been quite a long time since I had a private room with a sea view.

Camped down the beach from us, a group of three pretty Danish girls had not escaped Mike's notice. When we'd passed, they had all been lying out in the sun. We were gentlemen and proceeded past, discreetly distant, without ogling. We were sophisticated men of the world and didn't make a fuss about such things. Yeah, right.

Now, sitting together up in the taverna for supper, Mike leaned over and quietly noted, "They're even beautiful with their clothes on." The ladies in question were a few tables over, absorbed in their own conversation.

Coming in, we'd passed the table with Dieter, Edith and Anita whom we'd met earlier on the beach when setting up camp. They acknowledged us with raised wine glasses and a "*Guten abend*" from Dieter.

About half the tables were occupied. My informal census suggested about eighteen or twenty people were making the beach their home just now. A few others were staying in Nikko's bungalows behind the tavern. I liked the scene. Because we were spread out along the base of the cliff for hundreds of meters, nobody was on top of each other.

This afternoon had been a trip for me. I felt at ease with my nudity when I was alone or maybe with some friends jumping into a High Sierra lake, sunning and drying on great sheets of granite in the unpopulated mountains. But a public beach with others was a new deal. I'd come up out of the sea and strolled across the beach to my camp. Mike and Tony were sitting with two nude women and a nude man.

"Hello Vernon! Come meet the neighbors." My friends were also naked, sitting cross-legged on a sarong in the shadow of the cliff. A blue packet of Drum was laid out and the visitors were seated with them, happily rolling smokes.

Standing in front of five smiling faces, wet from the sea and stark naked, my first impulse was to grab my sarong and cover up. I noted the impulse. No need to act on it. In that instant of choice new doors burst open within me and a thrill, like going down the first big hill on a rollercoaster. Freedom. "Hello neighbors," I smiled back.

Dieter, Edith and Anita were the nearest camp to us, about a hundred feet down the beach. Dieter was lean and tanned, obviously tall and Aryan handsome. His long blond hair, stringy from being wet, hung well past his shoulders. Ice blue eyes and a strong, square jaw smoothed by elegant cheekbones and soulful expression. A Viking god on holiday. His large, uncircumcised penis rested on the sarong like a coffee table book.

Both Edith and Anita were striking, but quite distinct from each other. Edith was the athlete. Her body rippled with strength when she shifted sideways to meet my eyes. Blond, like Dieter, her long straight hair was pulled back in a thick ponytail. The amused expression in her green eyes told me she was accustomed to being admired. And why not.

Anita was softly beautiful, more delicate than Edith with Venus de Milo breasts and a sleek, sensuous body. Her fine, light brown hair was bobbed, setting off an elegant neck and heart shaped face. A sadness lurked in her hazel eyes, a grief maybe. I wondered where she fit into the Dieter-Edith picture. Her accented English was very sexy to me, exotic.

Dieter crumbled some hash into a large, multi-paper joint and the afternoon slipped by with a few swims, a siesta for me and some reading.

"Souvlaki?"

Mike's question pulled me back into the moment. I looked up into Nikko's smiling face.

"Yes, please, *perikalo*. Also rice and the zucchini balls."

Nikko nodded as he wrote the order.

My attention had been pulled away by a woman entering from the rear, through the kitchen. She had a few words with Marina, Nikko's daughter, who laughed and pointed to a corner table on the patio.

"What are zucchini balls?" Tony asked.

I pointed over to the table where Hillary and Christopher, the English couple, were dining. I'd shared a tumbler of wine with then before Mike and Tony made it up from the beach.

"Those round things they have there, deep fried. Shredded zucchini, feta and spices. I had one earlier with my wine. Really good, even if you think you don't like zucchini."

Tony grinned, "Aw yeah, that sounds good then. For me too Nikko. And if we could get this filled again?"

Nikko picked up our liter carafe, pouring the last splash into Mike's empty tumbler.

"Nectar of the gods," he intoned and made his way back inside to refill the flask.

The woman in the corner had removed her straw hat. Longish white blond hair cascaded down her back. She wore dark pants and a homemade looking purple vest over a white shirt. The back of the vest had a detailed geometric mandala embroidered in greens and reds and yellows.

Nikko's daughter brought out bread and half a liter of wine. They spoke again, laughing delightedly and nodding about whatever the subject was. They sounded so young.

Marina went back into the kitchen and the girl at the table opened the small, black case she had carried in. A glint of silver when she removed the ornate tube from the purple velvet interior, a flute.

"Maybe we'll have some music tonight, eh?"

Mike had followed my gaze towards the corner.

"Yeah, could be," I replied, noncommittally.

The flutist used a wire and cloth to clean the various tubes of the instrument, sipping wine and focusing on her labor. She happened to look my way when she snapped the case shut and I lifted my wine glass in a toast. She regarded me steadily for a long moment then lifted her glass back with the hint of a smile, a Mona Lisa smile. Marina reappeared with a Greek salad and she shifted her chair slightly to watch the sunset more directly. It wasn't a cold shoulder, but she didn't look back again. She didn't have to.

The cooking gear from our trek was coming in very handy now. It's amazing what you can do with a little gas burner and a couple of pots. The food at the taverna was brilliant but a little on the expensive side. On our third day, I made a marketing foray back to the port. Mike and Tony were sleeping in after a roaringly good night beside our little beach fire with Dieter and company. Mike overshot the mark with the retsina and lost his supper. Tony held it down, shouting encouragement to Mike as he washed himself off in the sea. It was pretty funny at the time. There was a good little open market near the pier and for a very few drachma I loaded up with some basics - oil and eggs, bread, fruit and veggies, rice, pasta and some dried soups.

On to Greece

On the way back, when I reached the top of the ridge I set down my bags and had a long drink of water. The breeze from the north had stiffened and I nearly missed the flute music floating in and out on the gusts. Away from the trail, down the ridge a dozen meters, a stone outcropping offered shelter from the wind. The girl from the taverna was playing <u>Bourée</u>, the Bach inspired flute riff Ian Anderson made famous on <u>Stand Up</u>. I hadn't heard much Jethro Tull coming across Asia. It was a welcome turn down memory lane and I held back, out of sight, listening.

She finished and it was silent, save for the wind through the herb garden of the scrub. I really did try to make a quiet exit but a roundish stone rolled underfoot and precipitated a dusty scuffle. Shit.

"Hello."

I turned to find her looking at me, wryly amused.

"Sorry," I managed.

"I heard you playing on my way back. I liked what you were doing."

"I'm Katje," she said simply.

"Vern, ah, Vernon. I apologize for disturbing you. I like to play alone sometimes too."

"What do you play?" Her accent was soft. Maybe German?

"Harmonica and, uh, recorder sometimes," I answered, then puffed up a bit, "They're easier to carry when I'm on the road." The last part made me wince inside. It sounded like I was claiming to be a musician when I wasn't.

Katje smiled then. She had very expressive lips, well formed, almost sculpted. I liked her pleasant, open face. Her eyes grabbed me. The big stupa in Kathmandu had eyes like hers, sweeping, almond shaped, almost Asian but electric blue. For a long moment we just stood there, the wind whipping our hair into our faces.

"Breezy," I said, to say something.

Katje looked down and then back up to me. I was taller.

"Is it windy where you are on the beach?"

How did she know I was on the beach? Oh, the bags of food. Why was I nervous?

"No, not really. The cliff makes a good break. Haven't you been down there?"

The Appearance of Things

"Yes, in the mornings. But not late, when the wind comes up like this."

"I have a room from Nikko," she added, "I'm not camping."

On the walk back, we trailed along together.

"An architect! That's cool. What sort of buildings do you do?"

Katje smiled. It was a pretty smile, bashful and playful.

"Maybe someday I'll do buildings on my own. I do industrial, what they call details and drafting. I work with a group in Hannover."

I spoke about the trip out from Indonesia and how I'd met Mike and Tony in Sumatra, how we'd banged into each other off and on.

"When we connected in Kathmandu and did the trek, that's when we started traveling together."

"I mostly like to be alone," she said.

Mike and Tony were up and about when I arrived back on the beach with the supplies. They had even collected a decent pile of firewood, replacing what we went through last night.

"Here Vernon, have a look," Tony grinned.

He unrolled a log of newspaper, revealing a large, red fish.

"Red snapper, I reckon," he said.

"A couple of fishermen came by in a little boat while you were over to the harbor. That guy Christopher said they come along every couple of days. Lot of people here buying off 'em. Good, eh?"

A small stone alcove between our two caves was the perfect kitchen space. We had the stove and our other gear set up from the second day, good for tea or instant coffee.

In the late afternoon, I made the trek up to the taverna to buy wine and refill my canteen at the spring. Katje was on the patio writing in her journal. We nodded to each other and I passed on into the interior. Nikko greeted me and took the empty bottles to refill while I replenished my water supply. I wandered back out to the patio and was about to sit at an empty table when Katje put down her pen and smiled over at me.

"So is it dinner on the beach or up here at the taverna?"

What I saw in her eyes caused something like an electrical discharge between my eyes and my groin. Wow!

On to Greece

I felt like my pupils must be fully dilated.

Resting my hands on the back of the chair opposite her, I tried to smoothly say, "How about the beach?"

She nodded an assent, but kept her eyes on mine. There was a crackling playfulness that somehow reassured and calmed me.

"When I got back, the guys had bought a good fish and collected wood for a cooking fire. Can I tempt you with wine, music and barbecue?"

"*Ja*, you can. Let me finish here and we will go back together."

When Katje and I walked into our site, it looked like a Thai fishing camp. Mike was seated on a stone in his plaid sarong, no shirt, tuning his guitar. Tony had his sarong bunched Indian style to look like baggy shorts. He was in Asian squat mode, his lean, bare back to us. Over his shoulder I saw the fish mounted on a long, straight metal rod. It was set in the sand, leaning over the small fire Tony was feeding.

"Look at you guys. I think I'm back in Phuket."

Tony turned and winked at us.

"Aw yeah, fish on the Barbie."

Then he registered Katje and straightened to standing. Mike strolled over holding his guitar, a somewhat wry expression in his eyes.

"Katje, my friends Mike and Tony."

"Hello," Mike in his suave mode, "We saw you last night at Nikko's. Hope you brought your flute."

Katje patted the sleeping bag she was carrying.

"Oh yeah, I don't leave my old friend alone."

He glanced down at the sleeping back and over to me.

"Well, maybe some music later then, if the spirit moves us."

Katje shrugged, "*Ja*, it's almost the full moon. We could do some howling."

The orange orb of the setting sun was just above the horizon when we finished eating. The red snapper had served us well. Tony was the fire master and was now adding a few twigs to bring the flames back up from the coals.

Fires are like magnets. Christopher and Hillary had drifted down as well as Dieter and the two girls. Katje was engaged in animated conversation with Anita down by the water's edge.

"Refill?"

I held the retsina bottle out to Mike, who looked at it ruefully.

"I'm taking it slow tonight, Vernon. I don't want to be wearing my tea again."

Tony laughed, "It sneaks up on you, doesn't it!"

He poured himself a tumbler and passed the flask along to Christopher.

We'd met him and Hillary our first night here, up at the taverna. First impressions were positive, an English couple that were erudite and well-traveled. I'd guess they were in their late twenties or very early thirties. Hillary had a languid, willowy grace I liked. They lived in Rome but not together. She had gazed at me meaningfully when she said "not together." It intrigued me.

Christopher was voluble and clever with a "just off the tennis court" breeziness. Thick, sandy blond hair and cheerful grey eyes added to the guileless persona. He seemed interested in everyone and everything, speaking at length with Mike, Tony and I. He was particularly interested in our journey from India to here.

"And Peshawar, that must have been quite a place, eh? Khyber Pass, loads of history there. Did you see much of a military presence, what with the Kashmir situation and all?" When I spoke of Fouzi in Afghanistan, he leaned in, eyes bright. "Really! Grabbed him just like that. What were the chaps like who picked him up?"

I asked about what he and Hillary were doing in Rome. The response was filled with effusive praise about the city and the people and the food but strangely opaque about them. After three days I had very little idea of what they were about. They were sort of there but not there.

"Guess they don't want to talk about it," Tony shrugged.

Guess I have a suspicious mind.

We built up the fire and Dieter passed around one of his super joints. Mike played guitar. I joined in with my harp on a few pieces. After the second joint, Katje was leaning against me, tracing down my open hand with the tip of her finger. She declined to take out her flute.

"No, too much sand. Another time maybe."

The fire was down to red coals and a few small yellow flames when people began leave taking, drifting back down the beach. The moonlight was brilliant on the sand, the calm sea a twinkling lake.

"Let's swim."

Katje had intertwined her hand in mine, wide, dark pupils in the moonlit night. A belladonna.

We dropped our clothes and walked into the sea, moonlight making our bodies look almost white. With a slight shock, I realized that in her baggy shirt I hadn't registered her lush figure. Her full breasts had a sensuous curve, nipples upturned and firm. We were past our waists in the cool water when I leaned down, caressing her breasts with my lips. Her hand pulled me in a bit closer and harder. We embraced, intertwining, kissing, sinking down under, when we teetered sideways and slipped under the water. It was a minor surprise. We came up laughing.

"It's beautiful," she said, running the flat of her hand across the shimmering sea. Looking at her there in the moonlight, she was beautiful.

Back at the fire, we rinsed and toweled off, warming our backsides beside the glowing coals. Mike and Tony had gone off and we were alone.

Wordlessly, Katje took my hand and we moved up to my private room.

The clink of a metal cup awakened me. Early morning sunlight reflected off the nearby sea, playing on the stone wall at the foot of our bed, a dance of golden light that could have been powered by my heart. We had explored and tasted each other, moving from love making to sleep and back again. A hungry passion released, we now lay side by side in the dawn light, touching each other gently, intimately, silently.

Another clink. I sat up and peered around the corner of the alcove, down towards the beach. Tony sat on the sand in his *lungi* shorts with a steaming cup and a cigarette, his back to me. Ripples and a splash in the near flat sea. Mike emerged naked and trudged up from the waterline to the fireplace. Picking up his sarong, he wiped down then tied the cloth around his waist. He said something to Tony and moved up, out of sight, to the kitchen alcove.

Katje stretched and pursed her lips into a goofy grin.

"Wake up swim?" she suggested.

We both walked down to the sea nude, again wading out into the water.

Tony nodded, "Morning," as we passed.

I dove down into the clear water with my eyes open. In fuzzy underwater vision, I could see Katje treading water and came up beside her.

"Good morning," I burbled.

Her eyes smiled and she burbled back.

"I need a coffee!" and stroked for shore.

Back at camp I passed her one of my sarongs and, slightly wrapped, we strolled over to the kitchen. Mike was tending a pot of near boiling water. He glanced over his shoulder at us and grinned.

"Wakie, wakie. Who wants coffee?"

Katje and I laughed, "We do, we do."

It was just instant coffee with sweetened condensed milk but it tasted like paradise.

After a shared breakfast of fried eggs, fried bread, banana and honey Katje excused herself.

"I want to go up to my room and bring down some things for the weaving." I had admired the wrist and ankle bracelets she wore. "I make them," she said, "Shall I teach you?"

I said "yes" of course. I liked her work but at this point she could have offered to teach me to cut out paper dolls and I would have been thrilled.

She headed off, down the beach and I cleaned up around the kitchen.

"Katje seems good."

Tony was poking around the fire area, cleaning up bits from our gathering last night.

"Yeah," I replied, "I'm sort of blown away at the moment."

"What'd you make of the story about Dieter?"

Katje spoke this morning about the Anita, Dieter, Edith triangle and it made me feel blue for Anita. They'd all been here for over two weeks and Katje had witnessed the unraveling as Dieter shifted his amorous attentions from Anita to her friend Edith. Everybody was trying to be open and loving but Katje confirmed what I thought I saw in Anita's eyes.

"She's thinking to go back early and just leave them here."

There was no mistaking Katje's annoyance with Dieter or her affection for Anita.

I replied to Tony's query, "I think Anita is really beautiful. I wouldn't choose Edith over her."

Not much of an answer but it was true. Mind states like wanting and love

On to Greece

and desire and anger and craziness were very much on my mind since leaving Manali. This morning, I felt an ease in my body and heart. It wasn't only the release of sex, although that was cool water for my thirsty libido. I hadn't been in a lusty encounter since Thailand but, maybe more important, since Manali. I went back to my sleeping area and wanted to inhale the bedding for the perfume of last night. Bunching up my bag into a sitting pillow, I tried to meditate.

The one that was excited and wanted and had an orgasm was me. The one that knew "I" was nothing, and being nothing, everything, was also "me." No problem. That was untroubling, a false conundrum.

Luang Pee had often spoken of big mind and little mind.

"When you look up to the stars at night and perhaps see arrangements, the Southern Cross or the Big Dipper, you know they are just names, conventions. There is not really a big dipper out there, any more than there is a "real you" in the constellation of arising thoughts and sensations. But once we see the pattern, it becomes very difficult to not see it. The big mind knows there is no dipper, the little mind cannot help but see it. No problem. What we really are holds it all."

"Meditation is the practice of being with what is, allowing the whole to be, without grasping or pushing away."

And that was the problem. It was easier said than done. I had to laugh at myself, thinking back over the last month. I felt so free and clear in Manali, and later in McLeod Ganj, a profound knowing that was so obvious I couldn't imagine how I missed it. Then a confrontation with border guards in Pakistan over cholera, a confrontation with a Palestinian over anti-Semitism, then a near knife fight in Herat over exchange rates and annoyance with a bunch of jerks in Tehran. Now I'm falling in love!

I read back in my journal to a quote I'd copied in Manali.

"It is in this fathom long body, with its perceptions and mind, that lies the world, and the arising of the world, and the cessation of the world, and the path leading to the cessation of the world."

Luang Pee and I spoke of this, after his Dharma talk on sexuality and being in the world.

"Well, Vernon, there is this body and mind for a time. It is the Dharma, your school. If you're going to be in school, you may as well take the curriculum."

That had made me laugh at the time. But increasingly it was all too clear "awakening" or "freedom" isn't an end point. It's the starting point for a lifetime of moment-to-moment choices. Wisdom is not conferred nor ignorance vanquished by just sitting on a cushion. For the rest of my life, the challenge was to respond appropriately.

I was reading *The Fixer* by Bernard Malamud. A character's comment leapt out at me.

"...and if you should ever get out of prison keep in mind that the purpose of freedom is to create it for others."

I felt like I'd been released from prison. What would creating freedom for others look like?

III

The weaving process involved a wooden ruler. It served as the working platform and my eight, thick black threads ran the length. The arrangement was not unlike the neck of a guitar, with the strings held taut slightly above the frets.

Katje demonstrated the basic moves of threading the colorful embroidery yarn back and forth, alternating over and under, and tamping down each row with a thin wood edge. The tamping locked each pass into the growing band.

"Yeah, that's it," she encouraged. "Pull the yarn a little tighter before you set it."

It became hypnotic, absorbing. She studied my labor and nodded approvingly. Two hours later, I tied the band I made around Katje's ankle. She tied hers around my left wrist.

"When it falls away, I make another," she smiled.

The solemnity of the exchange surprised me. We were lovers now and the little bands pulled us closer together.

My traveling companions had struck up a casual relationship with the Danish girls down the beach. Truth be told, Mike had struck up a relationship with Alana. Tony, Karolin and Mina were the loyal sidekicks. But nobody seemed to mind and we all enjoyed the fine life on the beach of Ios. The ladies spoke English fluently, a fact Mike commented on.

On to Greece

"Not so many speak Danish," Alana had reflected. "When you are a small country, it's that way."

Alana and Mike were fast friends. Like him, she was tall and elegant. Straight brown hair past her shoulders, generous lips and breasts, playful grey eyes and a ready laugh, she was very attractive. On our sixth night, she and Mike excused themselves early from our taverna meal.

"A walk on the beach and some stargazing," Mike had said.

In the slightly awkward silence after their departure, Tony cut down into a cube of roasted lamb. A fountain of meat juice sprayed out across Mina's supine forearm and she retracted it off the table in surprise.

"Hopah! Don't let it get away!"

Katje burst out laughing.

Tony looked mortified for a moment but then relaxed, the silence broken. He grinned sheepishly.

"Aw yeah, I've got a grip on it now."

Tony was comfortable but not intimate with the two women. They were tall, like Alana, and easily had six inches over him. Two beautiful Valkyries from the north.

"He's very shy, isn't he?" Katje had observed a few days after meeting Tony. By now, though, they liked each other. He would grin and turn red when she joked with him, but obviously enjoyed the interaction. He and Katje were also of similar stature. I could imagine that his reticence around the Danish girls was discomfort with their height.

While we finished our dinner, Karolin and Mina told us about Møn, the island they lived on in Denmark. Karolin's brothers owned a candle factory outside of Stege, the main town, and they both worked there occasionally. Alana too. All three were part of a nursing program in Copenhagen, a short drive to the north.

"You should come," Mina smiled. "The late summer is very good there."

"Yeah, yeah. Also my brothers always have work. You could work there," Karolin added.

In previous conversations, Tony had spoken of the need to find work when he and Mike arrived in Europe. The notion of living for some time on a beautiful Danish island, making candles and a bit of money had a definite appeal.

The Appearance of Things

The near constant breeze coming from the north hit the isthmus and was forced up and over the cliff beach. That conferred a tranquil, smooth surface on our little bay until the torrent of air descended again to the surface, offshore. In the afternoons white caps would often appear, starting about five hundred meters out and marching away from us toward the south.

On our seventh day a group of young Italian footballers showed up at the taverna around midday. Mike was on a water run and came back with the news.

"They're quite a jolly crew actually, really playing the Mama Mia routine for laughs. Have a little inflatable going, everybody taking turns on the foot pump."

"You mean an inflatable boat?" I asked.

"Aw, not a big thing. What we'd call a rubber ducky back home. They're going to row back around the point to the harbor."

The day was warm and still, the water inviting. Rowing sounded like a lot of work but I imagined it could be fun if you splashed around. Katje and I went back to reading and didn't give it much thought.

Maybe an hour later, I heard Tony say, "There they go."

I saw what Mike meant about them hamming it up with the Italian stuff. Getting all three of them into the petite raft was like the clown act at the circus. Laughing onlookers helped push them out from the shore, offering advice and encouragement. The would-be seafarers were waving back and blowing kisses.

I went back to my reading but after about fifteen minutes became aware of Katje staring out to sea and followed her gaze. The Italians had reached the end of the calm waters in our little bay and were approaching the point. The day still felt calm where we were, but wavelets on the sea beyond said the afternoon breeze was kicking in. They were moving in the opposite direction of their paddling, out to sea.

"The wind has them," Katje said, alarm in her voice.

Sure enough, they were now rapidly being blown south, away from the island. Mike and Tony joined us, all of us standing now at the edge of the water. The paddling had taken on a desperate edge, flailing against the push of the wind.

"What's south of here?" Mike asked, shading his eyes.

On to Greece

"Crete. About a hundred and fifty kilometers."

It was happening too quickly. The raft was fast becoming just a point on the horizon.

"Somebody better alert the harbor master. I'll go," Tony said decisively and set off.

"I'll come with you. We need more smokes and some Metaxa."

Mike strode over to their alcove and snagged his day sack, making haste to catch Tony up.

"Do we need anything else?" he called back.

"A pack of Gauloises for me," Katje called. The Drum finally ran out two days ago and we were smoking what was local.

We watched Mike and Tony climb up the cleft nearest the taverna. I imagined that others on the beach had similar concerns and the harbormaster would soon be alerted. Looking back out to sea, the raft was no longer discernable.

On Saturday night, our eighth on the beach, word went around that Swiss Pete was giving himself a birthday party up at Nikko's. His three companions, Damian, Inga and Maria made the rounds, asking members of our little campfire group to join them.

"The first ten liters of wine are on my Peter," Inga smiled, "then you're on your own."

Katje had only just finished another weaving and held it out. "Just in time for a birthday present." She waggled her head in the sweet way I found charming, almost Indian but uniquely her.

Tony appeared momentarily surprised. We both thought she was making the band for him.

Katje picked up on it and grinned mischievously.

"These aren't your colors, I've decided. You'll be more bright green and red."

"Aw well, I…I mean…"

He stopped, suddenly embarrassed then pressed on.

"Yeah, I like red and green. Thanks."

Katje winked at me and we shared a smile.

Up at the taverna, ten liters of wine later, I felt myself looking affectionately at the faces of our little instant community. It was intimate in the small room, even with the huge wine barrel looming over us. Hillary and Christopher were over in the corner, glasses poised while Pete finished his toast. Dieter, Edith and Anita were at the big table with Tony, me and Katje. Pete's friends, Inga, Maria and Damian sat with him at his table, their faces tilted up to him in tipsy affection. Mike was nearby with Alana, Karolin and Mina.

It still blew my mind that a little over a week ago I didn't know most of these people. And yet, here we were, sharing, laughing, celebrating one of us. Four of us if you count the Italian mariners. Pete had mentioned their rescue by local fishermen in his speech. Everybody had cheered and downed another glass of retsina. Maybe there was something in living naked on a beach together. Maybe our hearts were more naked too, naked and open to each other.

"And so, I wish myself a very happy birthday. Thank you for sharing it with me." Pete raised his nearly full tumbler to the gathering then polished it off in one great gulp. "*Yassou!*" he shouted and hurled the empty glass into the fireplace. I winced at the shattering explosion.

Inga, Damian and Maria rose from the table, toasted Peter and emptied their glasses. "*Yassou!*" they bellowed and three more tumblers smashed to bits in the fireplace.

Laughter and merriment as many others stood, finished their wine and moved towards the fireplace.

"*Óchi!* No!" I heard Nikko's strangled protest from behind the bar.

Too late and another six glasses exploded against the back of the fireplace, a few shards ricocheting back out on to the floor.

Katje, who had also heard Nikko, hesitated. Our eyes met and we understood each other.

"Happy Birthday Pete!" we called into the general mayhem, finished our wine and placed the tumbler back on the table.

Peter registered the anguish on Nikko's face and made his way over to the bar.

"Nikko my friend, I am sorry for the damage. Don't worry. I will make it good with you."

To his very Greek credit, Nikko lifted his glass to Peter, drained it and grinned.

"*Yassou*, Peter. Happy Birthday."

The next morning, Sunday, Katje and I joined Anita for a light breakfast up at the taverna.

"She's going back to Germany now. Dieter wants her to stay but she's finished with his game. Come with me. I know she wants to see you to say goodbye."

Over the last week, Anita and I had drawn closer together. Maybe in part, it owed to her wounding in the relationship with Dieter. She wanted to know that she was desirable, wanted him to know that others desired her. Several times we had been sunning nude on the beach, chatting a bit and reading. Out of the blue, she would lean across and kiss me. I didn't resist. Her lustrous tan body wafted the perfume of woman in the warm sun. It was very erotic.

"I like you," she'd whispered. "Your stories make me want to go and never come back."

Katje grew more passionate as well. Thinking back to how women seemed to gravitate to Mike, that he had some special quality that made him attractive to the opposite sex. I liked to think, to hope, that maybe some of that was rubbing off on me since we arrived in Greece. And I liked it.

I made my way back down to the beach when Katje departed with Anita for the harbor. Tony and Mike sat in camp watching me come.

"Hey, what's up?"

Mike spoke first.

"Well, we talked about heading for Athens when the money got low. I'm just about there. So is Tony."

Tony nodded in agreement.

"Yeah. For one thing, I want to get my funds, pay you back. Pay Mike back. And, I'm kinda ready."

I'd been watching the drachmas go as well but I wasn't too worried. The big tourist hotel in the village would change traveler's cheques. They charged five percent but forty dollars would get me thirty eight dollars' worth of drachmas. At our rate of spending, that was another week on the beach. And I liked how it was going with Katje. My rule of the road, "When you find paradise, stay awhile" was including the paradise I found in her.

The Appearance of Things

"Yeah, I get it. When were you thinking?"

Mike looked over to Tony.

"We were thinking of the day after tomorrow, Tuesday."

Tony spoke the unspoken between us in that moment.

"If you wanted to stay on awhile with Katje, we could meet up north. I'd leave the money I borrowed from you at the American Express mail."

I felt a twinge at the way he'd said the last part, and at the prospect of the three of us going apart. We'd been together on the road for quite a while. In my imaginings, it was going to be a real blast showing up in Europe together. It was like crossing the finish line. Now my heart wanted two conflicting paths. The here and now required a clarity I didn't have. When Katje and I gazed at each other, an electrical frisson coursed through me. She was intelligent and beautiful and sexually thrilling. Sometimes in our love making, we'd peer into the darkness behind the eyes, in breathless freefall. Was this just summer's wristband, lasting as long as it lasted and then falling away?

In McLeod Ganj, I'd snapped awake one night, a memory of the dream I had on the train. The old wise man had asked me what I wanted and I'd said, "To be happy." And he had gazed at me with my mother's eyes. The secret of happiness is to love and be loved. It was as simple and as difficult as that.

"Thanks Tony. I guess I haven't thought it through. I didn't expect to meet Katje, that's for sure. What's going on for you and Alana, Mike?"

"Aw well, they're all leaving on the morning boat tomorrow. Flying back to Copenhagen on Tuesday." He shrugged and looked out toward the horizon. "I reckon we'll see each other in Denmark. Alana has a couple of friends who are looking for a guitar player to join them. Maybe tour around a bit."

"There's the candle works too," Tony added. "The ladies reckon there's enough housing scattered around the property for us all. Could be good, eh?"

I nodded, "Yeah, could be good. It sounds corny, but let me meditate on it and talk to Katje. I was really looking forward to hitting Europe with you guys. Home of Drum and German beer, y'know."

About two o'clock Katje returned from seeing Anita off. We'd lain side by side in the sand for a time, in the silence that erupted when I'd spoken about Mike and Tony leaving on Tuesday. Katje now broke the silence.

"So, do you go with them?" she asked.

"I'm loving my time here. I think you are wonderful. Do you want me to stay on?"

"Whaa!" she exclaimed and sat bolt upright. She fixed me with an intense gaze. "Don't you do that! Don't you do a Dieter game!" Her blue eyes flashed, raw emotion rearing up. "You do what you want. You go or you stay because you want. Don't put it on me!"

She had leaped up then and walked out into the sea.

I lay back, feeling very stupid, and closed my eyes. The adrenaline rush had my heart beating suddenly faster. One long, deep inhalation and I started to follow my breath. Time to respond, not react. The cool, quiet place at the edge of mind began to unfold. Another long breath.

"You look a little burned." I opened my eyes and Tony was staring down at me. The shadows were longer. How long had I been meditating? Well, sleeping.

Sitting up, everything above my knees stung. My lower legs were ok but my face, chest and waist were throbbing with heat. Katje was nowhere in sight. I was relatively sun conditioned, but not enough, apparently.

"Ah!" I touched my upper left thigh and my hand felt like sandpaper on the stressed skin.

"Cool off time," I mumbled to Tony and made my way down to the water. I imagined I was giving off steam, a piece of hot iron dunked into a bucket. The relief was short lived for soon the stinging and throbbing returned, even though I was immersed up to my neck in the cooling sea. I'd never considered a sunburned penis but now found it unrelentingly unpleasant.

Back at the cave I applied some of the skin lotion I used after shaving. Some help but not much. My soft sarong felt protecting but I had to be gentle brushing off sand and even then, it hurt.

Katje walked into the camp shortly after, made her way over our alcove and picked up a few things. She didn't appear upset and said matter-of-factly, "I'll see you later." It was a general comment to me, Mike and Tony. She nodded and made to walk away, down the beach.

"Will you have dinner with me?" I asked tentatively. Katje stopped, her back to us, resting a hand on the stonewall of the cliff. "No, I don't think so. I need some time alone. Maybe I'll see you later." With that she moved off along the sandy shore, not looking back.

"What's going on?" Tony asked.

Mike did a double take, like he couldn't believe Tony was asking that.

"We talked about you and Mike heading up to Athens day after tomorrow. About whether I was going too."

"Aw yeah," Tony said, nodding and just getting the why of Katje's abrupt departure.

Later, I drank a little too much retsina around the fire. I guess we all did. Something good was coming to an end here. The Danish girls were over at the port tonight to catch their pre-dawn ferry. Katje stayed up in her room at Nikko's. We three would be leaving together on the ferry come Tuesday.

I didn't sleep well. The blow-up with Katje combined with the impossibility of physical comfort from the sunburn. I tossed and turned. It has been said that the worst time to take thoughts seriously is between two and five in the morning. I'd have to agree. And then, miraculously, just before dawn, I was awakened when Katje slipped into the alcove. Silently we embraced and made tender love, in more ways than one.

"I'm glad you came down," I whispered.

She gazed back at me. In the reddening dawn, she squeezed my hand. "Red sky at night, sailors delight. Red sky in the morning, sailor take warning." The eastern sky was blood streaked red, wisps of long, thin clouds catching and reflecting the coming light of the new sun.

"Think there's a storm coming?" I asked.

Katje shrugged, the hint of a smile. "It's just an old saying in German. Sometimes my father would take us sailing on the Kiel fjord. He always said that, no matter what the weather. How's your burn now?"

She looked at me sideways, a wry twinkle in her deep blue eyes. I snorted and touched my privates. "I thought I was pretty well sun conditioned after a week outside. Still hurts a bit."

We leaned into each other's naked body and kissed again. It was a lingering kiss, stroking the other softly. Pulling back, our eyes met. I knew it was a letting go. She was setting me free. We were setting each other free, wordlessly but certainly.

Mike and Tony concealed their surprise when we emerged from the alcove and sat down for coffee.

"Morning," Mike said.

On to Greece

Katje and Tony just grinned at each other.

It was a golden last day on the beach for all of us. Impermanence isn't always a drag. Sometimes it can be a reminder of the sweet, fleeing joy in being alive. We had most of the cooking gear packed up for our morning departure. It was Nikko's for our last supper.

"A toast of gratitude to Ios and Nikko," Mike raised his tumbler.

"*Yassou!*" we all said, but declined to smash our glasses into the fireplace.

Nikko had sent us back down to the beach with a couple of liters of wine.

"For singing and dancing together around the fire," he smiled.

During supper Katje had surprised us with her plans.

"*Ja*, Crete is a place I've wanted to go. And I can fly back to Germany directly from there so it makes more sense." It was her intention to grab the Friday ferry, making a direct trip from Ios to Crete.

The reality of our imminent separation had me feeling hollowed out. I supposed I'd be growing more sophisticated about leave taking but in fact it was proving more difficult. I left most of the retsina to Mike and Tony. Katje and I withdrew from the fire circle before it grew too late. There was still music and singing with Peter and his three friends. Dieter and Edith had literally drawn back into their cave since Anita departed, not from grief either. Around midnight, Katje and I treated ourselves to a night swim, refreshing and cleansing after some delightfully experimental love making.

"You know, at night, once you go out past your knees you're part of the food chain."

"Oh, stop it you!" she had laughed.

Another dawn and, later, coffee up at Nikko's. But the coffee was done now. Mike, Tony and I had our backpacks at the edge of the patio. A few others had drifted in as we ate and a round of farewells.

I looked back as we began our ascent of the little ridge trail. Katje was sitting at an outside table enjoying another coffee and cigarette, writing in her journal. I had her telephone number and address in Hannover. We'd see each other again, we both agreed. It had the aroma of a lie, designed to make us both feel better. I was leaving, she was staying behind, an "almost but not quite" affair.

Walking out to the pier, Tony and Mike were chatting amiably about our time on the beach and the time ahead. Mike was clear he wanted to reconnect with Alana on Møn, Tony enthusiastic about Athens and Germany. I knew I'd stop for a time in München to visit with Nancy, the wonderful older aunt of a woman I'd met in England. She was connected with the US military in some sort of intelligence capacity we didn't speak of and lived on a base within the city. We'd been fast friends since meeting back in early 1974. I'd written her periodically from my travels. She insisted I come and stay for a few days and tell her about my retreat up in Manali. An old Buddhist herself, she was one of the people Alan Watts would stay with when doing lecture tours in Europe.

The ferry horn blasted out three staccato bursts. A clackity sound from the shore lines being reeled in, a slight sense of movement and the pier began to recede. We were on our way. I joined my friends at the railing as we backed away from Ios, turned and began steaming northeast. There was Milipotas beach, still crowded with tents on the hillside. Our little beach had been much more to my liking. Gazing at Ios falling behind us, something gathered force in the center of me. It wasn't intellectual, something to roll around and consider. More of a growing, physical conviction, like being lost in the wilderness, a sense of having taken a wrong turn, moving in a direction that led to death rather than life. The further the island fell behind us the more an urgency, a near panic, engulfed me. What the hell?

A body memory, leaving Vientiane, leaving Hom. She'd be there when I returned. But she wasn't and I'd lost her.

Right now, a strangling sense of making the wrong choice again. I gripped the rail of the ferry.

"Hey, Vernon. Are you ok?"

Mike had placed a hand on my back and was peering at me with genuine concern.

"What?" I managed.

Tony came up too. My friends were looking at me like I'd had too much to drink and wanted to take the car for a spin.

"Are you ok? Your face is white."

"I just made a mistake," I whispered.

Looking up at them, I spoke with the conviction of realization.

"I just made a big mistake. I need to go back."

Mike grinned, "Bit of a swim I reckon."

On to Greece

I laughed. The suffocation and the panic subsided. So wild! My body made me know what my mind couldn't see. Take the curriculum, stupid!

"Oh boy. No, not a good swim back I reckon. But I'm getting off in Naxos and going back to Ios tomorrow."

Saying it, my chest expanded out to infinite. Freedom felt like this.

By the time we pulled into Naxos, Mike, Tony and I had worked out how we'd find each other in Europe. Tony would leave the money he borrowed from me in a letter at the American Express. Mike wrote out Alana's address on Møn and I gave him and Tony Katje Sommers address and number in Hannover.

"If worst comes to worst, send me a letter about where you are to Poste Restante in Amsterdam," I said.

We'd spoken of a pilgrimage over to England together to see how John and Louise were getting on. That still might happen.

At our harbor stop in Naxos, we gave each other hugs.

"Good on 'ya, Vernon." Tony smiled his big toothed grin.

"It's been a time, hasn't it?"

Mike's handshake lingered and we met each other's gaze.

"That it has," I agreed, "See you both again before too long."

There was no odor of disingenuousness in this parting.

I waved to them from the pebbly beach when their ferry pulled out of Naxos harbor and steamed towards Athens.

I was on my own again but feeling so whole. Sitting there atop my pack, I flipped small stones into the nearby sea. Ker-plunk! It was a cheerful sound. Ker-plunk!

The one who stepped off the plane alone in Singapore last year was me. I could touch that excited, fearful one, like a child I loved and cared for. I could put a hand on his shoulder, smile into his doubtful eyes and say in truth, "It's going to be ok."

Dinner was moussaka and a bottle of retsina at a nearby taverna. It amused me that the wine was not up to Nikko's standards. I'll have to tell him tomorrow, "Hey Nikko, not all Naxos retsina is created equal." When night fell, I just rolled out my bag right on the beach of Naxos harbor and spent a beautiful night under the Mediterranean stars, the gentle crunch of wavelets on the pebble shore for a lullaby.

The ferry from Naxos to Ios arrived at ten thirty in the morning. On my way past the little kiosk at the foot of the pier, I picked up a pack of Gauloises.

The morning air was still cool when I reached the crest of the ridge. Below, a bit of smoke rose from the kitchen area of the taverna. As fate would have it, on the way down I met Dieter coming up. His wide, handsome face burst into jolly grin and he grasped my hands.

"Werner, you are not supposed to be here!"

I returned his smile and winked, "That's what freedom is."

At that, he bellowed with laughter, "*Ja, Ja*, Ok! So we'll see you there."

I made my way down the hill to the taverna. In under the grape arbor I saw Katje as when I left, writing in her journal. She faced out to the southwest, not seeing my approach.

Removing my pack, I settled it down and stepped in under the arbor. She paused in her writing and looked up, out to sea. Then she turned and our eyes met. Neither of us moved or spoke for a long moment. I saw in her an avalanche of thoughts and feelings. In my chest an answering avalanche.

"Hi," I finally managed.

Katje smiled, "Hi."

Our eyes remained locked together.

"Feel like company?" I asked.

She slid the chair beside her out from the table with a foot and regarded me coolly.

I slid into the proffered seat.

"I came back," I said.

"I'm glad," she replied.

Epilogue

John and Louise made it safely to England where Louise delivered her girl, Samantha. They moved back to Australia in 1978.

Mike, Tony, Katje and Vern reconnected on the Danish island of Møn in the late summer of 1975. Mike made good as a guitar player with a local group that called themselves "Blum". All four worked and stayed until mid-Autumn at Karolin's brother's candle factory.

Mike married Alana and they have two children. They moved to Mike's Australian home in 1979.

Tony went back to Queensland, Australia after Mike's marriage in 1976 and pursued a career in what is now called "adventure tourism".

Vern and Katje went back to Hannover where Katje continued on her path as an architect and Vern worked as a carpenter in local trade shows. He also sold all of his silk bags at various street fairs in their travels around Europe. Vern returned to the USA in time for the 1976 Bicentennial celebrations on July 4th and departed for South America on July 10th of that year.

Katje Sommers joined him in Caracas, Venezuela and they commenced a two year journey that took them to Tierra del Fuego and back.

About the Author

Vernon St. Clair Castle is a third generation Californian, born in 1951. He grew up in Los Angeles, California and attended UCLA as a pre-med student and graduated with a BS in Zoology and minor in Biochemistry.

His family were ranchers in the northern reaches of Los Angeles County, but after the death of his father in 1952 his mother moved to the city where she worked as a designer.

After nearly a decade of travel and work around the world he married in 1984 and undertook the life of family and householder. The decade of travel included a formative period in Asia during the early 1980s when he explored the reality of becoming a Theravada Buddhist monk.

For the last thirty five years Vern has lived and worked in West Marin, California. He taught the sciences in both public and private schools until his retirement in 2013.

Currently he and his wife Renee, an encaustic and watercolor artist, divide their new "rewired" lives between Indonesia, Mexico and West Marin, California.

For more information, including a photo gallery, or to contact the author please go to www.vernoncastle.com

www.ingramcontent.com/pod-product-compliance
Lightning Source LLC
Chambersburg PA
CBHW081351290426
44110CB00018B/2348